Rosewood

The Full Story

By Gary Moore

"Each time, I want to know it all, everything. If I could just piece it all together, perhaps the things that people do to each other might make some sense."

—Edna Buchanan

"The world is not with you when you tell the truth. But God is for you when you tell the truth."

—Leroy Carrier

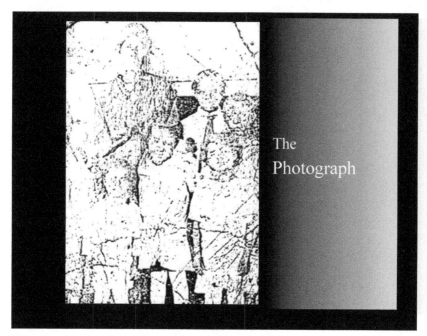

The
Photograph

The traveling photographer parked his Model T in the sand at the front fence, and Mama called the children together.

Minnie would have no memory of the sales pitch preceding the photo agreement, because she was playing house with Goldee in the back yard. This caused a problem when they posed. Goldee was wearing Mama's big shoes (being older, she got to be the Mama), and she refused to take the shoes off to get her picture taken. Goldee cried and threw a fit as the man stood there with his pan of flash powder, until they had to let her pose with the shoes still on. But the man said he would make up for it, by cutting off their feet. He climbed under his strange black hood, and there was a blinding flash.

The resulting photo was not perfect. Two of the faces, Rita's and Lonnie's, are lost in glare. Two other household members, Papa and Willard, are not in the photo at all.

And thus it becomes a symbol, reminding of the difficulties involved in traveling back into their world. The roadmap has to be pieced together slowly from bits and flashes—and, especially, from imperfect memory.

On the front porch that day they could not see that their world was about to end. Apparently this is the only surviving photograph of the community of Rosewood as it stood at a crucial moment, on the eve of its destruction.

Contents

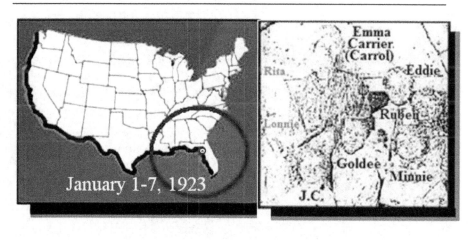

January 1-7, 1923

Emma
Carrier
(Carrol)
Rita
Eddie
Lonnie
Ruben
Goldee
Minnie
J.C.

Headlines

There was, to be sure, a word-picture of the event, traced out on wrinkled pages in the news—though these formed a hornet's nest of contradictions, fantasies, angry shouting, trumped-up myths—one more scrap of road map leading into the maze...

"FLORIDA RACE WAR BATTLE THROUGH THE NIGHT"

"...the negro and a number of his friends had barricaded themselves in a shanty on the outskirts of the town and defied any white man to come near them."
—*The Washington Post, January 6, 1923*

"....FLORIDA RACE WAR"

"Armed Warfare As Whites Attack Negro Community"
—*The New York Amsterdam News*, January 12, 1923

"VILLAGE RAZED IN RACE WAR"

—*The Chicago Daily News,* January 5, 1923

"NEGRO HOMES RAZED IN ROSEWOOD"

—*The New York Times*,
January 8, 1923

"ALL HOMES OF NEGROES ARE BURNED"

—*The Los Angeles Times*,
January 8, 1923

"Twenty-Five Negroes Barricaded in House, Defy Armed Posse and Open Fire on Whites...."

"...Officers to Aid in Quelling Rebellious Black Population"
—*The Gainesville Daily Sun*, January 5, 1923

"NINETEEN SLAIN IN FLORIDA RACE WAR"

"EX-SOLDIER IS HERO IN BLOODY RIOT
Makes Farm Hands Fight Back;
Had Just Come to Town; Called Chicagoan"
—*The Chicago Defender*, January 13, 1923

"CLASH BETWEEN WHITE MEN AND COLORED..."
"...NEGROES FIRED FIRST..."
"...PLENTY NEGROES IN PARTY"
—*The Ocala Evening Star*
January 5, 1923

"...a score or more of Negroes early to-day were barricaded in a house at Rosewood ...with hundreds of armed white men waiting for daybreak to attack the stronghold."
—*The New York World*, January 5, 1923

"In reality...between 70 and 250 people were killed in Rosewood..."
—*The New York Times online*, posted 1997-2015

(That a statement like the one above could appear in the *New York Times* online suggests the force of emotion pressing on images of racial conflict. The statement is a bizarre fantasy, but is asserted solemnly by the *Times* as fact. It not only wildly exaggerates but contradicts what survivor witnesses and supporting evidence verifiably and repeatedly said. Such lapses in evidence perception, even in forums with high standards of objectivity, form part of the mystery explored by this book.)

Introduction

In 1982 a solitary automobile pulled off a lonely back road. The driver stumbled out, soon off balance in high weeds. He peered uncertainly at the ground, as if searching for something.

It was an empty-looking spot, one more tangle of bushes and trees in a long wall of vegetation hedging the road. The two-lane thread of pavement was silent, devoid of traffic, running straight and level into opposite horizons, dwindling into humid haze.

This was swamp country, no hills or curves to relieve the eye. Once upon a time, a belt of towering subtropical jungles had lent majesty to this spot, but the lumber companies had come through, cutting in successive waves, leaving ruins and second growth. Sun-bleached cabbage palms still stood in clumps, guarding low thickets of fan-like saw palmetto. The intruder pushed back into the shadows.

Thus went the discovery of the atrocity at Rosewood.

The destruction of the community of Rosewood, Florida, during the mysterious week of January 1-7, 1923, has by now become an emblem in American history, showing how communal atrocities can be pushed eerily from public memory.

The Rosewood mystery had to be "discovered" sixty years after the fact, in 1982, because cultural denial had succeeded in blanking it out, hiding large traces to a startling degree. Official records and even general public memory were wiped clean. Only fifty miles from the site stood the 40,000-student University of Florida, but when the intruder drove to its prestigious P. K. Yonge Library of Florida History, he was told politely that no such incident had ever been heard of. Not even a legend or rumor had broken through. The completeness of the denial process invites strange phrases, along the lines of mass blindness or mass delusion.

From the very beginning in 1923, the Rosewood violence had fed off illusions. Then even after the destruction a stream of false images would continue rippling forward, not only into 1982 and the break with denial, but afterward. The three-plus decades of Rosewood publicity since 1982 have brought new waves of illusion, still rippling today.

A silent spot in the swamps has by now revealed a larger zone of fantasy belief in American information, where history meets the illusion-filled issue called race.

At midnight in the last moments of 1922, a small African American community of farmers, loggers and laborers lay sleeping in deep wilderness. Then came the week of January 1-7—and the community was gone. At the climax, hundreds of armed men were converging in a spasm of shooting and burning. But a few decades later in surviving official documents—paced closely by history and popular memory—it was almost as if nothing had occurred.

I was the intruder in the swamps so long ago, stumbling onto something beyond my knowledge. Meeting the six-decade-old riddles in 1982, I would then be drawn into three decades more of investigation. Putting the pieces together has turned out to be a bit more difficult than a puzzled intruder first expected.

That initial drive into the swampland came near the beginning of my journalism career. I had talked an editor into approving an aimless trip into a blank spot on the map, a remote area a hundred miles from the Florida city where I worked. The idea was simply to see what popped up, to probe for a harmless feature angle. And this, fatefully, meant open-ended questions, inviting undertones to bubble up. I began to hear secretive local tales, which seemed flatly impossible. Voices in the swamps said, guardedly, that six decades in the past an enormity had occurred—but was kept out of the pages of history.

The tales told of grotesque carnage. The tellers spoke fervently. But they were not eyewitnesses, and all of them were white—since only whites were left in the area. They said that the targeted black community was completely expunged, its inhabitants either killed or chased into parts unknown.

I had no way of knowing that the years had left layer on layer of misperceptions—or that I was becoming part of a new stream in American information. In the years since 1982, secretive cases of mass racial violence from the early twentieth century have repeatedly been unearthed and re-examined. And as with the harbinger case at Rosewood, which opened the way to others,[1] the publicity has erected a maze of myths. New technology and new sensibilities have synergized to probe back into a secretive chamber of the American past, the "Lynching Era," roughly the 1870s into the 1930s. But results have been mixed. Very real atrocities have repeatedly been cloaked in very dubious images.

4

As I peered into the palmetto thickets in 1982, shocked to find small bits of broken crockery and weathered brick in the sand, I was about to be pulled into a vortex of badly scattered clues—a puzzle whose pieces are still floating into view today. Through manic turns on the national stage, the Rosewood revelation has formed perhaps the single most publicized re-examination of a secret from the rural mists of the Lynching Era—in a case going far beyond the scale of an individual lynching, and taking an entire community as its target.

The process placing me as the recognized authority on the Rosewood evidence began with my 1982 Sunday magazine exposé in the newspaper where I worked, the *St. Petersburg Times*. In 1983 I took the still-emerging clues to "60 Minutes" and was background reporter on the segment that resulted. At that point I failed to guess how much patience would be required by such a cultural blindspot. A long slog lay ahead.[2]

Along the way in 1991-1994, the landmark Rosewood claims case brought a new publicity storm, marking the nation's first payment of government reparations on a Lynching Era atrocity.[3] I then served as consultant to separate Rosewood investigations by both the Florida Attorney General's Office and the Florida Department of Law Enforcement.

But the next media milestone did not involve me (as my skeptical comments may make clear). The $26-million big-screen motion picture on the case premiered in 1997. Logically titled *Rosewood*, it so badly distorted the 1923 events that the film was denounced not only by Rosewood survivors but by the author of a tie-in publicity book promoted with it. As ironies continued, that book also presented startling distortions, though distortions different from those in the movie. On the racially charged Rosewood enigma the public was left to view an enchanted forest of conflicting myths.

From the beginning in 1982, I was led behind the looking glass on Rosewood because I asked what seemed an obvious question: Where were the witnesses? I had accidentally met a unique window in time, for the Rosewood violence formed perhaps the last of the Lynching Era's large rampages, consisting of attacks on entire communities. In the early 1980s many lucid observers from 1923 were still alive, while the sheer size of the incident also meant a large pool of potential informants—if they could be found—and if the labyrinth of emerging testimony could be navigated.

The use of living witnesses would prove to be much more complex than simply quoting an old newspaper article or two, as history has often done on such cases. Looking through the eyes—and the flawed memories—of real people has required extensive additional effort. Corroborating documentation had to be sought, and there was the amazingly time-consuming task of collating and deconflicting the many contradictory statements.[4]

In the 1983 phase with "60 Minutes," resources from CBS News helped me find an ever-expanding number of survivors—as the world of memory, atrocity and illusion taught sharp lessons. At that point, the picture of the 1923 events was changing as the evidence pool grew more powerful, but the television script (which I had no hand in writing) wound up incorporating some tall tales. Then in the 1990s the process of warping the truth on a shocking racial issue would be amplified by the Rosewood claims case, and still more so by the climactic fantasies in the movie.

After 1997, as if exhausted by the movie's controversies, Rosewood excitement seemed to pause, but the lure of the old secrets was still strong, along with a disconcerting trend toward fantasy. In 2013, University Press of Florida, the most prestigious outlet for scholarly information in the nation's then-fourth largest state, was moved to recall and repudiate a book it had published that same year, a book built around Rosewood. The university publisher admitted "scholarly misconduct," which ranged from rampant plagiarism to bizarre imaginings dressed as history. The image of Rosewood floats in a very troubled informational sea.

The pivotal evidence on this hallmark case has come from its oldest and most credible eyewitnesses, African American survivors found in the 1980s. But the largest wave of media interest would arrive too late for them, not surging until the 1990s, after they had passed on. Increasingly, the only voices that were left belonged to informants who had either been small children in the 1923 events, with scarcely any real memories, or people who were not even born yet—though some were willing to fill in the gaps with dramatic stories suited to media appeal. The results are now scattered across the Web, sometimes presented in ponderous language, but enclosing the real events in fog.

So what really happened in 1923? What does the evidence say? The answers that have emerged—from all the voices together—are not suited to quick media melodrama. But with the puzzle pieces now finally tracked down and assembled, even the debunked illusions point to the one story we all know. This is simply a rough sketch of the great mystery, the face of real life.

Chapter 1: Lay of the Land

Minnie knew her cousin Sylvester mostly at a distance. He seemed a nice man, although, being grown, he shared few thoughts with a nine-year-old like her. Cud'n Syl lived just down the railroad tracks to the southwest, within hollering range.

Minnie Lee Mitchell had her own world —playing house or church in the back yard, or bob-a-needle or handkerchief-a-walkin'—or watering Mama's sweet potatoes and chufas, or filling the reservoir on the wood stove, or wielding a switch broom to sweep the sandy yard.

Through such ceremonies, she scarcely guessed how it would all turn out—how she and Sylvester, of all people, would be thrown together at the end. Two lonely figures would be at the heart of a human storm— as her wilderness community was attacked and destroyed.

Minnie Lee Langley:
    July 4, 1913 – Dec. 16, 1995
1920 Census:
    Household 113, Precinct 9,
    Levy County, Fla.
Maiden Name:
    Minnie Lee Mitchell
Interviewed:
    Moncrief Park, Jacksonville, Florida
    1983. 1993. 1994

Beside a vintage railroad that skirted a great swamp, she lived with her grandparents, James and Emma Carrier, calling them Mama and Papa. From their house she could look down the tracks and see where Sylvester lived. The view was clear both in summer, when fierce heat shimmered above dark railroad crossties, and in winter, when the bald cypress trees back in the hammock shed their fine needles, and the night roar of frogs fell mute, meeting short bursts of cold.

Minnie's front-yard picket fence faced one side of the railroad, while the house where Sylvester lived, less than a quarter mile southeast down the tracks, was on the other side, toward the tree-wall of Gulf Hammock, the great jungle where Minnie was forbidden to wander.

Bald Cypress

She knew that in times past a few more buildings had stood down there, in Sylvester's part of things. But through a period of two decades the community had fallen on hard times, under pressures not explained to Minnie. Cud'n Syl's place was left from the old days, when hopes had been higher.

She retained complicated feelings about that house, though not because of Sylvester. The problem was his mother, Aunt Sarah (Minnie's great-aunt, age fifty). A controversial figure in the community, energetic Sarah Carrier was loved by some, distrusted by others. There had been startling incidents, which not even the eyewitnesses seemed able to explain.[5] Like any community, Minnie's home had its share of personal mysteries—causing some gossip or chuckling tales—but certainly not seeming to foretell disaster.

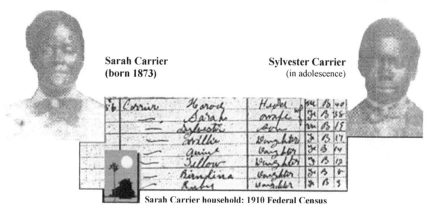

Sarah Carrier (born 1873)

Sylvester Carrier (in adolescence)

Sarah Carrier household: 1910 Federal Census

The house was Sarah's, while her son Sylvester lived there. At age 33 he had a room at the back with his wife Gert. Meanwhile, Sarah's touch appeared in front, in flowers on the porch. Ironically, that brightness recalled a lifetime of toil, for the flowers were planted in worn-out washtubs. Sarah Carrier worked as a laundress, ceaselessly forcing a soapy scrub board down onto the flat bottoms of metal tubs, until the dented metal strained, then gave way.

But Minnie's visits to Aunt Sarah's were not bleak. She liked playing with her cousin Arnett, Aunt Sarah's grandson. Arnett was born three month before Minnie, putting them both a year before the guns of August 1914, which brought World War I.

The bugle calls would reach even into those swamps, summoning people Minnie knew. After April 1917 and U.S. entry into the war, Minnie's young uncle, Aaron Carrier, would go away and then return with a forage cap and leggings. Records showed, too, that George Goins, married to Minnie's cousin Willie Carrier, was sent overseas—removing him from a communal trauma, a fatal shooting in church.[6]

In a tightly interwoven community, most of the people closest to Minnie were related by blood or marriage. Her playmate Arnett was George Goins's son, though by 1923, at age nine, Arnett was living with his grandmother Sarah. At least a third of the homes in the community held such adoptions, as "older heads" strove to mend family gaps, being forced to weave their own social safety nets.[7] Arnett, adopted like Minnie, knew his grandmother as "Mama," in the way that Minnie knew her own grandmothers as Mama and Papa.

When Minnie went to visit she liked to tussle and wrestle with Arnett. Quiet Arnett was quick with a throwing stick on rabbit hunts in the woods, but he didn't always win their wrestling matches. Stout little Minnie thought of herself as "fighty," a tomboy, not given to petticoat clichés.[8]

"Ironhead" throwing stuck, used by small boys across the South for rabbit hunting in the early twentieth century. (A heavy iron railroad nut was wedged onto a pointed stick for throw weight.)

She was not a cardboard cut-out ready for the fairy-tale version of history. Stubbornly unique, as filled with myster- ies as anyone, Minnie Lee Mitchell was born on the Fourth of July— without fireworks, and with hard times ahead. Her mother Daisy Mitchell did not survive the birth—as happened too often in their wilderness community. The childbed medicines supplied by the community midwife, Mary Ella McCoy, ran to dirt-dauber tea and spiderwebs to stop the bleeding, and could fall a little short.[9]

Just beyond the front yard and down the tracks, Aunt Sarah's house was no mere shanty. Sarah Carrier's half-acre lot was bought December 27, 1899, when her son Sylvester was ten.[10] It had seen many turns, as their fast-changing community reflected the journey of a wild frontier.[11] A number of the houses dotting this frontier were larger than one-story cabins, for abundant lumber afforded second stories This was a frontier not in the Wild West but the Deepest South—at the wild back door to Dixie called Florida.

Florida had become a state only sixteen years before the Civil War, when it looked a bit like a southern Alaska: hardly any people, hardly any apparent worth. "A land of swamps, of quagmires, of frogs and alligators," fumed Senator John Randolph at the admission.[12] Prior to some leaps of technology—notably the automobile and the air conditioner—the "Long Frontier" called Florida languished in the South's spooky basement, a state 900 miles long, 34 million acres vast—and 20 million of those acres were lost in bogs. Minnie was watching the emergence.

Aunt Sarah's house was tailored to the subtropical frontier, with a breezy shotgun hall and an upstairs hotbox mainly for night use, a kind of sleeping loft for children. "One story and a jump," the writer Zora Hurston had said of a house perhaps similar—where Hurston was born 130 miles southeast, on another part of the Long Frontier near Orlando.[13]

Sarah Carrier's house was better than some. An inside staircase, not just a ladder, led up to the sleeping loft. When cousin Arnett went upstairs to bed around 9:00 p.m., he met a nicely slanting banister rail, an angled landing halfway up, a kerosene lamp glowing at the top beside an attic doorway. In earlier years, Sarah's son Sylvester had slept up there, but by custom as a son grew up he might add an annex of his own to the rear. Facing a dogtrot breezeway at the back porch, Sylvester and his wife Gert had their own apartment.[14]

"'A Genius of the South'
Novelist, Folklorist, Anthropologist
1901-1960"
gravestone:
Zora Neale Hurston
born Eatonville, Florida

The resulting appearance could be confusing. If you passed the house in a rattling train coach out on the railroad, peering through drifting locomotive cinders and squinting past the shaggy cabbage palms in the front yard, this house could easily seem to be a full two-story affair. But the family knew the details. The upstairs portion was not broken up by room partitions. Up there, brass-knobbed dressers, gleaming mirrors and iron bedsteads faced white curtains and window glass in one big room, basically a furnished attic, with windows at each end.

The house was like Sarah herself—and her son Sylvester, and Minnie and all of them—a stubborn reminder of life's singularity, not easily packaged into fairy tales.

At Aunt Sarah's house, in all its riddles, the roadmap to atrocity would narrow down. This house would be ground-zero for the thing to come, as Minnie Mitchell met the horror of her ninth year.

"Fighty" Minnie did not forgive overnight, but the problem with Aunt Sarah had seemed to lessen with time. Domineering Aunt Sarah had softened, Minnie thought. And this seemed natural, since the community had gone down. People were moving out. A clique of popular church women used to buoy the spirits of outgoing Sarah Carrier, but now they were gone. Left in the remnant, Aunt Sarah had mellowed toward her remaining family. Or at least, so Minnie decided, without undue meditation. It was not something for a nine-year-old to puzzle over.

Minnie's life focused elsewhere—at the house she knew much better, up the tracks at the picket fence, where she idolized Mama and Papa. Their house, too, had a front porch looking out at the tracks, but from the other side, north of the railroad. There were chicken coops, a smokehouse, a back-porch pump. It was a larger house than Aunt Sarah's (all memories agreed), for Mama's and Papa's house was a full two-story, with room partitions upstairs. A chore that Minnie hated was making the beds upstairs (Mama being strict about the corners). As the little wrestler moved from room to room, grimly intent on rebellious sheets, there was no saying she was in an attic.

When reckoning came to all of this, the community's fate would be so shocking that it seemed to shatter even public perceptions. Private impressions would survive—outside the official silence of courthouse and history—but even there the truth was shattered. Those who did not actually experience the events, and only heard tales, would develop two opposite streams of false myth, in two starkly separated subcultures of believers.[15]

In one stream—among local white believers—the hard-working little place Minnie knew would come to be portrayed as a flimsy squatters' camp, or worse, as a grim outlaws' roost. Meanwhile the other stream began among some African Americans, but later swelled in a wave of re-examination in the 1990s. Then a rush of media fantasy reveresd the old slanders, portraying a miraculous lost paradise in the wilderness, allegedly a full-sized town with thriving businesses. This was as false as the idea of the squatter's camp. Minnie—and all the others with real experience of the place—recalled the in-between reality they knew.

As it stood when she was nine, the community spread across an area that can be plotted on U.S. Geological Survey maps. Two adjoining squares, each a mile wide, were formed by Sections 29 and 30 of Township 14 South, Range 14 East, of Levy County, Florida. Minnie's world was a two-square-mile expanse of scattered farmhouses.[16]

The dawn of 1923 found it arranged as a rural settlement, not a formal municipal unit. There was no downtown, no city limits or mayor or town hall. In better times there had been a start, complete with a town marshal, a one-man police force. But by 1923 the ex-marshal, Old Man John Coleman, was savoring his memories in his house back north in the woods.

As in the old days, the community remained unified by a name, as flowery as Florida. Just down from Aunt Sarah's house a small shed depot faced the railroad, presenting a weathered sign:

ROSEWOOD.

The eight letters held certain depths, shimmering like a two-syllable poem. But one message was obvious. Here was a frontier full of hope, praying for a beautiful flowering.

On its two-mile span of sandy soil, the community was defined by ownership of land. At its farthest western edge, Cornelia Carter cranked her wax-cylinder Victrola on a property of 80 acres.[17] From there the communal cluster spread east for two miles to its opposite margin, just beyond Aaron Carrier's small house, with its water bucket on a cramped back porch.[18][19]

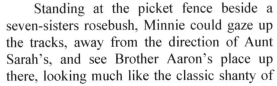

Standing at the picket fence beside a seven-sisters rosebush, Minnie could gaze up the tracks, away from the direction of Aunt Sarah's, and see Brother Aaron's place up there, looking much like the classic shanty of Dixie myth. Farther back, past Mama's chufa field for the hogs, widower Hardee Davis had another small cabin, smokier and mustier than Aaron's. But then back north or west, out of sight in the pines, lived the Halls, the Colemans, the Edwardses—all in two-story houses like Mama's and Papa's, flanked by fruit trees and livestock.

The list of holdings and residents was nuanced, riddled with exceptions, refusing to form an easily characterized pattern. The Halls, for example, lived in a two-story house but not in picture-book prosperity. Inside their grim old saltbox they had fallen onto hard times, and knew the pangs of hunger.[20]

Chufa

There were Carriers, Bradleys, Kings, Gordons, Goinses, Smiths, Haywards, McCoys, others. As distant threads of chimney smoke smudged the horizon, they

nut grass
ground almond
(Cyperus esculentus)

marked out an ancient pattern, that of the rural hamlet. It was bound together by the eight-letter name, by marriage and blood, by frontier necessity—and by one more point in common. All of the families named above, forming the great majority of the community, were African American.

They did not form a very large cluster of humanity, these land-owners, renters, leaseholders and miscellaneous die-hards. Apparently the full two square miles held no more than 22 African American house-holds in all, along with at least three households of whites.

But it was not size on the map that would give historic solemnity to this place.

It was the thing that happened to it.

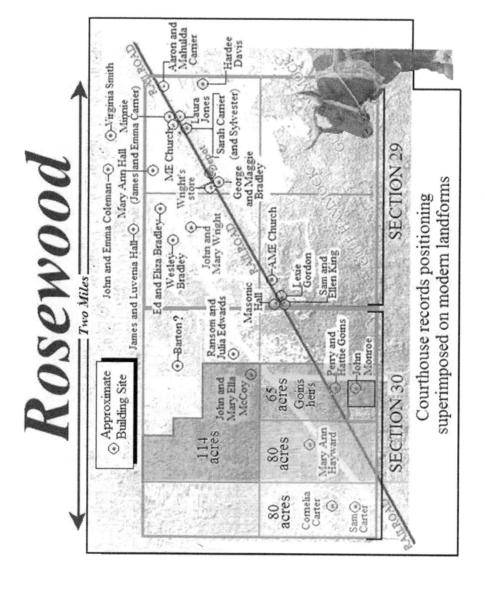

Rosewood

Two Miles

Approximate Building Site

John and Emma Coleman

Virginia Smith

James and Luvenia Hall

Mary Ann Hall
(James and Emma Carrier)

Minnie

Aaron and Mahulda Carrier

Hardee Davis

Laura Jones

Sarah Carrier
(and Sylvester)

ME Church

Wright's store

Depot

George and Maggie Bradley

Ed and Eliza Bradley

Wesley Bradley

John and Mary Wright

Barton?

Ransom and Julia Edwards

Masonic Hall

AME Church

Lexie Gordon

Sam and Ellen King

John and Mary Ella McCoy

114 acres

65 acres

Goins heirs

Perry and Hattie Goins

John Monroe

80 acres

Mary Ann Hayward

80 acres

Cornelia Carter

Sam Carter

RAILROAD

SECTION 30

SECTION 29

Courthouse records positioning superimposed on modern landforms

Chapter 2: The Company Town

Lee Carrier, age 22, is moving briskly through the dark, sure of his footing on familiar ground. The sand lane is clean but barely a ghost beneath his feet, lit by stars. Earlier the moon was nearly full but now is gone, having set at 5:50 a.m., according to the charts. That was around the time Lee was waking up, in a room shared with his cousin Bishop. Now both are striding along, having walked out across an L-shaped porch into pre-dawn starlight.

**Leroy "Lee" Carrier
born 1900 in Rosewood**

Nothing warns that in a few more days, Lee Carrier will be homeless and in flight, as his familiar life ends.

The coming day will be a short one, keeping winter's schedule, with official sunrise not coming until 7:26 a.m.[21] This is the first blush of 1923—dawn on New Year's Day, January 1—at a speck on the map that is Lee Carrier's home, Rosewood.

The pre-dawn temperature is about 56 degrees, Fahrenheit, the records show. Lee does not consider it cold. This looks like an ordinary Monday.

In a later age, an influential published account of the Rosewood events would claim to find cataclysmic weather at Rosewood on this date, January 1, 1923. The account (in 1996) elaborately described a bizarre ice storm encasing the site of the coming atrocity, as if in divine portent. Prefaced by the somber words "This much is known," the description left no doubt that it meant to be taken as historical fact.

And yet the ice storm was fantasy, reminding of the racially-loaded soft spot in public information that has continued to obscure the Rosewood events. False impressions have worked not only during the denial period of the pre-Civil Rights decades but even after modern revelation, as a sensitive subject has spawned excited myths. If a reader of the prestigiously framed ice storm were not acquainted with the testimony of witnesses like Lee Carrier (or the temperature records), there would be few ways to see that the epic weather image was in fact a mirage, part of a psychosocial fogbank blocking the view. [22]

Also at dawn, but in another part of Rosewood, a quarter mile distant, Lee Carrier's nine-year-old cousin, fighty little Minnie Mitchell, may not yet have thrown back the quilts. Downstairs in Mama's kitchen an iron skillet may be clanking and sizzling—bacon, eggs, grits, biscuits, syrup, clabbermilk. Nothing warns of the deep emotional scars about to come to Minnie Mitchell, Lee Carrier and many others—including a mysterious young woman who is not in Rosewood at all, but lives in the place three miles away toward which Lee Carrier is walking.

Lee's rapidly striding form passes a few lighted windows, in homes he knows well. There is no mood of impending crisis, all informants will agree. Today's walk is merely the ordinary hike Lee makes each morning —except, of course, for respites on Sunday.

Sunday, in his six-day work week, is the day to relax, when he can ease over to Old Man John Coleman's house to shoot crack-a-loop on the porch with the boys (that is, flipping pennies at a plank wall to see who can get the closest)—as they turn a skeptical eye toward church folk coming home from the shouting.

On this Monday's pre-dawn walk of nearly three miles. Lee shrugs off the distance. He enjoys these morning walks, with their camaraderie. Other figures emerge from the darkness and join the two cousins Bishop and Lee. A scattered parade begins leaving the home community, moving toward the nearest source of attractive weekly pay.

Their destination is a special kind of place, one more rare creature of the old Florida woods. Places like this were seldom seen by outsiders, and in later times they sank from the popular picture of the past.

2.87 miles

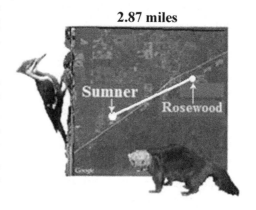

Sumner

Rosewood

The hikers are approaching a sawmill company town. This one is 2.87 miles from the heart of Rosewood, as measured from the Rosewood depot. They are moving toward a company town called Sumner.

Sawmill company towns were prominent from about 1900 into mid-century, as logging grew more mechanized and great forests were consumed. Rural and yet industrial, a company town would sprout suddenly in the wilderness, then as suddenly disappear, once its tracts of trees were gone. The company town of Sumner would live for 15 years, 1911 to 1926. It was built and largely owned by a single corporation, the Cummer Lumber Company.[23] Out of its steam-driven efficiency came perhaps 60,000 board feet of cypress lumber a day, covering acres of ground with planks, posts, beams and boards, in stacks rising more than 15 feet into the humid air.[24]

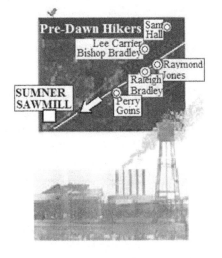

Onto these lumber stacks the Rosewood walkers would climb. Raleigh Bradley, Bishop Bradley, Perry Goins, Raymond Jones—and lately a younger initiate, 15-year-old Sam Hall. Each day, these Rosewood residents had to leave their shrinking remnant community for their work, moved by Saturdays at the pay office and the envelope sliding out through a barred window, proffered by a grouchy bookkeeper.

Not among the walkers is Sarah Carrier's son Sylvester. He has a different kind of job at home, working in the woods on his own. Lee sees his cousin Syl only in the evenings after walking home again. They get along well enough, Lee thinks; he views himself as liking Syl—though with irritated reservations. He finds Sylvester overbearing, bossy. That branch of the Carrier family is always trying to run things, the younger cousin feels. And in terms of Sylvester's mother Sarah, Lee's view is less moderate.

With remarkable force, he despises Sarah Carrier. Etched in his mind is the fateful Christmas years before, when the community seemed to blow apart. As with various others who survived to be informants in later decades, Lee Carrier was personally present at that Christmas pageant in the First A.M.E. Church—a moment of mystery that left the witnesses stunned, as George Goins was made an outcast and his brother Charlie a haunted fugitive. Angry rumors would be left to surround Sarah Carrier, George's mother-in-law. The blow had come so suddenly, so senselessly, that the community kept trying to puzzle it out, and there was talk about a curse.

Born in 1900, Lee Carrier started sawmill work as a child. The old mill in his community had still been running then, with its enticingly sweet smell. A specialized sawmill, it processed the aromatic wood of the swamp cedar, *Juniperus virginiana.*

Juniperus virginiana

Swamp Cedar
Red Juniper
Eastern Red Cedar
Pencil Cedar
Aromatic Cedar

Lee saw the last of those times, at a point when he was still so small that he was put to work catching cedar blocks flying down from a hopper. The heyday of Florida's coastal cedar boom was in the 1880s, when great cedar groves had darkened these lost shores, as if in the Black Forest of Hansel and Gretel. But by 1910, completing the witch's spell, the great groves were gone, clear-cut nearly to extinction.

THIRTEENTH CENSUS OF THE U

Leroy "Lee" Carrier in the Federal Census of 1910

The old sawmill that had stood in Rosewood was a relic from a vanished century, using ox and mule technology to extract logs from the swamps, rather than rails and steam as done by later Sumner. Still, the old Rosewood ghost had been like the later and larger operation at Sumner in one way. It was brief. There was Rule One of the timber booms: No timber town is forever, because its tract of trees will end.[25]

By August 1911 the Rosewood cedar mill was disassembled, its embarrassed old chutes and saws sold at auction.[26] An ox-and-mule community then stood marooned. Most of Rosewood's white residents moved out. More of its African American residents read a different kind of writing on the wall. Some owned land. They had something here. They hung on.

And thus it emerged—this last stand by the holdouts, an island of self-reliance—in its racial tightrope act, balancing over the abyss. Pressures on the dwindling hamlet rebounded within, as neighbor-on-neighbor feuds arose. Bursts of violent mystery lodged in record and reminiscence. There were not only shootings—as at church on that fatal Christmas—but also the other old standard of neighborly feuds: arson.

At Rosewood over the years after 1911, intentionally set fires struck at least two different churches, and by some accounts struck the community's school. Underlying rancors and perpetrators were seldom paraded in public, but no one blamed surrounding whites (who had their own feuds, duels and mysteries to occupy them). On a dangerous frontier, documents and memories captured only cryptic flashes of Rosewood's internal eruptions, often without explanation as to the tensions behind the acts. The Goins-Carrier incident at Christmas was verified by no known surviving document, although massively agreeing witness accounts left no doubt that it occurred. Here, too, was the power of a corroborated witness pool. If only paper sources were to be used to plot the history of Rosewood, and the labyrinth of living memory were to be shunned for its inconvenience, a turning point in communal life would be left outside the frame.

As Rosewood consolidated into a remnant community after 1911, whites in the surrounding woods looked on through the tunnel vision of the deepening segregation years. One captured the mood: "There was nigger houses all over these woods. Very few white people that lived up here. Everybody else had left because there wasn't anything goin' on... Moved to Sumner..."[27]

As Lee Carrier grew up, his life would straddle the divide between the old Rosewood, with its cedar mill and ox teams, and the new island of beleaguered independence. He moved up to a man's work, but could do so only by commuting to the new company town next door. In 1911, just as the Rosewood cedar mill died, its heir, bringing newer technology and going after a different species of tree, was springing up three miles away. The big Sumner sawmill, swelling like Oz out of sawbriars and rattlesnakes, formed a fortress of tram tracks, steam boilers and electric lights. Its house-sized steam skidders rolled out on rails into previously inaccessible citadels of jungle. They harvested not cedar but old-growth cypress, *Taxodium distichum,* the primeval giants of the deepest swamps. The new tools could root out these aquatic behemoths. And Sumner's saws waited to slice them up. Lee made his peace with the three-mile walk.

Bald Cypress,
Southern Cypress,
Tidewater Cypress

He would be a tireless worker all his life—though on the pre-dawn hikes he could still dream. If only he could have been like Old Man Coleman, a man of the real frontier days, back when the woods were still mighty—when they were not chewed up and hunted over as Lee found them. As far as the young admirer could see, Coleman had made his entire living off hunting and trapping—not just subsistence hunting but hard cash. A trapper in those days could stay busy in the Great Gulf Hammock, the fabled wilderness just behind Sylvester's house. More than five thousand acres of hanging moss and canopied rain forest cloaked a maze of swamps along the Gulf of Mexico: dangling air plants, cascading resurrection ferns, wild hogs in the palmetto clumps, sinkhole bass, panther, bear.[28] Coleman's day had produced professional hunters working for the commercial market. One such pair (whites in this case, with more range of motion than Coleman) had claimed to kill 1,300 deer over the course of two March-September seasons, sounding like the buffalo hunts of the Great Plains.[29]

Soon, as with the cedars, so went the game. After Coleman's generation it was severely thinned out.

In Lee's wistful view, it seemed the old man had never had to do a lick of time-clock work in his life. Hides and pelts seemed to have done the whole job of buying Coleman's acreage—and his two-story house, not poorly furnished, as all agreed. Even in 1921 (not far from the coming cataclysm), the Levy County tax rolls found the old hunter still owning a special possession—a prized hunting dog, pricey enough to be assessed at the courthouse. Like a ghost from the mists, the older man stood at the closing door, owning something more than a dog, something invisible that the younger man could only imagine. True, he had played his part in the destruction—but the ghost seemed to live on in him. When they shot crack-a-loop on Sundays, the wary old trapper usually won.

1921 tax roll – John Coleman's prized dog

Leaving the sand lane in the pre-dawn darkness, Lee's walking form veered onto the railroad. The tracks of the Seaboard Air Line led the band of walkers southwest through open country, toward the Gulf of Mexico six miles away. But long before any hint of salt breezes they would veer again, to the right, following a side track built for the log train of the Cummer Lumber Company. Sumner lay just off the main rail line, tucked into scrub to the north.

They thought little about Sumner's name, nor about the strange background hum in which it floated, a dream-like babble of wilderness rhymes. Cummer-Lumber-Company's-Sumner. The Humpty-Dumpty cadence went unremarked. It was happenstance—as familiar and uncontemplated as the one-word poem wedged into their own community's name. These were just accidents, freaks of the wild frontier.

Also incidental, as far as the walkers were concerned, was the calendar position of this particular Monday. This was New Year's Day, 1923. In many parts of America, folks were taking a holiday from toil. Across the South, ritual meals featured Hoppin' John or black-eyed peas for New Year's good luck. Even in towns rather nearby, just outside the great swamps and hammocklands known to Lee, some shops were closed for this day. But the deeper mystery land, home to the big trees and the company towns, had another set of rules. On New Year's Day you worked. No excuses about having stayed up last night to ring in the new—with a fruit jar of moonshine or, often, a hymn book. Many people in the wild places did do these things, either spending midnight in church (the New Year's "watchnight" service), or, less piously, going out at midnight with a festive firearm to blast drunkenly up at the moon. But neither kind of celebrant got a free pass from work the next morning.

The walkers—at least six of them—were soon passing buildings, entering Sumner. Nothing seemed amiss. All was quiet. Other men, a much larger number of them who lived in Sumner itself, were now leaving their homes to converge on the mill—in answer to a summons.

Perched high atop the mill's peaked roof was a squat metal gargoyle, a cylindrical steam whistle emitting a thunderous roar. At least six times each work day the whistle cord would be yanked. The first blast came well before dawn—not as a signal to the men but to their wives, the first shock troops in the day's battle of saws and log chains. The pre-dawn whistle called wives (and some sisters and mothers) to wake and stoke kindling into wood stoves, so the men could be fortified with breakfast. The moan of Sumner's whistle, as with many a big-city textile mill and foundry in those same years, could be heard for miles. Seeping across pine flats and bayhead thickets, it was faintly audible in Rosewood.[30]

As the walkers arrived, most of the men coming into the mill were African American like themselves. But the others lived inside Sumner, in a company-owned compound. This was Sumner's "quarters," made up of shanties, a larger barracks and a secluded, weatherbeaten dance hall.

By 1923 the racial division seen in Sumner's layout was part of a fixed tradition. A sawmill company town in Florida was going to have a large, racially segregated quarters for African American manual labor. And, sharply set apart, there would be a less populous area with better equipped homes in a smaller quarters. This other quarters was for foremen and skilled labor, who, by strict rule, could only be white.

In 1896 a U.S. Supreme Court decision had paved the way for a thousand-mile experiment that would cover the American South. The result, a regional system of social control, would last for three-quarters of a century, into the 1970s. This was "Jim Crow" racial segregation, built piecemeal as southern states passed many separate racial laws.[31]

In Sumner, where racial division showed starkly, there was no political fig-leaf claiming "separate but equal" treatment. It was understood that a black worker could not be promoted to foreman. Occasional whites might perform manual labor in mostly black crews, but African American laborers were forbidden to move up.

Cummer Lumber Company's Sumner
(author of map unrecorded)

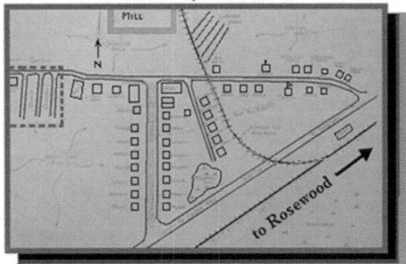

This hand-drawn map of Sumner as it stood in 1923 was apparently prepared for the Rosewood claims case of 1991-1994, though afterwards it was left unlabeled in a seldom-opened archive box. As publicity quickly faded, evidence in the claims case met no systematic attempt at preservation. The map (perhaps drawn from the near-encyclopedic memories of former Sumner resident Ernest Parham) became almost a throwaway.

*Sumner's African American quarters (**dotted line**) may have been larger than the map shows, for it held the majority of the company town's population, consisting of black sawmill laborers and their families. All of the **bold black lines** are imposed on the original map for clarity. Pencil markings in the original can still be seen faintly. The **curved line** is the sidetrack on which the Monday hikers entered Sumner from Rosewood.*

(Box 4, Exhibit 3, FAMU, Southeastern Regional Black Archives)

As dawn neared on Monday morning, January 1, 1923, hundreds of men were answering the Sumner whistle. Only a small percentage were white, holding better jobs as foremen or skilled craftsmen like carpenters or blacksmiths. Emerging from a quiet residential section laid out along a single north-south street, these whites defined Sumner's intermediate social tier. They were not the highest management, for the top brass lived just east in a few larger homes. The north-south quarters street was more modest in appearance.

At this street's lonely south end, and on the east side, stood a four-room house. It was much like the other four-room houses in the row: a back-porch faucet, a kitchen safe for blocks of delivered ice, floorboards bare but clean, a wood stove with a lifter handle for hot metal lids.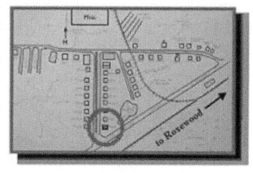

Exiled to the fringe of Sumner's activity, this house was the subject of some neighborhood gossip, but only faintly. People wondered about the young woman inside.

––––––––––––

The crucial house was not on Lee Carrier's route as he walked to the mill. By following the log train's sidetrack he moved at an angle to the white quarters street. The track, running northwest, and the quarters street, running due north-south, came close to meeting at Sumner's nerve center near the mill. This center was as much as a quarter mile from the south end of the street, where the unobtrusive house kept vigil.

The geography meant that out on the track, Lee and the other hikers had no sight line to the white quarters street. Even if there had been no intervening bushes and trees, the back fences of the quarters would have blocked the view. By chaotic chance at the beginning of a chaotic week, Lee Carrier narrowly missed being in the wrong place at the wrong time. The area of the ho use was about to become dangerous ground.

But Lee's good luck was a bad break for the prying eyes of posterity. Here was a careful, deliberative witness, and he had no view of the opening act in the play—a common difficulty in the examination of crowd events. Rare is the direct observer of the cataclysmic moment: the plunge of the knife, the tossed match, the squeezed trigger. There may be detailed and persuasive reports, but concerning things that are off to one side, or after the fact, or only overheard in passing. [32]

Core moments in a mob incident may be oddly intimate and unshared—screened by turmoil in a mass of distracted observers. The crowd event becomes a magician, camouflaging its secrets, gesturing grandly with feints and passes of the left hand—while, unseen in the commotion, there are the decisive tiny movements of the right.

The multiplicity of Rosewood informants again becomes important, narrowing the blind spots.

Minnie Lee Mitchell
ca. 1922

And not all would be left in the wings. A few—like Minnie Lee Mitchell—would live with memories of having stared point-blank into the hurricane's eye.

Minnie Lee Langley *
1994

Chapter 3: The Spark

*"The dream is the truth...
Then they act and do
things accordingly."*
—Zora Neale Hurston

The young woman in the last house on the street was not a social butterfly. In Sumner's white quarters she was more of a question mark—one more minor curiosity.

Her physical appearance seemed ordinary enough, at least according to the neighbors who knew her best—though others would grow more imaginative. The Rosewood week would lift this mysterious young housewife into the halls of local legend, and there she would have many faces.

After the January disaster, as traumatized residents of Rosewood fled to distant places, the image of the woman in the last house would haunt them—causing some to rework that image. Not all Rosewood survivors developed consoling stories about her (some, like Minnie Mitchell/Langley and Lee Carrier, seemed to feel no need), but believers did emerge. And as fate would have it, such beliefs would be the ones selected by larger belief in the publicity surrounding the Rosewood claims case of 1991-1994, as it made national news. Beforehand, the reworkings of her portrait had lived in private tellings that seemed to offer a kind of post-traumatic relief. But that was only among a few tellers, speaking to a few hearers. The 1990s spotlight seemed to find the drama in such stories so enthralling that it endorsed them as fact. Then, what might be called traumatic rescripting—or redemptive belief— swelled to reach out and persuade a national audience. A comforting screen of myth was provided not just for a few, but for society.

Her unremarkable appearance seemed to go like this: brown hair, rather thin, height about five-six.[33] Neither warts nor wonders were noticed by her real acquaintances—though one of them (a white child witness, not among the most reliable on some other points) recalled being disturbed by a coarse habit in the young woman, reminding of a hard-luck background. This story said that sometimes her lower lip bulged over a hidden lump, as she absorbed doses of nicotine the old-fashioned way, by dipping snuff.

As the moon went down at 5:50 a.m. on New Year's morning, 1923, her end house was left in January darkness, deepened by the silence of a winter's night, with no roar of frogs or insects, unlike raucous summer serenades. Thus she moved into a new year. She was 21.

Already married for a half-decade, she had two small children with her in the house, a toddler and an infant, both boys. Around the time the moon was going down, perhaps earlier, her husband, age 26, had risen in the dark. This was his usual way, for he worked a skewed shift at the mill. Moving out across the front yard and reaching a chest-high board fence, he opened the front gate, then turned onto a plank walk, walking north up the street. His wife was left behind with the sleeping children.

For a young mother this could be a stressful phase of life, when the three-year-old is into everything, but the infant still has to be watched. Two doors north in 1921, a devastating case of crib death had occurred, taking an infant only a few weeks old. Any mother nearby might naturally have some worries—though generally the street was quiet. Few Model T's came bouncing over the sawdust that paved the wide, carefully surveyed street, which tapered off toward thickets past her house. An occasional peddler's wagon might rattle by, as a farmer from the woods sold meat or produce to wives of the quarters personnel.

On toward 7:00 a.m. that Monday morning, multiple boots began sounding on the plank walk. White male residents up and down the street were going to the main shift, called by the roaring whistle. These were good jobs, the ones held by men on this street, foreman-level posts reserved for whites. However, the street's look of weathered stability covered a rootless truth. The street itself was a transient ghost, doomed as soon as it was born—for all the infrastructure of corporate Sumner—down to the house planks and water pipes—would be pried up, piled onto railroad flatcars and taken away. The removal would be complete by 1926, as Cummer Lumber move its operations to a new tract of virgin timber three counties away.

So there she was—in a more secure position than many people out in the woods, though not by much. As a child, the young housewife had apparently known painful poverty. By age 21 she was installed in the timber culture and its rural-industrial trade-offs. Other housewives up and down the street seemed to adapt sturdily to the movements of mill and crew, but there were doubts about this young neighbor. She was not a flamboyant caricature in her differences, but neither was she typical. She seemed nervous, stand-offish, aloof from the rest.[34]

At the edge of Sumner's small dot of civilization, her outrider residence was closely flanked by swamp, where small aquatic cypress trees grew too scrubby for the mill, but still erected a wall of gloom. Just beneath the sandy soil of the coastal jungles, enormous limestone catacombs could suddenly collapse, swallowing the surface soil. A shallow sinkhole had created the cypress pond at her back gate. Children from the four-room houses would wade out into the pond to catch minnows, though the mass of foliage covering the water hid deep shadows. Wild things were said to prowl out at night and steal chickens from yards in the quarters. Backed by this wall of darkness, she slept.[35]

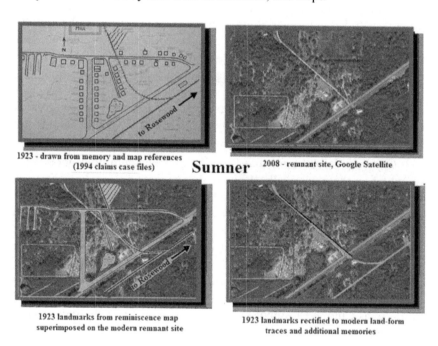

1923 - drawn from memory and map references
(1994 claims case files)

Sumner

2008 - remnant site, Google Satellite

1923 landmarks from reminiscence map
superimposed on the modern remnant site

1923 landmarks rectified to modern land-form
traces and additional memories

On October 4, 1922, she had borne her second child, three months before the fateful New Year's Day. As Monday approached, the infant was in a crib in a dark room. Whether there had been post-partum depression was one of many questions not publicly explored.

However, some form of psychological vulnerability was present. Whether it was germane to the coming emergency was another question.

The neighbors, at least, seemed to draw no connection between the two—between her puzzling ways and the crisis soon to come. She was a little strange, yes; but that was incidental. Such was the feeling.

Perhaps not even Dr. Augustus B. Cannon, the sawmill company doctor who lived near the head of the street, would have hazarded a psychological diagnosis. She was "peculiar, kind of," said a former neighbor, Frances Smith—offering the judgment reluctantly, meaning no disrespect. The phrasing was remarkably similar in two such descriptions, as separate witnesses struggled to describe the young wife's strangeness.[36] They liked her, they said, and would visit her, but other women kept their distance, feeling the young neighbor was "selfish"—or unneighborly, irritatingly withdrawn.

Apparently her four rooms and her sandy yard formed most of her world, guarded by the chest-high fence. One account, perhaps overblown, described neighbor children teasing her, tightroping along her fence-top and pulling leaves off her shrubs, just to taunt her—as they grew provoked in some way by her testy nervousness. The reality may have been less dramatic.

Up at the head of the street, past Doc Cannon's—too far to see from her house—an electric bulb is now glowing in the Monday moment before dawn. It lights the inside of the commissary, the sawmill's company store. The young clerk in there, Ernest Parham, is a keen observer. He does not know the young woman well, but, like closer neighbors, he has formed impressions. These will go with him into a far future age—when, still spry in his nineties, Parham will speak for the record.

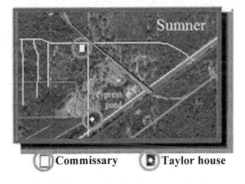

Commissary   Taylor house

He notices that the young housewife does not seem to appear in church (where he is the bell ringer, pulling the steeple rope). He sees her family's grocery shopping done at the commissary, but it seems to be conducted only by her husband, alone. This is a striking departure from the strict gender roles in the company town. The young wife is an absence, an unknown quantity, seemingly shut away from the world.

Parham once had occasion to go down there, chugging along in the commissary's stake-bed truck, delivering ice from the refrigeration machine at the sawmill, run off steam boilers. It was a routine ice delivery, one of the perks offered by the mill to the white quarters. She was polite. Opening the door, she showed him to the kitchen, where the big block of ice would go into the waiting icebox, safely separated from the wood stove. She was quiet, not saying much. Parham felt apologetic walking across her floor, it looked so clean.

In itself there was nothing special about a modest house in the woodlands having a scrubbed and bleached floor. But this particular floor seemed to draw attention. Neighbor Frances Smith also remarked on it, calling it the whitest, most bleached floor she'd ever seen, bleached white as bone. The young woman's four-room refuge seemed to be immaculate. But within it, a positive side of her appeared—according to the same two neighbor women who found her "peculiar." If you'd just go in there and take the time to get to know her, said both (in much the same way, though in independent conversations), she would open up and be nice as could be.

These neighbors had never heard of panic disorder, or its sometime correlate called agoraphobia, meaning a fear of leaving one's home and going into public places.[37] The panic attacks that can accompany panic disorder have been described concretely by a sufferer: "[The] fear can be so intense that you feel like you're going to die. Your pulse races, your heart pounds, you find it hard to breathe. You might even pass out."[38] In the narrower sub-category, agoraphobia, it's not unusual for outsiders to sometimes penetrate the sanctum of a housebound agoraphobic and express surprise. They sometimes marvel that the person shut up in there isn't so crazy after all, but seems nice as can be.

Perhaps none of this was relevant to the "nervous" young woman at the end of the street.

Born Fannie Coleman, she had grown up in the home of a transient laborer just after the turn of the century. Her marriage to young James Henry Taylor came on April 23, 1917, when she was younger than 17—and at a point less than a month after America entered World War I. Her new husband was apparently not called.

By everyone's description, James Taylor was a likeable young man—calm, easy to get along with, friendly and considerate—and with a secure future.[39] He was a millwright, a carpenter who repaired and built sawmills. Growing up in Levy County, he was hired at some point after marriage by Cummer Lumber, one of the largest corporations in 1920s Florida, for carpentry at their sawmill outpost in Sumner. This had put the young couple in their four-room, company-owned residence, with its cold running water in the back-porch sink, its stove wood and ice delivered from the mill—and even free sawdust to mulch the flowers, if you wanted it. There seemed to be no great fuss as a dark new year's morning crept toward dawn.

Two doors north at this moment, Frances Smith is dressing for work. Suddenly her attention is distracted. There is a sound.

Five years older than Fannie Taylor (and bearing a confusingly similar first name), Frances is assistant bookkeeper at the sawmill. In later life she will run a store. Living energetically past age 89, she will be found in 1982 in another sawmill company town, there to meet the prying eyes of posterity.

As Frances dresses on New Year's morning, 1923, a kerosene lamp is glowing. The Sumner mill's electric generator feeds streetlamps outside, looming over the street, but the wires don't reach into the quarters houses. To the northeast, the bungalow home of the top boss, superintendent Walter Pillsbury, does have electric lights, but in the lower social tier on the quarters street, luxuries are limited to another item. Through pipes under the street, the luxury of running water (cold only) is driven to the houses by gravity pressure in the mill's water tower.

Frances expects an ordinary Monday. If last night she made any kind of celebration for New Year's Eve with her husband, C. C. Smith, a mill oiler, it would escape later mention. This morning she expects to walk as usual up to the sawmill's business office near the commissary, and to follow orders given by the head bookkeeper, a man named Hill, not famed for social graces. Nearby, however, the chair of the bigger boss, Pillsbury, holds a nicer presence.[40] The dynamic but scrupulously ethical Walter Pillsbury seems to leave admiring recollections on all sides. The pay window in the office has

31

bars on it like a jail—and once in the past Pillsbury heard rumors that a hold-up was planned—but security is relaxed. A five-thousand dollar payroll might come off the train in a strongbox and then be counted in the office, with never a move to lock the door. At home this morning before work, Frances knows that her own door is in the same state, always unlocked.

She feels no fear as she stops for a moment in her morning routine, and wonders about the strange new sound.

By this point her husband and other men living on the street have gone to work. On this everyone will agree. When the moment of excitement arrives, only women and children are left in the houses. The layout of the company town is such that few industrial sounds intrude on the placid quarters. A pine grove screens out noise from the mill. Only if a particularly large or stubborn log resists the big saw does the quarters hear a scream—and even then faintly, like a blue jay's cry, or a lord-god drumming on a distant tree. This, indeed, was how the strange sound seemed at first, like some wild thing out in the woods.

Frances ventures out onto the porch, straining to form an impression from elusive cues. The sound is high-pitched, sharp. Then comes a visible form, pale in the poor light, just south. The movement is indistinct against the sawdust paving of the street. With a shock, Frances realizes that her neighbor, young Fannie Taylor, has run outside.

Interviewed six decades later, the former assistant bookkeeper had to be coaxed to continue the description. Fannie was crying out—but *what*, exactly, was she crying? Was she uttering words? When pressed for an answer, the 89-year-old narrator raised her eyebrows, still reluctant, and replied: *"A nigger! A nigger!"*

Thus it came. The 21-year-old occupant of the end house was crying out that she had been attacked by a black man—a stranger, she gasped, someone she had never seen before.

Her home stood less than a quarter mile north of the main line of the Seaboard railroad, where a freight train passed each day, aside from the nightly passenger train. Even so near the ends of the earth, at the meeting of swamp and Gulf, hobos riding the rails were a common sight, circuiting the timber jobs. And some of the hobos were Negroes. No one in Sumner seemed to remember any instance of such a drifter growing so bold as to break into the white quarters, but fear was in the air.

Only a month previously, on December 2, 1922, shocking news had come from another sawmill town, Perry, Florida, ninety miles northwest. A young white schoolteacher, Ruby Hendry, had been walking into Perry from her sister's outlying residence and crossed a low railroad trestle in isolated woods. She was found later that day with her throat slashed, the corpse badly battered. A massive manhunt became a racial frenzy. Clues at the scene were said to point to an assault by a black hobo, allegedly camping under the trestle. As whites flocked to the search for the assailant, at least three gruesome deaths of African Americans would occur, and buildings associated with black residents were burned. The event period would neatly cover a week, December 2–8, 1922. News from Perry raced across Florida by telephone and telegraph, reaching even the fastness of Sumner, coming in newspapers brought by train.

More generally, racial tensions had increased throughout the years surrounding World War I, for reasons as various as war fever, wartime labor shortages and black migration. Once more, the South's stormy experiment in racial segregation, begun in the late 1800s, had gone through a sub-phase, as racial violence peaked in 1919's "Red Summer" just after the war. With many of its outbreaks in the changing North, this was called the nation's worst period to date of urban race riots and lynching rampages, a poignant aftershock of "the war to end all wars." Newspaper headlines of the period took an older phrase to new heights, anointing eruptions of mob violence as "race wars," with an implication of national emergency, warfare in the streets.

Whether at the panoramic national level or the most local level in a weathered sawmill quarters at the ends of the earth, a wave of uncertainty was building toward the shock of New Year's Day, 1923.

In Sumner's white quarters, no one was so eccentric as to fear attack from the more populous black quarters of the company town. That concentration of African Americans was barely a stone's throw from the white quarters street, but few tensions were noticed. To both blacks and whites, the Monday emergency seemed to come out of nowhere.

The dramatic eyewitness account of that morning given by neighbor Frances Smith carries the customary witness baggage, the question of credibility. At age 89, how accurate were recollections six decades old, and formed during great excitement? This informant spoke crisply, with the appearance of alert precision, though she also spoke reluctantly when it came to the disturbing core events. On some points she was confirmed closely by other witnesses—but on some she was disconcertingly disputed. The contradictions were mostly on non-essential background details, but there were other shadows in Smith's telling, things harder to pin down, but still reminding that memory, as the courtroom experts like to say, is not a video camera.

For instance, Smith recalled that, upon seeing Fannie's distress, she resourcefully pulled a pistol from a drawer and took charge of the situation, rushing out with the gun as Fannie pleaded, *"My baby! Somebody save my baby!"* No one else would recall hearing of such daring intervention.

It was widely agreed that Fannie, the panic-stricken figure in the street, was so traumatized that soon she lost consciousness, though she managed to convey the bare outlines of a story. A black man had burst into the house after her husband had gone, she said; then he had knocked her to the floor to silence her. She seemed to describe an assault without a sexual motive, a reckless home invasion, as if in search of money, or just looking for food.

Hearing this while holding the pistol, Smith said, she gathered her wits and dashed into the Taylor house, not knowing whether the fearsome attacker was still in there. She said she quickly found little Addis Taylor, Fannie's baby, lying safely in his crib, whereupon she scooped him up and ran back outside with him.

All quite possible. But others, neighbors but not direct eyewitnesses like Smith, expressed doubts. They said that not only had they never heard of such a feat, but it didn't sound much like the personality of the quiet assistant bookkeeper they knew.[41] Was this anecdote an intrusion, one of the mystifying daydreams that can haunt very advanced age? Did it elevate an unwitting dreamer to a position of masterful control?

This difficult and perhaps unfair question fails to matter in one sense. No one disputed the bare fact that Smith was there. And by being there—in whatever role—she illuminates a question: Who, or where, was the attacker of Fannie Taylor? Answer: No one seemed to know.

Smith said that as she moved to Fannie's aid other women were coming out onto their porches, also drawn by the cries. According to the assistant bookkeeper, it was still dark or barely getting light. This, too, is puzzling, because the sawmill whistle was said to be timed to maximize the daylight hours of a short winter day, and the men were long gone. The timing of their absence seems to confirm that the reported home invasion would have happened in full light. But either way, a basic point remains. Whatever the hour, everyone agreed that the white neighbor women saw only Fannie—that they saw neither the attacker nor the attack.

Soon newspaper accounts, the only surviving written record of the moment, would construct a tighter scenario. The first adjustment would be almost unnoticeable: "Her screams after a time brought housewives in the neighborhood and the Negro escaped."[42] From such generality, impressions would grow that the brave ladies must have caught him in the act, driving him off. If so, then they would naturally have caught sight of him—confirming that he existed at all.

Any alternative explanation, asking whether Fannie's distress might have had some other kind of root, apparently was not contemplated by whites at the scene, perhaps simply for reasons of overwhelming evidence. On the one hand, those observers could easily have been influenced by excitement, but they also had access to details beyond the reach of later examination. At any rate, doubts did grow. As the week wore on and excitement led to catastrophe, skepticism toward Fannie Taylor's story would appear—especially as the intruder himself proved impossible to verify, seeming to disappear into the nothingness from which he had come.

The maze grows deep here—its shadow-play no easy caricature. The "obvious" answer may already be occurring to the reader—as it did to hurried or impassioned interpreters during the Rosewood claims case excitement of the 1990s. That obvious answer almost cries out to the shocked audience—focusing attention away from the magician's other hand.

Chapter 4: The News

The story of Fannie Taylor's distress took only a day to reach a wider audience, as it became published news. By Tuesday morning, January 2, it was greeting readers of urban newspapers across an area more than 200 miles wide.

Even this early in the events, a pattern of misleading media images was taking shape, to worsen as the week of violence worsened. No one dreamed, however, that such a process of false publicity might continue to echo much farther, into a far future age—our own age—when new bursts of media fantasy have fed off the old racial mysteries.

As the long parade was just beginning, on January 2, 1923, the first depiction could be seen in Jacksonville, the largest city of 1923 Florida, some 120 miles from the action described. The glimpse appeared on page eight of the *Florida Times-Union*, the Jacksonville-based newspaper which at that time was perhaps the most influential in the state:

YOUNG WIFE

ASSAULTED BY

NEGRO BRUTE

Cedar Key, Jan. 1—The young wife of a respectable white man of Sumner, a mill town, was brutally assaulted at an early hour this morning just after her husband had left for his work in the Cummer cypress mill only a short distance from the house. A knock brought the young lady to the door. She was knocked down by a burly negro and otherwise assaulted. Her screams brought the ladies of the neighborhood to her assistance....[43]

This drama has a remarkable lack of names. As if in a Greek tragedy, the players wear masks. The "respectable white man" (almost more prominent than the victim herself) co-stars with the "YOUNG WIFE," as they face off against the Evil One, played handily by the "BLACK BRUTE." There is even a Greek chorus of sorts, murmuring upstage: those stalwart "ladies of the neighborhood."

On the facing page in the *Times Union* that day, a cafeteria ad was caged in a bold black box, demanding attention as it promised service by black waiters: "BOYS TO CARRY YOUR TRAY." The visual coupling of "BLACK BRUTE" and "BOYS" on the double-page spread served as a blunt reminder. Daily newspapers in 1923 Florida aimed only at readers of one race.

As to concrete details on the Fannie Taylor incident, there were few. The story's dateline, "Cedar Key," supposedly told where the information had been gathered—but no actual reporter from Jacksonville seemed to have strayed into that far-flung boondock. Marooned on the swampy edge of the Gulf, Cedar Key was a decaying little port left from the cedar boom of the 1880s. Its strategic value in the news story was that it stood only about six miles from Sumner.

By about 1900-1910, once the area's cedar forests had been cut and new rail lines had bypassed the swamps, Cedar Key was left in quaint isolation, shrinking to a population of about a thousand by 1923. But, still clinging to a tidal island just offshore, it retained one claim to glory, continuing to serve as the Gulf terminus for the old rail line that ran through Rosewood and Sumner. Cedar Key's link to the mainland was formed by a series of low railroad trestles.

And above the rails ran a Southern Bell telephone wire. The few phones along the tracks were tied to this wire—a party line, meaning that everyone could listen in on everyone else—while all of the phones were tied to a central operator, who sat in Cedar Key.

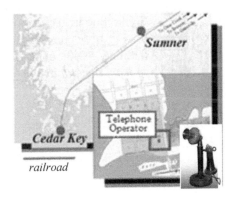

Long-distance calls made from Sumner—or from the one phone in Rosewood (at John

Wright's store)—had to run out to Cedar Key and its operator before they could be bounced back inland to the larger world.

It was a cozy set-up. The operator's plug-in switchboard hummed and crackled in her living room, where family members might jump to answer the magneto bell. There were no blinking plug lights, for the Cedar Key operator's cockpit was antique even by 1923 standards.[44] This was offset by intimacy. Neighbors who had no phone might come over and sit on the porch while their call requests went through.

In the Rosewood events, the arrangement would be more than a colorful detail. The Cedar Key operator (whose name neither reminiscence nor record preserved) was to become an amplifier—and distorter—of shocking images carried by her words of alarm.

A gossip center like the Cedar Key switchboard was well-suited to producing tips for newspapers. The operator had both the means to detect sensational intelligence and a tool for direct contact with distant newsrooms. In another part of frontier Florida, down the Gulf coast a bit in Bradenton, such a telephone operator had for years served as a sort of town crier. If a call came in with a fire alarm, she would reach outside her window and yank a rope, ringing the town's fire bell.[45]

Early telephone operator in Florida
(This was in 1902, but isolated
Cedar Key at this level in 1923)
photo: General Telephone Co. of Florida

In 1923, even if a newsroom rewrite man were to be far up the line in Jacksonville, he would find it no great trouble to ring up Cedar Key, thus to flavor his story with a local dateline—without having to directly say: *"Flash: This just in from our gabby operator, eavesdropping in Cedar Key."*

"A lie would make no sense
unless the truth were felt
dangerous."
—Alfred Adler

Chapter 5: Toil and Trouble

Because it's Monday, the old washerwoman
is due. On January 1, 1923, this is simply a
detail in the background. The white quarters
in Sumner, Florida, is focused elsewhere, on
an urgent alarm.

Across the early twentieth-century South, many housewives
took Monday as their washday, and two such lived in Sumner's white
quarters, where they contracted out the labor. A familiar figure could be
seen on Monday mornings, arriving at an outdoor washpot.

This washerwoman, an African American, seemed to some whites
to be a simple soul, her private life almost unknown to them. By week's
end she would be a tragic central figure in the Rosewood events.

On her weekly visits—always on Monday—this employee appeared
on foot out of blackjack scrub east of the Sumner quarters. Skirting the
wooded shallows of the cypress pond, she arrived at an open spot near a
back fence. There she broke kindling wood, then wedged the sticks into

growing flames, heating a black pot on a smoky fire. For
water she came through the back gate of an employer,
crossed the planks of a back porch and twisted a faucet
handle, thus filling a metal tub—for double duty. The
washing was done for the two households at once, as
sawmill paychecks enabled a life-changing convenience.

The two Monday employers lived nearly side by side, separated by
only one other residence. The washing was performed for Frances Smith,
the sawmill's assistant bookkeeper, and for her shy young neighbor,
Fannie Taylor.

The cost of the service was fifty cents a week, Smith would recall.
The laundress's total take, seemingly a dollar each Monday from the
two, could be compared to $1.75 a day paid to lumber stackers like Lee
Carrier—or, on the bottom tier of wages for men in the timber jobs,
perhaps a dollar a day for turpentine workers harvesting pine resin in
shadowy camps, like the camp on the other side of Rosewood.[46]

Sumner: quarters street for whites
(Buildings are magnified)

Over the years since 1911, when Sumner's white quarters had risen with the rest of the company town, daily life had carved out a lived-in appearance. Originally painted a stolid barn-red, the quarters houses had weathered toward gray. Fast-growing little eucalyptus trees had been planted, maturing to offer a little shade. Even the plank fence beside the Monday washerwoman told a tale.

Up until 1919 and the end of World War I, Sumner had been a different kind of place, an older-style frontier sawmill redoubt, not overly concerned about looking civilized. A rumpled bachelor mill boss had slept in a crude cabin, perhaps with the usual cans of kerosene cupping the bedposts of his cot, to keep crawling pests out of the sheets. Loose hogs had roamed muddy lanes, wallowing under the four-room houses and sending swarms of fleas up through the floors.

But as war pressures had eased in 1919, the nation at large was changing. In Jacksonville, 120 miles northeast, the millionaire Cummer brothers who owned Sumner had decided to dispatch a new kind of boss to run their jungle fortress. The energetic clean-up man was an old college chum of the Cummers, from years past in Michigan. This was the pensive, pipe-smoking administrator who still ruled Sumner in 1923, superintendent Walter Pillsbury.

In keeping with Pillsbury's new-style efficiency, a roomy, civilized bungalow was built for him in Sumner—and for his family. No more bachelor informality. Leaving behind a sedate city existence, Pillsbury brought his five children and his college-educated wife. As their big Buick arrived, it was soon followed by their parlor piano, enlivening the bungalow under the fingers of two daughters. Pillsbury was indignant about the hogs and fleas, and decreed that each house would get a chest-high fence—or at least, each house on the main street, the preserve of whites.[47] Thus arrived the proscenium arch for the Monday drama—Fannie Taylor's yard fence—with its role in the New Year's Day alarm.

The Smith and Taylor homes, of course, had histories of their own. Assistant bookkeeper Frances Smith found the washerwoman to be a painful reminder, linked to a moment Frances could never forget. One day in 1921 the laundress's scrubbing had nervously stopped, as she gazed at the Smiths' back porch. There in a crib lay Frances's new baby.

"That baby lookin' at me," the washerwoman complained—at least in Smith's recollection. "I think somethin' gon' happen."

Frances chuckled to herself. The superstitious old soul seemed to fear the evil eye. There was little choice but to move the crib. The moment seemed trivial—until events changed its meaning. Not long after that strange warning, at the age of five weeks, the baby passed away.

The pain of the 1921 crib death would revive more than a year later. In the tormented mind of grieving mother Frances Smith, the prophecy of 1921 would seem to merge with the catastrophe of January 1923—because the old washerwoman lived three miles up the railroad. Her Monday hikes to Sumner originated in the mysterious little place where Negroes lived, called Rosewood.

Thus, the great evil of January 1923 would seem to Frances Smith as if it completed the washday prophecy—for the tireless presence at the washpot would then also be taken.

The next view of the Monday mystery comes from another former neighbor. Interviewed in both 1982 and 1983, Edith Foster recalled her life in January 1923 as an extroverted adolescent, maiden name Edith Surls.

Edith, too, lived in Sumner's white quarters at the moment of Fannie Taylor's alarm. However, her vantage point was north of Frances Smith's and on the other side of the street. Living about midway up toward the commissary, Edith soon learned of the disturbing event, but could not directly observe it.[48]

Edith Foster
1982

Edith Surls
ca. 1924

Born January 29, 1907, Edith Surls was nearly sixteen as roosters crowed their morning greeting behind the fences, saluting a new year. Pert nose, bobbed hair, irrepressible drawl—she would remember herself as a restless sprite, often preoccupied with her boyfriend, broad-shouldered Roy Foster. As 1923 opened, Roy was running cargo errands for Cummer Lumber, shifting gears in the stake-bed truck. Before long he would move up, receiving a plum job in the company town, as "quarters boss." This was the company's enforcer in its African American quarters, a job with certain hidden layers. These, too, would play into the larger week-long mysteries.

Neighbor witnesses – approximate locations
(Buildings are magnified)

On an agitated Monday morning, as Edith learned of the excitement down at the Taylor house, she was bursting with curiosity. But her mother Elmyra laid down the law. This was adult business. It was all right for Elmyra herself to go down there—which she soon did—but in parting she snapped at the disappointed sprite: "You stay on that porch!"

It was no place for a young-un, this sudden clash of sex, violence and race. Word was spreading that Fannie said she was only beaten by the mysterious burglar, not raped; but the reality behind the rumors could be anything—and it was bound to be discussed at the crime scene.

Edith watched glumly as more liberated onlookers passed her porch, going to ruminate on the clues. Some would come back talking about neighbor Alma Murphy across the street, who took her sleuthing seriously. Spying a telltale footprint in the Taylors' sandy yard, they said, Alma feared the crush of onlookers might blot out this vital evidence, so she snatched up a wash tub and clapped it over the prize. Naturally, this bit of gossip focused on the main sensation, the crime itself, and thus ignored a trailing question: If the tub was there, where was the Monday laundress who used it?

Edith's mother soon gave her own report. At second hand, Edith Surls listened to an approximate repetition of what the attack victim, Fannie Taylor, was said to have told about the ordeal.

Sixty years later at age 75 (and in subsequent conversation at age 76), Edith Surls Foster would be a careful, grounded informant, whose stories corroborated closely with independent evidence on points that could be checked. She showed no warning signs of pseudo-memory or confabulation. Her version of Fannie Taylor's story was acquired indirectly, but seemed to reflect the general impression accepted by all the initial white observers:

Fannie is alone in the dark—except for the two sleeping children, her three-year-old and the infant in the crib. Her husband James, the easy-going carpenter, has left for work as usual, ahead of most of the other men. James's work, involving repairs to infrastructure, is performed before the mill cranks up in the morning. He is an early-bird worker, leaving home in deep darkness, perhaps around the time of the very first whistle, the one calling wives to get up and start breakfast.

But James's wife Fannie can ignore that call. Her husband's schedule sends him out the door without breakfast. He will take a break at mid-morning, once the mill is running, and come back home to eat then. Because of this schedule, it is possible that before dawn on the Monday in question, Fannie Taylor's state of consciousness was unlike her neighbors' in a main respect. She may still have been asleep.

In the story that soon enveloped the morning's events, the early schedule kept by James Taylor was stressed in a different way, to explain the seemingly inexplicable. The problem in the story was that the tight-knit, snugly-fenced mill quarters was deeply versed in the rancors of white supremacy, and was guarded by the horrific penalties of lynching. So why in the world would any black intruder take the risk of breaking in?

The special schedule offered a makeshift answer. The crafty intruder must have been secretly watching through the night, crouching in the woods that cloaked the cypress pond, waiting for some kind of opening. Suddenly he detects a change, a movement at the last house in line. That house is being left vulnerable, for its male protector has now walked out through the front gate.

In various ways the explanation grows thin. The streetlamps overhead were turned off at 10:00 p.m. to rest the generator at the mill, leaving deep darkness between the cypress pond and James at the front gate—not to mention obstructing fences and shrubs. The watcher would have had to be very astute. But then again, the moon… Could it be that James's exit was spied before the moon went down? The recorded moonset for that place and time was 5:50 a.m.

Possible—but again the emphasis on James's schedule seems misplaced. If all of the men in the houses were gone to work by the time the attack ended (when Fannie ran out into the street)—and everyone did agree that the men were gone—did this mean that Fannie was saying the attacker had stayed inside her house all that time—entering well before the other men left home (when only James was gone), but not leaving until a time when only women were left? That sounds like over an hour—a lengthy visit.

 But at any rate: Now she is alone, except for the sleeping children. And suddenly she hears a sound.

The sound is faint. But soon it becomes distinct in her awareness.

All of the stories—claiming to come from explanations gasped out by Fannie herself—present a process of growing perceptual acuteness—as if waking up. The telling by Edith Surls has Fannie hearing only one kind of odd sound, the main one. However, Frances Smith, who was closer to the action (and not entirely in doubt as to the reliability of her memory), portrayed Fannie in more detail, and said that in fact Fannie reported a sequence of puzzling sounds. The main one would be told by everyone, forming the next plot anchor: a strong sound at the front door. But Smith said this was preceded by a fainter preliminary intrusion, from a different direction. The first hint of trouble, Smith said, was a sound that seemed to come from Fannie's back yard.

Fannie thought it sounded like wood being broken, according to Smith: a splintering sound. Naturally, the puzzled hearer strove to make sense of this: *Why, it's Monday. A splintering sound must mean that the old washerwoman is back there, breaking sticks for the wash fire.*

No story would recall whether Fannie said she was waking from sleep as ambient noise became an issue. But there seemed to be a dreamy disregard, for Fannie well knew the schedule. The washerwoman arrived only after sunrise, logically waiting for light on the wooded path by the pond, as other evidence confirmed. It couldn't have been the washerwoman, not in deep darkness. And sure enough (continued  Frances Smith gravely) Fannie was dangerously wrong. The splintering sound had come from the devilish intruder. He was breaking slats out of that back fence to get in. Frances Smith described personally verifying this explanation. As the curiosity-seekers arrived in the aftermath, Smith said, she ventured out into Fannie's back yard to look, and saw the broken slats herself.

And now (with the quandary of the preliminary sound explored), the narrative as told by Edith Surls can resume—a more compact story than Smith's, describing only one sound, the main one.

Everyone would talk about this next part, the moment of horror and shock. Whatever the prelude, now in the darkened house Fannie's attention is drawn toward the front door. The sound there is louder, unmistakable. It may not be exactly a knocking at the door. Perhaps something more difficult to interpret. A scratching or bumping. The sound is so singular that, once more, the bemused hearer (whose state of wakefulness goes unquestioned by all the narrators) resorts to the fallback logic mode. She rationalizes. As when Sherlock Holmes eliminates the impossible and must accept whatever is left, however improbable, Fannie now dreamily compares the evidence, and accepts the unlikely. This front-door sound must come from her quiet husband James. Who else could it be? James must have suddenly turned playful, somehow doubling back from work to play a little trick on her. "You just as well to come on in, James," Fannie calls out boldly, seeming to forget her shy reputation. "I know it's you."

But the latched door makes no move. Now she's really curious—and dreamily unworried. So she walks to the door. And opens it.

And there he is!

The watcher from the woods has now lured her within reach.

He springs forward, silencing her with violence, beating or choking her, perhaps both. The struggle takes them to the floor. He is astride her—but only for a beating. The stories stress this. She insists that the assault was non-sexual. Whether out of discretion or accuracy—or for quite different reasons—Fannie says she was not raped.

But why, then, would the intruder break in at all? What is he looking for? Does he rifle the house for money—or for a hobo's desperate meal? Some stories suggested this, but uncertainly, as barely an afterthought.

Instead they focused on Fannie, projecting into the horrible feeling of being immobilized and trapped—although, to complete the plot, our plucky heroine will rise to impressive confidence again. She's about to turn the tables.

And here, a detour must again probe briefly into the background—this time meeting that faint hum heard throughout the Rosewood mystery, the lilt of semi-conscious poetry, making strange rhymes. Fannie's two small sons were creatively named. The second son, Addis, was not only "Added-to-Us," but his name rhymed with that of the three-year-old. That child had a name so odd that in adulthood he would hide it behind a nickname. The three-year-old, a boy, was named Bernice.

Pronunciation blunted this a bit (while also aiding the rhyme). In the family, the name was spoken as something like BURN-us.[49]

So now (returning from our detour) we can see Fannie turning the tables on her attacker. Seized by a sudden inspiration—though still lying helpless on the floor—the victim makes a devastatingly clever bluff. She cries: "BURN-us! BURN-us! Bring me the gun, and I'll shoot the ole black rascal!"

The attacker—previously so sly and fearless—now goes to pieces. He falls for the ruse, accepting blithely that an unseen rescuer (the poetically named BURN-us) must be old enough and large enough to save the day. Any such rescuer would have to have been hiding patiently all this time, right inside the house as Fannie lay in agony—though failing to act—until called suddenly to life like Golem. But now (the attacker has been tricked into believing) the shadowy Burn-us is finally aroused, and is ready to spring forth with a gun.

The intruder never guesses that Bernice is only three. He panics and takes off—though not out the front door where he has learned the route. Now he takes a different path, into the darkness of the back porch and out the back door, toward the woods. This, too, is an explanatory element. Fannie thus explains how the neighbor women, gathering in front of the house, see only Fannie in their moment of discovery. Naturally the victim has fled in the direction opposite that of her tormentor. This is why he is invisible.

Everyone sees her agitation. Led away and put to bed, the young victim seems out of her mind, hysterical with fright, and apparently with physical pain. It would be generally agreed that Fannie Taylor was never the same again, that this watershed moment left her in a heightened state of anxiety for the rest of her life. Mill boss Pillsbury, soon trying to juggle many demons during a mob-ridden week, would move the Taylors across the street to a new house, reportedly when terrified Fannie was unable to stand the sight of the old one. In the new house, it was said, James had to install bars on the windows to calm her.[50] Neighbor Frances Smith (with the questions about her own memory still in the wings) recalled accompanying Fannie after the attack and helping the doctor attend her. In that encounter, Smith said grimly, Doc Cannon did indeed find evidence of more than just a battering or choking. Smith said he saw indications of a sexual attack. Amid Smith's other questionable statements this could mean anything—a pseudo-memory or a hard fact. Still harder to pin down was what should have been Fannie's most public symptom. Were there visible bruises on her face? This was no subtlety. Yet no one seemed able to say anything conclusive like, "Yes, I saw a black eye."[51]

The laundress who came to Sumner each Monday was well known to nine-year-old Minnie Mitchell of Rosewood. The laundress was Minnie's great-aunt, Sarah J. Carrier. When walking three miles to work on Mondays, Sarah Carrier's starting point was her Rosewood home, the home with the attic-like bedroom and flowers on the porch—planted in worn-out washtubs.

When she would come to the Taylors' back fence, Aunt Sarah sometimes brought her youngest son Harry and two grandchildren as helpers. One of the latter was Arnett Goins, another sojourner who would survive into a future age and speak as a witness—as did the other grandchild, Arnett's older sister, Philomena Goins. They both agreed with employer Frances Smith about the general routine. All said the children helped on washdays, performing small chores—stacking firewood, feeding the wash fire. Philomena, age eleven in 1923, had an additional task, tending the white women's babies.[52]

Since 1910, at least six African American housewives in Rosewood had worked as laundresses. Most did so in Sumner, making the three-mile trip after the company town opened in 1911. One, Eliza Bradley, went not on foot but in a wagon, bringing loads of clothes back to Rosewood for washing and ironing by two adopted granddaughters.[53]

Sarah J. Carrier
née Sarah Lewis, ca. 1873
(photo ca. 1908?)

In the South of those years, even some white households of modest means were able to afford such service. The iconic image of the faithful washerwoman was so widespread that in 1956, as Elvis Presley rocked and rolled at a fairground in his old hometown, a new-style commercial laundry enshrined a reminder of the past, standing beside the park's entrance. A catchy neon sign displayed a silhouette of the faithful washerwoman, head rag and all, arms jerking tirelessly in electric flashes.[54]

More than 500 miles southeast at the dawn of 1923, Rosewood, Florida, had two-story homes but one-way traffic. No whites in Sumner were walking to Rosewood to wash. Later media portrayals, especially during the 1990s claims case publicity, sought to depict Rosewood in 1923 as a "prosperous" and "middle-class" community—which stretched the definition of middle class, while suppressing the pain of caste. Had the portrayals said "hard working" and "home-owning" they would have been capturing important truths, but passions on racial issues seemed to require extremes.

Sarah Carrier's real Rosewood projected illusions in many ways. Witnesses from within the community agreed that at home, this same laundress organized church pageants, played Methodist hymns on her parlor piano and presided over school picnics—while ruffling feathers with her domineering ways. But white employer Frances Smith could not imagine any such sophistication.

Smith responded to the description of Sarah Carrier's home life with an indulgent smile, conveying the message that a naive inquirer had been sold a bill of goods. Those stories were certainly not true, Smith said gently. The shuffling, mumbling figure who remained in the employer's memory—"Ole Aint Sarah"—could never have been so forceful and managerial. To the owner of the clothes in the washpot, the other life of the servant seemed impossible.

Née Sarah Lewis, Sarah Carrier can be tracked by census records back to age eight in 1880. She had not quite seen slavery, nor would she have many memories even of post-Civil War Reconstruction, which ended in 1877. She knew a more obscure transition time. In her youth, the old Florida frontier had been a live-and-let-live kind of place, with some breathing space for African Americans, even as whites fervently remembered the Lost Cause.

Sarah Carrier in the U.S. Census of 1900

But formal racial segregation soon swept the South on a wave of new state laws. One of the first, in 1887, would come in Florida. Already squeezed by timber economics, Sarah Carrier's wilderness community dealt with growing racial confinement. As segregation tightened, some whites in the woods muttered that if blacks were going to live out here at all, it should only be under strict control, in a company quarters. The old freeholds, they said, only spawned crime.

Familiar Icon
Gone With the Wind
Best Supporting Actress
Hattie McDaniel, 1939

When Sarah Carrier met the new year of 1923, at age fifty, she was not exactly the ancient fossil implied by her employer's sentimental phrase, "Ole Aint Sarah." At home in Rosewood she was called "Aunt" by Minnie for a different reason, as a real kinship label. But white usage in Sumner ran otherwise, preserving the jargon of slavery, which had said "Aunt Jemima" and "Uncle Ben" to avoid saying "Mr." or "Mrs."

On December 27, 1899, Haywood J. Carrier and his young wife Sarah had acquired the half-acre site where Sarah's flowers would still bloom on the porch in 1923. At the time of the purchase, the mid- to late 1890s had found the Florida frontier squeezed from yet another direction, by an old Florida demon, the weather. A series of disastrous winters in those years drove citrus growers out of northern Florida, hitting hard at a newly founded citrus haven called Rosewood. By 1899 land prices had collapsed. Less than two months after the Carrier purchase, a low temperature of two degrees below zero was recorded in northern Florida. A capricious environment was providing a side-effect, another breathing space.

The 1900 census found Haywood and Sarah Carrier with two of their children "at school." Their son Sylvester seemed to emerge with flowing penmanship. After 1904, daughter Ruby was sent across the state for a rare chance at post-elementary education, to Daytona Educational and Industrial Training School for Negro Girls. The family said that before graduation, however, Ruby Carrier heard a different drummer and went north, somewhat in the path of another Floridian. Like writer Zora Hurston, Ruby immigrated to Harlem in its Renaissance.[55]

Is Ruby Carrier here?
Mary McLeod Bethune
with girls from her school
at Daytona (ca. 1905)
*Florida Memory-State Archives
of Florida*

A world was hidden behind the image at the Taylors' back fence, where "Ole Aint Sarah" met the tubs.

———————

None of this, however, speaks to January 1, 1923, or answers the immediate question.

On this particular washday, was Sarah Carrier a witness?

Or in other words: Did the faithful washerwoman come to work as usual that day? With the back yard at the Taylor house soon prowled by angry whites, it would have been a logical day to stay home. And indeed, Frances Smith stated this categorically. She said that on the fateful Monday no washing was done: "She didn't come, no."

But there was another voice in the informant pool, telling a story of which whites like Frances Smith and Edith Surls Foster were unaware.

———————

The alarm raised by Fannie Taylor and the brutal attack she reported would be the trigger for the Rosewood mob violence of January 1-7, 1923. In some such eruptions, when masses of people have felt unified by emotion to the point of killing, it is not unusual for the trigger or precipitating alarm to come from a special category of initial participant, a community member who seems especially vulnerable or powerless, often a woman or a child.

Such a damsel in distress (or helpless child) can form an idealized object of rescue or revenge, calling into action a larger mass of (male) interveners, who, under private stresses of their own, may find glorious release as answering heroes.

The triggering figure—the mob's catalyst—will have been injured in some way by a demonic attacker—though this damage need not be visible. In some cases it might be starkly evident (as in Forsyth County, Georgia, in 1912, when a merciless rape and murder formed the trigger for a massive racial cleansing rampage). But under key circumstances the triggering injury may be only imagined (the Harlem riot of 1935 grew out of wildfire rumors about the beating death of a 16-year-old, which never occurred).

The power of imagination among potential mob avengers can reach extremes. In the village of Raxquiche, Guatemala, on April 22, 2002, a mob beat to death two indigenous neighbors, Roberto Chub and Luisa Che, on the charge of witchcraft, because a local resident had died of a gastric disorder said to come from a magic spell. This is not to mention the most famous such witchcraft accusation, in Salem Village, Massachusetts Colony, in 1692, when the triggering victim-accusers were young girls, ages nine to twelve.

The communal importance that comes to mantle a mob

Guatemala: Site of 2002 mob killing for witchcraft. The accused witches, Roberto Chub and Luisa Che of the Kekchi indigenous group, were both killed. The bare ground at left foreground was where their house was burned. *(photo 2003, Raxquiche, Guatemala)*

"Witchcraft in Salem Village"

Illustration of a tormented child accuser as imagined in 1876, nearly two centuries after the Salem trials.

catalyst figure can bring deeper mysteries. Under stresses unseen, some victim-accusers seem to seek out the starring role. Perhaps semiconsciously or entirely unconsciously, they may produce very convincing symptoms of injury that can be interpreted as evidence of monstrous assault. Real physical manifestations seen in the Salem witchcraft accusers, if explained today as hysteria or mass sociogenic illness, nonetheless point to a power in excited imagination that can go beyond what we might usually dismiss as fakery. As communal emotions rise toward readiness for a mob event, and a questionable catalyst offers proof of an attacking monster to hunt, there is the question of blame. Who really started all this? Was it the triggering figure, by producing required symptoms of injury? Or was it really the waiting interveners, by communicating their eagerness to accept such an alarm, few questions asked?

Victoria Price

Questionable accuser: the "Scottsboro Boys' Alabama, 1931

Repeatedly in such cases, mob eagerness ignores warning signs about the mental health or stability of the accuser. Not just hysterical involvement (as alleged after Salem), but other psychological or neurological distress—ranging from the hallucinations of temporal lobe epilepsy to the torment of personality disorder—may move an accuser toward seeing the required demon. By various routes, one anxious individual may enter a delusional state of alarm, thus facilitating others into a thrilling ritual of communal defense.

The result can seem almost mystical. The larger group, though stressed, might have difficulty producing an outright hallucination to excuse a rampage, but their receptiveness can seem to probe like water against a dam, until finding a weakest point in the community population, a distressed and perhaps marginalized neighbor, more vulnerable to visions than the rest—and thus able to cry: *"The devil is real! See where he attacked me!"*

This does not necessarily explain Fannie Taylor, by any means. But precisely a month prior to her terror and its symbolic moment—on New Year's Day—the shy young housewife and her community had received news of very real horror occurring ninety miles to the northwest, at the Florida town of Perry. Schoolteacher Ruby Hendry of Perry had been murdered and nearly decapitated in an apparent rape attempt, allegedly by a mysterious African American hobo. Whites in Perry had responded with a rampage against African Americans, climaxing in a live burning watched by a massive crowd, as if in a medieval witch hunt.

No direct evidence seems to show that Fannie Taylor a month later was somehow mirroring the Perry excitement, but the positioning was taut. As often happens after a mortified community covers the tracks of a mass rampage and its requisite catalyst figure, the evidence on Fannie Taylor has remained stubbornly vague, presenting a mass of questions without firm answers.

And this ambiguity, too, would have its echo. In later years it would invite less spectacular excitement, as a sequel of guesses, legends and rumors continued seeking to explain Fannie's screams.

Not until the 1990s, seven decades after the fact, would this current come back into full view, as if in a mass-media aftershock of the original Rosewood upheaval. By then a new political climate had outgrown the racist assumptions of 1923—but here, too, an excited atmosphere seemed ill-suited to fact-checking. Again came the ancient symptoms of witch hunting—not producing actual lynchings this time, mercifully, but still seizing eagerly on accusations that lacked evidence—including reversed accusations against the long-departed Fannie herself.

Amid the passions of the 1990s Rosewood claims case in the Florida Legislature, new interveners, indignant and enflamed, seemed to yearn to reach back through time and hunt their own form of witch. And in this rush, an old mechanism proved useful. Once again, rising emotion probed until a catalyst figure was discovered. A person emerged whose unusual mental state could provide proof that there was a witch.

There was a particularly sensational explanation that could resolve the riddles surrounding Fannie Taylor. The Rosewood claims case, 1991-1994, promoted this explanation fervently, by the simple device of screening out a large body of evidence that weighed against it. Then in 1997 the $26-million movie *Rosewood* took up the enticing explanation as its centerpiece, treating it as proven fact.

It was inviting in many ways, for in a general sense history provided precedents. Cases other than Rosewood showed the Lynching Era to have no shortage of incidents where such explanations proved to be true.

The 1990s consensus presented it like this:

Fannie Taylor was cynically lying about being attacked by an unidentified black stranger—because, secretly, her face had been bruised in a quarrel with an illicit white lover. Thus, she had to make up an excuse for her husband when he came home.

The dramatic appeal in this explanation is obvious. For an excited moment in the claims case period, the secret white boyfriend became too appealing to be questioned. Never identified by name, nor even tied to any scrap of biography, he was left to float vaguely in the public record, available for future enthusiasts to cite as alleged fact.

The thrill of this accusation gathered force in the 1997 movie, as a screenwriter added a flourish from further imagination, saying that the demonized target, Fannie Taylor, had not just one (imaginary) extra-marital lover, but was dallying with a series of such phantoms. No one in real life seems ever to have alleged these acrobatics, though the movie did base itself on another kind of scrap from reality.

There was the catalyst process. A crucial witness was needed to certify the witch—a witness whose private mental torments could be screened out of the public version of the story.

Philomena Theresa Goins, whose married name was Philomena Doctor, was born on August 28, 1911, in a delivery by Rosewood midwife Mary Ella McCoy.

On the one hand, Philomena Goins was blessed, growing up in a talented, dynamic Rosewood family, at least two of whose members would be professional musicians. But on the other hand there were family crises, even before the largest trauma in 1923. In an earlier year— not fixed by records but confirmed by multiple memories—Philomena Goins's father, George Goins, met disaster in the community's Christmas shooting in church. Her uncle Charlie Goins was ruined by the same incident, a blight on the most prosperous legacy in Rosewood, that of the land-owning Goins family. Three young Goins children, Philomena and two brothers, would grow up largely in the care of grandparents, Sarah and Haywood Carrier.

Philomena Goins Doctor was to become a vibrant, talented solo singer in her own right, performing in church, but adulthood also brought symptoms that shocked her family, including bedridden depression and shouting rage. Doctor's son said that once she reported seeing God standing at the foot of her bed, and that on another occasion, when he was in middle age, she attacked him with a belt. Her cousin Minnie called this "Philomena's ole mean"—a puzzling psychological pattern said to date from childhood.

I first met this informant in May 1982, failing to guess that I faced years more of learning how riddles of psychology can complicate memories of atrocity. It was in 1982 that I first heard about Fannie Taylor's alleged secret white boyfriend—and it made all the difference to hear it fresh, from its original source.

Ultimately, the large complex of later belief endorsing the boyfriend story seemed to track back to this one narrator—who had an authoritative credential. She said she had personally seen him.

Perhaps too credulously, I included Philomena Doctor's story as one more vignette in my July 25, 1982, article unearthing the buried Rosewood traces, though with a warning. At that point in the long process of penetrating a cultural secret, the evidence on Rosewood was still mostly hidden, leaving no way to either prove or disprove what Philomena Doctor was saying. I warned that such accounts represented personal points of view, and that readers would have to judge for themselves.

This was thin, I know, but was the best I could do at the time. I didn't realize that within another decade, in the 1990s wave of Rosewood publicity, the story would be resurrected after its teller was no longer alive, and thus she could no longer complicate the publicized picture.

Under the influence of startling new 1990s incentives, reaching up to $150,000 in individual claim payments from the State of Florida, the boyfriend story took on new life. By then much more evidence had come to light, repeatedly showing the boyfriend narrative to be unreliable in the extreme, but this met a seemingly irresistible pressure toward myths. There was Rosewood the lost paradise in the wilderness, Rosewood the apocalyptic massacre, Rosewood the place of angelic heroes beset by demonic villains—and Rosewood the racial melodrama, where all the villains had to be of only one race—which meant that a secret white boyfriend became necessary to the plot.

As to historical precedents, cases such as the Springfield, Illinois, race riot of 1908 and the "Scottsboro Boys" gang rape trial of 1931— only two examples—featured real events that looked much like the secret white boyfriend scenario. The pattern was simple. A hoax accusation against a black target was dreamed up as a cover, seeking to direct attention away from real misdeeds by an accuser who was white.

In 1908 and 1931, and on other occasions, persuasive evidence emerged that racial frenzies had been set off by accusational tricks. The accusers—typically white women or girls—told stories that seemed too pat. Mabel Hallam in 1908 was later said by news accounts to have invented a black rapist in order to hide a tryst with a white lover. Victoria Price in 1931 was clearly deceptive.

Nor was this limited to the Lynching Era. In 1994 a young white mother named Susan Smith told national television that an African American carjacker had kidnapped her two children. When confronted with growing evidence Smith confessed to an enormity. Her children were missing because she had murdered them. In 1989, male hoaxer Charles Stuart in Boston blamed the murder of his pregnant wife on a similar racial phantom, a mysterious carjacker, also allegedly black. When faced with evidence of his own guilt, Stuart committed suicide.

Springfield - 1908

Scottsboro - 1931

Many people, however, know this theme from another source, involving not a real case but an imagined one—in a landmark work of fiction. The almost biblically popular 1961 novel *To Kill a Mockingbird* hinged on a sub-plot that was seldom dissected for historical background. In ways, it resembled post-traumatic rumors that surrounded something horribly real, the 1934 Claude Neal torture-lynching in Florida.

The Neal case occurred near the Alabama state line at a time when Harper Lee, the future author of *To Kill a Mockingbird*, was living in southern Alabama at age eight. The novel did not resemble the real evidence from the Neal case, but bore a closer likeness to dramatically satisfying redemptive stories reported after Neal's death. Those stories claimed—on no proof that seems ever to have been cited—that the young woman Neal was accused of killing was really the person to blame, because, supposedly, she was seeing a secret boyfriend.

But this still doesn't answer the question. Did it happen in 1923? Was a secret lover behind the events at Rosewood?

One witness said yes.

There is no doubt that on some Mondays in childhood, Philomena Goins did accompany her grandmother Sarah Carrier on washday trips to Sumner. But the story she told me in 1982 was more specific than that. She described the particular Monday morning of January 1, 1923. Her account, printed in my article in 1982, went basically as follows:

Philomena and her grandmother Sarah are standing behind the Taylor house, washing. For some reason on this trip, unlike others, Sarah Carrier has brought only one child helper. There are no other witnesses.

As they start work at the back fence there is a minor distraction. Appearing from the woods, a visitor approaches. He says nothing to them, but enters the yard through the back gate, then goes into the house. He is not Mr. Taylor, because Mr. Taylor has already gone to work. However, since it is broad daylight—well up in the morning—one thing about the visitor is clearly visible. He is white. Indeed, he is Fannie Taylor's secret white lover.

After a while he comes back out of the house, still calm and unhurried. Without an apparent care, he saunters through the gate and disappears into the woods—though something has happened inside the house.

Shortly after the white man's departure, the two figures at the wash fire are astonished to see Fannie Taylor come running from the house, crying about an attack by a black man. There are bruises on her face, left by a lover's quarrel. She has created a cover story that she can tell to her husband, a way to explain the bruises.

On January 21, 1991, Philomena Doctor passed away. While she was alive, large difficulties appeared in her story about January 1, 1923, but after she was no longer on the scene the story was at liberty to change still further. Some of its contradictions were smoothed out by intermediaries involved in the campaign for reparations payments (culminating on May 4, 1994, when the Rosewood claims case won its victory). The public would see the boyfriend story only after it had been polished, and no hint was given about the mental state that had originally produced it.

In 1982 when I heard it, the story was delivered in bizarre bursts of shouting, as if the narrator sought to win acquiescence by force. Interspersed in the verbal barrage were equally startling intervals of boasting, such as a boast that the narrator weighed 249 pounds, and another announcing, for whatever reason, that her ancestors, though African American, had proudly owned slaves. There are theoretical ways to look at all this, involving post-traumatic stress fantasies, narcissistic precursors and grandiosity, but a less detailed impression might suffice. Whatever the cause, this was a profoundly disturbed individual, prone to flights of fantasy (It was true that her ancestors on one side had included moneyed landowners in North Carolina, where, before the Civil War, some wealthy African Americans did own others as slaves—but for a modern African American to be claiming this proudly, as a boast, sounded as disconcerting as the shouts).

The investigative problem—and the reason why I included Philomena Doctor's account in my 1982 exposé—was that early in the investigation there were few guides to probability. The Rosewood events held many twists that might look counter-intuitive, but were eventually proved to be factual. If firm accounting was ever to be reached on a serious atrocity, a claim of eyewitness observation could not be dismissed simply on smug assumptions. It would take years more of finding additional evidence to gauge the story in a systematic way.

After that process, the credibility can be approached from multiple angles. For example, also in 1982, Philomena Doctor claimed that during the Rosewood events she personally stepped over nineteen dead white men, who, she said, were killed by heroic black shooters. None of her relatives, in a better position to see, reported any such number, let alone claiming to have stepped over them. When I tried tentatively to give the benefit of the doubt and asked if Doctor might mean "about 19," her reply was scornfully dismissive—again in a loud voice, and amid cursing. There were exactly 19, she insisted imperiously, because she had counted them—though she said she was fleeing in terror at the moment of alleged counting. She seemed unaware that she was describing a case of miraculous hopscotch arithmetic, while all other witnesses from that moment, witnesses in her family, placed her in no position to be stepping over any dead men at all. In addition, no such whites had died or disappeared. Confirming this was one of the evidence points that would take years to pin down. The conclusion—that the pile was a fantasy assertion or confabulation—was not a cavalier assumption but the result of painstaking research, in which all streams of evidence kept leading back to the same place—the place suggested from the beginning by the signs of mental difficulties. And that was only one of the boasts.

In another, this informant said that the Rosewood events found her successfully enduring a period of concealment in the swamps that lasted for nine days, while she allegedly received no food or water the entire time: "The doctors say you can't do it, but OOOH, you can!" she announced theatrically, in a stage voice as if addressing a crowd, while emphasizing the alleged duration, nine days. In the real Rosewood events there was indeed a hiding period, and during it, this witness did verifiably experience terror and pain. That nugget was true. However, all the other witnesses—again including those in her family—agreed with an array of other evidence: the time span of hiding was two nights, January 4 and 5. And food was brought to them.

Whether the emotional problems suffered by this informant were of post-traumatic origin or dated from before the 1923 trauma, the void in credibility remained. Here was the least credible source among the Rosewood survivors, a towering exception unlike the others—but because her mental state seemed to seek theatrical extremes, this worst source was precisely the one taken as the standard of truth by the 1990s rush of belief. Posthumously, an afflicted source of extreme images was placed ahead of a multitude of honest and credible survivors. A sanitized ghost was anointed as authority.

Certainly, Philomena Doctor was a functional individual and not a staring zombie, but in her childhood at Rosewood she had endured life-threatening trauma. When traveling back into memories of that trauma she could behave—as some otherwise functional combat veterans can behave during flashback war stories—in a manner that looked insane. To argue about classifications such as psychotic, confabulational or merely defensive does not change the issue of credibility. Here was the mind that was the only proof in the world that there was ever a secret white boyfriend.

Life-threatening stress would come to Philomena Doctor on the night of January 4, 1923, in a manner closely linked to her story of the alleged earlier events of January 1 and the boyfriend. In the fires of January 4, she not only thought her own life might end but lost her beloved grandmother Sarah.

Such stress can have divergent individual effects. The extreme symptoms popularly associated with post-traumatic stress disorder don't come to every combat soldier. Among Rosewood survivors, none presented like this one exception. Others expressed their pain and loss, sometimes intensely, but in focused conversation, not in curses and raving.

The earliest distinct report of Philomena Doctor telling her story about the secret boyfriend placed its debut on Christmas 1949. It was said to come in a dramatic outpouring after a period of psychological depression that kept the teller in her bedroom for days.[56] There were Rosewood survivors who had never heard of any white boyfriend or any such story until I published it in 1982, though those survivors were older than Philomena Doctor and in Rosewood they had been better placed to hear adult gossip.

This is not to mention Fannie Taylor's white neighbors. For the boyfriend story to be true, the neighbors in Sumner would seem to have hatched a remarkably effective conspiracy. How else to explain the lack of rumors about Fannie as a harlot? The neighbors seemed to talk about a completely different kind of personality problem, her "peculiar" reclusiveness. Was she perhaps a reclusive harlot?

The Lynching Era's psychological effects remain unexplored in a nation that has been slow to examine even the original crimes. Any notion of post-traumatic coping mechanisms from the lynching years can be formulated only from glimpses. However, one such mechanism—appearing in a number of ways after Rosewood and arguably after other such incidents—can seek to medicate an atrocity's pain through extreme our-side/their-side simplifications: "our side" consists only of angelic heroes, theirs only of demons. In other fields of trauma this has been called "splitting." Philomena Doctor's shouts told vehemently of angels (our side) and demons (theirs).

From the start of the Rosewood events, demonization was practiced by whites—as "citizens" hunted "black brutes." But less obvious was a parallel on the other side, among potential mob targets. As the Rosewood violence sent shock waves through neighboring African American communities, the pain was deepened by a disturbing plot element in the events, the mysterious African American villain who had set the chaos in motion. This villain burdened an African American tragedy with an African American instigator, and folklore made adjustments.

An emotional drive to rescript this element could be seen most pointedly not in Philomena Doctor's story but in others—stories that had no secret boyfriend at all, and which Doctor apparently never heard. These other stories were told among African Americans just outside the crime scene, who, unable to examine any real evidence, could go still farther into re-imagining the disaster. These narrators also made the assertion that the attacker was secretly white—but they resolved the dissonance differently. They said that Fannie *had not known he was white—because he had blacked his face.*

In order to disguise himself while attack-ing her, they said, the white villain had done as the stage minstrels do, and had used burnt cork or lampblack to make himself look like a Negro.[57] The seeming implausibility did not seem to deter the tellers. Emotional pressures shaped the tale. The villain had to be white. No one said, *"The pressures of the past are intolerable and I must believe."* There was only the visible iceberg's tip, the story.

White minstrel performing fifty miles from Rosewood during January 1923
—Gainesville Daily Sun, Jan. 23, 1923

The face-blacking stories were told confidently, as with Philomena Doctor's story of the secret boyfriend, though lacking the additional cachet of her alleged eyewitness authority. Doctor said—emphatically and repeatedly—that she saw a white man of perfectly ordinary complexion, certainly with no face-blacking. To look at her story and the others together—as none of the tellers were in a position to do—is to meet their final refutation. The face-blacking stories can't be true if the secret boyfriend story is true, or vice versa. All of them—and still other variants besides—have the effect of disproving one another, and revealing psychological pressures to rescript an intolerable plot element.

As time passed after the Rosewood violence, not just African American culture but local white culture began to ponder the unlikeli-hoods in Fannie Taylor's alarm. But none of the skeptics were equipped by the knowledge of their place and time to probe into a deeper mystery, where the real probabilities pointed.

Instead, there was a parade of contradictory myths.

As one example, in 1967 a U.S. Peace Corps training camp was set up at Cedar Key, where swamps and jungles could approximate the challenges of Brazil, the eventual destination of the trainees. In the late 1960s cultural avoidance of the Rosewood secret was at its height, but the Cedar Key Peace Corps initiates stumbled onto local traces anyway (as recalled in more recent times by their instructor).[58]

These early discoverers reportedly did not attempt to formally restore the case to the historical record, but privately they were shocked, hearing Cedar Key tales about a cryptic episode of racial cleansing. One group was moved to make the incident the focus of a community survey training project, which gave them a chance to delve into the stories. A local pastor was said to help, though relations with other residents grew tense. Before leaving for Brazil, the outsider detectives were convinced, they had cracked the case.

They learned that, sure enough, the spark for the secretive Rosewood violence had arisen when a story about an attack on a white woman was fabricated—a cruel hoax. However, there was a catch. The Peace Corps sleuths became persuaded—and would apparently remain persuaded down to the present day—that the fabricated story, and the real attack on the white female victim, *came from her father.* According to confident local narrations that these visitors were being told in 1967, the sinister father figure lived in Cedar Key at the time of the attack (neatly giving prestige to the 1967 tellers of the tales, who also lived in Cedar Key). After that villainous father sexually assaulted his own daughter, the trainees were somberly told, it was he, the father—and not the daughter—who disguised the crime. The crafty father went running to Cedar Key, shouting that a black man had raped his daughter.

The Peace Corps inquirers apparently found no one who claimed to be a direct witness to any of this—nor apparently any black informants at all. Cedar Key, the all-white island town left behind at the ends of the earth, has long been an interesting hotbed of atrocity folklore, featuring assorted oft-told tales besides Rosewood. The repertoire tends to remedy communal  isolation by converting Cedar Key into a ghoulishly glamorous hub of imagined excitement. The 1967 sleuths (one trainee reportedly phoned home every night, never having been outside New York) met a flood of second-hand tellings, stories seeming to speak with great conviction. The inquirers had apparently never heard of the old American frontier mystery called "cracking" or backwoods boasting—with its confusing dimension of narrator half-belief. Also unknown to them were Rosewood's real witnesses and survivors from 1923, who were not traced until a decade and a half later. When found, none of those informants, black or white, said anything about a father being involved in the Fannie Taylor attack.

The Peace Corps trainees remained at a level of knowledge so vague that they never learned the initial attack victim's name; but, named or not, the real Fannie Taylor was not from Cedar Key and her father was not from Cedar Key. No one in 1923 would be remembered by real participants as running to Cedar Key crying that a daughter had been raped. The Peace Corps probe seems not to have found a material reality but an incredibly rich climate of confabulation—along with a more elusive possible companion: media fantasy.

The mysterious evil-father element seemed to arrive suddenly, living in tales for only a brief moment around 1967. Seven years later in 1974, an anthropologist would happen into Cedar Key and did hear remnants of the father story—but by then it was fading, forming an "alternative tale," mentioned only in passing.[59] More long-standing folklore (creative in other ways) seemed to be pushing the 1967 father into oblivion. By 1982, as far as I could see when I arrived, no trace of the father story remained.

In 1962, *To Kill a Mockingbird* was made into a blockbuster movie. In the 1960s both that cinema giant and another, *In the Heat of the Night,* were on the silver screen. Both films featured repulsive redneck fathers as racial villains.[60] *In the Heat of the Night* was such a sensation that it received five academy awards, then inspired two sequels and a TV series, while launching one of history's famous movie lines: "They call me *MISTER* Tibbs." Its plot featured an intrepid northern detective, a shrewd urbanite dropped into a secretive southern backwater, where the hero-sleuth defied backward locals and cracked a big local secret. *In the Heat of the Night* premiered in August 1967, in an atmosphere so emotional that its stars, Sidney Poitier and Rodd Steiger, were said to sneak into theaters in Manhattan to hear the cheering. As this film met the heartland in the fall of 1967, the Peace Corps arrived in Cedar Key. Racial tensions were so great that African American members of the Peace Corps team were partially sequestered in the town's

Island Hotel. A year later the Academy Awards ceremony that was practically given over to *In the Heat of the Night* had to be postponed for two days—because of the murder of Martin Luther King, with aftermath riots from which some American urban cores never fully recovered.

In the heat of this mercurial moment, the practice of blaming a white rural daddy had a certain celebrity. Some very sensitive radar in Cedar Key seemed to tune in dreamily to the spirit of the age.

But what, then, really did happen inside a four-room house on January 1, 1923? Who attacked Fannie Taylor?

There are the three main areas of possibility:

1) She was attacked by a real intruder, just as she said. Real crimes are often bizarre and may seem improbable in their clumsy surprises. There is material evidence in this vein, too, soon to come.

Or:

2) The redemptive stories got it right, and the attacker was secretly white, putting the truth somewhere in the motley line-up of the secret white boyfriend, or the face-blacker, or the incestuous redneck daddy— or still other folklore streams not given a hearing here (such as the-husband-secretly-beat-her-up). Perhaps the most extreme effort was published by the *Chicago Defender* in its Rosewood story of January 13, 1923, claiming (confidently) that the female accuser in Sumner, Florida, was herself non-existent, and that whites had made her up, too. As already said, the wide range of these contradictory stories tends to put them all in the same wan light.

But that still leaves Alternative Three—as now we come to:

3) The path of deepest mystery....

I should make it clear from the start that I don't think a complete explanation of the Fannie Taylor incident is likely to be found in the psychological phenomenon called sleep paralysis hallucination.[61] If the available evidence shows anything, it shows that the complete answer is likely to contain subtleties inaccessible to baffled examiners—perhaps a combination of factors, coming together chaotically—as often happens in real life, and especially in real crime. Perhaps the underlying reality was made up partly of a genuine intruder—and perhaps even partly of a disowned romantic secret in some unguessable way. But there may also have been a wild card in the deck.

Sleep paralysis, along with its panicked extreme, sleep paralysis hallucination, was unknown as a clinical entity in 1923. It was not a trendy topic until the computer age, as evidence increasingly suggested that something very old might be relevant to something rather more new—the new thing being the claim that certain people had been abducted by extra-terrestrials.

It was noticed, as stories of kidnapping by space aliens multiplied with the rocket age, that some of the stories seemed to be firmly believed by the victims doing the reporting. And some such victims seemed not to be psychotic or mentally disordered in any obvious way. Meanwhile, the setting for such abductions was often a bedroom. The victim wakes suddenly, finding that a horrific creature has crept into the room. This didn't apply to all the cases, but a theme emerged—pointing far back into history.

The modern reports bore resemblance to stories told centuries ago—when the sudden bedroom visitor was said to be not a spaceman but the devil, or a witch. The implication was that a universal quirk of psychology might be involved, an underlying constant down through time, but relabeled according to the demons of each age.

In this thinking, the intruder might not be material at all, but a warp in the interface between the mental and the material, a kink in consciousness. If this was so, one would expect to see the same kink manifested by humanity in general, in cultures around the world, though under local names. And indeed, Japan has a phenomenon called *kanashibari*, and China has *gui ya*—both sounding somewhat like witch abduction or UFO abduction. Other cultural traces were left elsewhere, some of them as familiar as the terms "nightmare" and "hag-ridden."[62]

In normal sleep, a kind of natural paralysis occurs, keeping us from flailing our arms and legs in a dream (sometimes a sleeping dog can be seen jerking its legs and whining as if in a dream-state rabbit hunt, when paralysis seems to partially wear off). Normally as we wake, the paralysis goes away smoothly. But there can be a hitch. Many people have had the experience of emerging into wakefulness but being briefly unable to open their eyes. This can grow more extensive, with the whole body refusing to move. If a sleeping brain remains deeply enough asleep to misinterpret such lingering immobility, panic can explode, blending real perceptions (or memories) from bedroom surroundings with the fantastic images of dream. Real sights or sounds—half-perceived from the environment, coming from outside the window, or from a ticking clock or sighing breeze—may be picked up and packaged into a new image, suddenly providing explanation: *Something is holding me down! What could it be?! What has been happening?!*

And then there he is.

Victims may insist afterward that their encounter with a demonic intruder could not have been a dream. It was too vivid, too horrifying, not at all dream-like. Too awake. Some sufferers never quite spy the demon visually (at the deepest level of hallucination), but are certain of having been held down by a presence, a sentience, *a something*. They may have heard breathing, or perhaps the rustling of bed covers (as ambient sounds, or the expectation of ambient sounds, turned into building blocks for the not-quite-dream). This is a very sketchy description of what is largely an uncharted realm.

The classic incubus painting:
"The Nightmare," by Henry Fuseli
—oft-reprinted as the modern age discovers sleep paralysis hallucination

Fannie Taylor's reported experience startlingly resembled known cases of sleep paralysis hallucination: 1) initial puzzled attempts at logical explanation, as the dreaming brain (not knowing that it is still half-asleep) applies waking rules; 2) The Sherlock Holmes acceptance of the implausible since no other explanation will work; 3) the initial incorporation of stray ambient noises; 4) the sudden perceptual leap as slight omens suddenly combine to form a demon; 4) a perceived "attack" that often involves choking and, primarily, a sensation that the chest is being suffocatingly pressed upon, explaining shortness of breath as panic or paralysis escalates; and 5) an insistence that this devil—or witch, or alien—is oddly cold, failing to take full sexual advantage—almost as if anesthetized. The match with the Fannie Taylor story is monolithic— seeming too great for simple coincidence.[63]

In China's *gui ya*, or "ghost pressure," a phantom presence is perceived as pressing down on the chest. *Kanashibari* in Japan ("to tie with an iron rope") finds a sinister ogre doing much the same, in an experience common enough to be discussed on Japanese talk shows. Thailand's victims are "ghost-covered" (*phi um*). The old word for "nightmare" in French is *cauchemar*—"trampling ogre." In Spanish a nightmare is a *pesadilla*, that which weighs down. German has *Hexendrücken* (witch pressure) and *Alpdrück* (elf pressure). In parts of the Caribbean there is an attack by a demon called Kokma, just before or just after sleep, involving pressure on the chest, great anxiety and an inability to move—though Kokma is not a witch, but the lingering presence of a deceased infant.[64]

Sporadic reports of being savagely beaten in such moments—or of being ridden through the night by a spellbinding witch—remind how deeply emotion and dream can reshape perceived experience.

But usually unexplored in discussions of this mystery is an historical no-man's land. What might be called a period of transitional demons stretched forward in time from the "witch craze," centuries ago, toward the techno-chic UFO reports of today. In that in-between age, the feared monster (at least in many American nightmares) was neither a witch nor an interplanetary troll. For roughly two and a half centuries there were nightmare visions spawned by slave insurrection panics—segueing into the "black brute" images of "race war" rampages and lynching. During those racial storms, the idea of mental-material interface was not exactly a hot topic. We have no way of knowing how many cases of alleged attack by black strangers might have involved waking dreams.

In 1907 journalist Ray Stannard Baker (one of the "muckrakers" and later a biographer of Woodrow Wilson) went south to explore the roots of the great Atlanta race riot of 1906. This was a lynching rampage involving frenetic, merciless attacks on random black targets, following a flood of newspaper reports about rape or rape attempts by African American drifters, allegedly committed against white women.[65] Baker did the rare thing, and

Ray Stannard Baker

Stanley Cohen

investigated. He found that some of the trigger attacks were gruesomely real (one white female victim lost an eye after being battered with a rock). But other accusations seemed to amplify a background reality seething with both fears and lesser crimes. The idea that a real context of danger could be—not entirely imagined—but grossly exaggerated, was articulated in later years by sociologist Stanley Cohen, in his formulation of a "moral panic."[66] In Cohen's view, a moral panic can feed off a real wave of crimes or other disruptions, but exaggerates them to the point of illusion, creating an urgent menace: *Demons at the gates!*

At the time of the Atlanta riot in 1906, the amplification involved intense imagination, as if in a waking dream. A white girl on a path met a black preacher and fled in terror, imagining attack. A white matron frantically phoned police about an intruder, then phoned back to say it was only a shadow on a window shade—though the initial report went into a newspaper headline anyway: *"Another Attack."* No one had heard of moral panic in 1906—or of panic disorder, or of "hypnagogic and hypnopompic during sleep paralysis." [67] Few signposts marked the paths, neurological or psychological, by which a hungry crowd might be supplied with a demon to hunt.[68]

Fannie Taylor may have met the old phrase "nervous breakdown,"[69] whether or not an intruder provided brutal input. Her neighbor Frances Smith recalled that through the rest of Fannie's life, until death from cancer in the 1960s, she would grow frantic if left alone. Edith Surls Foster also felt there was permanent emotional damage.

What really happened inside the house? I found both of Taylor's sons in adulthood, only to hear them confirm that they were too young in 1923 to remember anything. At every turn, the communal drama seemed to cover its tracks—making another kind of point.

To focus too intensely on the darkened house is to be fooled by the magician's left hand. What ultimately counted in the Fannie Taylor incident was the speed and fervor with which a waiting pool of witch hunters would take up the thrill of belief, dreamily disregarding any cautionary flags. The real action (the magician's disowned right hand) was not in the anguish of a disempowered community member who told a shocking story, but in a select population (not exactly the community as a whole) who were now empowered to new heights. They became pursuers of the demon—swelling into a heroic drama in their dreams.

Chapter 6: The Scent

Before noon on Monday, a black Ford Model T is bouncing over pale limerock road surface, as it rushes toward Sumner. The driver—a quiet, poker-faced frontier knight—is about to become chief investigator on the Fannie Taylor case.

Levy County Sheriff Bob Walker is at a career moment. By coincidence, as this January arrives, he has been in office exactly twenty years. And this New Year's Day is almost his birthday.[70]

Born January 6, 1869, he is graying a bit at age 53, having lived

Sheriff R. E. "Bob" Walker

through a great transition. Walker's twenty-year career path has led out of the old frontier—with its bear hunts and blood feuds—and into Florida's modern torrent. By 1923, any wagon smiths left from the old days have mostly retooled their sheds and shade-tree pulleys to become auto mechanics. The twenty-year leap has gone farther than the limerock ruts will lead the sheriff today.

In late 1902 his predecessor, Levy County Sheriff H. S. "Cap" Sutton, lost the big badge abruptly, being accused of kickbacks so greedy as to cast doubt even on a $30 carpenter's fee for a hangman's scaffold.[71] That scandal, and Sheriff Sutton's removal by the governor, caused Chief Deputy Bob Walker to move up—and then to keep getting re-elected by the jungled county's few hundred white male voters.

Generations into the future, people would still be talking about Bob Walker's big case of 1902, the Lewis case,[72] when a blundering double murder placed a bad blot on the good old days (as verified by the docket books). The nice old Lewis couple had been wreathed in gossip about savings hoarded in their remote home—less than twelve miles from Rosewood, near Otter Creek. Two hard-drinking young locals (whites, one of them a relative of the targets) went for the gold. The blood trail showed a pitiless pursuit from porch to hall, as the Lewises were clumsily finished off. The two cold-blooded bunglers were quickly arrested. A lynch mob closed in on their jail cell (without racial motivations; everyone involved was white).

Then came the magic. The mob found that the two prisoners—*Presto!*—had vanished from the jail. Out on a lonely creek bank (said the stories), Chief Deputy Walker was holding his gun on two forlorn divers, forcing them to dive down and haul up the stolen Lewis money, which they had stashed in the creek. The stories seem to wobble here, for in the records the bunglers apparently failed to get any money (though they might have been forced to dive for an incriminating weapon or two; reportedly they dumped their guns in the Waccasassa River). The stories said Walker let them choose: face mob torture back at the jail or cough up enough evidence to assure a quick legal hanging. The prisoners saw the point, opting for the legal hanging. Returning with the waterlogged evidence (of whatever sort), the quiet man wearing the star then faced the mob, as he rolled out one of his trademark peace-making speeches: *Look, boys, this stuff here means you can trust due process to do its job. No smart lawyer is going to get them off now. So go on home.*

Double hanging: Sept. 30, 1902.
Theodore Smith and Thomas Faircloth
for murdering Britt and Georgia Lewis.
Presiding is soon-to-be
ex-Sheriff H. S. "Cap" Sutton,
on his controversial gallows.
(State Archives of Florida, Florida Memory)

Whatever the specifics, the double hanging—a legal one (and apparently the last such legal hanging in Levy County)—would follow on September 30, enshrining Sheriff Cap Sutton's embarrassed gallows—and bringing fame to the chief deputy.

It was so long ago—that luminous triumph two decades in the past—as he now bounces toward what is to be the fateful replay, at the company town of Sumner. Assorted faint murmurs from 1902 will echo into 1923.

The title "Cap," for instance, was pinned onto Sheriff Sutton of 1902 in the old southern sense, deriving from "captain," the rank of tactical pivot in the Confederacy. Among the post-Confederate ruins, "Cap'n" took on a different sense, in a military make-believe of regional post-traumatic ritual, consoling the South's reversals. Precise in retooled meaning, "Cap'n" became the post-Confederate honorific for any white boss of a black work crew (which crew, playing the role of troop company, had best go along with Gilbert and Sullivan and salute). "Cap'n" made a matched set with "Colonel," which in the same regional stage play was granted to other dignitaries, also of no real military rank. The "Colonels," however, were up a step from mere Cap'ns, more on the strategic plane.

"They call me 'Colonel' largely out of respect," announced "Colonel" William J. Simmons, the man who revived the Ku Klux Klan in 1915.[73] "Every lawyer in Georgia is called 'Colonel,'" Simmons explained, "so they thought I was as good as a lawyer." Controversially, Zora Hurston praised this officers' club: "When the Negroes in the South name a white man a colonel, it means CLASS. They may flatter an ordinary bossman by calling him 'Cap'n' but when they say 'Colonel,' 'General' and 'Governor' they are recognizing something internal." Less indulgent was Mark Twain, who scoffed at "bogus decorations" making "every gentleman in the South a Major or a Colonel, or a General or a Judge."[74] (Symmetrically, Generals were few, but you could scarcely swing a courthouse cat without flushing out a Colonel).

The lynching-era white South was dispensing epidemic promotions, as if self-medicating a cultural wound. In "Cap'n" and "Colonel"—and in terms like "stockade" and "commissary," also grafted onto civilian life—some striking military tics patrolled the fortress of racial segregation.[75]

Bob Walker's old boss, Cap Sutton, took the title "Cap" to the limit, into a practice that formed an improvised substitute for slavery, known as convict leasing. Largely forgotten today but widespread in the South just after the Civil War, convict leasing was being used in

"Colonel" William J. Simmons at 1921 congressional hearing. His 1916 revival of the Ku Klux Klan was inspired by the movie *The Birth of a Nation* (background).

every southern state by 1900.[76] Cap Sutton was a local potentate in the buying and selling of county jail inmates. His basement lock-up, swarmed with mosquitoes underneath the courthouse, was a nexus for commercial transactions, as county government sold (or "leased") prisoners to private contractors, basically as temporary slaves. Most leased convicts were black.

Calling him "Cap" reminded that the sheriff was a crew boss. Young Bob Walker, second in command in 1902, was surrounded by shipments to remote plantations and timber jobs—though his next twenty years would see all that come to an end, at least in Levy County, if not in the worst pockets of Florida.[77] By 1923 most of the South would experience public outcry and reform on convict leasing, as each southern state replaced it with another storied institution. The successor would be the roadside chain gang, better known to modern times, with portraits ranging from *Cool Hand Luke* to Sam Cooke's lilting ditty (*...that's the sound of the men / workin' on the chain / ga-a-ang...*).[78] Chain gangs worked only for the government, not for private stockade owners, as had been the case in the worse phase that went before.

Indeed, the fat leasing fees of 1902 were what sank Cap Sutton, apparently tempting him to skim the profits. The new man, clean Bob Walker, then journeyed to middle age on a different ethic, He was still enclosed by racial segregation (re-elected each term in a white-only primary), but balanced on a rung somewhat above the old pit. Nobody said "Cap" Walker. This sheriff's twenty-year course would span the time when the South waked from at least part of the old dream, coming to view convict leasing, with its whipping bosses and flesh trade, as part of the barbaric past.

Reaching an age when fussy spectacles graced his official portraits, Bob Walker kept his distance from groups like the Klan, his friends would recall (and the grumbling of Klannish enemies seemed to confirm).[79] This was saying something. In that era one of the featured attractions at the Levy County Fair was a speech by a Grand Dragon.[80]

The quiet man in the Model T, now dodging ruts and grade piles as the steering wheel jerks irritably, knows that a trip like this one—this sudden alarm call to Sumner—could take him into the lion's den again, to meet the mob demons. So maybe he senses it, this twenty-year pilgrim: This week, they will get him.

Back-porch tales about 1902 would tell the rest of the story, the part the records ignored. There was said to be the secret trick Walker used to smuggle the two Lewis killers out of jail. Though that 1902 lynch mob had the jail surrounded, nobody minded when a wagon load of leased convicts went rolling out of the basement dungeon—since all the convicts in the wagon were black, like most lessees. The mob was interested only in finding two whites.

Into a far future age—the 1980s of blow-dry discotheques, voodoo Reaganomics and clunky green-on-black desktop computer screens—old-timers in those woods would be chuckling about 1902, and the way Chief Deputy Bob smuggled the two swamp rats out to the creek, right under the noses of the mob. Why, he disguised them as two more black convicts in the wagon—by blacking their faces.[81]

Now in 1923, the lease wagons are gone, but the aging sheriff is about to furl his magician's cape one more time. He will have to update his feints and dodges now, again facing superior mob numbers—and for a moment in this unfolding week, his bag of tricks will be enough.

Long ears flapping, sad-sack eyes squinting in the breeze, wrinkled mouth drooling a wet hello—there was apparently a passenger in the car with Sheriff Bob Walker as he rushed toward Sumner. The precise appearance is sadly lost to history, but the case would hinge on a dog.

At least three separate bloodhounds would be on the Fannie Taylor trail by nightfall on Monday, but two were specialists, brought in by train, remembered as arriving late in the afternoon.[82] In the meantime, first investigation seemed to fall to a more local dog, evidently brought twenty miles from the county seat by the sheriff. This dog, too, seems to have been a bloodhound, and not just some random redbone or blue-tick shooed from under a porch.

Bred to have some 230 million scent receptor cells, a good bloodhound could cost over $100 in 1923, more than the salary of a couple of convict road-gang guards for a month.[83] The nasal sensitivity of such a dog is said to be up to a hundred million times greater than a human's.

So what really happened in the Fannie Taylor attack?

It was time to consult the nose.

Almost immediately, the dog seemed to answer one question: Was there a real intruder? The initial answer was emphatic. *Yes!* A strong scent trail was picked up in the back yard. The dog followed it with great conviction—until things grew confusing.

Reconstructing any event through collaged witness statements can leave maddening gaps. The event sequence can become a snake in the weeds, starkly visible in places, but then disappearing at a crucial twist. Sheriff Bob Walker's arrival in Sumner with the dog was illuminated by no  surviving memory, perhaps because of crowd excitement.[84] This moment was a main piece in the puzzle, for the dog was about to become the chief accuser. But a question was left dangling. How was the bloodhound scented in the Taylors' back yard? What procedures—if any—guaranteed that the scent trail found by the dog was actually the right person's scent trail?

There were stories, very vague ones, saying that the "scent article" telling the dog whose trail to follow was an item of Fannie's clothing. But how carefully was this scenting done? Presumably the blouse or skirt held two different scents—Fannie's and the attacker's—so why couldn't it have held a third scent—for instance, the washerwoman's? No one, black or white, seemed to wonder about this. Perhaps it was precluded. At any rate, the dog would not lead to the washerwoman's house, so the issue seemed bypassed. For the moment.

Cummer company hotel, Sumner, Florida, ca. 1923

At the crime scene, the sheriff looked for a somber face shading under a low-brimmed, cowboy-style hat. This was Deputy Clarence Williams, the resident deputy sheriff in Sumner.[85] Williams was a new man, not so long ago appointed here and installed at the Cummer Company's hotel and boarding house. Monday's alarm may have found him in his bachelor's cubicle upstairs, where a crack of light shone from a bare electric bulb in the hall.

A network of such deputies lived in Levy County's remote outposts, especially company towns. In more ordinary villages a local deputy might be a part-time farmer, but in a company town there was the plum job, which the resident deputy got to pick. By firm custom in a company town, such an officer wore two badges at once, working not only as the government's enforcer, employed by the county as a deputy sheriff, but also as a private security guard, working for the ruling timber company.

Indeed, he was more than just a guard, for the deputy became the company's "quarters boss." The rule of law in Levy County, and across the timber jobs of Florida, was thus partly mortgaged. A local deputy also took orders from the company.[86] In Sumner, at least, the orders would be judicious, coming from reform-minded Walter Pillsbury, the Cummer superintendent.

Walter Pillsbury, Superintendent, Sumner

As Sheriff Walker's Ford rattled into Sumner, mill boss Pillsbury was part of the crime-scene equation. Apparently the only telephones in town sat in Cummer facilities—one at the pay office, one at Pillsbury's shady bungalow. The phone call bringing Walker from the county seat (a tiny crossroads called Bronson, more than twenty miles east), had to have come from Pillsbury's equipment.

The two powers at the scene, Walker and Pillsbury, knew that they walked a racial tightrope. The great majority of Sumner's population was African American, living behind the west fence of the white quarters street, in a larger, dustier black quarters. The men there, in shanties with their families or in a larger barracks for bachelors, made up nearly all of the mill's manual labor. Pillsbury depended on them—but whites out in the surrounding woods did not. Those whites lived hard lives on small farms, in the shadow of Sumner's prosperity,

If the farmers should grow enflamed by a sudden racial witch hunt, they might rampage through the black quarters. And then Sumner's work force might flee, leaving Pillsbury with a dead mill. He had reason to hope that the attacker of Fannie Taylor would be caught quickly, so that all of this—by whatever means—could be put to bed.

Pillsbury had only to think about Perry, Florida, a month earlier, with its spree of burning and killing spread across the week of December 2-8, 1922. Perry was also a sawmill town, though its rampage was different from Sumner's in one sense. At Perry, the triggering event had raised no questions about the veracity of the female accuser. The Perry victim, schoolteacher Ruby Hendry, was found slashed and beaten to death. Sumner's subsequent trigger was more ambiguous and puzzling, almost as if straining to echo the thrilling excitement at Perry.

The railroad trestle where Hendry's body was found ran over a blackwater slough called Pimple Creek, where her routine walk from a relative's house had caused a sudden encounter. Learning of indications that a black hobo had been sleeping under the trestle, crowds of manhunters spread out to terrorize African Americans through northern Florida and into Georgia. The whopping $425 spent on bloodhounds for the Perry hunt far exceeded the $50 that would be spent at Sumner/Rosewood a month later.[87] Perry's climax, a ritual live burning, apparently left no written documents at all, nor any preserved evidence that the man set on fire was really the killer of Ruby Hendry.

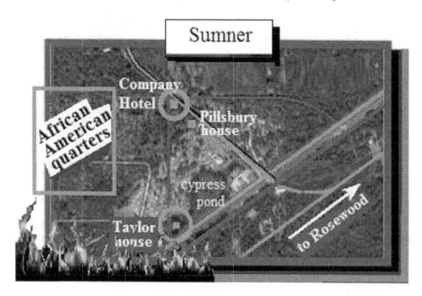

Such bursts of horror had flared across much of the United States in the brutalized aftermath of the Civil War, which ended in 1865. But by the 1890s the behavioral epidemic—the Lynching Era—was narrowing mainly to a core outbreak zone, the South, with its racial passions (relatively few African Americans lived in the North at that time).

There were assorted pressures. In 1910 the Rockefeller Foundation launched an ambitious, south-wide health campaign, said to finally liberate the region from infestation by hookworm.[88] Doctors contended that beforehand, this menace had been sapping the vitality and productivity from a staggering proportion of the southern population—as if a microbial face sat behind Dogpatch and Tobacco Road—with unknown whisperings to the mysterious Judge Lynch.

Hookworms and malaria mosquitoes were not accessible lynching targets, but discomfort could sometimes be displaced. Forty miles north of Rosewood in 1916, a mass lynching at Newberry, Florida, unfolded just as the town's economy was collapsing, taking it suddenly from boomtown to nearly a ghost town.[89] The issue of "social strain" as a hidden hand behind lynching patterns would be debated for generations.

This was small consolation to the man in the Model T, or his necktie-wearing ally in the sawmill pay office. Walker and Pillsbury could not look back on the totality of a great era of lynching—with its wave-like beginning and end, as if marking a fad or fashion. The Perry case of December 2-8, with its week-long ritual length, had enflamed a nerve, inviting emulation. A drumbeat of other cases in 1922 strengthened the call: a similar rampage in Kirven, Texas, lynchings in Georgia and Arkansas. At the one-month anniversary of Perry, two accidental guardians formed a thin line of defense.

ca. 1923

1982

Marshall Cannon

Sumner in 1923 was just big enough to have a barber. At age 23, the plain-spoken stylist had one chair, a pair of clippers and a pool table in the side room. On New Year's morning, 1923, the oasis run by Marshall Cannon was readying for its usual traffic in loafers and dispensers of wisdom.

Interviewed in 1982, still blue-eyed and blunt-spoken, the 82-year-old former barber (and former city councilman, by that time) would have no recollection of early alarm at his shop. His premises were on the outskirts of Sumner, well away from the back fence at the Taylors house. Intervening was a wide area of blackjack thickets, not to mention the dense trees at the cypress pond. Cannon worked in Sumner's secondary hub, a cluster of shops and houses outside the property owned by Cummer Lumber.

Where the side track for the log train went into Sumner from the main Seaboard line, it was flanked by an old wagon road curving up past the sawmill. This sandy lane held together a string of buildings rooted in Sumner's frontier past. In 1911 when crews had piled off a train to build the Cummer facilities, a tiny farming settlement had already stood at the spot, its pioneer families soon plugging into the new sawmill economy.[90] Their homes and stores remained in the area of Sumner's railroad depot. Larger than Rosewood's open shed depot three miles away, the Sumner train station came complete with a telegraph room and a young freight agent. Weathered neighboring buildings gave a village effect: Dorsett's meat market, Pearson's drug store, peg-legged Smallwood pigeon-holing letters at the cramped post office—and, parting the gooseweed nearby, there was Marshall Cannon's shop, steeped in the aroma of Lucky Tiger and Vitalis hair tonic, as the billiard balls rumbled and clicked.[91]

The first Cannon knew of anything amiss that morning, he said, was when he looked up in surprise. A group of men seemed to be rushing out of the scrub from the direction of the quarters, following a dog. Also drawn out onto a nearby porch was Ed Dorsett at the meat market. Cannon said the two of them ran out together, joining the chase, as it reached the obvious thoroughfare. Oil spots on the wooden crossties of the railroad seemed not to deter the sniffing nose. The bloodhound began following the Seaboard tracks, tracking the scent northeast toward the horizon.

Though Cannon could flesh things out with details, this same basic story was the one everyone told: the backyard scent, the strong trail, the swift passage to the tracks—and then straight along those tracks. But this left some puzzles. Frances Smith said that after the men gathered in the Taylors' back yard a woman like herself had no business being back there—and she wasn't aware there was any dog at all. But before the men arrived, she had seized her chance for sleuthing at the back fence. She clearly remembered seeing those broken fence palings, left by the man who crept in.

This sits uncomfortably with Cannon's telling. He said, with a little laugh, that the poor bloodhound got so excited by the strong scent in the back yard that it ran right up against the fence, and had to be lifted over clumsily like a sack of potatoes, then resuming on the other side. Cannon had the acrobatic fugitive *leaping over* a sturdily intact fence.

Both of these stories can't be true.

Moreover, there is Philomena Doctor's third version, telling of personally witnessing the intrusion while at her grandmother Sarah's wash fire. In 1982, Doctor emphatically described the intruder strolling peacefully through the back gate, then strolling back out the same way. She stressed his calmness, his arrogant unconcern—and his use of the gate. Her mystery man neither hopped nor broke the fence. Taken together, these three stories leave that passage in impenetrable fog. Somehow, the dog and the men found an escape route, and burst out to the railroad.

But one thing at the Taylor house was clear. The men did wait there for the sheriff to arrive. Nobody was going to jump the gun on the dog. Deputy Williams, already on the scene before the sheriff, may have kept them focused, but whites there didn't seem inclined to immediately go running through the nearby black quarters for random vandalism or revenge—not at this point. The intruder was thought to be a stranger— like the hobo under the bridge at Perry—and they wanted that particular stranger. In a world without public buses, hobos catching rides on freight trains were commonly seen, and many were black.[92] The "Scottsboro boys" in 1931 formed perhaps the most famous example—nine African Americans together, all younger than the age of twenty, riding in a single gondola car—until they were stopped and arrested for alleged rape.

At its outset, the Sumner manhunt seemed disciplined and rational, bent on catching one man, whom they hoped to quickly overtake.

———————————————

Twenty-two-year-old Lee Carrier of Rosewood, the stoic outsider who had walked to work before dawn, continued climbing the lumber stacks of Sumner through the day. He noticed little change in the routine, though some of the white personnel, the foremen and skilled craftsmen, seemed to have disappeared. Where had they gone? They weren't announcing their game plan to an African American laborer.

Still fewer signs were noted by Sam Hall, the newest lumber stacker among the hikers from Rosewood. Having turned 16 on December 5,

Sam was thrilled by his new job, with its special sign of manhood. Now he wears long pants, no more short child's knickers. And no more plodding child labor in the turpentine woods on the other side of Rosewood. Even the dangers of his new lumber-stacking job seem manly. One accident has already occurred, an older man hefting a big plank, not bothering to give warning as it flips onto Sam's ankle, the sharp edge skinning down his heel. Here was a red badge of courage, working through the day with blood in his shoe.

At mid-morning on Monday the whistle moans, "quartering time." Then it roars again at noon. No whites come roaming into the stacks to accuse the Rosewood hands of the attack.

Just south, among canned goods in the Sumner commissary, young clerk Ernest Parham is running the store, too far from the mill to see it through intervening pines. Today he has been left in charge of the commissary because its manager, Albert Johnson, has dashed off to join the chase.

Out on the railroad, short-stepping the crossties, barber Marshall Cannon has no idea who the quarry might be. But the fugitive seems close, judging by the dog. The eager nose does a dance, sniffing directly along the top of a rail, but occasionally darting off, then immediately back onto the rail again. "He's tryin' to walk that iron," someone exclaims.[93] This theory says that the runner knows a dog will be pursuing, so he's trying (ineffectively) to lift his scent off the ground, by balancing along the steel flange—though stumbling aside at times, with each of these stumbles followed neatly by the dog's nose—a standard ability in bloodhounds.

"The way the hounds traced his exact movements was a thing of beauty," marveled a Florida convict "cap'n" in the 1880s, describing the way a dog's nose re-enacted a fugitive's gyrations, even when the runner snatched a disguise outfit off a clothesline.[94]

That chase, however, made a second point. As at Sumner, the pursuit in the 1880s followed a railroad, but the 1880s fugitive logically darted among bushes alongside, trying to hide from view. The Sumner scent was described as going right down the middle of the tracks— almost flaunting the runner's visibility. And yet in houses along the way, no one seemed to notice anything unusual.

As the pursuers speed northeast up the tracks they meet open country, pastures and clumps of palmetto thicket. To their right is the dark mass of Gulf Hammock, laced with beards of Spanish moss and wild palms. Deputy Williams apparently sticks with the small group sweating behind the dog. The older sheriff seems to follow by car, pacing them on sand lanes.

Ahead on the horizon is a jumbled smear, coming closer, revealing human habitation. A rambling one-story home stands south of the tracks, facing across toward a deserted ruin. Trumpet vines or creepers curl around iron bars on a stern-looking but now deserted window. This was once the pay office of M. Goins & Bros. Naval Stores, a turpentine distillery operation—in fact *the* turpentine distillery in the area's African American history. Martin Goins, with his brothers and brother-in-law, were African American entrepreneurs working at the turn of the century, when the frontier was a different kind of place. Those times are ghosts as the dog appears—the old songs they sang at the Goins parlor piano, the ledgers and teamsters, the young ladies schooled at St. Augustine College, the starched collars and corsets—gone into a vanished past.

The dog is now delving into a veiled communal journey—as the pages before you seek also to do. At this house and its adjoining ruins, the manhunters have entered the leading edge of the two-mile communal area known as Rosewood.[95]

"Hattie," says the man in the cowboy-style hat and khakis, stepping onto the porch, "Have you seen any strangers go by?"

The caller from the posse is addressing Hattie Goins, the wife of Perry Goins, one of the lumber stackers who walked to Sumner this morning. Watching from inside the house is officious little Bea Goins, nearly ten years old. Tending her younger siblings, she considers herself already an adult.

Perry Goins
b. Oct. 4, 1884

Bea will recall only the one man, no glimpse of others out on the tracks, or a dog. Since turning nine she has washed and ironed. The younger ones are "the children" in her vocabulary. The caller she remembers could fit the description of Deputy Clarence Williams, but he could have been anyone, on a lone reconnaissance mission or a stop with the crowd. She notices no tone of accusation. The man seems polite. This branch of the Goins family is viewed amicably by both races, seeming to have eluded the community's cryptic feuds—which struck harder at Perry Goins's brothers, Charlie and George.

Work as a lumber stacker is a step-down from the Goins legacy of 1903, when Perry's uncle Martin was leasing eight square miles of pine lands to tap them for resin. The house sits on a 65-acre parcel that the family continues to own. As the Goins company faded by confusing turns, Perry tried market hunting for a while, ranging into the jungle behind the house for hides and pelts. But the wilderness was subsiding like the frontier economy. Over-extraction had thinned everything—the game, the trees, even the oyster beds out at Cedar Key. Those were so badly overfished around the turn of the century that years of recovery would be required.

Beatrice Goins Frazier
Feb. 12, 1913 - June 20, 1984

Perry Goins's wife Hattie knows the particulars, for her father is Old Man John Coleman, the aging trapper who caught the wave of virgin abundance at its peak, riding it into a two-story house on the other side of the community—and into the feuds. Little Bea Goins is not told that part of the story. She learns her lessons from other moments.

There are the visits from Aunt Sissy, another of John Coleman's daughters. Sissy, too (Virginia Coleman Smith), lives on the far side of Rosewood, but in a one-room cabin with rags burning at the door, smoking out the mosquitoes. Aunt Sissy sometimes teases Bea's mother for being too fussy.[96] Once when Hattie ordered her children to wear shoes, Sissy complained: "Why you make those children put on shoes? You tryin' to be white?"

Unremarked was the etiology of hookworm, the life-draining parasite that enters through the soles of bare feet. Bea took the lesson on more general grounds—one more view of the family, balanced by the good things, like wonderful old grandmother Coleman, Sissy's mother, laboring down the back path to bring a basket of fresh-baked cookies.

The man in khaki is soon gone from the porch. Hattie has told him the obvious: nothing has been seen. This morning has brought no ripple in their daily routine. No mysterious stranger has been spied. Inquiries of this type will soon spread through Rosewood and two miles beyond, into the railroad whistlestop called Wylly, where the area's sole remaining turpentine camp continues to smoke and boil. There, in one of the shanties belonging to M. & M. Naval Stores, Arthina Blocker, age eight, soon finds two white men at the door—asking about a mysterious fugitive. In this case they make a rather brusque search of the house.[97] Arthina is glad her brothers aren't playing in the loft and making suspicious noises. The men look nervous enough to shoot.

Up and down the tracks the ceremony repeats, always with the same result. What man? Where? The owner of the scent seems invisible.

As the dog continues northeast, leaving behind the Goins area, signs of a communal presence begin coming more thickly. Glimpses of plank walls and shingle roofs are set back from the railroad, nestled in hanging moss and trees. This is much like the quick snapshot view afforded to whites on passing trains, as they might briefly wonder: What is this mysterious little place the colored people have here, this Rosewood?

On the dog's right (as the manhunt pushes deeper into the community along the rails), a pale wooden box appears, moored on low brick foundation piers, topped by a smaller box—which is a squat church belfry, equipped inside with a pull-rope.

Backed into the shadows of Gulf Hammock, this is the First African Methodist Episcopal Church of Rosewood, on a triangular plot deeded in 1912. Its wider life is invisible to the search party: the Sunday school circulars mailed all the way from Nashville, Tennessee; the A.M.E. district office fifty miles up the tracks; the bishop's conventions; the melodious console organ filling the plank building on Sundays.

The songs are mostly gone now, along with other ghosts, though here the glow lingers, surviving beyond the death of the Goins turpentine distillery—and beyond the similar demise of the Rosewood cedar mill. The church marks out the fading transition, hope still alive: maybe time can stand still, just in this one pool of memories; maybe the old frontier can live on.[98]

The songs here, soaring up into the belfry, were strengthened by one solo voice in particular—that fellow with the knack, seemingly good at everything, the rich voice in the hymns—"Here Speaks the Comforter"— though also it is a voice that can ring more coarsely on summer nights, outdoors down at the depot as men gather to joke and talk. The one voice heard above the rest, as if still singing even there, belting it out, but by means of that other personal quirk—his strange, haunting style of laughter—like the laughing call of a lord-god bird out in the woods.

That laughing man, Sylvester.

The men with the dog, seeking no ghosts, are braced for quick capture. Some are perhaps thinking that at any moment the distant runner will be spied—whoever he is.

Already they have passed another wood-frame box, opposite the church across the tracks and just before it. Some in the posse may know details, that this is home base for Magnolia Lodge #148, a Masonic hall.[99] All of them probably understand its general nature; such fixtures stand in small communities throughout the woods of 1923—though this one has a distinction, being for Masons who are black, in a larger organizational stream long ago branching away from white Masonry. Predating governmental segregation, the Prince Hall Affiliation of the Free and Accepted Masons, initiating members who were African American, dated at least from the 1820s, with fainter roots in the 1700s. This building, pale like the church, is a two-story structure, but with a vaguely claustrophobic air, lacking windows in its upper half. Ritual architecture hides upstairs dramas—the parables of the sword and lamp, the all-night raisings. The lodge was sited here around the same time as the nearby church, in a combination storied in the black South of the segregation years: "church for the women, lodge for the men."

Here, too, was the hope for a new kind of community after the reverses around 1911, a community that might surmount the lack of any internal source of regular wages, relying on the farms and forest resources—while they lasted —and outside work for those willing to hike.

Through the World War years of 1914-1918, the community would continue to shrink—and on through 1920 and its post-war depression, the stirrings of Roaring Twenties recovery, the sound and fury of Prohibition, the distant Jazz Age. And perhaps only at odd moments pausing for the troubled question:

How will all this shrinkage finally end? At what lonely remaining cabin? In what kind of older head's last bedside whisper or sigh? In what obscurity of trumpet vine and crumbling porch?

Never thinking: No, not like this.

Straining at a martingale harness (to prevent the choking action of a collar), the dog on the tracks was presumably a rather typical bloodhound, in a line well established by the early twentieth century. Over many generations, genetic manipulation had produced a messy form of detective, whose over-salivating, drool-spewing lips reminded of maximized scent glands in the recesses of dewlap and shotgun nose. The sad red pockets under the eyes also spoke of this, to the extent that an occasional genetic misfire might be born blind.

That last nugget, the part about some bloodhounds being born blind, was told to me in 1996 by an ABC News producer, as we stood peering down a weedy lane, which formed the only remaining trace of the old railroad.[100] A tunnel of leafy shadows marked where the dog had gone. Now a new wave of excitement had come to a puzzling place in the swamps, as if something in the 1920s had refused to die, and was echoing—two new hunters squinting into the palmetto thickets, hoping to catch sight of something.

The men and the dog rush past the Masonic hall, the A.M. E. church and intermittent porches. Some of the buildings are boarded and abandoned, some still occupied. Looming ahead now is the historical key to the communal rune. A clearing in the bushes widens on the right, weeds and vines fringing a hardened mound of what looks like soil. But this is a refuse pile of sawdust.

When first formed here, this mound exuded sweet-smelling perfume, like the red-hearted trees from which it came, the cedar. As the dog passes, rusty metal spikes protrude from abandoned cement slabs, the remains of the Charpia cedar mill. Between about 1845 and 1911 this species of tree—*Juniperus virginiana*, eastern red cedar—was cut so heedlessly that by 1923 the few widely scattered survivor trees were deep in the hammock or on posted land, where a poacher could make a day's wages off a single filched log. The epitaph was phrased in 1954 by T. R. Hodges, a community leader in Cedar Key, in reference to both cedar and pine: "Today it is difficult to get anything larger than cord wood for a fence post."[101]

The dog rushes on, but now passes a more active spot, this time on the north side of the tracks. A railroad freight dock signals John Wright's store, the one commercial ember still glowing in the community. J. M.

Wright & Co. General Merchandise is set back in the trees, the fifty-year-old philosopher ensconced in there somewhere, the tall Sunday school teacher wife perhaps at the counter, the cracker barrels, bolts of cloth, floor bins, butcher paper for wrapping.[102]

In the quiet remnant community, a white-owned store serving black neighbors raises few questions. John Wright, the wry diplomat, hands out candy or scuppernong grapes from his vines to passing children, most of them African American. The dog passes on.

From Wright's, the community railroad depot can be seen up ahead: the open-fronted shed, the rain-washed sign with its eight letters in cryptogram array.

1) Cornelia Carter
   Sam Carter
2) Mary Ann
   Hayward
3) John McCoy
4) Perry Goins
   office (vacant)
   Baptist church
5) Sam King-Lexie Gordon
6) Masonic hall

7) Rob Ingram
   Will Ingram
8) A.M.E. church
9) Burns (vacant)
   white church
   George Bradley
10) Wright store
11) Wesley Bradley
    Ed Bradley

12) Carriers (south)
    Rosewood depot
    Sarah Carrier
    Laura Jones
    Aaron Carrier
13) Carriers (north)
    Coarsey (vacant)
    M.E. church
    James Carrier
    Sherman (vacant)
    Williams (vacant)

ROSEWOOD

→→→→→→
bloodhound's path on railroad

And then, still farther up, past the depot and the briars where there used to be more buildings, another jumble of roof shingles and shrubs coalesces in the humid distance: Sarah Carrier's house.

The front-yard cabbage palm, the yard fence now fallen away to leave one corner post still standing.

Is the homeowner in there now, on this washday gone bad? At the back of the house, down a shotgun hall, is the extra room they added as the last refuge for her son, Sylvester.

The dog shows no interest, passing Sarah Carrier's front porch without hesitation. Its trajectory seems to rule out a case of mistaken identity. If the dog were to be mistakenly following the scent of the washerwoman, surely it would turn aside at her door.

It seems to be following *someone*, without much doubt.

But who?

A single scent molecule striking a membrane in a bloodhound's sinus may conceivably produce a mental image as sharp as when a visual image strikes n human. Such a molecule may come not only from a quarry's "scurf" (a stream of dead skin cells trailing behind a moving body), but from shoe polish, sweat, even plant juices released by broken grass stems.[103] The idea of lifting one's scent off the ground to fool such a dog can be disastrously simplistic,[104] for the bloodhound will lift, too, casting for air traces. And yet again, the scent molecules and nerve impulses used in this process are not manipulable objects. Canine or not, this is an exquisitely *mental* dance, this nasal way of seeing, in its unknowable realm of bloodhound thought.

So it can fail.[105]

In cases where the bloodhound does *not* fail—the many cases when the nose wins the game and a desperate runner is found—the previously relentless canine sleuth may immediately lose interest in the chase, as if to say: *"Okay, game over."* Or, quite the contrary, a triumphant bloodhound may rush forward gleefully, licking the frightened quarry like a delighted puppy: *"Ha ha! Found you!"*

Media portrayals of the Rosewood events have repeatedly included an interesting hallmark of fantasy, the depiction of viciously snapping and baying bloodhounds. Real bloodhounds rarely even bark.

Chapter 7: Aaron's Ghosts

The strange sight—a lot of white men coming toward her up the railroad—has caught Minnie at the front fence, northeast of Aunt Sarah's house.

By now the group of manhunters that started at the Taylor house has grown. And not all are on foot.

Falling in with Sheriff Walker's car are other vehicles, including a prestigious one, driven by Edward Pillsbury, age 17. He is the impulsive, somewhat accident-prone son of Sumner's corporate ruler, sawmill Superintendent Walter Pillsbury. Meanwhile, by another mode of transport—on horseback—a turpentine foreman named Jack Cason has also galloped into the frame.

Nine-year-old Minnie Lee Mitchell does not hear the names. As she stands in the sandy yard near her grandmother's front gate, a comparison comes to her mind: an insect swarm, a hive, an anthill. The mass of men is "like antses"—though led by a dog.

Fourteenth Census of the United States: 1920

Household	Name	Relationship	Age	Color or Race
113 Carrier,	James	Head	54	B
"	Emma	Wife	48	B
"	Willard	Son	20	B
"	Wade	Son	17	B
"	Eddie	Son	15	B
"	Lonnie	Son	10	B
"	Goldee	Daughter	9	B
"	James Jr.	Son	6	B
Mitchell,	Ruben	Grand Dr	10	B
"	Lee	Grand Dr	8	B

No particular feeling of alarm will lodge in her memory—not yet. One of them comes to Mama at the fence, where Minnie stands in her customary guard position, close to Mama's skirts. The man says: "Emma has anybody come along here?" Again comes the response: No one has been seen. The question does not seem dangerous or menacing, merely strange, weighed skeptically by the small guardian.

She thinks of herself as "Mama's little shadow," unique among those of her household, distinguished by her fierce attachment to her grandmother Emma, to Mama. Half orphaned at birth by the death of her mother Daisy, then orphaned completely when her father, Theron Mitchell, stopped coming home from a work camp to the south on Crystal River, Minnie has fixed adoring affection on her substitute caregiver: tall, willowy Emma Carrier.

If Mama is away too long shopping in the buggy, fighty little Minnie indignantly scolds her on return, having worried so much. This reversal of roles, the scolding, over-protective parent played by the uprooted but irritably re-attached child, would be scrutinized by a future age, when an urbanized society began to worry about the latch-key kids of divorce. Minnie was a textbook example of what the pundits would call "separation anxiety."

The U.S. Census of 1920 was not perfect on the matter of that sandy strip in Precinct 9. The census taker was Alfred Dorsett, age 28, a white in a family with county political connections. Living three miles down the railroad in Sumner, Alf was the older brother of meat market operator Ed Dorsett, remembered as being in the 1923 manhunt. The gaps in Alfred Dorsett's census-taking appeared not only in Rosewood but in his hometown of Sumner, where he seemed to skip households here and there. Pushing into Rosewood among wary faces and ethnic dialect, he classified Minnie's older brother Ruben as a "Grand Dr" (grand-daughter), though in adulthood Ruben, a goofy bear of a jokester, would be strong enough to amuse turpentine cronies by lifting a Model T's back bumper to watch the wheels spin. Minnie received a scrawled abbreviation in the same census, a scrawl that may have said "Lee." She was also made a year older than her consensus age—and this gives pause. Her confirmably sharp memory does seem a bit precocious for a nine-year-old. It could be wondered whether she was really ten in January 1923. Her world in 1923 shimmers in reconstruction—never entirely blurred, but not perfectly sharp—like her scrawled label in the census.

Dorsett's visit, as he wrestled with his unwieldy census tablet, was in January of 1920. Now, two years later, it's January again—and again the official world of white men has come into Minnie's world.

Soon the swarm passes. The dog is impatient, straining along the rails. Southern manhunts often followed railroads because these offered a fugitive clear direction, unlike roads whose loops and bends could get you lost.[106] Just after passing Minnie's observation post, the hunt is almost at the point of leaving Rosewood entirely. Minnie stands near the community's inland edge, the northeastern edge, farthest from Sumner. Beyond her there are only two more homes in Rosewood in the dog's general path. Hardee Davis's pungent hermit cabin (he was known to stew up a skunk or two) stands back in the thickets behind Mama's field. But closer to the tracks is the home of a young married couple, Aaron and Gussie Carrier. Aaron is Minnie's uncle, the oldest son of her grandparents, James and Emma Carrier.

Past his house there are open fields, dwindling out of sight toward the shanties of Wylly and its turpentine camp, too far away to be seen. Whites are now arriving from that direction, too, converging with the Sumner whites coming from the southwest. Neither group has found any stranger. The riddle of disappearance is becoming acute.

Minnie catches only glimpses as the swarm diminishes toward Wylly. But then it does something new. The dog veers, suddenly leaving the tracks. The men go with it. This will form a high point in tales about the hunt.

Darting to the right off the tracks, the straining bloodhound crosses the railroad's grassy sixty-foot right-of-way, then reaches a house, the outermost in the community. Minnie knows it well. Outside is the small porch; and inside are strange olive-drab leg-wrappings, along with a little cap brought home from the great war.

Her uncle Aaron Carrier was born February 20, 1895, according to his U.S. Army service record from World War I. On a tense New Year's Day in 1923, he is 27. His small home faces the Seaboard tracks from the south, pointing its back porch into the secrets of Gulf Hammock. The positioning alone tells a tale—which now requires a pause (if the bloodhound can be frozen in mid-stride) for a little biography.

The family talked about how Papa—Minnie's grandfather James Carrier—had tried to keep his married children close, even architecturally. In years past, three small shanties had risen near Papa's larger home. Minnie was convinced that James Carrier himself had built these cabins, which may have been the case. In the community's first shrink-age from the freezes of the late 1890s, parcels of land had come available, even before the cedar and turpentine jobs went down, producing further shrinkage. The booms and busts of the Florida frontier formed an almost continuous roller coaster.

Minnie knew the three cabins personally: three wedding gifts. The first was given to Aaron, Papa's oldest son. It was the only one of the three still occupied on January 1, 1923. Less cheerful was the story of the second small house, given to daughter Daisy after she had married Theron Mitchell. That was where Minnie was born, not hearing the gathering storm of World War, as Daisy lost the battle with childbirth. Now at age nine Minnie can look out into bushes beyond Mama's fence and see the empty clearing. One day an accidental spark came along, finding the deserted structure, then removed it from the scene.

But then there was the third of the gifts, still intact in 1923, though empty. It had been the wedding present for James's daughter Beulah, when she married Frank Sherman the preacher. The family seldom called her Beulah, however; they knew her as Scrappy—not the best omen for the marriage. Mama had loved the choice of bridegroom, welcoming a preacher into the family, but within three years Sherman was gone, the cabin vacant. By then Scrappy had taken her two small children to Wylly, to live not in the old Rosewood freehold as Papa had hoped, but in one of the newer segregated compounds that were springing up throughout the woods, a company quarters.

Mama was doubly heartbroken, for Scrappy adapted to Wylly by working as a dancehall waitress, while living in the worst place possible—in the Wylly dancehall itself, with its harsh name that could be heard in other such places across the woods. Scrappy went to live in "the jook."

Minnie did not question Papa's original landscaping scheme, or its faint suggestion of a manor house flanked by slave cabins in a lost age. By the time she came along, Papa himself was almost a ghost. Minnie was present at his two cerebral strokes—not fatal episodes but leaving James Carrier partially paralyzed and barely able to speak. The crippled frontiersman had lived to see the one remaining wedding gift, Aaron's still-occupied shanty, meet the manhunt of 1923.

Less rebellious than his sister Scrappy, Aaron Carrier possessed one of the more puzzling temperaments in the community, viewed more as a gentle joke than a mystery. The family laughed about Aaron's courting days, just prior to marriage on December 20, 1917.[107] One night walking home, wearing his best suit, they said, Minnie's young uncle was gripped by a spell of panic, a wild fear in the moonlight. One minute he was walking peacefully alongside a hogwire fence, then the next minute— *there they were!*

Aaron had met the ghosts everyone talked about, the ones from the Civil War, left by the battle six miles to the southwest at Number Four Bridge.[108] And after the encounter, Mama's work was cut out for her. Her needle and thread had to mend the suit after its collision with the fence, so frenzied was Aaron's flight. When Minnie heard the story she did not think it was ridiculous to believe in ghosts, but she still chuckled a bit. Nobody else seemed to get carried away like that. It seemed unique, this tendency in Brother Aaron to panic.[109]

Cousin Lee Carrier agreed. Aaron seemed "scary," jumpy, as if someone had reset his carburetor to choke. Sam Hall said that the mystifying fits of panic were the reason for Aaron's early dismissal from the army in World War I. The records show only that he came home.

No outsider would be able to peer into a stressed stretch of woodland and take a psychological census of such individual quirks. Nor would any weather forecaster be able to say which of these stress points, if subjected to some sudden shock, might unstably converge into a larger pattern, and precipitate into the human weather of mass violence.

The manhunt was now proceeding so rapidly that little room was left to contemplate a coincidence. An invisible scent trail, over three miles long, was knitting together two individuals who, in their respective home communities, were both known for symptoms suggesting vulnerability to panic. If the entire week were to be viewed as a grand, unfathomable ecosystem of mass panic—including the kind of panic that kills—it had now somehow found its panic-plotted roadmap.

Minnie could see no details as the distant men poured onto Aaron's porch. Some whites would claim a closer view, though perhaps they were closer to the old tradition, the self-aggrandizing frontier boast—as they only fantasized being in the thick of things. Either way, any doubts about eyewitness authority were offset to a large degree

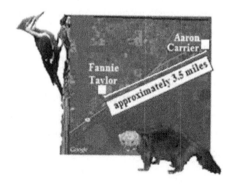

by uniform agreement. No one disagreed about this part.[110] The story about what happened at Aaron Carrier's house was accepted by even the sharpest dissenter on other matters. Philomena Doctor, despite her insistence that the scent really belonged to a misconstrued white man, and not to a black man, nonetheless agreed without objection on the core description of *how* this man was chased, whoever he was.

As to the nose, the bloodhound was too excited to stand on ceremony. Unconcerned about being polite, it rushed onto Aaron Carrier's small porch, then reared and threw its front paws on the door. Back down the tracks, as Minnie watched uncertainly from afar, she could have saved the men some trouble. She knew they needn't bother to knock on Brother Aaron's door, for no one was home.

The dog was pulled aside. The door was flung open. The dog then rushed into the house, once more dancing the meticulous bloodhound minuet, tracing out the actions of an absent party. Stories would vary slightly as to which objects, exactly, the dog sniffed out—ostensibly objects the owner of the scent had touched. He seemed first to have thrown himself down on a bed in exhaustion, then to have examined two household items, a pair of shoes under the bed (perhaps thinking to change shoes and block the scent?), and then an old shotgun in the corner—as if for a moment he grabbed up the gun, then reconsidered: *Would it only slow me down? Would it only provoke the hunters if I took a shot?* After such abortive feints (said the nose in its tracing), he then left it all behind, for next he fled out the back door—pausing only long enough for a gulp of water, having found the bucket at the back porch, cradled on its cooling shelf. The tales would preserve no musings about a familiar-looking *modus operandi*. As at Fannie Taylor's house three miles past, this house, too, was the most isolated one in its row, and the alleged route of intrusion came in through the front door, then out the back.

Things were about to grow too wrenching for Minnie to watch coolly. The swarm suddenly grew larger again, flooding back from Aaron's house—back toward where Minnie was standing.

What stayed in memory was a lone white man, seeming to get ahead of the rest, giving him a moment to urgently consult with Mama at the fence. Was this the sheriff? Sheriff Walker had known Emma Carrier for a long time. He had had long-ago dealings with this long-suffering household. But this time any conference came too late. Whoever the sympathetic presence was, he was quickly overtaken by his companions. Rushing past him into the yard, they barged into Emma's front door.

Apparently someone had told them what Minnie had known all along—that if they wanted Aaron Carrier, the place to find him was here, at his mother's house. He was in an upstairs bedroom. What Minnie did not know, however, was the counter-intuitive thing—that the men now storming through the yard did not think that Aaron himself was their shadowy fugitive. They thought only that he was a chief witness, perhaps an accomplice. Even in the tumult, none seemed to find reason to think that Aaron Carrier might be the runner from Sumner.

Their actions back at his house had reached a fateful finality. Beyond the telltale indoor dance, which ended at the water bucket on the back porch, the dog had leaped triumphantly into the sand of the back yard, still hot on the trail, signaling that the runner was once more running, now setting out toward Gulf Hammock.

But then came the glitch. The narrators loved this part. The dog "looked up"—meaning that it began desperately casting in the air for traces of the scent—because no scent was left on the ground. The annals of manhunting held many such moments. Though it was true that cheap tricks were unlikely to fool a dog (like sprinkling pepper on your tracks—or balancing along a railroad flange), it was also true that there was a limit. A half-century of such chases had immortalized an escape mechanism that could lift a fugitive into unsmellable safety. An accomplice could come along with a mule, giving him a lift, raising his scent up off the ground.[111]

Since no one can see into a bloodhound's mind, there is little way to reconcile the many tales of escape-by-mule with more modern exceptions, when verifiably a bloodhound has succeeded in trailing a closed automobile, or has traced a kidnap victim locked in a trunk.[112] The distinction may be that successful closed-vehicle pursuits are rare, and that in some modern cases, vehicle intervention does foil the dog. In the days of horseback pursuit, the mere height of a horse was said to be enough to lift the scent out of detectable range. And this height was negotiable. The device didn't have to be a horse or mule, exactly.

At the point behind Aaron Carrier's house where the suddenly confused dog was casting about, the pursuers looked down at the sand (so the universally-agreed narrative went). And there they saw it—the next clue. A wagon road snaked into the sheltering, seemingly limitless shadows of the Great Gulf Hammock. Perhaps carved into the sand were new wheel tracks. The obvious escape device was a wagon.

Whether or not there was hard evidence that now is lost, the majority of pursuers became firmly convinced. At Aaron Carrier's house, the sneaking fugitive had found help. Maybe more than one helper. Maybe a whole conspiracy—here in this nest of Negro mystery. Maybe one accomplice had run to get help, then had found an additional accomplice, who came back over here in a wagon, carrying the fellow off.

This theory was bad news for the most logical source of information about the alleged conspiracy, householder Aaron Carrier.

By this time—with a mere shift in a dog's confidence—the previously disciplined and controlled pursuit was turning into the thing that Sheriff Bob Walker had seen twenty years before. Modern images of lynching sometimes fail to capture the danger that was now arising—a danger not just to the primary suspect sought by a manhunt, but to African American bystanders along the trail—if the main target should disappear. Now somebody has to be made to talk, to tell where the mystery man has gone. Of course, a bystander might not *know* where he went—but then, torture could confirm that, too.

The three-mile run was shifting into an ancient pattern: a witch hunt—for lack of a better term. The insidious demon, vanishing so cleverly, must be found by proxy. And the witnesses must be pressured because they might be fellow witches, expendable in the name of public safety.

Out in the yard, Minnie could hear the men coming back down the stairs inside the house. They had found the upstairs bedroom. Shoved in front of them was the familiar figure, now captured. As they pushed him out into the sunlight she heard a voice shout, "Bring a rope!"

Again there was no chance to see the distinction. They were not going to execute such a star witness. He was the link who could keep the manhunt alive. The idea instead was to use a standard local torture technique, hauling up the accused accomplice and choking him until he talked. Choking with a lasso is such an effective persuader that it has been used to break wild horses. By contrast, an execution by hanging requires a sudden drop to snap the neck. They were going proceed more gradually, introducing panic-stricken Aaron Carrier to the terror of suffocation, as if by drowning (though they had never heard the tradecraft term of a later age, waterboarding).

No one would remember any effort to simply take the dog down the wagon road and catch up with the scent. Something of the sort must surely have been tried. But that tricky wagon driver had been thorough. In olfactory terms, the wagon had vanished. In later years, no one seemed able to cite any evidence showing that Aaron Carrier really did possess the knowledge they sought, but the theorists were unshaken. It must have been Aaron. He must have run to get the wagon driver. Aaron and the fugitive (whoever he was) must have been pals.

But even if Aaron Carrier was such a go-between, how would he know where the wagon then finally wound up, in all the vastness of Gulf Hammock?

On one point, at least, the evidence seemed clear. An emerging faction of torturers really did believe the logic they were constructing, though they were still not completely abandoned to frenzy. This was not a spree bent on torturing just anyone. They seemed to prize a sense of glorious purpose, of heroically solving the case. The intoxication of witch hunting seemed to be deepening, and cruelty was only a part of it.[113]

Mama is crying and begging. "Please don't hurt him, please don't hurt my son. He didn't do anything!" This fails. Then there is the last desperate argument. Minnie hears Mama cry:

"Please don't hurt him. He's sick."

Minnie knew little about Brother Aaron's heart trouble, though she had seen the medicine he took for it. The medicine was kept at Mama's house, in readiness for an attack. Why it was not kept at Aaron's own residence where he lived with his wife Gussie was not a question that seemed germane.

Minnie knew that Mahulda "Gussie" Carrier was a schoolteacher, and had taught in Rosewood's one-room school, which stood back north near the Halls. The school, like the community, had fallen on hard times, evoking sharply differing memories as to whether it was still open by 1923. "Gussie" Brown had first taught on the other side of the county at a sawmill town called Meredith, then married Aaron Carrier during World War I, when Aaron was called briefly to duty.[114]

Imaginative, nervous Aaron Carrier liked to talk about books and preaching. Tall, serious Mahulda ruled her classrooms sternly, and would one day be a school principal in the town of Otter Creek. But for Minnie the main fact was this: When the men came, Aaron was at Mama's because he was recovering from one of his attacks.

Heart attacks were well known in 1923, though cardiology was a new field. The modern era of epidemic cardiac arrests is sometimes said to have begun after World War II,[115] but by coincidence the crowd accosting Aaron Carrier reportedly included a woods farmer, Orrie Kirkland, known for cardiac difficulties. One of Kirkland's children recalled sadly that from an early age they had had to work, thus never going to school, because of "the heart trouble" that constrained their father. This seemed not to keep him, however, from the exertions of the manhunt.[116]

Minnie's understanding of "heart trouble" suggested that Aaron's latest episode occurred on Sunday night, December 31, 1922, though the household's routine seemed not to be disrupted. Typically, New Year's Eve found James and Emma Carrier's family in church, as Minnie sat sleepily through watchnight service. But she could not say for certain whether this New Year's Eve had unfolded in the usual way. She assumed it must have, since nothing unusual caused it to stand out in memory.

And where, by the way, were *all* the players that night? What had preceded Fannie Taylor's screams—whether the creeping movements of an approaching hobo or the first tremblings of a nightmare? In everyone's memory this prologue seemed to be a lost page—a night too mundane to be memorable—or else too personal to be explored.

Watchnight services were standard in early twentieth-century America, whether in the towering solemnity of Trinity Church in New York or woodland chapels like Minnie's. Many people rang in the New Year piously, in church. African American churches found still more meaning, recalling the thrilling watchnight of 1862, when freedom had come at the stroke of midnight, as Lincoln's Emancipation Proclamation was set to take effect on the first second of January 1, 1863.[117]

Exactly sixty years later the clock struck again. By then Rosewood's shrinkage may have made it difficult to get together a church congregation for watchnight. But somewhere in that darkness, by some means, a community member, Aaron Carrier, was said to go into crisis.

Minnie knew only that by Monday, January 1, her uncle Aaron was upstairs at Mama's, sick in bed—because of his attack. The patterning made a strange loop. On the same inscrutable night, at about the same time, the two symptom-rich endpoints of an ephemeral scent trail, Fannie Taylor and Aaron Carrier, were both suffering an "attack."

Aaron Carrier was a "tie chopper," according to his 1917 draft card. Surviving memories agreed, though calling him a "tie cutter." His daily occupation found him wielding an axe in the woods, as a freelance lumberjack. No woods boss was breathing down his neck, but there was no reliable company paycheck.

As railroads pushed through frontier Florida, their pathways continually needed repair. Metal rails grew misaligned and had to be pried back into place, and the wooden crossties beneath the rails were perishable. The weight caused splintering and sagging. Rot crept in. At many stretches, replacement timber was supplied on the spot, by an independent but threadbare class of men called tie-cutters.

On a roaring little gasoline-powered work cart, a "motorcar," a railroad section foreman would arrive with his crew. The foreman was always white, the crew typically black. Section crews, with their gandy-dancer work songs as they pried and heaved, became one more southern icon, not least in the pages of Zora Hurston.[118] The foreman would roll up to a neat ziggurat of squared logs that had been piled there by a sweating presence from deep in the woods, a tie cutter. The foreman would offer a price. Thus, at the edges of the economy, Aaron Carrier got along.

His tie-cutting camp in Gulf Hammock seemed to be the standard type, a lean-to shelter of palm logs and thatched fronds, with some barrels of flour or meal for nights by the campfire. And this was not an irrelevant detail. Such a camp could offer a secluded base for other activities. There were white woods farmers in the Monday posse who were particularly ready to suspect Aaron Carrier of conspiracy—because

they viewed him as a poacher of hog claims. They grumbled that he used tie-cutting as a cover for stealing white men's free-roaming hogs.[119]

Until 1949, the state of Florida was open range by law.[120] Stock roamed freely, no fences required, and you could own livestock without owning an acre of land. In the 1920s if a Model T carrying tin-can tourists were to venture onto Levy County's dusty branch of the Dixie Highway, it would meet "an area that serves as a range for isolated herds of semi-wild cattle and hogs," according to a federal guidebook.[121] And if one of those bony Spanish longhorns—or one of the bristly sows in a road puddle—were to be hit by the car, a woods farmer could make the driver pay for the damage, not vice versa.

Claimed hogs might look wild, but most had customized notches cut into their ears, each with an owner's special pattern, his mark, which was registered at the courthouse. Some hogs were also branded like cattle, but ear marks were easier. And ease was the problem. With a pocketknife, a thief could change a notch and then claim the hog had belonged to him from the start. The cryptic internal feuds in Rosewood strayed into accusations of hog theft, as did feuds in white settlements. "Many a man was killed over hogs in the woods," recalled ex-president pro tem of the Florida Senate Randolph Hodges, who grew up in Cedar Key. White-on-white was the dominant pattern in hog-claim controversies, but a racial overlay could turn things explosive.[122]

It was told how Orrie Kirkland's brother John had a place down Beck Well Road, just south of Rosewood in the mazes of Gulf Hammock. And there John, so the story went, began to miss some hogs.

The butchering place for the stolen hogs was found deep in the jungle. The thieves were then tracked to a camp, though at the moment of discovery no one was home. A food cache contained meal or flour, pale enough in color for the avengers to have a little fun. Similarly pale is strychnine, the active ingredient in rat poison, and this was poured in. There would be angry chuckling down through the generations about this trick. One day, they gloated, that fellow Aaron Carrier got powerful sick.[123]

Sam Hall, Aaron's neighbor just north, told much the same story, though from a different point of view. Hall confirmed that the whites had poisoned Aaron Carrier for stealing hogs, but said that the theft allegation was false, merely a suspicion. Hall protested: "They thought anybody in that settlement'd kill hogs." Aaron may have been lucky. In 1886 a hog feud in the woods of East Texas launched a strychnine ruse against an entire family, leaving three dead, others in critical condition.[124]

It could be wondered whether Aaron Carrier's "heart trouble" might be interpreted, with a slight shift in wording, as heartburn, including reflux attacks. Severe gastric damage can be one of the effects of strychnine poisoning, though another symptom is more surprising. As the toxin reaches the brain, strychnine can leave a lasting mark: a strangely heightened startle response, a hair-trigger tendency to panic.

Less than a quarter mile down the tracks from Aaron Carrier's residence was the back room at Sarah Carrier's house, lodging her son Sylvester. He, too, was a tie-cutter, eking out a living in the old hometown. In 1910, both young Sylvester and his father Haywood had had better work, with regular wages in the last days of the Rosewood cedar mill.[125] As recently as 1920, Sylvester had been drawing a paycheck in Sumner, as he and his wife lived in the company quarters. .

But storms seemed to follow the man with the startling laughter, and there was a quarrel—this time with a boss on the Cummer log train.[126] By 1923 the laughing man was back home again, running out of options. Like the back porch of his cousin Aaron, Sylvester's rear room pointed into Gulf Hammock, unclaimed land where a man could cut ties. Whether the two cousins, Aaron and Sylvester, did their tie-cutting together was not well remembered. But fatefully, whites in the woods tended to get the two of them mixed up, merging their images into a single suspicious shadow.

Chapter 8: The Fast Shuffle

He didn't try to be Wyatt Earp. His gun holster was barely a pouch, worn cross-draw style in front of bunched trousers, almost at the groin. A cheap strand of web belt held no macho cartridge loops, flaps, snaps or studs, let alone a gunslinger's drawstring.

The field dress of Levy County Sheriff R. E. "Bob" Walker was less formal than in his sit-down portraits.[127] In memories, the unpretentious sheriff sounded as though he made an art of fading into the crowd.

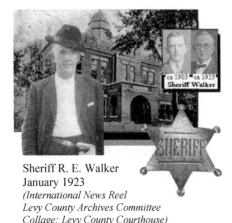

Sheriff R. E. Walker
January 1923
*(International News Reel
Levy County Archives Committee
Collage: Levy County Courthouse)*

At the home of James and Emma Carrier, as their son Aaron was taken into custody, the sheriff seemed to disappear once more. He and his deputy Clarence Williams were not among the clamoring new faction of interrogators. More impulsive souls were taking over now, challenging Walker's authority—and the quiet man was not jumping out in front of them with drawn gun.

The mob contingent now forming out of Walker's posse was laced with angry woods farmers, standing apart from the salaried, secure mill hands of Sumner. However, the less active onlookers from Sumner had a part in the show, projecting tacit approval. The mill personnel may not have been quite ready to torture Aaron Carrier personally, but they were eager for the answers that torture might supply, later statements made clear.[128]

Minnie watched as her 26-year-old uncle was taken down the tracks to a large oak on the other side, toward his house, a noose around his neck as he walked. The psychological effects on panic-prone Aaron Carrier were not noted. The plan was to haul him up on a low limb, feet just off the ground, and choke his throat shut until he talked. He had already given his denials: *I wasn't at home, I didn't see anything, I don't know anything, I saw no stranger, no wagon taking him away.*

To Minnie it seemed that such a stranger must surely exist—a flesh-and-blood black fugitive, and not a mirage or mistake. Hadn't the dog's nose said so? To think that all this might be a strange illusion of some sort wasn't in the playbook. Minnie's reservations lay elsewhere, in the matter of Aaron's alleged involvement. This mysterious black stranger had acted alone, she felt sure. He had simply broken into Brother Aaron's empty house, then had run out the back door.

For another sixty years—until I brought the witnesses together in 1982 and then again in 1983 for taping by "60 Minutes"[129]—the most generally reliable survivor-witnesses—notably Minnie Langley, Lee Carrier and Sam Hall—were unaware of Philomena Doctor's alternative story portraying a spectacular secret, a supposed white boyfriend as the source of the scent. When those survivors heard the boyfriend story in 1982-1983 it startled them. They couldn't flatly say that it was untrue, however, because of the larger problem. Since no bystanders inside Rosewood seemed to recall seeing anyone at all pass by, none could state flatly that they knew for sure that such an unseen presence was black.

After learning of Philomena Doctor's story, the other survivors began musing in surprise: *Could* he have been white? Nothing in 1923 had suggested this alternative to them (the idea would have seemed absurd at the time)—but then, what if he *was* white? The process of speculation—forming a maze of could-have-beens and might-have-beens—had been central to the Rosewood tragedy all along, enveloping baffled observers as they tried to make sense of murky developments.

On Monday at the oak tree, the air seemed to fill with exotic explanations of what had happened to the fugitive—or what *could* have or *might* have happened to him. The logic grew ornate.

The crafty fugitive *had* to have been a black crony of Aaron Carrier's, who *had* to have been an accomplice in the escape. Aaron *had* to have furtively hurried off to get still another crony, who owned a wagon, and then *must* have come sneaking back with the wagon in tow—to carry off the fugitive and hide the scent. All of this *had* to be true—not necessarily because of evidence, but because if it wasn't true, it would mean the fugitive had won the game, gotten clean away without a trace—and there would be no more excuse for the thrills of playing inquisitor.

They wanted a name. Who was the now-envisioned third conspirator, that wagon driver?

Illiteracy, moonshining and alcoholism wove into the resumes of the emerging interrogator group. Even so, there could have been solid clues egging them on. But whatever their reasons or delusions, their ceremony was about to come up short.

Veiled movements had been occurring at the edge of the crowd, especially among the parked cars—perhaps a raised eyebrow or two, a sidelong glance, evidently some instructions. Another of the often-seen elements in southern manhunts was about to emerge, again unlike some of the caricatured pictures in a later age.

With his horse tied somewhere near the oak tree, the sawed-off, barrel-chested fellow looked like he had wandered out of the wrong frontier, in the Wild West rather than the subtropical South.

Jack Cason, a stocky turpentine woods rider, was often seen on his cracker pony, and he had a reputation.[130] Some called him a killer. A niece pensively used the term "Napoleon complex," referring to his height plus his sometimes explosive temper. Such a hard case might seem ready-made for joining the rites of torture. This would be the cliché.

Cason's job often made him the lone white man in pine forests worked by crews of African Americans. A single chipper at a turpentine camp might work ten thousand trees, slashing the trunks to bleed out sticky

Woods rider
Levy County
ca. 1912
(Levy County Archives Committee)

resin. A woods rider checked and tallied such production, paperwork done in the saddle.[131] It was not a slave driver's job, and involved a certain amount of rapport.

Age 48 in the 1920 census, Cason had his own ranch and horse corral at Rocky Hammock, eight miles up the tracks beyond Wylly. But he, too, was not exactly Wyatt Earp. He had a wife, seven children and a brother with an adventurous streak, for the brother had divorced and then ran off with his wife's daughter, disappearing into the outlaw swamps beyond the county line, across the big river called the Suwannee. Like the black hunters of Rosewood, Jack Cason was a living bridge to the wide-open times of the old days.

A traveling photographer reportedly snapped this shot
of a "Mr. Cason" in Levy County in 1923.

Was this the Rosewood rescuer Jack Cason?

The affinity for children (one of the riders in the photo was said to
be aged ten) would have fit Jack Cason, who had a houseful of
children and stepchildren.

(Alachua County Historic Trust, Matheson Museum)

His face appears now as the torture stops. Cason is moving rapidly. Perhaps no one gets a very good view. More or less, he seems to step from behind the oak, then bares his gun, making his announcement. There will be no interrogation. Not here, not like this.[132] Quickly, then, the focus blurs again, panning to the next face in the crowd—or more exactly, to a blur of racing engine and fender metal.

———————————

At the moment of destiny under the oak, two giants of American fiction were still unborn. The Hardy Boys, that plucky pair of teen detectives in a flood of juvenile novels, would not be created until 1927.[133] But even in 1923 there were role models for youthful adventurers, and daydreams enough for two real chums, who on a chaotic Monday found themselves in the manhunt crowd.

They could have looked to various templates, ranging from the Baker Street Irregulars, scurrying after clues for Sherlock himself, to Mark Twain's Tom Sawyer, Boy Detective. Even the Boy Scouts, founded in 1907, were so steeped in crime-scene romance that Lord Baden Powell, the founder, ponderously set down instructions on how to be prepared if, perchance, a good Scout were to happen onto a dead body, left by some fiend.[134]

At the oak, a careening automobile has brought Edward Pillsbury, age 17, and his visiting crony, Bert Philips of Jacksonville, into a crime scene *par excellence*—though it is not exactly Hardy Boys material. The racial blood rite of a manhunt interrogation would seldom reach the library's juvenile shelf.[135]

As this Monday began, the two chums had been looking forward to a milder adventure. Bert had come 120 miles down the railroad to visit Edward for a New Year's turkey hunt.

Last night the young visitor had stepped off the passenger train after a jerky half-day's journey from big-city affluence, finding himself surrounded by the darkness of legendary coastal jungles. There a genteel sanctuary awaited, complete with parlor piano and mosquito-netted beds. Bert would bunk in the bungalow home of family friend Walter Pillsbury, the pipe-smoking sawmill administrator who was Edward's father.

As planned that morning, Edward hopped behind the wheel of the Model T reserved indulgently for the Pillsbury children. The two pals drove out in search of gobblers. But Edward's hand on the wheel was like a jumpy Ouija pointer, drawn magically toward anything adrenal.

It wouldn't be the first time. There had been the day with his sisters out at the Number Four Bridge to Cedar Key, when he had leaped impetuously from the driver's seat at a startling sight. A big gator was right up on land, sunning by a fence. In no time, Edward's hobnailed boot was planted heedlessly atop the scaly back, as he grinned and posed like Teddy Roosevelt with a trophy—until the thing whirled, latching onto the boot. The sisters watched in horror. A passerby—the mill's grouchy bookkeeper—had to play the role of Red Riding Hood's woodsman with the axe—though it was a gun in the bookkeeper's hand as he leaped from his own car, and the gator lost the fight.

Edward's impulsiveness left its share of tales. There was the day he was playing basketball so hard—pounding the clay court out at Cedar Key—that skinny Ernest Parham was fouled headlong into some wicked sandspurs on the sidelines. The wounded hand grew so infected that in a few days Parham almost lost it.

The prize-winning story, however, was more epic: Edward marching out alone to explore the great jungle north of Sumner—not Gulf Hammock to the south but the trackless mass of Suwannee Hammock, north toward the big river of no return, where the rails for the log train formed the only road. Edward left those rails, then got so lost that his failure to return by nightfall prompted an anguished all-night prayer vigil. The company town's small church, which his father Walter had built, grew filled with supporters. Walter Pillsbury rousted out Spearman the log train engineer, ordering him to plow up and down the jungle tracks in the dark, while the superintendent himself rode the cowcatcher in front, holding out the lantern, shouting to Spearman to keep yanking the cord, blowing the whistle—until Edward at last heard the tiny sound, faint in the inky distance, and was able to stumble out to the tracks.

Whether called accident prone, risk addicted, Type-T Personality (thrill-seeking) or simply a riddle, Edward Pillsbury was pulled into the whirlwind at the oak. Enter teen sleuth Frank Hardy, stage-left—with Bert playing Joe. Few eyes in the turmoil seemed to notice as the two arrived. No hurried conference would be remembered. The quiet man, Sheriff Bob Walker, seemed to appear on nobody's radar.

But the two adventurers did present the sheriff with some new possibilities. They were aloof from the passions enflaming the woods farmers, and to some extent were insulated from attack by their aristocratic status—while they possessed a valuable tool, a potential getaway car. Of course, the process could have been more accidental than this—a mere hyperactive blunder, more like the gator stunt. But none of those who caught glimpses could see the action as a whole. To peer in from several sides at once—using the seldom-compared viewpoints of widely differing witnesses—is to meet suggestions of a furtive chess move. Twitching in the background is the magician's other hand—the magician in this case being the taciturn, unnoticed sheriff.

Heroism is not supposed to be like this—the too-small Laurel-and-Hardy hat, the sagging cross-draw holster, the bug-eyed woods rider, the hot-rod rich kid out for the thrill—not to mention the racially minimized rescuee, who in the tales seems almost a forgotten afterthought.

In the moment, they didn't necessarily have the luxury of worrying about how it looked.

The would-be torturers are eyeing Cason and the gun, maybe thinking how easy it's going to be to outflank him—when suddenly they are caught from behind. A car roars into the crowd. Watching from a distance—and later hearing the recap from Aaron himself—Minnie would quizzically recall: "This boss man's son at Sumner, he was out there, Pillsbury. He got him, took Brother Aaron from them white folks, dodge him 'round. Him and somebody they run with Brother Aaron."

This was a crisp summary of what sources as diverse as the Pillsbury family and the foiled inquisitors would generally confirm. "Him and somebody" faithfully captures the dim image of the astonished sidekick, Bert.

Aaron Carrier's younger brother Lonnie, also in the household with Minnie, would say that Aaron had already been pulled up on the rope and choked when woods rider Cason pulled him back down. Things are still moving quickly—toward the next face in the crowd.

Deputy Clarence Williams, recently picked by Sheriff Walker for the plum job in Sumner, is like Walker, a man of few words—though with a bit more panache in his cowboy Stetson. The rescuers converging in the Monday fast shuffle suggest a general profile—these risk-takers, renegades and misfits. Williams, despite his star, is an outsider, unmoved by the neighborly rage thrilling through the woods farmers. Modern sociology has discarded a term that was used in the 1920s, "crowd mind." But whatever the crowd's outlook might properly be called, the rescuers seemed not to share it.[136]

Coming in at night to drop his hat by a lonely wash basin in his newly-occupied upstairs room, Williams is another adventurer. The farmers resent him for replacing a crony of theirs, the previous local deputy. Hard-boiled, compact (like his compact boss, Walker), Deputy Williams is a man who moves, not-so-secretly, outside even the law itself—because of the hallmark twist in law enforcement on the timber jobs.

It's not just that, as deputy-and-quarters-boss-at-once, Williams receives two paychecks, with corporate pay diluting his county loyalty. That's only the first step in his delicate position. Beyond is a special obligation known to any quarters boss of his day. Williams serves as both bouncer and bagman, supervising a low-slung, multi-roomed building nestled on the far side of Sumner's African American quarters.[137] As the local deputy and quarters boss, he rides herd over Sumner's jook.[138]

At each timber job or company town across the woods, the formula worked much the same, with almost cookie-cutter standardization.[139] According to corporate wisdom, if you wanted to keep black crews working in lonely swamps—and keep them from migrating north to vastly better wages—you had to provide a spectacular distraction, a place for conviviality, sexual adventure, razor slashings, shootings, euphoria and anesthesia: a black-only dance hall, where white clientele were forbidden.[140] Each company town called it by the same harsh, stripped-down name, "the jook." As a moonshine dispensary, gambling den and dance parlor, such an establishment was seldom if ever personalized with ornaments so cozy as a sign out front. Nothing said "Dew Drop Inn" or "Mac's Bar." Whatever the camp or town or quarters, it was just "the jook."

The basic contradiction—that the law was running such a place—assumed special poignance on January 16, 1920. On that date the Volstead Act took effect, ushering in the 13-year American experiment called National Prohibition. By the time Clarence Williams checked into his cubicle in Sumner, the sale and consumption of alcoholic beverages for entertainment was a violation of federal law. And yet his job was to oversee just such sales, in what amounted to an extra-legal exemption zone. It was not that jooks were hidden speakeasies or blind tigers, with peepholes or passwords. They didn't need to hide. Any child in a company town could point you toward the jook. Everyone knew it was there.[141] The rule of law turned upside down in Levy County—at the old southern crossroads of labor and race.

Jooks were furtive sore spots in the larger experiment, the southern racial segregation system, which had gained a three-decade lead on

Prohibition. Segregation and Prohibition—the two great "shuns" of American restrictive social engineering—collided in the shadows of the jook. Over and over, not only local lawmen but federal Prohibition enforcers ignored Florida's jooks, saying tacitly or overtly that African Americans were not covered by regular law. Timber companies wanted to keep black labor and yet not raise wages, so they offered this special perk—to blacks only—in the form of a company-approved (or company owned) hellhole, where the liquor business would not be raided—so long as only African American clients drank there.

Under the economic urgency of the timber jobs, Prohibition's ban on liquor was re-imagined, and was held to apply only to good white men, whose souls could be saved. A witness from the Newberry, Florida, mass lynching of 1916 remarked blandly that black folk in those days weren't thought to have souls.[142] Better known is the 1972 motion picture *The Godfather*, presenting mafia dons who supposedly okayed drug trafficking only in black ghettos, because (said Don Zaluchi), "They're animals anyway, so let them lose their souls."[143] As with modern convict road gangs obscuring the still larger but older enormity of convict leasing, few viewers of *The Godfather* grasped the still older idea of the racially-exempt jook. Deputy Williams was not just a sheltered bootlegger but the law in abrogation of itself. In 1921 the U.S. Bureau of Investigation, the forerunner of the FBI, journeyed across the big river on Levy County's edge, the dream-draped Suwannee, to invade the outlaw swamps on the other side. There a company town's quarters boss, its jook manager, was accused by an angry mill superintendent of pocketing $981.34 of the company's cut—a cut that was illegal in the first place under federal Prohibition.[144] The U.S.B.I. agents raised no quibbles about such corporate moonshine traffic. They wrote extensive reports, but on other issues.

Sumner's commissary clerk Ernest Parham (the basketball-and-sandspur martyr) would become a youthful sidekick of the tough-guy deputy, Clarence Williams. Parham watched one night at the hotel as the deputy prepared to slip out on an undercover mission. A wildcat moonshiner had set up in the woods and was horning in on the company's jook profits. To catch him, Parham said, the deputy disguised himself cleverly to look like a potential customer from the black quarters. The young sidekick recalled helping as Deputy Williams blacked his face.

At the Monday oak, the rescue is an outsider's game. Deputy Williams may have helped push Aaron Carrier into the back seat of

Pillsbury's car—or he may have dived in and gone with them. The trick is just beginning. The next part will be at journey's end, where the car is going.

As it roars away with Aaron Carrier inside, the mortified mob interrogators are more dangerous than ever. Now deprived of their preferred target, they are suffering painful embarrassment, and might decide to take it out on targets of opportunity. Aaron's mother's house, where little Minnie stands watching, is temptingly near. In the 1916 mass lynching at Newberry, forty miles north, two of the victims were women. It could happen—a danger that now shifts the focus to the next face in the crowd.

Left behind by the car is the graying, two-decade peacemaker, the sheriff, who now faces the task of placating the inquisitors. As if little has changed since the Lewis case in 1902, Walker trots out the conciliatory speech: *Now boys, this rescue is only a minor interruption, not a closing of the door. This valuable suspect has to be taken to a real jail, you know—but it's only three miles away, right there in Sumner.*

Walker doesn't have to spell it out. Tales told by the hearers themselves down through the decades would make it clear: they got the underlying point. The supposed jail in Sumner was just a crackerbox shanty, a holding pen for Saturday night brawlers from the jook. The crowd understood its vulnerability. They could go over there any time they chose and simply burst in, finishing with Aaron Carrier at their leisure. So for the moment they calmed down, lulled by the idea of "just taking him to Sumner."

Their interpretation of the message would be confirmed later that same Monday night, as their violence intensified. At that time the consolidating mob would take Sheriff Walker up on his implied invitation, and would rush to Sumner to drag Aaron Carrier out for torment. But the gesture only brought them up against the full beauty of the trick. For they found the Sumner jail empty. A bland-faced Deputy Williams greeted them there, alone, inviting them to come in and search, while tensely hearing their threats.[145]

The would-be interrogators had failed to guess, as the two Hardy boys sped away, that the automobile excursion would be longer than advertised. By Wednesday, January 3, the mob faction would grow so furious at being fooled that they sent a break-in squad twenty miles away to the county seat at Bronson, convinced that the disappeared Aaron Carrier must be hidden in the courthouse jail there. But again they would meet soothing words, and were invited in to search. No Aaron Carrier. No whisper of where he might have gone. The magic trick was complete.

Chapter 9: Gang Rape

A dawning Information Age—with its black funnel phones and racing Model T's—would continue taking news of the Monday events to a waiting world. First there was Fannie Taylor's alarm, and now the Aaron Carrier rescue has spawned a new drama to squeeze into the pipeline—though this brings up a question. Where, exactly, was this news pipeline located?

The telephone operator perched at Cedar Key was only a link in a chain. The real media action on Rosewood was fifty miles up the railroad.

Among verdant inland sandhills in the next county sat the nearest town of any size—and the nearest with a daily newspaper. The rising college town of Gainesville, with about 7,000 people in 1923 (but boasting of a round 10,000), was home to the *Gainesville Daily Sun*. Levy County, down in the coastal wilderness, lacked sufficient population to support a newspaper that came out every day, and got by on a shoestring weekly or two.

The *Gainesville Daily Sun* was itself no giant, employing a lone reporter, grandly titled "City Editor," but in fact a twenty-year-old college student. The *Sun* offered a Bible Thought for the Day, a regular column for the Boy Scouts and handy tips for farmers, such as how to kill hogs.

But this hometown voice—not the haughty *Florida Times-Union* far away in the big city of Jacksonville—would become news-central on the Rosewood events.

The *Sun* would be the main clearinghouse for information (and distortion) going out to other newspapers far and wide—first across

Florida, but soon with astonishing wider reach. Thursday night would see the week erupt into big-league bulletins, and the *Gainesville Daily Sun* would play wizard-behind-the-curtain, anonymously shaping images (and bewildering illusions) that went out to the nation, from New York to Los Angeles and Miami to Seattle.

The way such things worked was not grasped by many consumers of the news—in 1923 or today.

Snaking into a window or a chink in the bricks at the *Sun's* office, facing Gainesville's brick-paved Main Street, was a leased telegraph wire. This was not one of the public wires of Western Union, but a sinew in a separate great telegraph network. The *Sun's* wire was part of a 92,000-mile spiderweb owned by the Associated Press, a unique cooperative made up of 1,300 member newspapers in every corner of the nation (numbers are from the early 1920s). Every day in 1923, people coast to coast saw front-page tags announcing that news stories were "By the Associated Press," but few asked the particulars.

The 1923 *Gainesville Daily Sun* upstairs office as it stands today (long after the newspaper's departure)
Google Street View

The process in 1923 was crucially different from the still more immense Associated Press network today, and had some soft spots. Readers in 1923 may have assumed that intrepid correspondents—the kind who chatted with kings or dodged bullets in war—were out in the field in their trench coats, guaranteeing the accuracy of the news as they sent it in, but when a wire story in the Roaring Twenties came from a point of origin inside the United States, the source might be more humble.

The 1,300 member papers in the AP in 1923 (from the tiny *Sun* to the big urban Goliaths) used their telegraph network as a two-way street. While taking many items off the wire about news in distant places, they were also obliged by their AP membership to be senders, in the event that anything earth-shaking happened in their own back yards. The *Gainesville Daily Sun's* upstairs crow's nest, reached by outside stairs off a shadowy alley, contained keen ears that could interpret dots and dashes of Morse code chattering on the *Sun's* telegraph key—and there were nimble fingers, which, in the rare event of a local sensation, could tap the key to send news out. In that case, an AP story might emerge with little or no real investigation.

The "Black Brute" story in the *Florida Times-Union* on January 2, 1923, (Chapter Four) shows how the AP process could be strengthened a bit—if a newspaper took the time. Apparently the *Times-Union* conducted its own phone conversation with the (largely clueless) switchboard operator in Cedar Key. In the Rosewood coverage of January 1-7, this sort of haste was about as far as journalistic investigation went. As the violence snowballed and faraway newspapers weighed in, dozens or even hundreds nationwide would become involved. But almost all simply took the Associated Press version of events off the wire, apparently without checking. Apparently no reporters at all went to the actual scene. At the height of the Rosewood excitement on January 5 and 6, it could be that well over half the daily newspapers in America were running sensational Rosewood items—"Race War," "Burn Negro Houses," "Negro desperado," etc., But all of these tracked back to the AP wire, fed mostly or wholly by a modest upstairs office that was fifty miles from the action, in circumstances never examined in the shouting.

How many independent phone calls were made by papers like the *Times-Union* or the *Tampa Morning Tribune* is not clear, but there seemed to be few, and all seemed to tap into a few sources: the Cedar Key switchboard, the Levy County Sheriff's Department and the Cummer sawmill office in Sumner. Otherwise, the *Gainesville Daily Sun* fifty miles up the railroad was left to phone these same sources, digest some phrases and feed the wire. Apparently without any firsthand knowledge of a very confusing scene, the *Sun* used its phone and its telegraph key—and its standards of accuracy—to present Rosewood to the nation.

To large degree not just a single office but a single brain—in provincial seclusion—seemed at liberty to create for the nation a racial shadow-play, filled with sound and fury, sprinkled with some real facts, and weaving an imagined tapestry that repeatedly hid, changed or deleted the real events.

At age twenty, Truman Green, the "City Editor" of the *Gainesville Daily Sun,* kept a busy schedule. He was also a junior in Liberal Arts at the University of Florida, a new university in those days, rising less than two decades previously in a cow pasture a mile west of the *Sun's* office.

The university's five or six buildings, topped with medieval-style castle crenellations of brick fashioned by convict labor, marked out the "Baby University of the South," as its 1922 yearbook put the matter. Opening for classes in 1906 (and soon seeing a student riot complete with Confederate cannon), the new academy stood by the limerock road leading to the Levy County swamps—one more sign of Florida's emergence from the old frontier.

In 1913 one of the university's two dorms was found to contain malaria mosquitoes—ten per room. Florida was home to the oldest continually inhabited city in North America (old Spanish St. Augustine), but in 1923 was the "youngest and oldest state," in the words of an

Truman Green
City Editor

official state publication. The information climate surrounding Truman Green, cub reporter, was underscored in 1926 when the *Florida Historical Quarterly,* the state's keeper of historical standards, ran a scholarly article titled "White Man's Burden," revealing that the Negroes were predisposed to be cheerful.

Green was an energetic fraternity man, rising as rapidly as the castle walls. First editing a student newspaper, then the campus yearbook, he moved up to commercial journalism while still in school, as the one-man band at the *Sun.* The title "City Editor," when used at large urban papers in the 1920s, could sometimes mean a gruff titan barking "Get me rewrite," as Cary Grant did in the movies, but in the sweltering small dailies of Florida, the title was a quaint pretension, hiding the true meaning: "Our only reporter, who does everything."

Snatching up the black-tube phone to take down a society-page blurb from the garden club, pounding out an obituary if a funeral occurred, such a City Editor had little chance to write news, much less investigate it. In late 1922 the Sun front-paged a scolding piece about jaywalkers, who were scandalously flouting the law on sleepy University Avenue, a block from the office.

In the rare event of real action, such a city editor might receive a couple of sentences by phone, then "expand" them into a narrative, using assumptions to fill in the gaps. The process of expanding and imagining scarcely showed—or mattered—in a jaywalking filler, but a certain minefield lay waiting in larger news. Gainesville and the University of

Florida in 1923 were steeped in the racial segregation system (the university was all-white, as well as being all male), and the minefield lay in stories about race.

Truman Green's filter on racial issues could be gleaned from a series of stories in 1922, not simply ignoring or patronizing African Americans but nakedly ridiculing in print, the tone sounding a bit like college hazing (freshman "rats" on Green's campus had hard lives). On July 12, 1922, an African American woman in Gainesville's police court (also near the newsroom) was depicted pleading with the *Sun* reporter not to publish her name when she was fined for moonshine possession, for fear of her standing in church. The resulting article toyed laughingly with the plea, then printed her name anyway, as if to twist the knife. Moreover, the name was enclosed in playful quotation marks, as if it were a droll darky nickname, though it was apparently a name of record. This pattern of ridicule in the *Daily Sun* never aimed at whites, but repeatedly giggled at "chocolate-colored in-habitants" and "dusky sons of Ham."

Tuesday, Jan. 2, 1923

When the Associated Press of the 1920s used such small southern member papers for its coverage of local racial atrocities, the style of language was typically laundered to give the impression of terse professional-ism (any "dusky sons of Ham" became "negroes"—though with a small "n"). The effect was to discreetly remove outward signs that the picture might be less than reliable.

As Monday wears on, an oak-tree update apparently rings through to 219, the entire phone number of the *Gainesville Daily Sun*. The phone is customarily manned by the City Editor.[146] The rescue of Aaron Carrier is about to be re-imagined, so creatively that the printed result has to be teased apart to get to the nugget of truth—which for our purposes is verified independently by agreeing witnesses in later decades. It would be vanishingly unlikely that all such later informants, with their deeply differing attitudes and points of view, would be confabulating in unison. Their agreement points to the odd man out: the skewed picture in the news.

But the skewing brings a surprise. The real story of the Aaron Carrier rescue (as revealed even by hostile testimony) showed a redeeming streak in white culture surrounding the Rosewood violence. There was a strand of mercy —or heroism—mitigating and complicating the grim brutality. And yet in the white-controlled press, this vindication of whites is screened out. In the news, the rescue disappears—or is turned upside down.

The story is below. The dateline "Bronson" refers to the county seat of Levy County, twenty miles from Rosewood. A phone call may have been made from Gainesville to the Levy County Sheriff's Department in Bronson. The reader is invited to try and guess how the "two negroes" in this story are related to the verifiable events:

> **Bronson, AP, Jan. 1: Two negroes were in jail as suspects here tonight and sheriff Walker with bloodhounds and numerous posses was scouring the country for another negro in connection with an attack on the wife of a millworker at Sumner early today. The husband had left home for work when the negro appeared and knocked at the door, the woman opened the door and the negro struck her. Her screams after a time brought housewives...**
>
> **The negro believed by many to be guilty is making for Gulf Hammock, one of the most dense forests in Florida. The entire county is aroused and virtually every able-bodied man has joined the search.[147]**

Here is Fannie Taylor, obviously enough, but who are the two black "suspects"? They seem not to live in the same universe as the scene remembered by all the post-1982 witnesses. The news story has the crime being committed by at least three conspirators—two black accomplices and the main black rapist. The complicity suggests a shocking outbreak of gang barbarism. And the story makes clear that the two extra suspects are not just imaginary phantoms in some rumor mill—because they're not running around loose somewhere. In the news, they're safely "in jail," presumably at the datelined location of the news item, in Bronson, the Levy County seat.[148]

A different version of this story—appearing crazily on the same day in the same paper, the *Gainesville Daily Sun*—proceeded to change the geography, announcing that the two miscreants were instead "being held at Sumner last night." This second story placed great emphasis on that location. After the first statement—"held at Sumner"—it went on after two more sentences to again stress: "The negroes are lodged in jail at Sumner."

The illusion process here can perhaps be put into a single long hypothesis: In a confused burst, efforts by law enforcement to disguise the real location of a mob target seem to blend with something else, an eager newspaper writer's urge to inflate an alarm and imagine a black conspiracy, punching the old southern panic button about slaves in rebellion.

If this seems rather much, it's still not all—for there's still the question: Who are the two "suspects" held so firmly in custody? Who are these hulking brutes who helped their comrade in a nefarious, coordinated rape strategy?

Meet Aaron Carrier's wife.

Thirty miles up the Seaboard tracks at a rail crossing called Archer, the younger sister of Mahulda "Gussie" Carrier, Aaron Carrier's wife, looks out from her home. At the front gate, the younger sister is surprised to see Mr. Julius's Model-T taxicab. Usually that vehicle is slumbering down at the Archer railroad depot, waiting for the occasional fare. But now it is arriving at the house where Mahulda Brown Carrier grew up.[149]

The time of this arrival jumps the story ahead a bit. The younger sister, Theresa Brown Robinson, placed the arrival at just past sundown on Tuesday January 2, 1923, early on another short winter day.[150] The regular nightly passenger train, heading southwest from Gainesville toward the coastal swamps, has brought a passenger, apparently from Gainesville, twenty miles back up the line from Archer.

Mahulda Brown's parents live in Archer at the home where Theresa watches. The work ethic of this land-owning family could be seen in a carefully preserved Maxim's Penmanship handbook, used by Mahulda's father as he emerged from the enforced ignorance of slavery and taught himself to write. Mahulda was sent to a segregated school for African American teachers, then ran a schoolroom not far from Archer. Marrying Aaron Carrier in 1917, she moved to his isolated hometown, thirty miles farther toward the coast. Under obscure circumstances, Mahulda then taught in Rosewood through its twilight of decline.

But why—on this Tuesday, January 2, 1923—is she now suddenly arriving back at home, appearing on her parents' doorstep? Moving through the front gate from the taxi, Mahulda seems haunted, in shock. At the door she collapses into her mother's arms, sobbing, "Mama, they just done me all kind of way."

In bits and pieces, her sister Theresa learns that Mahulda ("Gussie") Carrier has just been released from overnight custody, where she endured third-degree questioning. The picture of that interrogation is faint, strained through Theresa's second-hand description. Mahulda says there was a railroad track, a chair, a gun—with the gun pointed at her head to make her talk. Theresa would notice that for a long period afterward Mahulda seemed to grow frantic at the sight of a gun, even a child's toy gun.

Mahulda assures her mother that no sexual improprieties were part of the ordeal. She says a police matron was posted with her during the interrogation, a chaperone. She also praises Sheriff Walker, saying that somehow he saved her. Whether the reality behind this was good-cop-bad-cop or another complicated bump-and-grab rescue by Walker, the gratitude was consonant with other expressions from Rosewood victims. Generally they viewed the sheriff as an ally in the Rosewood week, and a protector. However, that was behind the scenes. In public, the quiet, unadorned sheriff would meet a storm of criticism, notably from white voters. Taking hits from all factions, he was accused of concealing valuable witnesses from mob interrogators, but also of failing to do enough to stop the mob.

Most of the questions about Mahulda Carrier's captivity would remain unanswered. Who was pointing the gun? Where was the railroad interrogation? What did she tell them? How did she get there? How was she released?

Her fear seemed evident in the most important story she told. Theresa listened as her sister shakily described what happened on Monday morning inside the small house Mahulda shared with her husband Aaron in Rosewood, when disaster struck. At least according to one terrified voice, as recalled by one unsupported witness, there really was an intruder. His Rosewood intrusion was said to go like this:

It is early morning. Aaron and Mahulda are in bed—and they hear a noise. It seems to be coming from the front door. They can't tell exactly because they are secluded in the bedroom with the bedroom door shut. They are too terrified to go out into the adjoining room and investigate— though they realize that someone is breaking in. With increasing apprehension, they hear him going through the house. Somehow he never tries the bedroom door. Then he is gone. The sounds disappear out the back.

Mahulda's story, at least as her sister remembered it, managed to cover all the angles of self-defense. It exonerates the teller and the teller's husband of any involvement with the fugitive (they are only innocent bystanders), but also manages to leave the teller in possession of no dangerous information. She never saw his face, or any identifying details.

Once again, this strange will-o-the-wisp of a fugitive dissolves into nothingness. And it might be noticed that this story seems to directly contradict the one told by Minnie Mitchell, who recalled her uncle Aaron as being prostrate with illness that morning and hence at his mother's house—not at home in his own bed.

It also clashes, still more severely, with Philomena Doctor's secret white boyfriend epic, for Philomena was willing to throw Aaron Carrier to the wolves, directly accusing him of helping the secret white boyfriend to escape. What seemed important to her was discovering a white villain, at any cost, and then inserting him into the manhunters' accepted narrative of the vanished scent.

And this is not to mention a fourth contending version, the redneck daddy drama told to the Peace Corps in 1967 at Cedar Key. All of these competitors have the effect of keeping the crafty intruder beyond the reach of firm knowledge, as he morphs and multiplies.

As to Mahulda's interrogation on Monday night, some of the logistics can perhaps be deduced. The night train through Archer came from Gainesville. In the evening it did not go in the other direction from Bronson and Levy County. In Levy County, which had no police, it might have been difficult to find a jail matron as chaperone, but perhaps a bit easier in Gainesville. Despite the many missing puzzle pieces (and whether or not the matron was really just a fiction to tell the parents for propriety's sake), there are other clues in this direction. It is clear that, even at this early point in the week, the mayhem was spilling beyond timber country and into rolling farmland, to reach the college town of Gainesville.

As the county seat of Alachua County, just inland of Levy County, Gainesville was the logical source of law enforcement backup should the swampland's handful of deputies, constables and town marshals become besieged. It was long-standing custom to shuffle lynching targets furtively between county jails, playing cat-and-mouse with pursuing mobs. Events would show that Sheriff Perry Ramsey of Alachua County, a battle-scarred veteran, had entered the Rosewood dynamic as early as Monday, though under a public information blackout. Ramsey's red-brick jail, 47 miles from Rosewood and three blocks from the Alachua County Courthouse, had become part of the playing field— behind a veil of remarkably effective secrecy.

University Avenue, Gainesville, early 1920s, three blocks from the Alachua County Jail. *(Matheson Muesum and Archives)*

When Aaron Carrier disappeared from the torture tree his vanishing act was so complete that for weeks not even his family knew where he had gone. Some feared he might have been killed. However, Martha Pillsbury, age 14 at the time, the younger sister of risk-junkie Edward Pillsbury, would recall watching Edward's getaway car arrive—not at the Sumner jail but at the Pillsbury family's bungalow. Edward and Bert were said to race away from the rescue scene to seek advice from Edward's pipe-smoking father, Walter Pillsbury, the sawmill superintendent.

Martha had the impression that as her father leaned down to the driver's window, the dangerous passenger was hidden on the floor of the car. Walter Pillsbury seemed to be instructing the two Hardy Boys to take the rescued passenger to the county seat, Bronson. It was not a surprise to Martha that her father might work against a lynch mob, or would allow his son into such danger. Once as the mill's payroll shipment was due by train, the man in the necktie had heard some

Bonnie-and-Clyde-type bandit rumors and ordered the strongbox shipped instead to Cedar Key, where he picked it up secretly by car—wedging it under Martha's small feet on the front seat for camouflage. The flamboyant mill superintendent, by turns severe and courtly, was one more of the unusual characters drawn into the timber industry as it chewed through the forests. A former college baseball star and Spanish-American War adventurer, Pillsbury was a complicated base runner, not averse to bluffing the pitcher—though the coming week of violence would finally catch him, too, out in the open.

The getaway drive may not have been so simple, but recollection suggests an image: the two breezy Hardy Boys, amazed at their growing triumph, dusty tires crunching on the limerock road—as they glide past the Gothic brick parapets of the pasture-hemmed University of Florida.

At least two hours on Highway 13 would have been required to transport their passenger from Sumner to the final hiding place—not the Levy County Jail in Bronson but an hour or so beyond it. Whatever the intermediate steps and players, the end-point was Gainesville—though this was never known by the vigilantes back in Levy County. Years and decades later the would-be interrogators would go to their graves with the question unanswered. Where had Aaron Carrier gone? Minnie would later learn the answer inside the family, where eventually everyone knew. The tomb into which her uncle Aaron had disappeared—for days or weeks to come—was the red-brick jail three blocks from University Avenue in Gainesville.

Similarly, the principal rescuers would go to their graves without giving the location away, at least as far as any surviving informant has been able to reveal. The depth of the secrecy was majestic in its way— the ability to keep information so completely hidden among so many conspirators, all with knowledge, while this same information was being sought so fervently, and fruitlessly, by so many others.

In its way, here was a measure of the old secret South, that thousand-mile mystery land where so much could disappear—later to rise and spawn inflated legends and ornate conspiracy theories.

If this one rescue case were to be multiplied by the thousands of county jurisdictions across the hot-blooded realm, perhaps the secret of the South would not just be a secret of atrocity concealed, but also at times the reverse—of heroism standing against atrocity—heroism which perhaps could not be publicly revealed, because the game was too tight, the demons of mob vengeance too ready to spring if they learned the specifics.[151]

So no one could ever know. This was the way the shut-mouthed man in the Levy County sheriff's office seemed to want it. As with the tradition of legal-illegal jooks, official truth served as useful fiction. Sheriff Bob Walker had kept one step ahead of the whirlwind. For the moment. The week was young.

Through the week of dangers, the upstairs newsroom in Gainesville would keep pace. Soon to come would be news stories further expanding the illusion of a black gang conspiracy, built onto the original news image of two fierce black suspects arrested as if in uprising.

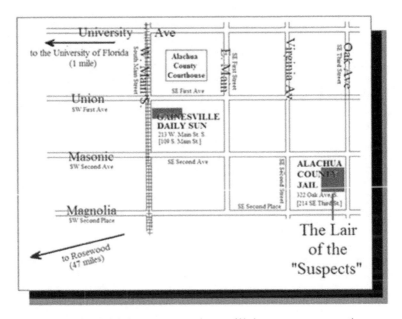

In the news, the initial two mysterious villains were soon to become three, four, *more!* By telegraph, this seeming proof of black conspiracy would go out across America—and indeed farther, into the future, where historians could find these mothballed news stories and use them, should they choose, to construct tidy narratives about what supposedly went on.

Hidden beneath the words was the irony: the murderous pair "in custody" were actually a panic-prone tie-cutter and his schoolteacher wife.

Moreover, the custody seemed to be largely for their own protection. No one at the scene, even the angriest self-appointed interrogator, accused Aaron Carrier or his wife of being suspects in the original crime, the attack on Fannie Taylor. Nor did the irony stop there. The two "suspects," once taken into custody, were not hidden in some shack in the swamps, but evidently were at 322 Oak Avenue South, Gainesville. The jail there was just down Masonic Street from the upstairs office of the *Daily Sun*. The "suspects," it seems, were only three blocks away from where their media masks were being made.

———————

Chapter 10: Bridge of Ghosts

I am at the site of Rosewood, in bushy scrub left by successive waves of logging.

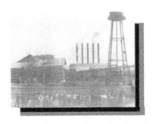

Cummer Lumber did not cut here, during its reign nearby in Sumner from 1911 to 1926. The Cummer saws went after the oldest, largest cypress giants in tracts of deep swamp. But other logging companies would fill in, taking one species of tree, then another—in a process going back to the near-extermination of the swamp cedar at the turn of the century, the veiled heartwood of the Rosewood riddle.

It was said that by the 1950s logging technology had improved to the point that the latest players could take even the saplings and splinters for particle board. A forest ranger near the site of Rosewood recalled a scene in a wasteland of fallen trunks as they were worked by a tractor-like gasoline-powered log skidder, one of the compact replacements for the old steam skidders and log trains of Cummer days. He said the driver of the skidder seemed to go into a frenzy of destruction, moving beyond work needs to ram and bulldoze even surviving cabbage palms that dotted the desolation, as if captivated by the thrill, like a mink in a henhouse, going after everything. Doubtless this was an exception. But whatever the less dramatic norm, the word "jungle" grew a bit outdated. The Great Gulf Hammock would survive in shell-shocked patches.

Now I am trudging through sand and dense weeds at about the spot where Minnie saw the men catch Brother Aaron (she didn't call him "Uncle Aaron," for reasons to be seen). Still dimly visible is the path left by the old railroad, though they pried up the rails in 1933, a year after this branch of the Seaboard quit running. The Florida Boom was in collapse by 1926, like a foretaste of the Great Depression, and the Seaboard line was deep in debt. At this stretch of former track not even wooden crossties would be left. The path is now visible only as a parting in the foliage, where hard-packed earth keeps out trees. At sandy spots you can see glinting black specks, the hard little cinders cast from locomotive funnels, as some white engineer gripped the throttle, some black fireman fed the roaring furnace (the arrangement was always the same, done according to the rules of the decades-long experiment called racial segregation, the only world Minnie Lee Mitchell knew).

But as to the exact spot where Mama's house once stood with its picket fence—or where Aunt Sarah's house once sheltered the back room for Sylvester—or where, exactly, Aaron's little cabin had enveloped the fugitive's vanished scent: those are harder questions.

The old property records are still on file, but they don't specify how the parcels interlocked. And at this end of the community any physical traces were literally bulldozed out of existence. Lingering foundation bricks and house sites were obliterated not by a mob but by later progress. In the 1970s an agricultural trend called pasture-leveling sought to maximize drainage by using bulldozers to scrape the soil. The effects extended even here, where a few pale tropical zebu cattle still shade under scattered cabbage palms—on leveled sand. Through various owners this part of the old site passed down to perhaps the most powerful politician in the area, former president pro tem of the Florida Senate Randolph Hodges. Now he has a hunting camp here, with a small block building for shelter. This site is his pasture.

Keeping our appointment, he walks out to the padlock on the aluminum gate, clicking it open to let me in. He wears unpretentious khaki, his woods clothes, as he recalls finding a few chimney brick in the bulldozed dirt piles. By now even those are covered by vines and clumps of palmetto.

Hodges himself was nearly nine when his daddy, also a power, a Levy County commissioner, gave a yes vote on Tuesday, January 2, 1923, to okay the rental fee charged for the manhunt's two extra bloodhounds, brought in a boxcar from a convict camp:

"...that Capt. H. H. Hinderson of Camp No. 17, Fort White RFDA, be paid the sum of

$50.00 for bringing to Sumner the Blood Hounds for chasing up the criminal that assaulted Mrs. Taylor at Sumner."[152]

Together with the phrase "Killed in the Riot" (scrawled on only one death certificate), the above 36 words (complete with the spelling of "Hinderson") form just about the only known official description of the Rosewood events that was allowed to survive on paper. The very idea of history, of keeping a record of all the ways the home folks might have been less than perfect here and there, was alien to this land—where a number of people couldn't read anyway. The default file cabinets were kept in a mental office of talk and tales, where old sins could squeeze into shapes preferred by the teller.

To challenge those understandings, I had only a narrow window in time. As I stood in the weeds in the early 1980s a great door was ponderously swinging shut, rumbling down on the baffled interloper, never to open again, ever, through all the ages. This was the door formed by the minds of the living witnesses. Its closing would be as permanent as the one-way flow of time. Or more specifically, of death. For they would all be gone. Very soon. All those highly imperfect vessels, carrying the truths that no one else in all of history would ever be able to carry. This was the only chance.

Randolph Hodges
1914 - 2005
(Florida Memory)

He had his own memories of it, of course, though as an eight-year-old in 1923 he had been isolated from the main action. The riot phase of the Rosewood events would emerge after Monday's first taste, to stretch through January 4-7, 1923. Young Randolph could view it only through the lens of gossip, as grown men talked, for instance, in Ben Roland's barbershop at Cedar Key. This was the town where his powerful family lived, headquartered in a big coastal stilt house, its twin peaks and broad, cool porch standing nine miles from the riot over on the mainland.

He is now listening to the underfed hippie-looking fellow, the supposed journalist he let in through the padlocked gate, as the fellow continues to get nosy about 1923, and asks: "In the whole thing, how many do you figure died?"

He gazes out into the sunlight where his pale cattle are drowsing under sun-baked palms, with maybe an egret or swallowtail kite floating against a backdrop of hanging moss. "I'd think maybe 75, or maybe a hundred."

"Really? Do you think it was really that high?"

He is pensive, deliberate, his face solemn: "You consider, there was killing all up and down here. I think so, yes."

Surely he must know that among older men who were actually near the scene at the time, none of them, not even the most chest-thumping blow-hards, ever got up the nerve to claim more than thirty or forty dead—and even that was empty boasting, a form of scorekeeping boast performed by whites, with no names of alleged victims, no specific identities to individualize the hordes of alleged black dead.

If tracked to the specifics, claims of a sky-high death toll looked like a form of white racial propaganda, mocking the assumptions of a later age, which would logically expect a hushed-up atrocity to have a hushed-up body count—so that the real number killed would logically be much greater than any number that the old white concealers might grudgingly admit. But the reality was the reverse. The real number of dead was small, then in tales was soaringly exaggerated.

Our side killed their side—with majestic effectiveness. We killed dozens of 'em. Run 'em all outa there. This was the spirit behind the tales, though often recycled through repeated tellers, until finally coming out in crocodile tears of regret and sympathy: *What a horrible shame it was that our boys were such formidable warriors....*

So now, as he says up to a hundred dead, is the seasoned politician just jerking the journalist's chain? Is he perhaps making fun (behind the studied poker face)—maybe making fun of city foolishness that comes prying into complexities it can never understand? Or is it politics on another plane? Does he take into consideration the possibility that in the changed climate of a new age, one way for an old southern politician to keep from getting pilloried as a racist is by exaggerating racism's bygone sins? Is he playing to modern yearnings to demonize the past?

The two figures—intruder and insider—squint out into the heat-shimmer together, looking not at one another but into the dazzling subtropical sunlight. No clue is there.

The answers lie in another direction. Lists made by survivor-witnesses, those who knew their home community the best, harmonize closely with the U.S. census and all other documentary indicators: As dawn broke on January 1, 1923, the entire African American population of the community of Rosewood was almost certainly less than a hundred.

And in the catastrophe of January 1-7, nearly all of that population got away.

But how could he be expected to know that? Those shadows fleeing into the night, going who-knows-where. The white cronies coming into the barbershop from the all-night ritual, giving the blow-by-blow, nobody taking notes, only the entertainment value. *Laid 'em out like cordwood. All up and down the road.* A barbershop orator overheard by an eight-year-old could get a mighty big ego boost from telling tales like that. The combat hero, practically pinned and ribboned. *Now listen, I hate to talk about all that killin', but...*

Gazing out into the sunlight across the pasture he says, well, there is one part of it that can still be seen: Right out there, that's where they played ball.

The hunting camp flanks a still-visible open space spilling toward Gulf Hammock. The position of this clearing in topographical and satellite maps suggests that it was indeed another of the communal anchors: the diamond-shaped ground used by the Rosewood community baseball team.

Every little crossroad had one, back in those days of Babe Ruth, Casey at Bat, the Black Sox. White communities played white communities and black communities played black communities, but they played. At Rosewood the diamond they used was behind Sarah Carrier's house, flanking the back room occupied by Sylvester. As 1923 arrived in the community's hard times, he had outgrown young men's things, and was no longer the team's catcher.

The shouting, laughing voice, like a blast of boiler steam, not solo hymns in church now but razzing and teasing the batter behind the plate, blasting out the words from behind the catcher's mask (with one hearer, Sam Hall, later making a stab at the exact words):

Th'ow it in here! They can't hit! Don't live on nothin' but fish and light bread!

Thus Sylvester was said to have shouted.

On practice nights, past twilight, till it grows too dark to see the ball, his younger cousin Lee Carrier loping through the outfield. Syl signaling Hoyt to pitch the drop-chute, or the dead-straight.

And Aaron at second base—if he doesn't get too scary and freeze.

Somewhere up the weedy dirt trace of the railroad, about in that pine clump over there, that was Mama's big house. And Aaron's smaller one floating well beyond, where they lost the scent. Mama screaming as they push him down the stairs.

Chapter 11: At the Store

Official sunset was 5:45 p.m. at
the weather post out at Cedar Key, as
Lee Carrier walked home from work
that Monday, January 1, 1923.[153]

Leroy "Lee" Carrier
1982

Leaving the lumber stacks in
Sumner, he moved into gathering
darkness—and mounting questions.

The familiar group of co-workers is now returning with him to
Rosewood—Perry Goins, stopping at the first house they meet, Raleigh
Bradley up the tracks, Bishop bunking with Lee back in the woods,
younger Sam Hall and Raymond Jones going farther up. They know little
about why the white foremen disappeared today from the lumber stacks,
leaving African Americans to continue working.

This sunset walk, as in the morning, again measures the level of
mob excitement at a point in time. Once again no one interrupts the
hikers, or accosts them simply because they are black. That phase of the
violence is still ahead—though tonight Lee will meet an omen.

His expression veiled in heavy-lidded eyes, he moves with an
athlete's ease, reflecting two of his favorite pastimes—hunting in the
woods and playing ball on the community team. Much of the rest of
community life he views through the skeptical eyes of an outsider.

Walking into Rosewood on the tracks, Lee passes between the two
pillars of the community in its twilight: the A.M.E. church on the right,
the silent Masonic hall on the left. His footsteps sound on a small trestle,
the rail bridge across a finger of swamp water from Gulf Hammock, just
down from the church. By this point word has reached him. Something
has happened to his cousin Aaron.

Ahead is the freight dock and plank walk at Wright's store,
promising the usual after-work relaxation. Lee can buy some cheese and
crackers, settle down on the steps of the store, watch the settlement's
sporadic parade. The cheese and crackers are no feast, but the big dinners
have ceased at Wesley's house where he stays, now that Wesley's wife
Virginia has joined the statistics on childbirth fatalities. For a generation
she was spared, through seven births, then fell in middle age.[154] Now

Wesley's smaller children are helped by sister-in-law Maggie Bradley. Lee, the solemn outsider in the household, age 22, fends for himself.

He wouldn't use the word stoic. If there is frost on the ground, it's not cold. If he eats only cheese and crackers, he's not hungry. He remembers real hunger from when he was a child, after his father Ransom Carrier died and his mother was left to work in Sumner as a cook, walking home to the children after dark with a quart can of leftovers. Those tears are cried out now. When he walks three miles to work, it's not far.

He looks askance at the loud branch of the Carrier family, up the tracks at Sarah's (he doesn't say "Aunt Sarah"). The exuberance at that house spreads a circle of stifling domination, he restlessly feels: their holier-than-thou solos sung in church, Sarah at the organ, Sylvester stepping up grandly to the rail—though Lee, like everyone else, admired the charms of Syl's laughing sisters, the ones who moved away. The talented star called Beauty (Lellon Carrier) would shout and razz the visiting teams at the ball games, back in the old days of better times. It echoes still in memory, after Beauty has left for bigger things.[155] Lee liked the good times, too—though some of those Carrier cousins could be like a long ground ball on rough turf, bidding the wary fielder to keep a close eye, tensed for the bad hop.

Approaching the steps at Wright's, he sees a changed atmosphere— not a dramatic crowd scene, but five or six whites are milling around. With Aaron now long gone, the information climate is spotty. Some of the whites who have come straggling into the manhunt by this point don't even know there *was* an Aaron Carrier. Some won't even know there was a Fannie Taylor. There is simply the core news—a fiend has struck, as reported by *somebody*. And hence the hunt. Does a man keep gaping at the bird dog once he's pointed the quail? No, he acts. No more information needed. In a storm of rumors some will get the idea that the rape victim was somehow the wife of storekeeper John Wright.

After the shock of the rescue there is the anti-climax—now no scent, no witness, no focus. Hovering on this knife edge are the tender mercies of target substitution. Prior to rescue, Aaron Carrier was fast becoming Candidate One in the category of substitute targets, a stand-in for anger at the vanished main actor, the original fugitive. Now the ball is ready to bounce again. As Lee approaches the steps of the store one of the whites suddenly glares at him, and says, "Well, we gonna get us a nigger."

The outfielder has a split second to play it out in his mind: *If you fight him you lose, if you run you lose, if you bow down you lose....*

Characteristically, he does not articulate this in melodramatic words, not even to himself. He keeps his eye on the ball.

But this one fouls out. The aggressor's companion pulls him back, calming him, saying (as Lee's memory has it): *"Oh, no, we don't want any nigger. We don't want the wrong man. We want the right one."*

In the ancient game now emerging—this drama or sport, whether called scapegoating, witch hunting, communal violence or simply riot— the initial reluctance is not unusual. The opening phase of aggression may be limited, selective. You can't yet go after just anybody—though certain targets might be okay. This phase will draw some blood of its own, but the full power will wait for the next big triggering incident, setting loose the big mysteries, those of random aggression. Then will come the time of escalation, when you *can* go after "just anybody." That trigger—the next-phase follow-up to Fannie Taylor's alarm—won't come until Thursday night.

Lee continues up Wright's steps. Inside the store perhaps a pressure lantern is purring, casting shadows on shelf and bin. The wry philosopher is there, age fifty—white store-keeper John Wright, settled into comfortable relations in a black world, finessing it so well that everybody, black and white, seems to have a complimentary word for John Wright.

Wright house, built ca. 1880 (photo 1982, house restored by Doyal and Fuji Scoggins) Site north of Wright's store

As Lee makes his purchase, any pleasantries mumbled at the counter soon fade. The men outside begin calling Wright to come out and join them. They urge him to take part in their manhunt.

A store in Levy County ca. 1923 (County Archives Committee)

The practiced diplomat never directly says no. He doesn't snap at them angrily, or retort that his sympathies are with the sheriff—and with mill boss Pillsbury and Cason—and with anybody else who has sense. The whites of substance here, the local managerial class, seem to view the attempt to torture Aaron Carrier as repugnant, a child's game of torment-the-cat. But Wright makes no speeches. Lee hears him fend off the invitation by using an excuse: "Naw, Mama's sick. She's at home."

He's pleading higher responsibility, saying he can't run out on his wife. Worlds are hidden in the way John Wright calls his wife "Mama"—old worlds, going back to tragedies at the turn of the century—in a verbal nuance picked up strikingly by Lee Carrier's memory.

And memory receives a second test here. Also on the scene is another later informant, Lee's younger colleague in the lumber stacks, Sam Hall. He has walked home to Rosewood at about the same time, and will also retain impressions. Neither Hall nor Lee Carrier will remember the other observer being present at this moment, though both seem to witness glimpses of the same event chain.

Sam's walk home has not gone directly to Wright's, for first he thought of trying the other social center, Rosewood's railroad depot. But on a tense evening the depot was dreary and deserted. Thus he doubled back to Wright's, still in search of a little conversation.

Arriving at the store he finds some whites gathered. They call out to the storekeeper from the yard, urging him to join the manhunt. Wright goes out onto the porch to deal with them. And he never directly says no.

But here the two memories diverge. Sam Hall recalls a material form of appeasement. In his memory, Wright ducks back into the store for a moment, rummaging under the counter for a usual item found in such stores. When he comes back out, Wright is carrying a shiny little "storekeeper's gun," the typical kind being a .32-caliber revolver. In Hall's memory, Wright offers the gleaming object to the insistent manhunters—as a loan, his gesture of support for the crusade.

Hall's recollection has him more dramatically acting out the core message: *I won't go out and kill innocents myself, but I can only resist to a certain point, and I have to show I'm not the enemy.*

The sixteen-year-old lumber stacker will recall gem-like detail, down to the nickel plating of the creamy pearl handle on the little break-back gun.

The two memories retain different elements, but encode the same theme: the white power broker shuns the growing mob appetite, but fears it. Soon (as both of these informants will know by the time they are declaring), this independent-minded storekeeper will shelter some of his African American neighbors, protecting them from mob violence. But he will not draw a gun against the mob. He will stop short of that, much as the maneuvering sheriff seems to stop short. Both memories, Lee

Carrier's and Sam Hall's, embody a cold realization: In the end, the authorities will not prevent the rampage; the law will bend; there is no refuge.

In the tense atmosphere, both memories may also have amplified the excitement. Small clues point to a possibility that both the aggressor at the steps and the invitation at the porch may have boiled down to a single individual, perhaps a taunting white youth from a household nearby in the woods. Perhaps not much of a crowd. But here too was a message: This was crowd enough.

Lee does not abandon his after-work routine. He has been throwing planks all day and is ready for a rest. Seated on the steps, he downs the cheese and crackers as usual. The straggling whites seem to disappear into deepening night. There is no memory of them leaving, but things grow quiet.

And at some point in this quiet, a new figure appears—not one of the lumber stackers, though the face is familiar. The confident gait and deliberate movements, the very dark skin. The face looms out of winter silence, no frogs or crickets now to sing back-up for that rich solo voice. Lee recognizes his older cousin Sylvester.

And Syl looks grim. He too has run into the manhunters today—or at least a story will say he did, a suspiciously vague story, as if perhaps stretching a rumor over unknown complexities. But whatever happened, it has now sent Sylvester Carrier to Wright's store, on a shopping trip of decisive effect—at least as Lee Carrier will recall it.

The story about Sylvester's encounter that day with the manhunters said that he angered one of them, causing a verbal response—and only verbal, reminding again that this is the restrained first phase of targeting. The offended white speaks sharply—but almost ceremonially, like a duelist primly slapping the glove. He declaims to Sylvester: *Be out of town by sundown, or we'll be back.*

Without doubt, during a tense period between Monday, January 1, and Thursday night, January 4, *something* did begin singling out Sylvester Carrier as a new mob target. The suspiciously vague stories may round out this shift with imaginings, turning a chain of subtle accidents into satisfying drama. As to first-hand observation, there is only the lone report from Lee Carrier, noting what seemed to be the result of the sundown challenge: the morbid errand at the store on Monday night.

Syl and Lee speak amicably. Lee does not harp on his misgivings about Sylvester, who, at age 33, has a way of bossing Lee around, trying to run things.[156] Lee still recalls the encounter in the past when Syl was gripped by needs unexplained. He snapped at his younger cousin: "Loan me ten dollars"—nearly a week's sawmill wages. Lee shrugged, "I don't have it"—whereupon he met Syl's other side, the history of quarrels and brawls. The older cousin exploded: "I oughta beat you,"

But he didn't. There were explosive words, but apparently no use of force. The connection between the two cousins runs deeper than that. They can still talk easily, especially about their common ground, their love of guns and hunting.

The golden afternoons, the muffled thunder of wings as the plump birds flush out and fly, like small chickens in their gooseweed dens, but fast-flying, low to the ground, rocketing toward palmetto clumps—like the hard line drive to the glove-tip that tests your whole machine. Now in these times the biggest game, the deer, is not so easy to find, as it was back in Old Man John Coleman's day. But there is still the sportsman's standard, flocking through the weedy open places, the quail.

Lee Carrier's love of quail hunting keeps him connected to the bossy household where Sylvester lives, the household of Syl's mother Sarah. To engage in that hunting, Lee borrows Syl's gun. Nothing works on quail like Sylvester's repeating shotgun.

It is a marvel, this gun. Men like to talk about Sylvester's Winchester .12-gauge pump shotgun, with its nearly unbroken stream of fire. Six shells in succession can be pumped into thunderous play without a reload—as such cannons have been doing since their introduction in 1887.[157]

The hunter in the background
"Bear hunt near Cedar Key"
Search for Yesterday, Ch. 15, p. 6
Levy Countyy Archives Committee
(photo ca. 1906)

Whites out in the woods called Sylvester Carrier a sharpshooter. In his complicated past he had tried his hand at commercial hunting. He was a guide for wealthy sportsmen in the depths of the hammock. His father Haywood apparently did the same.

African American hunting guides formed another forgotten motif of the Jim Crow South, their unheralded presence linking even to the phrase "teddy bear" (though that's down another game trail, soon to come). For now, suffice it to say that the gun came from his hunting days. And he was not stingy with it. Laughing, boasting, bossy Sylvester Carrier was willing to trust his prized possession to his younger cousin Lee. Many talked about the gun, but Lee knew it firsthand. The stoic outsider loved using it.

In the memories, Sylvester Carrier flashes like a bewildering prism, his contradictions and complexities sparkling until barely a silhouette is left where they converge—except for the one detail, the trait described again and again. There is the bizarre, triumphal, night-piercing laughter.

Perhaps the best portrait of the man now moving out of the darkness comes from Thelma Hawkins, who in Rosewood prior to about 1920 was Thelma Evans, one more adoptee, in her case shifted abruptly to the woods from a town over a hundred miles southeast.

Orphaned in the Florida town of Sanford, Thelma was adopted by her Rosewood aunt and uncle Ed and Eliza Bradley. They seemed loving enough, but she was put to work so constantly—in Eliza's home laundry operation—that Thelma could not join other children of the community in school. Escaping from the drudgery around 1920, going to the big city of Jacksonville, she became a maid for wealthy whites. After a long day's work she would make up for the lack of schooling, dragging herself out to a Jacksonville trolley line and going to night school, barely able to stay awake. The fierce effort showed to the end of her days, in crisp, carefully articulated diction.

Enjoying the family closeness when she was in Rosewood, but looking on the woodlands as a lonely place of toil, Thelma valued a special sanctuary. She loved the services at the First A.M.E. Church. And especially, she loved the magnificent hymns sung by the extraordinary voice. To her, his entire image gave a thrill—the perfect voice, the perfect sense of presence and command, even the perfect teeth, the perfect hair. The sensitive young girl had no illusions about this hard-working little settlement being a paradise, but, from afar, she kept a cameo in her heart, etched with the image of Sylvester.

Now in the lantern light of Monday night Lee is in the store, watching Syl gaze across the counter at Wright. Syl says something. Wright responds—with action rather than words. The storekeeper brings out an object, and it is not a little .32 pistol this time.

On the counter between them, Wright places a box of shotgun shells. Syl is making a purchase.

This moment, too, will engender many rumors—but among whites, not among African Americans in Rosewood. The white stories will be indignant. Why, that black demon Sylvester Carrier cornered poor Mr. Wright in the store and *forced* him to hand over some ammunition.

In the background of these stories one can almost imagine the store-counter diplomat himself, perhaps telling the tale in its original version, spinning it cagily to placate a white audience.

Lee Carrier, recalling firsthand observation, found no evidence of a dramatic confrontation. There seemed to be the usual friendly relations between Wright and Syl—though now under heavy emotional strain. Wright could have refused to sell Sylvester the shells for that formidable pump shotgun. Anyone could see what Sylvester was preparing for.

On the way out Syl pauses, speaking for a moment to Lee, one hunter to another, cradling the heavy little carton. If it holds the typical 25 shells, this means more than four reload sequences of six shots each for the repeating .12-gauge.

"I'm not gon' use the Winchester rifle," Syl reflects, as translated through Lee's memory. Syl is explaining why he is buying no ammunition for his other gun, which does not have a shotgun's wide scatter pattern. He says of the other gun, the rifle: "I got too many chances to miss with that."

The narrow bore of a rifle, able to propel only one bullet at a time, might only provoke an attacking crowd. Maybe you wound one of them, then the rest engulf you. But a .12-gauge pump with its spreading fire—that's something for everybody. Such a gun, if filled with double-ought shot, the big ones, would no longer be set for quail. Each of the big pellets flying from the red-paper tube could tear like a separate rifle slug.

Lee does not notice the size of the shot that Sylvester has purchased. Perhaps not the biggest. But big enough.

Syl carries the box into the night.

Chapter 12: The Carter

Wright's store, where Lee Carrier watches the passing parade early on Monday night, is not the main hub of mob activity at that moment. After sunset on Monday an excited new flashpoint will revive the manhunt, drawing searchers together at a point over a mile distant from Wright's. The shift could have left an opening for Sylvester Carrier to come to the store and buy ammunition.

The new spectacle, leading to shouts and then blood, will not involve Sylvester. Only over a period of days will he become an object of increasing crowd interest. On Monday night he is one more face in the background.

The new focus has erupted on an eighty-acre farm, one of the largest in Rosewood. Two homes stand there on land settled under Homestead Grant 13055, a relic of frontier days in the preceding century.[158]

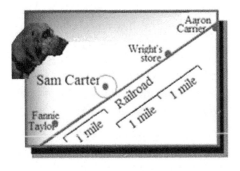

The location deepens the night's riddles. This new mob attraction stands on the extreme western edge of the area known as Rosewood, the edge nearest to Sumner. It is farthest from the Aaron Carrier action earlier in the day, which occurred at the community's far eastern edge. A process of excited deductions (or guesswork) has sent the searchers in a long backtrack, virtually abandoning the runner's established scent trail.

The details of this shift are lost in conflicting rumors, but by about 9:00 p.m. the picture will sharpen abruptly. At the eighty-acre parcel a burst of mob torture is going to draw a crowd, large enough to leave multiple surviving witnesses decades later. All of those observers will agree on their reason for being there.

They have found the wagon driver!

Aside from the general lore of such manhunts, saying that if a scent was lost there might have been a ride in some sort of conveyance, the actual evidence from Aaron Carrier's house would remain unclear. But on whatever basis, firm or flimsy, it was decided that the vanished runner was picked up by somebody's wagon, lifting his scent off the ground.

The two official investigators at the scene, Sheriff Bob Walker and his deputy, Clarence Williams, may or may not have agreed with this theory. They could have thought the evidence for it was obvious—or, quite the contrary, that the theory was daft conjecture. But their opinions appeared in none of the tales, as if they were determined not to be noticed. The dodge-and-switch tactics of crowd control favored by Sheriff Walker have now perhaps saved two lives on Monday, those of Aaron and Mahulda Carrier. But a larger wave is building.

So the question: Who is this sneaky wagon driver? Such an individual is now the only party, in all the wide world, who can put the manhunt back on track, by telling where the fugitive finally jumped down from the supposed wagon—so the dog might be taken to such a spot and put back on the scent. A lot of ifs.

The trail has now become airy, cerebral, deductive—not even tied to a scent trace any more. The inquisitor faction in the posse, self-promoted to the role of detective bureau, is increasingly taking control. In a swirl of woods farmers, hog hunters and the occasional reputation for moonshining, they have somehow come up with the answer they were after—the supposed name of the supposed wagon driver.

There will be rumors saying (or guessing) that Aaron himself supplied the name, or that it came from his terrified wife (the pattern of forced accusation in witch hunts was scarcely an innovation). But the real event chain at this point is mostly hidden by mob turmoil, like a scent trail trampled by a stampede.

At the edge of the eighty-acre farm is a small house, conveniently accessible. It is not on the railroad, which lies out of sight to the south, but stands beside a limerock road. The old vehicle track out of Sumner and Cedar Key creeps by here, snaking north toward the mossy plank ferry over the big river, the Suwannee. This road is the pale ribbon (bulked with some crushed shell from the Gulf) known as Highway 13, a road that will disappear in later asphalt decades. The small house takes commercial solace from Highway 13, for inside lives a wagon mechanic.

To many, the 48-year-old blacksmith in this house is a mystery—even in so basic a matter as his race.[159] Is he black? Or is he white? People looked at his features—and his mysterious background—and came up with radically differing answers. The classifications of Jim Crow racial segregation seemed to fall apart. Some black neighbors scoffed that this cryptic individual might as well be white. And yet all whites seemed to say he was black (with a nod or two toward "high yellow").

Meanwhile, a third point interposed. Everyone seemed to agree that he looked "like an Indian." The prominent cheekbones, the coppery skin, the stony gaze—these lay enfolded in his family riddles, which indeed cloaked all the western half of Rosewood, the square-mile area marked on maps as Section 30, where the blacksmith lived.[160]

Samuel S. Carter, apparently born in 1874, operated a small hand-cranked forge for heating and fashioning objects of metal—notably the flat iron tires or wheel rims of wagons. There was apparent aid from a pulley on an oak limb to hoist up the ailing vehicle. The solitary widower stooping over these flames was not known as the world's friendliest neighbor.

Whether actively scowling or peering silently, the coppery face rarely beamed a welcome to the occasional Model T on Highway 13. As far back as 1900, Carter had spent a year in prison for a shootout with his brother-in-law.[161] In September 1921 he was fined $75 for another violent offense."[162] Now a grown daughter sometimes comes to cook for him. A grown son has been in trouble. These eighty acres were homesteaded by his father Nebuchadnezzar Carter, whose widow still lives in a larger home elsewhere on the place. Less mysterious than her son Sam, Cornelia Carter listens tirelessly to "Nearer My God to Thee" on a wax-cylinder Victrola. She tends her fruit trees and, in the community tradition, cares for adopted grandchildren.[163]

Into this picture now comes a strange question, perhaps too trivial to mention, yet nagging in the wings: Could it be that the increasingly suggestible Monday manhunters have turned toward Sam Carter simply because of word associations?

The mere name "Aaron *Carrier*" points oddly toward this next target: "Sam *Carter.*" The two families in fact have no blood ties, but the names *sound* alike, creating a half-rhyme—and this rhymes farther. This wagon fixer is literally "a Carter." His very name says "wagon driver," as if tailored to manhunt suspicions.

People were accustomed to seeing stone-faced Sam Carter driving a wagon of his own—especially as his occupation modernized. By 1923 he had expanded his resumé into auto mechanics. Should the lonely reaches of Highway 13 witness a burst radiator or a stripped gear, it might be time to call the tow truck of the wilderness, meaning the blacksmith's one-horse wagon, the cart plied by Carter.

Possibly there was strong material evidence against Sam Carter that now is lost. But demonstrably the week of atrocity would produce other mob beliefs—some of them fatal—that rested on little more than dream-like mental associations. The explanation for this requires no mystical nod to a "crowd mind" or collective unconscious. A hive of interacting wildfire rumors did duty as the figurative neurons and synapses of group opinion. The week-long turmoil repeatedly used free association—and panicky, hair-trigger interpretations—as if mimicking a physiological impossibility, a collective dream.

By whatever logic, Sam Carter became a conspiracy theory's star player. *The running man has sought out a pal—Aaron Carrier—who then was urged by the runner to bring in another pal—Sam Carter—because Carter has a cart.*

Retrospect has to puzzle at the geography. In order to go and fetch Sam Carter, Aaron Carrier would have had to creep clear across the two-mile span of Rosewood, almost to Sumner. Nor was there any particular friendship between "scary" Aaron Carrier and scowling Sam Carter. They came from different worlds, in different parts of a strikingly divided community. No one would remember ever having seen them together.

But of course there were other possibilities. Could the answer simply have been bad luck? Did Sam Carter's wagon simply happen to pass by Aaron Carrier's back door at the wrong moment, when a stranger stumbled out of the house, asking to hop aboard?

The manhunters weren't splitting hairs. They had only one chance left to keep their pursuit going, and that was to make a wagon driver confess where the fugitive had been taken. So a wagon driver had to be produced. It did not help Sam Carter's case that other associations also lay in his background, negative associations. As a mob avalanche rolled toward the scowling blacksmith, the stage was set.

Section 30, one of the two map boxes roughly defining the area thought of as Rosewood (each box a mile square), contained the Carter place at the farthest edge of its box, the western edge. The adjoining box, Section 29 to the east, was home to the Carriers, the Bradleys and the heart of the community, centered around Wright's store and the depot. There in Section 29 were the area's oldest African American pioneer families, going back to slavery and the Civil War, before most of the 1923 residents were born. Those pioneer families, with their commercial hunters and woodsmen, presented a visible shared legacy, all being very dark of skin.

Their origins traced to the rail line through Rosewood, for it also was a pioneer, completed in 1861 to become the first railroad crossing the Florida peninsula, Atlantic to Gulf. For a brief period this would turn the Gulf terminus of that line into a wilderness boomtown, transforming a feisty little shallow-water port called Cedar Key. Soon thronged with schooners and steamships, Cedar Key became the southernmost railhead in a growing nation—for a moment. As soon as 1900 the prominence was a wistful memory, the frontier booms and busts leaving a trail of ruins. The proud old Florida Railroad, eventually demoted into a backwater branch of the Seaboard, kept many a secret.

The building of its final stretch of track, bridging the tide flats out to Cedar Key, was completed just as the Civil War began.[164] The rails were laid down by slaves, pushing through swamps and palmetto tangles. According to tradition—in an historical blank spot where no records seemed ever to surface—the slave laborers who survived to reach Cedar Key received their freedom as a reward.[165] Background clues—though no proof—suggest that these unnamed railroad builders might have included the first Carriers and Bradleys, among the original, very dark-skinned settlers of Section 29. Those surnames appeared suddenly in the first census after the war, the 1870 census. Before that, census lists did not name slaves, and the gap was too far back to be remedied by family stories. In 1870 the names bloomed up without explanation, as if rising from the earth.

But that was Section 29. Next door, the square mile covered by Section 30 displayed a different settlement history, a later one, not really beginning until three decades after the Civil War was over. At the end of the 1800s a new wave of settlers arrived, parceling up the woods in Section 30—and sharing a different kind of legacy.

Though African American, the families settling in Section 30 were light-complected, looking "like Indians"—or simply looking white, as some said. History books would take no notice of the mass movement that brought these families into a new beginning, on a 500-mile migration from the Carolinas into the malarial depths of Florida. But arriving with them was another of the folklore riddles of the South.

Since earliest colonial days, pockets of tri-racial population, including Native American ancestry, were noted in North and South Carolina or nearby, under a host of group labels: Melungeon, Croatan,

Lumbee, Black German, Black French, Brass Ankles, Portagee, "Cubans," "Turks." As the twentieth century dawned, racial segregation was closing around these unclassifiable population groups. The tri-racial settlers in Rosewood seem to have been moved to immigrate primarily by economics, as they sought frontier opportunity, but also in the air around them was the idea of escaping from segregation's new confinement. Frontier freedom was being sought by other African Americans in Oklahoma Territory, resulting in all-black towns. "Exodusters" were arriving in Kansas. Some went farther, taking ship to the old slave coast of Africa, sometimes at tragic cost, as they settled a U.S.-sponsored enclave named for freedom, Liberia. All of this frontier-seeking preceded the much larger Great Migration a generation later, when World War I's social forces would begin drawing perhaps a half million black southerners northward.

Rosewood became a sanctuary by stages. In the 1830s, even before it was born, a site fifty miles away was chosen by sugar planter and philanthropist Moses Levy for a utopian commune, Pilgrimage Plantation, where beautiful jungles invited retreat from the evils of the world. Levy had devised a plan to shelter persecuted European Jews, but the jungles were proving intractable even before the Seminole Wars destroyed his dream. After 1853, Levy's estranged son, financier and senator David Levy Yulee, would found the pioneer railroad out to Cedar Key, making the search for Florida paradise all the easier.[166]

Tri-racial settlers coming to Rosewood would use those rails at a troubled moment, when northern Florida lay devastated by severe winter freezes in 1896-1899. Here, too, a previous wave of dreamers was moving out, in the collapse of the 1880s citrus boom, to be replaced by a new wave in the form of moveable turpentine camps.[167] Most or all of the new arrivals in Rosewood were linked to turpentining, and to a central family with a frequently seen Melungeon or Croatan name: Goins.[168]

Southern Pines, North Carolina

Unlabeled photo in Goins family collection, said to be a possible depiction of Martin Goins.

Rosewood, Florida

Around 1895 in the compass-pointed town of West Southern Pines, North Carolina, a turpentine firm owned by the Goins family prepared to move south. As they financed this, they sold a swath of North Carolina real estate, 4,449 acres.[169] In Florida the firm would be known as M. Goins & Bros. Naval Stores, under chief entrepreneur Martin Goins.

Turpentining was by nature a migratory business, with any given tract of pines yielding resin for only about six to ten years. From its earliest colonial beginnings in the North, supplying tar and pitch for wooden ships and turpentine for paints and other uses, the "naval stores" industry had been working its way south down the Atlantic coast. Its nineteenth-century bastion in the Carolinas and Georgia (of the Tar Heels and the tar baby), had grown depleted of pine resin by the 1890s. Many turpentine outfits were moving into the previously forbidding forests of fever-ridden Florida, converting it by 1905 into the nation's top naval stores state.[170]

Typical turpentine camps used all-black labor with a few whites at the top, but an unheralded exception lay in M. Goins & Bros. Leasing eight square miles of pines near Rosewood in 1903, with a new distillery and quarters in Section 30 on Rosewood's southwestern edge, this was a business owned by tri-racial entrepreneurs. They specified to new neighbors that they classified themselves as Negroes.[171]

There were no memories of racial tensions as Martin Goins's niece Agnes (the daughter of his brother Ed Goins) brought her college education to the new family home in the wilderness. She also brought her piano, in this case not a basic upright as in some of the pioneer homes in Section 29, but a baby grand, confirmed by various witnesses. [172]

Eli Walden (right) with family

The moment was brief, the wilderness hard, and plagues appeared in paradise. Martin Goins was deceased by 1905. Brother-in-law Eli Walden, the firm's distillery technician, or "stiller," put on a brave face in a letter sent home to his wife—who refused to come south into the wilds:

> **"We have all the fish we want and Every thing fare fresh eating we want. I like this country very well...Mama, why don't you write oftoner then you due I have not received but five letters since I come out here...If you & the children was down here I would be so glad, for I can take care of you better here than I can there."[173]**

That was in 1900. Later that year, Eli Walden passed away.[174]

Many of their riddles would remain unsolved, even in family lore. Both Martin and a brother, Jean, pronounced their names as in French: "Mar-tine" and "John." If this had reference to their origins, the clues were lost over the years. More verifiably, older Eli had fought on both sides in the Civil War, enlisting as a white.[175] The name, "Goins," tracing back to colonial times, may have derived from Portuguese. Martin Goins's obituary in a North Carolina newspaper found a "Career Marked by Financial Success" while he "was of mixed blood, being a descendant of that Indian family, popularly assumed to stand for the old Croatan tradition" after "intermarriage...with the colored race."[176] Inside the family in Rosewood, stories told of ancestry leading back to the largest of the "Five Civilized Tribes" of the South, the Cherokee.

Their neighbors in Section 30, the Carters, were still more enigmatic, coming from South Carolina, where the Lumbee people formed a notable tri-racial population. Sam Carter's mother Cornelia was said to wear her hair in a long braid. Her late husband Nebuchadnezzar Carter, the homesteader of their 80 acres, was a cooper or barrel maker.[177] A typical fixture at any turpentine camp was its cooper's shed, surrounded by a veritable sea of wooden barrels. Metal barrel hoops would have required a blacksmith's touch, perhaps passed down to a blacksmith son. Isolated on his 80-acre preserve, Sam Carter gave few lessons in genealogy.

When people said Sam Carter was mean, they meant in the old-time sense—not necessarily cruel but dangerous, a man you didn't want to cross. "Sam Carter was mean as a circle saw," Sam Hall said, making the nuance clear. Some thought he could be nice enough—if you didn't give reason for the storm clouds to form. On Monday night he was profoundly alone.

"He wasn't a black man," said Pompey Glover, an African American in the Otter Creek area, where Carter once worked. "He looked more like a red Indian....Just like them big Cherokee Indians...You've seen them Indians, old long crooked nose."

For decades, white census takers labeled Carter as "B," black. White administrators, not as grudging as some of the woods farmers, tended to portray him generously, seeing a light-skinned black man who ran his own taut ship, on his own land, with no particular problems. But earthier opinions grew explosive, sneering about an outlaw, a "great big yellar nigger." Complicating things further were observations like those of Eloise King, age eight in 1923. Dark-complected herself but adopted by the tri-racial Kings, who were light, Eloise heard her father, Sam King, complain one day about that solitary misfit Sam Carter, who "didn't care too much for black people," because he "was a white man."

Nebuchadnezzar Carter had filed his homestead claim in 1897, when his son Sam was 23. A family tale from a white narrator went back farther—and more tenuously—to when Sam was a boy.[178] In that picture he is the pale, ordinary-looking playmate of a white boy, two Huck Finns on a live-and-let-live frontier, hunting rabbits with throwing sticks. But between boyhood and 1923 many things happened. A bronze-skinned frontier youth might have found himself on the wrong end of Jim Crow segregation laws by about 1900. In two  censuses, 1900 and 1910, something about Sam Carter's household made it one of the census taker's worst defeats, sprinkled with lame guesses and odd spellings. One son consistently came out as an illegible scrawl, except for the letter "G"—which a family document clarifies, showing that the son was named George.

From there the history deepens. On April 3, 1916, George Carter was sentenced to six months in the Florida prison system, for a form of crime later resonant at Fannie Taylor's hearth: breaking and entering. On October 8, 1919, George was found guilty again, this time for stealing and slaughtering a yearling bull or cow.[179] Lingering tales among whites notably matched the written record on this case, telling how the yearling belonged to Jesse Ford, an outlying resident of Sumner on a farm next to the Carter eighty.[180] But this was not the punch line of such tales. What kept the story circulating—for generations—was the *modus operandi* of the theft. As late as the 1980s, growling renditions could still be heard, telling how that savage thief had chased down Ford's calf on foot, then killed it with his bare hands. The file from 1919 stands by the folklore; Deputy J. L. Brish told a courtroom how George Carter "maliciously killed animal by beating, bruising."

Through obscure turns, George Carter's father, the blacksmith Sam Carter, became viewed by some as a criminal like George, with fewer records left to sort out the charge. Two different observers from those days—both white—recalled Sam Carter's reputation as a "pimp"—again in the old-time sense, meaning a criminal accomplice in general, not a procurer for prostitutes. Unsmiling Sam Carter had become known as a go-between, a one-way ticket, a smuggler who helped criminals get away. [181]

Was there a nugget of truth behind this? For instance, during George Carter's 1919 troubles, was he sheltered by his father? Sam Hall of Rosewood remembered a time, well before 1923, when the whites had done something terrible to Sam Carter, leaving him enraged. The whites themselves were more exact about it, saying that Carter was strung up to make him talk—in the way of the Aaron Carrier attempt but long before it.

The coming of night on Monday would lay a cloak of ambiguity over the manhunt's clues. In confusing darkness, assumptions came easier. And nightfall brought an old friend. Bottles or jugs of moonshine sloshed in the shadows.

Facing a crowd fortified by darkness, drink and dramatically growing numbers, Sheriff Bob Walker had now run out of tricks. Only once could he play the get-out-of-jail-free card—because the one successful effort, with Aaron Carrier, had made the crowd wary. They were determined not to be fooled again. At this early point Walker seemed to lose control of events, never to recover throughout the week. No one seemed to be making rescue plans for the wagon driver.

In Sumner, over a mile southwest of the Carter eighty, an empty Model T sits in the moonlight, facing the weathered planks of Sumner's hotel, the company boarding house. The parked Ford is a small one, a no-frills coup, only two seats. It is the personal vehicle of a hotel resident, Sheriff's Deputy Clarence Williams, who is busy elsewhere. Williams apparently left his car behind when he followed the dog on foot earlier in the day. After nightfall he is still out there, somewhere to the east.[182]

Though Williams is new to the coveted job of deputy in a sawmill company town (also making him company quarters boss), moonshine profits at the Sumner jook are evidently staying on track. The Sumner quarters boss before Williams was said to own not just one but two automobiles. The quarters boss coming after Williams will be photographed next to a car somewhat larger than a coup.

Tonight the rising moon is nearly full. Even before sunset at 5:29 p.m., the pale disk was up. But Williams's coup will get to rest only until just after 6:00. At that time, and at a point around the corner out of sight, a muffled click sounds in a padlock. The Cummer commissary, the company store, is closing for the night. If the low moon is gleaming picturesquely in the jug-top gas pump at the steps, this will not be recalled by commissary clerk Ernest Parham, age 18. He has more exciting things to think about as he locks up, now to face an intriguing evening.

Parham has been kept out of the action through the day, trapped in the commissary because its manager, Albert Johnson, pulled rank to run off and join the manhunt. Now the young assistant has marked the emergency by closing up early, not at 8:00 p.m. as usual. At last he is free to nose about. The skinny clerk (about 130 pounds) thinks naturally about his hero, Deputy Williams, out there on the job. Like a slim Sancho Panza to the deputy's Quixote, Parham lacks only a cinema casting call to play that sturdy role, the trusty frontier sidekick.

Rounding the corner of the hotel he is accompanied by another clerk from the store. There is the question. How to join a vanished manhunt? Reports through the day have been sketchy. The posse is over toward Rosewood somewhere. Moving across the spongy sawdust paving of the street, Parham spies the car.

Surely, says the young clerk's inner voice, the hard-running deputy will be fatigued by now. Someone should take him his car. By 1923 such cars no longer had arm-breaking hand cranks as in earlier years. Borrowing a ride was simple. The two explorers knew the key would be there, trustingly left in the ignition. And they knew Williams wouldn't mind.

The rabbit-ear levers of throttle and magneto are on the steering column. At Parham's touch, they find a spark. And just like that, the explorers are off, rolling across the limerock. The logical route east is Highway 13.

The moon is on its usual crazy-quilt schedule, a good three hours earlier tonight than it will be later in the week, on Thursday, when the really big moment will come.

Parham soon eases the throttle lever. Dark forms have loomed ahead, a line of parked cars in the weeds. He knows nothing of the Aaron Carrier events earlier in the day. That whole segment of the drama is now plowed under and unsuspected by new mob participants. Such transience and unawareness will occur again and again in a week of king-for-the-moment mob euphoria. Players will appear and disappear not in a unified plot, as a master novelist might wish, but in a jerky stream of one-time personal crises. Fannie Taylor is now gone, not to be seen again. There are new protagonists tonight—soon to disappear as well. Mass atrocity needs a continuity editor.

Parham is now approaching a segment of the action that has attracted white males from miles around. There are some rough-hewn stage managers for this moment in the show, but they appear only as glimpses or hoarse voices in the jostling crowd. They seem convinced that they know just what they're up to.

The coup rolls to a stop. It has met two lonely silhouettes marking time at the roadside, excluded from the main proceedings. Seated on the running board of a parked car, their feet on the rock road, the two outriders are talking quietly. Parham leans out, drawling helpfully to a familiar face: "I brought your car."

Levy County Sheriff
E. R. "Bob" Walker

Deputy Williams pauses from his conference with the other idler, who is apparently the sheriff.

One story about this night allegedly gave Sheriff Walker's own view as told in later years, saying that suddenly the sheriff felt two shotguns in his back and was told to stop his meddling. Another account was more of a swaggering boast, proud of the mob leaders who allegedly disarmed the sheriff: "Taken his pistol off, told him he could go on up if he wanted to, and look at it. He went up and looked at 'em."[183]

"It" was a spectacle that was unfolding beyond the parked cars, hidden by trees. Parham and his companion now leave the car, blundering forward on foot, pushing through the bushes. They are guided by bursts of distant shouting, as if approaching a ball game.

In command now is a group of intermarried woods families, threadbare but proud, their roots in the woods going back before the Civil War—and in some cases to Spanish Florida in the 1600s, when officials at St. Augustine groused about ragged, English-speaking interlopers encroaching on the lands of the crown.

On Monday night, January 1, 1923, one witness is a 14-year-old farm boy who lives west of Sumner. Fred Kirkland would later be a Florida game warden and, later still, a harvester of wild palm buds for sale at Cedar Key. He would recall his father, brother, uncle and cousins joining the 1923 manhunt, allegedly in leading roles—whether by way of frontier boasts or, quite possibly, in fact.

Looking back, the game warden had few doubts:

"They told Bob Walker, they dedicated one or two men to walk up to him. He was down there tryin' to compromise with 'em. And just about two thousand people told him to leave, and he wouldn't listen at 'em, so they just organized two people to go tell him. Said: 'Get out of sight in five minutes.'... You damn right he done it. Him and his deputy both, they was so scared, they had to go."

The "two thousand" was a recurrent element in the teller's narrative style, as the old frontier mixed boast with truth. Less boastful was quiet, watchful Ernest Parham, the 130-pound sidekick and commissary clerk. He knew of the woods families only in passing, as they would come into the quarters in wagons to peddle meat or produce to the housewives, or stopped by his counter at the company store.

Now, in the Monday moonlight, Parham pushes forward through blackjack tangles and saw palmetto. The shouts in the trees are louder. He lurches in surprise, practically tumbling into the circle of light and noise.

And there he is!

The light-skinned Negro, twisting in the air, boots kicking horribly, barely off the ground. This image would be told and retold. Some said he was choked on the same limb where he hoisted up his wagons. Others placed it to the south, down in the hammock. Everybody wanted to paint this picture, smudging and muddying the lines with each loving pass of the brush—although some of these word-painters, just as they said, were probably standing right there, watching the torture unfold.[184]

The hanging figure is writhing, gasping. Some will say he is tied hand and foot. Others that he was not. One detail—the reddening of blood vessels in the whites of the eyes as suffocation closes in—was told with a little too much glee, by a teller who snarled gloatingly about the "big yellar nigger." The forensic realities disappeared into pornography.

There was not even certainty about the source of light. Lanterns? Torches? Battery flashlights? Or perhaps the headlamps of somebody's Model T? This basic point seemed to register on no one. It was not a time for methodical observation—though on one detail all concurred.

Everyone seemed to hear him gasp out the big line—the one repeated carefully by all the tales (a repetition that was somewhat gratuitous, since centuries of witch-hunt torture had made it an immortal cliché).

At last they hear him cry:

"I'll tell you! I'll tell you!"

His larynx is ostensibly not so collapsed that he can't get the words out. He is dropped back to the ground, falling in a heap. What is he thinking? There would be third-hand rumors saying that when he was first captured, the captors were waiting in ambush for his wagon, then stepped out and pretended at first to be seeking only a tow for a stalled Model T—until he saw their weapons come up, and he growled, *"If I had my gun, we'd have a time."*

But then other rumors said they caught him sitting down to supper, and demanded to know where he'd been, and he growled: *Nowhere, I haven't been anywhere.*[185] Despite the fog at the beginning, on the matter of his capture, his final capitulation would always be told the same.

Now proceeding *en masse* on foot, shuffling over swamp holes and leaf mold in the dark, they make a crowded snake dance, composed of every white male curiosity-seeker and hanger-on who has been able to get to the show. The crowd is now moving, deeper into Gulf Hammock—because they have cracked the case.

Leading them is the haunted getaway artist himself, softened up now by choking. He is leading them to the magic spot where the runner left the wagon. Laced into the snake dance are the straining dogs (plural by this time). Their expert noses are being taken to the one place where, supposedly, they will be able to get back onto the precious scent.

In retrospect it seems senseless—but they were not in retrospect. Caught in the tumultuous moment they were both more informed and less informed than the voyeurism of later curiosity. As only one example of the quandary: If that magic spot out in Gulf Hammock, where the scent could be rediscovered, was really within just a couple of hours' walking distance from the string-up at Carter's, why, then, hadn't they just made systematic sweeps out there with the dogs in the first place, and found it the easy way? Such questions didn't seem to bother them. Maybe there were reasons.

But maybe, strange as it might sound, there was only that still, small voice—the one called mass delusion—reaching even to the last sober skeptic at the back of the crowd, who thought he was repelled by the craziness and was only along for the ride: the voice saying that maybe all of them were unknowingly much the same, and had no real reason at all....

Parham sees the fellow holding the rope. As they walk, one end of the rope is still around the neck of their guide, tormented Sam Carter. But the other end is held by a guardian. In the stumbling entourage Parham can't see the rope very well, or the holder. It's not the kind of situation to see much of anything very well.

But he can certainly *hear* the fellow, this rope holder. A stream of cursing is being directed at Carter. The fellow sounds drunk. Other witnesses would not remember a rope being held, but vividly recalled the loud cursing, coming from the one excited source. The blustering, boasting shouts seem filled with rage—or with an odd kind of self-importance. Parham knows vaguely that the loud drunk is from one of the woods families. Others are better versed. knowing his name. Soon—because of exploits this night—much of Levy County will know of him.

Bryant Hudson, born July 20, 1897, at a farm north of Sumner, is 23 years younger than Sam Carter, though life has weathered him a bit. By reputation a destitute alcoholic, a woodland drunk, Hudson is known to have no visible means of support, except perhaps a few roaming hogs. On December 17, 1921, he and a brother, Dave Hudson, age 28, were tried for attempting to murder a deputy sheriff with a knife. Local juries tended not to convict unless the crime was earthshaking, and the two brothers were let off—which left Bryant free to escalate just over a year later, on this Monday night.[186]

Five feet eight inches tall, light brown hair, blue eyes—he can be described from records, not just recollections, because in 1917, at age 19, Bryant Hudson entered a period of apparent stability. With the coming of World War I he joined the army, then re-enlisted in October 1918 near war's end. His military file contained no knife fights: "Service honest and faithful....Character: Excellent." When a former acquaintance was told of this profile, the rejoinder was not sympathetic: "He was one mean bastard." Fred Kirkland, a cousin, said flatly that Bryant was a drunk. In a way oddly like the target of his curses on Monday night, Bryant Hudson seemed to have no one in the wide world to say a good word for him.[187]

"Bryant was using all kinds of language," recalled Sumner barber Marshall Cannon, who stood listening in the Monday night crowd, flanked by his friend Ed Dorsett. Cannon thought he heard the drunken voice cry out: *"Let's kill the son of a bitch!"*

But the etiquette of first-phase mob aggression was still holding, with its qualms about target selection. The drunken shouter was taken in hand by cooler heads. Cannon heard them trying to calm Bryant down: *"No, let's go slow now. That nigger might know somethin' and we might get on his butt and get it out of him."*

Exquisitely obscured in that sentence is the word "might." He "might" know something. Cannon did not claim perfect memory, but his phrasing was succinct. He was suggesting that the crowd had not the foggiest notion whether Sam Carter really possessed any guilty knowledge. The age-old formula of witch hunts, passed down through slave insurrection panics into lynching, was again dunking the witch, to be satisfied with innocence if she drowned.

There were irritated glances at the drunk, Cannon recalled. Everybody wanted that fool Hudson to shut up. Then they reached the spot. The dogs—now including two state bloodhounds brought in by train—nosed about eagerly. But they were baffled. No scent. The thing grew prolix. There was said to be a second round of stringing-up and choking at the new site—until again there was the ageless cry: *"I'll tell you. I'll tell you!"*

Some stories said there were three sites, three chokings—and other tortures besides. At the last spot—whether second or third—commissary clerk Ernest Parham said he found a natural observation point, standing next to the most powerful man in the crowd. According to Parham, sawmill superintendent Walter Pillsbury was also keeping watch—not participating in the torture, but not interrupting it. Parham was an admirer of Pillsbury like many others. By the time he voiced his recollection he had long since been Pillsbury's loyal son-in-law, having married the boss's daughter, Sopha. He seemed unlikely to finger the superintendent falsely.

Parham made it clear that both of them, employer and employee, took a sane, business-like view of the unseemly mob.

But there was still the problem. If the fugitive wasn't caught, this kind of mayhem was likely to multiply, spreading white fury into Pillsbury's black work quarters, and ruining his bottom line. In Parham's telling, Pillsbury seemed to hope that the interrogation would work, that the white savages from the woods, however repellent, would get the truth out of this wagon driver— would shake loose the missing clue, and thus would bring the madness to an end.

Pillsbury was perhaps unaware of Sam Carter's roots. or that evidently they were Native American. No one remarked on a faint crossing of destinies, though Parham knew the background, as did everyone in Pillsbury's family. Within the family, it was a matter of quiet assent that the mill boss, with his dark, craggy features, was also Native American.

On December 27, 1882, a wandering New Englander named Edward Pillsbury says the vows of marriage, having left behind his birthright to plunge deep into the logging woods of Michigan, there meeting his new wife, Martha Howd, whose precise tribal genealogy would later be unknown, though likely Algonquian.

As to the wanderer, his last name was a famous one, known a full century later to an age of television, for the birthright he left behind was that of the New England flour-mill fortune, in a time long before its emblem would come to be a chuckling Doughboy.

In only a few more years this adventurer would pass away—and his wife as well—to leave their orphaned son, Walter, age six. From such shadows came the urbane, relentlessly energetic presence who, after many turns, would rule a Florida sawmill town.

Walter Pillsbury *was* the woods—was the moment when the great woods were coming down, both trees and tribes, crashing in a chaos of logs and epic personalities, the great dark mass giving up its ghosts.

The two dark faces—one gazing from beneath the brim of the neat fedora, the other hating the fact that he can now no longer scowl, but can only scream: *"I'll tell you! I'll tell you!"*

It catches them by surprise, the explosion.

Astonishes them. Deafening in its fury. Suddenly Hudson's ranting has stopped. And in its place—as their ears are ringing from the force of the blast—is the jumbled impression that one last exclamation was heard, something like: *"You son of a bitch, you didn't do it, neither!"*

Before this moment, Hudson had been holding a shotgun on Carter. After this moment, the crowd is gaping like the apostles at the Last Supper. The target now lies prone, without a face.

The barber and the merchant, Cannon and Dorsett, feel a wave of disgust. They can see that others feel the same. They are disgusted because Hudson has ruined the interrogation. He has "killed the evidence."

The identity of the shooter would be confirmed by Charlie Hudson, Bryant's younger brother, who was in adolescence and was left at home, but knew the story through the family: "My brother killed the first one." A cousin of Bryant's, Perry Hudson, said much the same: "My cousin killed the nigger. Bryant Hudson told me that." Cannon the barber named him as well, adding bitterly: "He killed the nigger, killed the evidence."

Charlie Hudson, younger brother of Bryant Hudson (photo 1982, Fraser Hale, *St. Petersburg Times*)

Parham said the crowd broke up quickly. Civilization was still out there somewhere, and might want to prosecute. A hard core of revelers may have stayed behind. Some may have pumped in more lead of their own, an old custom. "The same programme of hanging, then shooting bullets into the lifeless bodies was carried out to the letter," said a lynching account from 1892. In 1919, a reporter at a lynching in Mississippi used a customary viewing perch and recalled: "I had to drop from a tree behind him to escape bullets fired at his swinging body." After the Carter death a newspaper story said that it, too, was followed up this way—which could have been fact or imagination.

There would be stories about post-mortem mutilation and pilfering, but some of these were grafted onto the Carter killing from a completely different one years earlier, when another alcoholic woodsman, a hard case named Mannie Clyatt, had kept a lynching victim's ear.

Two business-like shadows, apprentice and master, now turn briskly on their heels, fleeing the scene of the crime. Parham will recall Pillsbury expressing the general sentiment. In the moment when they were all still gaping, Parham said, the dark man ruling the timber town breathed his regrets softly—though not regrets for the form on the ground. Parham heard the superintendent say: *"Oh, my God. We'll never know now."*

Just under fifty miles northeast, the city editor's phone is ringing. That thing in the swamps has blown. It has now caused a death. It is no longer just a racial manhunt sensation. Upstairs above brick streets, the *Gainesville Daily Sun* must piece together a larger narrative, using squawky bursts of phone conversation—amid thoughts of fame and glory as it alerts the wider world. The chattering telegraph key is ready to fill the Associated Press wire.

By Wednesday, January 3, the name "Sam Carter" will peer from a mystifying blurb, barely a sentence, in the *New York Tribune*, a lingering giant from an older newspaper age. A march of shadows now begins to go national, via telegraph. Back in Gainesville, a headline at the obscure point of origin carries a bit more detail:

SUMNER NEGRO SHOT BY MEMBERS
OF POSSE FOR ASSAULT MONDAY
Body of Sam Carter, 45, Found
Riddled with Bullets, Sheriff
Is Still Searching for Other Negroes

"Other Negroes?" Expanded now is the earlier hook, the uprising angle or gang conspiracy peg, started by distorting the protective custody process as Aaron and Mahulda Carrier became "two suspects," without revelation of who they were or why they were being held. Onto this, the new development is now grafted, the death of Sam Carter. The fictional uprising gang, first visualized on Monday, can now grow larger. Sam Carter is implied to be a *fourth* gang member—or a fifth or beyond (in addition to the two in custody, plus the "others" now allegedly being sought). Multiplying evil-doers are everywhere. Coherence collapses.

> "One negro is dead and two are being held for complicity in the assault upon a young white woman at Sumner early Monday morning, while posses headed by Sheriff Walker, is [sic] believed to have been the actual perpetrator of the crime. Sam Carter, age 45, was shot and killed by members of a mob last Monday night after he had confessed to have driven one of the hunted men several miles in a horse and wagon, officers stated Tuesday morning..."[188]

Apparently a line of type was dropped amid newsroom excitement, resulting in a kind of Freudian slip. As published, the line beginning "headed by Sheriff Walker" seems to ungrammatically confess that "posses" (in other words, the mob) "is believed to have been" the real culprit on the scene.

The gibberish was faithfully reproduced in some receiving papers as they pulled the story off the wire. Their failure to spot the gaffe could have come of bored routine or, quite the opposite, racial passion, as an editor skipped heatedly from image to image in the words, with little coherence demanded. Here in print lay a footprint of the Rosewood rumor process that could behave like the physiological impossibility, the dreaming "crowd mind." However it might be labeled, its tissue lay dried and mounted in smudgy marks on newsprint, as if pressed onto a microscope slide.

The old slave uprising panics, raging like fevers through diverse parts of the South before the Civil War, had fed on the idea of savage mystery, positing that the slaves might go primevally berserk, no logic needed. The outlook lived on in 1923. When the news could offer no reason or motivation behind its image of a budding Rosewood conspiracy, this was not disproof; it only underscored the danger. They were going wild, throwing off all reason. The apparent lack of motive in the multiplying marauders was grounds not for skepticism, but alarm.

In the main precedent for such alarms, the Nat Turner slave rebellion of 1831, the fears were all too drastically confirmed, as entire white families were killed. Panic then multiplied, and countless other rebellion conspiracies were only imagined. A century later in 1923, a reservoir of paranoid gullibility lay just beneath the surface in American society, and not just on race. A common rumor, repeated in public speeches and recalled by a later president (Reagan, from his youth in Illinois), told not of an African American but a Catholic uprising conspiracy. Every time a male baby was born to a Catholic family, said the rumor, a rifle was cached under a cathedral, for the day when the babies would all grow up and form an army, bent on taking over America for the Pope. A large number of people in the early twentieth century seemed to believe this was true. Fears also turned toward German-Americans during World War I, when some clandestine agents genuinely did work stateside for the German Kaiser, but many more innocents were suspected or attacked. The demon caught in the crosshairs could have many faces.

A final flourish in the Sam Carter news item deserves a moment of silence: "was shot and killed...after he had confessed." On the front page the case looks open and shut. This scoundrel freely admitted it: he really was a criminal accomplice. The story has no mention that he was tortured.

Chapter 13: Tuesday

On Tuesday, January 2, 1923, official sunrise came at 7:26 a.m. The house behind the picket fence was still in shock, as nine-year-old Minnie gathered chaotic impressions.

At this point, she knows only that her uncle Aaron has disappeared. At home no one seems to know where he went, or what he might be suffering. The next question is how far the violence might spread—and what this means for Minnie's "Mama," her grandmother Emma Carrier.

As the manhunt continues—now lacking both of its star witnesses, Aaron Carrier or Sam Carter—it might easily target Emma Carrier. She is Aaron's mother, and knows his comings and goings. And there is the Newberry precedent. On August 19, 1916, a similar mob pursuit forty miles north at Newberry turned on the relatives and neighbors of a fugitive, tailoring accusations and conspiracy theories to fit, killing six, including two women.[189]

Clearly, it might be better if Emma Carrier could drop out of sight for awhile. But where? Any hideout would have to be large, because Emma's household would have to come with her. Her four youngest children are still at home, plus the two grandchildren, Minnie and Ruben. What kind of place could hide such a crowd?

One member of the family has an answer. At some point after Aaron's disappearance, Minnie sees that a visitor has come.

The visitor is Scrappy, Minnie's aunt, who lives two miles up the tracks at the turpentine camp in Wylly. Scrappy (Beulah Carrier Sherman) is Emma Carrier's grown daughter.

Complicating Scrappy's plan, however—and any visit from her—are her living conditions. She is in disgrace. Scrappy lives and works in Wylly's jook, the dance hall at the turpentine camp.[190]

Mama is so opposed to such things that she forbids any kind of dancing in her home. If Minnie's clowning brother Ruben wants to dance the buck on the porch as a joke, he has to do it behind Mama's back.[191] Hard-shell Methodist Emma Carrier is tall, strong, patient and relentlessly disciplined. She has known many trials. Scrappy's path into the den of iniquity has been a hard one.[192]

Scrappy is undeterred. On the visit, she insistently tells Mama that there is a logical place to hide, with all the children, too—a place with plenty of room. Why doesn't Mama come and stay with her in the jook?

Minnie's memory would not retain the exact words in Emma Carrier's reply—or the exact mixture of anger and hurt. *The very thought! The devil's house!*

Scrappy goes back to Wylly in defeat, still the outcast. Thus a problem is left dangling—to play the devil later in the week.

Minnie is not as strict as Mama, and sometimes walks up the tracks to visit Scrappy, going in the daytime when the old jook stands quietly in its hungover vapors. It's an interesting old place, larger than Sumner's low-slung dance hall. Wylly's rambling, two-story jook is a bit large for a turpentine camp, and draws traffic from surrounding settlements. Set back out of sight in the trees toward Gulf Hammock, the Wylly jook offers a second floor with an impressive open area for dancing. Down below are the smaller rooms—a number of them, as Scrappy's invitation said—each neatly sectioned off, including Scrappy's room. Minnie likes to go by day and play with her young aunt's baby, not inquiring about the music of the night.[193]

As it turns out, the Wylly jook was one more ghost from frontier Florida's booms and busts. The land out of time called Rosewood, secluded at the ends of the earth, had grown entwined with an invisible presence, linked to the Wylly jook through the back door. Like any ghost, this presence had no material being at all, utterly no physical mass—and yet it had moved the world—for it was a form of poetry, a stream of rhymes.

It is 1851, a decade before the Civil War, as songwriting prodigy Stephen Foster delivers up his masterpiece—the soaring, sonorous, somnolent musical number with the geographical hook.

The song exalts an obscure river in Florida, which Foster has never seen and knows nothing about. He writes the song in his native city, Pittsburgh—way up upon the Allegheny. As he sought a centerpiece for his new hit, he simply picked the Florida river off a map, for mental reasons—because of the magnificent poetry in its name. He loves the sound of it, packaging so many meanings into one short sigh—a name that is swimming, swooning, swan-like...

Way down upon de Swanee Ribber....

"The most popular song in the world," would be one of the labels during its long decades of celebrity. Going global, this phenomenal song would be translated into many languages. Deep power seemed to lie in its core message, whispering that a dreamy southern paradise existed, a place symbolized by a mysterious river, which few hearers of the song would ever see.

...Far, far away. That's where my heart am turning ebber...

The spelling, too, was something of a screen, for the lyrics were not written in real black dialect, but in a makeshift used by whites on the minstrel stage, as they blacked their faces for a ritual that millions of fans did not see as bizarre. Blackface minstrelsy, with its dreamy disguise and signature Swanee song, would be one of the longest-running traditions in American-born music, lasting from the 1830s into the 1950s, amid triumphs such as the world's first talking movie ("Mammy" in 1927, with Russian-born Al Jolson in blackface); [194]the battle song of the Confederacy ("Dixie," taken from blackface in 1858); and the landmark number later borrowed into infamy, "Jump Jim Crow" (a frantic dance song made famous by minstrel sensation "Daddy" Rice in the 1830s). [195]

None of the other hits, however, were called the most popular song in the world. The song about the river was loftier, more sublime than all that—so effective was its depiction of lost paradise. The dream-place called "Swanee" became the oleo-curtain backdrop for school skits and movie bits, a shorthand name for the Lost South, where the slaves looked happy. The one song would spawn generations of spin-off songs, including the largest commercial success of George Gershwin's career, the spin-off song "Swanee" in 1919; and the drum-banger by Irving Berlin in 1910: "If you want to hear that Swanee River played in ragtime..." A dream-world had been compressed into a word. [196]

As this journey began in 1851, Florida had been a state for only six years. Its Suwannee River was a jungle question mark, guarded by swamps and plagues. But Foster's blackface sentiment captured a national mood. Following in only one more year would be Uncle Tom's Cabin in 1852, a still larger superstar, sometimes called the best-selling novel of the nineteenth century, and that best-selling book of any kind in that century after the Bible. A still larger dream-land of passions and controversies—called race—was probing at America's heart.

In 1851-1852, music critics complained that they couldn't get away from Foster's Swanee song. It was everywhere—crooned, choired, fiddled, whistled, hummed.[197] There is reason to wonder whether this Swanee mania may have helped inspire David Levy Yulee, in 1853, to begin plans for his pioneering railroad across Florida—whose weary tracks (subsumed into the Seaboard) would still beckon to Minnie Mitchell in 1923. The 1850s romance of the Swanee song would not have hurt Levy Yulee's efforts, conducted in Washington, D.C., to find investors for his romantically positioned new rail line, going nearly to the river's mouth.

After the railroad was completed in 1861 at Cedar Key, seekers were enabled to go and look for the magic river themselves. The ashes of the Civil War had cooled as Cedar Key entered its 1880s boom, and railway tourists could step off the coaches at a Cedar Key wharf on the Gulf. From there a stern-wheel excursion boat, the Belle of the Suwannee, took them the last few miles up the coast to the Suwannee's mouth. No roads reached such a wild spot, but from the steamer's decks the sightseers could gaze into moss-hung cypress giants. The railroad itself never actually met the Suwannee's banks, but back inland a bit it came close. Only about twelve miles lay between the Suwannee and the tracks at this near-point, giving it a certain prestige.

At the spot a tiny rail stop bloomed up, complete with an 1880s real estate concern, the Suwannee Valley Land Company (with the word "valley" finessing the inconvenience that the musical river was not right on the doorstep).[198]

It was generally a time of big dreams, swelled by North Florida's 1880s citrus boom, with dreamers coming to build a paradise of orange and tangerine groves among exotic jungle palms—until the 1890s freezes\, and low-wage turpentine camps came to occupy the ruins. The boom-and-bust whistlestop on the railroad saw it all—in the crosshairs of river, rail and song. Its name was Wylly.

In the 1880s, delighted visitors to Wylly might include hopeful citrus boomers or wealthy sportsmen seeking Gulf Hammock's swarms of wild game. Stepping off the train, they met a genteel little hotel, the Suwannee Inn. A gourmet chef supplied the fare for a spacious upstairs dining hall, whose impressive open space had a picturesque view of Gulf Hammock's splendor. Downstairs, guests found comfortable rooms.[199]

A generation later—after the freezes, the hurricane winds, the fevers, the new company towns and their quarters—the weathered old building still managed to stand. An accident of buried history had left the Wylly turpentine camp with an ornament. Ernest Parham, the hard-working commissary clerk over at Sumner, would make Saturday night change by driving the company truck to Wylly, hauling loggers from the Sumner terminus as they sought the area's hottest night spot, which nobody called the Suwannee Inn.

As Tuesday deepened, Minnie watched another parade—not whites with a dog this time, but a trickle of horses and wagons. The small, fighty face with its protective frown is peering over the picket fence at passersby who are African American, mostly men. The event drawing them has an aura of danger. They are going to the Tuesday funeral of Sam Carter.

One of Minnie's older uncles, Joe Robinson of Wylly, was said to recover the body, going out into the hammock where it was left. Few details of the funeral would be remembered. Back north of Minnie in a starving old salt-box house, little Wilson Hall finds himself left to watch over smaller children as his mother Mary Ann attends the funeral. At the cemetery an older gravestone mutely looks on, a slender obelisk marked by ritual symbols, a Masonic stone. Darkened by nearly two decades of jungle rain as it flanks the Carter funeral, this is the 1905 marker of entrepreneur Martin Goins, the lead partner in M. Goins & Bros. Naval Stores. His day is now gone—like the general store that once was operated by Wilson Hall's father Bacchus. That store had already closed when C. Bacchus Hall died in 1919, leaving the children to deal with hunger. In the Tuesday funeral for frontiersman Sam Carter, the old frontier is itself being buried.[200]

Roosters crowing, back-porch sinks sloshing, stove lids clanking, wagon hubs needing grease—naturally, no one would hold specific memories of the small sounds announcing the arrival of that Tuesday morning. In Sumner, dawn creeps once more through the quarters street for whites. In a house three doors north of the Taylors, little Billie Zetrouer wakes up on the floor, under a quilt.[201]

Ordinarily, such a Tuesday would find Billie at home, in her own bed on a struggling farm between Sumner and the Gulf. But yesterday, she understands vaguely, some kind of danger broke out. She will remember her mother piling the children into their truck, then driving them to safety inside the corporate fastness of Sumner. Billie is not quite eight.

Sumner, white quarters: McElveen house (Billie Zetrouer)

Her mother's sister Effie is married to Jason McElveen, a white sawmill employee, assigned to drive gasoline-powered work carts on the railroad. Through Monday night, Billie lies on the floor next to her mother, snuggled in the McElveens' four-room home—and shielded from nearby knowledge. She never guesses that just three doors south is the focal point of the danger, where the fiend has struck.

In the other direction, just up the street, Edith Surls, the 15-year-old pixie, is once more itching with curiosity. Word has spread about the killing last night. If only the grown-ups would let her go down there and see for herself, Edith frets, she could lay a question to rest. If she could just see him stretched out, then she could find out once and for all. The riddle keeps tugging at her. Is it really true what they say about the colored people, that when they die they turn white?

The folds of deeper irony in this particular case lay unguessed: even before death this fatality was viewed by some neighbors as white—though his killer saw him as black. And now, as if to complete the circle, the clues are erased from his face, since the shotgun fired at close range.

Billie wakes under the quilt, hearing voices. Grown-ups are in the kitchen talking. Uncle Jase has come home, arriving before dawn, apparently after staying out all night. With hardly any sleep, he will now have to gulp down some coffee and breakfast from the wood stove, then answer the shift whistle. No one explains to Billie that after Carter was killed, a late-night branch of the mob rushed to the Sumner jail (also not far from where she is lying) in hopes of dragging out Aaron Carrier, as they had been led to believe they could do—only to find him gone.

Billie's uncle Jase would say later that white mill personnel were posted as sentries around the black quarters through the night, guarding against such mob members. He said that was where he had been, standing guard. Still farther up the street, at its head by the hotel, this Tuesday finds clerk Ernest Parham back in the commissary. He hears that Pillsbury, the big boss, has laid down the law, telling his white employees that from now on they are to stay out of this racial trouble.

In the silence of the bungalow, no sound from the piano in the parlor, nor from the three family automobiles out front (though one is now cooling from the daredevil rescue run). Walter Pillsbury, father and husband, has had little sleep. The children are in their rooms. Seventeen-year-old Edward is now safe.[202]

Walter and Grace Pillsbury

Was it the right thing, that wild rescue, removing the mob target to Gainesville? Will it only blow up in his face? Despite a life of improbable adventure, the mill administrator is not a risk-junkie like his impulsive son. He calculates. And in the silence now, he prays. Witnesses can be dispensed with on this point. Praying was his way. Walter Pillsbury and his wife Grace were fervent Baptists, so fervent that they had already risked popular anger in the company town. By means of a puzzling managerial decree, and backed by his wife, Pillsbury converted the mill's recreation hall for whites into, of all things, a skating rink for children—thus pointedly ruining the floors and stopping the devil's curse, dancing. He is not a simple man.

Perhaps his favorite book (after the good one) is his richly embossed copy of Milton's Paradise Lost—not an easy read, and in the edition he owns darkened by large engravings of demons clamoring in hell. Those pictures have now come to life. He saw something like that last night.[203]

Billie cringes under the quilt, hearing the way the adult talk is going. In the kitchen her mother and Aunt Effie are pumping Uncle Jase for information. What has been going on out there? She hears his voice in the kitchen: "They hung him up."

A few hundred yards east, Marshall Cannon greets Tuesday in his shop, his barber clippers ready for the sheet on the chair. Cronies come and go, shooting the breeze—and expressing anger about how that fool Hudson ruined the interrogation.

Also at that end of Sumner is Drew Pearson's drug store, a realm of blood tonic, tinctures, salts, soothing syrup, morphine—and a ceremony which, according to memory, took over the premises on this tense Tuesday. Old Florida's courtroom hierarchy rested at its lowest level on a worthy called the justice of the peace. An accompanying phrase, "cracker-barrel justice," conjured images of such a figure pounding a gavel on a plank under a shade tree. But at Pearson's things were more civilized—in the pill-flanked courtroom of Justice of the Peace L. L. Johns.[204]

Boarding with a farmer in the woods, Johns has come today to set up at Pearson's for an inquest. A violent death cannot be just forgotten. An official opinion must be set down. Coroner's inquests in sawmill towns more often came on Mondays, addressing weekend killings at the jook, but whatever the crime scene, it had to be certified.

Crowning his dignity with owl-like spectacles on a George Washington nose, Justice Johns has kept a minor secret in Sumner: his first name. In all encounters he goes only by the initials "L. L." Arriving in the swamps as a sawmill security guard, Lottie Luconie Johns set his sights high and entered politics. Soon after 1923 he will be sheriff of all Levy County, besting Bob Walker in the election of 1924. For the old sheriff, the Rosewood atrocity will seem to begin a disastrous downhill slide, ending a twenty-year career.[205]

In December 1922, the month prior to Tuesday's session, Justice Johns reported collecting $27.13 in fines, though the Rosewood month, January, will see an uptick to $50, reasons obscure. Johns does not look complicit, however. As the violence skyrockets after January 4, the burly justice will be one more member of the managerial class who rejects mob violence. Some of the angry woods farmers will accuse him of sneaking treachery, in the form of helping people flee for their lives.[206]

Today the issue is more confined. In the death of one Samuel S. Carter, Johns's inquest calls witnesses. Just around the corner at

Cannon's barbershop, the name and deeds of Bryant Hudson, far from being a secret, are topics of ardent conversation, as the story of the Monday night shooter spreads across the county. It was possible that the Justice himself might have been standing in the Gulf Hammock crowd—since nobody wanted to miss that show. Perhaps most or even all of the white males in the drugstore courtroom were there, watching Carter die. Thus the drugstore verdict will neatly capture a world of rural secrets, showing how they could short-circuit the main tool of history, the written record.

The verdict on the Carter case that day, duly recorded and certified, was Death by Unknown Hands.

In living witness interviews outside the official record, Bryant Hudson was described by all concerned as the lowest of the low, and was defended by no one. Yet lynching's code of silence closed around even him, and never troubled him with prosecution. As with the legal-illegal jook just west of the drugstore courtroom, and its guardian bagman-lawman, there was a special meaning here to the rule of law.

In 1921 when Bryant Hudson was accused of trying to kill a deputy, local jurisprudence shrugged and let him go. Now in 1923 he is let go again. This would continue until 1931, when a brawl on a store porch sent him flying onto hard ground.[207] The rib damage then invited the bacterial reaper of the pre-penicillin age, pneumonia. By the time someone bothered taking him to a hospital, the most final of verdicts was well begun: death at age 34.

How Hudson's inner fires may or may not have related to his service in World War I would remain unexplored. *"Character: Excellent,"* said the service record from two successive enlistments. But the faceless ghost of Sam Carter would impose one more reproach, in the point-blank shotgun blast that reminded of Hudson's other service rating: *"Marksmanship: Not Qualified."*[208]

On Tuesday there was as yet no racial cleansing frenzy. The one death looked like an ordinary lynching—or ordinary enough, the execution being almost a blundering afterthought, not really a ritual lynching. As yet, a land of legal-illegal jooks and death-by-hands-unknown had not had to use its full genius for hiding the facts. But the time is coming, later in the week. The rest of the week's deaths would receive no inquests.

Such a lapse in legal procedure apparently caused belated discomfort, for nearly a year later some strange-looking death records on the week were grandfathered into official files by a new justice of the peace, R. Machen Middleton, after L. L. Johns had moved on to the 1924 sheriff's race and greater fame.[209] As instruments of avoidance the new scraps of paper were more artful than mere silence, for they looked certified, while managing to provide almost no hint that something large had gone on.

Chapter 14: The Convict

As Tuesday led to Wednesday and Thursday, January 3-4, 1923, uneasy quiet continued to envelope the two square miles known as Rosewood. Weather records from Cedar Key indicate some rain in the Tuesday-Wednesday period, but weather aside, a lull in mass violence is not unusual after an initial burst. The echoes may die away as if nothing else will happen.[210] Passions that have briefly rushed to the surface now hesitate, as if probing and testing for the next place to break out.

"NO FURTHER TRACE OF NEGROES WANTED FOR ASSAULT AT SUMNER"

Thus sighed the Thursday morning edition of the *Gainesville Daily Sun*. The media's ongoing spin—the construction of an apparent gang crime or group uprising—was still not abandoned. The lone attacker continued to undergo cell division ("NEGROES WANTED").

But this was wearing thin. None of the large metropolitan papers were going to look on the wire and pick up anything so bland as "NO FURTHER TRACE." The *Sun* soldiered on alone, bound by its local interest, but running out of ways to keep the uprising suggestion alive: *"Sheriff Walker and Posses Still Scouring Territory In Search Of Fiends."*

However, a new morsel now surfaces from somewhere. By Wednesday the disappeared attacker of Fannie Taylor is said in the press to have been identified—sort of.

He has still not been caught or even seen, but at least now he is tagged by public comment with a scrap of biography—which is going to grow. The start of this identification is preserved only in the newspaper stories, so the credibility is an open question. No informant in later years would have any inkling as to where the identification came from. On other points the press coverage was neither all true nor all false, but demonstrably mixed fact and fancy. The naming of the fugitive could be either—or both.

170

An example of the brief mention appeared in the *Tampa Morning Tribune*, perhaps coming off the Associated Press wire from the faithful crow's nest at the *Gainesville Daily Sun*. At a stroke, this identification conveniently links Fannie Taylor's attacker not only to Sam Carter (now newsworthy because he has suddenly turned up dead), but to Carter's stormy family life—a lot to pack into a few words. The entire media glimpse consists of only two sentences, embedded in a reference to Carter:

> **"His [Carter's] son was seen leaving Sumner shortly after the assault took place, in company with an escaped convict from a nearby turpentine camp. Members of the search party are of the opinion that one of these is guilty of the crime."**

Here is a lightning bolt. Suddenly two entirely new villains—a son of Sam Carter's plus "an escaped convict from a nearby turpentine camp"—erupt into the confusion. They will also disappear about as quickly from the news stories, without further explanation. The illogic is numbing. If the original attacker of Fannie Taylor did run from her house—leaving the scent trail that was the main evidence—then how could *two individuals* in Sumner be involved in this trail? Is someone saying that the scent trail was not the right trail? Did the two individuals leave *another* trail? And does this mean no scent trail was really left by a lone runner going to Aaron Carrier's house, and hence no wagon, and hence nothing pointing back to Sam Carter?

Unidentified Florida convict trusty, ca. 1920s
(photo: Florida Memory: State Archives of Florida

No one from the real events, black or white, would recall a sighting of two persons of interest. If they were "seen" leaving Sumner, this was an alternative scenario. Any alleged convict "leaving Sumner" in company with Sam Carter's alleged son couldn't possibly have been the runner. So what's the connection? Following the statement above, in the same news article, the *Tampa Tribune* also endorsed the core story about the lone runner leaving Fannie Taylor's house, more or less as in the witness memories:

171

"Carter, senior, became implicated last night when bloodhounds led searchers to a negro home several miles from Sumner. Members of [illegible phrase] party declared that the [illegible phrase] the home confessed to have hidden one of the fugitives until Carter drove him off in a horse and wagon...."

The article gives both of the conflicting alternatives together, as if the result makes sense. The newspaper images could seem a bit like the fugitive himself (Or two fugitives? Or more?)—flashing in many minds, but not very distinctly.

"His son" [Carter's alleged son] would receive only the passing nod above. After the main Rosewood explosion on Thursday night there would be a few more allegations about the vanished Monday attacker, but only alluding to a mysterious convict, alone. The riddle of Carter's companionable son would vanish, to be replaced by other mysteries— which also would soon vanish from the shouting.

Alas, Traveler, the trail gets a little slippery down this way—but it does call for exploration, because at the end, crazily, it may lead to a nugget of substance. There could have been an additional murder that was kept out of view. As already said, one of Sam Carter's two sons, George Carter, had a criminal record, and in 1919 had served a six-month prison term for killing a yearling cow or bull. Surviving court files confirm this background, though the news image of "his son" in 1923 gets onto softer ground.

There is the "nearby turpentine camp." where the convict supposedly escaped. Before about 1910, Levy County did have turpentine camps holding private stockades and leased convicts. But by 1923 the sordid old world of convict leasing had been eliminated from many parts of Florida, apparently including Levy County. Memories and records seem to agree that by January 1923 no turpentine convicts were being leased "nearby."[211]

Someone at a newspaper seemed to have imposed a leap of assumption, perhaps vaguely knowing the bygone cliché image of gloomy woodland lease camps, and dropping this in as a flourish— "expanding" the sparse information that was available—though no lease camps really were there. By January 6 the thinness would be underscored, for the story changed.[212] A new wire report—also garbled—placed the alleged escape not at a turpentine camp at all, but at a government road gang. This was a more plausible scenario, but so few details were given—not even the location of the road camp—that it, too, could have been imagined.

As the trail winds toward the promised payoff, distant on the horizon, it must now loop toward a witness—the one retrospective informant who can shed a little light on "the son."

Jason McElveen, white, the uncle of little Billie Zetrouer who sheltered in Sumner, was said by his niece to have links to the Ku Klux Klan. McElveen did not seem to deny this. He, too, would be an elderly Rosewood informant, though a defiant one, using explosive racist language and gloating about Rosewood's demise.[213]

No evidence of direct Ku Klux Klan involvement in the Rosewood events would ever surface (as explained later in these pages), but McElveen's leanings were important in another sense, in terms of his credibility as an informant. One story he told ran counter to his sympathies—perversely supporting his credibility on that point.

Living three doors north of James and Fannie Taylor in Sumner's white quarters, Jason McElveen was well set for mobility. In a land of swamps, a convenient way to get around was on the railroad, though not always on the trains. McElveen ran a "motorcar," not an automobile but a gasoline-powered work cart for rail travel. Cummer Lumber owned a fleet of loud little motorcars, with their lawn-mower pull ropes for starting. McElveen would recall overseeing the lot. Even allowing for neighborly chuckles about his reputation for boasting, he certainly did drive at least one. His account of Monday afternoon, January 1, 1923, generally agrees with other evidence.

work cart or "motorcar," 1938
(photo: Otis, FotoThing)

As noted, on Tuesday a scrap of county commission record confirmed that two extra blood-hounds were rented on January 1. McElveen supplied some back-ground on this, saying that he was sent in the motorcar to pick up the dogs. He described driving to Otter Creek, 12 miles up from Rosewood. Otter Creek was a logical node since the dogs (as shown by the record) came from a camp near the town of Fort White, whence they would have to travel on the Atlantic Coast Line railroad, which crossed the Seaboard tracks at Otter Creek. According to the cart driver, the sad-eyed canine detectives arrived at Otter Creek in a boxcar—but not until late Monday afternoon. Because of the delay, he said, it made sense to combine his Otter Creek mission with another one, also using the Atlantic Coast Line tracks. McElveen said the motorcar was switched onto the ACL and then ran southeast from Otter Creek into the southern end of Levy County, to reach a logging camp called Tidewater.

This trip was no lark. The driver said sternly that he was expecting murder at the destination, and he was ready to help. One of the reasons, he said, was that beside him in the vehicle sat

Remains of store - Otter Creek
(photo: Florida Trailblazer)

his neighbor from Sumner, James Taylor, still enraged by what had happened to his wife Fannie. And the other reason, McElveen recounted, lay waiting for them at Tidewater. A story had gotten out about Sam Carter's son, and this son was a logger at Tidewater. Whatever the climate of rumors at that moment, McElveen portrayed himself and Taylor as boiling with anger because the logger—Sam Carter's son—seemed to them to be Fannie's attacker.

There was the geography. If a wagon had wound its way east through Gulf Hammock from Aaron Carrier's house, the labyrinth of swamp trails might reach Tidewater on the hammock's far side—where a clever fugitive, anonymous in those distant parts, might conceivably swing aboard an ACL freight train in the dark and be gone. McElveen did not expound on the geography, or otherwise explain the evidence implicating the logger, but he frowned grimly as he said: "James Taylor woulda killed that nigger just like stubbin' your finger. Less than that even." Recollecting six decades later, this informant did not bother to give the logger a name, but dismissed him with an approximation, calling him "Sam Carter, Jr." According to the census and other records, Carter had two sons, neither named Sam. The logger would have to be one of the two.

In McElveen's angry telling, he and James Taylor climbed from the cart and marched forth to seek satisfaction—but were interrupted. The camp foreman, a white, suddenly was in their faces, waving a time sheet. He was showing them that Sam Carter's son—whichever son this was— had been at work in Tidewater since early that morning. He couldn't possibly have been twenty miles away in Sumner, on the other side of Gulf Hammock's maze.

Here the telling grows anti-climactic. McElveen shrugged that the two visitors climbed back into the cart and returned to Otter Creek. They agreed with the foreman. Sam Carter's son couldn't have been the attacker. The mob etiquette of first-phase aggression seemed to be holding again. These players, at this point, didn't like to see themselves as being frenzied loose cannons. Random strikes would later occur, but for now this was still a hunt, not an orgy. The target had to be the right one.

McElveen, with his racial slurs and disdain for "Sam Carter, Jr.," formed a persuasive witness for the defense. He certainly wasn't out to give the son any help. It's true that some boasting may have marred the description in some way, but when added to other puzzle pieces this account still leaves the newspaper story about Sam Carter's son looking empty.

Even a hostile witness seems to say that the report running in the papers on Wednesday had already been discarded at the scene on Monday.

But here our loop grows deeper. Whites close to the Taylor family would continue to insist, down through the decades, that at some point after the Rosewood week, James Taylor or his kin did locate the vanished Monday attacker, and allegedly they killed him, with no publicity. This, too, is a blatant boast, and perhaps an empty boast. If they killed someone, who was it?

In 1925 the adult heirs of Sam Carter were assembled to sign a deed, as the Carter 80 was sold.[214] Among those present was Sam Carter's daughter Pearlee, who was said to sometimes come and cook for him. And there was the widower of his deceased sister Janetta, along with Carter's still-living mother Cornelia. And there was his son George. Here on paper was proof that the bruiser allegedly tough enough to kill a sizeable animal with his bare hands had survived the fires of 1923.

But where was the other son? At some point before 1925, that other son was apparently deceased. Aside from the 1925 implications, a cryptic Florida death index notes the 1923 death of an individual who might be that son.[215] Is this the shadow fatality in the Taylor boasts? Did something terrible happen without public notice?

There are only loose ends in this direction, not answers. Of course, it might seem natural at this point to give the name of the missing son. But the chain of evidence, impertinently, continues to beg a bit more patience. To get to the name—circuitously—we turn now to the other half of the dangerous duo in the newspaper tale, the alleged escaped convict.

 When things blew up at Rosewood on Thursday night, January 4, and continued intermittently convulsing over the next three days, media attention would dramatically revive, bringing a need for the later news stories to summarize what had gone before. How had this great eruption come about? How did it all start? Some glances back at the Fannie Taylor attack were required—in a bit more detail.

The relevant dispatch would come on Friday, reaching newspapers nationwide on the Associated Press wire. This was the recap, again mentioning an escaped convict, that rectified the turpentine camp canard, now saying that the escapee came from a road camp.

Other evidence does seem to confirm that as 1923 approached, convicts worked from time to time on a new road through Rosewood (later to be Florida Highway 24).[216] The Friday dispatch simply said "road gang," without saying where, but it added a vital detail. It said that the county sheriff (increasingly desperate Bob Walker) had come up with the convict's name.

The isolated wisp of news story revealed that the hunted predator, this Jesse James of the swamps, this hunter of helpless housewives, was named Jesse Hunter.

Again, Rosewood's parade of whimsical names carries a suggestion of free association or semi-conscious poetry, bubbling from some fount unexplained. Now, in the litany of Add-Us and Burn-Us, Carrier-Carter, Cummer Lumber Company's Sumner and other rhymes, we have the Hunted Hunter.

Could this really have been his name? The obvious guess—that free association must have somehow twisted the outcome in the newspaper rumor mill—is given some support by one factor. No such "Jesse Hunter" has ever surfaced in any known independent document, official record or census sheet from surrounding Florida in the 1920s. Under the spelling in the newspaper dispatch, he seems to have no officially registered existence at all. Even a convict should have appeared in the records. A low-level county prisoner might have eluded the state prison register, but federal census takers routinely went to convict road camps and took names.[217]

Still—as elsewhere in the maze—it's not altogether that simple. There is the back door into confirmation, offered not by documents but by the testimony of the living witnesses.

And they do remember him.

"Jesse Hunter, big tall fella...gamble in Sumner and Wylly," mused Sam Hall, seated on his porch in South Georgia sixty years later.

"He had been stayin' in Sumner," said Lee Carrier. "...I saw him a couple of times."

Both Sam Hall and Lee Carrier, the two Rosewood survivor-informants best positioned for a view of Jesse Hunter's world, said he was real. They knew little about him, but both said they had seen him in passing in Sumner: a tall, rough figure in the fringes of the local underworld. They said he moved back and forth between the two underworld magnets, the jooks—that is, between the long, low cabin in Sumner and the doughty old two-story building in Wylly—meaning up and down the tracks through Rosewood. And if such an underworld figure sounds surprising in a regimented company preserve like Sumner, there is Zora Hurston to provide perspective, from her research into company towns and jooks elsewhere in Florida:

> **"The law is lax on these big saw-mill, turpentine and railroad 'jobs,'.... All of these places have plenty of men and women who are fugitives from justice. The management asks no questions. They need help and they can't be bothered looking for a bug under every chip...."[218]**

A jook's back room offered a card game called Georgia Skin, a kind of lethal blackjack, able to create a pauper or a prince at a stroke.[219] The trains brought a stream of drifters and gamblers, whether riding a Jim Crow coach with a cardboard suitcase or in an open gondola in the rain. Such a drifter might get pinched for a misdemeanor and clapped into a county road gang without many locals knowing about it. The wire-service story revealing the hunted Hunter threw in another specific. He was said to have become a convict by a common route, being charged with carrying a concealed weapon. Peaceable (and valuable) laborers weren't likely to be searched for the weapons carried by some of them—the little .32 in the overalls bib, the razor in the sock—but if a constable should want to convert a suspicious drifter into a thirty-day county ditch digger, a pat-down could often provide the rationale.

The January 5 wire story hinting at this—while giving little hard information—would introduce all of America to Jesse Hunter. Sent out on Friday and running on Saturday, January 6, the story appeared simultaneously on the front pages of both the *New York Times* and the *Los Angeles Times,* and in many papers in between.

> **"Rosewood, Jan. 5—(By Associated Press)—Armed posses of white men, numbering between 200 and 300, tonight were scouring the countryside for Jesse Hunter, escaped negro convict..."**

Now everybody knew Jesse Hunter—for an instant, before he was just as instantly forgotten. And of course, even if "Jesse Hunter, escaped negro convict" was quite real, he may still have been an illusion in another sense. He could have been really, truly, breaking limerock in a county road gang—and then could have really, truly escaped (perhaps in some sort of drunken confusion on New Year's Eve), but that still didn't prove that such an escapee, if one such were to be wandering around Levy County, was Fannie Taylor's visitor.

The Levy County Sheriff's Department appeared to be convinced, however. As this Hunter's notoriety was rushing coast to coast, a phone call reportedly came to the sheriff's office from downstate, originating in the Florida town of Lakeland.[220] Whether an all-

Rolling cage used in early Florida to house convicts at work sites

points bulletin had been issued for Fannie Taylor's attacker or there was other help, the Lakeland police announced proudly that they had caught him, the Sumner fugitive, who by then was famous. They had pulled him right off the train, they said. How they came to be convinced that it was the right man was a mystery that would swell with time, as a law enforcement team from Levy County was reportedly sent to get him.

Such was the urgency that on the long train ride apparently more than one deputy was assigned.

Then came the moment of truth. The Levy County deputies peered through the bars in Lakeland, scrutinizing the detainee. Then they turned back to the Lakeland police. And they said:

It's not him.

There is only a wisp of newsprint on this, too, but the arrangement of the information is compelling. At least one deputy seemed to be dead sure that the man in the Lakeland cell was not the elusive Jesse Hunter. The deputy seemed certain enough to be willing to embarrass his mission by coming home empty-handed. And this makes a point. Such a deputy would have to have known the escaped convict by sight (whether he was really named Jesse Hunter or something else), meaning that at least there was a real individual somewhere behind the name confusion.

Sam Hall went further, painting a word portrait of Jesse Hunter: "crooked, kind of mean, carried a pistol. It was out that Jesse had broke gang." However, Hall also added that in attacking Fannie Taylor, "all he was doin' was gettin' him somethin' to eat. He smelled the fried chicken cookin' for her husband. Took somethin' to eat and knocked the woman down."

All very nice, but a little early in the morning for fried chicken. Sam Hall was a careful informant on things he personally witnessed and knew, but in this case he was necessarily repeating from rumor—and from the newspaper reports —which contained both the concealed weapon ("carried a pistol") and the road gang escape ("had broke gang"). Where the fried chicken came from, perhaps only the rumor mill can tell.

"Hunter, who escaped from a road gang in Levy County, was accused in connection with the crime....Hunter was serving a prison term for carrying a concealed weapon."

This was how it appeared on January 6 in the *New York Times*, using the (apparently unchecked) wire-service story. When the *Times* then reworked the same phrase two days later, on January 8, a reader might have thought that now Jesse Hunter had been confirmed by two separate reporters, each looking at firsthand evidence. But it was all the same quick description, couched in professional-sounding language and apparently gleaned by phone: "Jesse Hunter, wanted for alleged implication in an attack on a young white woman at Sumner Monday."

The one wire-service mention that had gone out on January 5— perhaps the only origin of the name "Jesse Hunter"—was also reworked on January 8 in the *Chicago Evening Post*: "Officers are still without a

179

clue as to the whereabouts of Hunter"—as if this were independently obtained information, when it was really just a rehash with the name dropped in, and perhaps was rehashing what was originally one more jumbled mistake.

By 1923 the first tremors of the Florida Boom had begun, and even in the North Florida woodlands—where in fact the boom would never penetrate except in a hiccup or two—local boosters were tooling up as best they could to attract real estate treasure hunters. In Levy County this meant building a new road out to the Gulf beauty of Cedar Key.[221] By January 1, 1923, construction had already begun on Florida Highway 24, and work crews had set up around Rosewood. Sam Hall heard them blasting limerock out of a sink. A rock was said to come down and kill one of John McCoy's chickens. The remains of a borrow pit can still be seen at Rosewood's site. Standing at the picket fence, Minnie saw the trucks go by, over behind Mama's chufa field, where they were "buildin' that hard road." There was no way to misidentify the passengers of the trucks, since the convicts wore stripes. Minnie, too, heard the news account of Monday morning in Sumner, and she assumed it must be true—that a convict must have broken gang, then went in on a woman and fled up the rails, to find the home of Brother Aaron. If no living mortal would admit having seen his flight, this must have been because people were scared.

And so, Traveler, this looping trail has been long, but at last we come to the one name still missing.

Who was Sam Carter's other son?

What was the name of that son who seemed to disappear around 1923—and may or may not have met secret mayhem? To understand how his name may link to the fabled outlaw Jesse Hunter, one need only consult the Rosewood claims case of 1994 in the Florida Legislature, with its multiplicity of misunderstandings. In that case, a typed transcript rendered the declaration of one witness as follows:

"I reckon she said that Minea Hunting (phonetic) was in that house."

The word in parentheses, "phonetic," was inserted by the official transcriber, in an attempt to point out a dilemma. A court reporter typing the statement was trying to understand what the witness was saying, amid rural dialect and diverse confusion, and couldn't figure out how to spell that unusual name, belonging to someone called, approximately, "Minea Hunting."

Whoever Minea Hunting was, the witness seemed to be saying, he or she was in that house.

Here, the name of a non-existent individual has apparently been invented accidentally—after a drawling voice muttered: *"the man you're hunting."* But the point for us lies elsewhere: if such semantic creep could occur in the highest legislative body in the fourth largest state in the most powerful nation on earth, what about in semi-literate wilderness during a riot, with voices squawking through static on black candlestick phones?

Could "Jesse Hunter" be another "Minea Hunting"?

Might he, too, have been a slurred form of some covered-over original phrase or name?

On the one hand, we have that fearsome but stubbornly insubstantial outlaw Jesse Hunter, who no record nor all the mobs or posses of Jim Crow passion could ever find. And on the other hand, we have the mysteriously disappeared son of Sam Carter.

His name was *Jess* Carter.[222]

Chapter 15: Stranger in Paradise

L. L. Johns, the drugstore justice of the peace in Sumner, was independent of county government and its sheriff, Bob Walker. Sheriff Walker sent his cases to a county judge in Bronson, the county seat. Johns's smaller court, shining in the wilderness, was allotted a different kind of law enforcement officer.

L. L. Johns
Justice of the Peace
Precinct 9, Sumner

The legman for a justice of the peace was called a constable. The cracker-barrel-justice image, putting a justice of the peace behind a plank across two cracker barrels, included a second figure, a baleful bruiser standing at the end of the plank, keeping order: the constable.[223] In the sawmill company town of Sumner, Precinct 9, this was Constable D. P. "Poly" Wilkerson.

However, good old Poly, as his many friends knew him, was not just a head-busting goon. His complexity would become a key to the Rosewood puzzle.

Ostensibly, a constable working for a j.p. was a server of writs and a scourge only of small crimes. The law limited justice of the peace courts to misdemeanors. But this could be stretched. As Florida would enter a new boom period in the 1950s, buoyed by the spread of air conditioning, motorists from Long Island or the Loop might find that paradise greeted them with a sudden drop in local speed limits, where a backwoods justice of the peace had set a speed trap. When the trap was sprung, the fellow in your rearview mirror, cranking the siren, would be the constable. In earlier generations this kind of power had been still greater, and a justice of the peace might send his constable after the occasional African American stranger, who could be convicted of vagrancy, then profitably shipped off (or "leased") to a private convict stockade. Many such officials were above such tactics and made the best of hard circumstances, but Florida's justice of the peace system had its critics:

> "[T]he office is held in such low repute that the election is not contested. There have been instances of JPs elected by write-in votes—without their knowledge —merely as a prank. Jokesters have even

elected farm animals, bearing human
names; and some years ago a wooden
cigar-store Indian won the office in one
town.... One justice of the peace, over a
13-month period, earned \$4,533 from
'violations' at a single traffic light."[224]

Constable Poly Wilkerson—perhaps standing guard at the drugstore
inquest for Sam Carter on Tuesday, January 2, 1923—came from an old
family of pioneers. His father before him had been a justice of the peace,
presiding in the last of the cedar boom at the turn of the century. In those
days a courtroom had held certain difficulties for the hem of a lady's
long skirt. A brown scum tended to moisten public floors, left by spat
tobacco poorly aimed at sand in the spit box. By 1923, however, the
brown-scum days were gone, and floors were tidy—one more milestone
in the twenty-year passage out of the Florida frontier. But Poly
Wilkerson remained robust and rumpled like an old frontier fiddle frolic,
looking a little marooned in a brisk new age.

Like Justice Johns, Poly Wilkerson seemed to tell few people his
real first name. "Poly" was a nickname, and he signed documents as "D.
P. Wilkerson." Otherwise there are only hints. A kinsman of Poly's was,
neatly enough, also called Poly—and in that case the real first name was
publicly known. The kinsman's formal name of record was Poland Italy
Hathcox—and he had a sister named Cuba.[225]

Home-brewed poetry bubbled on the frontier like the wilderness
boasts and tall tales, as creativity raised its lonely wail. Poly Wilkerson's
two kinfolk, Poland and Cuba, took creativity to extremes, not only
named for nations but for a very narrowly rhyming *category* of nations,
tied to local farm products. Cuba tobacco, grown in northern Florida, was
at least daintier than the brother's evocation of Poland China hogs.

But Poly Wilkerson's nickname—whatever it was hiding—did not
mean "roly-poly" or simplistically obese. He was bulky, true, but more
on the muscular side. People wishing to portray him seemed to focus on
another trait, his robust, ruddy complexion. He was "red-faced," "rosy."
Hearty and florid, the constable seemed to fall somewhere between the
high jinx of a laughing frontier Falstaff and the stern lawman signed by
those terse initials, "D. P."

By the end of World War I he had done his family tradition proud,
holding three law enforcement jobs at once. He was not only district
constable but a local deputy sheriff in the county system, putting him

back under Sheriff Walker after all, while the deputy's badge conferred the third job, the plum, making him chief guard for the reigning timber company, its quarters boss.

So here, in short, is the fallen angel, a player already glimpsed in passing. By the dawn of 1923, Poly Wilkerson had fallen hard. Before the Rosewood events occurred, he had been fired from his deputy's job and replaced by the shut-mouthed new deputy-and-quarters-boss, Clarence Williams.

The fall of Poly Wilkerson was a story in itself, but for now suffice it to say that the Monday excitement found him side-lined, missing out on the biggest case in years. Now it was newly-appointed Deputy Williams, the bachelor in the company hotel, who would get the thrills behind the dog.

The loss of the deputy's star seemed to hit Wilkerson hard. There was the complication—not aired in public but not really hidden—of moonshine revenue at the jook.[226] Wilkerson's link to it, of whatever sort, was cut off by the firing. If he was no longer deputy, he was no longer quartersboss. Only one shred of authority was left to him, at the parallel court in the drugstore.

The fires of January 1-7, 1923, would seem almost diabolically contrived to lure in a desperate, demoralized constable.

Martha remembered her first sight of him, that strange man Wilkerson. It was just after World War I. She was ten. Until the war was over she had lived in the big family home in Jacksonville, in the city—before fate whisked her away to jungle adventure, along with her brothers, sister and two adventurous parents. Life was a whirlwind in the household of sawmill superintendent Walter Pillsbury, her father.

Martha Pillsbury Thompson
born Sept. 15, 1908

With the war ended in November 1918, the interests of the millionaire Cummer family retrenched from defense projects such as ship-building.[227] Walter Pillsbury, not only a managerial employee but a long-time friend of the Cummer brothers, received a new assignment, to be reigning potentate at a Cummer timber town, run and mostly owned by the Cummers, who had one of the largest fortunes in Florida. Before

Walter and Grace Pillsbury

leaving for Sumner, Pillsbury drove his family down to the Jacksonville wharf in their big Maxwell motorcar, then jumped out to stand at the gang plank, pumping the hands of doughboys returning from the war.

Daddy was like that, and not just because he had served in Cuba in '98. His reign in Sumner would find no one calling him Colonel, let alone Cap'n. No make-believe Dixie epaulets or drawling frippery sat on Sumner's new commander.

His roots were in the white-pine forests of Michigan, and in deep shadows: the dark Native American mother, the runaway Brahmin blueblood father—not really so odd a combination to wind up in a timber town, with its cast of exotic outsiders. In Sumner, Pillsbury's second-in-command was a Finnish-Swedish ship-jumper with a mail-order bride. Just below him was a yard boss with occasional paralytic fits and a severe stutter.[228]

The Pillsbury home in Jacksonville

Pillsbury exuded "demon energy," his assistant bookkeeper Frances Smith would recall: "You could just see the demon energy workin' in him." The necktie, the fedora, the air of command—and the sulfur match for the pipe, struck deftly on the seat of the pants. Nobody said "half-breed" to this man. It would only have sounded like jealousy.

After the wharf he sold the Maxwell, battening down for the move to the woods, buying Mama another kind of big car, the Buick, which seemed better for sand roads. For himself, Daddy bought only a little Ford—and another Ford for the children, with Edward the daredevil as chauffeur. Thus equipped, they rolled off to the ends of the earth, as Martha hung on.

1919 Maxwell

1920 Buick

As the big tank of an automobile slid into the new hometown, the Pillsbury children peered in awe: the strange little barn-red quarters houses, the fungus-soft sawdust streets. Their own bungalow was spacious, though Martha's window let in a mournful sound. The

Cummers were progressive tycoons, and their company hotel had plumbing. A shed at the back held a gang urinal, moaning near Martha's room at night as it cycled through automatic flush.

Their first days in the wilderness were marred by the great shadow, the worldwide pandemic of "Spanish flu," seeming to come home with the troops from Europe, and forming the deadliest strain of influenza known to modern history. Striking especially at vigorous young adults, the flu left tens of millions dead worldwide in 1918-1919, the numbers never firmly established. In early 1919 two Cummer sawmill managers, at both Sumner and Otter Creek, were knocked off their feet along with their families. In the new bungalow only Martha stayed well, the rest of her family lying prostrate for days. So it went across the woods. Three miles away in Rosewood, Ed Bradley's house found both its adults laid out, along with all the children but one, distressed grand-niece Thelma Evans, who tried to care for everyone:

"Told 'em use home remedies, lemon tea with boiled pine straws, put it in moonshine with a pinch of powdered black draught. Had to whip me to get me to drink it, with a peachtree switch."

In Wylly a man named Mozo failed to survive that flu, closing out his old Spanish frontier name. The Sumner freight agent Ben Darby lost his wife. Under the great shadow, the wilderness was not so far from the world.[229]

But Martha's family recovered. Daddy turned to his task, the bringing of a new age to the old frontier grime of Sumner. To fight against malaria mosquitoes from the swamps, a government doctor was brought in, Augustus B. Cannon. Buckets of minnows were dumped into the cypress pond to gobble up aquatic mosquito larvae.[230] Just west, another sawmill town, "the malarious town of Perry," became a poster child for the U.S. Public Health Service in 1920.[231] Pillsbury built the first church on Sumner's company premises—Baptists one week, Methodists the next. Sometimes the devoutly religious boss was the preacher.

Soon after the influenza passed, the bungalow received a visitor. The company quarters boss stopped by. Martha thought he seemed to bow and scrap clumsily to her father, who now held make-or-break power over this rough-hewn underling. To the ten-year-old city girl, the red-faced man looked almost like a clown. His crude, exuberant ways spoke of the old part of Sumner, the farm houses outside company property in the woods, where some of Martha's ragged new schoolmates lived. She failed to guess other colorful details. At home, the unpretentious quarters boss had a son nicknamed Monkey and a wife called Bob.[232]

But on his visit he came prepared with a gift—or proposition. Wilkerson offered to serve as a wilderness guide for the new managerial family, and take them on a Sunday excursion. He wanted to show off a special place of enchantment he knew, deep in the wilds. The idea was to make a two-car caravan, the Wilkerson family riding point in their own car, the Pillsburys following in the Buick. Soon Martha was bouncing along on safari, trapped in the parade.

Then there it is!

Wilkerson is now out of the car, standing proudly before a magnificent jungle grotto, showing just how rich his old frontier can be. This secluded natural wonder, a spring-fed lagoon in a great sinkhole at 29° 29' N., 82° 57' W.,[233] had been captivating outsiders at least since 1774, when explorer and botanist William Bartram found it by river in a Seminole canoe. After Bartram's book about his travels reached England, the site also went into the notebook of poet Samuel Taylor Coleridge,[234] and thus crept into what has been called the greatest dream-poem in the English language, Coleridge's drug-induced fantasy "Kubla Khan," with its "caverns measureless to man."[235]

Just below the sandy surface of Levy County, Florida, limestone labyrinths were pumping perhaps 100 million gallons of water a day into this moss-curtained well, burgeoning up into a surface jet or dome—water so crystal clear that in 1774 Bartram said he could see every mullet swimming in the depths, every tray-sized cooter turtle  gliding in waterweed on the bottom. [236] He thought the spell of the place made even the law of the jungle fall away, so that creatures normally predator and prey swam peacefully together. But then you didn't have to be in Bartram's dream—or Martha's—to come under the spell.

Sunset deep in summer, the light soft and gold, the big cypress trunks rising out of clear glass—as the hanging moss comes alive, wild laughter swelling, the flocks of lord-god birds coming in, roosting at this secret place, the big pileated woodpeckers, fire-crested, squadrons of them, bulky, ponderous like eagles, but making their taunting, laughing cries. Another explorer, Audubon, said that the cries of these birds could be followed only at the woodsman's risk, as they seemed to intentionally lure the unwary hunter ever deeper into the woods, away from safe trails...

The clarity of this spring-fed water, if you ease down into it, suffuses the swimmer with quiet euphoria, the feeling that the dream of paradise is real— here, now—in this curve of crystal and palm—the current then moving you gently out of the lagoon into a similarly transparent stream, still with the big turtles and fish visible all around, browsing peacefully— the stream floating you quickly to its outlet, ringed in distant cypress and palm, a vast theater stage, as if empties its clarity into the big river, the Suwannee.

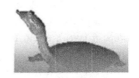

Apalone ferax
"Cooter"
(Florida soft-shelled turtle)

How did Stephen Foster grasp all this? In 1851 when he wrote "the most popular song in the world," he seemed never to have known that this same stream had already laid its spell on Bartram a century before, and thence on Coleridge after that. Did the dreamy minstrel poet somehow sense this, as he turned the echoes into the song?

Did he sense that at 29° 29' N., 82° 57' W., the muddy jumble of the visible world drops its charade, and what is solid admits the pretense, confesses that all along it has been dream?

Martha thought this was all very nice and when are we getting out of here? And why in the world did we follow this clown?

Chapter 16: Poly's Fall

"After dark, the jooks. Songs are born out of feelings with an old beat-up piano, or a guitar for a mid-wife. Love made and unmade. Who put out dat lie, it was supposed to last forever?...Dancing the belly-rub. Knocking the right hat off the right head and backing it up with a switch-blade....Maybe both get cut badly and back off. Anyhow, the fun of the place goes on. More dancing and singing and buying of drinks, parched peanuts, fried rabbit..."

—Zora Neale Hurston,
Dust Tracks on a Road, 1942

Missouri knew Poly, though not at the jook. Robert Missouri was a famously work-obsessed employee of the Cummer empire in Sumner, sweating in its shingle mill. Late at night after an overtime shift, walking home on dusty ruts in the black quarters, he would pass the Sumner jook, hearing the noise, not knowing what the bursts of shouting might mean, whether anger or jubilation. But noting the general force, the great babble, a vaguely menacing sound, like the shouts of the damned.[237]

Robert Missouri
in his eighties
(Levy County Archives Committee)

It was only gossip and custom that told him his friend Poly was in there—patrolling the customary quarters-boss domain—moving through the skin room for gambling in back, through the crowds on the dance floor, the bar. This was what a quarters boss did, the regular drill—though Missouri had heard (and not alone) that the rosy-faced man was getting a little carried away.[238] He had perhaps never heard of another *Heart of Darkness,* the one penned by novelist Joseph Conrad, or the novel's depiction of a quaint colonial slide, sometimes called going native. But Missouri heard people muttering, evoking the progression in all but name, that Poly had gone native.

Missouri was attuned to gossip, for he himself was an object of comment. People wondered, black and white, how a sawmill hand like Missouri, coming from the black quarters like everybody else, had scraped together so much money. Multiple witnesses would describe white foremen going to Missouri on occasion, seeking a quick payday loan.[239]

In a way this had started with the jook—though only in a backhand way. The shingle mill stood behind the main sawmill palace, enveloped in the droning sound of the planing mill next door. He had been drawing the same $1.75 a day as anybody else, stacking newly cut cypress shingles. But the man opposite him in the stacking line seemed to be out sick frequently, after nights at the jook. Because of this jook flu, Missouri would fill in—first a little, then entirely—as he took over both jobs at once, with a frenetic energy that moved the office to acknowledge it, allotting him more pay. Not the full double pay, equaling the two-man work he had begun doing, but $3.00 a day seemed a fortune.

The steady eyes sixty years later at his kitchen table at age 92, in the ghostly remains of the last Cummer mill town, the place to which the Sumner operation would migrate in 1926, once Sumner itself had cut its trees and shut down, all of it moving bodily to the new timber citadel three counties away, the place called Lacoochee. The amused smile as he looks back on it all, glad of the surprising visitor in the Lacoochee stillness, insisting on making a courtly offering from his refrigerator, one of the old glass-bottle soft drinks, like a man on a desert island in time, eyes far away.

It became a fire in him at Sumner, seeing that he could make money. To the double shift he added overtime. He found he could move still more shingles by improvising a special cart. The fire grew. He went out to Cedar Key on Sundays, buying pastries, oranges, peanuts—food he took back to the mill to sell—now turning lunchtime. too, into revenue. Then there was the selling of consignment clothes, sending off for samples from New York, taking the measurements, brokering the mail-order deals. His wife also began selling.

"Workin' night and day, the more I worked, the more I made, and I just went crazy at it."

Whites talked about the car, how he took $300 in saved-up nickels and dimes to a startled salesman in one of the towns and bought a Model T. The story inserts a false note of precision, based on people's vague knowledge that a Model T cost about $300 at the peak of its economy of scale. But Missouri himself could describe how the car was customized, and could quote the total cost: $468.

"Shipped it down in pieces, brought it on the train. Bought it in Cedar Key. Crank it in front. Had starter put on it. Ditch lights, drum headlights, green sun visor. I felt like I was king of the road."

The chuckling among whites about how he had supposedly dumped the coins in front of the car salesman was perhaps inspired by the way he made change at work, using separate pockets, keeping things straight as he peddled the pies and cakes.

"Wore a big canvas suit with five-cent pockets, ten-cent pockets, twenty-five-cent pockets, greenback pockets. Monday mornin' my wife would press out the bills...."

The lessons from Missouri weren't just about Poly. No matter how he worked in the shingle mill, there could be no promotion to foreman, not at Sumner. The idea was floated once by management and an ominous rumble came back from white labor: "If you're gon' work colored up here, you oughta work all colored" (recalled a white co-worker)—or in other words, a revolt was threatened if the job wasn't saved for whites, a walkout. He didn't dwell on the negatives. The census suggests he eventually left for Jacksonville for a time, and did get the promotion there.

I didn't know he was like Houdini, choosing by force of will to arrange his passage out of life itself to come on a symmetrical date. That he was shooting for his birthday as the date of his last day on earth— with the whole issue of whether this patterning was conscious or not conscious somehow left in the dust. He was lasting it out (as Harry Houdini the illusionist had lasted by force of will to die purposely on Halloween). Now everything was a choice.

One record said Robert Missouri was born August 14, 1891, another said August 13, 1891, another said August 13, 1892. Precisely in the blur of numbers he was splitting the difference: that one last knowing smile saying the world could be worked to his will. He was putting it in order, sitting there calmly with me, to last three more months, to die just about on his birthday, on August 15, 1982.

The mirror image, reversing the numbers even of the year—1892, 1982. I asked him if I could keep the old-style soft drink bottle as a souvenir, and I took it home, kept it for years, some gypsy journalist migration finally eliminating it in some forgotten box, maybe when the records were lost in the flood, maybe one day when I thought the whole thing was futile and the story could never be heard and why was I keeping these things? I wish I had it now. The precision in that calm smile, as if knowing how to structure even the end—though he couldn't possibly have known the full poetry.

That's my birthday, too.

———————————————

Like Martha Pillsbury, Robert Missouri did not see Poly Wilkerson as a snarling caricature version of the cruel quarters boss—or as a racist hater at all. Quite the contrary, Missouri thought that loose, hearty Poly had come to like *too well* his kingdom across the color line, in the jook.

Missouri's link to Wilkerson lay elsewhere. Everybody knew that Poly had a second life in commerce, for he also ran a dry good store beside his house, out in the cluster of shops toward the depot. The store was in partnership with Tom Holt (Poly's share supposedly coming through his wife), and some people called it Holt's store. But it was Poly's store to Missouri. The smiling face, the hearty greeting among the shelves of merchandise—that was Poly. They were both mercantile diplomats, working the loose ends, counting the change—and Missouri had the cash to be a paying customer, which didn't hurt the welcome, as Missouri bought such things as shoes for his daughter. But Poly seemed not to fixate on the sale. He seemed simply and heartily ready to talk.

As to the Sumner jook, Missouri knew the basics: five rooms, including a small one for ordering drinks, where the action could be controlled.[240] A larger ballroom had the dancing—much the same layout that white roadhouses would adopt after 1933 and the end of Prohibition—as whites also copied the name, but only to a point. The old company-town name, "jook," was pronounced in its heyday to rhyme with hook or crook. Post-1933 white usage would give this an uptight white twist, as if self-consciously protesting: "We're not copying black ways, just borrowing a bit." The new places for whites were called "juke joints," rhyming it with duke or fluke. The old jooks of the Roaring Twenties, defying Prohibition in company towns and plantations across the great thousand miles of Dixie, sometimes came equipped with a battered piano—a "jook box"— which name, soon pulled into the conveyer belt of electrical automation, would send the mystery word around the world.

Missouri did know, of course, that one and one did not equal five. The back part of the jook might be viewed as its nerve center, where they did the skinning. This did not mean prostitution (which had other arrangements), but gambling. The room or rooms for gambling offered

Georgia Skin, the card game of choice, drawing in cardboard-suitcase hustlers and hard-luck hobos on the promise—like the moonshine and the girls—that you can find paradise right now, tonight.

More often there was disappointed rage—at the bad card, the derisive remark, the swiped girl—and then the spilt blood for which the jooks were famous. "At the Jook, in the quarters," said a Levy County murder indictment in 1921, offering a rare example of the word being officially set down on paper, and not just spoken aloud. The court clerk in that case seemed to struggle with the oral relic, feeling moved to mark its special ambiguity, for the clerk Capitalized the word "Jook."[241]

Missouri heard the stories get specific, saying that Poly was growing too interested in the jook's waitresses. And that was not the worst of it. Clear over in Rosewood, Lee Carrier heard how Poly had lost a thousand dollars gambling at the jook.

That astronomical sum sounds suspiciously like the $300 car estimate, but whatever the real size of Wilkerson's losses, the stories were well known. A more general translation might move closer to the mark: lost a lot, lost everything. The red-faced player was said to have gambled away one of his two cars. The idea of a homeless black hustler fleecing a white bouncer with a gun might sound outlandish, but then so was the whole business, this idea of the legal-illegal jook. By definition the rules turned upside down. Sumner's white assistant bookkeeper, Frances Smith, might never have laid eyes on the jook (a place so near and yet so far, just behind the houses on the other side of the street), but Smith had heard another kind of folklore. People said that even the white bosses would perform the storied ritual, using lampblack or burnt cork to black their faces, thus to enter the forbidden underworld on Saturday nights, and taste the pleasures of the damned. The white intruders loved (the stories always added) to watch them dance. There was probably not a jook in the woods without its trail of face-blacking tales.

But whatever Poly was doing in there—and whether his exuberance could escalate to gambling mania—his hand was about to get called.

Perry Hudson, a more respectable cousin of avenger Bryant Hudson on Monday night, said he witnessed the moment of doom, happening to be in Wilkerson's dry goods store that day, when Sheriff Bob Walker stalked in. Hudson said he saw the angry sheriff fire Deputy Wilkerson on the spot. Explanations were not posted for public discussion.

Ernest Parham at the commissary, not much more jook-wise than Frances Smith, thought Poly must have been fired because he was riding the black labor too hard, playing Simon Legree with the whip. But in the black quarters, explanations tended more toward other kinds of riding: sexually, and with bets. Missouri was startled by the change.

When the job was snatched away, the hearty old Poly seemed to disappear. Now he sat for hours on his porch by the wagon road, staring, empty—"in a deep study." If he had indeed run up massive gambling debts, there would now be no more jook rake-off to hold them back. Events suggest that he knew he faced the loss of the store.

One day Ernest Parham saw the staring statue on the porch from a telling vantage point. Parham was riding past in the small Ford coup, as it was driven by its owner Deputy Clarence Williams, the man who had replaced Wilkerson in the plum job. Both occupants of the car felt the eyes on the porch turning to stare holes through Williams. The new deputy growled laconically as he drove: "Some day, that man's gon' kill me."

The shouts in front of the hotel now start suddenly. Parham is at the hotel, peering out. He sees that Poly Wilkerson has taken up a dramatic position in the hotel yard, drunk, apparently having wandered from his house down the wagon road. He is shouting for Williams to come out and face him. The stakes in such a confrontation could be judged by another parallel forty miles north at Newberry, this one in 1931, when two Newberry lawmen met like this—a loser and a replacement—and only one survived.

The new deputy is in his room upstairs as the shouting comes from the yard, but soon he is flying down the front steps, seeming heedless, getting just as close to Poly as apparently Poly had hoped, for Poly is the larger man. He readies to crush Williams as they go nose to nose. But before he can act Williams's gun is out, stabbing into the heavy midriff, the voice growling, *"If you move Poly, I'll kill you."*

How the witness, Parham, might have heard these words from the hotel is not entirely clear. But whatever the exact quotation, the shake-out remained. The big man was left to wander back down the road, now shorn even of his vengeful dreams. Nothing left now, less than nothing, the tidal wave of debt coming.

The timing of this scene is pushing close to 1923.

Chapter 17: Billy and Broad

Cornelia Carter (Sam Carter's mother)—"Private Laundry"
Louise Carrier (Lee Carrier's mother)—"Private Laundry"
Lydia Goins   (Martin Goins's widow)—"Private Laundry"
—1910 U.S. Census, Precinct 9 (including Rosewood)

At noon on Wednesday, January 3, 1923, Minnie takes no particular notice of a faint moaning sound, creeping northeast up the railroad. The big mill whistle in Sumner is wailing again, three miles away, marking the middle of another day.

Over there, 15-year-old Sam Hall in the lumber stacks is perhaps sauntering to the commissary for lunch—if he adheres to his favored routine—sitting on the drink box out back, not feeling himself to be exiled, savoring his proud new job. Inside, skinny, meditative Ernest Parham is behind the counter, two years older than Hall, clerking through his Christmas vacation from high school at Cedar Key. The big boss, Pillsbury, the man in the necktie, calculating board feet and railroad freight fees in the office just west, typically walks back to the bungalow for lunch, presiding over the picturebook wife, the four children, attended by a cook from the cookhouse out back. Within two more days Pillsbury will find himself escorting the cook back and forth to the black quarters with a shotgun for protection, as Sumner is overrun by angry whites from a radius of perhaps a hundred miles. But as late as noon on Wednesday, nobody seems to foresee the size of what is coming.

For Minnie, Wednesdays are washdays. Monday is the most popular day for washing ("No More Blue Mondays," purrs a 1923 ad for Weaver's Steam Laundry in Gainesville[242]). But Mama has set things up differently, making a clean sweep through the end of the week. After washing on Wednesdays, she takes Thursdays and Saturdays as her days to sweep the yard. Across the South in 1923 (and well afterward), isolated farmhouses tended to have yards of bare earth prowled by messy chickens—yards addressed by the sweeping of a broom, as if they were inside floors.

Minnie knows there are other schedules. Aunt Sarah, just down the tracks, not only walks to Sumner on Mondays, but, as Minnie understands it, also goes back to Sumner on another day, Thursday—

tomorrow. Sarah Carrier's Thursday washing is done for "the sheriff," Minnie notes, but this means the local *deputy* sheriff. The language of the old woods, with its boasts and rhymes, could sometimes seem barely removed from colonial days. A local deputy was a "sheriff" because his boss at the county seat was "the *high* sheriff," as if Robin Hood and Nottingham were just beyond Gulf Hammock.[243] Minnie was saying that on Thursdays her great-aunt Sarah worked for the family of Deputy Poly Wilkerson. Minnie knew of no grim mood at Wilkerson's, or that he had been fired. He was simply "the sheriff "—Aunt Sarah's employer on Thursdays.

At Mama's house, with its rosebush on the picket fence, only two girls are left at home to help with the wash, one being granddaughter Minnie. The other is Mama's youngest daughter Goldee, Minnie's play-mate, just two years older (so when playing house, out beside the chicken coops, Goldee gets to be the Mama).

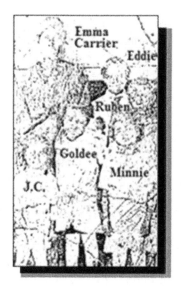

To help with the wash, Minnie and Goldee work the battling block, a section of log set on end. Mama boils the clothes, then deploys an axe handle to lift them steaming and dripping onto the flat of the block. Minnie and Goldee do the beating with flails, also made from axe handles. There is a technique. You have to roll the buttons under so they don't break. As with sweeping the yard, Minnie enters into the washing with a will. She likes helping Mama. The only chore that fills her with gloom is her wrestling match with the beds, when the big four posters won't let the sheets fall right.

The beds, the leather-bottomed couch downstairs, the buggy Mama drives on shopping trips, the console organ in the parlor that Sister Rita used to play—Minnie does not know the precise origins of some of these things, but she knows that Mama works very hard. Papa, age 56, is incapacitated by the strokes, able to limp along but unable to speak beyond a few words. Gone are his days as one of the community's commercial hunters—like his brother Haywood down the tracks, and old man Coleman, and big George Bradley near the depot, and others. They are silhouettes lost at the edges of a nation's parade: black hunters in a moment and in a jungle where no one came to record the history.

The deer hides and furs stacked up at the depot, going out by rail to distant buyers. Lee Carrier remembered one of the buying firms as "Montgomery Ward and them"—not a bad approximation of "Montgomery Ward & Co.," of Chicago. Ward was known for selling by mail-order through its catalogs, but since the 1880s it had also been buying the raw materials to manufacture some goods it sold, and furs and skins flowed in from far-flung woodlands.[244] There was money in hunting back then, before the hammock was hunted out.

Now Papa is like a shadow of the hammock: still present but ravaged. Tall, tireless Mama has eight mouths to feed. Papa sitting silently with the corncob pipe at night, staring into the fire.

The 1980s ballpoint pen, scratching furiously in the reporter's notebook, now pauses expectantly, as the gentle, elfin face—seeming the opposite of "fighty"—goes into that faraway look again, head cocked to one side, thinking back into the past that she loves to think about—as if it weren't sixty years ago, as if all that pain had never been—and there was only the time in Rosewood with Mama. "The chore I really loved," she confides, lingering with that wistful hint of a smile, as the eager pen hovers, waiting for it, waiting for that adorable detail that will surely make the whole melodrama come alive, as she continues:

"...was the skinning."

The pen is still poised—though in confusion now. It has scribbled its way into an unknown universe, not only long ago, and not only in the lost black world of the segregation years, and not only rural—but the world of the wilderness, the frontier, on the great battling block of American self-reliance. Now the pen continues scratching, but a bit less eagerly after the startling two words—"the skinning..."—as the writing hand wonders where all this is leading. But the destination is simple enough. It is leading to the ordinary reality of the bygone backwoods South—a place where one of the most joyous times of year, in households black or white, was the moment called hog-killing time. When they would throw down the corn, and the hungry animals, gobbling greedily, were too engrossed to flinch or flee as the axe came down on each in turn. The same big washpot bubbling—boiling the bristles off the hide; the lights, livers, brains, more private parts—these treasured with the bacon and hams, to make it a cheerful time of plenty, of full bellies, the blood and screams connoting festivity, like city folk smelling movie popcorn or new cars.

Skinning?

Papa trapped for fur, says the lovely faint smile. When he brought them home—before his strokes—he would let the two girls help. The easiest were the raccoons. Their skins came right off. But harder were the little otters. Maybe it was the waterproofing since otters live in water. Those skins were so hard to pull. It took both of them pulling together, Minnie and Goldee, as hard as they could. They loved helping Papa.

The jungles retained some wealth even as they retreated. You could still wait patiently for a gopher tortoise to leave his hole in the sand, and Mama knew how to cook them. Or you could stew the tender hearts of cabbage palms to make swamp cabbage.

Or you could sell the buds. Cedar Key, nine miles away among sea birds at the Gulf, had become only a shadow as well—the old 1880s railhead melting into gaunt shambles, the cedar boom gone, the big pencil factories on the Gulf that had used the splinter-free cedar wood, gone in the 1896 hurricane and never rebuilt, the schooners and steamers gone—even the old Belle of the Suwannee, beached like the skeleton of a stern-wheeled whale, cannibalized now for parts in the tidal mud, deaf to memories of the song.

But Cedar Key had one thing left. The Standard Manufacturing Company still chugged along in the quiet remains, because one vein of subtropical paradise could still yield up raw materials. The buds of cabbage palm trees produced fibers for merchandise that was shipped all over the country, in an oddly delicate epitaph. Cedar Key made whisk brooms.[245]

Papa would set aside a day—back in his strong times—and hitch the oxen, loading the cart with palm buds to take to Cedar Key. He had two oxen, Billy and Broad, grazing loose by the railroad—another form of ghost from nineteenth-century timber work, when cedar logs had been dragged by such beasts, not by steam skidders on rails— back in the days before mechanized fortresses like Sumner came to get the rest of it. Even little Minnie could hitch up an ox, and could steer it. Anybody could. Because with oxen you didn't really need reins, just words.

Ox used by an African American family in the segregation years
State Archives of Florida—Florida Memory

198

Talk to an oxen just like a person. No line needed. Come here, Bill. Come here, Broad. Gee meant right. Haw meant left. Hook a log and call him. Pull so hard till they get down on their knees....

It was open range along the railroad, causing the locomotive engineers to hate the times when some angry farmer would come out with the bill for the mangled casualty. She remembered when the train got Broad. Mama made the children go into the house because the other oxen nearby were doing something strange.

As they eyed the corpse, and saw the growling steel monster standing over it, they tightened into protective herd formation—as if no ages had passed since prehistoric bison and circling wolves. Minnie saw them sniffing the blood, bellowing, pawing the sand—before Mama

closed the door in the face of one more jungle mystery. Even after six or seven months had passed, if the humid air should thicken before a rain, so that smells would carry, they would catch it again, the ghost in the scent, and would start to bellow and stir.

Florida Memory – State Archives of Florida

 Playing house was not the best game. The best was playing church. They would troop into the back yard, sending the scandalized chickens into exile. A stick or mop handle was used to scratch out a big square in the sand. This was the church. Then rectangles for the pews. She didn't mind the fact that, along with Goldee and Lonnie and little J.C., she had to be the congregation, sitting on the sand in her pew. The starring role, the preacher, went to a live-wire fifth presence—up on the orange crate by the chicken coops, hollering his head off. In that direction lay natural talent, with far too much entertainment power to be denied. Nobody could preach like Ruben.

It could be wondered whether Ruben Mitchell, Minnie's older brother, might have had his own private view of his preaching performances. Tale after tale found a sly, mischievous sense of humor. Letting fly at his backyard congregation, he shouted about their doom in hell—as they clapped delightedly and said amen.

He was not yet as large as he would be in adulthood, when they would laugh about him lifting the bumper of a Model T. But in adolescence he was already the joker, seemingly immune to stuffy pretensions. Minnie laughed that he seemed able to go to sleep anywhere. One minute he might be mischievously dancing the buck on the porch, as Minnie glared with fighty disapproval, but then if Mama came out he would freeze and look innocent—and if this grew tedious he might be gone again, nodding off into dreamland.

Now the man with the camera, under the black hood, is cutting off Goldee's feet. He is holding up some kind of white powder in a pan. Ruben is posing just behind Minnie's ear, as she glares at the hood, fighty again, rared back in her wrestler's stance—though Ruben is determined to throw her off, make her grin. So he hisses to her, not thinking to capture unseen worlds. He is goofing on the strange man who came down the sand road in the Model T, as Ruben deadpans toward the lens, hissing in Minnie's ear: "Look at that kinky hair. He a Jew."

Emma Carrier/Carrol
born 1871

The real church, with the real pews, was of course more serious than the backyard version—and at times was seriously harsh. In public settings, Mama, so loving and caring, was painfully shy. She could teach Sunday school fine, but it was something else to stand up in front of the congregation. Rising to give testimony, she seemed to freeze, choking and stammering. This would have been no disgrace (Minnie knew how it felt to be shy) if not for the response. At such times a poisonous undertone of giggling might arise—certainly not from everybody, but from one special pew.

The sound tore at Mama's helplessness, cutting like a knife. It caused the protective little granddaughter to fill with disbelief and rage. Minnie could barely wait to get outside with Mama, where she demanded:

"Why you let Aunt Sarah do you that way?"

Tensions between two sisters,[246] living within sight of one another on a sleepy stretch of railroad, were of little interest to passing whites—whether passing calmly on dull errands and peering from the trains, or holding merciless torches for arson at the end. The complexities were ignored as part of an inscrutable subculture, its riddles indecipherable, unseen.

The one sister taller, thinner, older by three years—and far less at ease with a public audience. The other sister shorter, stouter, three years younger—and brimming with confidence. The second sister, the confident star, was filled with musical talent—and with theatrical talent, as proved by the beautiful pageants she directed in church. But as to the other side of that sister, the flashes of mystery, the relatives had only questions.

Protective little Minnie scolding still-mortified Mama once they get alone outside the church, saying why do you let your pushy younger sister be so cruel. Mama replying with that long-suffering look, saying a Christian forgives. To drive home the point, Mama takes Minnie back to the house, then hands her a plate of dressed meat covered with a cloth—for now it is Minnie's task, as penance, to take this plate down the tracks to Aunt Sarah, as a gift, a turning of the other cheek. Minnie grumbling to herself all the way down there, not at all convinced, wondering why Mama won't fight.

Sarah the beautiful pianist—with the beautiful children, now grown—now pianists on their own, beautiful singers, seemingly perfect at everything. Her son Sylvester, the man's man, not only the best solo singer in the church choir but the best shot on hunts in the woods. The Midas touch they seem to have, this one household of Carriers. Sarah in the popular crowd at church, surrounded by her close circle—somehow confident to the point of cruelty—as if above it all, disdaining the struggles of sister Emma—glowing, exuberant, nobody using the strange word grandiose.

The prism twists. All the eyes that see her in church—whether loving or hating her—seem never to see the further complexity—that there is yet a *third* Sarah Carrier.

These home-ground viewers seem unable even to imagine the shuffling, mumbling servant who seems to magically take over Sarah Carrier's persona at the washtubs and flat-irons three miles away. Of course they all know she is over there, washing in Sumner. But in their minds the dynamic church matron naturally remains the dynamic church matron—whether scrubbing or not. The radically different personality described by the white employers in Sumner does not exist for the hometown observers, could not exist. Mealy-mouthed, vaguely comic, harmless, muttering. In her home sanctuary it is seen by none of them, even those who hate her. The worlds are that far apart.

Chapter 18: Sending Word

It is now 5:47 p.m., the official time of sunset on Thursday, January 4, 1923, in the vicinity of Rosewood, Florida. Three days have passed since a preparatory moment, when, as lumber stacker Lee Carrier would recall, he watched his older cousin Sylvester buy shotgun shells at Wright's store.

Leroy "Lee" Carrier

For three nights, Lee will later say, Syl has now sat up with his gun, staying awake through Monday, Tuesday and Wednesday nights. If whites had threatened him on Monday, they were not following through. Stories about this passage leave the never-appearing whites unspecified —no names, no descriptions—as if part of this story might have been imagined after the fact, passing down to bystanders like Lee in traumatized rumors. Yet parts of it ring true.

Sam Hall heard much the same story about the night vigils—though he multiplied the one box of shotgun shells that Lee recalled seeing:

"Had two, three boxes of buckshot shells. Sot [sat up] for 'em two, three nights."

Lee compressed it into a kind of three-bar blues:

"They said they were comin' Monday; they didn't come Monday. They said they were comin' Tuesday; they didn't come Tuesday. They said they were comin' Wednesday; they didn't come Wednesday. He was sittin' on the porch, waitin'."

The younger cousin, Lee Carrier, did not claim to directly witness this vigil, but his memories of firsthand observation would resume just after nightfall on Thursday.

Again he has walked home from work. He is killing time before heading back to Wesley's and to bed (in a Thursday night time window apparently from about 6:30 to 8:30 p.m.). Now, once again, Lee runs into Sylvester. But this time Syl looks bad. Three nights of lost sleep have worked on him. He looks haggard, barely able to mope along. This is not the crowing, boasting Sylvester everybody knows, the domineering older cousin.

Each morning Syl has been dragging himself to work in Gulf Hammock, cutting trees for railroad crossties, despite the lost sleep. "I ain't had no rest," he complains to Lee. He says this vigil business is pointless. It's time to declare victory, to stop this stupid charade. *"They're not comin',"* he sighs, *"I can't get any work done. I'm goin' home to bed."*

Lee sums up: *"On Thursday night he had done give 'em out."*

The image looks simple enough—until compared to a second memory, which seems to contradict:

Since today is Thursday, Mama and her little shadow, the fighty protector, Minnie Lee, have pushed out into the thickets near the house, thus to obtain switch brooms. Grasping handfuls of leafy stems, they wrench them free and twist them together. The resulting brooms

are disposable. They will sweep the yard with these makeshifts, then Mama will take trash and brooms together into the field behind the house and pour on kerosene, leaning back quickly as the flames bloom up. Twice each week they do this, for Mama's schedule is strict. The yard is always swept on Thursdays and Saturdays.

Now night is falling on the sweeping. This moment comes at sunset. Minnie looks up from the faint grooves her switch broom is making in the sand. A visitor has arrived, a relative, walking out of the fading twilight. But it's not Scrappy this time—no well-meaning invitation for Mama to hide in the Wylly jook. This new visitor will speak to that same question, but more effectively: Where can Mama hide? If the whites are still looking high and low for Mama's disappeared son Aaron, will they come for Mama, too? The new visitor has a solution. Minnie naturally recognizes him. The visitor is Sylvester.

Stepping up to the picket fence, Cud'n Syl says to Mama:

"Aunt Emma, you better come on down to our house, cause it look like these white folks want to raise sand up here tonight. And I can protect y'all better up there."

"Raising sand" is another flourish of the woods, meaning what the oxen do in alarm, what the catch-dog does with the hog, the roosters do fighting. It means to cause a commotion, to kick up dust.[247] Sylvester is reminding Mama—as Scrappy had done—that if the whites come, there is only Papa's crippled form to protect her. Sylvester wants Mama—his aunt, Emma Carrier—to bring her household of children down the tracks to her sister Sarah's house, where Sylvester also lives.

And thus the contradiction:

Why would Sylvester be spreading alarm to Minnie and Mama— and taking on a new burden of protection—if his cousin Lee's memory was accurate, and Syl has now decided there is no real threat, and he is going home to bed?

The encounter Lee remembered would have come just after the one Minnie described (Lee would not be home from work in Sumner until after sunset). Could it be that Lee, a seasoned hunting companion, received Sylvester's most sincere strategic assessment, while the invitation to Emma, Minnie's Mama, was made more as a weary courtesy, which Syl privately felt to be unnecessary? Explanations might be tortured into any shape desired.

And what is this news Sylvester talks about? Is there some new bit of intelligence, revealing that the whites are coming after all?

The plot elements swirl together like debris in a tornado (where the occasional cow or smashed furniture might float lazily upward in defiance of gravity). Both witness impressions, Minnie's and Lee's, will in fact receive confirmation from the night's further events.

Just as Lee's story predicts, Sylvester will *not* be standing guard at his mother's house, but will be back in his room with his wife, apparently in bed. And just as Minnie's story predicts, Emma's household *will* go to the home of Sarah and her son Sylvester. Both witness accounts pass circumstantial tests, suggesting real observation. And hence the question: Could a crucial element be left outside both frames—a reconciling factor unknown to both witnesses, Minnie and Lee?

The communal tensions building from Monday to Thursday would be recalled in opposite ways in communities black and white. African American witnesses, including Lee Carrier, Minnie, Sam Hall and others, would recall messages of menace coming from whites, very vague but taunting ultimatums somehow transmitted to Rosewood.

But whites would describe an opposite kind of message, which they said came from African Americans, somehow summoning the whites—or allegedly luring them—to come to Rosewood and take action. Each stream was a vindication: *Our side didn't provoke this.* But, excuses and alibis aside, the two streams display a common thread. Both speak of messages. Both depict angry words of challenge and response passing back and forth between Rosewood and Sumner. Both say the other side "sent word."

Blacks would tell how whites (always unidentified whites) "sent word" that they were coming to get Sylvester. And whites, conversely, would tell how blacks (always unidentified blacks) allegedly "sent word" to the stalwart independent detective on the scene, the alert Constable Wilkerson, inviting him (they said), to come to Rosewood on some kind of law enforcement mission. There were assorted variations. But all implied a player just off-stage, a messenger.

> Lee Carrier: *"Then they started talkin' about, well, we're gonna get Syl next. They sent word....They sent word up there and told him he had to leave...."*

> Sam Hall: *"He [Sylvester] sent 'em word he was at home and he hadn't bothered nobody. Come on."*

> Charlie Hudson (white, brother of Bryant Hudson):
> *"This nigger sent 'em word: Come and get him."*

> Frank Coburn (white, resident of Cedar Key):
> Poly was *"invited to check up on things."*

> Woodrow Baylor (white): *"The colored people at Rosewood told this quarters boss"* to come to their location.

Everyone seemed to agree that some kind of "word" was being sent, though each side said the other side did it first. Were wildfire rumors merely imagining such back-and-forth traffic? Who might have carried such word?

Sarah Carrier, Sylvester's mother, allegedly arrived home in the same Thursday time frame as the two conflicting sunset scenes. Two later informants, Minnie and Sarah's grandson Arnett Goins, would agree that Sarah was washing at Poly Wilkerson's prior to her arrival back home. And everyone would agree on the next step. Just after that arrival, in the moonlight of Thursday night, Poly Wilkerson would certainly come to Sarah's. What is missing is the connection.

What could have happened at Wilkerson's to bring the ex-deputy following on Sarah's heels, after a lag of only a few hours? A hint came from Arnett Goins, the younger brother of Philomena Goins and backyard wrestling companion of Minnie Mitchell. For more than a decade, between 1982 and 1993, Arnett Goins would refuse to speak publicly about the Rosewood events, not relenting until after the death of his sister Philomena in 1991. Then, as publicity swelled in the Rosewood claims case, he came forward, declaring under oath in the Florida House of Representatives. He said: "They sent word by grandma, my grandmother, to tell Sylvester he was next...They said Sylvester was next if he stayed in Rosewood."[248]   A member of Sarah Carrier's

Arnett Turner Goins
April 18, 1913 –
March 24, 2002

household was saying she had become a messenger, a conduit for the tensions. This might be only a rationalization drawn from a rumor, but it shows signs of personal observation. As we near the eye of the storm, the winds grow disconcerting.

Chapter 19: Christmas

The role of Sarah Carrier in the prelude to Thursday night would later become deeply obscured by violence and pain—if indeed she played a preliminary role at all. Aftermath stories would mix bitter accusations with faint glimpses and mere imaginings. But in this confusion, survivors were reminded of an earlier incident.

Florida Memory
State Archives of Florida

A prior eruption of violence had occurred—very different from Thursday night's event, and yet with an undertone of similar riddles—as the same profoundly confusing community member was caught at center-stage.

The Christmas shooting in the First A.M.E. Church was years gone by 1923. Leaving no arrest record or indictment, it would slip into a calendar twilight zone, even its year of occurrence becoming uncertain in later decades, floating in mists of memory. That incident formed only a historical backdrop to a later Thursday night, but it, too, had involved bizarre twists, things no one seemed able to explain.

Apparently it was in the World War period, 1914-1918. Definitely it was before mid-1918. Witness Ernest Blocker was still a child. Eva Jenkins also remembered it. Others spoke of it generally. And some were right there, while being old enough—and startled enough—to retain detailed impressions.

Its roots can be taken farther back, to July 3, 1911, when the equipment from Rosewood's Charpia cedar mill was sold at auction. Thus ended the last twilight of the cedar boom, and with it, the old cedar sawmill community as it had been.[249] In 1911, Bacchus Hall's big store was still functioning,[250] and John Coleman's smaller shop. Buddy Williams and his wife Rita (Emma Carrier's oldest daughter) still had

Swamp Cedar

their shop just up from the depot. And Hall had a home-made cane grinding mill, its wooden cogs drawn in a circle by a plodding mule. The Rosewood post office would last until 1914, though operated by whites, its pigeonholes cobbled into the solid brick home of a last holdout family, the Coarseys, yankee dreamers from a still earlier boom and bust, the 1880s citrus boom.[251] In 1911 the southwestern flank of the community was still anchored by M. Goins & Bros. Naval Stores. Ed Goins, the surviving brother, was still nursing the family business along, though running out of pines.

Pinus palustris
Long-leafed pine

In those days, fully four working churches remained in the two-mile expanse, three of them churches for African Americans, one for whites. There was not only the A.M.E church (the long-term survivor in later years), but also an M.E. church called Pleasant Field near James and Emma Carrier's house, open since 1886— when the boom times had seemed forever. In 1911, the small Baptist chapel in Goins Quarters was apparently still attended, its bell mounted in the yard. And there was the school, a public school for African Americans. Its superintendent, farmer Ransom Edwards, lived not far away on acreage he owned, signing teacher paychecks in his precise hand.

Such pillars, it was hoped, might be enough to support a place of sanctuary, built around two main families, the intermarried Carriers and Bradleys.

One household of Carriers in particular stood out, steeped in confidence and talent.

In those days Lutie McCoy, in adolescence before she married and moved to Sumner, lived on the largest African American-owned farm in Rosewood, the 120-acre property belonging to her father John McCoy (later 114 acres, after minor cessions). Lutie had only admiration for talented Mrs. Carrier.

She loved Sarah Carrier's patience and skill, the way Mrs. Carrier would sit at the organ or piano and train the children for pageants in church. Such a wonderful lady. Along with fellow church leaders Mary Burns and Virginia Carrier Bradley, she was an organizing force. The community picnic ground was right behind Sarah Carrier's house, covered dishes filling long plank tables under moss-hung oaks. At these events two white faces also appeared, John and Mary Wright from the store. The picnics were for everyone. Any hobo walking down the tracks could come and eat his fill. In similar memories even Lee Carrier, the quiet outsider, laid aside his skepticism to soak up the good feeling at the picnics.

Also located behind Haywood and Sarah Carrier's house, convenient to the picnic tables, was the main attraction. At the ball field, a sense of community distinction deepened. Defeated teams from bigger places—Cedar Key, Chiefland, Newberry (points in the local black league)—were said to complain about wilderness Rosewood. It had an unfair advantage, they grumbled, out there in swamp seclusion, getting to practice all the time. The team itself said the secret was family teamwork, built around the Carriers and Bradleys.

But they also talked about a more elusive pride. This was not just the backside of some white town, but a black place of its own. Even the seclusion, facing into the waning majesty of the Great Gulf Hammock, seemed to foster a sense of being special.

At the ball games you could hear Beauty out there cracking (they used the old verb, "to crack," no strangers to backwoods boasting). Beauty Carrier, Sarah's vivacious daughter, would jeer and taunt the visiting teams. She was the one with the beautiful singing voice, on Sunday mornings enthralling the congregation in church—but then battering the visitors on the field.

Men would get dreamy-eyed sixty years later, thinking about her joking and prancing—soon gone, as the brassy voice tempted her toward wider fame. Everyone recalled how Beauty (Lellon Carrier) left home as a singer in a traveling show, while one memory held a scrap of name, saying that perhaps it was the famous Florida Blossom Minstrels.[252] Not all minstrels were whites in blackface. Beauty knew the tent shows that would launch some of the big names in the blues.

Her harmonizing sister Sweetie (Annie Carrier) was also soon gone, moving away from the picnic oaks. Sister Ruby, known as R.C., was gone to school over on the Atlantic, then to Harlem. When the eyes grew misty you could almost hear them back at the ball field tables under the trees, like lord god birds laughing loudly under the hanging moss—the cracking, boasting, perfectly-pitched children of Sarah Carrier.

The shock at the Christmas pageant seemed to write the epitaph to all this. "That finished tearin' up Rosewood," sighed Lutie McCoy Foster. Born in 1900, she would be able to describe the Christmas shooting in detail, persuasively

FLORIDA CHRISTMAS CHEER

Florida Memory
State Archives of Florida

supported by more fragmentary, mystified impressions held by others. However, not even Lutie knew the deeper layers, concealed in a web of feuds and grudges that precipitated the actions she watched. Those were grown men's things, not shared with a young girl. She saw the public face—in all its mystery, compressed into a blinding flash.

The metal plate reflectors gleaming behind kerosene lamps on the church walls, the swirl of organ music chording up into the shadows of the belfry—and the rich, sweet perfume of cedar wood: the big tree filling up the sectioned-off altar area by the pulpit, the fresh-cut Christmas tree, rising behind the chancel rail, suffusing the crowded room with aroma—at Mrs. Carrier's big show.

Mrs. Carrier has painstakingly trained the children for this, as any musical theater director might, seated at the small church organ to work them through the paces. (Was it by such rehearsals that her own children had become such extroverted performers? Or was it simply the same inner fire, director and progeny both that way all along, in the family gift?)

Lutie has listened as Mrs. Carrier taught this pageant's child players how to deal with an audience; those not on stage at a given moment are instructed to sit in the pews so the speaker can get the feel of addressing real hearers. Mrs. Carrier has polished the solo speeches, fine-tuned the dialogues, choreographed the moves—all according to guidelines.

The instructions come ready-made in quarterlies mailed from six hundred miles away at A.M.E. Sunday school headquarters in Tennessee.[253] *The Christmas crowd drawn as a result of these preparations will fill the collection plate at the pageant, enabling funds to go to A.M.E. regional in Gainesville, and thence to the bishop's office in Philadelphia. Momentary observers on trains that pass this spot may see only a small frame chapel in the woods, but it is not just an isolated wooden box.*[254]

As in any musical theater, the challenge of the pageant is to create combined delight for all the senses—not just for the ear, but also the eye—and here the challenge binds. The obvious solution, that of pleasing the eye with dance routines, is off limits here, because of Satan's snare.

The Sunday school quarterlies, however, provide for alternative visual entertainment, giving instructions on how to conduct synchronized marching, disciplined and chaste. Lutie is one of the beaming girls in white, not undulating sinfully as they move but marching crisply, in opposing lines that flow along the inside walls of the church, meeting first at the front, up by the beautiful tree, and then again at the rear, where, in the actual event, crowding standees will fill the door leading out to the railroad and the night.

Mrs. Carrier rehearses them to perfection, faster, faster, double-time, always in step.

Lutie is intent now, in the thrill of the big moment. The main pass in the marching is easy, where the two streams pass one another at the front. To make room for this, the church's front line of pews has been removed—requiring some forethought in a snugly-built structure. The pews had to be unscrewed from strips of small wooden lath on the floor. With this space cleared, only the lath strips remain, firmly nailed in place, forming slight ridges that are barely visible against the flooring. The girls easily step over these.

But another obstacle is more worrisome, also unseen by the admiring crowd, though painfully intruding on the performers. The second point where the streams converge, at the rear of the church by the door, has become clogged. The theatrical appeal has succeeded perhaps too well. Men not known for fanatical church attendance have been drawn to watch. The marchers are attractive, not infants but adolescent girls like Lutie, radiant in their white outfits trimmed in blue. The blue hems of their knickers are decorative, gathered tightly by elastic garters, now moving in beautiful harmony.

Lutie has been told that it is called marching the double cross, which soon resonates: Although each front pass by the tree goes beautifully, such success only brings uneasiness, for they know what will happen in the next pass, at the rear.

Back there, he is waiting. He's not a man she knows well, but naturally in a small community she knows his name, who he's married to. Lutie is from the light-skinned side of the community, in Section 30 toward Sumner—though she rarely thinks in such terms, or considers the conflicts that might move this man—who is still lighter of complexion than herself.

George Goins, heir to a dwindling turpentine fortune, will be classified in one record as white, others as colored. Tonight he is in a state not considered unusual for him. One recollection said tersely that he "would stay drunk." Lutie does not know the labyrinth of family emotion, or that his own children will be taught to call him not Daddy but "Baby George"—instruction apparently given by the complex grandmother raising them, Sarah Carrier. No one foresees the escape George Goins will eventually find, into the World War, where army documentation will conflict in classifying his race.[255]

Seated in the congregation is his older brother, steady and responsible Charlie Goins, the hope of the family, helping their father Ed in the last years of the turpentine firm, M. Goins & Bros. Naval Stores. In the church crowd, however, George is standing up, wedged in by the door. His isolation is doubly striking because family ties should have provided a front-row ticket. The pageant was organized not only by Sarah Carrier but by her similarly gifted daughter Willie. On September 29, 1910, Willie Carrier and George Goins were married. Sarah Carrier is George's mother-in-law.[256]

During the marching, it is not clear whether Willie or Sarah is at the organ. Perhaps Sarah is seated in a pew. Her son Sylvester is nearby.

Lutie does see that George is somehow a stranger at his wife's moment of pride. But he seems determined to spoil it. As the march carries Lutie toward him, she tenses once more. Sheltered in the press of bodies, he has taken to reaching out and hooking a finger into the blue-trimmed knickers as the girls pass, for a moment stretching the elastic tight, then letting it snap—trying to throw them off step.

But much worse, he soon escalates. Apparently tiring of furtive sabotage, the reeling figure pushes forward and staggers down the center aisle, boldly, forcing all eyes to turn, as if in some caricature of answering the holy invitation. The preacher watches helplessly, another of the old frontier Carrier brothers. The preacher is Elias Carrier, brother of Haywood, Ransom and James.[257] In this moment of joy and light, the interloper seems determined to tear apart the invisible bonds of community, to force things into sordidness and shame.

He comes to the wooden rail in front, his back turned arrogantly to the congregation—as he reaches across the rail, straining toward the tree, where brightly wrapped gifts for children have been hung.

In the way that he was plucking at hems before, now he paws and bats at the presents, seeming purposely to select the most cherished symbols of innocence for his defilement. The preacher, Elias, steps down from the pulpit. In efforts to defuse the situation he comes around in front of the rail, puts a fatherly arm around the intruder, trying to lead him away. And there is support. The predictable ally stands up, not fearing to get involved—the young man with the knack for everything, Sylvester. But in this story, Sylvester Carrier the prodigy is not center-stage. He is seen moving to help with George, then his image fades from recollection.

For suddenly it happens. Without warning, the preacher, Elias, lunges forward. George is by now enfolded in Elias's fatherly arm, so that as Elias jerks forward, George abruptly lunges, too, both toppling, caught off balance and going down. The crowd sees the force of the lunge knock both men to the floor, flailing and struggling.

Then it comes. They hear the scream—that unexplainable, unforgiveable scream—which they will talk about for generations. This split-second of action is so multi-layered that description of its facets takes much longer than the actual moment at the church rail. Instantly, the scream redirects attention, restructuring the way the tensed crowd interprets a chaotic image. An invisible storm of tensions, arising as two men face off, is suddenly translated into a unified form, which permits explosive release. What was at first merely potential in the image, only an anxious possibility, is turned into event. The worst fears are made into reality.

For she screams: "'Lias cuttin' George to death!"

They will remember slightly differing versions of the words. But the generality will be communal lore—in stories telling how panic seemed to rush far too quickly into the worst possible interpretation, inventing a threat, calling for violence when in fact none was required, squeezing out the most drama possible. They will wonder how this could have occurred.

Certainly, the peaceful preacher Elias was holding no knife. The scream—like a stage director—only caused them all to imagine a knife for a moment. The truth behind the lunging fall lay elsewhere—in the tiniest of details, unseen in the moment of magic.

As Elias Carrier had juggled the wobbling interloper, his forward-moving shoe had struck something with sharp force, something he could not see. An inch-high strip of wood lath was firmly nailed to the floor.

Failing to spy an obstacle where logically no obstacle should be, the distracted preacher was thrown completely off balance. His forward-moving foot was stopped dead, as if by Satan's stealth—while his body continued disastrously to move forward.

In an instant the crowd is unified by the emotional force, the scream. The room explodes. One figure, accustomed to command, leaps atop a pew, straining desperately to see George, to get the truth of this, to discover what really happened, to protect George. The older brother Charlie Goins, readied by mortifying suspense, is catapulted into action by the irresistible scream, the plea for intervention. Charlie is moved in an instant to disastrous guesswork—and he draws the gun.

"'Lias cuttin' George to death!"

Words cried only once, as if in reflex. Less than a breath. And yet seeming to orchestrate the entire vortex, all of them screaming in the roar of the gun. The lights going out—whether from percussion or deacons diving for the lamp stems. Darkness, screams, flight. Lutie is out on the railroad track, not stopping, still running even after getting away. Lee Carrier has taken closer comfort and dived under a pew.

No way to guess where Charlie went—though Lutie will find this out, too. Her father, the old-time associate of the Goins brothers, will now be sought by the desperate heir Charlie, briefly, as a way station in his flight.

Charlie knowing that his life is over now, running to John McCoy and borrowing the red horse. McCoy's oldest boy will ride after him on the mule so he can bring the horse back—once they get to the boundary line of no return, the point twelve miles north, the plank ferry crossing the blackwater Suwannee. Charlie then disappearing into the outlaw swamps on the other side, no indictment, no arrest.

Elias Carrier, said to be found on the floor, was rushed a long fifty miles to a hospital in Gainesville, but the bullet wound was fatal. In later years, at some point after the World War but before 1923, children would sometimes creep up to the back of the silent church on a dare, because it was said you could still hear it, that ghost with the special sound, the sound of a man falling down. They would creep slowly closer, terrified by the thought—then they would break and run, sure that they *had* heard it, bloom-bloom, the falling down. Lutie knew the open secret, where the vanished shooter had gone to escape arrest. But she also felt sorry for the poor red horse, brought back by her brother after the run, broken by the frantic speed of it, never to be the same again, the horse named Jinx.

Her metal chair sinking unevenly in loose sand in the yard of the Floyd Care Nursing Home,[258] as her eyes go far away, and she says, "That finished tearin' up Rosewood."

In the story of the scream, a voice was portrayed as packaging the tension, translating it into a sharpened, actionable form, a form that could move strong men to dispel nagging suspense—by plunging them ruinously into destruction. Lutie thought it might have been Willie who screamed, George's wife, Sarah's daughter. Everyone else seemed to agree otherwise. Bitterly, baffled by it, they said it was Sarah.

It was said that the bloodstain where he fell refused to come out of the floor, that if scrubbed it only receded deceptively for a time, waiting for the next heavy air before a summer rain, the thickening humidity when ghosts and smells could carry, then to bloom up again. Willie Evans, the grandson of the old school superintendent Ransom Edwards, did not know these tales, but had one of his own. Caught one day on the railroad by a sudden rainstorm, he took shelter in the church. To his surprise as he slipped into the silent building, he saw that someone was there ahead of him, the respected church leader Sarah Carrier, alone in the shadows. She was stretched out on a pew, as if exhausted by some strenuous labor, strangely asleep.

As Lutie marches just prior to the fatal moment, Lee Carrier is seated in the congregation—perhaps not quite old enough yet to have turned his back on the Sunday shouting—and at any rate drawn by the crowd.

Everyone has come to this big yearly event—Baptists, Methodists, backsliders, idlers, skeptics—and some whites—all of them taking in the show

In this crowd, Lee, too, watches as the moment unfolds—the unexplainable, unforgiveable scream, then instantly the explosion, the gun, the shouts—as more screams convulse the packed room. Somehow the kerosene lamps snuff out, increasing the confusion. In the dark he hears them running to escape into the night, as he dives under the pew.

At length things grow still. Still under the pew, he notices a glow. Someone has crept in and lit a lamp. He risks rising, peers over the polished wood. He is not surprised, seeing who it is.

She is at the chancel rail by the big Christmas tree, one of the old swamp cedars towering up into the ceiling shadows, festively hung with the gifts that were about to be given out to children when things blew up. The green boughs exuding cedar perfume, this lonely survivor from somewhere deep in the hammock, somehow missed by the clear-cutting that got the others—though found now.

In the glow she is leaning, reaching out, braced on the rail to reach the tree. He makes no sound as he sees her thinking that everyone has fled, so this can be done without observation. He has no doubt he is interpreting the scene correctly—for it seems just like her. He is certain that in the half-light she is plucking presents off the tree. And he knows she is not simply saving them—but, brazenly, she is stealing them. He is sure of it. Because she is like that. In his view there would always be something beyond explanation in his aunt Sarah.

Chapter 20: Going to Sarah's

At the picket fence at dusk, where they have swept the yard, Minnie hears Mama tell Cud'n Sylvester: Yes. She will come. Mama will bring her family down to Sarah's this Thursday night. But not right now, not right at sunset as Syl stands by the fence.

There will have to be a slight delay. It would have been more logical, as fears and warnings fly, to walk back with Sylvester right now, thus having not only his escort but the comfort of lingering daylight as protection. But Mama watches Sylvester depart alone, after telling him she will bring her household a little later.

Minnie knows the reason. Two of Mama's boys, her son Lonnie and her grandson Ruben, are not yet home from work. Both are in Wylly raking pine straw in the groves. Neither is older than 13. Mama won't leave without them.

Now it is dark—perhaps between 7:30 and 8:30 p.m. Lonnie and Ruben have come home. Their raking would have stopped at nightfall in any case, and they have had time to walk the two miles or so back to Rosewood. Mama assembles her stairstep household: little J.C., larger Goldee and Lonnie, Minnie, Ruben, still larger Eddy. There is the crippled form of Papa. And one more figure, a grown son, Willard, age about twenty but known as Big Baby, living at home because of an elusive mental disability—which later will take its place in the tale.

Minnie's recollection grows hazy on the two adults, Papa and Willard. Do they, too, walk to Sarah's, or do they remain at home? Both are background figures, largely silent in their difficulties. Minnie's attention is focused elsewhere, on the frightening darkness enclosing the walk.

A stairstep parade moves down the tracks, composed of at least seven forms. In daylight Aunt Sarah's house is within easy sight, but in darkness the trip seems to take forever. Every bush seems likely to hide a monstrous white man, ready to leap out and grab a nine-year-old.

Then the rush of relief. They are there! Aunt Sarah's flower planters and irritable little porch dog have never looked so good. Any bad feelings about this house are swept away. Nor does it matter that the house is dark when they arrive.

The occupants are already in bed. Aunt Sarah comes to the door in her nightgown. She looks tired, having been at work all day.

A different stream of stories would arise in the family of Constable Poly Wilkerson, also describing a preamble to the night's events.[259] Wilkerson's son James, age seven at the time, would say that an unnamed African American woman came to the Wilkerson home on the day of the disaster, not to do laundry but carrying a message.

This story fares poorly under circumstantial comparisons, conflicting with proven evidence on several points. But even if the messenger it pictures was only imagined or somehow invented (and this is not demonstrated for certain), an issue is still revisited—this matter of "sending word."

It was not unknown in the segregation years for southern law enforcement to cultivate informants in African American communities, sometimes choosing influential black residents. In the 1920s a Titan of the Ku Klux Klan, Judge Erwin Clark of Texas, testified: "If we anticipated there was going to be any disorder from a class, we would usually select a member of that class, a prominent, popular one, and instruct him to keep us posted."[260]

Poly Wilkerson apparently prided himself on his rapport in the black jook, and would know the informant drill. The story in Wilkerson's family about an unnamed female messenger does not prove or disprove that this was Sarah Carrier, but it does suggest that such message channels were not a novelty.

From the opposite perspective, inside Sarah Carrier's home, the whims of fate would leave three different informant views, those of Minnie (Mitchell) Langley, Arnett Goins and Philomena (Goins) Doctor. Despite Philomena Doctor's passion on other points, she seemed uninterested in painting a dramatic picture of a background detail, the atmosphere inside the house just before the main event. Mentioning it only in passing, she seemed to confirm Minnie's description, though here, too, with a haughty touch, portraying Minnie and Emma's household almost as beggarly poor relations, supposedly coming to

Sarah's house with no invitation at all, but showing up on the doorstep out of weakness: "They got scared and came down there." Sylvester's errand at sunset could easily have gone unmentioned to an eleven-year-old like Philomena. Minnie's detailed memory of the invitation was persuasive.

But more to the point, no one inside the house seemed to notice any atmosphere of siege. When Minnie arrived she saw no sign of Sylvester inside the house, and assumed he was back in his room with his wife Gert, in bed. Gert herself would later portray it the same way, as remembered by those she told. All accounts agreed that Sarah's daughter Bernadina, age about twenty, was at that moment in the front bedroom she shared with Sarah. Apparently Bernadina was not only in bed in her nightgown but already asleep. No one was recalled peeping tensely through the windows to scan for approaching invaders.

So what was going on? In this picture, was Sarah Carrier somehow pulling psychological strings? Had she first muttered to desperately needy Poly Wilkerson in Sumner that something looked bad back at her house, and would the valiant male protector come and check up on things?

And had she then come home to tell her exhausted son Sylvester that the mood of the whites looked bad, so would the valiant male protector go down to Emma's and gather in her brood? Either inadvertently or compulsively, had the elements been brought together for a spectacle? This hardly seems likely. The questions arise only because of the result—which looks improbable in the extreme, but undeniably did occur.

There was about to be an inexplicable coincidence. Though none of the players could see it, two simultaneous groups were converging on Sarah Carrier's residence from opposite directions, as if synchronized, though neither group seemed to know about the other. Emma's group was in fact walking into the crosshairs of destruction. And quite a different group—a group of whites—was making its way toward the same site of destruction at the same time, from Sumner.

On the face of it there is only the coincidence. Twist the prism and it can yield many possible explanations.

For example, could it have gone like this?

Out in the woods lurks an eagle-eyed white bystander. He has spotted a horde of black savages skulking into Sylvester Carrier's fortress. There are at least seven of the shadowy forms, walking right down the railroad tracks. God knows how many more might be coming—and with plans to do what? He hightails it over to Sumner, raising the alarm: Uprising! The blacks are gathering! But only one hero in Sumner is brave enough to listen. The spineless new sheriff's deputy shrugs it off. But another alert officer is more ready for action. Left out of the excitement until now, this officer still wears one badge, which can justify a manly intervention: the constable.

Twist the prism again and other hypotheticals can tumble out. The kaleidoscope of tension, motivation and coincidence glitters with possible ways to interpret the missing links—though all present a basic theme: The week's combustible fumes have reached flashpoint, scarcely needing a spark.

Chapter 21: Moonlit Ride

Minnie is with Aunt Sarah's grandchildren *in the darkened downstairs portion of the house. They can't yet hear it.*

But over north in the woods, her cousin Lee is more strategically placed. He has gone home to Wesley's and again is putting off going to bed. He relaxes on the front porch, unmoved by the sharp drop in temperature. Yesterday's recorded low in Gainesville was 64 degrees, Fahrenheit, but a front has passed through with

Leroy "Lee" Carrier

a touch of rain. Now, clear and cold under a brilliant moon, this night will dip to 37 degrees, and perhaps a bit colder in the swamps.[261] Tonight there will be frost, which can form just above the freezing point. The weather provides one more small trigger, stirring the blood. To stoic Lee Carrier, it is not so cold.

Also pulling at the trigger is the moon, official rising time 7:44 p.m. To the naked eye the January full moon can look larger than any other moon of the year, for a skewed orbit brings it slightly closer to earth. Six miles west of Lee's position the Gulf of Mexico is yearning. The tide is rising.

Wesley Bradley's house is not far from the wooded turnoff coming into Rosewood off the limerock of Highway 13, the automobile road from Sumner. The night is still. Something sounds in the crisp air, like a pond gnat buzzing in Lee's ear, tiny in the distance, chugging steadily along.

On the porch Lee says to his cousin Bishop, "Listen..."

As Lee Carrier hears a distant automobile in cold moonlight, another sound is beyond his hearing. A dull thud occurs in Sumner, three miles away. A stack of newspapers is landing on Sumner's railroad depot platform, heaved from the nightly passenger train. These are actually morning papers, arriving a bit late at the ends of the earth.

There is Thursday's disappointed headline, sighing about the manhunt: *"NO FURTHER TRACE"* of the *"Negroes"* (with the plural noun still hoping for a gang story). More tacit is a rebuke to Levy County's white manhood: *Is this the best you can do? He got away! (or: They got away!). Isn't anybody taking responsibility here?* The newspapers only underscore a mood. The car heard by Lee Carrier probably needed no prodding from the media.

He would recall a series of sounds, all faint, at the threshold of hearing. Prior to the one moving car there has been a mingling. Not one but at least two vehicles, perhaps more, have seemed to pull up to the turnoff from Highway 13, cutting their engines. "Why all them stoppin' up there," Lee says to Bishop. Then comes an interval of silence. After that the lone car starts up again, seeming to leave the others parked by the road. Only the one can be heard now, entering the confusing lanes of Rosewood, chugging south.

Though Lee can only guess about it, the driver of the car is not alone. This is Poly Wilkerson's moonlit ride, but it is not a solitary affair—which brings up another riddle, never finally answered: Has *he* recruited *them* to come on this expedition—or have *they* cajoled *him*, persuading Wilkerson to use his constable's badge to cover a plan that was not originally his own? The answers would be buried under carloads of excuses, alibis and attempts to shift the blame.

At least four other men are in the car—or on it, possibly standing on the running boards outside, gangster-style. The four, all identified later by name, are present beyond doubt.[262] There may have been more companions, but the image of a lone automobile—scarcely a parade or mob—is supported by other evidence. This was no large army. At the very most there were probably no more than fifteen of these travelers, and probably fewer than ten. And quite possibly there were only the five, a cadre later unable to hide their involvement and becoming publicly identified.

However, they did have some pseudo-companions. Later, some local heroes would love to boast about having been along on this big ride, but don't seem to have been there. After-glow tales told by wannabes—recited to closed circles of admiring relatives or neighbors (or to wide-eyed children) could proceed on a safe probability, thinking never to cross paths with the evidence. The boasters naturally assumed that any potential reality checks were forever removed, once all the African American witnesses had been attacked and chased into parts unknown.

Moreover, such boasting could ascend into a mystery realm where the liars weren't quite lying. Some of the false memoirs were apparently believed, not just by a campfire audience but seemingly by the tellers themselves. Frontier boasting and self-belief were once storied American folkways—preserved in code even by the phrase "Florida cracker." Originally not simply a reference to "whip-cracker," as romantics have maintained, this loaded phrase—or slur—reminds that frontier boasting was also called "cracking."[263] In an exquisite twist, the modern interpretation of "cracker"—imagining a macho hero cracking a bullwhip, when really the term meant "pathetic backwoods braggart"—is itself a form of cracking, a grandiose boast used to gloss an embarrassing reality.

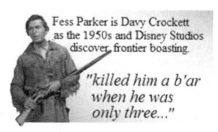

Fess Parker is Davy Crockett as the 1950s and Disney Studios discover frontier boasting.

"killed him a b'ar when he was only three..."

On the national stage, some of the notorious wilderness braggarts were half-mythical like Mike Fink, and some were frankly fictional like the Mark Twain characters, but reality lay behind them.[264] Against a backdrop of lonely woods, a loud voice might unleash a flood of ego inflation, as if to defy the darkness and cry: *"I exist! I am!"*

On a Thursday night this made for a crowded car—at least in imagination—as Constable D. P. Wilkerson drove through cold moonlight. That it was Wilkerson's car was later said by all. Of the two Model T's he was said to own as late as 1922, one may or may not have been lost to manic gambling. But at least one remained, along with the constable's badge. At the wheel now is the man of the hour, as if gambling to win it all back in one big stroke, doubling down, betting the farm.

But who is that riding beside him?

The companion with Wilkerson is not necktie-wearing Walter Pillsbury—though Pillsbury is linked to him on the job. Pillsbury, the boss in Sumner, has been preoccupied since Monday, running the sawmill full-steam to keep his employees out of the disintegrating manhunt. But any timber operation also has another branch. Sumner's sawmill necessarily depends on a separate sphere of activity out in the woods, where trees are felled for the sawmill to slice up. Out there, among screaming skidder cables and falling giants, things are not so orderly as at the mill. The few lost fingers at the sawmill can seem minor by comparison.

That other world, formed by Cummer logging crews, will seem to reverse Pillsbury's policy during the Rosewood week. Rather than keeping the loggers busy to forestall idle meddling, the woods operation stalls strangely all week. The cutting of trees seems to be put on hold, reasons not announced. Possibly tracts of cypress trees were becoming exhausted, or quotas were filled, but there were mutterings about the top boss of the logging crews.

A hard man in a hard job, logging superintendent Henry M. Andrews was particularly hated by African Americans. If a harsh Simon Legree were to be found in the Rosewood ecosystem, it could be here. On Monday, Andrews was said to send his white personnel out to beat the bushes for the fugitive, though this still did not explain the continued idleness of all the loggers, black and white. Working in a sealed environment of deep swamps, a woods boss had few outsiders looking over his shoulder.

As Thursday began to stiffen with cold, one of the loggers, foreman Perry Hudson, age 26 in January 1923, would remember squeezing in with about four other men in a car—for a hunting trip. The car did not belong to Poly Wilkerson and Wilkerson was not with this group. The hunting trip described by Hudson was a daytime affair, not going to Rosewood but probing north from Sumner. Hudson said they followed a road to the big river, the Suwannee, arriving near the Fowler's Bluff logging camp, where they went looking for deer.

There was a saying—Moon's up, Deer's up—  but they didn't wait for nightfall, or for the moon, to decide this was a bust. No deer were around. On the bank of the broad, dark river they put aside their guns and found a place to hole up from the dropping temperature. Forcing open a cobwebbed door, they pushed into a musty little den—an abandoned schoolhouse—where they played some cards.

These were white card players, not black sawmill hands in a jook, so their game of choice was not Georgia Skin. They played ordinary poker, penny-ante stuff, just an excuse to drink some moonshine. The story, with its growing level of alcohol consumption, raises a few questions of credibility, though other evidence does seem to confirm the basic theme, that a hunting trip occurred.

In the shadows of the mortified schoolhouse, Perry did not guess that he was twenty-four hours away from risking his life in a riot. Though he was a cousin of Bryant Hudson, Monday night's impulsive killer of Sam Carter, Perry Hudson took a different view of things. On Friday, January 5, as the week slid over the edge, he would side with law and order against a mob.

On Thursday, not knowing what lies ahead as he fans his cards, he is more preoccupied with his companions. One of them is another cousin, Mannie Hudson. Weathered and tough, Mannie is a bit more like Bryant in the alcohol department. Also in the card game are two loggers, Rogers and Purdee. But the fourth face is the one that will stand out in memory.

He is dark, like swarthy superintendent Pillsbury. Yet this fourth gambler is not of Native American stock as Pillsbury is said to be. He comes of old Florida ancestry in an exotic niche of history. His forebears fought against Native Americans, receiving government land as a reward.[265]

Seated behind his cards, he is no snob in a necktie. He has chosen hard-drinking woodsmen as companions, though he wields power they will never know. He is Perry's boss—and Perry is proud to call him a friend: woods boss Henry Andrews.

Born August 30, 1879,[266] logging superintendent Andrews is four years younger than his fellow administrator, college-educated Pillsbury. In the opinion of commissary clerk Ernest Parham, who would see Andrews only in passing, he is a "high-type man" like Pillsbury, classy, self-possessed, at home with responsibility at the executive level.

In the dark schoolhouse or elsewhere, Perry Hudson thinks of the logging superintendent as likeable, a fine man to work for. Some other whites say the same—though at times choosing their words carefully, using wary disclaimers such as "a good provider for his family, but...."

Neither Parham nor Hudson has heard a nickname used among African American loggers, with enough currency for even children to repeat it. The critics call him "Boots," saying that Andrews kicks his men.

> *"He was a devil man. Not only black but everybody was scared of him."* —Pompey Glover

"Just hard. He was a really likeable man, but he was just tough."
—former Florida Governor Charley Johns

"He was a lover of his children and his family, but as far as everything else, you see, times were different back then. They worked for small wages, and you had to drive them. He drove those work crews....You had to be mean to work those people the way they worked them. They were literal slaves. When they got movin' they didn't quit till they fell in their tracks."—L. W. Norsworthy, son-in-law

"Andrews kicked a many people out there in that log camp."
—Lee Carrier

"Kick him? White and black...He wasn't <u>playin'</u> bad. He <u>was</u> bad."
—Sam Hall

"He just didn't beat up colored. He'd beat up white, too."
—Robert Missouri

"He loved to put his feet on people."
—Minnie Lee Langley

"He was a bad 'un...He would beat and kick Negroes."
—Philomena Doctor

"(Made his crews load) *32 cars of cypress a day. If they didn't load 'em (they had to keep working till they did). Made 'em load 'em that night. Chastise you with his foot."*—Pompey Glover

There were whites, too, who seemed to hate Andrews, especially the side of him that appeared while drinking. Perry Hudson recalled growing uneasy as talk in the schoolhouse took a turn. They should all go over to Rosewood, somebody was saying. They should put some bite into this manhunt thing.

He recalled no plan any more specific than that. By the time they were climbing back into the car, Hudson said, he had made a choice. He told the driver to drop him off at a logging camp on the way back to Sumner, opting out of the newly planned trip. Sixty-one years later, alone in a wheelchair in a fly-blown house on a deserted dirt road, with yellowed newspaper on some of the windows, Perry Hudson grew distraught at the memory, chastising himself. Why hadn't he found a way to talk them out of it, he said. Why hadn't he stopped them? He recalled that a second deer hunter, Rogers, also chose to bail out and not make the additional trip. A third man seemed to drop out later. The car disappeared toward Sumner. Verifiably, two of the travelers named by Perry Hudson would somehow find Poly Wilkerson.

It was a night for adventure, cold and sharp under an enormous moon. Decades later people would still marvel at the brightness of that night, saying you could have picked up a pin off the ground. A nebulous cloud of stories—clouded by boasts—suggests that several prowling drivers, in different cars, may have run across one another that night by coincidence, as the pull of the weather brought them nosing toward Rosewood. There was the tipping point: The search for the Monday fugitive could now be officially declared dead—and cold, bracing air is calling for bold deeds.

One of the alleged deer hunters who finds Wilkerson—or is found by him—is Mannie Hudson. Not only the cousin of Perry but the older brother of Bryant, Mannie knows the Monday night story with family intimacy. He is not as widely despised as Bryant, but is not a saint, and inspires the odd moonshining or hog hunting tale as Bryant does.

As 9:00 p.m. passes and Wilkerson's Model T leaves the turn-off to enter Rosewood's sleeping expanse, Mannie might be squeezed onto the backseat or the running board. But he would not have been in the seat of honor beside the driver. The most prestigious man on board reportedly carries a shotgun, a natural weapon to have brought from a deer hunt. Riding with Wilkerson, and probably sitting next to him, is the slayer of cypress giants, Henry Andrews.

"...the dark Minorcan, sad & separate
Wrapt in his cloak strolls with unsocial eye..."
—Ralph Waldo Emerson, in Florida, 1827[267]

The family name was originally Andreu, reaching the Florida frontier in 1768. The rocky Mediterranean island of Minorca, 250 miles off the coast of Spain, was briefly a British possession. Eight shiploads of Minorcans were recruited to become colonists for another brief British foothold, Florida.

For two centuries beforehand, a *castillo* at St. Augustine had ruled the mostly empty wilderness of Spanish Florida. As this expanse turned British, the 1,403 new colonists (Minorcans and some Italians, Greeks and French) were dumped into a starving indigo plantation owned by a British entrepreneur. Dr. Andrew Turnbull had built a coquina-rock castle in the dunes, and ran his plantation as a private nightmare.[268]

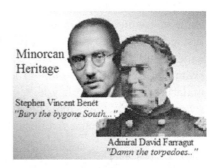

Minorcan Heritage

Stephen Vincent Benét
"Bury the bygone South..."

Admiral David Farragut
"Damn the torpedoes.."

Turnbull's colony, New Smyrna, lay seventy miles down the Atlantic beach from St. Augustine, lost in mangrove swamps and marked by whippings and mass executions. A rescue operation in 1777 brought the last tattered Minorcans into St. Augustine refuge, in a group of fewer than 700 survivors. A half century later, philosopher and traveler Ralph Waldo Emerson would find them still there, as he fled New England's winter for his health. His note about "the dark Minorcan, sad & separate" matched his view of the old Spanish capital—a "dilapidated sandbank," though its "air and sky...are delicious."[269]

Emerson had met a breathing space in the Seminole Wars, 1817-1858 (sometimes called the costliest Indian conflict in U.S. history). But the Andreu/Andrews family was more involved, following a martial tradition among Minorcan settlers that would extend to Admiral David Farragut in the Civil War and the military family of poet Stephen Vincent Benét—also descended from that small cadre of 700.[270] Seminole War service would leave the Andreus with a government land grant, where they settled at a spot some 75 miles northeast of future Sumner and Rosewood.[271]

Log skidder
early twentieth century
(Levy County Archives Committee)

By 1910, descendant Henry Andrews was running a steam log skidder, a smoking tyrannosaur on rails, in the no-man's-land swamps just across the Suwannee from Levy County. The local census taker called Andrews a "foarman." By 1920 he had logged the Pocotaligo swamps of South Carolina—in a spot so remote that a special strain of malaria was wreaking havoc.[272] The man on the skidder knew the great secret places of the South, hidden from the porch-swing perspective of small towns. A steam skidder's taut cable, pulling great logs to a rail

"Logging Old-Growth Cypress," WPA mural
U.S. Post Office, Perry, Florida

spur, tended to mow down everything before it—bushes, palms, non-commercial trees—leaving wastelands that mirrored the empty scars left by timber towns when they moved on. The work was violent by nature. In the Civil Rights Era in Mississippi and Louisiana it was the piney woods logging belt, down toward the coast and Florida,[273] that became the stronghold of the Ku Klux Klan. Imperial Wizard Sam Bowers (the real face of *Mississippi Burning*) suggested a direct link to logging violence in his 1965 "logging letter."[274] A 1920 timber company pamphlet was more poetic:

> *"...spectacular and strenuous activity...Horses and men rushing to and fro; seeming in constant and imminent peril from falling trees; giant logs with skidder cables attached, plunging through the undergrowth on their way to the skidder, there to be tossed into the air and whirled dexterously into place on the log cars; the 'boom-boom' of*

*falling trees, the roar of steam exhausts, engines puffing,
workmen shouting warnings and instructions ...makes the
forest seethe with motion and resound with a confusion of
noises.* "[275]

Florida timber bosses like Andrews became legends, though not of
the Paul Bunyan type. The tales told by loggers and settlers (the narrators
were often but not always African American) had villains but few heroes.
There was Cap'n Brown of Dixie County (W. Alston Brown), or the

photo: Levy County Archives Committee

shadow-boss Bully Bob (gunned down in a revenge fable, last name
apparently Sullivan). Pictured with his billy club and pitbull, there was
Cap'n Roddenberry (first name John).[276] The names and deeds could mix
and switch around, leaving mostly questions. Once in a while came a
lightning stroke of documentation, as in the court records of 1923 itself,
when logging boss William Fisher of Putnam Lumber was pried from his
Dixie County camp and charged with murder.[277]

More often it went like this:

*At dusk, capping a beautiful rural Florida day, I am speaking to a
former local official, a white official. We sit placidly on his yard bench at
the edge of the Great Gulf Hammock—or what's left of it. Some majesty
remains. This magic time of day, twilight, is marked in the middle
distance by a small swamp drama. Slender shapes float delicately into
the open air from the wall of trees: graceful birds of prey called
swallowtailed kites. Long wings flashing—black and white, black and*

white—they make low, slow, lazy passes over the clearing, almost touching the grass, as they pounce on field mice.

The former official is asked about logging boss Henry Andrews, whom he personally knew, long ago as an adolescent. His face takes on a strange expression. He suddenly says to turn off the tape recorder. He doesn't want his name tagged to this. The button clicks. The machine goes helpless on the rough wooden bench, as he slips into it: the dream-universe of the woodland tale.

He tells it somberly, as absolute truth, a scene that he personally witnessed. But in some way it is clearly the great mystery, the frontier ceremony of cracking—not presented exactly as a boast in this case, but given extra force as a sad and reluctant lament.

He tells it as a double whammy—for this is actually two tales chained together, each so like the other in underlying elements (if you were to view them in the spoilsport yankee way) that it has to be wondered just how deeply into the subconscious mind this well bucket has dropped, and how these symbols are operating. Could these two tales be true? Could their central figure—this fine family man, this corporate executive, viewed as decorous and responsible by so many friends and associates—could he really be this bad? At the very least, the telling proves one point. It proves how much this extraordinary individual could engender hatred. If he is being lied about here, it is a lie born of seething contempt.

The teller is going back to the old days, when he was the son of a storekeeper in Otter Creek. Non-company stores in timber towns were outside the favored loop. Lumber companies sought to recoup wages paid out by having employees shop close to home, at the company's own store, its commissary. This larger pattern of the

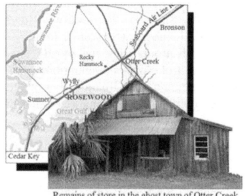

Remains of store in the ghost town of Otter Creek
(photo: Florida Trailblazer)

times *("...I owe my soul to the company store")* was not always a caricatured debt-bondage trap. The shiny commissary under Walter Pillsbury in Sumner was apparently a taut ship, raising no issues. But the spectrum went downhill from there, and companies did not welcome private competition.

The boots of Henry Andrews are now sounding on a plank walk. He comes into the store, the one owned by the father of the teller of the tale. At age fourteen, the teller himself stands near the counter, watching. The father is behind the counter. The man coming in the door, Andrews, is at this point running not only a logging quarters in Otter Creek but an adjoining crate mill. He has a commissary or company store to look out for, clouding his view of private merchants.

Superintendent Andrews faces the storekeeper across the counter, then notices a coincidental movement. Any such store is going to have certain appliances—one of which now perches on a barrel top or counterpane. There is always going to be the storekeeper's cat, keeping down mice. Andrews has noticed this cat. It sits within arm's reach. On arrival, the visitor had seemed to have no particular plan, but now is working by inspiration, his actions shaped by this happenstance, the cat.

He picks it up. And opens a pocketknife.

The storekeeper is a calm-voiced fellow, molded by the old frontier, where you didn't let your tone of voice give away your hand. The storekeeper does not change expression as he asks, mildly:

"What are you fixin' to do with that cat, Henry?"

The logging boss then replies, just as mildly:

"I'm fixin' to cut its tail off."

Then something happens. Very rapidly. Again an item comes from standard inventory (the prop table for the narrating playwright telling the tale). Another appliance (besides a cat) that a storekeeper is always going to have is typically kept out of sight. Now the merchant's hand comes up so quickly from beneath a sheet of butcher paper under the counter that the little .32 revolver seems almost to materialize by itself, its shiny muzzle coming to rest against the forehead of the man holding the cat. The voice of the man holding the gun remains mild, as if wondering about rain:

"If you cut the cat's tail off, Henry, I'll kill you."

The man with the knife smiles faintly, and lets the cat jump down.

Thus went the first tale.

Now, in the second tale, it is night—Saturday night in Otter Creek, and men are roaming the sawdust streets. But soon they flock to a pool of lantern light on the store porch. Something is happening, a fascinating entertainment. One man has grabbed and pinned another, and is holding his neck in a hammerlock, displaying him to the crowd, while laughing drunkenly. The holder is white; the captive is black. The latter is one of the drifters drawn to the jook, on nobody's payroll, fair game for a little prank. The holder is the big boss, Andrews.

The Ruins of Otter Creek

This tale leaves a deeper subtext unspoken. It makes tacit reference to a widespread folk saying in the woods, uttered by whites with ambivalent fondness, like naming a sports team after a conquered tribe.

The teller of the tale doesn't have to fill this in, because the tale embodies it for him. The man tightening the hammerlock in the tale is playing on this deeper context. Again—as with the cat—there is an aggressor with quick hands. And again he holds the target dexterously, using only one arm (as with the cat), while the free hand goes for a weapon (as with the cat)—though in this case the weapon is better than a pocketknife.

The free hand brings up a pistol—though gripping it in an inventive way (as with one-handed opening of the pocketknife on the cat). The gun is gripped by the barrel, and thus is lifted high in the air, imitating the use of a tool the aggressor knows well, a logger's axe. As if the barrel were an axe handle and the gun butt the blade, the holder lifts and then chops down, lifts and then chops down, repeatedly, each time connecting with a dull, sickening chunk—though only glancingly. There is more of a chipping motion than a direct hit—again and again. He is skinning the sharp edge of the gun butt down the side of the captive's head.

As if a tree were being barked, he is attempting to chip off a small piece of scalp. Unspoken is also another stream of lore, from the Indian wars, the old Seminole conflict, a stream told and retold at frontier campfires, imputing to both warring sides the creative use of skin, especially scalp. And deeper still, farther back, is the nightmare colony, the Minorcan ancestry of the man in the lamplight, some of those

Minorcan slaves forced to whip one another, or to endure an African whipping boss. Such things, so impossibly distant, come closer as the teller goes into that strange place of the great frontier, the waking dream, the thing the city folk can never understand, so they call it a tall tale.

And now success! The man chopping down with the pistol has at last achieved his goal. The human tree is glancingly barked, a small piece of essence pried off the skull. He lifts it, the limp crimson shred, holds it aloft jubilantly. He laughs to the crowd drunkenly. He glories, afraid of nothing—glories in taking them farther and farther into the place where few dare to go, the forbidden land of completely unbridled desire, of yearning, magic, sorcery, savagery—the place of the mob, of dreams—as the man holding the red fragment aloft cries:

"Got to have me a little nigger wool! Got to have me a little nigger wool on Saturday night!"

Now he has completely fixated their gaping attention, the obscenity complete, the monstrosity of the tale and the monstrosity of the pictured man made one—monstrous imagination, monstrous reality—the monstrosity of the saying and the yearning of the lonely woods, all resolved, converted into unity.

For he has eaten it.

The horrific stories are themselves like an axe, bludgeoning the hearer—converting the audience into the obscenely immobilized cat, into the unspeakably defiled drifter—and thus distracting the audience from the poverty of new elements from one story to the next. There is the texture of a dream, which finds no need to apologize if a knife turns into a gun butt, or a captive cat a captive drifter. Some flourishes of detail are needed, in the way that a dream or a novelist needs details, smoothing it out to look like real observation.

Either way, the teller wins the game, and makes his point: If a man who had somehow moved people to tell such tales—for whatever reason, true or false—if such a man were suddenly to materialize in the moonlight of 1923 in the front yard of a family of African Americans, expectations inside the house might grow intense.

Minnie hears it now. Out in the moonlight, there is a car.

Chapter 22: Man

"....the crime...is said to have resulted in Carrier saying his act was an example of what the negroes could do without interference. The white men went to Carrier's home last night to see if Hunter was there, and to warn Carrier against further talk of that kind."

—*New York Times,* Jan. 6, 1923

Sylvester Carrier
in adolescence

He would be famous for a moment.

Sylvester Carrier, seemingly a minor figure in the first part of the Rosewood week, would reach center-stage on Thursday night. By Saturday, January 6, his name would be greeting readers of the *New York Times.*

Much of the image was fantasy. The passage quoted above was so blatantly fantasized that the *Gainesville Daily Sun,* where it apparently originated by telegraph, had to issue a sheepish retraction locally, confessing some of the mistakes ("We Were Misinformed," mumbled the local headline on January 13)—but this never reached the countless readers nationwide who marveled at the wire-service story.

Through the magic of the telegraph wires, readers of the *Los Angeles Times* saw his mysterious name at the same time as those in New York—as well as readers in Chicago, Dallas, Seattle, Memphis, Omaha, Denver, New Orleans, and on and on.

It was an evocative name, poetic, so to speak—*this Carrier, this man of the woods, this savage Sylvester.* The *Washington Post,* using an early bulletin to get the jump on January 5, added spice to the name by crafting a special tag: *"Sylvester Carrier, negro desperado."*

But generally the wire-service copy was left unchanged, evidently presented by receiving papers in the same form that it came in over the wire, tracking back to the upstairs office in Gainesville. A memory from the *Gainesville Daily Sun* of that era, the 1920s, recalled its telegraph key as being innovatively equipped.[278] To amplify the clicking of dots and dashes in Morse Code, the *Sun* veteran recalled, a hollow metal sounder had been rigged up from office flotsam, using a red Prince Albert Tobacco can.

BANG bang BANG bang bang BANG.

The desperado was an acoustical essence, dancing in electrical clicks—and in aromatic pipe blend.

The *Washington Post* saw the urgency. This desperado was waging a "FLORIDA RACE WAR."[279] The underlying theme, as old as slave insurrection panics in colonial days, had been boosted by \World War I, with its heightened excitability.

"During the first postwar years," wrote historian George Brown Tindall about that moment in race relations, "newspapers North and South reported rumors of plots, revolts, and insurrections." The summer of 1919, just after the war, "ushered in the greatest period of interracial strife the nation had ever witnessed"—twenty-five race riots counted nationwide by year's end, including the "Red Summer," which referred not to Russian Bolsheviks or the Red Scare, but to blood-stained American racial clashes.[280]

"Sylvester Carrier, negro desperado" floated in that haze—one more mystery name in the news, to vanish in the next press run. The scraps of narrative that brought him into the Rosewood news picture are so confusing—and so divorced from the reality shown by agreeing witnesses—that they require a pause here for decoding, as if teasing apart crumbled parchment in the Dead Sea Scrolls.

The passage quoted at the beginning of this chapter forms a hive of mystery phrases:

"Carrier saying his act was an example."

And "to see if Hunter was there."

And notably: "talk of that kind."

Full Name: Henry Sylvester Carrier
born 1890
This photo was made long before 1923. By the time of the Rosewood violence, Sylvester Carrier had apparently reached the age of 33.
(*Photo: Rosewood claims case files, Southeast Regional Black Archives*)

No real Rosewood survivors seemed to hear of such nefarious goings-on. Either all of those informants were covering up at the same time, in the same way, or something was wrong with the news.

The phrase "talk of that kind" in the wire story meant talk of a rebellious, violent or brutal kind. It was a quick way to put a gloss on Poly Wilkerson's moonlit ride, which would wind up at Sarah Carrier's doorstep in a disastrous explosion. In the news, this ride became heroic, a respectable investigation trip by whites, who were simply forced to check out a black desperado spouting "talk of that kind.'

But the desperado could also be construed as making menacing boasts—which brings up the question: Could there have been a nugget of truth behind this mask, too?

"Syl was kind of loud," recalled neighbor Sam Hall, introducing another cycle of stories about how Monday led to Thursday. Hall said that during the Monday-Thursday period, Sylvester did indeed make one of his trademark, taunting boasts, which Hall rendered as follows:

"Well, now, you didn't ax me nothin' 'bout him. If you'da ax me about him, I'd a told 'em he's down there."

. When I first heard those words I stared blankly. What did they mean? Hall obligingly rephrased, using slightly different words, now saying that Syl boasted:

"They didn't ax me nothin' about it. If they'da ask me, I'da told 'em where he was."

A translation may peek from a second stream of stories, told among whites. These said that Sylvester's mother Sarah did some of her Sumner washing off-site, taking laundry home to wash. The practice was known from earlier years when Sarah Carrier's in-law Eliza Bradley picked up wash in a wagon, though imputing it to Sarah is more doubtful. True or false, however, the story may capture something.

A white woman has come to Sarah's to pick up her laundered clothes. And there she runs into Sylvester. This, says the tale, is when he blurts it out—the strange statement about knowing where the manhunt fugitive was hiding.

But why would Sylvester Carrier say such a thing? Missing from the tale is his motivation. The white tellers needed none. Here was a crazy, unstable Negro, willing to say just about anything—which only made him more dangerous.

Could something real lie hidden behind this rumor? Could a real white woman, nervous or pompous, have been chattering away at Sarah's house, venting about the disappeared Monday fugitive? Could she have grown so offensive—or perhaps merely so comic—that a laughing, boasting hearer decided to jerk her chain a bit? There was, after all, the oral universe called cracking. Might the boast have come with a droll raised eyebrow, hinting at the joke, but unnoticed by an anxious hearer? Was there a "Florida cracker" here—but not a white one?

Could Sam Hall's mystery quote be translatable like this:

"Well, those manhunters were so busy bothering everybody around here that they couldn't find their noses with both hands. They should have come and asked me. I could have set 'em straight."

Did the rumor—and the false face in the news—capture a glimpse of real personality?

KA-KA-KA!

They talked about that laugh. Sixty years later, after many cares and years, when posterity finally came asking for specifics, Rosewood survivors gamely reached back in time as they tried to reproduce the sound of it. How does one describe a man with a strange, explosive style of laughter?

KA-KA-KA!

On the depot platform at night, as men would gather to pass the time, the mutter of voices would be pierced by that trumpet: Like a great dark bird composed only of sound, swooping up from the mass.

KA-KA-KA!

That loud Carrier voice, as if determined to show that the sheer joy of life, the triumph, is beyond any wound the world can dish out. Sometimes it was at the ball field behind Sarah's house, the dark figure crouching in the catcher's mask, hunched behind the plate (the most dangerous position, and the one calling the shots, directing the pitcher with the hand signs)—as he cries out through the mask:

"Th'ow it on by him! He cain't hit! He got a hole in his bat!"

And at game's end, once the visiting team has been taught a lesson, the laughter keeps on:

"Ya'll can't play ball!"

Thelma Evans, not knowing him very well, the shy city girl orphaned and sent to live with her Bradley grandparents on the lonely farm—finding her pool of comfort in that voice, as it turned solemn for the Sunday hymns:

"Here speaks the Comforter, tenderly saying..."

239

How could he be all these things—star singer, star baseball catcher—and star hunter, the best shot with a gun?

This was how they viewed him, not myth-making sentimentally but shrugging mundanely. The laughter seemed born of some inner precision—the knack, the knowingness—sighting down the gunsight at the quail, hitting the musical pitches on the wing.

People didn't put it that way—this thing called talent. As in Beauty and Willie and Sweetie, his singing sisters—or Sarah herself, directing the show. His younger brother Harry, still living at home in 1923, would one day make a living as a musician, as Beauty did. What was the force in this one household? The others viewed it as special. They wondered about it.

Draft card:

Henry Sylvester Carrier
Born Sept. 7, 1892, in "Rosewood, Fla."
Employment: "Tie Chopper" in "Rosewood"
for the "See Board Airline RR."

The misspelling, "See Board," was not his but came from the Sumner draft registrar in 1917. The birth date, for whatever reason, disagrees with all census records. Apparently his real birth year, the credible one for various reasons, was 1890. But he did sign the draft card, adding an extra flourish on the odd part, that first name he never used, the name most of his neighbors had never heard, Henry.

Again the small clues. When his sister Willie named her first son Arnett Turner Goins in 1913, the nod suggested two bishops. Willie's mother Sarah had, in impressionable youth, known of A.M.E. Bishop Benjamin Arnett, a national figure, so admired that in 1898 he was chosen to administer the oath of office to President William McKinley. The other bishop suggested by the naming echo, Henry McNeal Turner, would in 1883 become the first head of the A.M.E. church to be elected from the newly emancipated South, and soon denounced Jim Crow racial segregation.[281] Sarah's first son—whether born in 1890 or 1892—came in the time of that bishop named Henry.

Almost immediately the young woodsman, Henry Sylvester Carrier, seemed to grow away from the first name, dropping it even as a child. It was not loaded like the middle name, which could have been just a local borrowing, but perhaps was picked specifically for its Latin portent— suiting word to context: Sylvester, Man of the Woods.

As with gun sight or song line, something seemed to say that the whole name had to scan, the measure rhyme out, the first part resonate heavily enough to balance the symbolic heft in that last part, the similarly loaded surname, Carrier.

And whence came *that* poetry? The family's surname led back into silence. From the islands? From the slave block? Borrowed from the Carrier logging equipment company? From the Jim Crow patronage custom in old Florida that gave African Americans the job of mail carrier? Or, perhaps, as with the Latin middle name, might it have gone deeper than that, into inner fire: a name picked intentionally because it sounded right, because it carried an idea?

The name Henry, lacking such internal weight (no matter how pious its original intention), would be disowned twice—not only pushed aside by the rich middle name, Sylvester, but also by another tag in his portfolio, an entirely made-up name pinned onto him by his family as he grew up, a nickname.

In the 1930s, when the survivors were still struggling with their loss, a young girl heard them talking about him—that mystery hero gone from their midst—and she thought they were admiringly calling him "the man." But that was not it, not exactly. Sylvester Carrier's real nickname was not as easy or colloquial as that. Not as accessible or flat.

The nickname from childhood had perhaps emerged laughingly, to brace him against all those extroverted sisters—but it then grew with him, seeming right. Those closest to him would continue using the nickname into adulthood.

They called him "Man."

Without the "the."

The laughter at the depot at night, fixing attention on the star at center-stage—never the tiny voice lost in the wilderness, but grandiose, like the ghost parade of frontier titans, the Paul Bunyans, Pecos Bills—and John Henrys. But then also more than them, bigger and better—because after all, those heroes were just air, made-up myths, mere marsh gas born of cracking. But not him. For he could bleed. He was Man.

It would seem fated, that he could go out no other way, to become nothing at all in the end—so that he could be all of it, lifted to Olympus or Valhalla in their minds. In exchange for that prize you had to become nothing that could live or breathe, slipping sideways into the epic world of giants, where you could never die—but could never again know, think, feel—or laugh. Because now you were just grandness in the minds of other people.

The Carrier, The Comforter, Man of the Woods.
"Sylvester Carrier, negro desperado."

Already in childhood the jubilant personality seemed to be formed, at least according to one tale. There was the day young Sylvester "crowed up as his daddy," making an impertinent remark. His father, the logger, sometime preacher and commercial hunter Haywood Carrier, was not amused. In response to the bumptiousness, "his daddy knocked him cold with the water bucket."[282]

 The 1910 census found both Haywood and young Sylvester working at the Rosewood cedar mill. When that mill disappeared in 1911—like all the cedar mills—the youth-no-longer-called-Henry found himself to be obsolete. He was skilled in the old technology, using oxen and mules to drag logs from the swamps, a world that was being replaced by steam and rails.

"Syl cut cedar," said Sam Hall, who grew up hearing stories about the vanished time:

"He was a teamster. Do more with a pair of mules. If they balkin' in that swamp, send for Syl. Take his whip, tap 'em on the leg, pop that whip, walk 'em. GET outa here. Jump WALK. Rough mud. Bogged to the knees. Get 'em to prancin'."

The records from 1911 showed Sylvester Carrier owning four animals, two mules, two oxen.[283] An ox was better in the mud than a mule. There were woods bosses who would torture their oxen for the last ounce of pulling strength, but Syl was said to have a lighter touch, coaxing them to do their miracles—after which, though, would come a less subtle trick, the trademark victory dance, the humble nod to the rival team.

"KA-KA-KA! Ya'll ain't no teamsters!"

Then it was gone, a phase of his life vanishing with the cedar and the mill. On August 12, 1911, he went to the Gainesville National Bank and mortgaged the four draft animals. By then he had had his first arrest, on May 9, 1911, for the cryptic crime of selling alcoholic cider—perhaps meaning "buck," the dishpan beer brewed from fermented corn soakings.[284]

If he had overstepped some deputy sheriff's bootlegging turf, the records failed to say so. The jury said not guilty.

Worse news for the Carrier family came on August 19, 1911. Rosewood's A.M.E church burned to the ground, amid signs of arson.[285] Sylvester was not involved, but fingers pointed toward John Coleman, the crusty trapper who didn't much like the church scene. Then stronger evidence surfaced, pointing to a fired church treasurer, Richard Williams (the troubled brother-in-law of Sam Carter). In both arson trials, of Coleman and then Williams, the jury said not guilty.

The feuds grew daunting in their convolutions. Sylvester's name was seldom mentioned, but the maze closed around him. Lutie Foster said the Baptist church in Goins quarters was also a victim of neighbor-on-neighbor arson, and that an attempt was made even against the Rosewood school. Minnie agreed about the school, saying the burning temporarily forced classes to move. Schools made tempting targets for wilderness rancors, and again there was a parallel forty miles north, a feud among whites in Newberry, destroying a white school there.

On February 15, 1912, Sylvester Carrier, age about 22, would have been keenly interested when land was deeded for the new A.M.E. church, to replace the one in ashes.[286] This hope was what deepened the pain of the later Christmas shooting, explaining Lutie Foster's lament, "That finished tearin' up Rosewood." The Christmas shooting meant that the new church, too, had fallen to the old wrath.

On November 6, 1912, Sylvester Carrier married—though not to Gertrude King, who would be his wife as 1923 arrived. An earlier wife, Mattie Smith, somehow disappeared, according to his statement before a judge on March 16, 1916, when he reported her abandoning him for parts unknown. The plea was necessary for a one-party divorce, granted two months before he then married Gert King in May 1916.

Gertrude King Carrier Johnson in later years (ca. 1940s?) married Sylvester Carrier May 18, 1916
Collection of Marie Ames

The next court appearance was a year later, for "animal mark changing," meaning the theft of one of John Monroe's hogs. The former teamster then became Florida Prison System innate 13175, a leased convict, assigned to a logging operation in the badlands across the Suwannee.[287] In Rosewood that year of tragedy left few clues as to how the pieces meshed. John Monroe's wife Sophie died in 1917, along with her cousin Agnes Marshall, both on the same day.[288]

There were dimly remembered chapters. His fist fight with Elijah Green left no recollection even as to motive, only a scrap of blow-by-blow narration: Green seizing the advantage, jumping atop the Carrier prodigy, pinning him and then continuing to pummel—until Gert approaches with the garden hoe, coming from behind, chopping Elijah aside—though Elijah then boasts anyway, marching down to the depot, pacing back and forth before the crowd, shouting: *See this blood, I brought this with my natural fist!*

"He liked to crack, and fight, too," mused Sam Hall. The visiting ball teams might try to return the cracking, but to no avail. The voice in the catcher's mask would just laugh back: *That's the way lies gets out! You boys, you can't play no ball!*

This is not a tale of heroes or demons, as believers on either side might wish. But it is, among other things, an attempt to glimpse the invisible thing that the tales kept dancing around—the magic within—which in the end would not step aside, or shut up, or bow to the inevitable certainties in the dying sanctuary of the dying woods. But instead it kept maneuvering, this magic, kept twisting stubbornly into the last shrinking space available—as on Thursday night, when he would find a certain cubbyhole under the stairs....

Chapter 23: All at Once

They are downstairs when they hear the car.[289] The sound is somewhere out in the moonlight between the railroad and the house. Minnie, inside, finds no sharp-eyed sentinels at the windows of the parlor, no one at all standing guard—an important detail in view of later legends. She sees only a less dramatic action. As the sound of the car is heard, she sees the door of the front bedroom swing open.

But first, to visualize this, we need a floor plan:

The front door of Sarah Carrier's house opens onto a kind of crossroads, not exactly a vestibule but a point where you can walk in four different directions into the interior. To the left, as you come in the front door, is the parlor with its upright piano (where Minnie now stands in the dark with the other children). But if from the front door you look straight ahead past the parlor, into the second arm of the crossroads, you see the shotgun hall leading back toward the kitchen and the back porch. Out of sight back there, the hall reaches the dogtrot breezeway tying Sylvester's and Gert's add-on back room to the main building.

And then there is the third arm of the crossroads. If, still standing at the front door, you look just to the side of the hall, a bit to the right, you see running alongside the hall a route that goes upward. This is the stairway with its banister rail. That side of the hall is walled off by the staircase, with a small firewood closet cut into the casing under the stairs. These stairs reach a landing halfway up, then angle to a landing at the top, lit by a lamp on the wall, at a door into the unpartitioned attic where the children sleep.

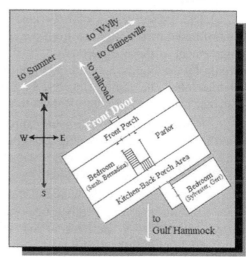

Downstairs Floor Plan
Sarah Carrier Residence
(approximation from witness statements)

This still leaves the fourth path. As you come into the house through the front door you can also turn hard right—into the doorway to the front bedroom. This bedroom, anchoring the corner of the house on the ground floor, faces onto the front porch, with a window on the porch's western end. When the car is heard, this is the bedroom door that Minnie sees opening.

The figure emerging from the bedroom is Bernadina. Standing at the door (and looking half-asleep) she is Sarah's youngest daughter, age about twenty. Mother and daughter sleep in that room, in the same bed, perhaps on a mattress stuffed with Spanish moss, another standard of the woods. Bernadina is in her nightgown, apparently having been roused from sleep by the sound of the car. She seems to have dozed off without much alarm or feeling of suspense. The stories about Sylvester standing guard night after night begin to sound questionable here. At least on this particular night (and in accordance with Lee Carrier's separate impression), Sylvester does not seem to be pacing the premises.

Communities black and white would tell opposite tales about this moment, each group painting boastful images of heroic soldiery by the home team. Whites would say that their brave boys were up against a sinister black army inside this hellish house. But blacks also would boast—about the valor of the same supposed army—which in fact was not there.

The distant tellers of both kinds of tales were repeating rumors, uninformed by descriptions from the real witnesses inside the house. The agreement of those witnesses on the basic situation is tight, leaving little room for doubt. In a sense there were three houses: the mythical house in white tales, the mythical house in black tales, and the less dramatic silence of the real structure, known to the witnesses caught inside.

Bernadina is holding a lamp, apparently having lit it in the darkened bedroom, now bringing it with her to the door. She seems to be sleepily curious, wondering what kind of visitors might be out there.

Again and again the events of the week will involve a half-conscious mental state sometimes called "hypnopomp" —a state occurring when a person is waking, but not fully awake.

Bernadina squints in bafflement, raising the lamp. But Aunt Sarah seems to have a much better understanding of the arriving automobile. She hisses angrily to Bernadina: *"Put out that light!"*

Minnie sees no more. With the other children she is shooed upstairs by Mama—that is, by her grandmother Emma Carrier, Sarah's older sister. In Minnie's last view of the downstairs area, there is still no sign of Sylvester. He and Gert, in their room at the rear, must surely have heard the car. Gert herself would later tell stories confirming the obvious, that at that moment she and Sylvester were in the back room—apparently in bed. Gert, too, was in her nightgown.

The rush of children into the darkened attic leaves Minnie with no sharp impressions—except on one point. One of the children is already up there, having preceded the others before the excitement. Everyone knew that the arrival of Mama's household would make Aunt Sarah's sleeping loft a crowded place. So one guest dispensed with stuffy ceremony, going immediately upstairs to bed, claiming his spot.

Minnie's brother Ruben, the buck-dancing joker and backyard preacher, has had a hard day today, raking pine straw in Wylly. And now the strange trip to Aunt Sarah's has meant still more weariness, walking after dark. When the group arrived, Ruben did not bother socializing but disappeared up Aunt Sarah's stairway, then fell out on a bed. Late-comers would have to pile in where they could.

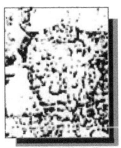

Ruben Mitchell
ca. 1922

Now the others, having been sent upstairs, do push in. Ruben doesn't bother waking. That he is really asleep—and not just playing possum—will soon be shown for certain.

For Minnie, time begins to stretch out. Nothing seems to be happening. Gone is the fear she felt while walking down the railroad. She is snug inside the house now. That sound outside, it was just a car, some kind of adult business. She is in bed, her shoes off, perhaps in her nightgown—though not quite drifting off. Her mind races, filled with a familiar theme. *Where is Mama right now? What is Mama doing down there? Wouldn't it be nice if she could come upstairs? Isn't there some way to be with Mama?*

With or without her separation anxiety, Minnie Mitchell is now in a blind spot, unable to see any activity either downstairs or out in the yard where the car has arrived. Her focus is inward, fretting about Mama. Still, the drama downstairs is not entirely masked. She hears snatches of at least two voices from the ground level, calling cryptically to one other—apparently one voice calling from outside the house, the other answering within—and only a thin plank wall between them.

The less distinct voice is Aunt Sarah's, perhaps entirely muffled, perhaps shouting something simple: *Go away! We're in bed!*

Apparently Sarah Carrier has instructed Bernadina to climb back into bed. Events will show that Sarah has now climbed in with her—as if the shadowy visitors outside could be dismissed like tiresome neighbors, to be brushed off with a shout: *Can't you see it's late? What are you thinking?*

In Minnie's impressions only the second voice sounds clearly: a man's voice, calling Aunt Sarah to come and open the door.

"Sarah!"

This was apparently Poly Wilkerson.

The man who would have been sitting next to Wilkerson in the car is now in the yard. Logging superintendent Henry Andrews is standing somewhere behind the big constable. Nearby are Mannie Hudson and at least two others, who apparently joined the party among the darkened mysteries of Sumner. One is Mannie's cousin Bryan Kirkland—not to be con-fused with Mannie's brother Bryant (with a "t") from Monday night. The new player, Bryan, is a compact figure, less than five-feet-six, gray eyes, blond hair. He is subject to rather exact description for the same reason as Bryant: military service records. Leaving the army a week after World War I ended in 1918, Jennings Bryan Kirkland would be one more veteran drawn into a post-war wave of racial confrontation.[290]

Levy County World War I recruits
(Levy County Archives Committee)

But also arriving with the car is a less tested adventurer, a young lumber inspector from Sumner. His name of record is Minor Studstill, but everyone knows him as Cephus. By age 23, Cephus Studstill was foreman over a black crew, as the rules of segregation kept African Americans from promotion. Whites in Sumner would wonder how Cephus, a quiet, business-like presence, became involved in a moonlit ride.[291]

The chicken-and-egg question remains: Did woods boss Henry Andrews, returning from the deer hunt and not ready to go home, recruit a reluctant Poly Wilkerson, while also pulling in a sawmill hand, Studstill, who happened to come along? Or was it Wilkerson who recruited Andrews, after some kind of veiled encounter with Sarah Carrier during the day? Andrews, for one, had a special reason to be interested in Sylvester Carrier.

A lumber crew boss in Levy County
(Levy County Archives Committee)

Of the 471 Levy County residents recorded in military service during World War I, only twelve were noted as fatalities, including four African Americans.[292] In 1918-1919 most came home. In Rosewood, children were told that such activity explained where Sylvester Carrier had been during that time, for he seemed to disappear from the community. It was explained that Cud'n Syl had been in the army—like George Goins, like Grover Coleman (another of old man John's sons), and like Syl's cousin Aaron (until Aaron's early return under a psycho-medical cloud).

But in Sylvester's case the war story was a blind. The government business taking him away from home had classified him as Prisoner 13175, during his five months as a leased convict in a camp beyond the Suwannee. Imprisoned at the same time was his father Haywood, Prisoner 13196. Both were convicted on the same charge, "animal mark changing," in the theft of a hog whose owner was also African American, neighbor John Monroe. The make-nice stories saying that Sylvester was away at the war left some questions unanswered. Puzzling irregularities can be seen in the records of the two court cases sending father and son away. A possibility is opened that the two Carriers might have been framed and hijacked into convict labor in response to the war's local labor shortage.[293]

Or was it the other way around? Were two Carrier masterminds to blame for a world of missing hogs, with the law simply focusing on one of the cases for courtroom convenience? The clues could mean anything. As the two men were swallowed up by the trans-Suwannee no-man's land, this veiled time period concealed even the basic nature of their deeds, good or bad. Haywood would return to Rosewood only briefly, if at all. He was then said to go away preaching, with few details preserved. At home in Rosewood he was well established as a lay preacher, one of the untrained part-timers customarily serving woodland chapels. Without doubt, some kind of deep psychological forces were at work. All tellers would agree that after the additional shock of 1923, Haywood Carrier seemed so overcome with grief that he "lost his mind." He was described as wandering blindly, sometimes unclothed. His side of the Rosewood puzzle was left still more deeply in shadow. Sylvester, however, would emerge from the trans-Suwannee ordeal to seek familiar ground. He came home, then was hired by Cummer Lumber in Sumner.

The work he found was steady but harsh. Sylvester became a logtrain fireman, tossing scrap wood into a sweltering locomotive furnace as the Cummer log train ran loads from Suwannee Hammock. By 1920 the fireman's job had enabled him to move with Gert to a small company-owned house in Sumner's black quarters.[294]

Then came the fight—one more riddle, and barely a silhouette in the mists of memory. This time, laughing, outspoken Sylvester Carrier came into conflict with a boss, a logging supervisor. And once more the story was apparently laundered when told to children—though this time for dramatic effect. And apparently as children hearing it grew up, they added to the punch. The result would be like a thrilling silent-screen western movie, with a cliff-hanger brawl on a moving train:

EXTERIOR, DAY, cue furiously jangling piano: Sylvester-as-Tom-Mix physically kicks hated villain off thunderously roaring locomotive....

In these tales the punchline is a triumphant kick, an epic flourish. The oppressive villain is booted into painful oblivion.

Tom Mix

However, Lee Carrier, who was old enough to hear an adult version of the story—and from Syl himself—said the fight was less dramatic, a verbal quarrel and not a brawl—which was bad enough. Sylvester lost the job, and with it the company house in the quarters. This was when he and Gert moved once more, into the back room at Sarah's. Retreating to the refuge of his birthplace, he would approach age 33 as a freelance tie-cutter in the woods. His cousin Lee said the supervisor in the quarrel was Andrews.

The cinematic Tom Mix version of the story was too vague to name the boss, but it, too, suggested Andrews by indirection. Since kicking was allegedly the style of employee relations favored by Andrews, the tale implied poetic justice.

The moon is up now, enormous, silvering the wiregrass in the shadows of the yard, etching the scaly trunk of the old cabbage palm in front, creeping toward the porch swing in its dark porch cavern, clutching at the washtub flower planters chastened by the chill. The man stepping from Wilkerson's car carries a loaded shotgun, shells unspent. No deer today. He knows this impudent fireman, this Sylvester, just the sort to be holding criminal secrets about a disappeared fugitive.

And, fugitive or not, there is the moon, possibly the grudge, possibly the alcohol. Time to skid this log.

> *"'Hello, there! Call your dogs!'*
> *That is the regular way to call in the*
> *country because nearly everybody*
> *who has anything to watch has*
> *biting dogs."*
> —Zora Hurston, 1942[295]

The insignificant-seeming wild card in the coming explosion at the house is now perched on the porch. But it is not quietly perched. Adding its infuriating racket to the tensions, Aunt Sarah's protective little porch dog ignores its humble name, Shant Tail. There is nothing shant or scant about the insanely roaring sound.

Minnie hears it from upstairs: *"Shant Tail a-raisin' sand out there."*

It is not a cute little dog, in the best of times. Minnie avoids it. Like an ill-tempered symbol of the haughty ways at Sarah's house, Shant Tail does not rush to make friends. Here in the woods, dogs are not lap companions—though Aunt Sarah has spoiled this one, feeding it choice table scraps. Shant Tail sulks among the red-veined coleus leaves that spill from washtub planters. The snarling little sentry seldom leaves the porch, still less leaving the yard. These limits define its safety zone for making ferocious criticisms of passersby, roaring like a demented little lion at anyone unlucky enough to walk by on the railroad.

Minnie knows not to pet the scrawny little thing.

It bites.

There are now at least fifteen people in the house. The first eight live there: Sarah, Bernadina, Sylvester, Gert, Sarah's youngest son Harry, plus the three grandchildren (Philomena, Arnett and their smaller brother George, called Buster). The rest came from Emma Carrier's house, at least seven of them: Emma, Minnie, Ruben, Eddy, Lonnie, Goldee and little J.C. Uncertainty surrounds another two, the largely silent, disabled adult males in Emma's household: her crippled husband James and her grown son Willard, with his nickname "Big Baby."

If they also came to Sarah's, the total number of occupants is brought to 17. Except for this small margin of error—15 or 17—memories from inside the house will agree unfailingly, while making no apparent effort to emphasize or force the point. To the occupants themselves, mere counting scarcely seemed a matter of dramatic interest. It was a bland background detail, as obvious as the walls and floor. Other mysteries would multiply epidemically at this house, but the basic number of people in it would be well confirmed.

And this matters—for it measures the degree of fantasy in the public picture that would close around the crime scene—as newspaper articles and rumors created a mirage:

> **"...the negro and a number of his friends had barricaded themselves in a shanty on the outskirts of the town and defied any white man to come near them."**
>
> —*The Washington Post,* January 5, 1923

This was the uprising fantasy, able to float freely in the absence of independent investigation at the scene. It was the accusation that such a house could be an armed fortress, packed with sneering black rebels.

Multiply this fantasy by a thousand incidents—or ten thousand—and it might begin to suggest the fog of belief that could envelope a thousand-mile mystery realm, that of rural southern lynching. The *Washington Post* of 1923 was not the paper it would become under later ownership. In 1919 it had been accused of intentionally helping to start

252

one of the era's "race wars."[296] In 1923 it tweaked the Rosewood information coming over the Associated Press wire to maximize possibilities for white anger—though the bulletins needed little help in that regard. So dramatic was the first Rosewood wire story used by the *Post* that, symmetrically, it was published in both Washingtons, following telegraph wires across the Rockies to climb into the *Seattle Post-Intelligencer*, also on January 5:

> **"...a score or more of negroes early today were barricaded in a house at Rosewood."**

The word "barricaded" could evoke World War I trenches or rebel slaves holed up in a barn with knives clenched in their teeth (and for any Gettysburg drop-outs, "a score" means twenty).

> **"...a score or more of Negroes early to-day were barricaded in a house at Rosewood."**
> —The *New York World*, January 5, 1923

There were slight changes in style from one newspaper to the next, like "today" becoming "to-day." And dots and dashes coming off the telegraph could cause minor spelling errors. But in essence the stories in all the different receiving papers were the same story, just one, generated by a heavily fantasizing source who in the stories themselves was never formally named. The effect was fleeting, the impressions soon to be replaced by tomorrow's mysterious stories about other distant and never-seen places. There was no knowing how much of a boost was given to a certain kind of mass belief.

> **"...a score or more of negroes early today were barricaded in a house at Rosewood."**
> —*The Florida Times Union*, January 5, 1923

In the excitement of the image, as concerned whites found their fears made flesh, the precise number of fierce black rebels inside the house could float as well, even within the same newspaper.

> **"They found about twenty-five negroes gathered in a house."**
> —*The Florida Times Union*, January 5, 1923

"It later developed that 21 heavily armed negroes were in the house."
—*The Jacksonville Journal,* January 5, 1923

"Five to sixteen negroes were said to have been barricaded in the place at that time."
—*The Jacksonville Journal,* January 5, 1923

But what was motivating these fierce rebels? What was their intriguing biography? Public information had no need to investigate. Believers could consult their own prior beliefs.

"Twenty negroes barricaded in a house."
—*The Ocala (Fla.) Evening Star,* January 5, 1923

"25 or more heavily armed negroes are making a stand here in a small hut".
—*The St Augustine (Fla.) Evening Record,* January 5, 1923

"In one house, they found about 25 negroes."
—*The Tampa Daily Times,* January 5, 1923

"...about twenty-five Negroes heavily armed in one house..."
—*The New York Age,* January 13, 1923

Somewhere at the center of this belief-storm was the upstairs crow's nest in Gainesville, telegraphing the mirage to the nation. Another recollection from the 1920s veteran of the *Gainesville Daily Sun* recapped the standard operation called "expanding"--that is, taking a scrap or tip from the phone and imagining details that might logically surround such a scrap, then dropping these in as if they had been observed.

"I think there was an awful lot of exaggeration and imagination in those stories. A good news man back in those days could take a couple of facts and make a full-column story out of it. That was the art of writing and expanding ...There

254

really wasn't much big news....A lot of those
stories were expanded."

> --John Paul Jones, 1920s *Gainesville Daily
> Sun* employee, later City Editor of the
> *Palatka (Fla.) Daily News* and manager of
> the Florida Press Association, interviewed
> 1994

A history of the Associated Press recalled that before the Civil War
this technique of imagination—"to 'blow up' the story into several
hundred words with whatever 'details' came to mind"—was so prevalent
that when reformers sought to replace it with fact-based reporting there
were misgivings. It was feared that "editors did not know the difference
between real and imaginary news."[297]

The evidence on Rosewood, shedding light backstage behind the
image, reminds that such "blowing up" continued after the nineteenth
century. Nor was it confined to rural Florida. "Getting out the *Paris
Tribune* each day, I soon found, was primarily a work of the
imagination," wrote William Shirer of a 1920s publication in Europe run
by the *Chicago Tribune*. Shirer called the technique "expansion."[298]

It wasn't exactly lying—if you added only bland, neutral details—in
the way that a high school essay might use desperate expansion to fill up
space: "His name was George Washington. And he had a nose. And it
was big. And he had two eyes."

But if "the art of writing and expanding" were to become harnessed
to the passions of racial projection, it might not be so hard to spy "25
Negroes, heavily armed."

On January 13, 1923, the *Gainesville Daily Sun* would expose this
process in its retraction editorial: "WE WERE MISINFORMED."
Apparently by then Sheriff Bob Walker was so incensed by illusions
coming out of the *Sun* in next-door Alachua County that he forced it to
recant—at least on some points. The wire-service bulletins had defended
the whites at Sarah Carrier's house as being there justifiably—even
nobly—because someone had supposedly told them that the Monday
fugitive could be caught on the premises. Even if such a tip had been
heard it would have been no excuse for nightriding—but in fact (as the
Sun was forced to confess) there was no such tip. The January 13

correction admitted: "No one believed that the negro wanted for the crime was in the house."

This also hinted at an answer to a question. What were Poly Wilkerson and Henry Andrews planning to do as they drove toward Rosewood that night?

Answer: maybe there was no plan: *It's a beautiful night, we're drinking, let's go to Sylvester Carrier's house—and see what happens.*

That mysterious flash of lamplight winking for a moment inside the house. Wait! Now it's gone! What was it? What did it mean? What's behind those dark old planks?

Whether or not a mysterious meeting had occurred in the daylight hours on Thursday between Sarah Carrier and Poly Wilkerson, now, at night, her house proceeds to ignore him, presenting a mute facade. He approaches the steps. Apparently Wilkerson manages to get up into the dark cavern of the porch. The front door is locked.

"Sarah!"

By whatever chain of causation, the disgraced lawman is left with this one big chance to prove he can solve the case after all. But the scene greets him with mortifying resistance—and some of this resistance is more active than the silent planks.

If only that damned little thing would shut up.

Do the furious little teeth actually make contact, finding juicy flesh? Or do they only threaten to?

Minnie hears Shant Tail down there, raising sand. Then suddenly it stops. In that split-second everything is in turmoil—because the end of the barking is simultaneous with that other sound, much greater, the one that immediately cues a disastrous symphony: BAM.

Apparently a pistol shot, apparently from Wilkerson.

The uprising image in the newspapers would chastely omit this piece of the action—along with many others—as if the dog had never existed, as if the peaceful white men were simply walking up to the door, bouquets of roses in hand, in all innocence, to ask a few harmless questions. Off-stage, some local whites were more forthright.

Ernest Parham: *"I know the dog was killed when they walked up."*

Fred Kirkland: *"One of 'em killed the dog in the yard."*

Jason McElveen: *"Poly Wilkerson shot a dog inside the yard."*

If Wilkerson's pistol was the gun that fired, he may also have whirled in the disoriented moment of recoil. A grim piece of evidence suggests this.

Caught off balance in the darkness of the porch—perhaps when bitten—the big man twists, immediately firing again, releasing a second shot almost at the same time, because a second source of aggression has reached his confused mind—in the form of a wall-muffled but shouting voice.

Was this how it went?

Facing the porch is the window to the front downstairs bedroom. The shade is drawn. The room behind it is dark. Two occupants are in the room, Sarah Carrier and her daughter Bernadina, both in bed, facing the window. Certainly not sleeping now, but terrified, immobilized.

The grim piece of evidence is formed by the mysterious accuracy of the second shot. Through a drawn shade the shooter could not have seen into the room, even had it been lit—and yet the aim is uncanny. Of course, it could have been a miraculous accident. But more likely the shooter was very near, just outside the window on the porch. And even in that proximity, the bullet still had to cross the darkened room.

It seemed to be aimed toward the sound of a voice.

Did she cry out? Did she shout almost against her will in the fear and indignation—at the sudden realization of the loss of her beloved pet? In the painful years to come there would be too many burdens for such small questions. Few comparisons would be drawn to another time years before, and the stories about the scream in church.

It is now the last gate at the last path to the last washday. The flower planters on the porch await the night's coming frost. The years of shoulder and forearm bearing down, forcing out the grime, the shuffling, mumbling disguise. The accumulated years of abrasion—washboard banging over and over against the bottom of the tub in the scrubbing, strongly enough to wear it thin. The exhausted tubs watching on the porch.

It was a direct head shot, incredibly precise under the circumstances, as if following something. Perhaps the voice. Only one person was then left in the bed to feel the terror, the warmth soaking across into the gown worn by trembling Bernadina.

Gone now, the shadow at the wash pot that could not have existed at the piano. Gone is the light at the piano that could not have shuffled at the wash pot. Gone the mysterious tension in between.

Gone is Sarah Carrier.

There could be no pause to mourn. Even in a minor tavern brawl the throwing of one punch can cause a blizzard of flawed observations—and this was no tavern brawl. Spilling into the moonlight now is an ant heap of interacting movements, a spaghetti bowl of near-simultaneous reactions, all these participants acting at once, mocking the very notion of cause and effect—and especially, mocking the notion of linear narrative, the satisfying illusion that A-then-B-then-C equals the story of what went on.

Poly has disappeared into the shadows of the porch. *What is he doing in there?* The men in the yard aren't too drunk to be nervous. Perhaps keenly thrilled, or perhaps grasping the possibility of danger— perhaps lusting for it, longing for a little resistance to spark a fight. Or perhaps they are already glancing about anxiously for possible cover. But mostly: every fiber of auditory nerve listening, tensed for the cue, preparing to react instantly to that one kind of sound, the one that can kill.

BAM!

AND IT HAS COME! *AMBUSH! SNIPERS!*

When Poly went up onto the porch he was probably not so clairvoyant as to explain to them beforehand: "Now listen here, I'm about to shoot the little ole dog, so don't get all excited."

BAM! Then suddenly again. BAM! The neurological tripwires snap—and not just among the men in the yard.

The two worlds, black and white, are meeting now at the exquisitely thin divide, separated by a plank wall. Outside, white moonlight is rapidly filling with cold illusions. Inside, the crowd under siege is in dark mystery, invisible in there, their physical contours unguessable from without.

But then comes the break. A flash of action appears at a window.

Movement! Look, the sniper! Perhaps the sequence was more subtle than this—and perhaps the response was more callous than just a reflex action. The gun might have raised not in a nervous flinch but a gleeful burst of sadistic target practice.

But at the center now is the one figure upstairs who is oblivious to it all, able to sleep through anything. Or almost anything. The sound of the car was barely a nuisance, something for busybodies to get upset about, bound to work itself out if just left alone. Even the shoving and pushing of the latecomers as they piled into the bed—hardly worth waking up for.

BAM!

Thirteen-year-old Ruben Mitchell apparently never consciously decided to sit bolt upright in bed—because he was not awake. As the world exploded he jerked up and sat blankly, unable to orient, directly in front of the window, staring down dreamily into the yard.

THERE! IN THE WINDOW! A SNIPER SURE ENOUGH!

The shot is not from a pistol this time. Apparently three shotgun pellets find him, two tunneling under the arm, which apparently is upraised in sleepwalking awkwardness, as if to say, *Stop! Stop!* The other pellet reaching the face, burrowing along the line of the jaw.

But they are not big double-ought pellets. That would have torn deer meat to pieces. These are just enough to bring a deer down. And the pellets themselves are not the worst of it. They had to get through the window. Astonished, still in the dream, he faces obliviously into the shattering glass. With Harry, Sarah's youngest son, Minnie crawls desperately to him, trying to pull the frozen figure away from the window and to the floor. Somebody finds a towel, soaking up the blood. Despite three gunshot wounds, Ruben Mitchell is not hit fatally. Showered by flying window glass, he has lost an eye.

In later years, meeting the inevitable questions about the eye, there would be the deadpan expression, the blank suppression of any mischievous grin—as in the days of the backyard orange crate and the fires of hell. Perhaps at first humbly refusing to talk about it at all, saying the memory is too painful—but then, perhaps, allowing himself to be persuaded, revving up to reveal the awful majesty, the raging fires of Armageddon, the story that keeps even his white bosses spellbound: how Ruben Mitchell's entire family was mercilessly killed, the bodies piled in a ghastly heap, massacred to the last child, with him helpless on the bottom, left for dead.

And that, says the solemn teller, was what happened to the eye.

Apparently a mere shotgun blast could not kill something in Ruben Mitchell.

The phrase "contagious shooting" (or "target panic") gained prominence in 1999, when a hail of bullets in New York took the life of Amadou Diallo, an immigrant from West Africa. Though unarmed, Diallo was killed in a dark alley by four New York police officers who fired a total of 41 rounds in his direction, reportedly in the space of no more than four seconds. The seeming viciousness of the overkill caused large street protests, though the shooters sought desperately to explain. The police said they had faced a split-second decision when a suspicious figure began reaching for his pocket.[299]

The word "panic" in "target panic" can be misleading. Such a shooting results from a decision, but in a hair's breadth of time, preventing analysis. Accumulated assumptions—and fears—can substitute as criteria for the decision. Apparently, on that night in 1999, when one officer fired the others had to decide instantly whether he had good reason for firing, a reason that perhaps they weren't in a position to see—as they entered a growing—but amazingly brief—frenzy.

Minnie, listening in the dark, in bed, hears the explosion that ends the barking of the dog, but not as a chain of two shots—because it is *larger* than that. It sounds like many guns at once, not just one, a roaring wall of sound. The other two witnesses from the attic seemed to have similar impressions.

Additional evidence also pointed to a generalized burst of shooting. A neighboring household reported a piercing shriek, thinking a child might have been hit. But in the rear room of Sarah Carrier's house, invisible to the children upstairs, an adult witness was on hand who would recall being the source of the shriek.

Whites in the yard watch a pale, ghostly figure leap from the rear of the house and dash toward the woods. Gert Carrier is in her nightgown. She will later tell family and friends that her husband Sylvester instructed her to run and save herself.[300] In order for Sylvester to move forward into the main house for defense he must cross an exposed area, the short breezeway. A shrieking escapee leaping into the moonlight could serve, however accidentally, as distracting cover.

Gert would describe to others how she shouted over her shoulder to the whites as she ran, begging them not to shoot her. She reported hearing shots, aimed either over her head or at her, or perhaps fired at the house by shooters unaware of her. She sought the safety of nearby thickets with such force that when she reached other witnesses she was cut and bleeding. Rumors said she had a flesh wound from gunfire, but the actual witnesses said not.

The roll call inside the house has now changed: one escaped, one wounded, and one forever gone. The living occupants of the building now number between 13 and 15.

Apparently the oldest individual in the attic is Eddie Carrier, age 17, the third oldest son of James and Emma Carrier, making him Minnie's uncle. At the beginning of the generalized volley, as Ruben was bleeding on the floor and Minnie and Harry were trying to help, Eddie took other action. Heedless of his own safety, he apparently stripped a mattress from a bed and flung it over the smaller children, trying to shield them from bullets.

But now silence. The gunfire has stopped. The children in the attic don't dare move. Gert is gone. Sylvester has apparently reached the main house, though no one upstairs knows that. The lone voice, the one outside in the yard, now begins again.

"Sarah!"

Wilkerson is seeking some kind of response. Tales among whites will proudly feature this as white gallantry, a gentleman's call for women and children to come out and receive safe passage through the ranks of the noble white warriors. Such pretension was not unknown in nightriding events, the attackers viewing themselves as knightly heroes, solicitous of the weak. Of course, these particular Sir Galahads had already shot a dog—and did far worse, as the front bedroom attested— but if logical consistency had been their specialty they would not have been there in the first place. Everyone agreed that Poly—or someone—

did call to Sarah, seeming not to grasp the chilling irony, that he was calling to the dead.

From the tangled heap of puzzle pieces another detail emerges, seeming to confirm that Sarah Carrier was deceased by this point. In the silence of the lull in the shooting, Minnie finds herself near the door to the landing at the top of the stairs. A tall, pale specter appears. Bernadina is still in the bloody nightgown from the bed downstairs. She has crept up the stairs to the attic. Either the terror downstairs has sent her to look for companionship or, like Eddy, she is thinking first about protecting the children.

Standing at the attic door, Bernadina is sobbing. Minnie hears her but has edged to the door for another reason. In memory the conversation sounds like code.

Bernadina sobs: *"Mama dead."*

Minnie replies: *"Where Mama?"*

Minnie's anxiety is not eased by the sight of Bernadina's nightgown, with its dark stain. On a larger journey through this night there will be no chance to change clothes, and other witnesses, too, will see Bernadina in the bloodstained gown. Some whites will later insist that mean old Sarah Carrier (suddenly demoted from the status of trusty servant) was killed only because she was loading the gun for devilish Sylvester. The actual witnesses present a story with many weaknesses, but not here. It is almost certain that Sarah Carrier was killed by sudden ambush at the outset, not in any kind of equal combat. One more embarrassment arises for white fantasies about a big Negro uprising and white heroes in a car.

Minnie moves past Bernadina to the top of the stairs. The greater concern fills her mind. *Where is Mama?* Where is her grandmother Emma Carrier?

None of the other children in the attic would have dreamed of going down the stairs at that moment, into the guns of the attackers. But, they later agreed, a lone exception did do just that—an obsessed little protector, unmoved by anything a later age might say about separation anxiety disorder or its parent-like role-reversals.

Throughout the chaotic tapestry of this night, driven individuals would answer improbable calls from deep within their private worlds—which then would cause chaotic effects in the public world.

"I had to get to Mama...I figure me and Mama go down together."

Still barefoot, she would not remember the stairs being cold. Nearing the bottom step, she knew that just to her right, through the downstairs bedroom door, was a horror not to be contemplated, as shown by Bernadina's gown.

And yet that same bedroom would be the logical place to look for the one adult female still crouching in the darkness. *Where is Mama?* Momentum took Minnie from the bottom step toward the worst possible destination, the front door—the thinnest spot in the wall between worlds.

She could not know that just beyond her nose—only inches away, but in the other world outside—two white men on the porch were peering in bad light, scrutinizing the latch, sizing up the hinges—opting now for Plan B. They had given up on chivalrous shouting, readying now to try something more direct. Facing impossibilities, Minnie froze.

And again the world exploded.

She is thrown off her feet, finding herself flying backward down the hall, quickly coming to rest in a confused heap of arms and legs at a new location, wedged into a lightless opening.

The small firewood closet cut into the side of the stairs is like a doll house for dwarves—and now a crowded doll house. In it entrance, she finds, the arms and legs are not all hers. She has flown backward into the firewood closet because she was yanked.

She is pressing against him, squeezed with him into the mouth of the cubbyhole. If a perfect sniper's post had been devised for a marksman covering the front door, offering least exposure of the marksman, it might have been designed like this. The firewood closet faces the hall and the hall runs toward the front door—so that a gun braced on the closet frame means that practically all of the shooter's body can be sheltered back in the closet, behind the bulk of the stairs. To her dying day, more than seventy years later in a joltingly different world, Minnie Lee Langley will remember the words breathed into her ear as the hand came out of the darkness to drag her back, when the world was about to explode. He said:

"Come here and let me save you."

In the moment of the combat soldier—when the world becomes luminous symbol and things seem suddenly to shimmer with dreamy coincidence—the problem is not that you're dreaming but instead the deeper mystery—when the rush of real, material events *becomes* a flood of symbol, when *something else* appears—with people saying later it was just adrenaline.

She doesn't have to be told whose hand it was that grabbed her, as he now crouches with her in the opening.

She is on her knees by the closet frame, facing directly toward the front door. And immediately the world again explodes—only this time in a crash of latch and hinge, as the front door is broken down.

For an instant she sees the large man fully etched on the moonlit space where he has broken through, stumbling forward in his momentum, lunging, reeling. And she does not think in the darkness that there is no way the moonlight could have gotten in here to illuminate him like this, or that now it is something else that is lighting him up, every mole and freckle, bright as day. She feels the trigger-guard pump, slamming furiously against her shoulder, and will remember no sound.

Chapter 24: The First Battle

Winchester Model 1887 Repeating Shotgun
Weight: 8 pounds
Length: 39 inches
Fire Mode: Lever Action
Capacity: 6 shots without reload

On Thursday night, Sylvester Carrier would engage in at least two and possibly three running firefights. This was to trigger the week's most intensive phase, that of riot. There would then be symbolic murder of bystander targets and forced de-population, subjecting a community to racial cleansing.

This second trigger on Thursday night (Fannie Taylor's alarm on Monday being the first) came at the point where violent pressures at last brought violent resistance, in this case clearly in self-defense.

The first segment of the Rosewood events, January 1-4, remained at the level of selective targeting, with some familiar components: manhunt, torture-interrogation and extra-legal execution (the latter not exactly a ritual lynching). In that earlier phase, a chief assumption was that white aggressors, viewing themselves as valuable defenders of public order, need have little worry about any harm to themselves.

But if that expectation were to be violated—if violent resistance were to injure any of them—their grandiose picture of themselves was primed to feel doubly outraged at the affront.

On Thursday night, the banished constable Poly Wilkerson and the controversial logging boss Henry Andrews would take the events across this threshold. Their acts—and injuries—would unleash a rush by others, escalating into the second phase.

This idea of a second phase in lynching violence is often obscured in stereotyped images of the era. Focus has been on the first or selective phase: the lone target in the noose on the tree, the grim circle of vigilantes. Everyone knows that picture. And indeed the second phase, worsening the violence into a communal pogrom, was more of a rarity. But its menace remained, deeply evident to southerners who were black.

In a way, the cliché picture that admits only the lone noose forms a subtle slander against African Americans who avoided challenging lynch mobs. The cliché hides the size of the thing they were avoiding—not just lynching, with its narrowly selected targets, but generalized racial rampage, which tossed aside fig-leaf claims to civilized behavior and targeted anyone who came along—if they happened to be black (or sometimes if they were whites viewed as helping blacks).[301]

The second phase at Rosewood would never quite swell into the perfect storm, or genuinely deserve the word used in killing fields worldwide: "massacre." The term "massacre" implies a mowing-down of multiple targets at a stroke. This never came to Rosewood.[302] Its second-phase eruption would be tentative and fitful, producing a short chain of isolated shootings, as overwhelming numbers happened onto targets of opportunity. This, too, traced out a classic form, though one less epic than massacre.

These second-phase bursts at Rosewood looked much like the ordinary mob cowardice seen in many riots. In Rosewood's riot phase such cowardice, preening itself as being great courage, would repeatedly find victims who were over the age of fifty, and who were simply too slow to get away.[303] The mob fury was hesitant and incomplete. It only probed toward the grandiose vision embodied in the ageless phrase "Kill them all."

At the turning point into this shift, naturally it would be preferable to consult many witnesses, thus to offset the observational flaws in any one. But mass violence seldom considers the convenience of the investigator. In the heart of Rosewood's turning point—in the roar itself— there would be only one surviving pair of eyes to capture impressions, the overburdened eyes of a child. As often happens with real people in real violence, what Minnie Lee Mitchell saw would not be well suited to narrative clichés.

So for the moment, as we approach the blinding flash, it might be best to drop back a bit—deep into the outfield. Another pair of eyes exists there, capturing a broader background—eyes accustomed to gauging the tricky hops of grounders, and the soaring arcs of fly balls.

Lee Carrier, outfielder on the Rosewood baseball team, would always remember a hallmark moment long before 1923, framed by dark pines in the turpentine woods. It was a baseball story only in the larger sense, plumbing the mysteries of eye-hand coordination.

The date blurred in recollection, but it was in the transition times when things were hard. Loggers and sawmill hands like Lee Carrier looked down on dipping and chipping in pine groves for turpentine operations, doing the sticky, bottom-tier work of harvesting resin. From the time he was ten, Lee had done sawmilling when he could. Even as a child he had stood at a chute and caught small blocks of cedar at the old Charpia mill.

But now, in the changed time of this recollection, the cedar mill is gone. The year is somewhere between about 1912 and 1918—no more specific than that. By whatever route of desperation or routine, the Rosewood boys are now out there somewhere, working the turpentine pines, in a group of varied ages. Lee was born in 1900. His cousin Sylvester is a decade older. Syl also is there.

The pine forest has the look of a park, its ground clean and open between scaly trunks, not tangled with under-growth. This is the way of great woods, and especially jungles like the Great Gulf Hammock, just south of the pine groves in question. In mature forest, thick overhead canopy can

Turpentine forest, this one in Mississippi, 1930s
(photo: "Old New Orleans" http://www.thepastwhispers.com)

screen out sunlight and reduce bushy ground plants. But in a turpentine grove there was artificial help. Each spring, as resin in the pines grew more fluid and signaled another work season, access to the trees would be cleared for chippers and dippers by intentional burning. Torches were applied to bushes and briars, a process that explained why in winter children were hired to rake pine straw. This flammable material was removed from around the trunks of valuable trees, giving the flames of springtime less chance to consume the trees with the bushes.

Lee and his companions are now surrounded by the result. They can look away off into a shadow-world of strobing tree trunks—where tricks of distant vision will shape this tale.

Suddenly one of them freezes. It's Syl. Peering into distant half-light, Sylvester focuses on something no one else has seen. The memory is enlivened by no cameo details, no recollection of Sylvester's appearance at this moment—or whether a faint, mischievous smile might have appeared.

As he hisses to them:

"Who got a gun?"

It was a natural assumption. Even in a small turpentine crew, at least one member was likely to be carrying some kind of pistol. The woods were lonely—and not just in the Robert Frost sense. Long swamps intervened against outside help, should there be a quarrel, or perhaps an enemy in ambush. Some men liked to carry protection. This world was not the unarmed black South envisioned by stereotypes of Delta plantation sharecroppers—and indeed the stereotype was invalid even there.[304]

Now, by speaking only four words, Sylvester has brought the group to gather around him, claiming leadership once again. On the one hand, he has directed their attention to a distant spot among the trees, barely visible from where they stand. And on the other, somebody does fish down into an overalls bib or pants pocket, and then passes the gleaming object to Syl. It is the predictable kind of gun, a little .32, mostly good for making noise.

Syl says: *"See that rabbit?"*

On hearing this, the group ripples with amusement—not because they can't see the tiny speck, once it's been pointed out, but because of the implied boast. The speck can be made out because it moves now and then, slowly grazing from point to point, like an optical mote quivering on the field of vision. They are laughing because Syl has made his intention clear. He means to shoot that mote, at that distance, using this wobbly little gun.

 In this tale, unlike those that tell of his teamster prowess or baseball skill, he does not make the trademark crowing boast. He never exults, *KA-KA-KA! Ya'll ain't no shooter!* This tale (like its teller) is quiet, focused in huntsman's reverie.

Saying nothing more, Sylvester now pours his being into aiming mode. He seems deaf to the chuckling of the companions, as if the only two inhabitants of the entire lonely universe are himself and that distant dot—all other illusions in the great game melting away, narrowing down to the one completely imaginary line: target to eye.

CRACK!

And they laugh some more. Naturally, the wary little dot in the distance is only startled by the noise. It runs off, so nonchalantly that it doesn't even bother to run very far. At a place still within sight among the pines it settles down to amble and browse again, as if thumbing its nose at the impotent figures far away, not even afraid. No surprise here. There are trick shots that just aren't possible, no matter how confident you are.

But the world of focus that Syl has composed—just him and the dot—is not relinquished even now—as if the chuckling companions still don't exist. Even in defeat, he addresses his closing remark not to them, but to the only thing existing in this focused world, the object of desire. In that flippant way of his, as if confidence alone could bridge the gap— as if it could undo time and space, overrule a thing already over and done—he breathes:

"You may run, but you hit."

This makes an even better joke, and they laugh still more—until the distant dot seems to grow uncertain in its grazing, and then falls still.

When people talked about the best shot in the community, they usually didn't mean his skill with a back-pocket pea-shooter. At home at his mother's house, Sylvester Carrier kept a commercial hunter's collection of tools, including the gun of local legend, recalled in countless tales.

The actual gun said to have been used by Sylvester Carrier on January 4, 1923, apparently photographed January 7.

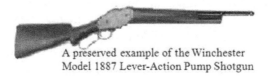

A preserved example of the Winchester
Model 1887 Lever-Action Pump Shotgun

By the whims of fate—and the caprices of crowd control—his Winchester .12 -gauge pump shotgun would be one of the very few objects from the Rosewood violence whose image crept into a photo, its authenticity persuasively verified.[305]

The circumstances of the photograph belong to a later chapter, in the way that an earlier one has already shown cousin Lee Carrier borrowing the gun to shoot quail.

Lee could describe the .12-gauge pump with his own kind of persuasiveness. When asked about second-hand stories claiming that the owner's name— "*Sylvester*"—was carved dramatically onto the stock, Lee grew puzzled, ransacking his memory. At last, trying to be helpful, he said that maybe, if all those people knew the signature was on there, it must have been hidden on the stock somehow—since he personally had never seen any sign of such a thing. This kind of frankness is not the mark of a confabulating witness.

A .12-gauge pump shotgun is crucially different from the break-back, double-barreled variety that many people associate with the word "shotgun." Double-barrel shotguns were already becoming outmoded as far back as 1887, when John Browning invented the Winchester lever-action pump.[306] The resulting pump shotgun was a single-barrel affair, but with a devastating stream of fire. Six shells could be fired in succession, no pause to reload. You had only to keep flip-cocking the lever that was built

into the trigger-guard, like *The Rifleman* of vintage TV—though as the TV title pointed out, Chuck Connors's fancy gun was a rifle, shooting only a single bullet at each pull.[307] The 1887 introduction of lever technology into the shotgun—a gun that could send many pellets at once—produced a repeating cannon.

And even that was a passing phase. Browning would refine a more logical kind of pump, a slide, hugging the shotgun's barrel and traveling along it. Premiering in 1893, slide-pump shotguns soon swept aside the initial lever guns, which had become back items by about 1901. A Levy County story said that Sylvester Carrier's lever gun was a relic from his days as a hunting guide, allegedly one of the gifts bestowed in Rosewood by wealthy visiting sportsmen. In this case, however, the donor was local, according to the tale. He was said to be: County Commissioner W. R. Hodges of Cedar Key.[308] Whatever the truth, there was the general fact that long before 1923 hunters who could afford the investment were moving up to the new slides—while the old lever guns had lost none of their basic power. One of them might have been handed down.

Pry and shoot, pry and shoot. As the pump of such a gun snaps one shell after another into the chamber, the wide scatter pattern clears a path.

As the moon rose on January 4, 1923, the Beer Wars in Chicago were also rising, to festoon the Roaring Twenties with images of gangsters blasting away while hanging onto running boards and careening in speeding cars. Those warriors were said to prefer pump shotguns to the famous tommy gun. The Thompson submachine gun was quick but not as all-encompassing. It was not the door-maker, the wall-buster, the crowd-cleaver. Whether held by Eliot Ness or James Bond, the pumpgun had many names.

In World War I, the military model of the .12-gauge pump was the "trench gun."[309] You leaped into an enemy trench and walked forward, cleaning it out—with such

The Trench Gun
World War I military model
of the .12-gauge pump shotgun

force that the government of Germany seemed to feel it was worse than poison gas, lodging a formal protest against the .12-gauge pump as a violation of the rules of war. Police of the era gave it another name: the "riot gun." At night the man—or crowd—meeting this weapon might have only a blink of time to marvel at the full effect, being not only hit but blinded, as the muzzle flash lit up the world.[310]

She was absolutely certain. It was a repeating rifle, and not a shotgun. She had grown up in a woodsman's home, knew Papa's guns. Everybody knew how a rifle cocked and fired, levering in the shells with the prying action of the trigger guard. A repeating rifle was not at all like Papa's double-barreled shotgun.

She would become indignant, sixty years later, if someone should suggest that the gun she knew in that blinding moment had been a shotgun, and not a rifle. It was as if they were saying she was not really there, not really a witness, that she didn't feel the lever action beating against her shoulder. Her memory was such a vulnerable possession, hers alone to defend, supported by no one else, certified by no document at the courthouse. The world could try to talk the matter to death if it chose. She didn't care. She was adamant, not budging an inch, scoffing sarcastically: How could it have been a shotgun? Why would a shotgun shoot like a rifle? She knew what she felt striking her shoulder that night. She didn't claim to have seen it, didn't have to have seen it. Because it was beating against her.

In her insistence—as if still alone back there in the dark—Minnie Lee Langley stamped credibility even onto the mistake.

No deafening sound in her ears, no cold on her bare feet. The familiar tricksters of perceptual narrowing came with the combat stress. A nine-year-old girl with ear-splitting thunder inches away from her head, and before her face the sudden lightning flash on the astonished target, the very moment of death—this formed a fragile lens. She had not been positioned to see the preparations, the big man out there on the porch, gathering his weight to swing into either a latch-busting rush or a door-stomping kick—hovering, hovering out there, all that lifetime in his tottering form—his cars, his family with their frontier names, the debts in the storekeeper's ledger, badge, jook—tilting exquisitely onto the one foot, off balance for the big moment now, then hurling himself into the black mysteries on the other side, betting the pile.

Again the parallels, but this one like a ghost.

On August 18, 1916, the red-faced district constable at Sumner, Florida, Precinct 9, could not have failed to hear that gore and glory had come to another district constable only forty miles to the north, in the precinct of Newberry.[311] The events of 1916 were to climax in a multiple lynching, but at first there was only the one death, which would trigger the others—the death of a white constable, killed by a black man. Hearing about it forty miles away, Constable Poly Wilkerson might have felt the pull to go up there himself, as hundreds of others were doing. A moonshadow beckoned even in the names: the martyred constable at Newberry was not named Wilkerson, but close. His name was Wynne.

The issue of traumatic emulation, or copycatting, leads into some of the deep shadows of criminal affairs. It asks whether a riveting, vividly envisioned event can become a kind of dramatist's script, lying dormant in the mind but sharpening with emotional pressure, until at last, at some breakpoint of anxiety or pain, the script bursts to the surface—perhaps not entirely as a plan, but as dim choreography—moving from the level of daydream into material act, as the mental script is played out.[312]

In 1916 the woods around Newberry had grown tense. There was talk about a rash of livestock thefts, striking at free-roaming hogs. This was an old problem, going far beyond racial issues (in the 1930s when Newberry saw one white lawman kill another, it was apparently over stolen hogs).[313] However, in 1916 race had become the focus.

George Wynne
Constable, District 6,
Alachua County, Florida.
killed Aug. 17, 1916

An isolated community of African Americans was said to be sheltering a theft ring, at a spot called Jonesville, six miles from Newberry. A prime suspect was identified, but managed to slip away to Jacksonville, eighty miles northeast, then was somehow picked up by city police there. This meant a call for Newberry's constable, George Wynne, to go to the city and bring the prisoner back by train, more or less a full day's round trip.

The ride home gave time for undisclosed methods of interrogation, which proved successful (at least according to the only published version of the story).[314] It was said that by the time constable and prisoner stepped out onto a depot platform, the prisoner had fingered an accomplice. But by then it was late at night. The prisoner was handed over to a sleepy county jailer. The train had arrived in Gainesville, the home of the *Gainesville Daily Sun*. By way of the Atlantic Coast Line from Jacksonville, Gainesville was as close as Constable Wynne could get to his home base in Newberry.

With his prisoner delivered, Wynne found himself pondering his important new lead, the revelation obtained on the train. But he was now in a sleeping town in the middle of the night, still some 18 miles from home. Then came a break. By whatever means—pre-arrangement or accident—two residents of Newberry popped up at that hour, in a position to help out.

The two were coming from a deer hunt, in a car.

The details form a strange foreshadowing of 1923. One of the deer hunters was a leading citizen—not a logging superintendent in this case but a Newberry pharmacist, Lem Harris (the coincidence grows stranger, for he was called "Dr. Harris" in Newberry, while, six years later, some whites referred to woods boss Henry Andrews as "Doc").

As in the deer hunt alleged to Andrews in 1923, it was not unusual for such trips to close with a little alcohol,[315] but there would be only one record of the 1916 hunt, an article in the *Gainesville Daily Sun,* painting a picture that was saintly, no alcohol mentioned. For all anyone could say in a later age, that word-picture might have been scrupulously accurate— or it could have been more like the *Sun's* later coverage of Rosewood.

In the 1916 events, a moonlit ride to disaster would result, and the *Sun* would portray it as a sober, serious law enforcement mission. Quite possibly it was. But six years later Constable Poly Wilkerson's ride of 1923 would be portrayed in much the same terms by the same news outlet, and in that case the newspaper would be forced to admit its mirage ("We Were Misinformed" on January 13, 1923).

On an August night in 1916 the car, now carrying two deer hunters and Constable Wynne, moved from Gainesville toward Newberry on a pale rock road framed by hanging moss. The moon was full—or it looked full, though technically it was two nights past—just as the moon would be on Thursday night, January 4, 1923. Even the day of the week struck an eerie chord. This was Thursday night, August 17-18, 1916.

As they drove, it was later said, an idea took shape. Their route passed a turn-out to a wooded lane leading into the isolated community of Jonesville. The newly revealed accomplice, the alleged hog thief fingered by the prisoner on the train, was a resident of Jonesville. So why not make a short detour? Why not go and arrest him right now, no matter how late the hour, so he won't have a chance to run?

In the *Daily Sun's* 1916 report this background had to be part of the package, because otherwise the story raised a difficulty. Why, in the middle of the night, at a secluded woodland settlement of African Americans known for hunting and guns, would some white men suddenly arrive in a car?[316]

Constable Wynne and his two helpers located the moonlit home of the suspect, though after parking in the weeds they still had to climb a couple of fences to get to the doorstep—just two of the visitors now on this final foray, going on foot to the house: the constable and the "doctor" (the pharmacist). The third man stays with the car. The suspect in the house is named Boise Long, later to receive a desperado's description: "mean disposition...dark, bumpy skin, round face and stubby moustache."[317]

The darkened house in Jonesville looms up. No sound. Dr. Harris goes around and covers the back door. He is only barely able to hear snatches of Wynne hailing in front, through the latched front door: *"Boise, is that you?"*

Then shots. Harris dashes back around. He finds the front door open. Constable Wynne is inside, lying on the floor. Standing over him is the suspect Boise Long, holding a gun. Harris holds out his hands desperately in an effort at defense, but Long shoots him, too. The third man out at the car, G. H. Blount, hears the shots. Rushing to investigate, he now finds both Wynne and Harris on the floor, bleeding badly, but still alive. Boise Long, the shooter, has fled—somehow having been wounded as well. Wynne is said to have gotten off a shot as he fell—which would mean Long was already wounded when he succeeded in shooting Harris.

The two injured whites are somehow dragged back across the two fences by Blount. Dr. Harris's wounds are severe, but not fatal. Wynne has guessed his own fate. He was hit in a vital organ, the liver. He gasps to Blount in the moment of discovery: "I am shot. Help me to save Harris. I am going to die."

The valor in those words, relayed by newspaper coverage, could not have failed to strike deeply at a district constable living just forty miles to the south. By Friday morning, August 18, 1916, crowds of whites were searching for the vanished Boise Long, seeking revenge. Soon killed were six of Long's relatives and neighbors in Jonesville, five hanged together, including two women. The site would retain the name Lynch Hammock. Boise Long was caught on the other side of the county, arrested, convicted of murdering the constable and also was hanged. Confirmed incident death toll: eight.

For Poly Wilkerson forty miles away, no newspaper eulogy would have been needed to capture the similarity. The man on that floor might almost have been Constable Wilkerson himself, but for the grace of God. There was even the same triple star. Wynne, like Wilkerson, was both a constable and a deputy sheriff at once, while also serving as Newberry's town marshal, conferring a third badge. Wynne's newspaper obituary was a bugle call: "One of the most alert officers...a terror to evil-doers...."

At the opening of the twentieth century an unknown number of African American settlements stood in the Florida woods, holdovers from Civil War Reconstruction and the dying frontier, as they met the pressures of codified racial segregation after about 1900. During August 19-21, 1916, as a result of the Wynne-Harris shooting, the settlement of Jonesville would meet a mass attack, in a type of incident whose numbers were never systematically counted. The term "ethnic cleansing" was unknown in 1916, apparently not used in the United States until the 1990s in news reports from far away, in disintegrating Yugoslavia. As the Internet age brought growing awareness of bygone rampages in the American lynching era, it was argued that Yugoslavia's term was a poor fit, since it implied government power behind the cleansings. "Racial cleansing," rather than "ethnic cleansing," was suggested as a better label for the American variety of mob de-population.

In the moonlight on Thursday night, January 4, 1923, a few men in a car at Rosewood would not likely have been planning to destroy an entire community. They certainly were not planning to sacrifice themselves to get the ball rolling. But their joyride would have that effect—when it blew up in their faces. This would call out crowds of other men through Friday, Saturday and Sunday—as if to finish a half-dreamed work of art, begun by the few pioneers in the Thursday night car. The riot phase would stop short of the most grandiose extermination fantasy—the one embodied in *"Kill them all!"*—but a throng of cleansers would still demand to keep it up until they were rewarded with closure of a sort, enabling them to live out a slightly less ambitious fantasy, with its own motto: *"Clean them all out!"*

Constable Poly Wilkerson's script was shorter. Already in the opening scene he seemed to totter on a cliff—if stories about debts from secret gambling at the jook were true. He still had one automobile on the 1922 tax rolls, but the faucets of bootleg revenue had been turned off, his children's upturned faces now haunting him, no hope to give them. Under such pressures, was there conscious emulation of Wynne in 1916?

Or was it something deeper, in some mental cavern measureless to man? If an individual were to be in an impossible position, would it be so impossible for him to follow, knowingly or not, a faint treasure map stamped into memory six years in the past?

Not the temptation to *be* Wynne. But to be *better* than Wynne. To play the same blind hand Wynne had been dealt, but more triumphantly—to bravely barge into the same kind of moonlit puzzle trap, on the same kind of darky's porch, at the same kind of house—*and beat the house.*

To gamble big. And win.

———————————

Remembering no sound, seeming to feel no strangeness in describing a large firearm exploding so near her head that a grown man in such proximity would have wished for earplugs—she made no effort to excuse the logic. Because she didn't care. Didn't care if you didn't believe her, wasn't going to say things you expected to hear, just to make you believe her. Wasn't going to agree cagily that it might be a shotgun and not a rifle just so she could sound convincing. Because she knew.

She couldn't say much about how the man fell, apparently not considering that her only illumination in the darkness would have been the muzzle flash. Some whites later said Wilkerson was found slumped in a corner just inside the door. Some liked to clean it up and say he fell back onto the porch, dying not by a black man's shotgun but by breaking his neck. However the consensus said, as with Sam Carter on Monday, that the shot was in the face.

Robert Missouri at the shingle mill saw the wagon go by the next day, carrying Poly's casket to Shiloh Cemetery. He was sorry for his friend Poly, who seemed a good sort. But Missouri was working that day (no surprise, since he was always working), and at the funeral he would have been of the wrong race. The Wilkerson family would lose the dry goods store as the debts came in, the widow forced to stack scrap wood at the mill. They, too, faced long, hard years of privation.[318]

D. P. Wilkerson

> Date of death: January 4, 1923
> Date of birth: "Not known"
> Cause of death: "shot by unknown part [sic]
> in Levy County riot."
> —*Death Certificate, File No. 774.*
> *Florida Bureau of Vital Statistics*

When last I looked, you could still go out through the gooseweed and blackjack to the old Shiloh Cemetery, in the scrub near the site of vanished Sumner—where new settlement continues to spring up, also using the name Sumner. At Shiloh some of the graves were still neatly marked and maintained. Others were disappearing in the sand. A rotted wooden stake had once been a cross, the arms having fallen away. Some homemade grave borders were marked out, touchingly economical, formed of large conch shells brought from the Gulf, or pulled from the ancient Indian shell mound at Number Four bridge out to Cedar Key. The shells were weathered and bleached white by the sun, like souvenir-stand mementos of sunny Florida lying in some flower bed up north. Maybe Poly's grave was one of those. Somebody probably knows, behind the screen of sawbriars and secrets. It would probably be worth it to find out. Why doesn't anybody find these things out?

From her kneeling position, facing the front door without time to move, it seems a continuous stream. The furious mechanical banging of the hand and the gun pump on her shoulder seem not to stop. Nor does the stream of men rushing into the door, as it quickly frames the next one. There is no need to break down the door now. This one falls on the porch.

Henry Martin Andrews
Time of death: 11:00 p.m.
Date of birth Aug 30, 1879
Cause of death: "Gunshot wounds, killed instantly"
—*Levy County Health Department, residual record*

In the *New York Times* of January 6, 1923, he was "Henry Andrews, superintendent of the Cummer Lumber Co., at Otter Creek"—while the same story elevated his comrade to mercantile stability, describing him as "C. P. Wilkinson, a merchant of Sumner." The dots and dashes of the telegraph key left only slight ambiguities to be misinterpreted in an unfamiliar name, which should have read "D. P. Wilkerson." Some other media seemed to misinterpret dih-DAH-DAH-dih, apparently thinking it must have been DAH-dih-dih-dih, for they called him "Boly."

The biographical phrases were references to Wilkerson's share in Tom Holt's dry goods store and Andrews's management of the logging quarters and crate mill at Otter Creek. The "merchant" line might also have been influenced by Sheriff Bob Walker shouting to a reporter on the phone: *He wasn't one of mine! Don't say he was a county deputy! He wasn't a deputy! No longer in the employ of the Levy County Sheriff's Department. Nossir. Not carrying our authority at all. If you have to say something, say he had a store.*

So, of the men who stepped onto the porch, here was Number Two.

And if you counted from Monday, here was Death Number Four.

Sam Carter, Sarah Carrier, Poly Wilkerson. And now Henry Andrews.

Each one a world.

Rushing onto the porch, the dark man who ruled great steam-driven palaces called log skidders, mechanisms that the complacent world using the lumber would never see. Descendant of Indian fighters, heir to

Minorcan slaves, knowing bloodshed's secret heart, where it becomes metaphysical—whether or not he ever actually lifted a bleeding scalp to fantastically blend all the weary racial emblems into one: the scalped black man being literally eaten by the dark white man.

And at the other end of the scale, knowing the messy way that real business has to get done, the reconciliation of board-feet quotas with broken legs and water-rotted feet and swift kicks. As of January 1, 1920, and National Prohibition under the Volstead Act, a nation was straining to confine the poison that could move such a man. But nobody doubted he still drank.

It was summed up by Robert Missouri, the smiling, triple-shift workaholic in Sumner, who was careful to say only good about everybody (and who spoke only good of his friend Poly), but who nonetheless drew the line when it came to mention of Andrews. Then, Missouri lost the smile: "He just didn't beat up colored. He'd beat up white, too."

Henry Martin Andrews
"Logging Supt.".
Date of death: January 4, 1923
Age at death: 44
Cause of death: "shot in Homicide killing instantly"
—Death Certificate, File No. 768
Florida Bureau of Vital Statistics

In the 1930s, novelist James Street said you could ride the train east from New Orleans clear across the Mississippi coast—in the direction of Florida—and see little besides wasteland, dotted with stumps and "a chain of dead towns"[319]—timber ghost towns—as if a great hurricane had razed the coastal woodland South, though this was a human wave, the storm surge of the steam log skidders. "There has never been a more short-sighted or destructive method of logging," wrote forestry expert James Fickle of the skidder boom that swept the South after about 1900—when the Cummers and other little-known giants were beginning to dismember Florida.[320] A newspaper echoed: "What trees they didn't cut were ripped and torn by the high-powered skidders"[321]—a wave moving so quickly and unstably, leaving so little culture, that no chronicles would arise, no romantic outrage or public romance of any kind, as the jungles gave way across the South: everybody needed the wood.

The great jungles would go as if they had never been, no history of the violent storm, no picture, no song, no Uncle Remus or Swanny Ribber, no King Cotton or Ole Cotton Fields Back Home—though perhaps the vaguest of wonderings, now and then, as to what might have stood in all that empty space.

And yet, even at that, the answer was in there, coiled inside the name, the lost world crammed into the grain of sand.

Rosewood.

"Two white men are dead...," the *Seattle Post-Intelligencer* is now telling its readers, on Friday, January 5, 1923, as it nods toward cryptic hysteria in very distant swampland. "Two white men are dead...," agrees the *New York World* (since all are using the same Associated Press dispatch). "TWO WHITE MEN KILLED," say headlines across Florida.

No, No, No!

(But this is the smaller, more fragile voice...)

She knows what she saw, and she won't budge an inch.

She insists, avows, hotly maintains: It was a lot more than just two.

As if sixty years later Minnie Lee Langley is still kneeling in that darkness, her face still held toward the revolving door of death, she doesn't care what you think of her credibility. She's not trying to persuade. "And the next one jump up there, Syl shot him, too." Then another one, and another. They fell, too. They kept coming, and he kept knocking them down.

In the "race war" wave around the time of World War I, an echo often followed the killing. The phenomenon could be called scorekeeping, "a feeling that the score must be kept even—that is, on an eye-for-an-eye basis," as it was put by African American journalist Roi Ottley.[322]

In these pseudo-war riots, ethnic death tolls were repeatedly treated like sports scores, testing which team could run up the highest tally, which race could kill the most members of the other race.[323] It was not a very pretty form of grandiosity, and this form of racial cracking was heard not only among white braggarts but among African Americans, though they were typically the target group. Rather than denouncing the phenomenon of killing in general, the cheerleaders—of either race—strained to prove that Our Side was the best at doing it.[324] Historian John

Hope Franklin noted it after the mile-square Tulsa riot of 1921, when "the collective wisdom in the black community" included an insistence that "many more whites were killed during the riot than any whites were willing to admit."[325]

Boasts by whites about supposed great numbers of hidden black dead *(Our side is much better at killing)* were mirrored morosely by many blacks with an opposite claim, alleging that there were hidden crowds of white dead *(No, our side is much better at killing)*. This post-traumatic pattern appeared after Rosewood as it did after Tulsa, Wilmington, Elaine, Chicago, East St. Louis and other landmark events—as if great mounds of corpses could be hidden easily by the other side as it rigged the score, with no funerals, no outcry from the kin.[326] Post-traumatic grandiosity seemed to find mounds of invisible corpses easy to imagine.

So the question: Did this mean that fiercely honest Minnie Lee Langley was in fact merely a scorekeeper? Was she simply imagining all those dead white men? She certainly had the post-traumatic credentials, losing her home community to a storm of racial violence. Did she really see a parade of men rushing the house and then falling down—"a lot more than just two"?

Again, the clues are in the newspapers—though deeply veiled. As Thursday night bulletins poured from the upstairs office in Gainesville and fed the Associated Press wire, the blizzard of words grew frantic. Markers in the dispatches suggest that the bulletins were going out roughly once an hour from midnight on. In that furor, the clues ran like this:

The Washington Post:
"Gainesville, Fla., Jan. 4—Three white men...are dead..."

The Atlanta Constitution:
"Three White Men...Dead in Outbreak at Rosewood..."

The Los Angeles Daily Times:
**"BY A.P. NIGHT WIRE --"GAINESVILLE (Fla.)...
Three white men...are dead...as a result of an outbreak
at Rosewood, three miles from Sumner..."**

So what is this? Later, by the end of the week, all public accounts would firmly agree that only two whites were killed: Wilkerson and Andrews. So who is this third dead white, reported in the heated wee hours of Friday morning? Was he dragged off and hidden so tricky

281

whites could deprive black shooters of their rightful score? And if this happened, might many more dead whites have been hidden as well?

In the Thursday night moonlight just prior to the explosion, logging boss Henry Andrews was flanked by a less prestigious figure. There was the other deer hunter. Whatever the truth about their trip to the Suwannee earlier that day, Mannie Hudson was present beyond any doubt at Sarah Carrier's house. A sometime farmer in the woods, he was the older brother of Bryant Hudson from the Monday murder of Sam Carter. A still younger brother, Charlie Hudson, was left at home and would later confirm what other evidence also said, that on Thursday night Mannie was at Sarah Carrier's front porch—and took a load of buckshot in the face. A little farther out than Andrews, he may have fallen near the steps—though still in a position to be seen with ghastly clarity by a little girl peering out.

There was a deeper bit of unpleasantness here, not easy for the white heroes to confess. Not all of the companions of Poly Wilkerson and Henry Andrews were hit like Mannie, and the more nimble ones were soon in a hurry. Apparently they fled in terror—leaving Mannie for dead, without venturing near the porch to take a pulse.

It would be a cold night. The frost that formed by morning would not be gentle on an immobilized casualty lying on an exposed porch. But the bodies on the porch were left where they lay: Wilkerson, Andrews— and apparently Mannie Hudson (whose death certificate, issued in 1942, shows clearly that he did not die in 1923). Perhaps, as frightened as the rest of them, he refrained from groaning for help as he lay there, fearing to alert the army of black savages thought to be in the house.

As his luckier companions rushed back to Sumner, they cried that the blacks were up in arms—which distracted from the untidiness. To admit that they had abandoned their dead was bad enough, but they had also abandoned their wounded. Word poured out by telephone and into the newspapers: *Worse than we thought! Three of them killed!* This misimpression, at least, was brief. By dawn the bulletins were going back down to two white deaths. As the smoke cleared, Mannie Hudson would be duly listed by name as one of the wounded. But by then media across America had said three dead. And why should they retract? Why trouble their readers with mere quibbles from a remote swamp?

By dawn—after other veiled events—apparently a crowd of white reinforcements grew large enough for someone to risk tiptoeing onto the silent porch, and discover Mannie's heartbeat. His family was sent for.

Rushing to Sumner, the family found him at Doc Cannon's, barely alive. It was a serious wound, said to keep him at Cannon's for a week.

Jim Turner:
> "He was just a regular old reprobate, drunk...[working] just a day now and then...He just looked like a pretty tough drunk."

Fred Kirkland:
> "...not too much of anything, mostly got drunk, hunted."

John Yearty:
> "Mannie was a bad drinker, wore overalls [and one day a female relative said]: 'That ole drunk, what I wanta speak to him for?'"

Around midnight on May 18, 1942, near Otter Creek, a vehicle came to an abrupt halt. Unlike his brother Bryant, who had lived to age 34 in 1931, Mannie Hudson would survive to age 47. Stories portrayed a one-vehicle accident involving alcohol. The death certificate was more forensic: "Head & Body crushed in Truck wreck."

Newspapers across the land had pronounced him dead two decades too soon, but the nightrider had caught up. To a nine-year-old girl staring through a darkened doorway, he might easily have looked dead, falling horribly, lying horribly still. And he was not the last.

To see just one man blown to bits in your face might give nightmares to a nine-year-old. To see three shot down in succession might easily blur in traumatic memory—translating as "more than a couple, too many to count." However in this case things were apparently simpler than a traumatic illusion. She saw a parade of them falling because they really were falling.

A special kind of mental state is required for a person to flatly report a flagrant fantasy as personal observation. Most people, even if severely traumatized, seem not to enter such a state. As Minnie's family later marveled at what she had lived through—and knew the evidence making it clear that her story was true—her story seemed to acquire a shadow. Minnie's cousin Philomena had had no such dramatic experience, according to the family members, though at some point, perhaps much later in life, Philomena developed a narrative that might be viewed as a competitor to Minnie's. Throughout the long years after the disaster, that narrative was not shared with Minnie, but was told to selected younger relatives, some of whom (according to one of them) were instructed sternly not to ask questions. This was the narrative I heard in 1982, which had Philomena personally stepping over 19 dead white men, and counting them one by one as she ran. In a large enough pool of survivors perhaps it is inevitable that this kind of riddle will appear. But it is not likely to appear in many of them—as at Rosewood it did not.

Like all of the Rosewood survivors save one, Minnie (Mitchell) Langley showed no sign of such a psychological extreme. She felt crushed by the losses of 1923, and arguably never recovered in some ways, displaying deep sadness if not depression even in advanced age— but those effects only served to underscore a great gulf, separating emotional pain from the mysteries of clinical disorder.

Minnie said: *"I believe if I wasn't right there to see it, and see him—Cud'n Syl, shootin' those people down—I would have got over it better. They were fallin' like birds in that door. It kind of got next to me."*

The next two birds were Bryan Kirkland and Cephus Studstill. They were quicker or more cautious than Wilkerson, Andrews and Hudson— but not quick enough. In Minnie's unshakeable description of more white men than just two being mowed down—and more than just three—she described not only carnage in the door and on the porch but out in the yard, a kind of shooting gallery image, as if ghastly tin ducks were darting back and forth and flopping down when shot. *"He saw one 'crost the yard, and he shot that one down."*

Not much cover was out there, besides an old cabbage palm near the porch. The palm was at least thick enough to hide a shoulder or two, because of its boot—another poem of the woods. As a wild cabbage palm grows and sheds fronds, its trunk becomes encased in a shaggy husk left by fallen stems. This is the "boot." The boot encasing the palm in front of Sarah Carrier's house would grow famous.

As the night of battle eventually passed and banal aftermath set in, there would be sightseers among the ruins. A main attraction was the old tree's boot. It drew the eye, chewed as it was by shotgun fire. Self-appointed crime-scene technicians pondered it gravely, stroking their jowls, formulating theories: *Must have been a mighty fierce shooter, to cut up the old cabbage tree like that.* However the theorists were stumped by one thing, the angle of fire. Judging by the way the boot was lacerated, the shooter seemed to have been positioned low, seemingly too low to be at a window. Some of the wizards thus concluded that he must have been shooting from *under* the house. Inadvertently, these mistakes, too, seemed to confirm Minnie, for they pointed toward the answer the wizards failed to grasp, the firewood closet.

Boot or not, it must have seemed scant shelter to young lumber inspector Cephus Studstill—especially if his war veteran companion, Jennings Bryan Kirkland, was trying to squeeze in as well. Minnie knew that not all of the men in the yard were killed: *"When they crossed that yard (they) had their guns like they was huntin' rabbits or coons or possums....I could see 'em, mumblin' and whisperin' and goin' on."*

Both Kirkland and Studstill were later formally reported as being wounded that night, though in Studstill's case, at least, it was not serious. He was seen the same night at the Sumner hotel, his arm in a bandage after an out-patient visit to Doc Cannon.[327] Neither of these two visitors was wounded too severely to get away. But at first, in the panic behind the boot, the priority would have been to dive for cover.

There were the racing emotions of first horror—two strong leaders lying unbelievably dead on the porch, in an unspeakable pile with the motionless Hudson. Both of the men with lesser wounds, Studstill and Kirkland, would reportedly describe struggling to hide behind Sarah Carriers' front-yard cabbage palm, as buckshot tore into its bark.

And there was more company—of a sort. As boasts came in from other claimed participants that night—some of them certifiably fantasizing, and perhaps all of them—the poor palm tree began to look like the skinny oak in one of those old cartoons from the early days of animation, where countless sneaky, big-nosed redskins in war paint keep tiptoeing up to disappear behind the same pencil-thin trunk. If all the boasts were true, it was a crowded tree.

———

Then it was over. She recalled: *"Didn't take that long."* White narrators agreed. *"I heard it was over pretty quick,"* said Perry Hudson, cousin of both Mannie Hudson and Bryan Kirkland. Lee Carrier described Sylvester as logically expecting such brevity: *"You wouldn't think it would last too long."*

One box of shotgun shells, 25 shells in a box.[328]

The battering motion that had been slamming Minnie's shoulder now stops. Like a bugle sounding retreat, she hears a faint voice somewhere out in the yard, rendered by memory into her own approximation: *"Let's go! He's done kill all of us up!"*

Whatever the words, the action was plain. The battle was a rout. The surviving whites left quickly, nursing wounds. She heard a car crank. Apparently it was Studstill, fumbling at the throttle lever with his wounded arm. Back north, Lee Carrier soon heard engine noise again—but then a crash. He later heard from whites that Studstill had lost the struggle with his nicked arm and ran the car into a tree, then leaped out and continued the flight on foot. Lee mused in his stoic way: *"They was scared out there. The two baddest mens was gone. It scared them, I guess."*

Also in that stretch of woods, Ed and Eliza Bradley heard footsteps and cries, as if from men running. Back in Sumner at the big fireplace in the Sumner hotel, Ernest Parham looked up to see Studstill climbing the stairs, his arm already bandaged—and not even bedtime. The next morning Martha Pillsbury saw Studstill fidgeting nervously in the dining room of the bungalow where her father, top boss Walter Pillsbury, was finishing breakfast. Employee Studstill was said to penitently give the boss the play-by-play on last night's moonlit disaster.

By then the word was out. *Of course, the heroes had had no choice.* They just naturally had to abandon the three bodies (one not quite dead)—because it was all so sudden.

It would not have been easy, back at Sumner, for such heroes to face the two widows and their horrified children. How to soften the blow?

Ambush! Treachery by the blacks! Uprising!

The reality—that drunken folly had consumed two heedless aggressors—was not exactly what you would say to the next of kin. Whites in Sumner and far out into the woods soon thrilled to a rumor fit for the silent screen, packed with white heroism, high drama and black betrayal. Local mainstream culture generally accepted this story, apparently never confronting the completeness with which it had embraced a delusion.

Responsibility for the episode was effectively reversed, shifting the blame onto the targets. Especially at upper levels of power and sophistication some whites did seem to comprehend a less palatable reality—but even then only in snatches. Some expressed shock at the violence and spoke sympathetically of the Rosewood targets, but still tended to swallow large chunks of the uprising fantasy, even as they considered themselves as being too enlightened for cheap mob anger. This was the old secret of uprising panic rampages. The mainstream could view itself as having righteously rejected the "hot heads" or "outsiders" who acted out the savagery, though in fact a mainstream consensus may have enabled it, because the mainstream believed the myth of blame:

The nightriders were making a polite, orderly law enforcement visit, knocking respectfully at Sarah Carrier's door. And they did it at that odd hour only because the trusty old servant had urged them to do just that. The crafty witch, she had actually invited them—knowing she was luring them into a trap.

The rumor—like any good delusion—didn't need to say why. It didn't matter why. Strong emotion could fill in the blanks. What mattered was the indignation, the haughty sense of wronged heroism, as martyrdom transfigured a band of bullies in a car. The automobile visitors had entered the miracle play of whiteness, in which Our Side can do no wrong.[329]

White resident of Sumner:
The deputy sheriff was "tryin' to talk one of the leadin' black people up there into helpin' them catch the guy."

White resident of Cedar Key:
The "sheriff" went to a house in Rosewood and was "killed when he's invited to check up on things."

White resident of the woods:
"The colored people at Rosewood told this quarters boss that they have him up there" (meaning that Wilkerson and Andrews were supposedly invited to Sarah Carrier's house to pick up the Monday fugitive).

The peaceable visitors were simply standing there, waiting at the door—*when it happened! Ambush!*

A nefarious black trick had drawn officers of the law into a deadfall—because...

...There didn't need to be a because. Obviously if the savages did it they had a reason—but an inscrutable, savage reason. They were plotting something big and horrible, trying to get the law officers out of the way first, so they could roll through the countryside, etc., etc., etc.

The suspension of disbelief—the thrill of Our-Side-Must-Be-Right—was such that the story could be believed even by narrators who admitted, with a shrug, that the first shot had certainly come from a white, and killed the dog. Savoring this colorful detail, such stories made the small confession without apology. But then as the narrative spread, the dog, too, would be laundered out. An ethnic fairy tale was polished and sharpened, to appear in its grandest form only after meeting the professional polishers, those in the newspapers.

"NEGROES FIRED FIRST," exclaimed the Ocala, Florida, *Evening Star,* sixty miles east, on Friday afternoon, January 5. By then the wire service stories from Gainesville were taking the reversal of blame nationwide. The *Evening Star* added flair with headlines of its own: "PLENTY NEGROES IN PARTY."

Across the nation, great urban dailies would present this image of rebellion and ambush as hard fact—minus the killing of the dog, much less Sarah Carrier. In yellowed news clips, then on microfilm, and finally in digital glow, the story of black treachery in the news clips would become the only written description produced in 1923 itself—a description available to any historian who might wish to source an impressive-looking footnote to a prestigious publication. And any such footnote, in turn, could be re-quoted by historian after historian, to form a supposedly documented picture of a time of secrets.

There is no way to know how deeply such a process may have led us astray on other incidents from the Lynching Era (just as 1923 left no way for its newspaper readers to see how they were being led astray while the events were actually occurring). We can't see what surprising twists of reality might lie hidden beneath the accretion of lynching fantasies—twists perhaps not suited to political agendas either left or right, twists simply different from the easy pictures, more subtle or ornate, more human—but still twists that are essential to understanding the dynamics of what really went wrong.

Minnie gazed at the doorway framing the dead. She would not recall looking up at Sylvester. Again, memory would retain only a voice, burned into recollection like a hot iron in soft wax—though the sound of the gun was not remembered at all.

He says:

"Go on back upstairs with the rest of 'em."

Crouching at the firewood closet, she has had no time to think about him, to envision what his movements might have been before he was astonished to find a small human form in his gun sight. He would have known, before he grabbed her, that his mother was dead. The numbness of the previously unthinkable was already operant. It could have been he who pried Bernadina from the blood-soaked bed, perhaps in the first rehearsal of the phrase: *"Go on upstairs."* The downstairs was being cleared for action. When a nine-year-old form then blocked his line of fire he may have guessed that there were only seconds left. The crowing, boasting mind could have spared a split second to wonder if he was being a fool, exposing himself to snatch her back. Now it is everything at once, not just self defense. Because now his mother is dead. Now it is all symbolic, the battle that no living flesh can win, wondering for a split second at the price he is now called to charge—and pay—the incredible meaninglessness, since the perimeters of the battle zone can only expand now, to consume all the community; no mortal could defend it all. Wondering, perhaps throwing himself into the astonishment of it, marveling that he is now already dead.

It has toppled over the cliff into the larger script now, the one the newspapers call race war, and that the old South of slavery used to call putting down insurrection: the near-instantaneous response of white culture as it pours forth crowds of avengers, protectors, crusaders and general drunks, tossing them into the stampede. Nobody has to be told the next act in this play. The children upstairs do not need it spelled out. White men have been killed. It is like having intimate prior medical knowledge of how snakebite progresses as you watch your arm balloon.

It might arrive in a few minutes. Or perhaps a few hours. But this is all the death dance now. It will certainly come. This thing at the door, this incredible elimination of everything that the first impulsive rush could throw, this is only a distorted interlude.

Following it will be something much larger. And the knowledge of this has force. Throughout the community there is panic, houses emptying in fearful flight. In the grip of such terror only one adult who was inside the house, Bernadina, has gone upstairs to the children. At least in Minnie's admiring recollection, Sylvester makes no move to help the children escape. And Gert has already fled.

Emma, Minnie's grandmother, Mama, is apparently still in the house but will escape alone, finding her way to Wright's store. She has two buckshot wounds, not life-threatening but deepening the fear. The words from Sylvester are like a judge's sentence, a farewell: *"Go on back upstairs with the rest of 'em."*

For seven decades she will cherish the memory of how Sylvester protected her. When I first heard it—in 1983 after I finally located her in Jacksonville—I thought I must have misunderstood. Patiently, she walked me through it again: *"When Cud'n Syl grabbed me [he put] the gun over this shoulder."* She pointed to her shoulder. She didn't understand why I was lost. I thought surely she must have meant that he pushed her behind him, to protect her in the firewood closet as he fired.

Didn't she really mean that *he* was behind *her*? Her patience grew thin. She was hurt and offended. Was I doubting her word?

"Yes, he was," she snapped back, meaning: *"Yes he was behind me."*

She emphasized: *"I could see the gun on my shoulder."*

In February 1994, Minnie Lee Langley's formal testimony to the Florida Legislature would say much the same: *"Syl put the gun over my shoulder. They kicked the door down. Syl let him have it. He killed them."*

The child intruder in the gunfight had been positioned in a way that could be construed as a shield.

This is not the tale of heroes, or of demons.

This is the forbidden roadmap to something else.

Chapter 25: Man Down There

Carry out, carry over, carry through

Carry me back to Old Virginie

Eight plus nine equals seventeen, carry the one

Carry on, raising sand

Tote that barge, lift that bale

Typhoid Mary

Logging equipment, refrigeration, postal service, sea power

The world on his shoulders

To Minnie the truth seemed obvious. The whites had come to Aunt Sarah's with plans to commit a massacre. They were going to kill everybody, all the Carriers and Bradleys, children and all. Poly and Boots were plotting a diabolical frenzy of child-shooting and wholesale extermination. They were planning to go house to house. So first they had to knock out the main obstacle, the leader, the best shot in town. This why they came to Sylvester's—only as a first stop. It was only because of him that all those people were saved from certain death, only because of his courage. This was how it looked to her, in post-traumatic echoes down through the years.

"If Cud'n Syl hadn't been in there we'd all been dead."

Sam Hall, too—though no great fan of the Carriers—would agree on this frightening scenario: *"If it hadn't been for Syl, they would've killed 'em all. They went down there to kill 'em."*

Was this possible? Was it likely? These questions were not asked. Once the killing had started the most demonic explanation was set in stone—with the demons defined by whose side you were on. Neither whites out in the woods, spying a demonic black uprising, nor the fleeing black targets with their profound conviction that Boots and Poly had come for insatiable massacre, ever got to learn what the other side was really thinking.

Hall's conviction came largely from gossip. Earlier in the week a neighbor, elderly Julia Edwards, had visited Sam's mother Mary Ann Hall. *"Old lady Julia came by and told Mama they gonna kill out all the*

Bradleys and Carriers." The pressures of fear and rumor were already working. "Old Lady Julia," a kindly neighbor loved by all, was remembered by another resident, Nettie Smith, as bringing provocative predictions to the Smith household as well. Two sharply defined groups, blacks and whites, seemed to be behaving and believing like nations mobilizing for war—each spying plans of apocalyptic massacre being hatched by the other.

Minnie climbs the dark stairs, again alone. In the attic at least one window has now been blown out. Mute forms are standing or crouching, barely shadows in the sharp chill, gazing at her. She can think only to report on her original mission, numbly.

She says: *"I ain't seen Mama."*

The mute forms have been affected in various ways. Seventeen-year-old Eddie, at the outset so heroic, tossing a mattress over the smallest children to shield them from bullets, heedless of his own safety, now has changed. He sits like a statue, staring into space. The others begin asking him what to do. He seems uninterested, almost asleep.

Harry, Aunt Sarah's youngest son, creeps to a window and looks out, then rushes back to Eddie, trying to break the spell. He cries: *"They gone, Eddie! They gone!"*

Minnie and Bernadina join Harry, all now tugging at Eddie. This is no time for staring. The next act of the play is very near, the big one that they all know is coming, the massive wave of retaliation. *There are white men dead on the porch.* If some magic has produced a temporary lull in the action, the opportunity must be seized. Bernadina pleads with Eddie: *"Mama's dead. They gone. Let's get out of here."*

Then suddenly the lunacy of traumatic shock seems to grow epidemic, to spread. For now it is Bernadina. She stiffens, staring into space. The tugging at Eddie stops. She seems to have seen a ghost. Or heard one. In the blood-stained nightgown she freezes, then gasps:

"Listen!"

The children also freeze. What does she hear? It is faint, coming from outside—in a place beyond the yard. Out in that direction seepage from underground limestone labyrinths has formed a small slough, a thread of water they call the branch. No one has ever bothered clearing the bushes away from the branch, so a thicket hugs its slight depression. If a marksman were to be seeking a logical ambush point outside the house, there to lie in wait for an arriving army, he might choose the thicket on the branch.

The children now hear it, too. That sound. Barely more than a thought. Battlefield survivors could have told them that shock and horror can seem to shatter something beyond perception, something that underlies perception: the construction of meaning. As in near-death or massive injury experiences, consciousness explores new rules. The world reconfigures, right before your eyes, creating encounters too gem-like and grossly symbolic to be real. And yet they are real. Solid as rocks. Solid as your hand. This is not the tunnel of light but the flood of coincidence, when ordinary, familiar objects manifest in sequences too packed with meaning to be accidental—"the wink of God," some say— just letting you know he's watching.

Or as if waking awareness itself were in essence a dream. Perhaps anyone facing death has known it, the stressed combatant gazing in bewilderment at the flashing, swirling, taunting hints that *everything* is imagination—the drowning swimmer's whole life in an instant, making a mockery of time.

They could scarcely mistake it.

"Listen," said Bernadina.

Then she said:

"Man down there laughin'!"

That blast of sound, his very spirit turned into something that had no material existence at all, merely auditory shock waves, reconfigurations of the air.

KA-KA-KA!

Wild—maniacal-sounding now, under these circumstances— exploding up away from everything that could be logical or sane.

Minnie has no doubt: *"I heard him laughin'. We heard him down there laughin'. But that's the last time we heard him or seen him. We heard him laughin' down there on that branch.*

"He say, HA! HA! HA!"

His world is gone. His mother is dead. He has won the unimaginable victory and lost all. *The absurdity!* Because he has won, he knows, the retaliation is likely to consume the community as a whole. Victory and doom. As if his entire lifetime had been directed toward this one drowningly compressed instant—when it is revealed that he has lived out the name.

Man, the Carrier.

So now he is free, out of the trap—escaping not into the woods but elsewhere, into the sideways world, the Valhalla and Olympus of myth, immortal now, paying only the small price of being trapped in other people's minds, in their myths, wholly converted to thought, image—in a realm of perfection that all along his love of perfection seemed to seek.

"Listen!"

The children are about to dash into bone-chilling cold and terrifying darkness—in their nightclothes, barefoot, on a night that is beginning to bring frost. They will cower shivering in the woods while expecting at any minute to be found and killed. They don't reflect on the faintness of the sound, the elusiveness of the laughter, in an atmosphere of shock so intense that one of them can only sit and stare. They don't think of the possibility that the sound might be—not exactly an auditory hallucination—but something less easily defined: the explosiveness of revealed meaning, so deep, so searing, that it exceeds the bounds of what is and is not materially real.

They hear Man.

Down there laughing.

Eddie revives. Blinking at Bernadina and Minnie, he seems to wake from the dream. His confidence returns. He thinks of a plan: *"We can go out that back way."* He is going to lead them down the stairs and out Aunt Sarah's back door, avoiding the front porch. There are dead white men on the front porch. Any whites left as watchers might be out there hiding. This is the sequence that would be accepted as true by all of them. Philomena's later story of stepping over nineteen dead white men—on the front porch—could be told only to people who weren't there.

On the stairs the barefoot procession is halted suddenly by another sound—not laughter this time. They have rushed down too quickly. The youngest child, George "Buster" Goins, has been left at the top, peering down at them, wailing, too small to make the steps. They rush back and scoop him up.[330]

The tunnel of hallway looms downstairs. Minnie sees moonlight flooding the back yard. She keeps to the dark side of the house, leaping from the back porch. Her legs pump furiously for the woods, almost feeling the bullets of the white men as she crashes into deeper darkness, hitting the briars. A straggling platoon: Bernadina, Eddie, Harry, Lonnie, Philomena, Goldee, Arnett, little J.C., even smaller Buster. And there is the stocky form with the towel, blood now crusted on Ruben's lost eye. And Minnie. Eleven of them, stumbling in the vines. They are now out of the "death house," as a newspaper will call it. Nothing ahead or behind. The night is only beginning.

Chapter 26: To the Woods

As he hears it, Lee Carrier is in bed. The sound of gunfire is coming faintly across the woods. Though he had heard the car go past earlier, moving in the direction of the railroad and his aunt Sarah's house, he had to think first about work in the morning. The incoming car passed at bedtime, around 9:00 p.m., and he has to get up before dawn. Tomorrow is one more day to make the hike with Bishop, the younger cousin sharing the room with him. No memories from the community would recall efforts by anyone to creep through the woods and see where the car went—despite suspicions.

Lee's view is confined to the house. After the car passed, Bishop's father Wesley Bradley, head of the household, began pacing fretfully, no explanations offered. Wesley is a logger for Cummer Lumber, one of the big men who goes into the cypress swamps for a week at a time. He is also still grieving for his wife Virginia, recently deceased. In the vague stories surrounding his nephew Sylvester earlier in the week, Wesley was said to express fear that disaster was coming.

Hearty and exuberant, Wesley Bradley is also deeply religious. While his wife Virginia was alive there were ceremonial family dinners on Sundays; children were not allowed to run and play outside on the day of contemplation. Virginia's Sunday cooking was done on Saturdays, a daughter recalled. Like various households in Rosewood, this one seemed aloof from the communal tensions and feuds, and was followed by no stories of hostility or violence.

At one point a bedroom at Wesley and Virginia Bradley's house was kept free for visiting preachers, or for the occasional higher church official, making rounds from Gainesville or Ocala. One day at Sunday dinner, facing his many children, Wesley captured his personal blend of piety and gusto. Peering down the table at his rapidly eating son, Donarion, he exclaimed with a laugh: "Son, you don't just eat like a *preacher!* You eat like a *Bishop!*"

The laughter going around the table certified it. Throughout a long life and even after migration north to Harlem, Bishop Bradley would be thought by most people he knew to have no other first name.

Though he is a decade older than Sylvester Carrier, Wesley is perhaps Sylvester's best friend. Lee Carrier would recall that early in the week of violence Wesley urged Syl to leave town for a while, until tensions cooled. Later years would see stories contending that friends like Wesley

Donarion "Bishop" Bradley later years in New York *(Southeastern Regional Black Archives, FAMU)*

went farther, and in a thrilling show of solidarity they stood with Syl against the Thursday night foes—forming the "army barricaded in the hut." Lee's closer view of his uncle Wesley, finding him at home during the shooting on Thursday night, was consonant with other real observers. Still other accounts, within the Carrier house, drove the point home: the solidarity stories were fantasies.[331] Wesley Bradley had other responsibilities that night: his children.

The federal census of 1920 found "West" Bradley with three small children still at home, as memories agreed. His wife Virginia then died in the birth of a subsequent child. In addition, three adolescent sons live with widower Wes Bradley, including Bishop. The nearing prospect of a racial rampage gives reason for anxious pacing.

Lee woke quickly at the sound of the shots. Throughout the community people were leaping from bed—apparently primed for flight response—as they threw on their clothes and dashed into the darkness, leaving their homes unattended. In northeast Rosewood where the shots were audible, the reaction was remarkably consistent, described by witness after witness. Houses emptied with speed approaching reflex action. Everyone seemed to know the drill. At one of the farthest points, Rosewood's largest African American-owned farm may have been out of earshot. The John McCoy household on their 114 acres received word by other means, according to McCoy's daughter Lutie. She said that white storekeeper John Wright slipped off from the center of the action, apparently driving his Ford, and came to warn the McCoys.

The lynching-era ritual of "going to the woods" seemed to date from Civil War Reconstruction, forming the flip side of the word "nightrider," both terms born of night attacks by white vigilante groups. On the night of January 4, 1923, the first sounds of an automobile entering Rosewood were not taken as a portent of massacre. But as its engine cut off, a new reality was about to be signaled by the next sound, gunfire.

Shooting was the warning sign for the breakdown that the newspapers called "race war." Something more than a beating or brawl was now announced, something more final. If a gun had been fired by a black man at a white, a small army of whites would certainly be following to retaliate—or a large army. From Rosewood's neighboring houses no one could see what had happened around 9:30 p.m. at Sarah Carrier's, but if a white man had been hit, or worse, killed, no household was now safe. War refugees anywhere face a worst-case scenario, so dire that the worst possibility has to be treated as the operant truth. If rumors say the hordes are just over the hill, you can scarcely afford to wait around for responsible confirmation. You flee—not knowing if they are really there. You flee while there is time.

In the black South of the Lynching Era, the idea of concerted self-defense at such times was often discussed, and sometimes was practiced. But the odds were poor. The overwhelming numbers in a retaliatory white mob could go beyond gale force, and it was absurd to shoot at a hurricane. The reason for going to the woods was to stay out of sight, to remove oneself from the list of possible random scapegoats who might satisfy mob pretensions, on a bet that by morning it will all be over. One's home, in this equation, was left fearfully exposed, on another bet—that things would not escalate to arson. The insecurity was profound.

As the distant gunfire crackled, the sound of Wesley's pacing in the other room seemed to cease, again with no word to Lee. Wesley had apparently grabbed up his smallest children—Lee Ruth, Ivory, Clifford and Wesley James—and was half-herding, half-carrying them out of the house.[332] Bishop, sharing the room with Lee, leaped from bed and barely took time to dress, displaying a speed that to Lee seemed astounding. Lee was left blinking in the dark. The stoic outsider, raised largely as an orphan, had missed being initiated into the drill.

Farther back in the woods, crotchety Ransom Edwards, old pioneer and once the community's school superintendent, now takes his time. Packing a trunk for his wife Julia, he loads it into a wagon and hauls it into the woods—then he returns home, refusing to leave his residence unguarded. A younger neighbor, Virginia "Sissy" Smith, hears the alarm in her smoky cabin where the only beds are wooden shelves along the walls. She gathers her three small children, Nettie, Gilbert and Johnnie, and rushes into the night. Farther west the McCoys, reportedly warned by storekeeper Wright, are packing a wagon. The Perry Goins household is in flight.[333] Sixteen-year-old Sam Hall is at home in bed. His mother Mary Ann shouts up the stairs: *"Sammy! Sammy! Get up!"*

Lee Carrier finds himself alone. He tries to be methodical in the crisis. Thinking ahead, he dons an extra pair of wool socks. No way to know how long he might be out there. The dual movements—an influx of avenging whites and an outrush of fleeing African American residents—is considered inevitable by all, once whites have been shot at or hurt. The only question is how large it will get. A little whooping and hollering? An isolated case of torture or beating here and there?

This was about how Lee gauged it, in his ignorance of the drill. The idea of anything larger—of something horrendous being done to the community at large, by whites he knew and seemed to get along with— this seemed unthinkable, like hail stones in an earthquake. To the east, Sam Hall, also young and optimistic, expects much the same—no more than a night in the woods, then back to the normal routine. Older residents like Wesley Bradley apparently have deeper knowledge. Both Sam and Lee will walk to work in Sumner the next day, Friday, as if it were all over and their lives could go on.

Finding himself in front of Wesley's house in the moonlight, Lee stands in puzzlement. What now? There is a feeling of abandonment. Where is everybody? Of course, there is the option of now finding a cold little thicket and bedding down, but even the stoic finds the temperature a little sharp for that, while rising adrenalin keeps him  restless. So there is always the fallback, the usual center of activity at Wright's store. It will be closed at this hour, but Lee starts toward it anyway. Walking the sand lane beside Wright's hog-wire fence, he spies a light. Wright's house is set well back from the store, and behind the house is a shed. In the shed a lamp or lantern seems to be flickering. Stoic outsider Lee Carrier is about to learn that going to the woods has strict rules.

———

The panic has two halves, white and black. In the confusion of darkness and rumors, counter-intuitive as it might sound, white households in the woods are also feeling panic, though events will prove that only black households are in danger. The same unseen blacks who in reality are now fleeing for their lives are envisioned murkily by many whites as massing for some kind of never-specified attack. A generalized panic is developing, laced with delusion and fed by a vacuum in reliable information. The nearest daily newspaper, the *Sun,* fifty miles away, cannot fill the vacuum because it has joined in the panic mode. Law enforcement can't provide real information because it is busy trying to hide mob targets behind cover stories and denials. No island of objectivity is left in public information—a lack which prepares the way for a hole in history, a blank spot that will be impossible for posterity to penetrate in the absence of any official or reliable descriptions—unless posterity can find a way to consult the only guide still left, the confusing maze of living memory.

Charlie Hudson, white, age 14, the younger brother of Mannie and Bryant, watches white women running to one another's doorsteps, anxiously inquiring for the latest on the rebellious black hordes, who are expected to roll through the countryside at any moment. If they have already done the unthinkable, ambushing poor Poly and Andrews—*what might they do next?*

The reversal of blame is a reversal of fear—up to a point. Whites do not seem to be pouring from their homes to sleep in the woods as done by African Americans in Rosewood. The white panic is more of a strange tremor, not so far removed from being an excited thrill. This has the delicious urgency of emergency management, but in a bubble of frantic make-believe.

One white, woods rider and gunman Jack Cason, has already surged to prominence on Monday in the rescue of Aaron Carrier, but then fades from the radar screen of recollection in the lull of Tuesday and Wednesday. Now, on Thursday night, he is spurring back—again for rescue and damage control. At Cason's home in Rocky Hammock, his young son Lloyd is left to be the proud sentry in his father's absence, peering into the dark for any hostile movement. But movement by whom? Lloyd's memories would become a measure of the white echo panic. While his father is in Rosewood trying to protect African Americans from whites, Lloyd has absorbed the idea—from neighbors or even from his excited father—that it is the blacks who are attacking. When Lloyd stands at his father's horse corral, scanning the night for signs of hostile approach, he is trying to catch sight of sneaking black uprisers.

And some whites go farther, into the behavioral hallmark of mass panic known as mobilization. On the Gulf at Cedar Key, fisherman Allen Faircloth will describe loading his family into a wagon and fleeing town, because nearly half of Cedar Key's population is black in 1923. Faircloth fears they will catch the contagion from those Rosewood outlaws—and that the Cedar Key blacks will also go berserk, erupt into savagery, rise up. The fisherman hears that the Rosewood bunch has already killed the sheriff himself. Now the sneaking black allies in Cedar Key are plotting to burn down the town.

Cedar Key resident Naomi Tooke Dorsett, also white, says much the same, recalling that her family became so convinced by uprising news from Rosewood that they piled into their fishing boat and put out into the Gulf, like Noah in the flood. But panic mobilization can have two faces, the passive (flight) and the aggressive (striking at the menace). Cedar Key neighbor Frank Coburn finds himself hitching a ride in a parade of automobiles leaving Cedar Key early Friday morning— not fleeing from the envisioned black horde, but sallying forth to smite it. The Cedar Key motorists see themselves as reinforcements, aiding brave whites at Rosewood, who are said to be besieged by black guerrillas. The reinforcements don't sally until dawn, however—because they fear snipers. At the bridge linking Cedar Key to the swampy mainland, Coburn will recall, the cars had to pause ponderously for inspection, conducted by newly self-appointed town guards. A car-by-car search is made-car for the sinister jugs of gasoline, envisioned in the burning-down-the-town rumor. Though this angry string of cars is clearly filled with whites—and is going in the wrong direction for any Cedar Key sabotage—the teller of the tale seems to find the whole thing perfectly reasonable.

Cedar Key resident Joe Wilder will recall the fear shown by white women and girls left at home by the outgoing motorcade. A mischievous boy is said to duplicate the Fannie Taylor routine, making suspicious-sounding noises at a front door—only to get his due when the door flies open. A frightened girl inside points a rifle into the prankster's face, ready to blast away at black marauders.

All such stories are suspect to a degree, and probable only to a degree. None can be used as final evidence of what was materially occurring at the time—for they demonstrate a deeper implication, that local culture in general—down to the coldest skeptic laughing at the crowd—had entered a shadow-play of make-believe. For a moment, all the white believers could play Home Guard, could be adrenal and important, steeped in the thrill of insurrection fever.

The stories displayed a flaccid ambiguity, blurring their blame reversal. Were the panicked whites really afraid of being butchered by (fleeing) blacks? Or, more realistically, of getting caught in the shooting as whites attacked blacks? Or, perhaps, were they afraid of the crossfire as the two sides clashed equally? The answer was perhaps all three. The essence was a free-floating fear of what *might* happen, jelling into wildfire rumors about what supposedly *had* happened, and what allegedly *was* happening.[334]

On July 2, 1917, one of the worst race riots of the century, in East St. Louis, Illinois, found entire communities of whites reportedly fleeing en masse— though the reports had an unsettling vagueness.[335] Were those whites really only *poised* to flee? The flight, or half-readiness for flight, was due to fear of invading black armies—which

Springfield, Illinois, *Republican*
July 3, 1917

were imaginary. The reality was that in that charged moment of the East St. Louis race riot, African Americans were being butchered by whites, as a "race war" unfolded. Some newspapers applauded the brutality, one going so far as to say that the attack on blacks came just in the nick of time, barely foiling an enormous black conspiracy that had supposedly been set to massacre thousands of whites on the Fourth of July (naturally this vast plot could not be proved later by any public evidence, because the timely white butchery destroyed any sign of it). The East St. Louis reasoning seemed to go something like this: Whites were not, in fact, massacred on the Fourth of July, so this proved that whites were right to have performed massacre themselves, as a pre-emptive strike, foiling the (imaginary) massacre by the Other Side. A historian marveled: "A mighty black army was seen everywhere."[336]

The delusions at East St. Louis were taken farther by the best known African American newspaper of the day, the *Chicago Defender*. Seizing on the black army imagined by whites, the *Defender* then turned it into a boastful emblem of black solidarity.[337] The non-existent battalion was not only embraced as being real, but was described in thrilling detail by the *Defender*, as a news item, as if that army really was marching through Illinois cornfields. Both races were producing delusions that might seem too ludicrous to believe—if viewed from outside the bubble of belief.

Lee moves toward the glint of lantern light in Wright's shed. He hears voices, then peeps inside. John Wright, the wry white storekeeper, is not present in the shed. The tense figures crowded there are all African American. Lee feels a rush of relief. These are familiar faces. He doesn't guess what is out of line in this picture, not at first.

Stepping into the dim light, he mutters hello. Soon he will learn that "going to the woods" in some ways resembles a ghastly game—or, in the minds of the pursuers, a sport.

As the post-traumatic psychology of lynching and its "race wars" has eluded systematic examination, so, too, has the fearfully closed world represented by going to the woods. This American folk pattern, enduring at least from the 1870s into the 1920s, would go as unanalyzed by social science as the upholstery inside a UFO. In this direction the Rosewood witnesses provide a corroborated picture of behavior motifs seldom if ever explored before—one more rebuke to the clichés and melodramas erected by society around a time of secrets.

The underlying structure of "going to the woods" remained hidden from public scrutiny because those involved wished it to remain hidden, notably its most powerful participants. A foretaste of this came in the Aaron Carrier rescue on Monday, but here the picture broadens. Left out of American discussion on lynching (among many such gaps) was a disorienting complication. The depths of the Jim Crow South could conceal a response pattern faintly resembling the underground railroad of slavery.

Whites reading newspapers in distant places might see "going to the woods" as merely a sudden disappearance, a chaotic dive into the pines, but at Rosewood, at least, striking segmentation appeared in the escape movement, as it purposefully sought clandestine way stations. Four main escape routes led to four improvised sanctuaries. In essence, each of these was a no-fire zone set up on the property of a power broker who was white. The four operators of the refuges were acquainted socially and in business, in a world where most business was not aired in the newspapers.

Storekeeper John Wright was the first of the four. The shed behind his house, found by Lee Carrier, had become a makeshift tornado cellar against a human storm.[338] Unlike Lee, older Rosewood residents seemed to know immediately about such refuge. Lee found that Wesley Bradley's four youngest children were already there at Wright's—though Wesley himself had slipped out again. This, Lee would learn, was because of the rules.

Before exploring those rules (and they were coldly simple), the list of protectors continues. The second sanctuary was on the premises of another white businessman, two miles northeast of Rosewood at Wylly. There, the hiding was done in a pine grove owned by M. & M. Naval Stores, the property of Daniel P. McKenzie, a future Florida legislator.[339]

Photo said to be of John Wright in his youth, ca. 1898
(Levy County Archives Committee)

Geography determined which refugees sought which refuge. Those in areas closest to Wright's went there, but farther up the railroad, flight tended to find McKenzie's. Still others farther north, such as Virginia Smith, made a longer loop to the third node, some ten miles northeast. The third white provider of riot sanctuary was the volatile horseman Jack Cason, at his corral in Rocky Hammock.[340] Even as Cason's son Lloyd kept a sharp eye out for black rebels, he was watching frightened African Americans come in who were fleeing from the real dangers.

D. P. McKenzie
(Florida Memory/State Archives of Florida)

This then left the fourth sanctuary, sought by those on the west side of Rosewood, the area of pale-complexioned residents nearest to Sumner. That refuge was in Sumner itself. Specifically, refugees were channeled to the cook house behind the bungalow residence of the most powerful white in the area, sawmill superintendent Walter Pillsbury.[341]

Wright, Pillsbury, McKenzie and Cason moved within a matrix of triage and unappealing choices, a hidden thread in the white South of the Lynching Era. Their side of things (and certainly not all leading whites took these risks) was kept out of the newspapers, for the simple reason that publicity might bring mob retaliation against them. Here, too, the Rosewood witnesses cast harsh light on the kind of convenience-driven history that depicts atrocity from neatly packaged news clips. The convenience begins to look like describing a shark by its visible fin.

Invisible in written records was a morbid choreography of escape, whose dance steps reached toward the absurd. By Friday, dislocated African American women and children at Wright's were said to move from his shed out into his fenced yard, under instructions from Wright to stay inside the fence. White rioters were presumably within sight and were looking for black targets to shoot, but no attack came. The game had placed Wright's property out of bounds—as if a referee were watching with a whistle.[342] The eerie semblance of chalk lines suggested not just sport but something deeper, the pretend-world of children at play.

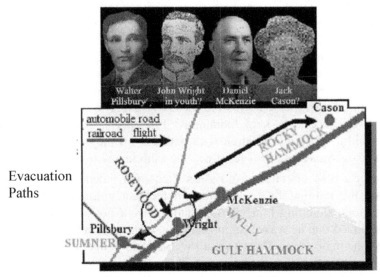

(collaged photos: Jerry Peterson Collection, Levy County Archives Committee, Florida Memory-State Archives of Florida, Matheson Museum and Archives)

But for all this to work, a main rule had to be followed, which Lee Carrier was about to learn in the shed. The four referees—Wright, Pillsbury, McKenzie, and Cason—imposed a restriction. Only women and children were allowed into their sanctuaries—in order to leverage the mob's pretensions to gallantry. Since attacking vigilantes saw themselves as protectors of order, they ostensibly were looking only for ferocious male uprisers, men or teenaged boys. Some in the mob were quite capable of shooting a fleeing woman (this, too, was coming), but only in sordid secrecy, and not if their noses were rubbed in it publicly—at least in the Rosewood version of this game.

The Rosewood violence was rural, remaining vastly more limited in its destruction than urban riots of the same era, which occurred in crowded caldrons like East St. Louis in 1917. There, African American women were randomly tortured and killed. But at Rosewood the nervous referees were able to protect their no-fire zones simply by discretion, as if an unspoken reproach said: "Are you really such a worm as to kill the helpless?"

Wesley Bradley, age 44, had stayed at Wright's only long enough to drop off his four children, and perhaps have a grim word with John and Mary Wright. Then he had to hit the road, moving into a second track in "going to the woods" —a track reserved for adult and late-adolescent African American males. The rules painted a bulls-eye on these residents, declaring them to be in open season. If a man or older boy were to be found in a sanctuary, mob avengers might resent the breach of etiquette and start shooting. Levels of security seemed to vary. Two of the sanctuaries, McKenzie's pine grove at Wylly and Pillsbury's cook house in Sumner, were not as public as Wright's. Women and children there were anxiously kept hidden. At Pillsbury's, frightened mothers were said to gag their children with petticoats if they started to cry and make dangerous noise—so scant was the faith in any rules.

Lee's rush of relief in Wright's shed soon faded. As he sat down among the familiar faces he began to feel uncomfortable. The others grew quiet, shunning him. No one had to say it out loud. With a start, Lee realized that he wasn't supposed to be there, that he was unlike them in the one major way. They were all women and children. He was a male youth, a potential bringer of disaster, like a carrier of disease.

Young Sammy Hall hears his mother's voice anxiously waking him, then notices the sounds, the jerky distant hammering of gunfire. Rushing downstairs to join the rest of the family, he flees with them into the moonlight—not a methodical flight in this case but more like the stock image of panic. The Halls leave so quickly—as with the attic refugees on the stairs at Sarah Carrier's—that one is overlooked. Counting heads at the edge of the woods, they see that little Mary Hall, age three, has been left in her bed. They rush back for her. By then, Sam's older sister Margie is so frightened that her perceptual processing rebels. Dashing through the woods, Margie will recall, she suddenly freezes. Right in front of her is a bright light. The white men! But she looks again and sees only darkness. The light was apparently imaginary, a product of panic.

In Wright's shed as Lee absorbs the rules, he watches an agitated figure arrive. Gert Carrier, Sylvester's wife, has not stopped running since leaping from the room at the back of Sarah's house. Finding the shed at Wright's, Gert excitedly tells her story, despite bleeding welts from her dash through bushes and briars.

Her narration—a woman's story told to other women—only reminds Lee of his discomfort. He rises, slipping back out into the moonlight, again alone. What now? Sleep is out of the question. There is one more source of possible companionship. He begins the two-mile walk to Wylly.

This hike takes him through the vicinity of Sarah Carrier's house, but he hears no more gunfire. He does not think of detouring to see what assistance might be offered. Whatever is happening with Sylvester is not his affair. The opinion seems general. Those in the best position to know do not depict Sylvester Carrier as being surrounded by neighborly solidarity.

Allen Stephenson:
>"He was the bravest of all that was down there, and he was the only one. They was all runnin' for their lives."

Margie (Hall) Johnson:
>"If there had a been three black like him, they woulda did some damage there. But there was just him one."

Lee Ruth (Bradley) Davis:
>"Papa (Wesley Bradley) told me...I don't think nobody was with him."

Arnett Goins:
>*Q: "How many people in the house could use guns to ward off the whites from the outside?"*
>
>*A:* "Wasn't nobody in there shooting, wasn't nobody in there shooting, but Sylvester..."
>
>*Q: "But Sylvester was the one doing the shooting?"*
>
>*A: "He was the one doing the shooting."*

Lonnie Carrol (Carrier):
>"He was the onliest one that would fight to try to save himself—Sylvester..."

Lee Carrier:
>"The people wasn't there <u>to</u> fight back. They all gone."

Though perhaps Minnie said it best:
>"If he wasn't there to back us up, we don't know what we woulda did, 'cause none of the Bradleys or nothin', they all took to the woods. They left Cud'n Syl to fight the battle by hisself. I don't know why, but they took to the woods. Nobody help him out at all."

Lee soon finds himself among the dirt lanes and shanty roofs of M. & M. Naval Stores in Wylly. The grimy little settlement is not sleeping. Instead of darkened windows and latched doors there are people standing expectantly at doorways, dressed and ready to run.

The game is on now—everyone knows this—the big game of white retaliation after a racial confrontation. Rosewood has become a general target. But how far will this targeting spread? Will Wylly be factored in? The figures in the doorways have their coats on. Lee hears them talking about something called a race riot. As they scan for signs of attack, their owlish stares look ridiculous to the stoic outfielder.

An ex-resident of Rosewood, Annie Blocker, known as Sis, lives in the Wylly quarters with her children. Lee is friends with Sis Blocker and moves toward her comforting presence. But as he enters the quarters, the moment comes. A child runs from the direction of the railroad, shouting: *"Sis! Sis! Sis! The people's up there on the other end, and they're comin' up this way!"*

He has no time to decipher the meaning. Residents seem to pour from the shanties. Wylly, too, is "going to the woods." Another view will be preserved from inside the Blocker house. Little Arthina Blocker recalls her mother lining the children up like a schoolteacher at a

Abandoned turpentine cabins

fire drill, then marching them out to shelter. But this is only precautionary shelter. Wylly's danger is not yet proven. The Blocker family will spend the night under a railroad trestle, then go home. Wylly will be spared by the storm.

A question remains: What had sparked the alarm Lee observed? Who was "they" in the phrase *"They're comin' up this way...?"*

In this case, the sudden bright light that was seen was apparently no hallucination. Stories had it moving rapidly down the railroad from the northeast, the direction of Otter Creek, toward Wylly and Rosewood. This light seems to have been the headlamp of a motorized railroad work cart, one of Cummer Lumber Company's small "motorcars."

By now the lone telephone line along the railroad is busy—a party line, leaving no conversation in privacy. In a turpentine camp at Lennon, almost to the Alachua County line, a woods rider named Bud Campbell will be recalled growing exasperated. His phone is constantly ringing, the party line going mad. Each phone subscriber hears all the rings, each time any phone is called.[343] Campbell's niece, Lillie Washington, would describe him giving in to curiosity: the discreet lifting of the earpiece from the hook, the furtive palm cupped over the mouthpiece to block the sound of the listener's breathing, and—as easy as that—a wiretap is plugged into a world of gossip. Campbell hears a frantic woman's voice: *Have you seen my husband? What's this they're saying about my husband? Please tell me what's happened to my husband?"* The woman seems to be making call after call, phoning everywhere. *What's happened to my husband?!*

This is said to be the wife of the logging superintendent, Cuba Andrews—also a distant relative of Constable Poly Wilkerson. Henry Andrews has three small children at home. His wife seems to struggle to get behind the rumors and discover his fate. By phone and otherwise, grim news is pushing toward the logging quarters managed by Andrews at Otter Creek, where his white foremen are also listening.

The old man has been cut down, ambushed, killed out of the blue. The blacks have gone berserk. He's lying out there, exposed on that porch!

The quickest way across the Rocky Hammock swamps from Otter Creek to Rosewood is by rail. And if there are no trains, there is the motorcar. Yank the starter cord and the greasy thing snarls like a wildcat. Stories will tell how they piled on. Maybe more than one cart. But maybe just one, groaning under a Keystone Kops pile of excited humanity. Wylly fails to guess, as it stands on their route, that the onrushing intruders with the bright light have no interest in stopping for mischief along the way.

He's lying out there?! Nobody's got him?!

The second battle is about to begin.

―――――――――――――

Chapter 27: Left Behind

By 11:30 p.m. on Thursday night, white Sumner is stunned. The hush of disaster fills stricken parlors. *Two brave men! Gone!*

An agonized widow or sobbing child is unlikely to be told: "Well, you know, your loved one went on acting like a drunken bully until it killed him." White society fills with white lies. *The heroes were blameless! They were ambushed! They were only trying to uphold the law! They had even been invited! Why, they were lured into a trap....!*

So they must be avenged. At first the avengers move in shadowy knots and bunches, sometimes one group apparently bumping into another in surprise, fumbling in the darkened lanes at the scene. Not until morning will the flow become a flood.

Among the many undercurrents in this, one was nowhere visible on the surface. Superficially, it hardly seemed relevant. And yet it was a central fact of life in Sumner, Florida:

Sumner itself was dying. Indeed, it was already dead. The Cummer Lumber Company, that rhyming-named empire run by Michigan-born logging tycoons, had set the schedule for Sumner's funeral. Its timber tracts in swamps along the Suwannee were nearing exhaustion, and a plan was already established to move to a new headquarters three counties away.[344]

Any company town was a walking ghost, lasting little more than a decade in many cases, as lumber companies bought stands of timber, then cut them and moved on. Sumner, built suddenly by Cummer crews in 1911, was slated to be completely gone by 1926. Its successor town, quaint-sounding Lacoochee in Pasco County, ninety miles southeast, was already up and running by 1923, processing a new tract in the Panasoffkee swamp area. The old mill at Sumner was aiding its own demise, feeding lumber into the building of Lacoochee, whose bigger and better mill was touted as being one of the first all-electric sawmills in the South. Fast disappearing was the cumbersome old age of steam.

By fits and starts, both personnel and equipment were being pulled from Sumner and installed at Lacoochee. Fannie Taylor and her husband James would soon move there, to be found in Lacoochee by the federal census of 1930. Neighbor Frances Smith would be positioned to see Fannie's lingering emotional distress, for Frances, too, would move to Lacoochee with her husband Charles, a sawmill oiler.

Saucy Edith Surls, growing up, would marry her brawny Sumner beau Roy Foster—who would be quarters boss at Lacoochee. Robert Missouri, the smiling, relentless workaholic, not only wound up at Lacoochee but, into his nineties, would continue living in its ghostly remains, after the big mill itself had long ago died, playing out the formula in turn.

And there was top boss Walter Pillsbury—also soon moving to Lacoochee, and into a bigger house, more than just a bungalow this time, with a convenient clay tennis court.

After 1926, the site of Sumner would revert uncannily to bare pasture. Even the water pipes that fed back-porch sinks were packed onto railroad flatcars. Like a traveling circus but with stumps, the gypsy culture's tents would soon furl.

There was pain in this shut-down—but not so much for the mill hands. Their steady paychecks and borrowed housing would continue, simply moving to a new location. The losers in the timber game were farther out in the woods —among locals who relied on Sumner's cash flow, their wagons creaking into the quarters to sell produce, beef or seafood from the Gulf. Small independent stores, run by pioneer families and dependent on the mill payroll, dotted a swath that extended out to the Gulf at Cedar Key. Southern forestry historian James Fickle wrote that the timber industry of those years "had its greatest impact" on those who were "left behind."[345]

It's no revelation that mass violence and group hatred can be used to dramatize a slow burn of panic felt by marginal or "left-behind" populations. There are ways to punish the uppity outside world: the hillbillies in *Deliverance* grabbing urban campers, the ghetto rock-throwers engulfing a strayed motorist, Luddites spiking the infernal machines. Terrorism expert Jessica Stern extended the definition to jihadists, vengeful as they "feel left behind by modernity…feel they can't keep up."[346]

In Sumner this was no vague abstraction. The woods farmers were staring abandonment in the face. They could only guess about the further step. Only a few years later, in 1932, even their backwater branch of railroad would cease to function, completing their shipwreck at the ends of the earth. In a cut-over jungle of stumps and malaria mosquitoes, few tourists were going be peeking in.

The last passenger train leaving Cedar Key July 7. 1932
(photo: Florida Master Site File)

It would be the woods farmers, not secure Sumner mill hands, who tipped the scales of the Rosewood week, first in the manhunt and then after Thursday in revenge for Poly Wilkerson and Henry Andrews, as this became racial cleansing. Stories would claim that mysterious outsiders were to blame, but there was no shortage of boasts by the home team.

In all this, it seemed a mere coincidence that 1923 looked a bit like a rehearsal for 1926. A community was scheduled formally for disappearance in 1926, and in 1923—as the corporate axe hovered—the drama of communal disappearance was acted out.

A tableau of town destruction was imposed ritually, but now with the script rectified, to put the left-behinds back on top, no longer to be kicked around by timber millionaires in fancy cars, but now wielding the intoxicating power of destruction themselves—sacrificing somebody else's town.

The view could be broadened. Sumner's left-behind woodland was but a micro-vortex in a great swirling backwater long famed for acting out left-behind woes: the low-wage South.[347] If a region-wide weather map could be drawn of lynching storms, each of them, of course, would be unique, born of special local conditions and events. And yet the basic winds, the storm fronts of displaced frustration and symbolized rage, would appear again and again, as if isobars might be plotted on a chart.

The arrival of a new year, 1923, drew Sumner's attention to the calendar, with its reminder of the countdown to 1926. Then the suspense was suddenly interrupted, as if by a scream in church.

Chapter 28: Footprints of Panic

While running for her life, Minnie Lee Mitchell could not see her growing fame. She had become one of "Twenty-Five Negroes Barricaded in House"—murderous cutthroats, lying in wait to "Open Fire on Whites..."

5 DIE SUMNER RACE RIOT
TWO WHITE MEN AND THREE BLACKS ARE SHOT TO DEATH

Rosewood, Three Miles Out of Sumner
Is Centre of Trouble
Arising From Case of Assault

Twenty-Five Negroes Barricaded in House, Defy
Armed Posse and Open Fire on Whites, Killing Two, Wounding
Several

Entire City of Cedar Key Up in Arms
Sheriff Ramsey and Many Others Respond to Call of Levy
County Officers to Aid in Quelling Rebellious Black Population

This word-picture greeted readers of the *Gainesville Daily Sun* on Friday morning, January 5. The week had now gone over the edge.

As in some other rampage escalations of the era, this shift was triggered by mysteriously suicidal meddling, conducted by a few would-be heroes in a car—perhaps drawn to the call of sadistic glory, but then consumed like moths in a flame. Many more moths would now seek revenge.

The kind of triggering role played by interveners Henry Andrews and Poly Wilkerson could vary with circumstances. In the Tulsa race riot of 1921, initial disastrous intervention came not from the population that

313

had the power, but from an opposing force. A group of armed African Americans rushed to Tulsa's courthouse square, answering a threat that later shown to be largely imagined. Though of a different race than Wilkerson and Andrews, the Tulsa interveners, too, seemed almost to insist on suicidal escalation of a crisis, which had originally been limited and manageable.

Much more typical in the time of lynching were glory seekers from the powerful white camp—and results tilted only one way. No matter who might have pulled the incidental trigger, it was white fury that would be released, under white supremacy's protecting umbrella, as response by whites brought the voracity of rampage.

The Friday headline put it simply. A "Rebellious Black Population" has arisen. The old rhythms of slave insurrection panic can still roll, even in the modern Roaring Twenties.

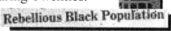

As Friday deepens, the footprints of mass panic will spread across a core geographical area with a population of more than 15,000 whites, mostly up and down the Seaboard tracks. It is a strange beast, this panic—living only moment to moment in excited rumors and speculation, swelling in stray bursts, dissipating suddenly as new information comes in to beat back the temptations of delusion. But in the Rosewood case, at least, the footprints of this exotic beast were captured for examination. As if preserved in plaster casts in a museum drawer, the signs of mass panic can be viewed in the surviving newspaper articles.

Here, staring from the yellowed old news clips, is the denizen that lacks even an adequate name. Mass panic? Contagious delusion? "Symbolic community scare"?[348] No wonder such storms of panic can

314

slip through the cracks of history as if nothing were there. Illusion and mirage are the thing itself, leaving tidy documentation at a loss.

When last we saw Minnie Mitchell, age nine, she was in the cold moonlight of Thursday night, leaping from her aunt Sarah Carrier's back porch. Stretched before her was Rosewood's silent baseball field to the south, and more distantly the tree mass of Gulf Hammock. Prior to reaching that jungle, however, she would find smaller thickets and dive in among the vines, sticking close to the other combat-shocked children, led by older Eddie and Bernadina. The children had now passed into the blank side of history, the side not penetrated by dissertations with neatly packaged written sources.

Dazed little Philomena, struggling to carry her younger brother Buster, whose tears from the stairway confusion are not dry. Unflappable Ruben, the backyard preacher, now finding that some of life's absurdities exceed even his droll gift for satire, as he deals with literally blinding pain. Bernadina in the stiffening russet stains on the gown. Quiet little Arnett, the rabbit hunter and future baseball star, too shocked now to absorb the sense of helplessness that will later haunt him, when he will think back about this night, and how he ran in panic. Not like a man, he thinks—some-thing to push from his mind. Post-traumatic coping by his sister Philomena will take a different turn, not into Arnett's solution of silent avoidance, but using more assertive blockage, re-scripting the flashback war story, imposing a glorious inner drama onto harsh memory—though never enough. It will never blot out the shock, the thought of the red pillow on the downstairs bed.

Present in the group fleeing from the house

Eddie   Ruben

Goldee

James, Jr. "J.C."

Minnie

Also in the group but not pictured:
Carrier family: Bernadina, Harry
Carrier/Carrol family: Lonnie
Goins family; Philomena, Arnettt ("A.T."),
Giorge, Jr. ("Buster")

At some level, many local whites seemed to know that the twenty-five rebel cutthroats in the news hid a reproachful reality. Boasts by assorted white fabulists would tell how they personally dashed into the death house and saved black children. This was laughably untrue, since the tellers demonstrably were not there, and whites who *were* there were afraid to get near the house, even to rescue their own dead, and (one) wounded. The children had to rescue themselves. Still, the tales made another kind of confession. Outside the house, awareness did dawn at some point that inside there might be children.

As Minnie's bare feet left the back porch, she could not see a figure who was simultaneously in flight. Young lumber inspector Cephus Studstill was headed almost as furiously in the opposite direction. While still in the attic Minnie had heard the car crank, apparently Wilkerson's car, seized by Studstill for strategic retreat—despite a .12-gauge pellet or two burning in Cephus's arm. With difficulty he would get home, along with wounded Bryan Kirkland. If an unknown number of other spur-of-the-moment nightriders had arrived with them (a small number if not zero), they also trickled back to Sumner.

No known memory or even a legend would find the chastened heroes (whatever their number) admitting their own debacle. Instead what was recalled (by whites (for only whites were in this loop) was the improved version of the story, spreading as a wildfire rumor.

The home team has not lost after all. Because it was tricked. Our boys were decoyed to that house by devilish old Sarah, so her barricaded uprisers could shoot down the flower of white manhood, taking out the first line of white defense.

While the adrenaline is pumping it is apparently unnecessary for the stories to make much sense, or even to agree with one another. The newspaper headlines embalm this, too. Rather than an appeal to logic there is a non-sequential adrenal mass, offering little more information than the command adrenaline makes. *Act! To Arms!*

Among the hieroglyphs is: "Entire City of Cedar Key Up in Arms." Why doesn't the headline say "Entire City of Sumner"? Again the Cedar Key telephone operator offers the most convenient eyes and ears (or just ears) for remote sensing by distant journalists, as they enter the coastal jungles only in their minds. Apparently the operator grows excited. The clues suggest that after lunging for her living-room switchboard she is pulled into the communal drama.

If, in Sumner or Otter Creek, the increasingly distraught wife of logging boss Henry Andrews is making use of the telephone to pin down rumors about something having happened to her husband, this will be known to the operator in Cedar Key. In Sumner, both Pillsbury and Deputy Williams will have had to phone up Sheriff Bob Walker in Bronson, the county  seat, to consult on the new Wilkerson-Andrews emergency. And the Cedar Key operator will know. Nobody else can turn that crank and make that magneto bell ring.

There were the backdrop memories from Cedar Key: Frank Coburn, Naomi Dorsett, Allen Faircloth, Milt McCain, others. The tough old island town apparently received the news around midnight. As a fishing enclave—and with ancestry as a hard-drinking frontier seaport and boomtown—Cedar Key was a place where you might stay up late, waiting for the tides, unlike sleepy mainland farmers. Around midnight there is talk, movement, whites turning out for the alarm.

Suddenly decaying Cedar Key is no longer left behind, but is on the front lines, helping save the white race. Its slow-motion death over the years is no longer the main menace, for a more exciting menace has stepped in.

The emotions were heartfelt and not cartoon caricatures, but these real emotions were directed at a menace which, impertinently, refused to materially exist.

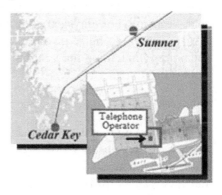

The blacks have killed the sheriff! (Never happened). *The blacks cooked up an ambush trick!* (Never happened) *They have all along been buying up a gallon of gas apiece so they can run wild tonight and burn down the town—just like the slaves at Charleston!* The hordes were just around the corner, just out of sight.

For years, as its isolation deepened, the island town had displayed a mad genius for believing in scare legends and frightening fantasies, as if knowing it was too far out in the tide flats for outsiders to come and check. Standard stories ran the gamut from the Massacre At Number Four, to Chasing Out The Mormons, to Henry Plant's Curse—stories too ornate for exploration here, but similarly woven. Imaginations seemed to be primed.

The skulking beast that is mass panic is not a screaming frenzy as in a cartoon, but at Cedar Key the footprints grew numerous. An adrenally heightened tendency to impulsive interpretations seemed able to hear a rumor and leap to conclusions. For comparison, a look might be taken at one of the most notorious panic stories of the twentieth century, the Halloween 1938 response to Orson Welles's *radio verité* program "The War of the Worlds."[349] Aftershocks from that mystery extended into social science, as scholars argued as to whether radio listeners really did panic, or whether newspapers and even sociologists accepted exaggerated illusions about the illusions.[350] The shape-shifting beast of belief, peering from the cavern of reality construction, can confuse many a sage.

For example, what about those Cedar Key stories spying guards on the bridges in the Thursday night alarm? Were the guards really there? Or was the real nature of the panic more subtle than that—causing not physical mobilization (real guards), but bizarre pseudo-memories (imagining the guards)? Or did both occur together?

Old Cedar Key

Around midnight on Thursday night, at a spot 57 miles from Cedar Key, a sleepy upstairs office comes alive. Perhaps at the *Gainesville Daily Sun* a lone night owl is on duty. Downstairs a room-sized linotype machine clanks away, croaking out harsh lullabies to a pressman on a stool. Now comes another footprint—but not in the *Daily Sun*:

> "First word of the trouble came from Cedar Key, about 10 miles from Rosewood, shortly after midnight."

This sentence, sounding much like the *Daily Sun's* headline ("Entire City of Cedar Key Up in Arms"), appeared at the same time but ran in the *Florida Times-Union* in Jacksonville. The information apparently came first to the *Sun* by phone, then bounced to the *Times-Union* by telegraph. The sequence is suggested by another footprint as the excitement grew—a wild spoor indeed The *Times-Union* went on:

> "The *Gainesville Sun* was requested to start for Rosewood immediately with as many men as he possibly could get together."

Try reading that again. The incoherence here, in all its glory, emblazons the fog of mass panic. No firm image can be focused upon in the words above. There is nothing to easily remember or responsibly document—because the English language breaks down. The sentence is gibberish. It makes no sense. Yet it stares soberly from a newspaper page, using sternly formal vocabulary, as if it must surely be saying something.

Perhaps here, too, the excitement of racial panic caused someone in the office to drop a line of type, or to leave out a scrawled line of pencil writing while feverishly translating dots and dashes off the telegraph. But in the heat of the moment the message makes another Freudian slip. The suddenly-important upstairs office is personified as a kind of supernatural being—  "he"—as if the *Daily Sun* itself were an avenging angel, poised to swoop down from the clouds—at the head of a trumpet-blaring heavenly host containing "as many men as he could possibly get together."

The dropped line is in fact trying to say that the county sheriff based in Gainesville, Sheriff Perry Ramsey of Alachua County, is the rescuing angel. But even after that glitch is remedied, the footprint still remains in another way, also suggesting irrational excitement. Newspapers like the  *Times-Union* did not give out advertisements for rival papers on the front page. Here was the *Gainesville Sun* getting a free ride. The alarm bells of Negro Insurrection were apparently ringing loudly. The cry for help had to be rushed into print, no matter what it said.

There were other signs. Even if the world were ending, county sheriffs in 1920s Florida did not contact one another by using a newspaper intermediary. Here, too, the *Gainesville Daily Sun* (or some suddenly-thrilled sentry there, manning the graveyard shift) was catapulted into Olympian importance. The Associated Press had strict rules against member papers strutting their names in wire copy. The daily flood of AP stories was supposed to look like the work of one large, seamless machine—"By the Associated Press"—with no obvious reminders of bush-league origins. Through war, pestilence and famine this rigor seldom relaxed. But in the first moments of 1923, amid the white South's "race war" fears, the footprints were getting sloppy—and the *Sun* slipped its name into the wire copy.

The line about Cedar Key suggests a sequence. The Cedar Key operator is suddenly swamped with calls asking her what is going on. She hears distraught Cuba Andrews pleading on the phone: *"My husband drove over to Rosewood..."* She hears the cryptic emergency conferences of law enforcement—which, of necessity, must be *very* cryptic, owing to the party line, on which everyone with a phone can listen. Many of those listeners will in turn be calling in to the operator. Cedar Key's love of scare stories intrudes—stories about blacks buying a gallon of gasoline apiece. The frantic operator hears other stories spreading from Sumner, saying that law enforcement has been mowed down cruelly by black conspiracy. They are ready to roll like Nat Turner through village and farm.

She acts. We have the footprint. Someone in the midnight panic zone phoned clear to the next county, Alachua County, to plead for reinforcements—in a doubly unorthodox way. Perhaps the Cedar Key operator was accustomed to talking to the *Sun*, sharing local news. Somehow, when a plug was stabbed into a hole in the central exchange switchboard in Gainesville, the hole was Number 219, the news number for the *Sun*—which soon was cranking out a telegraphed story featuring the *Sun* itself as the hero of the piece. Sheriff Bob Walker of Levy County would not have been pleased with this circumvention of his authority. The hyper-ventilating urgency—and perhaps a plea from the operator in Cedar Key—can be heard in another of the Friday headlines:

**"Sheriff Ramsey and Many Others Respond to Call
of Levy County Officers to Aid in Quelling Rebellious Black Population"**

It looks as if "Levy County Officers" are themselves pleading for help. But are they? Or is the phone call from a third party, insisting that Levy County's finest have now been shot down or run off, and white rescuers must respond? Either way, the cry is raised. A "Rebellious Black Population" needs "Quelling."

Below the headline in the story's main text, African American participants in the events disappear into a formless blur, without names or input as witnesses (though this version remedies the heavenly host glitch):

> **Two white men and three negroes are dead and a number of white and blacks injured as a result of an outbreak at Rosewood, three miles from Sumner, Levy county, late to-day and early tonight, according to reports received here late last night by telephone from Cedar Key.**
>
> **The dead are Boly Wilkinson [sic] of Sumner and Henry Andrews of Otter Creek, both white, and three unidentified negroes.**
>
> **The reports added that the population of Cedar Key was aroused and that many armed men from there were planning to go to Rosewood. The Sun was requested to ask Sheriff Ramsey of this, Alachua County, to go to the scene with as many men as possible as it was feared the situation, already beyond control of the Levy County authorities, would grow worse.**

Even with the footprints measured and cataloged, the largest distortions remain concealed, for they occur by omission. The story omits all fumbles by Our Team (the whites)—such as the shooting of the dog, the rout of the nightriders, the murder of the laundress in her bed, the signs of drunken target panic. In the process, ironically, it misses real action that could have helped its bid for sensational thrills. The only town it depicts as being "aroused" is Cedar Key. In reality, communities up and down the railroad were sending white rescue parties, though no one was recording this in print. On this point the only footprints are in the muddy ground of living memory. Around midnight two main forces were closing on Rosewood, from the direction of Sumner and—more formidably—from the company town of Otter Creek.

Chapter 29: The Last Stand

By midnight on Thursday night, the children in Sarah Carrier's house have all fled. For purposes of looking back into the night's events this closes a curtain. After this point, the inside of the house can supply no more direct eyewitness testimony. Behind a screen of rumors and fragmentary clues, the night is about to witness the last stand of Sylvester Carrier.

The backdrop, as it begins, is grim.

Downstairs in the front bedroom, probably still on the bed, is the stiffened form of Sarah Carrier. On the porch, just outside the shattered bedroom window, two more bodies can be seen only barely, those of Constable Poly Wilkerson and logging superintendent Henry Andrews, lost in caverns of moonshadow. From the perspective of the yard the porch might seem heaped with carnage, for a third figure is stretched somewhere near the steps, the hard-drinking woodsman Mannie Hudson, apparently so motionless that his panic-stricken comrades have left him for dead. He will stay at his involuntary sentry post until morning.

Gone from this backdrop is Emma Carrier, Minnie's grandmother. At some point, either in the shooting or in the shocked silence just afterward, Emma has fled, apparently alone, as Gert Carrier fled earlier. Emma, more heavily burdened, has at least one flesh wound.

Now only one certainly known living occupant of the house remains. Somewhere on the scene is Sylvester Carrier. When he sent Minnie upstairs to join the others he seemed to her to be unhurt. Then shortly afterward came the ghostly laughter, floating up from outside, as if grasping the absurdity of the doom. Stories later told by whites suggest that after the house had emptied the defender came back to it, making his last stand within.

Minnie recalled only silence surrounding her flight, as she and the others avoided the dim light of the moon: *"We jumped down off the porch, walked 'round the dark side....We ain't seen nobody or heard nobody when we left."*

A story cherished by the white rumor mill would depict the retreat of the nightriders as an orderly affair, leaving behind a watchman to monitor the field, supposedly hiding in the bushes.[351] The watcher soon harkens. He sees menacing movement. Sure enough, those black savages are slipping out the back of the house, barely visible in the moonlight—for they are seeking to surround the watcher and murder him, like poor Wilkerson and Andrews. He has no choice (he explains nobly in the tale) but to flee like the others, finding himself vastly outnumbered.

By midnight, the Cummer logging quarters in Otter Creek knows that the big boss is dead.

Or perhaps not quite dead. Perhaps he is only wounded on that devil's porch, and can still be rescued. They begin piling onto the gasoline-powered railroad motorcar—or perhaps more than one motorcar.

One tale, dim and perhaps imagined, said the riders grew numbed with cold, rushing twelve miles through frost-nipped air. The story said that on arrival in Rosewood they built a bonfire on the railroad, within sight of the "death house."[352]

The fierce old building had already consumed a previous expedition. Any white man now planning to creep near it would have to wonder, very specifically, whether he wanted to die. The Otter Creek group—and any others from Sumner or elsewhere who might have joined them—could only guess about who or what was hidden inside the house. The number of black casualties there was unknown, and the number of potential shooters.

A newspaper report apparently referred to this Otter Creek group (though in a muddle, merging it with other scenes) when it said that one Henry Odom was wounded at the house, and somehow had come from Jacksonville, 120 miles away.[353] No known record has ever confirmed the existence of such a participant. Additionally, an oral story put an Otter Creek resident named Wainwright in the group, having him, too, crouched for protection behind the crowded old palm tree in the yard.[354] No other names would surface. The Otter Creek effort would remain more secretive than Poly Wilkerson's confident preliminary.

This is no drunken lark or entertaining bloodhound chase. Deaths have occurred. They want those bodies.

As they finally close in, the shotgun replies, reportedly firing from inside the house. The Odom story has Odom leaping impulsively to a window, shining a flashlight for his comrades to shoot at a black marksman inside. The figure deftly wheels, shooting Odom in the neck, knocking him back out into the yard, leaving him badly wounded. Did this really occur? The veil is thick. Another story has the inside shooter retreating up the stairs as he fires. All of this could be moonshine.

The overall result, however, was proved by an unavoidable detail. As badly as the Otter Creek visitors would have wanted to retrieve the bodies on the porch, they couldn't get them. Everyone agreed that Wilkerson, Andrews and Hudson were not carried away until next morning, when daylight brought a larger crowd. Apparently the Otter Creek group was driven off, grumbling that this would have to wait for dawn.

By all indications, the defender has triumphed again.

This deeply concealed event would seem to be Sylvester Carrier's most dramatic victory—not just the rout of a few drunken joyriders but the defeat of a determined attack force. And it leaves no picture. The central act of the play is a void, a blacked-out game, a vague bumping of the stage furniture behind the curtain.

Legend will fill in the spaces.

———————————

As Sam Hall hears his mother shouting—*Sammy! Get up!*—the gunfire is distant but distinct. Listening from the groggy edge of sleep, he hears a pattern. Moving toward the stairs in his family's bare old saltbox house he continues to think about it. He thinks he can make out different kinds of guns.

First, there is a resonant booming, seeming to indicate fire from within the house, as if in an echo chamber (like a sound made in a barrel, he thinks). But there is also a sharper, thinner cracking, as if these are shots from outside ("out in the element"). He draws a picture in his mind of the two sides, attackers in the yard, defensive fire coming from within.

But the echoing and booming, seemingly from within the house, offers a second complication. It seems to result from two different defensive guns being fired, not just one. Sam will think harder about this later, as he hears the stories. There is yet another major chapter in what will become an underground Rosewood epic.

Some African American narrators, unheard by whites, would say that Sylvester Carrier was not entirely abandoned in the house. True, these informants agreed, the logical candidates for neighborly solidarity had all fled. But there was allegedly a lone exception—who by his very nature did not do things logically.

These stories depicted nothing so grand as the army of black rebels imagined in the newspapers. The new player on the stage is a riddle all by himself. Whether he was really in the house at all is an open question—but there was certainly a sobering precedent. At least once before in his life he had bucked the tide.

———————————————

The second son of James and Emma Carrier—younger than Aaron, older than Eddie—was named Willard.

Born at the dawn of the twentieth century, Willard Carrier would appear in the censuses of both 1910 and 1920, both times living at his parents' home, household 113. The censuses, however, failed to agree on his age, a key point in his history of sudden panache.

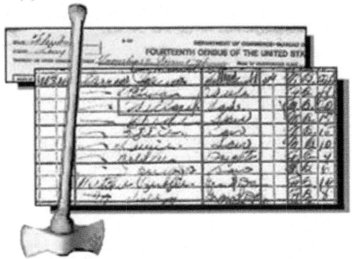

In 1920, according to that year's census, he was twenty, but the 1910 census said he was six. And in 1908 a news story had him as being six then, too—when he made big news.[355]

The 1908 explosion was long gone by 1923, but in it he was apparently around eight or nine, making him about 22 in January 1923. The age factor was blurred by something else. People knew Willard Carrier by a nickname, in reference to his deeper mystery.

"Big Baby, his mind was bad," said Thelma Hawkins, who grew up just north at Ed and Eliza Bradley's house. "Big Baby...He stuttered when he talked," said his brother Lonnie.[356]

Sam Hall, as usual, perceived a subtle distinction: Big Baby "wasn't ever just like he ought to be," and yet he "had good sense."

Descriptions of "Big Baby" Carrier, Willard, the second son of James and Emma, suggest autism, a word unknown in the woodlands of 1923. Some forms of autism bring severe speech repetition and a stuttering effect, and stuttering was often remarked in Big Baby. Another symptom came closer to the popular picture of "Rain Man" autism. For long periods he was said to sit on his parents' porch and stare into space—as he apparently absorbed startling knowledge.

Complicating Willard Carrier's childhood was Rosewood's boom time before 1911, as both a cedar mill and multiple turpentine camps brought unpredictable activity. A typical turpentine camp was "primitive, isolated, lonely, destructive," and Rosewood apparently had three such camps at its height before 1908, one of them using leased convicts.[357] [358] [359] Just up the railroad in those days was another cluster so violent that lawmen were said to keep their distance.[360] An immobilized child on a porch was facing a turbulent world—though he could also witness some frontier self-defense.

Rosewood's commercial hunters, fur trappers and hunting guides included the Carrier brothers, James and Haywood, living within sight of one another beside the wilderness railroad. James, Willard's father, was "a mighty man," in the words of another son, Lonnie.

Lonnie recalled how his father would appear at dawn from all-night hunts in the woods, a deer slung over one shoulder, his shot sack stuffed with smaller game. Lonnie watched one day as a wounded deer ran out of the woods and tangled in the fence at home, then was killed by his father. A white man arrived on a horse, shouting that the deer was rightfully his because it was his shot that originally wounded it. But James menacingly leveled a shotgun, forcing the horseman to gallop away. Whether Willard was a quiet observer in the background of this scene, no one would recall.

It was May 11, 1908, when the reckoning came. A court record would survive, supporting a less formal newspaper story, and the family passed down stories of its own. A group of young men, neighbors, came walking down the railroad, apparently in a reckless mood. They spied the motionless figure on the porch.

These were not strangers, for they knew his symptoms.[361] Savoring a chance to be cruel, one of them stepped up to the fence, shouting comically, imitating Big Baby's tortured speech.

Stories in the community would focus on what happened next—an event that left people gaping—with fewer comments on the prelude of cruel bullying. One story put it on a Sunday, the day off in a six-day work week, perhaps meaning afternoon drinking (just down the tracks in those days stood a sawmill jook at Lukens, bustling not only on Saturday but Sunday nights).[362] But the calendar was unkind to this explanation. May 11, 1908, was actually a Monday.

At any rate, as the taunts came insistently across the front-yard fence, the bully won the game. The small target was forced to leave his place on the porch, and he disappeared into the house. The tormenters apparently lingered, perhaps still mocking. Thus they saw the small figure reappear, standing in the front doorway. And he was carrying something.

The shotgun barrel came up level, the long weight braced against the child's form. Then suddenly a 28-year-old man at the fence, Warren Coleman, from a hunting and trapping family back in the woods, lay dead.

One of the tellings about this was a remarkably taut poem, only eight words:

"Little Buddy tease him. Big Baby kill him."

There was reason to wonder about a secondary mystery, one often seen in the autistic spectrum, a gift sometimes called savant syndrome. The sufferer, cut off from everyday skills by neurological blockage, somehow acquires genius-level ability in very narrow but spectacular domains—perhaps mathematical calculation, or photographic memory, or musical composition, or a camera-like ability to draw and paint.

Willard Carrier's life had exposed him to a local form of artistry. He evidently knew the gun.

Court proceedings came on May 25. Against all the caprices of time and basement storage, the actual indictment against Willard Carrier would be physically preserved, surviving into the cyber-age tied up in dusty string: "*State of Fla. v. Willard Carrier*...willfully and of his malice aforethought ...with a certain shot gun...a mortal wound did inflict." Ten witnesses were named. Less formal was the story in the *Levy Times-Democrat*, a weekly newspaper printed at the county seat, marveling at the deed by "the little Negro boy...about six years old."

It can happen. On October 29, 1997, a child named Nathaniel Abraham, not quite 12, lifted a stolen .22-caliber rifle in Pontiac, Michigan, and killed an 18-year-old stranger coming out of a convenience store.[363] Only a year later the Jonesboro, Arkansas, school shootings produced perpetrators aged 11 and 13, killing five, wounding ten.[364]

The family stories told of Big Baby's reaction. Once the bully was dead, they said, Willard just sat back down on the porch and resumed staring, as if nothing had happened.

In the 1980s this would be strangely reprised. An elderly white informant from the Sumner area, a woman, recalled a story she had heard as a child, about her father's service as a deputy sheriff. The story said that one day the deputy got a call to go to Rosewood, apparently a rough little Negro place, since a man had just been killed there. But, the teller puzzled, the story insisted that the lawman was in no hurry, saying the killer was not going to flee.[365] And sure enough, the teller puzzled further, the criminal was sitting right there on a porch, waiting.

The woman seemed not to guess that as a child she might have picked up only half a story, leaving out the punchline about the shooter's age. To her it became a different kind of instructional tale, explaining why, one week in 1923, her familiar white culture had seen the necessity of burning down a dangerous outlaw's roost.

In reality, a slow-burn of internal violence did burden a small community in the woods. But as with Big Baby, the reality was unlike the monstrous menace envisioned from afar.

Judge Ben Friedman peered at a small defendant in 1908 and declared the murder indictment "no bill." Big Baby was released to the custody of his parents. In 1923 he was still there. Like his brother Aaron and his cousin Sylvester, he cut railroad crossties in the woods, while living at Mama's and Papa's house along with Minnie, who liked him.

It could be wondered whether in 1908 a fast shuffle had occurred, and perhaps the real shooter, defending a child against an adult bully, was the hot-tempered father James Carrier. Was the blame really shifted onto the silent child in order to seek the lightest sentence, after everyone agreed the tormentor had it coming?

No trace of gossip hinted at this. There were no dissenters; everyone agreed: It really was Big Baby.

As a much larger explosion neared on Thursday night, January 4, 1923, Big Baby again faded from view. Most members of his household walked down to Aunt Sarah's house, but there were the two question marks. Memories varied on the two silent figures, James Carrier (Papa, age 56) and Willard (Big Baby). Did they go to Sarah's or not? They seemed to be everywhere and nowhere. Both were disabled, and both were adult males who might have shunned a women-and-children refuge at Sarah's. Any number of factors could have muddled them in memory—which freed up Big Baby for the biggest story of all.

Once again in the hour of need, the sleepy Man-Child wakes, throws off his dreamy staring—and towers again as in 1908, ready to strike at the bullies. In his mysterious mind it is as if no time has passed. Once again he will ignore overwhelming odds—as he stands with Sylvester.

This, more or less, was the drift of the story, which was told only among certain African American narrators, and was apparently unknown to whites. In white circles there was a bit of gossip suggesting that gunfire might have come from Sarah Carrier's back door, foiling attackers who sought to encircle. This could easily have been Sylvester, still in the battle after the children had fled, making a *beau geste* with his six-shot cannon, running back and forth in the hall from front door to back.

Or it could have been Big Baby.

After all, implausibility is not disproof in this case. The hero has done the implausible before. But as the most ardent versions of the story continue, question marks multiply.

As Big Baby stands with Sylvester, he shoots valiantly, but at last the numbers are too great. He is overwhelmed. Then the martyred Man-Child meets the next phase of the apocalypse, as the house is burned down around him. His charred corpse is unidentifiable in the ruins, enabling the trick.

Cleverly, the body is disguised to fool the attackers, so they will think they have won their trophy, and that Sylvester has been killed. Big Baby's corpse is arranged so that they will think it is Sylvester lying there dead—thus providing cover for Sylvester to escape, in complete secrecy. No matter what the official voices say, Sylvester, the Protector, did not really die on that cross of porch and hall. We won! He lives!

Thus went the story, more or less.

Willard Carrier did disappear on that Thursday night, January 4, 1923. For an extended period afterward his niece Minnie was among those thinking that he must have been killed. But in later times, as painful exile took Minnie into foster homes and turpentine camps, there came a knock at the door. She could scarcely believe her eyes. Standing before her was her long lost uncle, Willard.

In his halting way, Big Baby explained to her that he had been badly frightened after the January 1923 events—so frightened that he fled to a place where no one seemed likely to find him, up the Suwannee to the state line, there to find a logging job in the deepest of the swamps, the one called Okefenokee, at the Suwannee's source.

Apparently Willard Carrier really did live through the Thursday night explosion. The story saying otherwise seems to have been one more fantasy, a post-traumatic rescripting told among survivors who were small children at the time of the events, cut off from contrary evidence—though this story had a long reach. The 1997 film *Rosewood* [366] would use the disguised-body story as if it were proven fact, in a screenplay woven of such luminous stories: the secret white boyfriend, the Masonic intervention, the Rosewood paradise, others—while excluding the most credible survivor testimony with its disproof of the myths. Cinema seemed drawn to a Rosewood of magic—a painfully wished-for Rosewood—as it buried the Rosewood of fact.

But with that said, Minnie's proof of Big Baby's survival left a loose end. *Why* was he so frightened in the wake of Thursday night?

Did he flee that far away, and have so little contact with the rest of his family, simply because the night was shocking? Back in 1908, the sound of gunfire hadn't seemed to shock him much. Did this imply that on the night of mystery, January 4, 1923, Willard Carrier really did do more than just watch?

The darkness in the house was deep, and Big Baby was not given to explanations. The children in the attic could not see downstairs, and Minnie, even when she was downstairs, could not see up—where a second gun might have operated in the attic. Nor could any of them see who might have crept into the house later, arriving for the larger battle after they were gone. The last word goes to another family member, tormented by a disability of his own—cerebral stroke—which had stricken him by the time posterity came asking for his observations.

Lonnie Carroll, Willard's younger brother, used his father's preferred spelling of his last name, instead of "Carrier." Lonnie, too, was in the attic that night. Sixty years later he fought the demons of stroke-induced aphasia to force out the words, as he said:

"Big Baby done a lot of shootin'."

Chapter 30: First Flames

More than a half mile southwest of Sarah Carrier's house another residence faces the railroad, occupying a plot of 4.65 acres near the First A.M.E. Church.[367] The owners are Sam and Ellen King, living there with a small daughter, Eloise. The 1920 census lists this as Household 108, without mentioning the family portraits over the mantelpiece, the picture of Jesus, the long front porch with cracked planks, or the pedal sewing machine in the side room, where Ellen does seamstress work.[368]

As midnight brings the first moments of Friday, January 5, white avengers are trickling into an apprehensive settlement, at first only a few men probing through the woods, wondering what to focus on, what kind of action to take. These could be enraged stragglers from the original rout at Sarah Carrier's house, or frustrated Otter Creek veterans of the second defeat. In this murky moment no one hears a snap. An invisible bough has been bending as the week progressed. Now, at the King house, it breaks. This will begin the hurricane phase of mass atrocity, when selective targeting swells into random expression of group hatred.

Ironically, the King house stands on an invisible boundary, the north-south section line that separates the two halves of Rosewood, its dark- and light-complexioned halves.[369] To the east are the Carriers, Bradleys, Halls, Colemans and others who are dark, going back to the earliest pioneers.[370] But the Kings are later arrivals, drawn to these palm-lined jungles in the 1890s with the Caucasian-looking Goins family—coming from origins cloaked in Cherokee tales and strange old ethnic words like Portagee and Melungeon.[371]

Next to the Kings, just up the railroad, is the home of a 55-year-old widow, Lexie Gordon, who has similar roots.[372] These two homes—and the nearby church—will mark the breaking point.

Little Eloise King has heard no gunfire tonight. She sees only a faint hint that something is amiss. Her father Sam King, a logger with Cummer Lumber, has stepped out for a moment, an odd thing to do at this late hour. For some reason, he has walked up the tracks to Wright's store.

Eloise is accustomed to isolation. Up the tracks, Minnie and other children view Eloise as something of a hothouse plant, a spoiled little princess. Eloise enjoys the image. Her adoring father, so strong that he can fell large trees, would never dream of spanking her. She thinks  smugly to herself: *He would sooner break the switch.* Sam King has indulgently opened a small charge account for his saucy daughter at Wright's, so she can buy candy. Their home is dotted with trophies—the toy stove, the tiny carriage—gifts for Eloise at Christmas.

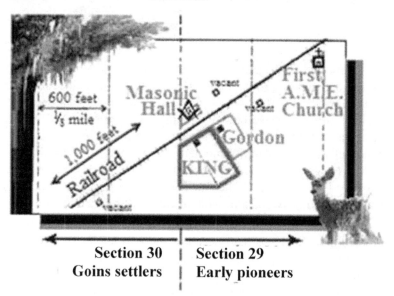

Section 30 | **Section 29**
Goins settlers | **Early pioneers**

Once on Christmas Eve, hearing a sound in the parlor, Eloise peeked toward the chimney. She was startled to see two booted feet dangling there, after a furtive performer had climbed right up into the grimy flue, and now was kicking his boots theatrically in the fireplace, pretending to be Santa. Someone was going to great lengths to intrigue the little princess. She smirked and went along with the act, knowing it was Daddy.

Other children are allowed to come only to the gate of the King home, not into the yard, though there is an exception to the rule. A little white boy, Rob Ingram, lives just back in the woods to the south. In the morning Eloise's mother drinks coffee with Rob's mother. Like suburban housewives on a rotating schedule, they go first to one's house, then the other's. Rob Ingram is accepted as an appropriate playmate.

Eloise, fearing no punishments, makes a game of seeing how far she can push her mischief—though one day this backfires. "Don't drink water behind Rob at the pump," her mother warns sternly, explaining that Rob has caught whooping cough. So if Rob drinks from the hand pump in the backyard as they play, Eloise is not to follow. She then mischievously creeps out to the pump and does just that, to prove she can. The results would later seem  sadly logical to her (as it seemed logical to her that whooping cough might be carried only by water and not general playtime contact). Soon she was coughing. It grew worse. Her father was frantic. Walking out to the railroad with his gun, he searched until he found a large crow perched on the tracks. The glistening bundle of feathers, still trembling after the shot, was brought back to breathe its dying breath into Eloise's open mouth—the treating of like with like, hoarse cough with hoarse croak. And sure enough, she got well. This seemed logical.[373]

In Eloise's mind none of these adventures, nor her isolation, related to the pressures of the larger world. For more than two decades, racial segregation laws had been tightening in the South, marking off the regional experiment with the sarcastic name, Jim Crow segregation. As it fenced off the thousand miles of Dixie, Eloise was shielded from such thoughts.

Some people said that her light-complected parents, as well as Lexie Gordon next door, might as well be white—that they were just "going for colored," pretending to be Negroes.[374] But the Kings firmly considered themselves African American—and perhaps also Cherokee, Lumbee, Scottish Highlander, Portuguese or any of the other components in the old tri-racial riddles. Their only child, Eloise, was in fact adopted. She had come from the dark side of town, and knew this comfortably. Originally she was a Carrier, born to Ransom and Louisa Carrier, and thus a sister of the orphaned outsider Lee Carrier. Eloise, unlike her adoptive parents, was dark. Seeing no problem in this, she felt an indestructible shelter of parental love.

 Their house was not a two-story structure, but its long wrap-around porch pointed back to a smokehouse and garden space. In the far corner of the four-acre lot were hogs, penned, not roaming wild on a woodland hog claim. Loggers like Sam King were proud of their pay, and Sam had added enterprise income. On Sundays, his one day off, he sometimes cranked out ice cream in a salt freezer, then sold it at Wright's. There was also the thumping rhythm of Ellen's foot on the cast-iron pedal of her sewing machine, bringing in seamstress income.

.Their life was not perfect. Despite the friendship of the wives, a quarrel developed between Sam and Rob Ingram, the father of Eloise's playmate. The hog pen was at the back of the four acres, the usual arrangement, confining the smell, but it was hard to see what went on back there. The hogs seemed to disappear. Sam blamed the white neighbor. There were words. It was no novelty for hog-theft accusations in the woods to point to the largest racial group, the whites.[375]

The quarrel passed. On the long porch she felt no loneliness. There were companions. She conversed with her little dog—or with a still smaller face darting among the porch planks, the old black snake. There were tea parties to be held with the blacksnake, as she fed it cornbread—to the horror of her mother. It was not that a harmless rat snake might bite, but that this, too, involved sympathetic magic,[376] joining spirit to spirit. After Eloise had unwisely made contact, you couldn't kill the snake. *Kill the snake, you kill Eloise.* Eloise heard this and gazed back skeptically—as at the boots kicking in the Christmas chimney and the warning about whooping cough. What could possibly  go wrong? From her porch throne she could wave at the passenger train. And Bryce, the jolly Santa Claus of a train conductor, would wave back. This world was forever, too secure to end.

Why is Daddy gone? Why did he go up to Wright's store so late? It's not even open.

As a lumberjack for the Cummer corporation, Sam King is under the command of logging superintendent Henry Andrews—though with a distinction. Most Cummer loggers live in company quarters at Otter Creek, or at the Fowlers Bluff camp on the Suwannee. But King and one other logger, Wesley Bradley, live in their own homes in Rosewood, outside company control. Each Monday before dawn they hike into Sumner and catch the log train. This takes them another twelve miles or so into the Suwannee swamps, where they camp through the week, usually returning home Saturday night. It is not unknown, amid the pressures of production quotas, for the loggers to stay out several weeks at a time.

Sam knows the logging personnel who bunk at Otter Creek. He rides the log train with them. He knows the white foremen and others who apparently have now come down the tracks in a work cart. Conceivably, he might be in a position to walk up the tracks this night and act as mediator. Not very likely. But then nothing is very likely tonight. For unstated reasons, Sam King has walked up into the dark side of the community, an area where flight to the woods has already begun, women and children crowding into Wright's shed. But this evacuation has not yet generalized. The panic has not reached the side of the community where the Kings live—not quite yet. It would be an under-standable thing, for him to go up there and check on the disturbance.

Then he is back.

Bursting through the front door, gasping to his wife:

"Ellen, we better get out of here."

"What we gon' do?"

"Ain't nothin' to do but to take to the woods."

Someone seems to be coming just behind him, moving down the railroad. Sam and Ellen throw a coat over Eloise. She is still barefoot, rising from bed. Sam pauses for only one thing, to dash next door and shout a warning to neighbor Lexie Gordon, urging her to run as well. He then grabs Eloise as he and Ellen dash out the back. Reaching the trees behind the house, they pause and look back. From somewhere out of sight there are voices, apparently in front of the house. "Sam! Sam! We know you're in there! Come on out!"

Whoever it is, they know Sam King well enough to know where he lives. She thinks she glimpses them. She thinks some are on horses.

Then the shots, fired into the silent house. Then the flames.

And that is all. No further details.

As this next phase unfolds, no surviving memory will be able to reveal the thinking of the perpetrators—or to tell who those perpetrators are.

The cavern is deepening now, the bystanders falling away. Increasingly, the only witnesses left on the scene have much to hide. The answers to the questions—*Why here? Why now?*—remain the private possessions of those with the least reason to talk, the doers of the deeds, in their eternal courtroom lament: Your Honor, I wasn't there.

The opening burst of destruction will be confined to a narrow strip along the railroad, probably less than a quarter mile long, around the King and Gordon homes:

The pedal sewing machine in the side room, the chimney where the Santa Claus boots kicked, the pictures of the Last Supper and the Crucifixion over the fireplace, the toy stove and miniature carriage, the Victrola playing "Just a Closer Walk With Thee," the family portraits gazing down from parlor walls. She hears her father speak to her mother softly as they watch it burst into flames:

"Oh, my God. Baby, your stuff is gone."

If the Otter Creek visitors, defeated at Sarah Carrier's house, have now turned their anger onto substitutes, new arrivals on horseback could have joined them in the dark. Or, later events suggest, other horsemen—notably the woods rider Jack Cason—might even have been trying to stop them, though Eloise heard no argument, only the taunts and flames.

Once the arson threshold has been crossed, there are targets on hand that are not houses. The initial rampage area contains two larger buildings, the remaining anchors of communal life. There would be reports of the church bell ringing—though apparently not in alarm. Perhaps euphoria and sarcasm mixed together as an arsonist found the bell rope. Eloise was just down the tracks, also hearing the bell.

The plank church with its small belfry, opened in 1912 as the successor to the church burned in 1911. The echoing shouts of praise, the visiting preachers sleeping in the spare room at Wesley's, Virginia cooking the big dinners in advance on Saturday because the Lord's Day is for rest. The discussions of whether it is a sin to dance. The celebrity preacher coming one day from Gainesville in his baby-doll slippers that the men joked about, the shouts so smooth that women swooned and men fought off the sin of jealousy. The backsliders at Coleman's playing crack-a-loop and cutting their eyes at the high and mighty. The worn hymnals. *It is well, It is well with my soul.* The district conventions at Gainesville or Ocala, the soaring organ music, the voices beautifully raised, Sarah beaming at the smartly stepping marchers, the Easter passion play, crepe paper barrel hoops held up by beaming children spelling out E-A-S..., the influx from the other church up the tracks in the customary southern-style split of feuding congregations. *Come Ye Disconsolate. Brighten the Corner Where You Are.* The stinging lye smell in the last wisp of smoke from the neat square of white ash.

First African Methodist Episcopal Church of Rosewood.

Feb. 15, 1912 – Jan. 5, 1923.

R.I.P.

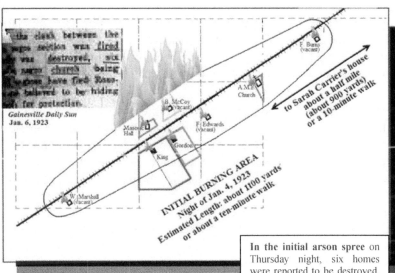

Gainesville Daily Sun
Jan. 6, 1923

INITIAL BURNING AREA
Night of Jan. 4, 1923
Estimated Length: about 1100 yards
or about a ten-minute walk

to Sarah Carrier's house
about a half mile
(about 900 yards)
or a 10-minute walk

In the initial arson spree on Thursday night, six homes were reported to be destroyed. Evidence suggests that in addition to the King and Gordon homes, the other four targeted houses were already vacant.

Land records in the area did not specify house sites within parcels. In the map above, house placement is derived from informant memories collated with data in parcel records.

The second institutional target, also a pale plank building, is similarly easy to find. It stands across the tracks from the church, but down a bit to the northeast, its one-acre plot forming a skewed parallelogram. The building itself is distinctively turned, its board facade facing not southeast toward the railroad but due east, in the direction of the ancient mysteries. Silent in the night, looking particularly blank and blind because of its oddly windowless upper story, the building projects a vaguely fortress-like appearance, like a stockade with loopholes instead of windows—not an unusual arrangement for a backwoods Masonic hall.

Magnolia Lodge #148, floating in the African American stream of the organization called the Free and Accepted Masons, acquired its one-acre plot on March 23, 1910, as the cedar mill was about to close and the community it supported was dying.[377] The Masonic hall formed an anchor for a new kind of community, in the separate stream of Masonry that was African American. A meeting room on the ground floor was used for public events—sometimes dances, but later as a subscription school, after the community's one-room public school for African Americans had apparently closed. Children who could afford the fifteen cents a week came to be taught in the Masonic hall.[378]

The upstairs portion, however, went by different rules, off-limits to all but initiated men, no women or children allowed. The darkened theater maze for initiations, the lobed pillars, the tyler's sword, the all-seeing eye. The awe of the journeyman as the sword probes, the invocation of Solomon, the secrets of pharaoh's tomb.[379]

Eloise would watch at night as Daddy went over there to the raisings, carrying a plate Mama had cooked because he would be gone all night. This was all that could be known of the inner things, when someone was raised, undergoing the harsh interrogation for the third degree. Masonic code phrases extended across the land—"on the square," "past master," "getting the third degree."[380] On the old frontier if you arrived new at a place, not knowing who to trust, you gave the hand sign (looking like you were merely scratching your ear, should an unknowing cowan or outsider observe it). When you shook hands there was the grip, the concealed greeting of the widow's son.[381] Lodges of white Masons—in the other stream—stood in Cedar Key, Otter Creek, Bronson. You could go anywhere and find the Craft, though divided into the streams, black and white.

Eloise was no stranger to the ground floor of the Rosewood lodge, the public part, for she attended its subscription school. There had been a series of teachers, including college-educated Agnes Marshall, one of the Goins daughters. After Mrs. Marshall's death in 1918, Aaron Carrier's wife Mahulda was said to teach in the school. At some point a smaller building, a one-room public schoolhouse well to the north, between the Hall and Ed Bradley farms, had fallen into disuse, growing cobwebbed and musty like the abandoned houses that were beginning to dot the two-square-mile area of communal contraction.[382] Sitting in the subscription school in the Masonic hall, Eloise did not feel the decline. She could look out the front downstairs window and wave to her mother on the porch at home, just across the tracks.

The 1890s turpentine migration had brought not only Agnes Marshall of North Carolina and her grand piano, but her entrepreneur father Martin Goins, the lessor of eight square miles of pinelands for M. Goins & Bros. Naval Stores.[383] By the time the Masonic hall was sited in 1910, Martin Goins had been deceased for a half decade. But he, too, was a Mason.[384]

Child-sized writing slates, blue-backed geography books, the substitute teacher rapping your knuckles if you spelled wrong, arithmetic at the board, the history of how we came from Africa. Gone were the teacher paychecks from the county, signed by Ransom Edwards the superintendent of the old public school.[385] On October 14, 1911, a newspaper at the county seat summed up the pressures on such schools under the segregation system, noting: "Salaries: male teacher $59.34, female white: $44.84, black: $30.75." [386]

There would be no one to say who applied the torch to the Masonic hall, as if the two-story plank building walked into the flames all by itself, no human hand to help it. No labyrinth of motivation was confessed, just the sour smell of the completeness, the neat square of ash.

Magnolia Lodge #148, F. & A. M.

March 23, 1910 – January 5, 1923.

R.I.P.

The community is now deeply wounded. Its two institutional pillars, already strained, have been eliminated. The intention is clear. Moving toward reality now is a dream of grandiose simplicity—the idea of cauterizing an envisioned ethnic wound, deleting the bad seed, creating blissful racial consistency: *running them all out of there.*

The implementation will come in ragged bursts as it meets logistical difficulties or opportunities. As Friday morning dawns, most of the buildings in the community are undamaged, being missed by the tentative euphoria of the first spree.

"Additional ammunition has been ordered from Gainesville, and Sheriff [illegible] Walker told the Associated Press tonight further trouble appeared imminent. Relatives of the slain negroes are believed to be armed and are

expected to cause trouble if overtaken by the whites.

"During the clash between the races the negro section was fired and virtually was destroyed, six houses and a negro church being burned...."

—Gainesville Daily Sun, Jan. 6, 1923

This glimpse has apparently come from Sheriff Bob Walker's voice speaking on the phone: "six houses and a negro church being burned." Accuracy does not seem a primary concern. Someone—either the sheriff doing the talking or the reporter doing the listening (and translating)—has wound up implying that the "six houses and a negro church" made up the entire community: "the negro section was...virtually destroyed."

Readers are led to believe that a small shantytown section of a white town was the only target, and that this "negro section" consisted of only about six homes, elimination of which means that the whole place was "virtually destroyed."

As the telegraph wire spread this view, an editor three thousand miles away would further refine it. *The Los Angeles Times* (quoted below) made the tiny shift of "during" to "following," and, more importantly, changed the phrase "virtually destroyed" into flat dismissal: "the negro section was fired and destroyed." The confusion could have originated as Sheriff Walker hoped once again to calm down the mob, by insisting that there is now nothing left to destroy. Or, less nobly, it could reflect the Our Side mentality of a white reporter (Any atrocity committed by Our Side couldn't possibly have been very large).

"Additional ammunition has been ordered from Gainesville and Sheriff Walker said tonight that further trouble appeared imminent. Relatives of the slain negroes are believed to be armed and are expected to cause trouble if overtaken.

"Following the clash between the races, the negro section was fired and destroyed, six houses and a negro church being burned. All negroes have fled Rosewood and are believed to be hiding in the woods for protection."

—Los Angeles Times, Jan. 6, 1923[387]

Mainstream history would be too overworked to look very closely at this *trompe l'oeil*. In the 1960s, historian George Brown Tindall tackled the information gap on the Lynching Era in his landmark survey work, *The Emergence of the New South* (1967). He was faced with trying to do justice to the great thousand-mile stretch of mystery land over multiple decades. Even so, Tindall did manage, rather heroically, to squeeze in one of the very few mentions of the disowned Rosewood atrocity, while historians in Florida were essentially burying the case. However, the local denial had kept contextual information out of the available record and thus still snared Tindall in the end, for his 1967 overview of the Rosewood incident would be expressed like this:

> **"...at Rosewood, Florida, where a white mob in search of an alleged Negro rapist ran amuck through a Negro community, burned six houses and a church and left five Negroes and two whites dead."** (p. 155)

In other words, Tindall's research had happened onto the one newspaper mention that told of the initial burning spree on Thursday night. Apparently feeling unable to check its accuracy by looking further, he endorsed that story as unquestioned fact—and as being the whole story. Simply by thumbing ahead a couple of days in the same newspapers, he could have seen larger reports showing events soon to follow. Instead, Rosewood was left to look like a six-house blip, with no further damage. The historical silence on lynching was so large that even methodical inquirers were liable to the illusions.

And Tindall's one-sentence mention formed the *best* history on the Rosewood blind spot. It was a rare if not unique exception to the solution offered by more local academia, that of complete suppression.

But what, then, was the reality behind those "six houses"?

The old cedar mill area around the King and Gordon homes held at least four residences that were vacant and boarded up by 1923. The departed householders were Frank Burns, Fred Edwards, Benny McCoy and Will Marshall.[388] The shells they left behind may have tempted the torch (and perhaps a moment of silence is deserved here for an object never announced; in one of those houses, under a cobwebbed sheet, stood the late Agnes Marshall's grand piano).

343

So now the count rises to five homes initially burned, if we include the King home and the four vacant residences, plus the church (the Masonic hall went unmentioned in the news item). However, the news may have wobbled into accuracy here, with its "six houses...burned." There is one more house still left to examine. In the initial target area along the railroad there were two homes of African Americans, not just one, that were still occupied. They stood side by side. In one lived the lumberjack, the seamstress and the little princess.

And in the other, the widow.

It made a nice Sunday drive from Sumner, only a couple of miles, going over to Lexie Gordon's house to buy buttermilk. This was an accustomed outing for some of the old pioneer whites in Sumner. The jersey cow owned by widow Lexie Gordon of Rosewood was a prized possession, supplementing her garden. She, too, had met the community's long slide. Lexie's husband Minner Gordon was gone (the records may have misspelled his first name). A son-in-law had been there to help for awhile, but by 1923 the married daughter and her husband had moved away.[389]

Lexie, age 55, made a vivid image in memory. There was her size—short, feisty, energetic. But more arresting was the other detail, the hair. Her hair was bright auburn-colored, red, and was worn long. A lingering outrider of the Highlander/Melungeon/Cherokee/African mysteries from the Carolinas, red-haired Lexie Gordon was another resident who eluded the racial categories of Jim Crow.

Eloise King next door felt sure that Miz Lexie was white. The federal census classified Lexie Gordon as neither "B" (black) nor "W" (white), but as "Mu," meaning "Mulatto." Like the Kings, the Goinses and others around her, she was trapped between worlds.

Apparently at least one grown daughter, Fonnie, still lived with her. Other children and grandchildren—and the son-in-law—had lived there at one point, but as Rosewood shrank, the household dwindled. When a cry of alarm rang out on Thursday night, January 4, 1923—from Sam King or whatever source—the Gordon household (perhaps consisting of only two adults by that point, mother and daughter) was reportedly thrown into turmoil. The stories were vague, but agreed on one point. Lexie was seriously ill in bed, unable to run. The folklore diagnosis was "typhoid-malaria fever," a catch-all that could mean anything, but probably meant simple malaria, the strain of non-cerebral malaria found in much of the South in those days, and especially in Florida. This was *Plasmodium malariae,* much less fatal than the plagues of the Equator such as *Plasmodium falciparum,* which still kills millions today. However, even this "mild" form can be curse enough—perhaps feeling like a bad flu if the victim is a strong adult. In the very young or the malnourished or the old it can mean the end. At best there are wracking cycles of chills, fever and severe aches.

It was said that when the alarm rang out she gasped helplessly to the others (or perhaps to just one other, the frightened daughter Fonnie), allegedly saying: *Run, leave me here, I'll be all right, I can't do it, save yourself.*

The torches didn't know that only one occupant remained in the house. The porch was collapsing in flames. *Look! In the backyard! There's one now!* The tales had her stumbling into a bush, or trying to hide under the house, or cowering under a quilt, or—in one sensitive rendition among some whites—fumbling at the door of an outhouse. Perhaps nobody knew. Perhaps nobody besides the one hero, squinting into the dark as the gunsight triumphantly finds the fierce black rebel combatant—whose blurred form is strangely pale, for some reason, flickering under the moon.

Beyond doubt there was at least this one witness, because somebody did open fire. The shooting could have been a clumsy mistake, soon plunging its perpetrator into remorse and horror—or it could have been done out of merciless glee. Perhaps the shooter had no illusions about firing at some fierce black rebel, but, in a secret moment when no one else could see, perhaps he found a helpless middle-aged woman, fully viewed and recognized, to be an enticing target.

There was the story that the shooter walked up to the corpse and broke down in tears, seeing what he had done. And another story saying that a vengeful white youth had once been told to stay away from one of Lexie Gordon's light-skinned daughters, and in the moonlight he got even. Braggarts found it irresistible to fill in the gaps, no knowledge necessary.

On the ground lay a small, pale, aging figure with flowing red hair, whose crime was that she was sicker and slower than anybody else.

Whatever the effect on the shooter, it was not strong enough for public confession.

Death Number Five has occurred.

Sam Carter, Sarah Carrier, Poly Wilkerson, Henry Andrews.

And now Lexie Gordon.

This killing was the lone example in the Rosewood events of an atrocity folkway that had grown notorious in the "race war" era around World War I. The fame surrounding this technique was spread especially by news coverage of the East St. Louis race riot of 1917.

The ritual was simple. You set a house on fire with the occupants inside, then as they run out you take potshots.[390] In East St. Louis this grew horrifically epidemic, and news of it joined with stories from other riots to tempt new shooters into trying out the script. If an aspiring champion of the white race were to be daydreaming on a store porch one day, pondering the challenges posed by dreams of mass extermination, a stray bit of instruction might stir: burn and shoot.

After the Rosewood events there were white gossips who told how this technique was used with massive success at Rosewood, allegedly causing pro-cessions of black men, women and children to be mowed down.

Aside from the internal contradictions that such stories often displayed, there was a more serious difficulty that they had never expected to face. Such white storytellers thought of the decimated black population as being faceless and uncountable, an amorphous horde— which could be lied about as one chose. It seemed unthinkable that such phantoms might someday be traced—or, still more unthinkable, that tracing might show nobody as having disappeared.

The Rosewood in these boasts was not the six-house "negro section" that was minimized in the news, but was the opposite. In the boasts, great rows of homes were on fire, great crowds of bodies falling to the skillful guns of white marksmen. The Home Team is racking up quite a score.

The tales, like the perpetrators on the ground, were inflated with mob grandiosity, beneath which lay an inglorious truth. At Rosewood, burn-and-shoot worked a total of one time. The reason was simple. After that first time, all potential targets took note and were gone, fleeing into the woods. From then on, the houses that were burned were empty. The lone exception was left to her inconvenience, as auburn hair spilled across the sand.

The temporary rebuff of the Otter Creek group at the Carrier house would be irrelevant to the final outcome of the night. This final outcome was never in much doubt, because of the force of numbers.

Bands of whites would continue arriving in Rosewood in the dark, then by daylight. The first large mass would be the vaunted motorcade from Cedar Key *("...the population of Cedar Key was aroused and...many armed men from there were planning to go to Rosewood...")* This safari would arrive a little late, waiting for dawn in fear of World War I-style snipers, and thus, embarrassingly, they would find no battle left to fight.

Cedar Key fish packer Frank Coburn dives from the car to flatten behind a log in the area his companions have told him is Rosewood. All of them are prudently ducking for cover as they leave the cars, dodging the snipers—which, very luckily, seem not to be firing. Then nothing. The snipers are very crafty, seeming extremely well hidden. His sharp-eyed comrades find a solution. They think they spy movement in bushes and shadows and manage to get off a few shots. But even those comrades are now invisible, disembodied, crouching somewhere in the dark. They are flagged only by an occasional stream of cursing that floats up, making some kind of claim to importance. Once, however, there is something concrete to focus their attention. A pathetically fleeing hound dashes through, perhaps suddenly homeless like its masters. It searches in confusion for what was lost. Then the roar of gunfire, the strangled yelp. The heroes naturally chafe in the darkness at the frustrating waste of their skills. But there are always the dogs.

By mid-morning more lines of cars are coming, this time from the other direction in Gainesville, fifty miles away—and from still farther up the line near the town of Starke, the family home of Henry Andrews. Whether or not rioters arrived from as far away as Jacksonville, as some stories said, the radius of participation certainly extended for a hundred miles.

Friday will now finish the business at Sarah Carrier's house—or what is left of that house. The descriptions necessarily come only from whites—in much the same way that eyewitness descriptions of lynchings came only from whites, and seldom from African Americans. The heart of the crime scene now has two main kinds of players, the compromised and the dead. The descriptions are suspiciously vague, bristling with contradictions that sound like alibis. Still, many will show agreement on at least one basic element at this point, an odd detail in the wings. In tale after tale, no matter how they differ otherwise, the final episode at the Carrier house involves a bed.

These are the tales about the death of Sylvester.

The massive gathering of whites after daylight finds the house obedient now, offering no more resistance. They decide to inch forward. The boldest man shows his mettle, and peers into a window. At this window a ghostly light had been seen.

The intrepid spy solves the riddle. Inside that room, sure enough, a lamp has been lit—a strangely brazen and unconcerned lamp, seemingly indifferent to outside surveillance. Next to the lamp is a bed. And on that bed lies a man. All the stories agree that the figure on the bed is a man. They never say it is a woman, or that she was shot through a window shade in cold blood. On many other things they disagree, but it is always a man.

Some say the man on the bed is already dead. Some, that he is only badly wounded. In the latter version the intrepid spy at the window turns out to have a gun, and he aims expertly, plugging the prone figure right in "the burr of the ear"—which does the trick. Now he is really finished.

But other stories don't find him in the house at all. The bed becomes only symbolic, formed by the hard ground—for the prone figure is now lying outside the house in the bushes, where presumably he tried another of his ambush tricks. But now, too, he is still alive, prone because he is badly wounded, so badly wounded that he can move only one finger. The small movement is unmistakeable, like pulling a trigger, showing the crowd just what he means. Even as they gather around him, he is showing his evil intent. He would still be shooting if he could.

All of these stories also agree on one more thing, the identity of the prone figure. He is Sylvester Carrier—or Carry, or Kerry, or Kearn—or even Carter—for the tellers aren't very careful about pronouncing the name. In all the stories the crowd is massive. He is not laughing now. Life ends.

Sam Hall creeps out of the woods. It is just after daylight on Friday morning, a little later than his usual hour of waking. The worst of the rampage seems to be over, he thinks. He makes it to the railroad, seeing no threat. He begins the usual walk to work at Sumner, as on any other day.

The other Rosewood lumber stackers seem to feel much the same. Lee Carrier, Bishop Bradley, Raleigh Bradley, Perry Goins—all will walk to work today—without being molested. The other-worldly rhythms, horror mixing with banal calm, will now continue—typical of mass violence, not to mention war. Not only are the walkers not molested, but they don't particularly try to hide. The orgy of shadows in the night is gone. The full random phase of violence, unable to maintain its force, now squeaks and falls back down a notch. In a sense, the whole movement toward randomness has only been a partial widening of selective stages. The bulls-eye has always been restricted to blacks (or in Lexie Gordon's case, targets who can be defined as black).

Sam links up with his regular walking companion, Raymond Jones.[391] As they walk southwest down the tracks they reach the middle of Rosewood, then suddenly they hear a roar. It is far behind them, back up toward Raymond's house. Even now they see no necessity to hide, but stand peering up the tracks curiously, trying to see what it was.

Up there is Sarah Carrier's house. Many guns seem to be firing at once—the old sign-off for many a lynching.[392] Hearing the stories later, Hall will feel sure that this firing of many guns can only have been one thing, the finishing-off of Sylvester Carrier.

Apparently all residents of Rosewood who were over the age of twelve at the time of occurrence, and were in the best position for firm knowledge, would accept flatly, as one accepts the rising of the sun, that Sylvester Carrier really did die that day, and did not escape. To them the evidence seemed over-whelming, impossible to avoid. It was not just that the sheriff displayed Sylvester's gun to a camera (still trying to prove that it was all over and everybody should go home).[393] It was that *everything* said so. There were many indicators. Sylvester's widow Gert would remarry, still describing Sylvester in glowing terms but never dreaming of doing anything so crazy as going to look for him. Because he was dead. An African American gravedigger who knew him would report recognizing the body.

By itself, 1923 Florida Death Certificate 775, "Sylvester Carrier," is not absolute proof. Unfortunately, the Rosewood death certificates form a dodgy mass of irregularities, too many irregularities for them to be accepted at face value. After all, this was the lynching-era South, where official truth could become quicksilver. But on the other hand, the Florida Bureau of Vital Statistics was not simply a facade. The document is at least persuasive *partial* proof. And when combined with all the other proofs and indications, the word "probability" does the UFO dance: It is indeed possible that a UFO could land in your backyard—if you care to define possibility in that sense—but it is not very probable.

All of these indicators, however, could be re-imagined.

As with the secret white boyfriend in the story about Fannie Taylor and the all-powerful freemasons as a device to explain Aaron Carrier and Sam Carrier, the rescripting process would embrace the death of Sylvester, to produce a scene that was luminously dramatic but evasively vague, lacking in specific names or details, unsupported by any direct evidence—and evidently suited to post-traumatic emotional needs. This was the larger theme using the alleged death of Big Baby, whose body was said to be switched. Rolling into the 1997 film *Rosewood,* the refined version lacked only a studio pitch line: Sylvester secretly escapes to live happily ever after, in a place far, far away.

After all, he had the knack, the magic.

If anybody could do it...

As with other Rosewood rescriptings, the escape story took various forms, each depending on not being compared to the others, since they contradicted. If they couldn't all be true at once, the possibility that one of them might somehow be an exception became increasingly small.[394]

The stories discovered special circumstances to explain how everyone in a position to know could insist that the Protector was killed. Besides the Big Baby device, there was the workhorse explanation in the other tales: the Masons. So secret were the Masons, and so powerful, that they could do anything—and no one would ever know.[395] It was the Masons who put him in that fake coffin, who switched out Big Baby's body, who took the fleeing Sylvester to the boat on the Gulf, who sent him to New Orleans—or to Houston, or South Florida—or to Kentucky in one story, for whatever reason. Wherever nobody could go and look and thus disprove the story—maybe he was there.

History provides other examples of didn't-die-after-all rescripting, ranging from Jesse James to John Wilkes Booth to Emiliano Zapata in the Mexican Revolution. The hard-pressed believer group, badly in need of hope, might consist of defeated ex-Confederates (James and Booth), or defeated *campesinos* (Zapata)—or they might be traumatized survivors of the lynching years. Zapata was ambushed and killed on April 10, 1919, before numerous eyewitnesses, including an anguished *Zapatista* major who described the death in detail, after the body was put on public display.[396] But as more years passed—and the original hard evidence began to look distant and dim—admirers began deciding that Zapata's displayed body must have been a fake, or that a certain birthmark was missing, or a trademark crook in the little finger was suspiciously straight.

He lives!

And if contrary evidence intruded, there were special circumstances that neutralized it. The crafty hero, Zapata, had escaped to a place far, far away, where no one could ever check. One story had him moving clandestinely to the desert sands of Arabia. Less ambitious was John Wilkes Booth, who was said by grieving southern admirers to have secretly escaped only to Booneville, Mississippi. And as to Jesse James, wherever it was he had disappeared to, he had just faked his death, fooling the illegitimate yankee lawmen. The theme was not new. The ending was unsatisfactory. It needed a little work. This theme, indeed, was old.

In the newspapers, the last stand of Sylvester Carrier floated in a blur, like the painting in the opening scene of *Moby Dick*, when Ishmael enters a rooming house by the wharf and squints at the painting on the wall. The painting is so murky that he can barely tell what it depicts. But maybe it's a picture of a whale.

When the newspapers depicted "Sylvester, negro desperado," the desperado was not alone. There was his army of fellow rebels, barricaded in the house with him. So what happened to *them*? As far as could be told from the news, on Friday they were still right there, inside the "shanty," banging away at white besiegers.

> **"The negro and a number of his friends had barricaded themselves in a shanty on the outskirts of the town and defied any white man to come near them."**
> —*The Washington Post*, Friday, Jan. 5, 1923

> **"21 heavily armed negroes were in the house."**
> —*The Jacksonville Journal*, Friday, Jan. 5, 1923

> **"A score or more of Negroes early to-day were barricaded in a house at Rosewood...with hundreds of armed white men waiting for daybreak to attack the stronghold."**
> —*The New York World*, Saturday, Jan. 6, 1923

> **"NEGROES ARE BARRICADED IN CABIN AT ROSEWOOD"**
> —*The Sanford (Fla.) Daily Herald*, Friday, Jan. 5, 1923

"PLENTY NEGROES IN PARTY"
—The Ocala (Fla.) Evening Star, Friday, Jan. 5, 1923

Perhaps it was no wonder that a historian in 1967 looked no further into the newspapers than the initial Thursday night burning spree, and then took it as the whole story. To look further—if one has no independent witness testimony as a guide—is to find a jumble of images flickering like marsh gas.

Perhaps, then, it's not so surprising to again hear the background hum. The intruding poetry could be explained as coincidence, stress, creativity or reality construction, but the rhymes remain. Could whole masses of people fixate so intensely that their shared drama kept dreaming up puns?

He was Sylvester, man of the woods.

Carrier of their pride. Carrier of the germ of doom.

Would he rise?

Oh, yes, he Rose. Yes, he wood.

Chapter 31: Crow's Thrice[397]

On the sand road south of the tracks the troop in
nightclothes makes a ghostly parade, darting into
the bushes at the sight of approaching headlamps.
This road is not the larger limerock track that is
under construction north of the railroad, running
basically parallel to the tracks (the future Highway
24). This is a smaller lane, "the back road,"
skirting Gulf Hammock past Aaron Carrier's
house, going toward Wylly. Even here, and even at
this late hour, they meet occasional cars laboring
over the ruts. Things are popping now.

The eleven figures in the parade range in age from toddler level
(George Goins, Jr., "Buster," who is being carried) up to Bernadina, age
about twenty.[398] There are Eddie, age 17; Harry, about 14; Ruben, 13;
Lonnie, about 12; Philomena, 11; Goldee, about ten; Arnett, nine; little
J.C., about six; and Buster, about four.

And Minnie.

Though many or most of them are barefoot and barely clad, in
temperatures now dropping toward freezing, they are taking the long
route, not following Gert Carrier's earlier flight to Wright's. They are in
too much trouble for that. White men are dead now, and this parade of
refugees was intimately involved. When Gert fled at the beginning this
had looked like just another nightriding attack—bad enough, but still a
quantum level below the next step, that of white men being killed. Now
they are hurrying northeast toward Wylly, where they have family.

Minnie glimpses other fleeing forms. She thinks she recognizes
Marion and Donarion, the teenaged Bradley brothers, known as Bishop
and Soda.[399] They don't stop to help the children from Sarah's. Minnie
doesn't fault them. "They passed us goin' to Wylly. They was tryin' to
save their own lives." Panic is in part defined by a breakdown in social
consideration, a frenetic focus on self-preservation.[400] Minnie was only
beginning to feel something that would deepen with the night: a sense of
being abandoned and betrayed. The feeling was already compressed into
the central moment of symbolism in the week, the split-second encoding
it all:

The maniacal laughter, the upraised cry—

...forsaken me!

Reaching the Wylly quarters, they make their way to the cabin occupied by Minnie's young uncle Wade, former catcher on the Rosewood baseball team, current driver of a stake-bed turpentine truck used by M & M Naval Stores. Wade Carrier is the older brother of three of the children who are with Minnie, Lonnie, Goldee and J.C. As recently as the 1920 census, Wade was still living at home with his parents James and Emma. On September 23, 1922, he married.[401] Now he lives with his bride in the turpentine quarters.

Again Minnie feels a rush of relief as she reaches safety. They burst through the door at Wade's. She thrills at the thought of the joyful hug he is going to give her. She envisions his tearful delight at finding them safe and sound.

But instead, he barely speaks. Wade and his wife have heard about the dead whites—and perhaps have heard things Minnie fails to guess. The turpentine camp owner, future Florida legislator D. P. McKenzie is working against the riot, but he has apparently spread word to his employees that it is too dangerous to harbor evacuees in camp. Any who arrive are to be redirected to the secrecy of McKenzie's pine groves. To Minnie it looks as though she and the others are untouchable, tainted by something too poisonous to permit association. Wade seems distant, even irritated.

Minnie hears: *"Y'all can't stay here."*

In seventy-two more years of life, she would never quite get over the feeling, or feel quite right toward Wade.

But mercifully, not everyone in Wylly turns away. A new face slips into the cabin. There is Scrappy.

Beulah Carrier, Wade's sister and Minnie's aunt, is again living up to her nickname, getting into scrapes that others fear. The Magdalene of the family, working in the Wylly jook, is reaching out. Minnie is hugged and consoled as she longed to be.

Thus comes the operatic tableau, the fallen woman and the stairstep parade of untouchables. Leaving the cold welcome at Wade's, they follow Scrappy as she leads them back out into the night, this time to the pine grove, the makeshift hiding place. The tallest form in the parade, Bernadina, is still in her blood-stained gown. Ruben is learning to turn his head to see. Little Buster is still being carried, Goldee and Philomena and Arnett are in varying stages of shock. Their bare feet dance between numbness and excruciating cold.

354

e

Minnie is gnawed by an all-consuming thought: *Where is Mama?* She will have no word for another day and a half, not until Saturday.

Scrappy is accompanied by a male companion, someone Minnie has never met. She does not consider that this man might be a go-between sent by McKenzie, the camp owner. The two of them, Scrappy and the man, take charge of the escapees—or some of them. The three oldest boys, Eddie, Harry and Ruben, ages about 17, 14 and 13, now have to follow the sanctuary rules. They disappear from the group, to find other shelter wherever they can. They are old enough to be classed as combat-aged males, and would be eligible targets. Their presence at the sanctuary would only jeopardize it. Ruben, with the towel on his crusted eye socket, receives no exemption.

This is another reason why the two Bradley boys failed to stop and help the smaller children. It would have been inconsiderate to stop, would turn them all into eligible targets. The role of male protector is turned on its head.

As they cross the railroad, a distant twinkle appears far down the tracks in the direction of Rosewood, seemingly the glow of flames. It could conceivably have been the fabled bonfire of the Otter Creek visitors, or perhaps the intensity of the King and Gordon fires combined to be seen far away. But to Minnie and the others, a different answer seemed certain, that it was their own house, Mama's and Papa's big house, now meeting the fate they had begun hearing about.

They freeze at the sight. Scrappy cries out, starting to rush toward the distant glow, forgetting about practicality or caution, desperate to save something. The man pulls her back, saying to think about the children. She stops, then resumes her task.

Scrappy will stay with them through the night in the pines. She makes a fire but keeps the flame small, hiding the light, feeding in sticks and twigs as hours pass. The uncontrollably shivering children are told to lie down and place their feet toward the fire. Tomorrow, Sis Blocker in Wylly will return to her home in Wylly—after overnight refuge beneath the railroad trestle—and will cook for them. Scrappy will bring them the food. Friday will seem endless as frost melts back from the ground. The pine grove offers no distractions from the fear and pain and cold.

In this fashion, Minnie Mitchell will survive.

Chapter 32: Road Shadow

Prior to Friday, January 5, 1923, the automobile road leading into the Levy County swamps from Gainesville was a quiet affair, tunneling under moss-hung oaks, kicking out an occasional limerock clod at an otter or wild hog. Few of Gainesville's 7,000 residents ever found reason to push into the gloomy coastal wilderness just west, with its shadowy work camps and reputation for swamp violence.[402] But on Friday, traffic increased.

This road (later Florida Highway 24) would be the conduit for Rosewood-bound vigilantes, rioters and general excitement-seekers, drawn by news of Sylvester Carrier's Thursday night stand. The *"Rebellious Black Population"* in Friday morning's newspaper was "Beyond Control of Levy County Authorities." White Gainesville had no way of knowing that the violent "population" consisted mostly of one man, Sylvester Carrier—who had not fired first, who was avenging the murder of his mother, and who, by Friday morning, was no longer in the game. Newspaper readers saw a situation more or less like this:

A gang of black savages went after a white woman back on Monday, then grew so vicious by Thursday that they killed two lawmen coming to get them. And now, crazed or arrogant, they're holed up in an outlaw's den, openly defying white authority.

In Gainesville and surrounding towns, such images were producing an emotional change, diagnosed neatly by the *Gainesville Daily Sun*—though not in the news pages run by young City Editor Truman Green. Each day a separate page in the *Sun* was reserved for its highest-flown flights of oratorical prose. This was the editorial page, displaying the paper's official opinions, and written by an orator *par excellence*. The editorial page editor was also Gainesville's premiere elder statesman.

"The horrible affair at Rosewood," wrote "Colonel" Robert W. Davis, "threw us all into a fever of excitement." [403] The felicitous phrase "fever of excitement" hinted at unseen depths, as a special mental state was stealing over the college town.

Davis was known for capturing the gist of things. "The most flowery speaker, the best word painter and most pleasing orator the state has ever produced," thrilled the *Sun* in 1922, as a get-well bouquet when he was ailing.[404]

An attorney by trade (with his shingle still hung out at age 73, just around the corner from the *Sun*), he had barely missed being elected Florida governor in 1904, and had served in both the state legislature and Congress. His lofty military title—once more— was honorary gloss in a haunted southern culture nursing its ghosts. But "Colonel Bob" had the credentials that counted. Though never a real officer in the military, he had enlisted at age 14 as a boy private in the Civil War. When he launched into one of his famous impromptu speeches—as he did one day at an awed courthouse in Liveoak—his tributes to the hallowed Confederate dead made grown men weep (the grown men said).

"Colonel" Robert Davis
Editorial Page Editor
Gainesville Daily Sun

This was not a gold-plated race-baiter along the lines of Governor Ben Tillman of South Carolina ("Pitchfork Ben") or Senator Tom Watson of Georgia ("lynch a few"). Colonel Davis was an old southern sentimentalist, giving tearful praise in print to his "Old Negro Mammy...on the plantation way back yonder."[405] He even threw rocks at a cherished southern rite, hunting, when he penned two separate editorials quixotically slamming hunters for shooting at helpless birds (and muddling the facts on the hunting laws, as oratory swept him away).

But even this gentle spellbinder found the Rosewood uprising illusion all too believable. Its imagined ambush of two brave white lawmen made the old Colonel "too indignant just now to write with calm judgment."[406] His word "fever," ("lynch fever" was a variant) made a convenient tag on an otherwise unnamed inner condition, arising when excited images demand excited action ("war fever" was also still lingering from World War I, when militant U.S. Ambassador James

357

Gerard had threatened to use "lamp posts" for "hanging" disloyal German-Americans, and mobs sometimes took the advice).[407]

In his "fever," Colonel Davis was certainly not insane, and yet he was admitting that he had lost it in some way, was beside himself. He had entered a psychological realm of makeshift labels: witch hunt, accusation frenzy, rogue prosecution, riot, "rush to judgment."

The swampland—so near and yet so far from Gainesville—seemed a natural place for jungle uprising. Those were not "civilized town Negroes" down there, but wild Africans eking out turpentine work, or chopping down trees in the muck.[408] They might easily succumb to a national trend. Wire-service items in the *Sun* told of racial conflict across the nation.[409] "Race wars" were epidemic. And now it had come home, landing on Gainesville's doorstep—to then climb back into the wire for other distant readers: *"RACE WAR...Florida Town is Scene," "FLORIDA RACE WAR."*[410]

Chicago's "race war" of 1919 had found shooters massed behind street barricades as if still fighting in France. On July 22, 1919, the *Washington Post* had helped provoke a "race war" in the nation's capital, using pseudo-military language: "It was learned that a mobilization of every available service man...has been ordered for tomorrow evening...The hour of assembly is 9 o'clock and the purpose is a 'clean-up'..."

Friday morning's plea in the *Gainesville Sun* sounded much the same: *"Citizens of this place appealed to Sheriff Ramsey of Alachua County of Gainesville shortly after midnight to go to Rosewood with as many men as he could gather."*

Some had already departed, aiming to *"Aid in Quelling Rebellious Black Population." "Armed parties from Gainesville began to leave...in groups, by automobile..."*

Two blocks northeast of the upstairs office stood the unofficial nerve center of Gainesville—not the courthouse but a comfortably spacious building opposite it. Baird Hardware had begun as a mining supply store in the area's 1900 phosphate boom, then blossomed into a department store selling a little of everything. It was the gathering place in Gainesville. The clerks knew customers by first name. And Baird's was especially known for catering to Colonel Bob's nemesis. It specialized in hunting gear.

On Friday morning, this largest retail outlet in Gainesville was said to experience a rush, as men heading for the swamps bought new weapons. A special hunting season had opened, with its own form of "buck fever." A tale portrayed brown paper wrapping torn hurriedly from the new purchases as flivvers sped toward Levy County, the scraps swirling like confetti in a parade.

Passing the gates of the University of Florida and leaving town, an intermittent convoy poured into the woods, where turpentine camps slumbered in the winter off-season. By noon, cars were coming from a wide area. The target community stood mute and still, depopulated by the flight of Thursday night. This was less a war than a game—or a hunt.

Each new squad of hunters probing down the Gainesville road could only conjecture about what they might find—what chance for glory, novelty or war stories to take home. The lapsed inhibitions of riot did not form a raving frenzy, but there was still the change, the "fever"—a willingness to act on forbidden impulse.

One story, true or not, preserved a jovial, gloating tone. A would-be warrior festively hails a friend: *"Come on, let's go to Rosewood and kill us a nigger."*

Around 1:00 p.m. on Friday, a lone figure stands beside the Gainesville road, silhouetted against turpentine pines. The spot is about a mile northeast of Bronson, the county seat of Levy County. This is more than twenty miles northeast of Rosewood, and twenty-five miles from Gainesville in the opposite direction.

In 1923 Bronson was barely a crossroads—a few houses and backyard orange trees, a small county courthouse under great oaks and hanging moss. The jail in the courthouse basement no longer used hammocks as in pioneer days. There was a hotel, a couple of cafes, a Ford dealership, a Masonic hall. The 1920 census found Bronson with a population of 799. The state census of 1925 would find it shrinking to 493.[411]

The pedestrian standing just outside town is a puzzling sight in one way. He is African American, and on this dangerous day few African Americans are venturing onto this dangerous road. The county's black population, numbering about 4,000 out of 10,000 total residents, is scattered over a wide expanse. But word has spread quickly.[412] White men have been killed. Rampage is sure to follow. The lone figure seems not to have gotten this memo. Dust from passing cars drifts toward him off the limerock paving.

Name: **Mingo Williams**
Residence: **the L.W. Drummond turpentine camp,**
          Bronson, Florida

There will be stories about this roadside shadow, and these too are puzzling. Faint intimations suggest he may be impaired in some way, perhaps mentally retarded, hence failing to grasp the drama closing around him. On most days he is an unnoticed brush stroke in Bronson's background, forming a certain kind of southern roadside icon, like a weathered plank tacked to a pine reminding that Jesus Saves. He is the unknown wandering darky, the Old Black Joe.

Turpentine's off-season offered the winter job of raking pine straw, but at children's wages. As an alternative, there was a low-grade task called scraping. The resin inside the pines grew thick and unworkable in winter, but a few scab-like traces remained hardened onto old cuts in the bark.[413] This crust could be scraped off, sending flakes into a metal box or tray. It was not coveted work. There were suggestions that he was scraping.

Whatever the task, Mingo Williams had picked a fateful spot for it, not just on the wrong road but at a gateway of sorts. At this point on the road, just short of Bronson, a slight slope descends from scrubby sandhills into darker, more imposing flatwoods, as the road meets the coastal lowlands, giving the feel of entering a place of jungles. Upon reaching this point, rescuers in the Friday parade might logically have started to look sharp, scanning the landscape for the "Rebellious Black Population."

Date of birth: **August 7, 1866**
Age: **57**

With the exception of Sylvester Carrier, age 33, all African Americans killed in the full riot phase of the Rosewood events (January 4-7) would be in their fifties. Sarah Carrier was 50; Lexie Gordon was 55. On Friday the list was not quite yet complete, but the pattern would persist. The killings were of people who were immobilized in some way, making them easy targets. Sarah Carrier was in bed. Lexie Gordon was nearly too sick to move.

Mingo Williams is primed for fame. By midday on Friday the telegraph key twenty-five miles from his roadside position will be chattering once again, upstairs in Gainesville and two blocks from Baird Hardware. Editors nationwide will receive notice of a new development in the growing Rosewood sensation. A thousand miles northeast, above the clamor of Times Square, a larger and louder machine, a Morkrum telegraph printer, is taking dots and dashes off the wire, feeding words to the *New York Times*:

> **"This afternoon, the body of Mingo Williams, negro, was found on a road about 20 miles from Rosewood. He had been shot through the jaw."**

Beyond this skeletal level of knowledge, there would be only gossip. *They say the car pulled over, that the driver was on a crowded front seat, that he leaned out the window and asked directions, luring the fellow to the car.* Then the carnival, the thunder.

Some said that afterwards they put the corpse head-down in a turpentine bucket as a trophy beside the road. Some said the car continued into Bronson and found a café, so they could boast a little. Some said it was target practice, trying out newly-bought guns.

One story specified names, claiming to identify two of the shooters, saying that they were an auto mechanic and a restaurant owner, both from Gainesville. Unfortunately, soft spots in the accusation leave it at the level of rumor. The Rosewood week was continuing into its time of anonymous killings, the victims seeming to fall as if by disembodied magic, killed by no one.

Imagination took up the slack. Over the years, local narrators would claim (always vaguely, offering no supporting details) that as whites drove toward Rosewood, ghastly multitudes of black bystanders were mowed down on the roads. Tellers of these tales were always white, impressed by the prowess of white shooters.

"They killed a lot of niggers up in Wylly," announced an elderly sage—though he knew little or nothing about the community of Wylly, while acquaintances chuckled that he was known for something else, attention-seeking bluster, the art of the "cracker" in its old sense. As to Wylly's real residents, the African Americans who lived in its turpentine cabins seemed to find no indication that anyone there had disappeared.

The unavoidable conclusion in this vein, that no such deaths occurred in outlying areas like Wylly, is not simply a guess or an official gloss. Since the Rosewood atrocity was exhumed in the 1980s, extensive tracing and multiple lines of evidence have repeatedly told the story.[414] The supposed expert on Wylly's alleged carnage, spinning tales on a porch, belonged to a special informant niche, containing only a minority of white informants but a loud one. He was not interested in the dead having names or faces, but dismissed African Americans as a class.

Black communities in Bronson, Otter Creek and elsewhere in Levy County presented not even rumors of any Rosewood-related disappearances. It was in white culture, with its sense that African Americans could drop like flies and not be missed, that the black death toll took on epic proportions—in stories laced with gloating, or, more innocently, relaying boasts heard from others.

There was a further demonstration. After the Rosewood claims case won its victory in 1994, the State of Florida widely publicized an offer of money payments to anyone who could show that a family member had met violence in the Rosewood week.[415] This was a new approach to the old lynching secrets, and it produced results. A large number of new claimants appeared, insisting that they or their relatives had lived in Rosewood. Some of these applicants were genuine, some were dubious and were paid anyway, and many were disproven by agreeing testimony from the real residents and by documentary evidence. But the point here is that not even in that rush—when even flagrant hoaxers received a chance to say anything they chose, and had incentive to do so—did anyone allege even a single death in an outlying community.[416] At last, the vast-roadside-slaughter stories, told about alleged deaths outside

Rosewood, would prove to resemble the burn-and-shoot stories told about alleged deaths *inside* Rosewood.

In each theme, the nugget of truth seemed to reduce not to a crowd, but to a single tragic individual.

The burn-and-shoot stories boiled down to Lexie Gordon.

The outlying-slaughter stories were similar. They boiled down to one man, the roadside shadow, Mingo Williams.[417]

There was a proper victim category for Mingo Williams, but it was not in a Rosewood "massacre" that never occurred. The Jim Crow segregation years produced a separate form of atrocity, requiring no riot. This was the dimension of Three-R killings: Random Roadside Racial. Not lynchings, at least as usually defined, these impulsive homicides suggested more casual sadism, in a wreath of lynching-style excuses. They, too, were sending a message, warning the target population to stay in line—so why not have a little fun in the sending? Roadside shooters could see themselves as keeping up a slow burn of terrorism for white supremacy, the way lynching did, just without the crowd.[418]

It could happen on any dark night, or in broad daylight—the anonymous thunderbolt from a passing car, the glove-box pistol or hunting rifle pried from behind the seat. And obviously it was not entirely random. Targets were selected from within the excluded group, minimizing the fear of consequences.

This other enormity failed to create spectacles as lynching did. But if the death of Mingo Williams were to be multiplied by all the lonely roadsides and all the local experimenters in the thousand-mile mystery land of Jim Crow—then the killing field might be vast.

Alachua County Sheriff Perry Ramsey

It was a Friday full of mysteries, as the Gainesville road grew filled. The Alachua County Sheriff's Department in Gainesville would keep no record to show who, exactly, had headed for Rosewood in the sheriff's brigade. The mere existence of such an expedition is known only from the *Gainesville Sun*, and it named only two participants. Naturally, one was the head man, Sheriff Perry Ramsey, an old veteran of frontier days like his colleague in Levy County, Sheriff Bob Walker. But the second name told a different tale.

> **"...Chief Deputy Dunning and several automobile loads of deputies and armed citizens were preparing at 1 o'clock this morning to leave immediately for Rosewood."** [419]

The mention of Deputy Frank Dunning sent a *sub rosa* message to Gainesville readers, for many knew the background. Dunning's inclusion in the motorcade was only symbolic, for he was severely disabled. Six months earlier, on July 5, 1922, he had reportedly answered a public nuisance call in a remote part of the county, and then, reportedly, he discovered a family of "Negro Moonshiners," who resisted arrest with gunfire, badly crippling him.[420] Thus went the story in the *Sun.* No other source would be left to posterity for an independent look at the evidence.

During the *Sun's* Rosewood coverage, the "fevered" mind of Colonel Davis on the editorial page was dwelling on the Dunning case six months earlier, and on cases still farther back. Davis made reference to more than a decade of local black-on-white shootings of officers, deepening his Rosewood rage.[421] Seemingly without reflection—in the grip of his "fever"—the Colonel leaped to the conclusion that the latest ambiguity, that of Poly Wilkerson and Henry Andrews, must be more of the same. Viewed through the lens of the "fever," these two fallen whites must surely have been sober lawmen, methodically carrying out an official mission (and not drunken meddlers who killed a woman in bed, then blundered into a shotgun).

"These officers in Levy County," wrote the Colonel in righteous wrath, meaning Wilkerson and Andrews, "were trying to do their duty just as Officer Dunning of this county was trying to do his duty when shot almost to his death by negroes barricaded in a house..." [422]

It was true that in northern Florida since 1912 at least ten white lawmen or civilians accompanying them had been shot by African Americans, causing at least seven deaths. However, the Colonel's "fever of excitement" screened out complications. Among other things, he was taking his information from a badly flawed source. The public appearance of those incidents came from newspaper coverage, itself a mix of fact and "fever."[423]

The series of officer casualties seemed to begin spiking on May 11, 1912, when Alachua County Deputy Sheriff Charles Slaughter and a backup man, F. V. White, were both killed in the later-familiar way—while raiding an isolated home.[424] Another deputy with them was wounded. Two African Americans, Cain and Fortune Perry, father and son, were apprehended, tried and then hanged for the killings. On May 14 the *Gainesville Daily Sun* (back in a day when neither Colonel Bob nor City Editor Truman Green were on staff) raged that

Alachua County
Deputy Sheriff
Charles Slaughter
(Florida Memory
State Archives of Florida)

the unsuspecting white lawmen had been intentionally lured into "an atrociously conceived death trap" by the black shooters. The *Sun* exclaimed that those 1912 killings were coldly planned in advance by a conspiracy, abetted by "others of the negro race."

Then came the trial. The surviving deputy, J. A. Manning, the wounded man—certainly no apologist for the shooters—gave trial testimony that left the *Sun's* conspiracy story in ruins. All of the trial witnesses, including the two men soon to be hanged, seemed to agree that the black men at the house had in no way lured the lawmen into a trap. The African Americans at the house, drinking heavily, were apparently caught off guard by the raiders and reacted chaotically. Neither the *Sun* nor the trial seemed to mention a latent thread, the widespread custom that involved local law enforcement in places like jooks. Information reaching the public lacked any discussion of possible turf wars over bootlegging. And perhaps none were there. At trial the surviving deputy characterized the raid as a fishing expedition in search of concealed weapons. Whatever the subtext—and however warranted or contrived—the testimony showed that the newspaper had leaped to a racist conclusion, accusing targets of being targeters and imputing conspiracy, when the real initiative had come from whites.

Such reversal of blame was apparently not an isolated exception in the local press. A long-standing fever could be seen. The shootings of officers between 1912 and 1923 did form an urgent sequence and race was a factor, but the published picture was shaped to a simple message: Our Side Can Do No Wrong, because we are safeguarding the ramparts of racial segregation.

By January 7, 1923, the *Sun's* editorialist seemed to be drawn into the thrilling endeavor of hating a demon—in this case, hating demonic Sylvester Carrier and his "heavily-armed" fellow uprisers, who, in Colonel Davis's view, had lured white "deputies" to their doom. Unlike in 1912 or the 1922 case involving Deputy Dunning, the *Sun* was now deepening the angry dream. At Rosewood it not only blamed the targets but created imaginary deputy badges to excuse the aggressors. Within a week the Colonel's certainties would again be in ruins, steamrolled by contrary evidence from real officers in Levy County. This time there would be no trial to air the facts as in 1912, only the *Sun's* January 13 retraction: "We were misinformed."[425]

The "several automobile loads of deputies and armed citizens" that the *Gainesville Daily Sun* placed in the Rosewood excursion bring up various questions. Across the South and elsewhere in the nation, Sheriff's departments have often kept lists of private citizens who agree to serve as special deputies in emergencies. Such lists have sometimes been partly honorary, rewarding political supporters who like to play cops and robbers—somewhat in the way that the Florida governor's special colonels could play soldier.[426] Whether Friday's "armed citizens" came from a special deputies list was not mentioned in the *Sun*, but such a list apparently did exist. Of the two men alleged as killers of Mingo Williams, one was said, by a separate source, to be on the special deputies list.[427]

Questions about mobilization lists remind that after 1920 a large mobilizing presence had entered Florida, in the form of the Knights of the Ku Klux Klan, Inc., headquartered in Atlanta.[428] On Monday night, January 1, 1923, a Klan parade down Main Street in Gainesville moved past the *Sun* office, introducing this new presence to the town, and announcing that a local chapter had been formed, Alachua Klan No. 46.[429]

It should be pointed out that this happened *after* Fannie Taylor's alarm, so the Monday events at Rosewood were not a matter of Klansmen rushing conveniently from a parade into a posse (as still more media myths have alleged, by mistakenly moving the parade back a day to New Year's Eve).[430] Nor were these Klansmen involved in the Monday night killing of Sam Carter, for they were busy fifty miles away at that moment, marching in Gainesville.

But their display in Gainesville was impressive. Some eighty hooded marchers carried "blazing white crosses. and numerous banners" past a large crowd. Nine days later, both the mayor of Gainesville and its police chief would endorse a ceremonial whipping conducted by the Klan.[431] At the *Sun,* Colonel Bob kept up a pattern of excited ambivalence—first applauding the New Year's parade in print, but then later denouncing the Klan—which would earn him a strange footnote in history. Today the Web is sprinkled with an allegation from the 1990s Rosewood media rush, claiming that the *Sun's* editor publicly admitted being an actual member of the 1920s Klan. When traced, this statement leads back to an enthusiastic academic paper, whose purported source for Davis's confession turns out to be non-existent.[432] Uncomfortably, the Rosewood revelations were also revelations about a certain vein of historiography in Florida, which for decades had kept the atrocity a secret in deference to politics, but then by the 1990s, under new political pressures, seemed to switch with similar responsiveness to an opposite pole, bringing fantasy exaggeration.

"Colonel" Sam Salisbury
(photo: Orlando Police Dept.)

Between 1920 and 1925, as Ku Klux Klan influence peaked nationwide, a number of Florida's municipal governments seemed to become Klan strongholds. A former police chief in Orlando, Sam Salisbury (another honorary "colonel"), was a mob leader in the Ocoee riot of 1920, and claimed that most law enforcement officers in his area had Klan ties.[433] At Ocoee, as at Rosewood two years later, two white interveners were killed and this formed a trigger for wider rampage. But the 1920 case provided another kind of glimpse. One of those fatalities, though wearing no insignia during the attack—no hood, mask or robe—was shipped for burial to a distant spot, Stone Mountain, Georgia. The deceased apparently had no kin there, but Stone Mountain was the Klan's ritual commemoration site, convenient to Atlanta headquarters and draped in solemn lore.[434]

The Knights of the Ku Klux Klan, Inc., was born in 1915. At that time its ancestor, the post-Civil War Klan, had been dead for forty years. At first the 1915 revival seemed to remain inside Georgia, with minor spillover to Alabama, but in the summer of

> **ORGANIZING KNIGHTS OF THE KU KLUX KLAN**
>
> **Organization Granted Charter by Superior Court of Georgia**
>
> Atlanta, Ga., Aug. 4.—Work of organizing branches of Knights of the Ku Klux Klan throughout Florida already has been started and is progressing rapidly it was announced today. Organization work already has begun in Jacksonville, Palm Beach, Daytona, Hastings and several other points, it is said, while inquiries regarding preliminary organization have been received from Lakeland, Palatka, Bartow and other points in the state.

Apparently the first announcement of the Ku Klux Klan's arrival in Florida
Bradford County Telegraph (Starke, Fla.)
August 20, 1920

1920 the new organization's founder, "Colonel" William Simmons (no real military rank), consigned his creation to multi-tiered marketers, who peddled ten-dollar Klan memberships nationwide, with a four-dollar sales commission.[435] Within a few months new chapters, or klaverns, were visible in Florida. Kleagles (membership salesmen) met success as far away as Oregon. In Florida's largest city of that time, Jacksonville, penetration of municipal institutions was flaunted. To dramatize a burning-cross parade, streetlights along the route were switched off.[436]

In Gainesville, however, Sheriff Perry Ramsey did not join with the city's police chief in cheering for the Klan. Nor did Ramsey's colleague in Levy County. Sheriff Bob Walker was said to be a firm Klan opponent.[437]

In the Rosewood events no hoods or robes were reported by anyone. Nor was any other indication of Klan conspiracy, though individual klansmen must surely have been drawn into the Rosewood crowds on Friday. Moreover, the 1920 Stone Mountain burial, documented but not publicly explained, reminds that wheels could turn unseen.

By sunset on Friday, January 5, the whites converging on Rosewood would begin to display a crude organizational structure, if only for a moment, using a base camp at Sumner.[438] Not even a rumor has ever alleged Klan involvement in that process. In later years an unconfirmed report would describe a Florida Klan mobilization procedure called the Fiery Summons, allegedly able to call together large numbers of men in a short time. But all of these threads—including the squadrons of faux colonels—serve only to remind of underlying fevers. Various informants from Rosewood and Sumner, of both races, told stories describing local Ku Klux Klan activity in their area at various times, but none pointed to January 1-7, 1923.[439]

The killing of Mingo Williams left almost no information. The only accessible clue to his deeper existence lay in a pathetically small scrap of evidence: his name.

Or that is, his two names. Putting aside for the moment the pedestrian surname, "Williams," there remained two richly suggestive signposts. One was the resonant first name, "Mingo." And paired with it was a less formal label, a nickname, not listed on his death certificate. Both pointed into a maze of shadows.

On its face, the word "Mingo" sounds Native American, The Seminoles, the most famous Native people in Florida, were present in Levy County before their forced removal in the 1840s, leaving place-names like Atsena Otie (cedar island) and Waccasassa (place of cows). However, the name "Mingo" doesn't seem to come from the Seminoles. It was apparently one more transplant in Florida's land of runaways.[440]

The notion of Florida runaways or fugitives whispers in the very word "Seminole," for it is a slurring of the Spanish word *"cimarron,"* meaning fugitive or runway, the Seminoles being breakaways from the Creeks in Georgia. In the 1700s they migrated into what had become an empty quarter in northern Florida, where the earlier Timucuas had been depopulated.[441] Group after group would leave faint epitaphs in words and names.

The name "Suwannee" was similarly honed and polished, coming originally from "Rio San Juanito," but then passing into pijin-Creek,[442] until at last the sounds flowed melodically, perfect for a song.

Obviously, the first name of Mingo Williams can be followed at least back to August 7, 1866, when his death certificate says he was born.[443] But before that are mists. The death certificate was written in Bronson on a standard paper form, with blank spaces for background on the deceased, but the Bronson examiner scrawled on these blanks: "Do Not Know."

In another direction, one of the "five civilized tribes" of the South was a people called the Choctaws, living in Mississippi but forced west to Oklahoma in the 1830s—though a few escaped to Florida. The Florida Panhandle's Choctawhatchee River is named for them.[444] This obscure trace was the most probable origin of the name.

The word "mingo" is prominent in Choctaw. It means "chief."[445]

In the long travail of the segregation years, a number of black southerners sought a kind of conceptual refuge, envisioning descent from Native royalty. "I am the only Negro in the United States," joked Zora Hurston, "whose grandfather on the mother's side was not an Indian chief."[446] Even in Rosewood itself the motif could be found. Desperate widow Mary Ann Hall, living back north of the railroad, quieted hunger pangs in her children at night by telling them enchanting tales, revealing that once upon a time she had been a Seminole princess, but was stolen in infancy.[447]

In the 1920 federal census the only name even remotely resembling "Mingo Williams" in the Bronson area attached to an aging bachelor who bunked with another bachelor. Hints raised a faint possibility—very faint—that the two might have been "conjure doctors" or back-porch sorcerers.[448] These were mysterious figures (Hurston, again, is the authority), who sometimes mumbled and wandered in their private worlds.[449] Could he have been a "chief" in this sense? A chief of magic? Doubtful.

In the years since I stumbled onto the Rosewood enigma I was haunted by Mingo Williams—because he was faceless. There seemed to be no way to bring a bit of humanity to his senseless murder. The more I dug for his biography, the more elusive he seemed.

Informant Jim Turner, white, aged 14 in 1923, was living in Bronson when the killing took place. He remembered the way people said the old Negro was shot down. But the name on the death certificate, "Mingo," was unknown to Turner. He said people in Bronson knew the mumbling old soul by a nickname—a strange one, recalled in slightly different forms. Another informant, knowing still less, thought vaguely that the nickname might be "God Knows." But Turner seemed to know the story in more detail, and he said the lowly outcast was called "Lord God."

In old Levy County this was pronounced with a bounce—not LORD GOD (with equal stress on both words, as a preacher might have it), but LORD-god. stressing only the first syllable. This bounce applied only in a special way, when the phrase was being used as woods lore.

People knew routinely that the LORD-god was a kind of bird—and only one kind. A LORD-god was the big creature with the red top knot and the crazy call. Naturalist John James Audubon had noted this bird's maniacal-sounding laughter "even in the wildest parts of Eastern Florida."[450]

The LORD-god was the big phantom, *Hylatomus pileatus*, the pileated woodpecker.[451] Using this as a man's nickname begins to sound less like lordly respect, and more like a snide giggle.

That crazy peckerwood......

When I was a child I stood at times by a big picture window and pulled musty books from a shelf, not knowing what these parental heirlooms might mean, but curious.

One book held me strangely, though I couldn't understand some of the big words, and I grew impatient with the run-on sentences, which seemed to say nothing. But there was a resonance, not least because the man who wrote the book had lived only fifty miles from where I sat, and received the Nobel Prize on the year I was born.

I managed to glean that the book was about a boy, who was lost in a great jungle. I didn't understand that the jungle in the book had once existed practically on my doorstep, before clear-cutting swept it away.

The boy was lost after coming into the jungle with men on a hunt—a bear hunt, seeking a specific bear, a monster, larger than any other, a bear that was half-legend. When the boy wandered off and grew lost he suddenly felt a presence, something looking at him. He then made a leap of faith, laying his gun on the ground and hanging his compass on a bush—so that nothing on his person would smell of metal. Because he knew that the presence he felt was the great bear, like the soul of the wilderness, come for unfathomable encounter. He made the leap of faith so the bear would show itself.

And then the great shadow appeared, gazing at him.

371

And that was all. No action whatever. No excitement, no drama. How could such strange and musty old words hold me like that?

The cycle of stories from William Faulkner followed the boy in the woods into adulthood and then old age. [452] I couldn't understand why the boy grew up to sacrifice his privileged birthright, his inheritance, to live in a small house that was barely a hut. I dimly gathered that it had something to do with race, and the wound of race, some wrong that could never heal, unless somebody sacrificed something.

Years later as an adult, long after stumbling into the Rosewood labyrinth, I was standing in a public library and happened to pull a book from a shelf, spying the old title that had held me in childhood, wondering about it. What did all those big words really say? Would I be able to decipher them now?

I scanned down the page and found myself reading something that in the intervening years I had completely forgotten. When the boy feels the presence of the great shadow, knowing it has come to look at him, he knows this only because the forest suddenly grows quiet. Prior to this moment the woods had been ringing with a steady sound, a drumming, the sound of a bird hammering on a tree. Then this stops. That is the signal. The book identifies this signaler as "the big woodpecker called lord-to-god by Negroes."

All that time, digging for Mingo Williams, and I didn't know I was digging for my own past.

As when they say time compresses into a drowning instant, I saw that when I was a child with the book the spiraling nautilus shell was somehow already formed—as if already I was in Levy County, Florida, looking for what I didn't know was myself, the ghost questions from childhood.

The strange harmonics in the shadow man, Mingo Williams, led on until the unwary hunter was lost. In the book the boy was taught his woods lore by a hunting guide, a dark woodsman, partly descended from slaves but partly from Chickasaw chiefs, the *mingos*— for the Chickasaws spoke basically the same language as the Choctaws. The book called him Sam Fathers, this dark woodsman. First published in 1935, the story was said to have been written in the late 1920s, perhaps germinating in 1923.

It occurred to me in the search for Mingo Williams that the bird was like an animal spirit guide, a *nahual.* And I didn't want to be equated with such a guide—this uncomfortable creature, always battering, battering, tirelessly digging away. But over the years the bird kept crossing my path, until at last it seemed right—that I had become that digger, that hammerer, wanting the secrets, not caring if I was lost.

The crazy red topknot, the maniac's laugh. No other species of woodpecker has that crest and laughs that laugh. By contrast, the similar-looking ivorybill woodpecker (the still larger species now extinct) also had a crest, but made only a muted cluck as its call—no loud mirth. The full picture, laughter and all, fits only the one species, *Hylatomus pileatus,* the bird that haunted Audubon.

Though it does have one more name.

Woody Woodpecker is also the lord god—complete with red topknot and crazy laugh—Huh-huh-huh-HUH-huh! No other species fits the loony cartoon. And indeed it was comic, my bouncing through the old southern secrets, hammering away at sunny Florida, digging, digging. Wanting that vortex of mystery, seeking it through the lens that was available, the great wound, the lost wilderness, not even knowing what he meant by that bear.

Huh-huh-huh-HUH-huh!

KA! KA! KA!

Chapter 33: Paradise Lost

Before dawn on Friday, Lee Carrier rises stiffly from the spot where he slept in the woods. He shrugs off the cold with his usual disregard— though he is glad for the extra pair of wool socks he thought to put on at Wesley's. The first rays of sun are not yet glittering on the frost in the wiregrass, but the early whistle in Sumner is moaning.

In the dark he hears no more shooting. The woods give no sign of frightened movement as in Wylly the night before.

He starts to walk. A paycheck is coming tomorrow. Saturday will bring the fortnightly encounter with the iron-barred window at the pay office. His hike reaches the side track into Sumner and he strides north toward the mountains of stacked lumber. But he finds that the night's disaster is not easily ignored.

White-run Sumner has become a natural gathering place for arriving white rioters. Groups are camping at their cars. Some wander the sawdust-paved streets. None accost Lee as first light shows him entering the gate of the lumber yard. The Rosewood rampage will be oddly ambivalent throughout, restricted by unpredictable whims.

But in distant newspapers this "race war" has reached official status. In California—a state where wide-roaming Lee Carrier will one day roam—morning paper deliveries are moving down the Hollywood Freeway and out dusty paths like Wiltshire, a boomtown lane among oil wells. Readers of the *Los Angeles Daily Times* are three time zones away from the Sumner swampland, but are instantaneously linked to it (or to an illusion of it) by the telegraph wire. As Lee walks through the pre-dawn darkness this Friday morning, Angelenos are already seeing the headlines: "RACE WAR... Florida Town is Scene."

The story is so big (or for a moment it *looks* so big) that the *Times* in Los Angeles, like the *Times* in New York, will run updates for three successive days. A Los Angeles headline writer gets creative: "POSSE HUNTS NEGRO MORON." Lee Carrier, keeping his work schedule, does not see himself as the undramatic reality behind the dancing images.[453]

Despite its news classification as a race war—a classification applied to Rosewood in Los Angeles, New York, Chicago and elsewhere—the incident is limited. This is no Tulsa race riot, such as Oklahoma endured in 1921, when apocalyptic-seeming fires gutted more than thirty city blocks. Nor, on Friday, has Rosewood reached the scale seen in 1920 in Florida itself, with the burning out and driving away of the black population of Ocoee, Florida, a citrus town near Orlando.

Sumner waits. The arriving whites have come to find targets, and their gathering place is ominously near the largest concentration of African American residents in the area, Sumner's black quarters.

If Monday night saw nervous guards posted around that quarters to protect Sumner's valuable asset, its manual labor, now things are much worse. Buildings in Rosewood have been burned. Two whites are deceased. Similar circumstances—the killing of two white vigilantes in 1920—were enough to set off the Florida cleansing at Ocoee.

It's a tense gamble for the man at the top, Walter Pillsbury—who in his strict Baptist piety is not a gambling man, though the former athlete knows the calculus of stealing second base. Pillsbury's long-ago stardom in bush-league baseball rides strangely now on his starched collar, his dark, chiseled features locked into command mode. His underlying conflicts will be revealed by a private letter written days later, on January 9,[454] but witnesses see only the outward calm. The craggy face eerily resembles a later emblem —the giant stone memorial in South Dakota depicting Crazy Horse. Pillsbury's Native roots are probably not Sioux as with that chief. The specifics were apparently buried with his mother Martha.[455]

Whites streaming into Sumner have not guessed that women and children escaping from Rosewood are practically under their noses, seeking refuge in Sumner's company office or hiding in the lumber stacks, as Pillsbury rechannels them into his cook house. His wife Grace, age 37, is smuggling food to the terrified hiders. Daughter Martha hears drunken whites in passing cars shouting and whooping. A wrong step and Pillsbury's empire is a house of cards.

"Alone and without guide, half lost, I seek What readiest path leads where your gloomy bounds / Confine with Heaven."
—the voice of Satan, speaking to Chaos, *Paradise Lost* [456]

On quieter nights at home, as the piano was being played by Sopha or Martha (commercial radio was only two years old), the screaming saws would grow distant. At such times, he might open the book. He was an intense man, and the intensity moved from ledger lines and log chains into his reading at night.

The book was not the Bible (his impassioned first choice), but it served as a companion volume, a kind of guide. He would pry open the embossed leather cover and gaze for hours into ornate print and florid lithographs, which graced his 1884 special reprint of Milton's *Paradise Lost.*

This epic poem of the striving soul, framed by hellish fiends in dangerous darkness, seemed to hold him fiercely with its revelations of the cosmic drama. The original ten books of *Paradise Lost,* issued in 1667, were reverently condensed two centuries later into this one slim family heirloom, republished when Walter was nine—two years after his father, the wandering Pillsbury flour-mill heir, passed away at age 35.

One of the few pools of wired illumination in Sumner was in the mosquito-screened bungalow. The book swam under an electric filament bulb. By this light he scrutinized writhing monsters in full-page etchings drawn by master illustrator Gustave Doré. There was winged Satan, brooding, seated alone on a bleak crag, hunched like Rodin's Thinker.

Far below are the palm-lined jungles of paradise, calling to the lonely thinker at the top.

...such a numerous host
Fled not in silence through the frighted deep
With ruin upon ruin, rout on rout,
Confusion worse confounded...
　　　　　　　　—Chaos, speaking to Satan,
　　　　　　　　　Paradise Lost

Name: Walter Harlan Pillsbury
Age: 47
Address: Superintendent's residence, Sumner, Florida,
　　　　　no house number or street name necessary.

College luminary in Michigan, trust-fund orphan, baseball star, volunteer in the Spanish-American War, log sawyer, Baptist preacher and founder of churches. King of a sawmill town.

Few accuse him of being a simple man. Born in the North Woods near the logging town of Cadillac, he has become a dance-hating Baptist in somewhat the Southern Baptist way. With his wife Grace, who shares his faith and fervor, he arrived in Sumner to find two shocking dens of iniquity roaring away. One was a dilapidated dance hall for black labor, the jook. The other was a recreation hall for less numerous white foremen and craftsmen such as sawyers and smiths. They, too, had their dances, their fiddle frolics.

Half of this double equation, the jook for blacks, was untouchable under corporate rules. The jook had to be there, an enticement to hold manual labor (and thus keeping pay scales down to the thrifty southern level). Not even Pillsbury's piety could dismantle the jook, ruled by quarters boss Poly Wilkerson (though its white ingredient, Poly himself, might be extracted).

Riding the wave of National Prohibition in 1919-1920,[457] the crusading managerial couple, Walter and Grace, turned their attention to the sins of whites, mirroring Prohibition as a whole in its quiet exemption of company-town jooks for African American labor. The white rec hall was doomed.

To avoid direct battle, the Pillsburys converted the hall to a skating rink for children, ruining the dance floor. Some patrons seemed less than grateful. The boss built a replacement, a church.

For nearly a decade previously, the company had not mixed business and faith; any whites seeking services could ride north to Shiloh Church in the woods. Pillsbury's combination chapel (Baptists one week, Methodists the next) found his devout family on the front pew. Brooding among corporate crags, he is a man of his moment: the Progressive Era, the Anti-Saloon League, Idealistic President Wilson, Teddy the Bull Moose, the War To End All Wars. Time to clean up the world.[458]

A simple man? There was the time he impulsively waded into a swamp to pluck a water lily for his beautiful wife; the laughing times he carried the children to the circus in Gainesville. And there was the day when, solemnly, he was peeling an orange with a pocket knife outside the bungalow, and issued a warning. As an unbroken spiral of orange peel circled toward the ground, he was speaking to his adolescent daughter, who had found romance. She had been seeing a boy who lived in the quarters, A. J. Studstill, the younger brother of Cephus Studstill.

Moonlit trysts had occurred on the sweetheart swing in the side yard. The man peeling the orange told his daughter to pause and remember that A. J. was not of her social class. "You see that pine tree over there?" said the voice, as recalled by the hearer. "From the top of that pine tree down to the ground, that's how far you are above A. J."[459]

Clenching the pipe in his teeth, striking the match on his trousers, keeping the spiral of orange peel unbroken—he did not shrink from managing things.

Scant attention turned to his Algonquian riddle: the tomahawk nose, the almond eyes, the deep-hued skin. The week of atrocity—January 1-7, 1923—would echo the songs of dying wilderness: the mysteries of Mingo, the scowl of Sam Carter—and the power of Pillsbury. The racial cleansing had this other background hum, the faintest of funeral drums.

It is before noon on Friday as Lee Carrier and his co-workers in the Sumner yard are told to take a break. Their white foreman, Troy Jones, calls a meeting in the stacks, where the mountains of planks keep them hidden from outside eyes. By this point the crowds of arriving whites have begun focusing attention on the yard itself. The cry in the newspapers—"25 Negroes Barricaded in House, Defy Armed Posse and Open Fire on Whites" [460]—is twisting into a new theory.

The murderous black uprisers from the house have not really disappeared. They are <u>right here</u>—in Sumner, sheltered by Cummer Lumber—because they are Cummer employees.

Pressure is building toward the previously unthinkable, an attack on the company. Now, just before noon, the cliques of arriving white rioters remain undecided, still getting their bearings. There is time for the Cummer company to maneuver.

All or almost all of the lumber stackers called to the meeting are African American. The great majority live just southwest of the yard in the Sumner quarters. But at least six, including Lee Carrier, live farther away in private homes in Rosewood.

Lee begins to feel that in this meeting he is the focus of some kind of investigation. Foreman Jones stands apart, casting an eye toward the Rosewood laborers, while saying something to the big boss, Pillsbury. The dark man in the necktie follows the foreman's gaze.

Lumber stacks in Dixie County, late 1920s
Florida Memory, State Archives of Florida

This trouble is like a wildfire. It must be contained. For the moment it has been confined to Rosewood (before noon on Friday, the Mingo Williams killing has not yet occurred near Bronson). Jones and Pillsbury know in vague terms that five deaths have occurred. And two were whites. Mob fury is going to want a higher vengeance ratio than this.

The arriving avengers want those cutthroats, the rebels, the ones that were barricaded in that house. Thus far, only one of them has been put on the list of the fallen: the renegade Sylvester. There have to be more of them still loose, running around somewhere.

For a hundred miles around, belief would be widespread among whites that the house really did contain a band of merciless black shooters. Though many whites were shocked and saddened by the white rioting, they often accepted its core premise of black conspiracy. The actual rioters could feel this as majority support, seeing themselves as simply being more courageous than the timid majority, who saw the menace but wouldn't plunge the knife.

In the lumber stacks no one, neither Pillsbury, Jones nor Lee Carrier and his colleagues, was in a position to see what really had happened at the mystery house. Pillsbury, with his Michigan accent and college education, did not seem to believe that all of his Rosewood employees had been shooters in the rebel stronghold. But, as on Monday night in the judging of Sam Carter, he did not seem to *disbelieve*. The overall illusion of a houseful of shooters remained. *Maybe some of them...*

Lee watches the yard foreman draw Pillsbury's attention to three laborers—one of whom is Lee himself. The other two are the Bradleys, Bishop and Raleigh (the latter from the George Bradley household near the Rosewood depot). Multiple memories will agree on a background detail. Jones, the foreman, was another of the minor mysteries in the timber town's haven for outsiders. His speech has a pronounced stutter. Lee hears him say: *"Uh, uh, uh, Mr. Pillsbury, I-I-I don't think Bishop was in it. But Lee and Raleigh might have been in it."*

Lee can't believe his ears. Among last night's cold choices it never occurred to him to meddle in other people's business or go to the aid of his beleaguered cousin Sylvester. And now this. He is accused of it anyway. His mind goes back to the past, the time when he and Raleigh questioned foreman Jones's tally of their work hours, then went to the office and complained. Lee sees it now. It branded them as troublemakers. Jones has it in for them. That must be it. Angry workers make angry shooters.

Pillsbury raises his voice to address the group. He announces—sympathetically—that all of the Rosewood laborers are to continue at their jobs until just before quitting time. And then, for their safety, they are to leave the yard by a back route. At the front gate a white crowd has begun gathering, passing the word that prime Rosewood targets are going to be walking out through that gate at day's end. Obviously a trap is being set—a chance for a little mob interrogation, which might make the rope tricks on Aaron Carrier and Sam Carter seem tame. Pillsbury is helping them evade this.

And there his help stops—for he also falls back on the new rules, those of going to the woods. The Rosewood hands are adult males, meaning unprotect-able mob targets, not to be sheltered by sympathetic whites.

After leaving company property, the Rosewood workers are told, they are not to come back. Ever. They are being fired and banished. Pillsbury is apparently putting himself in a position to placate the mob, to keep them from attacking his black quarters—by telling them he has done everything humanly possible to make sure no men from Rosewood are sheltered on company land. The Rosewood hands have been offered a small gesture, but at the cost of their livelihoods. (One, Perry Goins, will be rehired in later months—small comfort to the more thoroughly banished others).

Sam Hall, standing in the lumber yard with Lee, will remember the helpful warning: "Boss man told us, when y'all leave this evenin', all y'all go together. Don't go the way you came." But Hall, too, would remember that after this last leaving there was to be no return, that now he was on his own.

The meeting is adjourned, leaving shock and suspicion. Lee approaches the yard boss, Jones, reminding him of something. The Rosewood hands have not been paid. They are owed for two weeks' work and payday is tomorrow. If they leave for good today, how will they pick up their checks? Lee can scarcely go to the pay office and argue his case. The way is barred by the mob.

He recalls saying hesitantly: "Mr. Jones, can you get—I'm tryin' to get my money."

And he will recall Jones responding sympathetically: "Yes, Lee, I'll go get it. Just as soon as they get the time made up."

Jones is saying that he will see whether the office can issue the paychecks early and send them out with him. Just before the noon whistle, Lee sees him walking back. Memory bitterly emblazons the broken speech pattern:

"I-I-I I'm sorry, Lee. I couldn't get it."

The head bookkeeper at the pay office, the grouch named Hill, is notorious at the company hotel for exploding at breakfast if his eggs aren't cooked just so. Lee doesn't see a rigid personality but a bottom line. Cummer Lumber is ejecting him for something he didn't do, and is keeping his money to boot.

Jones's stammering is lost in a larger sound. As the foreman turns away, the noon whistle blows, freezing the moment in Lee's recollection, marking the coldness of a workplace he thought he knew and could depend on.

After nightfall, again making his way to Wylly, he will then go north on foot, walking two nights and a day, fearing capture at every turn. He will walk way up along the Suwannee River, as if pulled into the song—*All up and down de whole creation / Sadly I roam ...All de world am sad and dreary / Ebrywhere I roam* [461]—the fake dialect words perhaps suiting the irony. Striding up by the river and then far back around to reach the home of his long-ago estranged mother, his feet by then almost too sore to walk. In the roar of the last memory he could still hear his final words just after the foreman turned away, spoken only to himself.

"I ain't got nothin' down here."

Not until 1983 and on-site taping for "60 Minutes" would he see the site of Rosewood again.

At about the time of the noon whistle, Mossy is three miles away, watching an automobile depart. Mossy is Lee Ruth Bradley, age seven, born February 21, 1915.[462] In the departing car is her protector. Lee Ruth is one of the women and children who took refuge through the night on the property of John Wright, the white storekeeper. Now, in the nervous anti-climax of midday, Wright is driving away. Like Pillsbury three miles distant, he is adjusting his tightrope.

Lee Carrier's depiction of Wright on Monday, furnishing shotgun shells to Sylvester, agreed with more general recollections. Lilly Washington, who lived in Rosewood until around 1920, phrased a consensus among African American observers: Wright was "for the Negroes." At age 52, the owner of J. M. Wright & Co. General Merchandise was siding with his black neighbors—but carefully.

As shooting erupted on Thursday night, a separate memory from Lutie Foster placed Wright in motion, going to warn the isolated McCoy farm of the danger. He may have made other rounds. And possibly he did more. In the darkened "death house" as Sylvester Carrier lay dying, someone seemed to creep in and light a lamp—someone also able to take word back to the white information loop, telling them the number of dead inside the house, and the condition of wounded Mannie Hudson (these details, reflected in the wee-hours wire bulletins, had to come from somewhere).

This someone seemed also to be a party who disdained the fallen attackers, not bothering to drag them off the porch. Of course, the mystery visitor could have been Sheriff Bob Walker, working in his usual stealth mode. Or it could have been Walker and Wright together. But the clues suggest solitude, pointing to the nearest, quietest white resident in the vicinity, the wary storekeeper, on the tightrope alone.

Whatever Wright's movements during the night, it is daylight now, a morbid Friday. Potential targets are crowded into his premises. In his balancing act he turns again to placate the other side. Mossy knows where he is going in the car. Everyone knows. Wright and his wife Mary are driving over to Sumner, attending the funeral of Poly Wilkerson.

As he walks through the gate to the car, seeing Mossy and her sister Ivory, he scolds, "You stay in this fence." The rules of going to the woods, which allow Wright to leave his sanctuary unguarded this way, have a precedent. The whites probing through the community are veterans of hunting camps and November deer seasons, where manliness is proved by killing a buck, an adult male deer, and not a doe or a fawn. They know the mysteries of "buck fever," the novice hunter's hysterical freeze-up upon spying the big prize, the virile buck. The sufferer of buck fever may experience violent trembling, or at times almost a trance or fugue state like sleep-walking—as adrenaline marks a test of the soul.[463] Nobody calls this test "doe fever." The proof is in going after the adult male, manhood to manhood (with no need for the other manhood to be dangerously shooting back).

Mossy sees them passing and is terrified. The car carrying her protector bounces over rutted sand and is gone.

When John M. Wright first came into the wild frontier he was a railroad section foreman, another outsider. Arriving in the 1890s, he found a placid little oasis of citrus groves, fringed like a postcard with hanging moss and wild palms. Spacious new homes with gingerbread porches were occupied by optimistic northern transplants, whites, from New England and as far north as Canada.[464] The old jungle railroad had brought them in the time of rebuilding after the Civil War—not as political carpetbaggers, exactly, but as Florida's longer-term staple, seekers of sunny paradise.

White railroad section foreman, African American crew
"near Rosewood," ca. 1890s *(Levy County Archives Committee)*

African American woodsmen were entering the records at the same time, perhaps having arrived as railroad labor,[465] but then carving out farms, working timber jobs, hunting game, founding churches and stores. In the North Florida citrus boom of the 1880s, even quintessential northerner Harriet Beecher Stowe moved to Jacksonville. "The little lady who wrote the book that started this great war" launched into a romantic post-war career, shipping her orange crop to the world. [466]

The woods came to be dotted with fine homes, perfumed by orchard blossoms in spring. The fancy wooden gingerbread on the porches was a signature flourish of the 1880s, made with emergent technology, steam-powered jigsaws. New citrus towns received poetic names: Citra, Orange Springs, Orange Park (Stowe's haven), Fruit Cove, Melrose—and of course another rose-word, factoring in the roseate heartwood of another boom item, the timber of cedar trees. None of it seemed doomed. The new section foreman, Wright, would watch the boom collapse.

In retrospect, the citrus rush after the Civil War seemed strangely blind to the whims of North Florida's weather. For perhaps a decade or two winters might be mild, but this was still mainland North America, not the deepest, steamiest Florida peninsula.[467] The 1890s brought the reminder. Disastrous freezes ran from 1894 (ten degrees Fahrenheit as railroad water tanks became icicles) into the "Great Arctic Outbreak" of 1899.[468] Northern Florida was ruined economically, and changed permanently. Citrus-growing was pushed far south, below the frost line around Orlando—into new towns with defiant fortress names—

Frostproof, Winter Garden, Winter Haven. Left-behind northern Florida displayed a moonscape of withered groves and abandoned homes.[469] Strong men were said to go gray overnight, or died of the shock. Wright, the migratory foreman, was reportedly rooming in the Rosewood home of old Charlie Jacobs, the citrus community's leading light. Jacobs suffered a stroke in the crisis and lay dying. A national financial crash had come in 1893. A Gulf hurricane in 1896 rounded out the curse, destroying Cedar Key, leveling forests miles inland to Rosewood.[470] Clear-cutting had already thinned the cedar forests. Paradise had turned.

Charlie Jacobs had ridden high in the 1880s. Rough-hewn but prospering in his new citrus town, he took a desperately impoverished child bride, a castaway of the wilderness thirty years his junior.[471] The stories said that Wright, the young boarder, found the haunted young wife caring for stroke-ravaged, freeze-ruined Jacobs in his last days. The old man was said to grow delirious in his gingerbread palace, raving in the halls. Records told the rest.

In January 1923, the big steamboat of a house that looked down on Mossy Bradley as she stood in the yard was Charlie Jacobs's old castle, standing near the store that Jacobs also built—before the young widow, released by death in the ruins, had married the newcomer.

Wright, the survivor, did not come out unscathed. His new bride Mary bore two sons, but both died in infancy. The newcomer would become the scarred, saddened sage behind the store counter. Arnett Goins, the grandson of Sarah Carrier, born in 1913, liked the old white man at the store, who always seemed to be giving out candy or cookies for children to eat on the way home. White children walking over from Sumner felt the same. "He was kind. He encouraged people," said the Sumner mill boss's daughter. "A kind, big-hearted man," said Ruth Kirby, daughter of Rob Ingram near the Kings. Philomena Doctor, no apologist for whites, reserved one of her rare compliments for her neighbors the Wrights, saying they weren't like the rest, but were "pretty nice people/" A halo of fond stories followed the wary diplomat—and this description needs saying.[472]

The reason is the 1997 movie *Rosewood*, which, for unknown reasons, took special aim at John Wright. Though the survivors of Rosewood uniformly portrayed him positively, the image of the kindly storekeeper seemed to somehow irritate the creators of the film, for they reshaped John Wright—while using his real name—to present him as a repulsive degenerate, the opposite of what witnesses portrayed.[473] The film's opening scene is so disconcerting that some audience members giggled nervously. White storekeeper "John Wright" is shown as a depraved sex fiend, grunting clumsily in a pornographic encounter (despite the film's self-congratulation on its human rights solemnity). The movie presents Wright as a simpering slug who forces sex onto an adolescent black store clerk (an imagined character, dreamed up for the sex angle). The degenerate's pants drop toward his ankles. He expresses his lust bestially, pinning his victim in a standing position (the screenwriter's prior credits were said to include such human rights masterworks as *Sorority Pink*). The John Wright in the movie is so greedy that even when he improves a bit and helps some Rosewood residents to escape the mob (in a warped nod to the real events), the movie-Wright disgustingly tries to extort a fee for the service. These images came from no witness, black or white. They came, for whatever reason, from the minds behind the film.

Going farther, someone in a train of production assistants and studio lawyers apparently conducted enough research to discover the greatest pain in John Wright's life, the loss of his two sons in infancy. The screenplay toyed with this—but not for audience appeal, because audiences couldn't possibly have known the joke. The script brought Wright's two lost sons back to life and age-progressed them into adolescence, turning them, too, into tools for demonizing the chosen target. The movie-Wright is shown abusing and degrading the two sons, slapping one of them drunkenly. In what looks like a twisted insider's prank, smirking in the editing suite, a man's ghost is forced by movie magic to betray and debauch his own pain and love.

Why would they do this, these untouchable tormenters in movieland?

But then, why would a mob attack a helpless community in 1923, at no risk to itself?

Perhaps the two questions aren't so far apart.

Amid the tensions of Friday afternoon, January 5, 1923, the funeral of D. P. "Poly" Wilkerson did not ease the situation. Assistant bookkeeper Frances Smith attended the funeral oration at Shiloh Cemetery, her memory held by the preacher shouting over the grave. The unshaven circuit rider happened to be in Sumner for a revival, she recalled. Smith watched spellbound as drops of brown tobacco juice fell from the shouting lips onto the coffin.

It seemed a symbol. Things had broken down, craziness had taken over. All this meanness and mischief—her own washerwoman now dead, trusty old Aunt Sarah Carroway. This riot was the work of outsiders, she felt sure, loose cannons like the circuit preacher.

She envisioned the new arrivals as wild men from the deepest swamps, festooned with long beards—maybe not actually seeing them, but hearing that they've come—swamp rats from that awful place beyond the Styx called Suwannee, the no-man's land, Dixie County.

Back among the lumber stacks, Sam Hall and Lee Carrier face their fears. Quitting time is nearing. Each of them will recall his apprehension. Their exile from the company is sealed, but at least there is the escape plan. Out at the front gate as quitting time approaches, cars can be heard cranking, seeming to anticipate the shift whistle, warming up for the chase—cars perhaps newly arrived from the funeral, filled with rage. Following the escape plan, the Rosewood hands slip out the back, under the trestle for the Number One tram. With no time to think about bitterness, they focus on staying alive.

A back path loops through the woods—and not a secret path. Anyone could be out there. Soon they hear sounds. Darting into the bushes, they watch the path from concealment. A walker draws near, but the sounds are labored, as if someone were staggering.

Both informants, Hall and Carrier, will recall the same moment, in the same way. The stumbling figure lurches into view. Someone in the group whispers: *"Look, there's old man James Carrier."*

The 56-year-old hunter, crippled by stroke, is making his customary difficult progress, dragging a partially paralyzed leg, holding a twisted arm against his back. His whereabouts during the preceding hours would never be established. Some said he was present in the "death house," witnessing Sylvester's first clash. But some said he stayed home, in his own house up the tracks, not coming with his wife Emma to the refuge at her sister Sarah's. Whatever the preamble, blurred by deep remorse in the recollections, James Carrier is now terribly alone. Apparently he is trying to reach his married daughter Rita Williams, who lives in the Sumner quarters.

As his younger neighbors watch, according to both informants, he never becomes aware of their presence. What happens next will haunt them.

Someone hisses: *"Leave him. He'll slow us down."*

Then nothing further occurs. They remain hidden. He pulls himself along.

Then he is gone.

They have no way to know that James Carrier is headed for his own moment of coast-to-coast fame. Another wire-service story will soon be streaming toward newspapers nationwide, carrying another mysterious name, which distant readers will never be able to connect to a face or a personal history. As with his nephew Sylvester, James Carrier is about to ascend among the peaks of Olympus, the mercurial peaks of public myth, where his material existence, with its complicated facts, will be replaced by immortal description.

But that will come on Saturday.

Now it is only Friday, as observations under intense emotional pressure squeeze out intense images—the intensity of the combat soldier who watches the commonplace become epic, because each rock, each tree, now binds into the choice of life or death.

Luminous tempera paintings on pasteboard hanging above fireplace mantels are coming to life: Pillsbury's Pilate, Sylvester's Rising—and now Gethsemane's turning away.

Quitting time. The roar of the big whistle. At the front gate, the crowd is hopping mad. *Tricked again!* The realization creeps in slowly, obvious only as the last black lumber stacker trickles out of the stacks— and no Rosewood suspects have appeared.

Again there is the riddle of selectivity. The whites at the gate could have grabbed any of the departing black laborers as scapegoats, disregarding whether they stood accused of anything. But apparently this level of ferocity is elusive. Locals in the crowd, knowing the Rosewood workers personally, have evidently promised to scrutinize each emerging face, as if repeatedly counseling: "No, now wait. Not him, not yet. Those Rosewood outlaws haven't come out yet. They'll be out any minute now."

When mass violence moves from selective to random targeting, a perfect extreme can never be reached. If targeting were to grow perfectly random, berserk rioters would shoot one another, would shoot at anything, would shoot themselves. Self-evidently, some level of calculation remains. Now at the lumberyard gate, whites certainly aren't shooting other whites. They seem to pardon even adult black males—if those males come from outside the demonized target zone—that is, if they are judged not to come from Rosewood.

Cummer Lumber's management seems aware of this reservation. Pillsbury didn't tell *all* his workers to sneak out the back way. Only the Rosewood hands, at least six in number, were advised to use the escape route. Perhaps nervously, but unharmed, the many black employees who live in the Sumner quarters have filed past menacing white examiners—presumably

Cummer Lumber Company and elevated tram. Sumner
(Levy County Archives Committee)

sorely embarrassed. If local braggarts had done a little cracking—*I know them Rosewood villains, known 'em all my life, I'll point 'em out*—the boasters now look less than shrewd, having let all the blacks file out, then peering like quizzical raccoons into the gloom of an empty yard.

As on Monday when a similar crowd let Aaron Carrier slip through its fingers into the hands of rescuers, there has been a humiliating fast shuffle, a betrayal. The authorities aren't playing fair. And this time the betrayer is the company.

It's the Cummer Company that has pulled this switch—pulled this scab off the old wound. The company from the big city with its slick ways, its tricky account books, its fancy talk, sucking the woods dry for the almighty dollar—defiling good white men's territory, bringing in all these blacks as labor, keeping this hellhole quarters full of dangerous savages and crime. This should be a white man's woods.

It's the greedy company that says by 1926 they'll leave the stumps and thank you very much, that Sumner will be packed up and moved to the next county until they cut the trees down there, too. The company is too big for its britches. Somebody should teach it a lesson.

In a few hours, as dark falls on Friday night, this feeling will become action.

With Rosewood turned into a ghost town by Friday afternoon, that ground offers no targets. The crowd will have to shift its focus if it is to continue fighting for justice—or glory, or fuel for its fever. Somewhere in the confusion such dynamics are discussed. No situation report comes from within the mass, but soon their action will be concerted. Does an angry fist pound on a cracker barrel? Do voices clamor by lantern light?

Apparently they continue thinking of themselves as a law enforcement posse, couching the logical next step as a continuation of the hunt for criminals. Where would those Rosewood rebels from the death house be hiding—except with other blacks? And what is the only place where blacks would be concentrated enough to provide such shelter? Where but the Sumner quarters? The next target of rampage is clear. The quarters must be combed. There must be a shanty-by-shanty search.

A new goal now welds them into fleeting organization. By nightfall they will fix on a demand. The company must allow them to go through the quarters and count heads. House to house, all respectable. Like the visit from Poly and Boots was respectable.

Just outside company property, a vigilante command post bustles, in the cluster of shops down by the railroad depot. Battle lines form— though not between races now, but between factions of whites. The secure, regimented Cummer Lumber employees have become repelled by the violence. But some of the old pioneer whites in the woods have found a cause. Along with a collection of sympathizers from afar, they are ready to roll the dice.

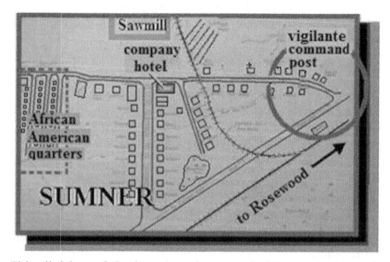

This division of factions is only general. Many woodsmen have stayed home, disdainful of the mob's pretensions. Some, like horseman Jack Cason, have actively resisted. But others seem thrilled to be part of something grand. For decades afterward they will nurse grudges, grumbling that they stood, on that grand day, for right and justice.

By around 9:00 p.m. it is clear. They are going to move. A unified rush is going to be made from the command post onto company property. The plan is to enter near the hotel in an irresistible mass, sweeping into the black quarters beyond.[474]

Again the maneuvering. As happened with the planned ambush at the yard gate at quitting time, now the showdown march is plotted and planned a little too obviously. The company gets wind in advance, mapping a counter-plan.

Pillsbury glares at his loyal white employees as they stand before him in the lobby of the hotel. The big hunting-lodge fireplace is solid like the company. The short man with fire in his eyes now goes far out on a limb, beyond employee relations, asking for their all now, as with the bugles back in Cuba. There is the battlefield harangue. *Will you stand with me?!* He puts his power on the line. Are they ready to walk out into the street and face down the mob? They know it means risking their lives.

The lobby explodes with activity. Commissary clerk Ernest Parham, age 18, finds himself cradling an old squirrel gun. Others get weapons as they can. Pillsbury is marching out the front door, down the weathered hotel steps. They follow him, dizzy in the light-headedness of combat, wondering if they're going to die. Feet on the spongy sawdust paving, they string out and block the street.

The night is chilled. Electric streetlamps powered by the mill's steam generator cast harsh shadows. Where the streetlights dwindle down the road, the railroad depot is too far away to be seen. Parham can make out a crowd of men coming from down there, rolling under the lights. Pillsbury is in front. Behind him is the big logger Perry Hudson— cousin of Mannie and Bryant, friend of Henry Andrews. The crowd coming toward Hudson's gun probably holds some of his kin.

This moment will be invisible in the newspapers.

A railroad sidetrack cuts across the sawdust paving in front of Pillsbury. The mob reaches the line.

He cries, *"Another step and we'll shoot!"*

Parham wonders specifically whether he is going to die. The crowd under the streetlight ripples. They are murmuring angrily. Then it stops. And it begins to fall apart. The vigilantes are not going to face gunfire. The black quarters area in Sumner, out of sight to the west, stands in suspense. Even in victory its powerlessness has been underscored. But it is spared.

Parham feels the incredible relief, the soldier's astonishment. Perry Hudson treasures another kind of feeling. The fiery superintendent in front of him misses no detail, turns to the big man, saying quietly, *"Hudson, I knew you'd do."*

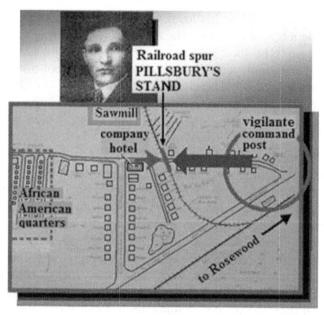

For a second time the threat of deadly force has been used against a mob.[475] The first was when Jack Cason threatened to shoot if the Monday interrogators moved toward Aaron and Mahulda Carrier. Both times, the stand worked.

But apparently, these will be the only times.

_____

Chapter 34: The Sergeant

Not until the peak riot period, January 4-7, would the name "Rosewood" begin appearing in distant newspapers. Earlier in the week, items about the emerging events had lumped together the varied geography as "Sumner."

The hands typing the stories—screened by anonymity and far from the events—seemed to map the scene by guesswork. Some reports took events that had happened at Rosewood and moved them to Sumner. One account moved the killing of Sam Carter to the county seat at Bronson, more than twenty miles away.[476]

Now a new incident phase, that of rampage, brought its first wire story, a piece sent "shortly after midnight" on Thursday night. At least two other such items would be transmitted in the pre-dawn hours Friday. Small clues suggested how information was flowing to Gainesville from Cedar Key:

In the *Los Angeles Times,* page 1
(dateline Jan. 4, published Jan. 5, 1923)

> **"The Gainesville Sun was requested to ask Sheriff Ramsey of this (Alachua) county, to go to the scene with as many men as possible..."**

In the *Atlanta Constitution,* page 1:
(dateline Jan. 4, published Jan. 5, 1923)

> **"Gainesville....The reports added that the population of Cedar Key was aroused and that many armed men from there were planning to go to Rosewood."**

In the *Florida Times-Union,* page 1:
(dateline Jan. 4, published Jan. 5, 1923)

> **"Gainesville, Jan. 4—(By the Associated Press)... according to reports received here late tonight by telephone from Cedar Key."**

Clues also pinpointed the times, when the stories were composed and sent out over the wire:

"shortly after midnight"

> **"First word of the trouble came from Cedar Key, about 10 miles from Rosewood, <u>shortly after midnight</u>..."**—*Florida Times-Union*

1:00 a.m.

> **"...automobile loads of deputies and armed citizens are preparing <u>at one o'clock this morning</u> to leave immediately for Rosewood..."**—*Tampa Daily Times*

2:20 a.m.

> **"The situation <u>at 2:20 o'clock this morning</u>, had resolved itself into a state of siege. The negroes were in the house, apparently well supplied with arms and ammunition..."**—*Florida Times-Union*

The upstairs office in Gainesville didn't seem to be getting much sleep. Besides the wire dispatches, the *Sun* ran local versions on its own front page:

> **"The Sun was requested to ask Sheriff Ramsey of this, Alachua County, to go to the scene with as many men as possible as it was feared the situation ...would grow worse."**
> —*Gainesville Daily Sun,* Friday, Jan. 5, 1923

> **"Entire City of Cedar Key Up in Arms"**
> —*Gainesville Daily Sun,* Friday, Jan. 5, 1923

> **"Call of Levy County Officers to Aid in Quelling Rebellious Black Population"**
> —*Gainesville Daily Sun,* Friday, Jan. 5, 1923

A large part of the core message lay in the fantasy uprising:

> **"They found about twenty-five negroes gathered in a house. Andrews and Wilkerson started to enter and were shot to death without warning."**

The rare opportunity provided by the Rosewood witnesses—that of probing behind news coverage from the Lynching Era from an independent point of view—reveals (at least in this prominent case) a pattern of illusion going beyond a few tweaks and shadings.[477] And this does not mean the lapses we met in earlier chapters. The show is just getting started.

The old technique of journalistic "expansion"—adding imagination to a few skeletal details—would find raw material in the three initial wire service stories sent out in the wee hours on Friday. These would provide building blocks for what would be towering castles in the sky, seen in slightly later stories. The initial building blocks, hinted or implied in the wee-hours bulletins, consisted of the following impressions:[478]

1. The original attack on the white woman was a gang affair.
2. The gang, including outlying members, then took refuge in a house—quite a sizeable gang.
3. There, they ambushed two legally assigned white officers.
4. And these virtuous lawmen had come on a peaceable mission.
5. But were lured to their deaths to get them out of the way.
6. So the black rebels could run wild and take over.

This palette of impressions would be unified neatly on Friday afternoon in the *Jacksonville Journal,* an evening paper newly revamped in 1922, under a rather famous new editor and owner. Richard Lloyd Jones used his middle name prominently, as if to remind of his still more famous cousin, Frank Lloyd Wright. Indeed, the architect of modernist innovation had designed his cousin Richard's unusual manor house, known as Westhope.

As the name suggests, that home stood a thousand miles west of Jacksonville. Richard Lloyd Jones had come east to take over the *Jacksonville Journal* from his home base in the

Richard Lloyd Jones, *Jacksonville Journal* and *Tulsa Tribune*

oil boom city of Tulsa, Oklahoma, where his situation had grown a bit tense. Critics (including a National Guard commander) said that Jones and his flagship Oklahoma newspaper, the *Tulsa Tribune,* had helped set off the Tulsa race riot of May-June 1921.[479]

"To lynch Negro tonight," the *Tulsa Tribune* was remembered as crying invitingly on May 31, 1921,[480] in an editorial seemingly written by Jones himself. This had helped to provoke a racial confrontation when in fact there had seemed to be no real danger of a lynching. Jones's editorial voice (reprised by a distinctive hairstyle) displayed a flair for theater. Like Colonel Davis at the *Gainesville Sun,* Jones was a student of crowd emotion and impassioned oratory, capped by an "irascible temper" that "made him many enemies."[481] No soulless hack, however, he put his audience rapport to work by part-timing as a Unitarian preacher, reprinting his sermons on his editorial page. A year and a half after this thunder had met race-riot disaster in Tulsa, Jones's *Jacksonville Journal* waded into the Rosewood mirage:

"Since Monday this section of Florida has been stirred as a result of an alleged criminal attack upon a young white woman at Sumner. Three negroes are alleged to have taken part in the attack ....A party of citizens came here from Sumner to investigate. In one house, it was said, they found about twenty-five negroes, heavily armed. Andrews and Wilkerson started to enter the house and citizens said they were shot without warning."[482]

Such intermediate repackaging of the image helped build the larger castles to come. Another such summary was in the *Ocala Evening Star,* a hundred miles southwest of Jacksonville. More rural in outlook than the urbane Jones (who co-owned nine newspapers across the nation),[483] the Ocala outlet added peppery headlines: "NEGROES FIRED FIRST," and (in case you missed the point) "PLENTY NEGROES IN PARTY."

But a third *Evening Star* headline took the prize. "NEGROES SLIPPED OUT IN THE NIGHT." This might be translated as a sheepish shrug: *Well, nobody actually got a look at those fierce black rebels, but we know they were in there somewhere.*

In 1920, Florida's violence at Ocoee had featured similar shrugs from cheerleading newspapers, as they explained why a sensational uprising event seemed to produce no rebels who could ever be found. At Ocoee, an ostensible stronghold full of black shooters turned out to be empty. Media in nearby Orlando announced that this was because the crafty rebels had sneaked off during the night. Persuasive evidence has shown that the Ocoee phantoms probably never existed.

The *Ocala Evening Star* report bears reading in context, as preparation for the larger leaps soon to come:

CLASH BETWEEN WHITE MEN AND COLORED IN LEVY COUNTY

Two White Men and Several Negroes Killed And Most of the Village of Rosewood Burned (By Associated Press)

Firing at Rosewood, two miles from here, where more than a score of negroes were barricaded in a house with hundreds of armed men besieging them, ceased shortly before dawn and had not been resumed at 8:00 this morning. Intermittent firing through the night could be heard distinctly here.

TWO WHITE MEN KILLED

....[There are] two white men dead and three wounded...a hail of bullets penetrated the walls of the structure...bodies of Henry Andrews and Poly Wilkerson were recovered this morning. Volunteers entered the yard under the guns of the negroes and recovered the bodies without being fired upon. They were brought here.

Parties of armed men continued to pass through here this morning, en route to the scene.

...The fighting began last night when a party of men approached the negro house in which it was believed the men were hiding who were implicated in an alleged attack on a white woman of Rosewood recently.

NEGROES FIRED FIRST

...It is believed that many other casualties will result ...With the exception of three buildings, the entire village was burned by a mob at daybreak, according to reports received here.

PLENTY NEGROES IN PARTY

The fighting began when a party of citizens from Sumner went to Rosewood seeking a negro alleged to have attacked a white woman there

Monday and were fired on by twenty negroes
barricaded in a house.

NEGROES SLIPPED OUT IN THE NIGHT

...established a cordon around the house and
opened fire....Several left to replenish the
supply....the negroes escaped, leaving the bodies
of the two women and one man in the house. ⇐
Bloodstains indicated several had been wounded.

NEGRO VILLAGE BURNED

...the mob began firing buildings in the
village...While the village was in flames it is said
many of the whites fired upon negroes fleeing
from their homes.....

The illusions weave densely, but a pause might be taken for "the
bodies of the **two women**...in the house" **(box and arrow above)**. Here
was a stumper. One of these female fatalities would have to be Sarah
Carrier. But who was the second?

Answer: Red-haired Lexie Gordon has been cured of her malaria.
She is no longer too sick to get away. As the cowardice and cruelty of
her murder is kept from sullying a picture of white heroism, newspaper
magic has managed to pluck Gordon's body from her own yard and
move her to the rebel house, where she now looks rather like a
combatant, who was asking for it.

World War I, with its homefront hunger for
news, had seen a proliferation of evening newspapers
like the *Ocala Star* and the *Jacksonville Journal*.[484]
They encouraged leisurely reading, as men put their
feet up after a hard day, or women sat down from the
dishes. There was room to develop a plot, to enthrall
the armchair traveler.

At some point on Friday, someone in the wire-service network
seemed to grasp this opportunity. The scant Rosewood details that had
already gone out over the wire were then massaged into something new.
Up to now the unspoken news angle had been white supremacy cheerleading, but sensationalism could be punched up in other ways. The
image of barricaded black uprisers was crying out for elaboration, while
it was becoming more apparent that the attacking whites might not be
complete heroes. Such dynamics could produce a romance for the

evening papers—and to get it, no reporter had to endure mosquito bites or briar scratches at the crime scene. The art of "expanding" a phrase into a full column could supply the legwork, resulting in what might be called The Story Of The Hut.

On the one hand, this was one more repackaging of the uprising, but it had such verve and such reach—touting an imaginary band of brothers to the far corners of America—that it would unleash the floodgates of far more inventive newsroom imaginations. It said:

> **ROSEWOOD, Fla., Jan. 5 (By the Associated Press)—Hundreds of citizens early today were preparing to renew their efforts to smash a barricade behind which 25 or more heavily armed negroes are making a stand here in a small hut. Two white men are known to be dead, three wounded, and a score or more blacks are believed to be slain in the fighting which took place early last night.[485]**
>
> **Deputized posses and citizens said to be numbering in the thousands were pouring into this village early this morning. Automobile after automobile heavily laden with armed men have arrived, some coming from a distance of about 75 miles.**
>
> **All night long citizens surrounding the hut kept up a heavy fire, and at intervals volleys of lead were fired from behind the barricade. At the first break of dawn the whites were preparing to rush the house from all sides. Authorities believe that unless the negroes surrender 'they will be smoked out.'**

This narration is so artfully compact that, again, itemization is helpful:

1. "a barricade behind which 25 or more heavily armed negroes"

2. "are making a stand here in a small hut"

3. interveners "numbering in the thousands"

4. "All night long citizens surrounding the hut kept up a heavy fire"

5. "volleys of lead were fired from behind the barricade"

6. "unless the negroes surrender 'they will be smoked out'"

At a stroke, Sarah Carrier's split-level home is collapsed into Uncle Tom's Cabin, while Sylvester's solitude balloons into Nat Turner's horde. But there is a difficulty. This exercise in fiction-writing calls for rich descriptive detail, and the previous brief wire stories—the building blocks—could provide few such flourishes, because reporters didn't go out there. Even under pressure, the building blocks offer little to be "expanded."

Thus the deception process is still somewhat restrained—at this stage. It is not quite ready to invent galaxies out of fairy dust.

But that is coming. The journey of The Hut has now begun—an epic journey, which, at last, will span resistant decades to roll into a new age that considers itself above all that sort of humbug. This stream of fantasy will continue creating new shapes—and new lies—among the glowing screens of the cyber-age.

En route to such a destiny, the next step in the process now moves outside the Associated Press network. In 1923 that network was overwhelmingly white. But the nation had 113 newspapers published by and for African Americans, according to the U.S. Department of Labor in 1922[486] (It was an elusive issue; another study counted 252 such publications in 1922).[487]

Some of these papers, though starting small, had developed continental reach and large revenue streams. Nearly all were weeklies, not dailies. Based mostly in the Northeast and Midwest, they had grown with new racial ghettos since the Great Migration of World War I.

As white-run media excluded or caricatured African Americans, black weeklies came to have important influence in their markets. The largest went beyond urban readership and passed hand-to-hand in rural cafes, stores, churches, lodge halls and barbershops, especially in the South, where the mainstream competitors bristled with "black brute" language and white supremacist ranting.[488]

For the black weeklies, however, a difficult challenge was posed by lynching coverage. Readers naturally looked to them for an alternative to the racist minefield in white-authored wire stories, but how could the information be obtained? Sending a reporter into a remote southern outback was expensive—and far worse was the danger. However, the prohibitive expense and phenomenal risk of lynching investigation could be outflanked.

Weeklies, with their delayed deadlines, could receive daily wire-service feeds and apply expansion techniques of their own—which techniques could grow especially inventive, owing to cultural pressures on the target readers. These readers were severely constrained from going out and independently checking the facts, while meeting reasons to welcome an emotional sanctuary in print. Here, too, the Rosewood evidence illuminates a dimension seldom examined.[489]

On January 12, 1923, the *Baltimore Afro-American,* a leader in the weekly niche, published its reworking of the wire-service piece about The Hut. Though this story had started as a panic piece for whites, spying black troublemakers, it could be adapted to a different purpose. In the *Afro-American,* The Story of the Hut became a boast about the valor of the elusive rebels. Expansion techniques now moved into heroic intensity, interrupted by almost no facts from the real scene:

DEAD AND HURT NUMBER 22 IN FLORIDA RIOT

Armed Warfare as Whites Attack Negro Community
Following Escape of Suspect
Numerous Instances of Heroism as Men Defend Homes
Against Savages

Rosewood, Fla., Jan. 9 (Crusader Service)—Eighteen white and colored men and women are known to be dead and many others wounded in a savage mob battle that has raged here since the evening of January 5th, following an attempt by a mob of lawless whites to take the law into their own hands in the case of a colored man accused of attacking a white woman.

Hearing that the accused man, Jesse Hunter, was in hiding in the village of Rosewood, whites from the neighboring towns invaded the Negro section and attempted a house-to-house search. They were met with a hail of bullets at the first house they came to. The inmates recognizing the belligerency and lawless

401

composition of the howling mob did not wait to ask for an explanation of their visit. They opened fire and prepared to sell their lives dearly.

...At this point Negroes from other houses came to the aid of their besieged brothers and a rude barricade was thrown up and loop holes made for rifle fire. Negro ex-soldiers put their knowledge and experience gained in France to use in the service of the Race and an effective defense was soon organized.

The whites, reinforced, came back, 600 strong, and a battle royal developed....Robbed of their prey and not anxious to face the lions at bay, the most cowardly part of the white mob set itself to the safer task of destroying the undefended Negro residences and the village church and lodge buildings.

....[The defenders bore] comparison with many of the bravest feats of the colored soldiers on Flanders fields, and forged another link in the long chain of evidence to show that the Negro has at last decided he can fight his own battles...

Finally, their ammunition almost exhausted, the little band decided to emulate the action of the "Guards at Cahill" and with clubbed muskets, made a rush through the besieging forces and breaking through sought the refuge of the surrounding woods.

Amid the thrill of eighteen (non-existent) dead on Flanders Field, the imagination process here seems so unconcerned about any factual connection that it misses an opportunity. It leaves out the initial Thursday night aggression by whites—the killing of the dog and the murder of Sarah Carrier. Though exalting the African Americans supposedly barricaded in the house, the *Afro-American* has them firing first, initiating the combat. This was how the white racist fantasy on the telegraph wire had presented it, and that core was borrowed and left intact.

The Hut's journey has now fused together deceptions coming from both races, as each side draws its favored conclusions from what was basically the same original (and false) image. Embedded deep inside the *Afro-American's* war story is its "nut graf," journalistic parlance meaning a summary paragraph or theme statement (boxed above):

"Negro ex-soldiers put their knowledge and experience gained in France to use in the service of the Race and an effective defense was soon organized."

Here, the reversal of truth and fantasy comes full circle—because the real Sylvester Carrier, a bit distant from France, spent World War I not as a soldier but as convict lease prisoner 13175.

 "War fever" was much discussed on the American homefront in World War I. Its fine line between patriotic sacrifice and mob hatred grew complex in domestic racial controversies. The overarching issue, a siren call of glory in disregard of the cost, was phrased in a later era by war correspondent Chris Hedges of the *New York Times*:

"War's simplicity and high (provide) the chance to exist for an intense and overpowering moment. Many of us, restless, unfulfilled, see no supreme worth in our lives. We want more out of life. And war, at least, gives a sense that we rise above our smallness and divisions."[490]

As in military propaganda, the *Baltimore Afro-American's* fever, lingering four years after World War I, portrayed not only imaginary heroism but imaginary atrocities by the enemy. Continuing beyond the passage quoted above, the story  declared that "two Negro women were attacked and raped between Rosewood and Sumner. The sexual lust of the brutal white mobbists satisfied, the women were strangled."

No real survivors recalled any event even remotely resembling this. In the real world no evidence at all, not even dim rumors, told of a double-rape-strangling (or a single-rape-strangling, etc.). These images weren't lifted or expanded, but were cynically or heedlessly foisted onto readers from sheer fabrication. The psychological overlays come so thickly that examination begins to seem voyeuristic, an intrusion into mysteries meant only for believers. An original white-spun lie has now redoubled into the force of a wish-fulfillment dream.

And the journey is still only beginning.

On that same week, the same story, with much the same wording, ran in another major weekly for African American readers, the *New York Amsterdam News*—with more changes.[491] In the New York paper the death toll side-slipped, going from eighteen unspecified fatalities, as in the *Baltimore Afro-American,* to eighteen dead *whites* in the New York version (plus four deaths of blacks, the story said). The home team is rolling now. Score: 18 to 4.

Along the way, both the *Afro-American* and the *Amsterdam News* would unknowingly slander two real African Americans, Aaron and Mahulda Carrier, the terrified couple whom the Levy County sheriff had taken into protective custody. The original racist wire-service portrait of them, sans names or gender, was also lifted into the black press— unchanged from its original white media disguise. "Two negroes have been arrested on suspicion of the alleged attack on a white woman and taken to Bronson," said the two northern weeklies. Insinuation of a gang rape was preserved without question. Once again, the frightened tie-cutter and his schoolteacher wife are phantom suspects.

Not all black-oriented publications did this on Rosewood. Another, the *New York Age,* was associated with James Weldon Johnson, a former State Department official, the head of the NAACP and a laureled author and poet—who also was born in Florida. When the *Age* ran its report on Rosewood, it scrupulously adhered to the information received from the Associated Press, adding no fictional soldiers or "lions at bay." But, dismally, this meant that the white racist distortions in the original wire stories were allowed to go unchallenged, as if they were true. The grim result suggested that taking the high road, and refusing to insert home-team war propaganda for an African American audience, could mean serving as an unwitting mouthpiece for the other side, for white propaganda slandering blacks. Readers of the *Age* learned that "three Negroes were accused of having taken part in the [Monday] attack" on a white woman, that the Thursday nightriders "found about twenty-five Negroes heavily armed in one house," and that two whites were killed in what looked like a cruel ambush by blacks.

And the journey of The Hut still has far to go.

The most influential African American weekly of the 1920s—and the most controversial—was the *Chicago Defender*. The *Defender* was said to circulate more than 100,000 copies a week as 563 newsboys sold it on the street. Extensive rail deliveries and pass-alongs were said to extend its reach to 600,000 readers, particularly in the Deep South.[492] Poet Langston Hughes (a *Defender* columnist) called it "the journalistic voice of a largely voiceless people." The *Defender* called itself "The Mouthpiece of 14 Million People."[493]

Robert S. Abbott

The *Chicago Defender's* founder and publisher, Robert Abbott, had developed an information market so lucrative that he was known as the nation's first black millionaire, owning a red-brick mansion and two chauffeur-driven automobiles, a Duesenberg touring car and a Rolls-Royce.[494]

In the World War I era the *Chicago Defender* periodically faced complaints that it was inventing some of its news, but these protests were often mixed with racism and were seldom examined by historians. Indeed, some historians have used news reports in the *Chicago Defender* as valuable tools for describing lynching atrocities. The *Defender's* stories displayed vivid, startling details that no other news outlet seemed able to obtain.[495]

In the Rosewood events, the *Defender* had seemed badly scooped by the *Baltimore Afro-American,* with its war heroes in the swamps, but the next day brought an answer. On January 13, a front-page Rosewood story in the Chicago paper pulled out the stops, carrying a wealth of detail seen nowhere else—because the story was a hoax. The Chicago story was an oblique reminder that the Baltimore offering had been incomplete. It had failed to include a main plot element. The *Afro-American*'s fictional expansion had lacked a central hero.

The *Defender* found him. It revealed to readers that the protagonist in the Rosewood drama was epic indeed—and he was no obscure woodsman named Sylvester Carrier.

Sylvester, the real-life central figure, was deleted entirely from the *Defender's* web of imagination, as if any hint of reality might get in the way. Instead there was miraculous coincidence. The hero of the Rosewood events, the *Defender* proudly announced, was actually from Chicago. The miraculous coincidence found him traveling in the Florida swamps just as trouble broke out—whereupon he saved the day. Glamour enfolded this avatar, for he was also "the representative of a Chicago motion-picture house."

Nobody seemed to laugh.

No real survivor from Rosewood ever heard of such a traveler, or anyone remotely resembling him. All of it was made up, not simply an exaggeration but a fantasy, presented as hard fact. Since few living witnesses from lynching atrocities would be consulted in later years, the

Chicago Defender of the 1920s would rarely be challenged by history on such hoaxing—and has repeatedly been treated as an historical source.

The January 13 story on Rosewood resembled the real events only in a light sprinkling of place names, easily culled from the wire and woven into what was otherwise a dream. Nearly everything was fake, though presented sternly as news.[496]

NINETEEN SLAIN IN

FLORIDA RACE WAR

EX-SOLDIER

IS HERO IN

BLOODY RIOT

**Makes Farm Hands Fight Back;
Had Just Come to Town;
Called Chicagoan
By EUGENE BROWN**

Tallahassee, Fla., Jan. 12—Fought to a standstill, repulsed, defeated in his own bailiwick, the Southern lyncher has fled from an open attack against Race men and women at Rosewood, where 14 whites were killed, and resorted to guerrilla warfare, sneaking out in parties of death at night...

In this flood of words, the "EX-SOLDIER" (and movie representative) who is promised by the headline does not appear in the body text until paragraph five:

Ted Cole, former sergeant in a pioneer infantry regiment which saw service in France on the lines and behind the lines, led and inspired his brothers in blood against the murderous mob.

Having wandered far from Chicago, this commando finds himself coincidentally in Rosewood, tapped by fate:

Soldier Different

The soldier Cole seems to have been a bird of passage. Little is known about

him in Rosewood, Gainesville, Sumner, Bronson or any of the surrounding towns. He seems to have come quietly at an opportune time, and then to have vanished.

Aside from the geographical anchors—Gainesville, Sumner, Bronson—the Ted Cole fantasy seems almost to taunt readers for their gullibility.[497] The story mentions an attack on a white woman at Sumner, but even the mere existence of the woman is dismissed as a lie told by whites. Not bothering to accuse Fannie Taylor of being a liar herself, the *Defender* takes an easier route and banishes her from reality: "There is even now some doubt as to whether she exists." In much the same way, the real Sylvester Carrier is banished and the fabricated Ted Cole is parachuted in as a substitute, battling through a Rosewood Armageddon in Robert Abbott's mind.

Abbott's biographer, noted African American editor Roi Ottley, described how the *Chicago Defender's* publisher would sometimes attend the Chicago Civic Opera House in his Rolls-Royce while carrying a silver-headed cane. Ottley wrote that friends there were unsettled when Abbott sometimes spoke loudly in foreign-sounding gibberish, pretending to be visiting royalty from Africa.[498] The imposture was presented in the biography as a mystifyingly serious effort, not a passing joke. In the pages of the *Chicago Defender,* a larger imposture pattern had found an influential channel. As in the white-run media, the face behind the news could sometimes be as interesting as the printed product.

A thousand miles south of the *Chicago Defender* in late January 1923, an eleven-year-old girl, newly entered into refugee status, remained in the grip of severe trauma. And at the same moment, stacks of *Defender* editions were making their customary trip south in railroad baggage cars for marketing in Florida.[499] It is not specifically known whether someone in the chaos of Philomena Goins's new exile in Gainesville said something like: "Here, want to read about what happened to you?"

But there are some hints in this regard. The startling narrative told in later years by Philomena Doctor, née Philomena Goins, may have been related to media influence, through the *Chicago Defender's* hoax story about Sergeant Ted Cole.

That story's January 13 headline announced "Nineteen Slain." Six decades later in 1982, Philomena Doctor described personally stepping over 19 dead white men on a front porch, though her family members agreed they all fled out the back, leaving no chance for the miracle arithmetic. To dispel any doubts as she told the story, Doctor did not fall back on the authority of her own observation, but invoked a higher power. The number nineteen was open to no doubt, she said angrily, because "it came out in the paper."

The alleged author of the Ted Cole story, Eugene Brown, was placed by its dateline as supposedly writing the story in another boilerplate locale, the Florida state capital, Tallahassee. Unfortunately, Tallahassee is more than 130 miles from the site of Rosewood, an impressive distance over which to shout out an interview that the story described:

How Cole Pleaded

...**One old man told me how the ex-soldier pleaded with these people to defend themselves.**

"Fight," the old man said the veteran urged. "Do not be afraid to die. Go on an´ give up your life. What does it matter? Be sure to take your enemy with you when you go."

Then my informant told me of how Cole had told them not to expect anything from being humble *[words left out of original text]* **commanded them to come together and fight off their oppressors, making every bullet count. Several had remonstrated with the soldier, believing him to be hot-headed and young. But his way finally prevailed.**

When it was known that the mob actually was coming, the men went off

> to get their rifles and shotguns. Cole
> told them how to do, selected a house
> on the outskirts of the town, protected
> by the woods. He led them into this
> seeming ambush, a blockhouse, and
> there they awaited the coming of the
> mob. The women offered to help the
> men fight. They, too, locked themselves
> up with their husbands. Some of the
> villagers refused to join the plucky
> band. The loss of their homes by
> burning and ever-lasting fear is now
> their reward.[500]

The "old man," cited by the *Defender's* reporter Eugene Brown as "my informant," did not exist—unless a large crowd of real African American witnesses were all lying at once.

Possibly, Eugene Brown himself did not exist. The *Defender* had a far larger circulation base than twenty-year-old Truman Green's one-man newsroom at the *Gainesville Daily Sun*, but Abbott, too, was a hands-on director. In the Ted Cole hoax, the publisher who spoke in gibberish at the opera, pretending to be foreign royalty, may have been speaking to readers directly.

In that story, an eagerness to urge other people to throw away their lives stares from the page. NAACP board member Julius Rosenwald grew so appalled by Abbott's mysteries that his reported characterization does not bear reproducing here.[501] Marrying a woman thirty years younger than himself in 1918, Abbott reportedly required her to call him only "Mr. Abbott" throughout their decade and a half of marriage, even in the bedroom. After divorce, a second wife, with a twenty-five-year age gap, was also required to say "Mr. Abbott."[502] The ethnic passion in "*...fight off their oppressors, making every bullet count...*" paired privately with the choosing of these wives, both of them so pale that they were sometimes thought to be white.

Even a preliminary survey shows that Sgt. Ted Cole of Rosewood was not an isolated example. A separate issue of the *Defender* carried a story on Rosewood's Sam Carter—also fictionalized.[503] Later in 1923 Abbott touted an alleged black version of the Ku Klux Klan, to be called the L.L.L. ("only by invitation" for "lucky individuals").[504] In 1917 he embraced a theory that Mexican revolutionary Pancho Villa was secretly black.[505] The Waco, Texas, spectacle lynching of 1916 was fictionally transformed by the *Defender*, and the Longview, Texas, race riot of 1919 was largely caused by a slanderous article in the *Defender*.[506] Perhaps its most notorious coup was the invention of a fake atrocity that enflamed Chicago's 1919 race riot.[507] An exception to the general historical silence on the *Defender* noted its "tradition of publishing exciting falsehoods."[508]

In graphics as well as text, its pages suggested a wish-universe predicated on desperation, with large ads promoting skin whiteners, hair straighteners, miracle cures and get-rich-quick schemes. An anxious audience, trapped by ignorance and oppression, seemed to be viewed as willing to accept large doses of absurdity, if the results could bring a brief illusion of relief.

The collision of news and truth in the Lynching Era brought many twists. In 1918, Abbott and the *Defender* were sued by the Hearst media empire for, in essence, stealing the design and front-page logo of Hearst's *Chicago American*.[509] Abbott was accused of trying to trick his readers into believing that the *Defender* was part of the Hearst chain, and as such a bearer of Hearst prestige. The court agreed with Hearst. The *Defender* was forced to drop its front-page Hearst-style eagle emblem.

But that was not the twist. At that time, the Hearst organization itself was also being sued—and also for stealing.[510] The Associated Press took its 1917-1918 lawsuit against Hearst's International News Service to the U.S. Supreme Court, claiming massive pirating and relabeling of AP wire dispatches. It charged that Hearst representatives were "bribing and corrupting employees or members of the Associated Press."[511] Here, too, the court agreed; Hearst was ordered to stop. Meanwhile Robert Abbott complained—also with reason—that his own work was being pirated by the Associated Negro Press.[512] The journalistic world surrounding the *Chicago Defender* was not a perfect place. There were certainly brave and principled individuals who went to great lengths to produce objective, accurate news. But they were not the whole story.

More than seventy years after Sergeant Ted Cole battled his way through the *Chicago Defender*, he would be revived. By the 1990s, the January 13, 1923, issue of the *Defender* lay in an obscure microfilm grave, but some determined tomb-raiders were at hand, conducting story research for the 1997 film *Rosewood*. That film left few doubts that it sought to be taken as a serious embodiment of history. At its climax a documentary-style screen note underscored the solemnity, and promotional materials did much the same. The creators made it clear that, despite a little dramatic tightening here and there, they were out to tell the deeper truth.[513]

The tightening, however, was not small. Sgt. Ted Cole—who never existed anywhere in real life, in any form—was discovered by the moviemakers in the *Chicago Defender's* mothballs. Out of the musty old verbiage, the fictional titan was picked to become the movie's hero, its dramatic centerpiece, complete with supporting flourishes from the *Defender* hoax.

Transferred intact into the film is the ex-soldier's arrival in Rosewood as a mysterious stranger (a "bird of passage," as the *Defender* put it). His supposed memories of heroism in World War I are stressed in the movie as he nostalgically contemplates his war medal. But, tartly, the movie also borrows the fictionalizing process as a whole, and gives the hero a new name. As if "Ted Cole" were a little pedestrian, a labyrinth of cinema creativity gives the Cole character Sylvester Carrier's real nickname, "Man."

The movie turns this into a surname, spelled "Mann," so that characters in the movie greet the war hero monosyllabically, calling him simply "Mann" (echoing the way Sylvester's real family members called *him* "Man"). Meanwhile, Sylvester himself also appears in the movie— called "Sylvester Carrier" in the script—but as a different character, demoted to a supporting role, now a placid but plucky "music teacher."

No one seemed to laugh.

"Mann," the valiant (and non-existent) ex-soldier, rides into the movie in a cloud of cinema clichés. Like the Lone Ranger, he appears on a trusty wonder horse, which horse, clairvoyantly, obeys complex voice commands. The *Chicago Tribune* called the results "Hollywood hooey," but many reviewers seemed thrilled.[514] Peppered in was a cavalcade of real Rosewood names—Minnie, Sarah, Emma, James, Fannie, Poly, Aaron, Philomena, Sam Carter, Sheriff Bob Walker—and John Wright.

As with Sylvester the re-imagined "music teacher," the names were grafted onto invented personalities and events. The nickname "Scrappy" was borrowed from its real owner—a brave, conflicted jook waitress in Wylly named Beulah Carrier Sherman—and in the movie "Scrappy" was pinned onto an opposite, an imagined angel who was a mild and virtuous schoolteacher, with crisp elocution among raptly listening children, as

"Scrappy" taught them—not useful school subjects—but dreamy, movie-style fairy tales. How such an ethereal saint would come to have the nickname "Scrappy" was not explained.

And soon, sure enough, Scrappy-The-Miracle-Teacher fell in love with Ted-Cole-The-Miracle-Mann, and in their love scenes they barely held hands, so perfect was the virtue in paradise.

It was a long journey from that imaginary "hut," but the dilemma of truth in racial controversy was not confined to 1923.

———————————

*"Then Joshua burned Ai,
msking it a ruin forevermore, a
desolate place even to this day."
—Joshua 8:28*

Chapter 35: The Bargain

The Sanctuaries:
 a cookhouse in Sumner, Cummer Lumber Company
 a yard shed in Rosewood, J. M. Wright Genl. Merchandise
 a pine grove in Wylly, M. & M. Naval Stores
 a horse corral at Rocky Hammock, woods rider Jack Cason

The sanctuaries were spread over a distance of more than twelve miles,
though no geographer was mapping their configuration for the
edification of history. No newspaper or official record gave any
indication that they existed at all. The Rosewood sanctuary network—
four improvised havens for dispossessed women and children—
represented a deeply secret conspiracy, though not the kind of lynching-
era conspiracy painted by clichés. Klan huddles and necktie parties were
only one side of the old South's clannish secrecy. Also out of sight were
the furtive handshakes and backroom conferences that sought to impose
damage control.

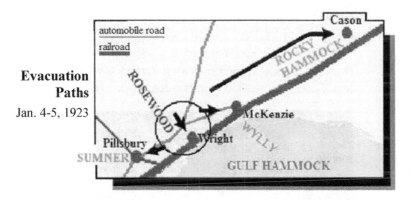

After Newberry, Florida's rampage and mass lynching in 1916, a
witness account said that a number of African Americans took refuge
from the mob violence on the area's largest plantation, run by widow
Fannie Dudley, whose family had ambiguous ties to the lynching itself.[515]
In 1906, the Atlanta race riot produced a flood of reports telling of

prestigious whites sheltering black neighbors or employees; Atlanta journalist Joel Chandler Harris, who compiled the Uncle Remus tales, was said to harbor several people fleeing from that riot.[516] These stories, even when supported by massively agreeing testimony from Rosewood, still leave a great gap in knowledge about the larger regional picture. How often the sanctuary pattern may or may not have been repeated is unknown.

On Friday, January 5, the hundreds of whites converging on Sumner and Rosewood evidently felt themselves to be answering a call—in some cases quite a direct call from a newspaper, pleading for their help in "quelling" a "rebellious black population."[517] Perhaps others had been invited by the Alachua County Sheriff's Department, or conceivably by some hidden Titan of the Klan. But for most, it was probably informal, a call made by rumor and impulse.

For some, there was doubtless a sadistic kick, perhaps for others the thrill of the hunt. And many came for vengeance. Relatives of Henry Andrews crossed seventy miles.[518] And Fannie Taylor's in-laws (or at least one of them) still wanted blood. Rumors also told of visitors from the town of Perry, more than a hundred miles across the Suwannee no-man's land, where passions were still enflamed by the straight-razor decapitation of Ruby Henry a month earlier. This was a lot of mob anger to be managed.

The Referees:

      Walter H. Pillsbury, sawmill superintendent, Sumner
      John M. Wright, merchant, Rosewood
      D. P. McKenzie, turpentine camp owner, Wylly
      Jack Cason, turpentine woods rider, Rocky Hammock

The network of sanctuaries and referees is now known at all only because Rosewood's African American survivors were found in a later era—and were asked the simple question never posed by official truth: *"Where did you go?"*

The managers themselves took the secret to their graves. In the segregation era, when the Florida Legislature was notoriously dominated by a rural clique called the "Porkchop Gang," it was said that the state's destiny was often decided not publicly but at discreet meetings in a fish camp west of the capital.[519] This was the kind of handshake world the referees knew. Among the porkchoppers was Florida Senator Randolph Hodges,[520] whose father worked crews of African American labor in Cedar Key in 1923, and might have been hard hit if the Rosewood violence had spread. Another legislative Porkchopper was Will Yearty, who in 1923 was a store owner and county commissioner living at Otter Creek—also warily watching the mob, monitoring for signs of spread.[521] Even Charley Johns, the state governor known for a 1950s McCarthy-style witch hunt seeking communists and deviancy, had earlier links to some of the Rosewood players through the Seaboard railroad.

But caught in the action itself were the four. They were white business owners or managerial personnel tapped by circumstances—or by self-interest, or Christian mercy—to step glumly into a position never labeled in public, but here called referee.

On Friday, most of Rosewood's infrastructure had not yet been destroyed, though its ground remained prohibitively dangerous for residents, since wandering whites felt justified in shooting. The women and children who were huddled in the sanctuaries could not safely go back home—not now, not in a few days. Smokehouses and root cellars were being looted, livestock and appliances carried off. There were the stray shots at dogs.

No record would tell how they communicated across the twelve miles—three miles from Pillsbury to Wright, two more from Wright to McKenzie, another seven or eight to Cason. The party line telephone in Wright's store was out of the question. In a time of emergency like this, secret listeners on the line would be legion. Storekeeper Wright had a Model T and could drive to McKenzie's on one side and Sumner on the other, as on Friday when memory caught him driving to the Wilkerson funeral. And Cason was on the horse—a hefty ride from Rocky Hammock, but he seemed to keep popping up. By this point, Bob Walker's badly overwhelmed sheriff's department was invisible in the memories, but was also somewhere on the scene.

By some means the result emerged. Whether over bourbon or a dipper from the water bucket, whether scuffing a boot on a noonday porch or gazing morosely out into the night, someone came up with a plan. The evolution of the decision is one more blank spot in a chain of blank spots. Perhaps the very first firebug or firebugs, unidentified at the King and Gordon homes around midnight on Thursday, had been trying intentionally to provoke this sort of plan. That initial spree had hit buildings in a confined area along the railroad, failing to move up the tracks where it might have met white resistance at Wright's store. Nor did it reach north into the woods where other snares might have waited in the dark. It was only a taste, that first spree, but it gave notice: *We can do anything we want.* This was the kind of threat answered by the plan.

Of course, the ultimatum might have been delivered overtly. By Friday night the mob had coalesced into organized action, confronting Pillsbury's mill hands at Sumner. A vigilante committee of sorts seemed to appear.[522] There was a command post—or at least a hang-out area—among freehold

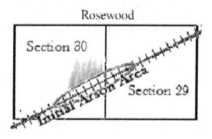

white-owned shops near the Sumner depot. Hence it could be wondered: Did the revolutionaries send a manifesto to Pillsbury, stating a demand: the complete de-population of the target community three miles to the northeast?

Did they say: *Get 'em outa here—or we'll do it?*

Probably not. The dance was of another type. The destruction continued swelling until resistance made it stop. If the government, state or federal, had sent troops (as rumors and newspapers speculated might happen), the violence could perhaps have been stopped after Friday night, when the attackers were kept from storming Sumner. But to stop them entirely—that is, to have soldiers guarding the remaining homes in Rosewood—would have brought up the rest of the lynching-era equation: African Americans throughout a wider area were in a vulnerable position. If white attackers were squeezed out of their preferred target zone, they could easily displace onto substitute areas, creating untold misery—and ruining business for leading whites, by driving off labor. The managerial thinking in response to this dynamic would speak through action: *They have to be granted some kind of prize, something that satisfies their dignity, so they'll go home.*

The obvious prize seemed beyond saving at any rate. The remnant homes in Rosewood were already partially doomed by economics, even if there had been no mob. They hovered in the dying of the old woods, with no internal source of regular wages—walking ghosts, no matter what (it could easily have been said).

The childhood home loved by Minnie was already slipping over the edge. In 1922, unknown to a nine-year-old, desperate Emma Carrier seemed to have trouble paying her property tax.[523] The torches of Thursday night found some homes already unoccupied, vacant shells. So was this how the thinking went? *To sacrifice a place already doomed is not so great a harm.*

Such grimness would be hidden in a later period of Rosewood excitement, the media rush in the 1990s, when audience appeal was sharpened (and the Rosewood claims case was boosted) by depictions of the lost community as a kind of economic Eden, "a thriving...black town" of robust economic promise. This was a mirage—much as in 1923 the twenty-five-black-rebels-in-a-hut had formed an opposite mirage in a different age. A nation of vibrant but volatile diversity was undergoing fashion changes as to what was "right," "accurate"—or even real.

"a thriving, upper middle-class community"
—*Tampa Tribune*, 1993

"a once-thriving milltown...home to some 400 residents"
—*Gainesville Sun*, 1993

"a fully functional and economically viable black community"
"by 1920...a number of small, black-owned business enterprises"
—*The Historian*, 1996

"300-acre plantation [in a] thriving black community"
—*Chicago Tribune*, 1997

"a thriving town...of African Americans who ran local businesses"
—*People* magazine, 1997

"economic stability, through...small business"
—*American Historical Review*, 1998

Transforming desire into official-looking fact even in historical journals, a prevailing climate spoke loudly in its era—simply by avoiding the evidence. No longer, as in 1923, did mainstream media spy a grim little hellhole of crazed brutes—a picture accepted nationwide in its day, with no recorded objections. By contrast, the psychological projections of the 1990s were gentler, sacrificing only a feeble victim called history.

The Florida Legislature's academic report of December 21, 1993, still attracting Web surfers today,[524] multiplied Rosewood's population to six times its actual size, a lapse admitted later by the authors of the report, though in a manner discreetly kept from public view. That exaggeration was mild compared to some portrayals of the lost paradise. A "Black Mecca" was similar to "what Atlanta is today," with "manicured lawns."[525]

The reality, confirmed by all the survivors, was that Rosewood had no more than 22 still-occupied African American households, and perhaps as few as 18 or 20. Today this is generally accepted—after the moment of excitement has cooled. At least seven of those households were supported by jobs in Sumner, jobs that would end with the scheduled departure of the mill in 1926.

The significance of the Rosewood racial cleansing was not limited to geography (Ocoee in 1920 was apparently larger; Tulsa in 1921 was tremendously larger; and globally the competition was vast). Rosewood's significance lay in part in the unique witness evidence revealing it—and also in something else. The witness evidence, in its turn, has unmasked a complex of public fantasy increasing the landmark stature—a complex ranging from 1923 mob and media imaginings to those of the 1990s wish list and now beyond.[526] A small site of atrocity has become a large lesson in mass belief.

———————————

As Minnie shivered uncontrollably in McKenzie's turpentine grove she could only wonder if she would live through the night. Then word came—in the depths of Friday night or the wee hours Saturday. *There would be rescue!* Again she thrilled with gratitude and relief. Yet she saw older women crying. She wondered why.

If a wildfire were to strike the woods, from lightning or some cow hunter's flipped cheroot, the only protection might be to set a backfire, removing the tinder in the inferno's path. And this meant marking out and sacrificing a designated area in that path—a triage maneuver, writing off the strip that can't be saved. They left no records to say whether this was the direction of their thoughts.

———————————

"The conductor sings his song again:
The passengers will please refrain—'
This train's got the disappearing railroad blues."
—*The City of New Orleans,*
Steve Goodman

He was not a man of tragedy, though he was willing to lend a hand in tragedy if he could. The jovial train conductor, William Crighton "Kay" Bryce, could easily look like the happiest man on earth.[527]

Some might think, naively, that riding back and forth on a train all day could get a little old. But not Bryce. The clickety-clack was his heartbeat—clear back to the old childhood plantation—and no small plantation at that. The child of wealth had waged a running battle with maternal fears, for he had the terrifying habit of trotting along beside the moving cars and hopping on. Knowing the stories about amputated legs, his mother had at last belted him bizarrely into a girl's long petticoat, thus to restrict his running and jumping, the family stories chuckled. But one day she looked out and saw the petticoat fluttering in the breeze, the boy still in it, as he perched again on the brakeman's step.

The family tales were as jovial as the man. At age 48, Bryce was one of those fellows—like Walter Pillsbury in Sumner—who seemed to live out his dreams. When the big, bold conductor ambled down the aisle to stamp your ticket, it was natural to think he had to do this for a living. The truth was other-wise. He did it for love. Like countless country boys of his epoch, Bryce loved the far-off whistle. Family tradition portrayed his ancestors as being so wealthy that they had deeded the land that would give rise to the Georgia capitol building in Atlanta. True or not, the size of Kay Bryce's later legacy made it sound believable.

The old backwater branch of the Seaboard Air Line through Rosewood--155 miles from Fernandina just above Jacksonville down to Cedar Key—could almost look like *their* railroad, a Bryce project—because large Bryce homes stood at either end. Near the northern terminus was an entire town named Bryceville—in the old plantation style, built on or around Bryce property. His nearby industrial base was Kaytown, turpentining and sawmilling. Then far down at the southern end of the tracks in Cedar Key was his other castle, all three stories of it, looking out over Cedar Key's small beach area.[528] The windmill rising behind the three-story Bryce manse serviced its luxury fixtures. You had to have water pressure to have an inside bathroom on every floor. At one point his turpentine camps were said to be strung out in a pattern that paced the line. There were investments in sponge fishing at Cedar Key, banking, ranching. After about 1918 the three-story beach house stood neglected as he focused on Kaytown and Bryceville. Then in the summers he rented it out as a vacation hideaway for friends, the Pillsburys of Sumner, so the children could get away from the sawdust for awhile.[529]

As a passenger train conductor, the moneyed minion was not just a hobbyist but had a rolling principality. It was the conductor of a train, not the engineer, who bossed the operation, like a ship captain on the high seas. Carrying out telegraphed orders from a dispatcher, the conductor ordered the coupling or uncoupling of cars, marshalled his squad of brakemen and porters, gave instructions to the baggage master, the fireman, the engineer. Punching tickets was only the public face.

Some kind of adventure always lay waiting. The days were gone when there was much venison to buy from dark hunters like James Carrier at the Rosewood stop, but he could always signal the engineer, saying to throttle back as he dropped off a little something for Emma,[530] knowing how it was with James and the strokes. Multiply such variations by all the houses, depots, whistlestops, peddlers, potentates, poets, pawns and kings. He liked the train.

But this week's schedule was bleak.

On Monday night, New Year's, his train pulled through Gainesville at about the time the Alachua Klan paraders were getting the bed sheets ready, ten blocks north of the depot. The old iron horse was gone before the parade could begin, shuddering down into the coastal swamps—but then it passed through Rosewood at just about the time when a shotgun blast in Gulf Hammock struck Sam Carter. Three nights later on Thursday night, under the big, cold moon, the stiff-billed conductor's cap was pulling into overnight berthing at the end of the line, near the wharf at Cedar Key, at about the time that Sarah Carrier's house was erupting in gunfire, nine miles inland.

By Friday morning there would never again be a lonely little princess on Sam and Ellen King's front porch to wave at conductor Bryce—because there was no more porch, no house. The daily departure of the passenger train from Cedar Key occurred before dawn, taking the cars past the King and Gordon homes as the ashes were still smoking. Out there somewhere, Lexie Gordon was still lying on the sand. The perpetrators themselves may have stood along the tracks, gazing vacantly up at the conductor.

Bryce worked black crews on his farm and was a man of segregated society. His porters on the train were African American, like the fireman in the locomotive at the furnace, though by rule the engineer was white. And the ruling conductor was white. Bryce's train had the standard "Jim Crow car" up front, where you had to ride if you were black. It was not in the back as in a bus, because in a train the least wanted spot was in the noise and cinders up by the locomotive. Jim Crow was his world. The shanties on the sprawling Bryce plantation looked like southern shanties anywhere.

He knew, too, that the jungle frontier was dying—and may have guessed that his own passenger route would not last much longer (waiting only for the Depression to shut down this branch of the Seaboard). He had perhaps expected to watch Rosewood, with its rich old memories, continue to sink peacefully into the forest floor. But he also reads the newspapers. He knows what a race war is. And now it has come.

Now, on Friday night, January 5, Bryce's train is moving southwest on the trestles over the Gulf tide flats toward Cedar Key, probing into the sea air in the dark—at roughly the same moment when Pillsbury and his sawmill militia, back inland and north of the tracks, are facing down the mob. By this time the situation is clear—and the choices. On each run since Monday the lover of trains has watched the tensions build, perhaps thinking: *Never here, it can't explode here, too quiet, too peaceful here.* But now it's a wildfire. Requiring damage control.

The four shut-mouthed white referees have their hands full. They can't play host forever. You don't tell it to the newspapers or over the telephone party line, but it has to be worked out—in conference with the fifth referee. One more cryptic knight on the southern checkerboard.

The fifth sanctuary will be the train.

Now comes the second rescue that is not told in public (the larger sequel to the rescue of Aaron and Mahulda Carrier on Monday). With no formal record of this action—and certainly no description by the lock-jawed referees—there is little way to assess a key ingredient, the real extent of its valor and heroism. Possibly the five conspirators did not see it as being so valorous, but simply as sad work—tense, dangerous, dirty, dicey business, something to weigh on a man. The old frontier boom shouldn't have ended like this, in such shame.

Maybe he knew as soon as word came about Poly and Andrews that it was over now, that it would come to this decision. Some knew, some didn't. Lee Carrier and Sam Hall, very close to the action, and yet far enough away for the shooting to sound like distant tapping, thought it would likely be a one-night ordeal, back to normal in the morning. They were too reasonable to encompass the reality, to think their world could end.

The state governor, Cary Hardee, was asked on Friday if he would send the National Guard. Mysteriously, a newspaper story reported that the governor then received a telegram from Sheriff Walker asking him *not* to send troops.[531] The background would never be revealed. But once that line had been drawn in the sand, it was time.

5:30 a.m.: Daily departure of the Seaboard Air Line passenger train from Cedar Key

On Saturday morning, January 6, in darkness before dawn, the old snake moves even more slowly than its usual crawl. There are orders. The pickups are to be sternly selective. No adult black males will be allowed on board. This run is for a special category of passengers. There are pre-arranged sites for stops, some of them guarded by a growing body of whites like Jack Cason, who oppose the mob. There, boardings will occur, as occupants of the sanctuaries are brought out into the open. With anguished mixed feelings, women and children will climb into the fifth sanctuary.[532]

The time has come to remove the targets to more distant places of safety. If all goes as planned, the mob will cling to its pretense of chivalry, and thus will not interfere. It is not shouted about that the essence of this plan is appeasement, with appeasement's price. Rather than using the power of the law to restore order forcibly and drive out criminal aggression, the aggressors are being left unmolested, and will receive their consolation prize. The physical infrastructure of the target community is to be surrendered to them. The last of the mantelpiece tempera paintings now also comes to life: the sacrifice.

The impulse toward racial cleansing has won out, within a designated zone. The African American presence in this designated area is removed, leaving the cleansers with a sense of accomplishment and glory. The rescuees will be taken fifty miles up the line to Gainesville, and in some cases farther, to Kay Bryce's plantation at Bryceville.[533]

Most will never see their homes again. It could be called rescue. Or it could be called de-population. But it did not protect the property left behind.

Land ownership was not formally stripped by this action. Some dislocated African American property owners would continue paying taxes and holding title to their Rosewood land for years to come, into a time when passions cooled sufficiently for some to make bizarre, nostalgic visits back from places like Jacksonville or Miami, to see the old jungle-choked ground that they had no further reason to inhabit. Ellen King, widowed by her husband Sam's heart attack (they said he worked himself to death trying to build back what he had lost),[534] would hold title to her 4.65 acres at Rosewood through the Depression and World War II, mailing in the property tax each year from the Miami area, until it was hard to remember why. On July 31, 1952, she sold.[535]

But most others were harder pressed. As the Florida Boom had brought land fever even to the backwoods in 1924-1925, most of the dispossessed sold to whoever would buy, perhaps at a loss. Some of the transactions showed irregularities, though the meaning of these was unclear.[536] One of the buyers, John McNulty, was listed as living in Ohio. A common story about Florida's 1925 real estate bubble was that two-thirds of the buyers were absentees, buying by mail.[537]

Around the world, the face-off between official authority and mob power tends to bring a dismal decision process. Instead of the brave stand—as with Pillsbury's brief stand in Sumner—there is often a demoralized assessment that a mob can only be contained, not controlled. The mob demands a trophy to prove its potency, in the form of a successfully ravaged victim.[538] In some lonely times and places, the sacrifices are terrified individuals—the hunted witch or witches—left to be torn apart as the unspoken price, which is paid to mob "fever" by reigning authority, in its bargain. Perhaps the tempera pictures on the mantelpiece are not so far from this.

Nervous official power can accomplish the bargain tacitly, by confining arriving troops or law enforcement to the perimeter of a riot zone, or simply by delaying their arrival—while inside the ring of fire the mob is allowed to go on, lynching or burning, though confined to the core sacrifice—which later may be found in ashes (or, if the sacrifice is more corporeal, may be found hanging there). As a next step, authorities may round up a few symbolic suspects accused of rioting, to send a message that these authorities are all-powerful in the long run. But this—in the ancient mob triage formula—is preferably done after the crowd has wandered off or grown tired, and the danger of further explosion is past.[539]

Or alternatively, no one may be arrested at all. This was the case at Rosewood. Either way, later public statements from officialdom may offer a helpless shrug. *We came as fast as we could; we can't do everything.* The process was enshrined in the 1992 attack on truck driver Reginald Denny in the Los Angeles riot, with its more than 50 dead.[540] A news helicopter shot live video clearly showing the faces of rioters who were mercilessly beating Denny into a state of lasting brain damage, one weapon being a large chunk of cement. No police came. Rescue was performed finally by a group of shocked African Americans watching the drama at home on TV, as, aghast at the lack of response, they rushed there themselves to pry the victim away. After court proceedings, all but one of the clearly televised attackers went free.[541] The legal system did not say, in so many words, that if a large enough population rebels, the priority is to somehow squeeze the passions back into the box. The law defers to fears for public safety—or simply to fear.

The Bargain: White men have been killed in an outlaw's roost; hence the price must be levied on any Negro accused of this effrontery, as well as on the physical structure of the community where it occurred. All of these designated sacrifices—any accused men plus the community as a unit—are forfeit to vengeance.

And in exchange for this, everyone else at the scene will be allowed to escape with their lives. The open season on rampage killings, such as those of Lexie Gordon and Mingo Williams, is now closed. These bursts will cease.

Perhaps it was only an organic, *de facto* bargain, unspoken and never sealed with a handshake. But the result remained.

In pre-dawn darkness, frightened children and weeping women are emerging from cramped hiding places. At John Wright's, they file along a plank walk to a freight platform. Near Wylly, Minnie has spent two shivering, terrified nights in the woods. Now she stumbles aboard, grateful for the box lunches handed out by Bryce the conductor. Not until arrival in Gainesville will she be reunited with Mama. Emma Carrier, a particularly dangerous person to rescue—an adult from inside the "death house"—has been taken out separately by car. Emma is under particular threat because the proof of her presence in the house is inescapable. She carries one or more buckshot wounds.

The numbness in Gainesville brings realization. Mama has lost everything she owned. Living on the charity of relatives, Emma Carrier will try to keep the children together. Her physical wounds seem small, but she weakens. Within a year, by age 53, she will be gone. Minnie will live as a bitter waif, drifting among relatives in turpentine camps.

In the 1997 motion picture *Rosewood,* the train rescue received another of the movie's action-thriller upgrades. The non-existent ex-soldier hero, complete with war medal, was depicted blazing away with his trusty six-gun from the back of the fleeing train, firing at howling rednecks who are chasing like wolves in their Model T's—as the rednecks fire, too, seeming monstrously determined to kill the women and children on the train.

But they get no chance. The movie hero is picking them off in droves, not the Lone Ranger now but the big Duke, making three-at-a-time Injun shots. The harsh real-life nature of the train rescue is transformed in this climax into something looking horribly like a joke. And indeed, the surrender of reasonable examination to mob fantasy can often look absurd, like something in a bad joke—if you're not the witch being burned.

The newspaper fantasies of 1923 are relatively easy to unmask, once independent evidence can be brought to bear for comparison to their false contentions. But what if the more familiar world around us, right now, were to find its own mob voice, using the favored medium of the moment, and in the favored moral fashion of the age?

How would we know?

Conductor Bryce also appeared in the movie, real name and all, and was treated rather nicely—though with an unintended nod to me. One of my early errors as I investigated Rosewood—an error I corrected long before the movie came along—had accepted a passing tale saying that Kay Bryce's brother, John Bryce, was also involved in the train rescue, putting a second kindly conductor into the evacuation. As it turns out, John Bryce wasn't there. Notwithstanding, the creators of the film apparently discovered this old clinker in my earliest work and were charmed by the cozy brother act, without bothering to check. So John is in the movie rescue, too.[542]

Also appearing in the movie was a minor character named Minnie, though only in the background. She was eclipsed by a more theatrically appealing child heroine, whom the movie dutifully named as Philomena—presented as a calm and even-tempered witness to history. Buried behind these images were two staring, haunted forms on a depot platform in Gainesville, the real little girls.

Chapter 36: Jump Jim Crow

Listen all you gals and boys,
I'se just from Tucky-hoe;
I'm goin' to sing a little song.
My name's Jim Crow.
W'eel about and turn about,
And do jis' so.
Ev'ry time I w'eel about
I jump Jim Crow.

> —*song "Jump Jim Crow,"*
> *apparently first performed by*
> *white dancer T. D. "Daddy" Rice,*
> *pioneer blackface minstrel,*
> *1830s, Bowery Theatre, New York*[543]

Minnie would watch Papa sitting up late at night, smoking his pipe, staring into the fire. After his two strokes, James Carrier was perhaps thinking back to years when he had stayed up for a different reason, checking his traps in the woods, hunting by moonlight, coming home at dawn laden with game. Records traced him back to 1870, finding him in Rosewood at age four. Record-keeping was sketchy. Rosewood's notary public in those early years was community founder Charlie Jacobs, who signed one document as "C. M. Jacobs, No Tree Republic."[544] Big Charlie's accidental poetry managed to parody the great drama shaping hunters like James Carrier: the razing of the woods.

In 1886, James married tall, shy Emma Lewis,[545] as he was becoming the woodsman and commercial trapper known to future witnesses. Professional hunting called as well to his forceful brother Haywood, who on Sundays was known for his passionate lay sermons in church. In-laws George Bradley, John Coleman and others followed the hunting path

Conuropsis carolinensis
Carolina parakeet

The five-thousand-acre jungle called Gulf Hammock, a gem of northern Florida's transitional climate belt, teemed with vanishing exuberance—perhaps still the occasional bright green Carolina parakeet pecking at a cypress pod; the dwindling flocks of carrier pigeons, the great ivorybills (similar to but larger than the laughing lord-gods)—and even improbable beasts like the "dog-killer" or tayra, a sort of hot-country wolverine (confirmed as late as 1941).[546] There were coastal red wolves and pint-sized Florida panthers.

They said the last bear was trapped out of the hammock around 1916. A news item found a youthful sheriff, Bob Walker, still bear hunting in 1908. This was six years after President Roosevelt's news-making "teddy bear" encounter in a similar jungle, among canebrakes on the Mississippi River. The 1908 Sears, Roebuck catalog flagged the hunting and trapping market: "We operate the largest fur coat, duck and leather coat and working clothing factory in the United States."[547]

The frontier Florida of James Carrier was stocked with carbon bisulfate powder to keep the bugs out of rank-smelling hide rooms, and the bundles went north by train. "Genuine Black Raccoon Muffs," "Genuine Plymouth Buck Gloves," crowed Montgomery Ward.[548] It all had to come from somewhere.

As the sun rises on Saturday, January 6, 1923, stroke-disabled James Carrier has apparently spent a cold night in the woods. The whistle of the pre-dawn passenger train is long gone, with its mournful load on this day, the women and children bound for exile. A night has passed since sunset Friday, when lumber stackers concealed in the bushes watched the handicapped hunter struggle along the back path. By now those stackers, including Lee Carrier and Sam Hall, are miles away on their own exile journeys, on foot, grappling with their sudden status as untouchables. In a distant meadow this Saturday at dawn, Lee Carrier's striding figure freezes. Throwing himself to the ground, he flattens in the weeds as an armed white approaches with a dog. He braces to rise desperately and fight the gunman if the dog should catch his scent. All whites are alert for the Rosewood uprisers now. But this one passes. At last Lee gets up again, and strides on. Far behind him in the vicinity of Sumner, the refugee who can barely walk, James Carrier, is even more alone.

Coffee is boiling in riot camps around Sumner. At the company store, with its faint odor of gasoline at the front steps, punctual commissary clerk Ernest Parham once more clicks open the padlock, opening for business as usual on this Saturday. Still lingering is the thrill of surviving last night's mob showdown. Rows of canned goods gleam in dawn shadows.

As the day progresses, the usual buyers of cold drinks and a nickel's worth of cheese will mingle with hard-eyed newcomers, strolling up to the counter past the jug-top gas pump and the two spittoons. These out-of-town avengers give no sunny greeting to the nervous young clerk—this lackey of corporate power, fronting for the greedy company with its jook and its quarters, in this stronghold of African crime. A stone face presents itself to Parham at the counter, demanding to buy shotgun shells. Parham obediently pushes the box of 25 weighty red tubes across the counter. The fellow scoops up the box and stalks out, glaring defiantly, no payment offered.

When James Carrier passed the lumber stackers on Friday he was apparently trying to reach Sumner's black quarters farther west, hoping for shelter with his daughter Rita Carrier Williams. But she is in little position to help.

Tall, graceful "Sister Rita," former organist at the Rosewood church, used to rehearse at home on her mother's parlor console. But in the Sumner shanty of her married life the beatings began, the private rages of her husband Buddy. At last she had taken the route of last resort, trying to flee where Buddy would never find her, crossing the Styx called Suwannee, taking the plank river ferry with its stolid boatman, disappearing into the outlaw swamps marked off as Dixie County.[549] People could have told her what was waiting over there. Rita was snared by one of the slave camps, of a type that would put Florida once more into national headlines when the pattern was exposed. Revelations about Dixie County's forced labor abuses would erupt in April 1923, only months after the Rosewood explosion—bringing another Pulitzer Prize to Ralph Pulitzer's *New York World*, as it pegged the slaving story to Florida's flair for denial: "A million people have been either ignorant of the system or have closed their eyes and ears to what was going on about them."[550]

The Dixie County labor practices were unknown publicly when Rita became a captive. Family members fearfully crossed the river to bail her out, in a maze of peonage ploys on the order of "surety bonds" and "foot speeding" fines. Minnie gathered only that the fee was paid to someone in the place with high fences. Defeated, the escapee was then brought home—once more to Buddy. As dawn came on Saturday, January 6, 1923, she was still living there. It was not the kind of personal history to encourage a new round of risks, as Rita Carrier Williams found a twisted figure at her door.

The scene now replays: the seeker of sanctuary, the carrier of the virus of blame, the danger posed to reluctant relatives. Again, as in the Wylly quarters two nights before, the refusing family member is not only fearful but under corporate orders. Any Rosewood evacuee found in the Sumner quarters is to be handed over to the company—for deposit in the cook house if the party is a woman or a child—but, in the case of an adult male....

This was the dilemma—now falling to the dark man in the necktie.

Superintendent Walter Pillsbury has won his Friday night battle, but the slate won't seem to stay clean. Keeping things clean has been his rule—building the yard fences to keep out wandering hogs, building the church for wayward souls, shutting down the unclean dance hall for whites—even cleaning the air, stamping out malaria mosquitoes with coal oil poured on the breeding places in puddles and ponds.[551] And there was the firing of Poly Wilkerson, cleansing the white stain from the black den, the jook.

The forces of chaos can be managed. He can reason with the vigilantes, using his bargaining chip, the announcement that his quarters area is clean, that it is harboring no adult males from Rosewood. By now even the cookhouse has been emptied. His exhausted wife is no longer smuggling food to the hiders. The assistant bookkeeper has gone home. The suspicious-looking lumber stackers from Rosewood have all been fired (with perhaps no one troubling to tell him that they went away unpaid).

Sumner has been cleansed. All ties to Rosewood are eliminated.

Then the shocked face of the daughter of James Carrier. The crippled hunter facing her.

The family will recall how Rita dutifully notified Pillsbury. A newspaper story will say much the same.[552] The glimpses grow scarce. The weary superintendent has spent the night waiting for the rescue train, perhaps with little or no sleep, knowing that if the drunken whoops from passing cars should turn into gunfire, his wife in the cookhouse could be in the line of fire.

In Saturday's sunlight, mill hands are trooping to the office to be paid, peering through the burglar bars at the sourpuss accountant who thumbs the envelopes. At some point the higher man who sits nearby, Pillsbury, comes into possession of the unwanted secret.

The figure at the shanty door lurches and groans, barely able to speak, releasing an aphasic explosion of monosyllables. The stain on Pillsbury's clean quarters has now come creeping back, ruining the bargain.

The crippled old man has to be put somewhere. There is Sumner's small jail, the shack that holds occasional weekend brawlers from the jook, sobering them up for Monday's whistle. He is stuffed in there, flanked by the ruts and outhouses of the black quarters, not far from the jook.

Speech aphasia, a sequel of stroke, is a disruption of language centers in the brain. It was given the name by physicians in France around the time that James Carrier was born.[553] Apparently after the strokes he can still think and understand with at least some clarity—can helplessly watch his own struggle—but less intact is his ability to put thoughts into spoken words, and perhaps to comprehend the words of others. With effort he can force out some halting phrases, making a confused burst.

Gossip among whites will translate this a bit.

"An ole crazy one" has now been caught. Why, he's the brother of that main rebel Sylvester (the gossip promotes him from his real kinship position, that of uncle).[554] Here's a hot suspect, all right, probably one of the very ambushers who shot down the two brave lawmen.

The makeshift army camping at Sumner has by this point come perilously close to indignity, facing the thought of going home empty-handed, with no thrilling exploits to describe. Who wants to tell the admiring nephews and nieces about getting outsmarted and wandering around?

But at last, redemption! One of the main rebels has been caught! This tough old renegade is holding precious information. He can tell where all those other rebels have gone, in their crafty invisibility.

In a delusional sequence rarely questioned even by moderates among the observers (as with Sam Carter on Monday night), the new captive is assumed to know it all—because they need him to know it all. The wisdom of the heroes is now validated. There *is* an uprising. And this old bird can tick off the names, finger all of the black rebels who were behind that tricky Thursday night barricade.

Some would hear that an angry crowd cornered Pillsbury. Perhaps they asked if he was willing to get his quarters burned down over a crazy old murderer. He knew he was not Pilate, that he was of the other tribe: Daniel in the lion's den, the faithful servant with the talents, the good son in the robe. The gargoyle images in the handsome book, the brooding of fallen angels. Why would things not stay clean?

The next glimpse is far, far away, on a Swanny River flowing through the telegraph wires. A new wire bulletin—retooling the geography a bit (and otherwise enhanced)—will find its way into the Sunday *New York Times*:

> **Carrier had returned to Rosewood this morning and appealed to W. H. Pillsbury, Superintendent of the Sumner Cypress Company mill there, for protection. Pillsbury locked him in a house in the negro quarter. Later, however, when a new clash became imminent, the negro was turned over to twenty-five or thirty men.[555]**

When a sufferer of aphasia tries to speak, the result may be "stereotypy"—a fixation on a single word or phrase. A landmark patient in the 1860s, who gave rise to the word "aphasia," tended to repeat the syllable "tan," saying it over and over. A half-century later in Sumner, Florida, a handier diagnosis was shuttling through the white rumor mill.

> *That old crazy one, he egged 'em on. He taunted 'em, that shameless rascal. They tried to ask him civilized questions, and he threw it back in their faces. He shook his fist at 'em, dared 'em to fight, kept wavin' that crazy hand over toward Rosewood, wantin' to draw 'em into an ambush all over again, and he kept sayin': "Come on! Come on!"*

Neither the white gossips nor the white-run newspapers would mention, in their tales of mob virtue, that this dangerous cutthroat had any *kind of disability. The story was cleaned up to hide the fact that he was* crippled. To reveal the pathetic extenuating circumstance, in rumors or in print, would be to reveal the full degeneration of the tormentors, whom both the gossip and the printed words, quite the contrary, chose to flatter:

SEVENTH VICTIM
OF ROSEWOOD RACE RIOT
NEGRO MAN RIDDLED WITH
BULLETS WHILE STANDING
OVER THE GRAVES OF THREE
OTHER VICTIMS

REFUSED TO GIVE NAMES

Admitted That He Was in House
From Which Death Dealing Volley
Came That Cost Lives of Two
White Men...

Rosewood, Fla.—(By the Associated Press)—A new grave was dug in the negro cemetery at Sumner near here late today and in it Sheriff Elias Walker placed the body of James Carrier, whose death at the hands of several white men.... [556]

To be precise, James Carrier was not the seventh but the eighth fatality, if Sam Carter on Monday night is included in the count. Possibly this eighth death did occur in a graveyard as the news said, but if so, it was in Rosewood, and he was taken there from Sumner. The three other African American victims inside Rosewood may already have been interred by that point—in the Rosewood cemetery. They were Sarah Carrier, Lexie Gordon and Sylvester Carrier, killed in that order on Thursday night and Friday morning. Sam Carter was buried separately on Tuesday, when conditions still permitted a funeral. The process by which James Carrier may have arrived at a graveyard prior to death was apparently not something that "Sheriff Elias Walker" seemed to explain to the press (and Walker's name was rendered almost accurately; "Elisha Walker" was Sheriff Bob Walker's name of record).[557]

The James Carrier news story, like others that week, followed some of the rules of military propaganda, though this was propaganda with a difference, not military but ethnic propaganda, cheering for an ethnic side. In military propaganda the hat trick is to use accurate, verifiable background details but to weave them around a falsehood that is harder to spot: a falsehood of theme. The site and date of a battle might be reported with painstaking accuracy, but an abstract theme—such as who massacred whom—may be turned on its head to blame the enemy. This

433

can be done simply by omission, leaving no visible lies to be caught. If our side loses a battle and our dead are clearly lying on the field, with their weapons, the weapons can be omitted, to produce a devilish massacre of unarmed prisoners by the other side. Omission alone was able to rework Rosewood's Thursday night shootout, leaving out warts like the shooting of the dog. The theme being promoted in the Rosewood wire stories was group virtue, something to give white readers a boost. The wrong kind of facts might muddle the show.

James Carrier's last moments were doubly suited to this. Unlike the Sam Carter killing earlier in the week, riot escalation has now left no uninvolved spectators at the killing. The show has become private. Apparently no one present considered himself innocent enough to later tell the tale. Perhaps the secretive audience consisted only of "several white men," as in the one report—or "twenty-five or thirty men," as in another.[558] Perhaps it was not a crowd but a few cronies. Not even legend would be able to look into this closed circle and check. No specific killer of James Carrier would ever be named.

Though there is a clue.

Name: Patrick I. Taylor
Date of birth: July 23, 1902
Age in 1923: 20
Features: "Brown eyes, black hair,
ruddy complexion"
Height: Six feet, two inches[559]

In the remnant boomtown of Cedar Key, with its singular reputation for left-behind violence,[560] one figure stood above the rest, literally. Taller than most people around him, though lean and lanky, Pat Taylor was barely voting age in 1923, but was on his way to being Cedar Key's most feared Saturday night brawler.[561] In a communal home of gloating ghost stories and atrocity chic, Taylor would be chosen as town marshal, Cedar Key's one-man police force. Still later, in 1932, another law enforcement leader in Cedar Key, Justice of the Peace T. W. Brewer, would be sentenced to life in prison for murdering three men in the town jail, one of them apparently burned alive.[562] It meant something to be the law in Cedar Key.

Pat Taylor came from a solid family of carpenters, which included his solid, dependable brother James.[563] The tall brawler had a special interest in the Rosewood violence, for he was the brother-in-law of Fannie Taylor in Sumner. But Pat's brother (Fannie's husband James) was said not to drink or even chew tobacco. Pat, by contrast, had found alcohol, and the battle call of the mean drunk.[564] A remembered conversation had him toying with thoughts of clean-up:

"I was gonna kill that man."
"How come?"
"Cause he was just no good."[565]

Assessments were diverse.

Jim Turner:
"I guess you'd call him the black sheep of the Taylor family."

Woodrow Baylor:
"Pat drank a lot and would get rowdy when he drank."

Allen Faircloth:
"Pat Taylor was a big man....He was a good man."

Fred Kirkland:
"Pat Taylor was a good friend of mine. He was about seven-foot. But he wasn't as big around as you. Now if you wanted to fight or anything else, that's all you had to ask. He's ready. But he wouldn't pick a fight."

The witness ambivalence (all of those above are white) continued with Randolph Hodges, who was just under nine years old in January 1923 and was living in Cedar Key—later to grow up and become a power in Florida politics.[566] Hodges watched as his beautiful and violent hometown, "the town that refused to die," shrank around its memories. In such a setting, he viewed Pat Taylor as "a good friend," though he said he once saw the tall friend draw a gun, shoot a man and then shrug nonchalantly: "I didn't kill him. He's too sorry to die. He'll get up in a minute." Enhanced or not, the impression was not isolated. Narrators seemed to find a certain coldness.

For decades after the Rosewood events, Cedar Key seethed privately with Rosewood atrocity stories, brought out on occasion like family heirlooms. Often in these stories the star was Pat Taylor. If you asked a teller for a perpetrator-name from Rosewood, it tended to be Pat's, as if a killing machine had stood over heaps of corpses. Typically, such tellers expressed revulsion and dismay at the homicides being described—and yet there was a fascination, an ease with which exaggeration was accepted to pump up the thrill. Pat Taylor began to sound like a Babe Ruth of murder, running up quite a nice score for the proud home team.

 Some discussions placed him in the Rosewood violence with a sidekick, Punk Hudson, a rough cob who ran a few hogs in the woods.[567] An acquaintance mused: *"Punk was just as lazy as he could be, a good old Joe to talk to, kind of comical like."*[568] In Cedar Key's mental wax museum, two horsemen rode through the Rosewood apocalypse, Pat and Punk.

Almost certainly, these two individuals did commit some kind of crime or crimes in the Rosewood events. The wealth of tales didn't come out of nowhere. But a favorite story about Pat Taylor—and the only one known to put him in a specific Rosewood crime—turns out to bear the earmarks of myth. This was The Story Of The Otter Creek Bridge.[569]

In terms of geography, the area around Otter Creek, twelve miles up from Rosewood, formed a natural chokepoint between swamps. Its dry land narrowed to a strategically placed bridge near a turpentine settlement called Ellzey—a logical place for vigilantes to lie in wait for Rosewood refugees trying to move inland. The Otter Creek Bridge Story, however, did not pause for real Rosewood details as portrayed by witnesses, like the rescue by train. That rescue would seem to make the notion of a chokepoint or strategic bridge a bit irrelevant. The story was undeterred:

The lanky terminator, Pat Taylor, is now crouching in wait, hiding at the Otter Creek bridge. Like the companions crouching with him, Pat knows that hated Rosewood inhabitants, now fleeing for their lives, will have to cross this bridge.

And sure enough, a target appears. A small, disoriented figure creeps onto the span—a black child, alone, glancing about fearfully. He spots Pat. Immediately, the desperate refugee turns to flee, as Pat's friends watch in horror—for they see the look in his eye. "Don't do it, Pat," the virtuous companions plead. ("Say it ain't so, Joe" was the nationally repeated line from the "Black Sox" baseball scandal of 1919.)[570] In the tale of the bridge, civilized white society in Cedar Key is shocked, shocked, by their demonic home-run hero.

And this is because he ignores the pleading, and he shoots. Fatally.

"Why, Pat? Why?" cry the comrades as the child lies there. And here—not in the alleged killing itself—lies the punchline of the story. The reply reportedly given by homicidal stringbean Pat Taylor would become one of the heirlooms in Cedar Key's oral attic, for it incorporated a code phrase.

Pat reportedly explains his lack of mercy by retorting:
"A nit'll make a louse, won't it?"
Or as given in another version:
"A goddamn nit makes a louse, don't he?"

Before deconstructing this phrase—with its brutal universe contained in a grain of sand—the evidence behind the tale should be put in perspective. Repeated tracing, using multiple evidentiary streams, has shown again and again that no African American children disappeared that week in Otter Creek, or anywhere around—or were locally alleged, even dimly, to have disappeared, or to have been hurt or killed. Nor did any of the Rosewood survivors hear of any child running off and disappearing from among the Rosewood refugees. There were rumors that reached some survivors about deaths of children, but these consistently traced back to false assumptions made amid the chaos, such as stories about Frances Goins or Eloise King. Though portrayed in occasional gossip as tragic fatalities, both those parties turned out to insist, once they were located in later years, that they certainly were not deceased.[571]

In Otter Creek's African American community, concealing the pain of a child's death would not have been as easy as white braggarts seemed to imagine. Among local African Americans not a hint—nor even a baseless legend—seemed to claim such a thing. Moreover, whites living in Otter Creek in 1923 also had their tales—and these were the opposite of the bridge story. They described a feeling of relief when Otter Creek was spared the violence that enveloped Rosewood, as the mayhem failed to spread. These whites, too, saw no Otter Creek deaths.[572]

However there was a nugget. During the first week of 1923, Otter Creek did witness the funeral of an African American infant, apparently a crib death from natural causes. This infant would not have been old enough to run across a bridge, but even so, could there have been a funeral procession? Might it have crossed the bridge? Would this have been nugget enough to feed imagination?

More significant is the heart of the tale, embodied in Pat Taylor's alleged retort. The phrase "Nits make lice" was far older than Rosewood, and was well known in Pat Taylor's world. Its use in the tale refracts the heart of the Rosewood riddle.

"Nits make lice" is an expression of an extreme fantasy, whose essence is the Final Solution.

Nits, the eggs of lice, are used as a symbol to say that in some situations sympathy for the young is out of place.[573]

Nazi death camp

The phrase portrays a hated group of humans as insect-like pests, on whom sentiment is wasted. To exempt the young in such cases would be like coddling mosquito larvae. It's meant to sound harsh.

Perhaps the first warrior associated with such words was Oliver Cromwell, leading England's Puritan revolution in the 1600s. Stories have told of Cromwell burning a church in Ireland where Catholics had taken refuge, killing them all, including children. Cromwell was said to answer his shocked compatriots by retorting: "Nits make lice."

It is documented that Cromwell did speak of his lack of mercy at some Irish massacre sites, most famously Drogheda.[574] But not even tireless researchers, including stern critics of Cromwell, seem to have found any record of him using the specific toxic phrase.[575] As with Rosewood and Pat Taylor (though on a vastly larger scale), the phrase seemed to be used more in speaking

Drogheda

about Cromwell, to convey a sense of monstrosity, than in speaking *by* Cromwell (though there were recollections that his soldiers used the phrase). Far from Cromwell's battles, stories from frontier Tennessee that were handed down through the culture of the Cherokees said that Indian fighter John Sevier also took up the cold words. Again there is little traceable support.

The phrase is a receptacle, using myth to capture a theme.

Whatever the vocabulary of Sevier, the Indian wars did nurture the impulse behind the words. General Phil Sheridan may or may not have said in 1869, "The only good Indians I ever saw were dead,"[576] but his actions spoke for him. His subordinate general, William T. Sherman, wrote: "We must act with vindictive earnestness against the Sioux, even to their extermination, men, women and children."[577] Sherman was better known for his Civil War march through Georgia, which he foreshadowed in a letter to his wife in 1862, advocating "extermination" of southern whites, "not of soldiers alone, that is the least part of the trouble, but the people." [578]

The more compact way of expressing extermination—"Nits make lice"—was reinforced in American memory during the same period. On November 29, 1864. Colonel John Chivington, a controversial "fighting parson" in Colorado Territory, led some 675 temporary U.S. volunteer troops and others in what became known as the Sand Creek Massacre, as they attacked a settlement of Cheyenne and Arapaho. The majority of those killed were women and children. Estimates of the number have varied widely, most going over 100 or higher, while frequent and extreme mutilations were verified—not least by anatomical souvenirs brought home and flaunted in Denver. Within a year Chivington was called before official tribunals and news reports led to nationwide revulsion. Again, proof of any real use of the phrase was tenuous. A single witness testified that three months prior to Sand Creek, Chivington had spoken the phrase in a public speech. The monstrosity of the massacre then made it an emblem, a way of characterizing almost unutter-able evil.[579] The mysterious "fever" that had seized John Chivington received a makeshift diagnostic label. Civilization lacked any systematic way to classify what Chivington had done.

Sand Creek and massacre survivor
*photos: Denver Post; U.S. National
Park Service, Sand Creek Massacre
National Historic Site; painting of
massacre: Robert Lindneaux.*

Still later, as the Jim Crow segregation system[580] was paralleled by uprising panics and "race wars" that extended beyond the left-behind South, a farther-behind outcrop called Cedar Key nursed its atrocity boasts. The phrase lived on—whether linked to an actual bridge at Otter Creek or a bridge in the mind.

The boy-on-the-bridge story enabled narrators to have it all. They could nobly abhor the killing of children and yet suggest a yearning toward the unspeakable extreme (by the fact that the tale was apparently an invention, and hence invented for a reason). In 1923 the population of Cedar Key was more than one third African American; by 1982 the island town would be all-white. That journey of racial exclusion was not accomplished just by the Rosewood cleansing—which was confined to a community nine miles away—but certainly Rosewood played a part.[581]

Seven years before Pat Taylor's Rosewood mysteries, Allied diplomats exchanging notes in World War I had protested the extermination of Armenians in Turkey. However, international law offered no special category to capture the enormity. In the 1930s came Stalin's mass deportations and forced famines, the Rape of Nanking by the army of Japan, detailed plans for ethnic cleansing in the Balkans. What did one call things like this? Not until the climactic surge, followed by the Nuremberg Tribunal looking back into that Holocaust, would a word, newly coined by author and jurist Rafael Lemkin, come into currency.

The impulse embodied in "Nits make lice" then became a formal classification:

Genocide.[582]

The Rosewood atrocity was limited to two square miles of cleansing and a scattering of homicides, never reaching full rampage level, let alone the world-scale solemnity of massacre. It was nowhere near the universe of genocide. Yet beneath its material surface lay an invisible world of thought and desire. Thoughts about large possibilities clearly grew tempting for an elated moment, groping their way forward until they met cultural resistance, or ran into personal inhibitions or logistical stumbling blocks. The self-appointed army of 1923 was testing the possibilities, as countless others have done throughout history. How far could the grandiose dream go in the real world, at a time and place that found defenses weak?

These were large worlds to lie nestled in a little phrase.

But what, then, of Pat and Punk, the two horsemen of the swamp apocalypse? Were they really just two local loafers, harmless and blameless? There was the motorcade of vigilantes that went out from Cedar Key just after dawn on Friday—to then supposedly remain in the field through the next night. In that crowd, where were these two? What *did* they do? Participation in the killing of Lexie Gordon seems to be ruled out. Cedar Key was not "aroused" until after that occurred—and it's a long nine miles inland to Rosewood from Cedar Key. True, there could conceivably have been involvement in finishing off Sylvester Carrier on Friday morning. But for various reasons this, too, seems unlikely. And Mingo Williams was killed in Bronson, thirty miles from Cedar Key, with no Cedar Key residents in evidence.

However, one possible victim is more likely.

Somebody self-importantly interrogated and then murdered James Carrier. It didn't happen by itself. Somebody killed a helpless man whose handicaps made him as vulnerable as a child. As the struggling 56-year-old waved his one good arm, somebody pulled the trigger. On the one hand, the Pat Taylor stories are without a specified victim. And on the other hand, a specified victim lacks a known killer.

There would be no day in court for Cedar Key town marshal Pat Taylor.[583] The questions hang in the air.

Around the year 1830, and at a place far from Florida, Thomas D. "Daddy" Rice began pleasing rowdy audiences at the Bowery Theatre in New York, as he debuted a new kind of act.[584] Rice was a white hoofer and singer, and had taken up a growing idea. With makeup, he could blacken his face and assume a new identity on-stage.

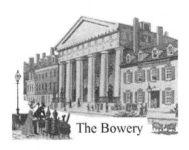

The Bowery

Thomas Rice
as Jim Crow

Such were the beginnings of minstrelsy, at first disdained by highbrows as "Ethiopian songs," but soon becoming "the favorite amusement of millions of Americans."[585] After Daddy Rice helped show the way, there would be stage extravaganzas with crowds of whites clowning and capering in disguise. The trademark white holes for eyes and mouth formed "the minstrel with the honey mouth."[586] Rice himself performed a frantic-looking shuffle-dance, while reciting a little nonsense song called "Jump Jim Crow."

Stories had him explaining that his Jim Crow character was modeled after a real person, not just an arbitrary fantasy ("based on a true story" is not a new hook). Supposedly a tour of Kentucky Derby country had taken Rice to Louisville, where he met an African American stable hand.[587] Besides other tribulations, this lowly figure exhibited a physical impairment. The alleged stable hand had a disability, forcing him into jaunty, jerky motions, as if flapping his limbs, half paralyzed. Hence, said Daddy Rice (at least in the tales), Louisville folks referred to this dark, flapping fellow as Jim Crow. But he was still happy, and showed Daddy a crippled little dance.

W'eel about and turn about,
And do jis' so.
Ev'ry time I w'eel about
I jump Jim Crow.

The rest is history. The raves and applause for the Jim Crow character mock the simplicity of terms like "ridicule" and "sympathy."[588] Was the character being loved or reviled? Or was he being elevated into a realm ill-suited to rational discussion, the realm of emotional distancing, of saying (in no conscious way), "How wonderful that we, here in the audience, are us, and not the afflicted Other."[589]

Whatever the source of appeal, it seemed potent. Rice crossed the Atlantic and jumped Jim Crow for British aristocracy, receiving more rave reviews. Britain was said to experience "Jim Crow mania."[590] The flapping, disinhibited Jim Crow had become one of "the two most popular characters in the world," puzzled the *Boston Post* in the 1830s (the other contender was Queen Victoria).[591] In America the dream-like name seemed to be everywhere—but more so in the North, the epicenter of the Jim Crow craze. And it was in the North that another modern marvel was coming onto the scene: the railroad. Near the peak of Daddy Rice's fame, this new form of transportation was changing the nation, and would further enshrine Jim Crow.

In 1841, nearly a generation before the Civil War, Massachusetts prohibited African Americans from riding with whites in its new railway coaches.[592] The massive experiment that was legally mandated racial segregation did not begin in the South (which in 1841 still had slavery as its prime segregation tool).

Railway passenger coach 1848

(A History of the American People, by Woodrow Wilson, 1901)

African American train passengers in Massachusetts were relegated to special cars, soon called "Jim Crow cars," since everyone knew the Daddy Rice character.

The use of such segregated coaches was not banned in Massachusetts until after the Civil War, in 1866.[593] By that time the white South had lost slavery and was more disposed to take up the old northern experiment of segregation by race. At first the new southern segregation was brief, occurring only in 1865-1866, before Reconstruction intervened and occupation troops from the North enforced more open practices. But in 1877 the troops went home. "Jim Crow cars" then appeared on southern passenger trains, in Tennessee after 1881, in Florida after 1887, in much of the rest of the South by 1891. From 1890 to 1896 the practice underwent a test in the U.S. Supreme Court and was ruled constitutional.[594] All of this, then, prepared the way for the biggest push, the social engineering that would go far beyond the fits and starts that had been segregation in the North before the Civil War. The thousand mile exception, Dixieland, would be fenced off by procedural walls, rigidly in place by about 1900, then to last more than a half century, into the fires of the Civil Rights Era in the 1960s.

The name born in the 1830s was long-lived, going onto the train cars in 1841, then around 1900 getting a new lease on life as a larger symbol. The term "Jim Crow segregation" was applied to the South's emerging racial system as a pejorative, borrowed from the old train cars, as critics sought to capture the system's grotesqueness. It had been a northern phrase, but the southern experiment retained an essence, an intimation of wings restrained, beating against the cage.

Thomas Rice as Jim Crow

The frantic face of Jim Crow was offset in minstrelsy by another side, a sentimental one, rising at times to weepy magnificence. The star number here was the song about Rosewood's own Suwannee River, the Stephen Foster hit of 1851.

Perhaps the power would have been lessened had Foster not gone about it backwards—first dreaming up

The movie, 1941

443

the somnolent melody, then looking for a two-syllable river name to fit into it.

Peering into the mysteries of the South, he experimented. "Way down upon de Pee Dee Ribber"? (South Carolina lost out). "Way down upon de Yazoo Ribber"?[595] (The river in Mississippi buzzed like a kazoo). He wanted the sound eternal.

Then a map revealed a tiny thread, reaching only from the mysteries of Okefenokee Swamp on the Georgia line down into other swamps on the Gulf of Mexico, near a spot called Cedar Key. Nearly the entire length was within the then-mysterious wilderness state called Florida.

But the remoteness hardly mattered (or the squeezing to get the required two syllables). For he had found the magic <u>sound</u>. Foster may never have learned that this was really a gibberish word—or an inadvertent poem--fashioned by many lips for nearly three centuries from at least three different languages, bubbling up in a no-man's land at the ends of the earth. What mattered was the swan-like, swooning symbolism that all those minds had somehow managed to impart to the word, forming an incantation that could evoke dreams.

Rich in graceful, riverine associations—swan, swim, swirl, swoop— the sound was gently hypnotic—soothing, smoothing, swooning—a name remarkably encapsulating the sunny, sleepy, sweltering region that Foster, the northern boy from Pittsburgh, loved to dream about. The word was a cryptogram, encoding the languid southern drawl.

Long after Stephen Foster's death, as Jim Crow racial segregation arrived, white America seemed to love the song all the more, as attested by the spin-off hits of Irving Berlin and George Gershwin. *"Swanee! Swanee! How I love ya, how I love ya, my dear ol' Swanee!"*

It was the lost river of the soul.

Blackface minstrelsy left its coded traces. The racial slur "coon" may trace back to "Zip Coon," a snappy minstrel number with the lyrics "possum up a gum tree, coony up a stump"—the buried source of the song known today as "Turkey in the Straw."[596] The big minstrel hit of 1858 was only slightly topsy-turvy, pairing the words "Dixie" and "frosty"—before rising in 1861 to lead the charge as the battle song of the Confederacy.[597] Like the love of blackface exhibited by Confederate soldiers singing "Dixie," the later labeling of the Jim Crow segregation system might seem illogical. Future schoolchildren might wonder. *Jim Crow? What could that be? Is it a person, a thing, some kind of strange bird?*

The music is playing again—far, far away. Now the old hunter is soft-shoeing it lazily past the smoky limelights on the stage: dark denizen of dying woods, tottering, flapping the one good arm.

Florida Death Certificate 777-1923 is on the theater marquee, explaining that he was "shot by unknown parties." Every census since 1870 confirmed that James Carrier was a Florida native, but his death certificate switches his place of birth to South Carolina. His occupation, listed by the certificate as "laborer," is true enough, though obscuring his commercial hunting and the building of a farm. And as if to further enfeeble him, his age is also revised, from 56, the verifiable reality, to 67.

The creativity in the death certificate is such that it becomes an inadvertent poem, even giving him an imaginary name—or a nickname, apparently never used by him in real life: "Jim."

In official typescript he merges with the image that passed his house each day in the passenger train, the Jim Crow car.

"*FULL NAME:* Jim Carrier ."

Chapter 37: Arson for the Camera?

Age: **46**
Born: **Taylor County, Florida**
Name: **Cary A. Hardee**
Office: **Governor of Florida**
Term: **1921-1925**
Background: **Self-taught schoolteacher,**
    self-taught lawyer, self-taught banker[598]

The silver hair and gold-headed cane were familiar sights among the shady sidewalks of downtown Tallahassee, the capital of Florida, population about 5,000 during his term.[599]

Governor Cary Augustus Hardee could be seen strolling under mossy oaks, his walking cane tapping smartly on mossy bricks. The southern gentleman image had been carefully cultivated. Hardee's pioneer parents were not poor, but he was not from wealth on the scale of Kay Bryce the hobby train conductor. One of ten children on a farm in deep timber country, he had started his climb as a teacher in a one-room school, then "read for the law" by age 21, then taught himself banking in a tiny town on the Suwannee, just upstream from Levy County.[600]

Hardee was Transition Florida, the rural mediator standing at the cross-roads as old frontier violence met the traffic jams of the Florida Boom, one of history's signature financial bubbles. By the end of Hardee's term in 1925, paradise-seekers were flooding into Florida from as far away as Britain, drawn by the promise of riches in South Florida real estate, especially the new paradise called Miami. Pop culture received the term "swamp lot."[601]

The governor's home area of timber camps was far north of Miami, barely a fly-speck in a 900-mile-long state, but its violence became a major publicity headache. First there was Rosewood in January 1923, then in April 1923 the same wilderness zone (covered by three isolated counties: Levy, Taylor and Dixie), produced the Florida slave-camp scandal known for its symbolic victim, a white youth named Martin Tabert.[602] That was in Dixie County, facing Levy County across the Suwannee.

446

In 1921 as Hardee took the oath of office, the powder keg called Dixie County was not quite ready to blow—because in 1921 Dixie County was still being created. The new county was carved out of wild terrain without a single incorporated town, though it was dotted with isolated camps specializing in holding timber workers by force, through peonage, convict lease, vagrancy arrests or other means. A black resident from those times, veteran turpentine chipper Cliff Clark, recalled a Dixie County

Martin Tabert
died Feb. 1922, Dixie County
(Florida Memory
State Archives of Florida)

crossroads being labeled "Burnt Nigger."[603] Much of the county's land surface was owned by a single corporation, Putnam Lumber Company, whose reputation was not as admired as that of Cummer Lumber across the river.[604] Accusations against Putnam personnel in 1923 included

The end of Dixie County's cypress giants
(Florida Memory-State Archives of Florida)

murder, torture and miscellaneous horror, shocking not only Florida but the nation, as the scandal reached out to involve officials in Tallahassee.[605] Nestled on the symbolic "Swanny" and named Dixie, the new county stronghold of substitute slavery was rolled out on Confederate Memorial Day—its official founding on April 25 hitting the newspapers on April 26, Dixie's day.[606]

By 1928, federal agents would send Dixie County's newly minted sheriff to prison.[607] In the spring of 1923 an editorial cartoon in a national publication showed an embarrassed Governor Hardee trying to explain the mess.[608] Distant news consumers perhaps recalled that this was also the same general area which, only months prior, in January 1923, had produced a frightening racial image—that of 25 black rebels barricaded in a hut. Governor Hardee's role in the Rosewood affair was similarly murky:

MAY CALL TROOPS

TALLAHASSEE, Jan. 5— Governor Hardee when informed by the Associated Press here early today of the racial outbreak at Rosewood immediately made efforts to get in touch with authorities at Rosewood to determine whether troops would be necessary to restore order. The calling out of units of the Florida National Guard depends on how serious the civil authorities view the situation, the governor said.[609]

GOVERNOR HARDEE IS ADVISED THAT RACIAL TROUBLES ARE AT HAND

Tallahassee, Jan. 5—(By Associated Press)—A telegram was received at the governor's mansion late today from the sheriff of Levy County declaring that the racial disturbance around Rosewood had quieted down to the extent that it was believed that local authorities had things under control...[610]

Such scraps in newspapers form the only surviving record that state government took any interest in the Rosewood events. Official files left no trace of government action or inquiry. In dealings with the State Archives of Florida this particular governor was so discreet—as the Florida Boom poured both chaos and money into his state—that no work records of any kind were left by the Hardee administration. As his legacy to public truth, Hardee bequeathed only a cryptic scrapbook holding a few press clips.[611] Nor did any personal papers or correspondence seem to survive among members of his family.[612] As he had created himself, so Cary Hardee seemed to erase himself. The tracks were washed remarkably clean.

If the governor had called out the Florida National Guard on Friday or Saturday, January 5 or 6, the remainder of Rosewood might have been saved as a standing community. Little Minnie Mitchell might still have had a home. As late as Saturday the final arson spree had still not come—the last act in the play. But (at least as it was made to appear) the telegram from Sheriff Walker sealed the bargain, shrugging that all was well, letting the governor off the hook. As the newspaper story explained, a local sheriff's request was required for the Florida National Guard to be deployed. Whatever the hidden side of Walker's telegram, the end was now assured.

There were rumors claiming that Governor Hardee was involved in the train rescue, not physically but with input into the plan. This was possible, in the way that anything is possible in a rumor. No real evidence appeared.

Rosewood's homes, churches, lodge property, barns, livestock, chickens and crops were effectively surrendered to the mob, along with whatever else the vigilante force could burn, break or steal. Stories would tell of whites dragging a mule to a well in the vacated community, killing it and then toppling it in, seeking to poison the water, to make the place permanently uninhabitable as if sowing the ruins of Carthage with salt. No resident witnesses were left to say whose mule this might have been, or whose well. The circumstances suggest the well and blind mule at Mary Ann Hall's house, where her late husband Bacchus had run a wooden cane-grinding press. Little Sammy Hall had once been the sleepy rider on that mule, mounted to keep it shuffling in endless circles, drawing the wooden arm of the grinding cog, as Sammy batted flies in the heat. Sleepier, sleepier, sleepier—then BANG. And he was on the ground, waking rudely from the dream.

The impulse to gawk at disaster sites is not new, though in pre-electronic days it required some transportation.[613] In the 1920s as today, storms, wildfires and miscellaneous cataclysms could call out straggling crowds to poke through the ruins, as they pondered the whims of fate. A 1936 tornado in Mississippi, reportedly killing 200, was said to bring out more than 100,000 sightseers on a single day. By coincidence that was in my birthplace, years before I was born, though an infant named Elvis Aron Presley was on hand, rocked in a storm cellar. A news photo from the aftermath of that Great Tupelo Tornado showed flatbed trucks hired to bring in the crowds of curiosity-seekers, as what might be called a "fever of excitement" drove the death toll still higher—for one of the sightseeing trucks overturned.[614]

This dimension of human experience (perhaps not so far removed from the 25 savages barricaded in a hut) would also come to Rosewood. On Sunday, January 7, the last gasp of the tragedy would find local white residents taking afternoon drives.

As Sunday morning began, the desolation was still partial. The community's main church and lodge hall were gone, along with the King and Gordon homes, but farther out in the woods and farther along the railroad there were apparently no ashes. A number of farm houses were still intact. Not even Sarah Carrier's bullet-riddled home, the "death house," was in the small initial arson area. It seems to have met Sunday as a ghostly war trophy, still standing. But all of the homes were now gloomily deserted, and word of this had spread. From a radius of at least twelve miles, white sightseers could now come to take a look.

In this about-face—from alarm to idle curiosity in practically the blink of an eye—the preceding uprising panic looks doubly confusing. For a moment—on Friday and Saturday, and perhaps mostly on Friday—whites as far west as Cedar Key, as far north as the community of Janney and as far east as Rocky Hammock had feared that fierce black rebels in Rosewood might break out and storm through the countryside. But by Sunday the fears seemed to be gone. Like the riot itself, the panic manifestations had the look of theater, inviting impassioned hisses at the villain or trembling at the monster—but then you can button up and go home. In this "race war," one side was suffering a real attack, but the other side seemed to receive the thrill of *feeling* attacked, without the inconvenience.

Sunday morning, January 7, brought an accustomed rhythm, as people went to church. Perhaps some of the rioters camping around Sumner failed to attend (amid moonshine hangovers), but much of white society worshipped as usual. Then Sunday afternoon beckoned. The strictest hard-shell Methodists might forbid recreation on the day of rest, but others were more at liberty. A six-day work week put gold in Sunday afternoon. There was the old routine from horse-and-buggy days, the Sunday afternoon drive and picnic, now harnessed to the automobile.

By the Sunday afternoon of January 7, vacant Rosewood was a kind of tourist trap, any danger now so forgotten that women and children piled out of arriving cars. One child, peering from a car window, would in later years be sure that he saw a white looter engaged in strange parody, donning an item seemingly filched from a residence, a woman's Sunday hat.[615] The defenseless buildings invited creativity.

And this was about to receive some help. The last act in the play is now opening. An unusual form of sightseer is about to join the gawking.

"Seventy years of a man's life.
That's a lot to get in a newsreel."
—*newsreel reporter in Citizen Kane*

 Into the mass of parked cars and Sunday drivers, a more business-like presence intrudes. This contingent, consisting of one or more individuals, is not local. There is perhaps a crew of several men, or perhaps a solo artist. Such crews had a trademark way of dressing—the cap worn backwards to accommodate the lens, the short, blousy golf knickers ready for unpredictable action. This crew (or lone wolf) would be accustomed to thrills and spills, perhaps at the far corners of the earth.

Though drawn to the spot by the early warning system of the Associated Press wire, the newly arrived presence has no connection to the AP. They (or he) represent a rival sector of the 1920s Information Age. Unlike newspaper or wire-service reporters, who can spin imaginative descriptions of a place like Rosewood without ever going there, these new arrivals cannot afford to stay desk-bound. Today, Sunday, they are a bit late for the main action, but they are forced by their job to push into the crime scene.

Rosewood now meets the infancy of video. The visiting presence is from William Randolph Hearst's movie news service, known as International News Reel.[616]

There were said to be some 18,000 movie theaters in America in the mid-1920s. All were silent, using printed captions to narrate soundless film, but most offered an extra. As a warm-up before the main feature, they showed newsreels, flickering cinema collages of news events of the day.[617] The appeal of newsreels was that they captured real life, not rouged and powdered actors on a cardboard set.

But somebody had to go and get those slices of real life, dragging a big mouse-eared movie camera to bizarre or dangerous spots, where visuals could be maximized.

Nationwide, six newsreel studios were producing footage in 1923, giving rise to a Roaring Twenties icon, the daredevil newsreel cameraman, with one eye winked shut as he hunches at the lens—or perhaps even dangling from a high bridge to get the killer shot, which on occasion might kill the cameraman, too.[618] Such a daredevil—or daredevils—did documentably come bouncing into Levy County in search of the uprising announced in the news. Presumably in a cloud of dust, but with almost no paper trail, this expedition would remain as anonymous as a spirit of the night.

But it was there—because it left pictures. And those pictures were accompanied by a few penciled notes. From one more angle now, the secret in the swamps yields up a few more clues.[619]

"When Charles Foster Kane died, he said just one word: 'Rosebud' "
—newsreel reporter in Citizen Kane

The power behind International News Reel, William Randolph Hearst, was the castle-dwelling tycoon caricatured in the 1941 motion picture *Citizen Kane*. Indeed, that movie ("the greatest film of all time") was a parody that mimicked newsreel footage, and was put together by an actual newsreel crew. There was much to parody. By the end of World War I, Hearst's corner-cutting journalism had caused his International News Service to be banned from European nations. He was also entangled in the era's landmark information battle, as his corporation was sued by the Associated Press for stealing its news dispatches. But Hearst's newsreel crews, like his controversies, continued to push forward.

"Good. Rosebud. Dead or alive.
It'll probably turn out to be quite a simple thing."
—*newsreel reporter in Citizen Kane*

Miles of newsreel footage were feeding into theaters by 1923. Much of it was soon thrown away. If Hearst's crew in Rosewood took moving pictures, no one in a later age has been able to find any surviving trace of that film. Under the pressures of Rosewood's modern publicity, video experts have searched 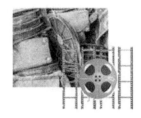 the archives of the world—and the screen always comes up dark: no Rosewood movie clips from 1923. Perhaps this stubborn riddle will be cracked by some future Web wizard or vault gnome. Could there be a lost treasure trove of Rosewood video?

But in the meantime, the International News Reel presence at Rosewood did leave something else. Someone did point a camera and snap—obtaining not movie footage but still photographs. This is certain because some of those stills have survived. In 1923 the process of distributing news photos was painfully slow,[620] but by mid-January, International News Reel was offering its Rosewood shots for publication. At least five can still be seen today.

"THE SCENE OF FLORIDA'S NEW YEAR RACE RIOT—THE MORNING AFTER"

On January 20, 1923, the caption above appeared in *The Literary Digest,* one of the news giants of its day. As a weekly magazine, the *Digest* could wait for the Rosewood stills to creep through the pipeline. It chose to publish two of them—though neither gave much insight into the events. In one, a few sightseers are visible, mostly male, standing where a house has been burned. The ashes form a jumble, nearly featureless. What looks like an iron bedstead lies half-collapsed in a dying puff of smoke. The only other discernible household object seems to be a tin washtub.

So was this Sarah Carrier's house? Was this bed (in the center of the photo), the one where she died? Or did the flames bring an upstairs bed crashing down to ground level? And if this was a washtub (foreground), was it where Sarah drudged out her fiftieth year?

Text in *The Literary Digest* suggests that this may indeed have been her house—though also endorsed is the uprising illusion from the wire-service stories (the text subtracts five uprisers from the 25, as if to seek a happy medium):

> "The ruins of the house near Rosewood, Florida, in which twenty armed negroes fought off a band of white men searching for a negro who, it is said, had attacked a white woman."

Since the ashes and ruins are a grainy blur in the photo, its focal point devolves onto a burly white man looking down at the debris. Possibly middle aged, he wears a short coat, lace-up leggings around the cuffs of his trousers (customary to keep out subtropical ticks), and a Stetson-type hat. He is seen full-length, facing away from the camera. No Rosewood witness has been able to identify this mysterious Everyman. Other gawkers are distant, barely lumps.

The vagueness brings up a possibility. Could this photo be a fake, only claiming to depict Rosewood? Silent newsreel crews were notorious for faking their shots—and the corporate culture of the Hearst  organization was not known for pious restraint.[621] In any of the newsreel studios, if a crew were to be, say, rushing to shoot a burning barn, but then learned en route that the fire was already over, there was the temptation to recruit a couple of local swains as movie stars, then smear ash on their faces as they play fireman for the camera.[622] In 1915, *The Literary Digest* itself published an exposé of newsreel fakery in a World War I battle. The footage showed soldiers bravely crossing a river under fire, artillery shells exploding in the water around them. But the explosions were made by air bladders;

the battle was a sham. No newsreel caption said so, but a future age might appreciate those air bladders—as marking the birth of cinema special effects.[623]

At first glance the Rosewood photos suggest authenticity. Pine foliage, hanging Spanish moss and what appears to be a Florida cabbage palm all fix the climate zone. And if a crew took the trouble to get to the general vicinity, it wouldn't have been much harder to get to the site itself. Why go all the way out there and stop a mile short?

But there is more than one way to fake an image. The second extant photo shows a small shanty, resembling descriptions of Aaron and Mahulda Carrier's house. A lean-to porch supports a wood-shingle roof. The plank walls, unpainted, are darkened by age. And these details are visible because in the photo the shanty stands intact, with no visible damage—yet.

With remarkable efficiency, the picture tells a complete story: before and after. Both the intact house and the doom awaiting it are captured in the same picture, because the shutter is snapped as a thick plume of smoke is billowing from the roof. This arson case is just starting. The timing of the photo approaches the miraculous.

Somehow, this genius of a photographer has arrived at precisely the right moment, despite untold transportation difficulties in the crossing of tank towns, mud holes and swamps. A world is caught in a flash: *Here is a Negro shanty. And it is burning.*

Also approaching the miraculous in the photo is another point, the absence of human figures. Who set this fire? The photo gives no hint. There is only the shanty—forlorn, unattended—as if the fire were occurring by spontaneous combustion on some unpopulated planet.

Unspoken is the question of how many jolly arsonists might be crowding right around the tripod, just outside the frame. After all, *somebody* set this blaze. And such a somebody would want to stand and watch.

The implication is dismal. Could the last act in the Rosewood drama have been more than just figuratively theatrical? Was it possible that the last standing homes in Rosewood were burned on demand, because the camera needed a shot?

In this question, a much later offering, the 1997 movie *Rosewood*, with its "based on a true story" cachet, takes on historical perspective. From 1920s Hearst to 1990s Holly-wood—and into a new millennium—a small place in the swamps has produced a river of questionable images.

If one's attention is focused on believing the myths—that is, on trying to prove that the demonic uprisers existed in physical reality (or their opposite, the angelic paradise), then one never gets to wonder about an intriguing possibility, those invisible arsonists giggling around the camera.

After all, if this should happen to be a staged burning, posed for the camera, who would tell? Print reporters weren't out there investigating. And the Levy County Sheriff's Department seemed a bit star-struck. Two of the five known Hearst photos show local whites posing cooperatively for the camera. A third shows only one poser, Sheriff Bob Walker. All seem to enter into the spirit of the photo-op.

In the only contemporary written record of the Rosewood events—the dubious series of wire-service stories—the newsreelers are never mentioned. This is not surprising, since Hearst and AP were bitter enemies, but the result is a parable about the arsonists just outside the frame. There is no confession of what is left out.

And with this said, the story can now return to the wire-service dispatches:

**LAST NEGRO HOMES
RAZED IN ROSEWOOD**

Florida Mob Deliberately Fires
One House After Another
In Black Section

NEGROES HIDE IN WOODS

456

Authorities Now Believe Race Riots
Which Caused Seven Deaths
Have Come to an End

ROSEWOOD, Fla. Jan. 7 (Associated Press)—Twelve houses, all that remained of the negro section of Rosewood following the clash between whites and blacks on Thursday night, in which seven were killed, were fired by a crowd of white men here this afternoon and burned to the ground. The houses were fired, one at a time, while a crowd of between 100 and 150 men looked on without making an effort to extinguish the flames, according to Levy County authorities. All of the negroes were hiding in the woods, where they went late Thursday night after the clash.[624]

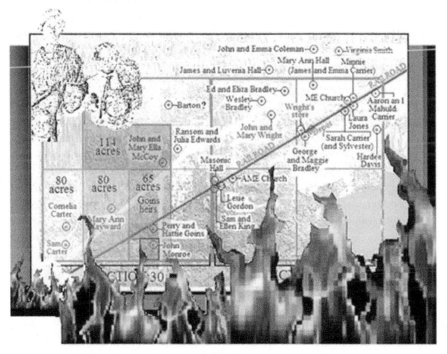

Seen or unseen, the houses fall one by one.

The Hall house with the mule-driven cane press; the Coleman home with the old man's prized hunting dog—and a parlor piano; Aaron Carrier's shanty with its souvenir cap and leggings from World War I; James and Emma Carrier's house with its seven-sisters rosebush on the front fence; Wesley Bradley's house with the wrap-around porch; widow Laura Jones's little house with her sugar cane patch on eleven acres; the cabin of old hermit Hardee Davis where wide-eyed children watched him stew unlikely game; Virginia Smith's smoky hovel where children slept on shelves against the wall; the two-story Hayward house on its eighty acres, holding another of the parlor pianos; the rambling Perry Goins home, a vestige of vanished family wealth in the defunct M. Goins & Bros. turpentine operation; John McCoy's home with the scent of jasmine shrubs around the front porch, where a well bucket drops down into the limerock; Cornelia Carter's big house on another 80 acres; and the vacant home of her son Sam.

Also reportedly burned were Rosewood's two remaining black churches, both of them nearly unattended. The small Baptist chapel with its bell on a stand in the yard would no longer brood in the deserted Goins turpentine quarters. The Pleasant Field M.E. Church, sturdier, founded in 1886, equipped with a small organ but moribund after a long-ago congregational quarrel, would no longer stand near the home of James and Emma Carrier.

Mama's youngest, little J.C., would go up into the plum tree on the side of the house when the night passenger train was coming, not to wave at Bryce the conductor in the dark, but because of the big halogen headlamp, lighting up the end of the house toward Wylly where the plum tree stood. J.C. leaning out and making the shapes of flapping birds and barking dogs with his hands, projecting the shadows on the wall for the rest of them sitting down there enjoying the show. Ruben on the orange crate playing preacher; Goldee in the big shoes playing house; going out with Papa in the ox cart to cut palm buds; the little bucket under the back porch pump for watering the sweet potatoes; going out with Mama to get the switch brooms to sweep the yard; hating to make the beds upstairs; wrestling at Aunt Sarah's house with Arnett. Barely a chance to look back.

The number of buildings confirmably destroyed fails to tally exactly with the newspaper reports, but the difference is small. Now the curtain is descending. The news finds fewer temptations to go off into new visions.

As to who, specifically, burned the buildings, no names have ever surfaced, nor the alleged methods of arson. On many points the legends about Rosewood grew loud and boastful, but not here.

Witnesses would agree, however, that one category of building was spared—buildings owned by whites. Left standing were Rosewood's open-fronted railroad depot, the many-roomed home of George and Maggie Bradley (rented from white owners and left from the days when it had been Ford's Hotel), a Baptist church for whites across from Wright's store (attended by the Wrights and others).

The Wright house, left intact in 1923
Florida Master Site File
Florida Division of Historical Resources

Also spared were the big store itself, J. M. Wright & Co. General Merchandise, along with Wright's gingerbread steamboat of a two-story house. Similarly exempt were the two homes of white brothers, Will and Rob Ingram, near the King and Gordon ruins.

Even with regard to black-occupied households, the destruction was not systematic. Not every single home was burned. Besides the saving of George Bradley's house on the grounds of white ownership, there was a more striking exception. At the fringe of the area of destruction, at least one African American-owned home, though considered to be in the Rosewood community, apparently remained unmolested.

Elderly, cantankerous Ransom Edwards had once been the superintendent of Rosewood's segregated public school. His wife Julia had been one of the loyal domestic servants beloved by whites. On the farm they owned, the Edwardses lived in a two-story house flanked by scarred orange trees that had made it through periodic freezes. Ransom Edwards seemed irritably aloof from a community embroiled in feuds, as he and his wife cared for two orphaned grandchildren.

Perhaps this house, isolated from the rest, proved difficult for the arsonists to reach. Or perhaps it was spared on purpose. Could some unknown white have intervened? There were stories suggesting this.

The Edwards home remained so little damaged that months later the elderly couple returned, unhampered, and tried to set up housekeeping again, unlike their exiled neighbors. The de-population had this omission. The Edwards's grandson Willie Evans came with them, and his testimony is persuasive. Evans said he was surprised to find that among the scenes of devastation there was also another house, farther out in the woods, that was left undamaged. That was the home of elderly James and Luvenia Hall, though they had fled and did not return. For the Edwards household, return was grim. Without a surrounding community the elderly couple found it impossible to hang on, their grandson said. They soon moved out for good, going far down the Gulf coast to the town of Bradenton.

After that the picture was complete. An experiment in racial cleansing had reached its end.

Chapter 38: The Mass Grave

So now the Rosewood question—the kind of question that follows any secretive atrocity. After all the cover-ups, boasts, myths, tricks and illusions have been peeled away, what was the real number of people killed? In the Rosewood violence of January 1-7, 1923, how many people died?

To seek an answer, any reasonable inquirer might turn to the most prestigious news medium in the nation, long established as the newspaper of record on American events.

"In reality," explains the *New York Times* online (not in the 1920s but in an Internet post today) "between 70 and 250 people were killed in Rosewood."

Try reading that again.

"In reality, between 70 and 250 people were killed in Rosewood."

The statement requires a moment of contemplation—like finding a kangaroo in your living room or a purple cow on the roof. If you have read the pages here, the post in the *Times* online might seem to come from a different universe. Who are all those extra fatalities?

 The assertion was written in 1997, but has remained on the *Times* site ever since, unretracted and apparently still endorsed, as if to remind how small bits of insanity can appear in quite functional humans. Of course, the word "insanity" overreaches. But could the *Times* statement point to a kind of non-clinical craziness, something that surrounds us all the time, even in enlightened settings? Could it be a footprint of deluded mass belief, the spoor of an elusive "fever"?

At this writing, anyone who turns to the Web for an authoritative look at the Rosewood death toll, then logically tries the keywords "New York Times" + "Rosewood" + "killed," will be waylaid by the startling kangaroo quoted above, which the *Times* online presents gravely as being verified fact. As in the media fantasies of 1923, with their 25 phantom uprisers, the *Times* fantasy of today might seem too demented to exist—if it weren't right there in print.

The "between 70 and 250" statement, with its interestingly wide point spread, gained entry to the *Times* online in a review of the 1997 film *Rosewood,* as a summary that now remains posted for the benefit of film buffs and video store patrons.[625] But this kangaroo statement is not presented as anything so easily explained as a recap of the movie's imagineering. Quite the contrary. In somber wording, it purports to give the "known facts" about the real history that lies behind the movie's plot, hence its lead phrase, "in reality...."

As carping as my comments might sound, I am doubly well placed to speak up here—because the fantasy in the *Times* goes farther, and cites itself to me. Mercifully, it avoids using my name, but calls me "the reporter....who stumbled across the old story and began investigating." It says that this intrepid soul (everyone agrees this was me) located the survivors and interviewed them, whereupon (the *Times* alleges) those interviews produced the astronomical body count, with its daffy endpoints, 70 and 250.

To say this never happened seems inadequate—like sputtering that *The War of the Worlds* never happened, and that Martians didn't really land in New Jersey. Nothing I have ever said about the Rosewood death toll even faintly resembles the fantasized count in the *Times* online. Apparently the writer, one Michael Rogers, a contract reviewer, was in an interesting state of excitement—a "fever," if you will. And in fairness, this would seem to have been encouraged by the movie *Rosewood* and its horrific images of (largely imagined) racial killing. But whatever the psychological influences, the writer's mind seemed to kick into a violent daydream, which kept rolling beyond the false attribution to me. The piece also goes on to say that those "known facts"—that is, fatalities supposedly numbering "between 70 and 250"—were similarly stated in a legislative report on Rosewood in Florida. Oops again. In the real world, that report was very specific on the death toll. It flatly states, just as I do: "eight deaths." [626]

Quite a difference. The eight fatalities described in the pages here— Sam Carter, Sarah Carrier, D. P. "Poly" Wilkerson, Henry Andrews, Lexie Gordon, Sylvester Carrier, Mingo Williams and James Carrier— seem to be the only deaths that the incident directly produced (with some reservations about that missing son of Sam Carter).[627] The evidence always leads back to this compact number: eight.[628]

How then, could the *New York Times,* still the meticulously fact-checking information leader in the most powerful nation on earth, discover dozens if not hundreds of imaginary dead? There are two possibilities. One, I might be a sneaking liar and racist concealer who won't admit the truth. But if not, the second possibility is that something less definable is at work, something able to push excited mirages prominently and without much challenge into public discourse, especially on the subject of race.

The footprints here point toward a realm argued endlessly in psychology, the realm of the subconscious mind. By 1997, the Web and the media were thronged with retrospectives not only on Rosewood but on a larger case from the same era, the Tulsa race riot of 1921. On Tulsa, too, 1990s excitement was creating highly questionable new characterizations of the death toll. Some of those Tulsa number allegations were similar to 70 and 250.[629] The 1990s Tulsa discussion placed those numbers before the public in a feverish haze—which arguably could have prepared the way for the next leap, the subconscious one at the *New York Times* online.

Only a profoundly unconscious process would seem able to reach into a mental soup bowl (where perhaps the Tulsa allegations vaguely floated) and transfer these free-floating bits from Tulsa onto Rosewood—using utterly no supporting evidence from the material world. Simultaneously, this dreamy borrowing process seemed to pin the result onto real sources that could be checked, but which were excitedly *not* checked—that is, pinning them onto me and onto a legislative report in Florida.

Evidently, various *Times* editors who were supposed to watch for just such whoppers found these particular whoppers somehow unquestionable—in a process that supposedly can't happen at the *New York Times*. Yet it did happen. Thus the importance. How did this kangaroo in the living room get there?

Does this process reveal a psychosocial zone of excited misperception on certain matters of intense emotion? And in this case, at the *Times* specifically, is the panic button the issue of race?

If the 1997 movie helped inspire the imagination process at the *Times,* some possible mechanics might be noted, for the movie also grossly exaggerated the Rosewood death toll, and used a grandiose point-spread—though the movie used *different* fantasy numbers. The *Times* portrayal was not simply quoting an inaccuracy from the movie, but was reaching into the brain of its writer, and there apparently dredging up a dream.

The movie's death toll numbers came in a prominently displayed screen note, informing audiences that "the survivors...place the number" of people killed at Rosewood "anywhere between 40 and 150."[630] Here was another daffy combination, and a double illusion—for the information in the movie's count was not only inaccurate but misattributed. The real survivors, the people who had lived at Rosewood, never said either 40 or 150, or anything remotely similar.[631]

The movie, too, seemed to be reaching into the private world of its creators, on a "fevered" expectation that viewers might be similarly excited, to the point of never questioning.

The *New York Times*'s illusional range, still more surreal at "70 to 250," suggests lapsed critical monitoring on the scale of "buck fever," the deer hunter's elated breakdown in the moment of truth, plunging the perceiver into a spell of absence, almost a blackout.

And yet a long list of editors and gatekeepers must have signed off on the *Times* extremity. This was not a private sleepwalking episode. A mass of people seemed to buy into the absurdity, as if in delusional consensus. The questions sound more and more like earlier Rosewood media mysteries in 1923—though adapted to newer political sensibilities.

Repeatedly the Rosewood evidence shows how large numbers of people—and impressive centers of authority—can see, almost before their eyes, a dance of fantasy shapes, even in the presence of disproof.

"GRAVES OF THE COLORED VICTIMS"

The caption above was published to describe another of the International News Reel photographs (see preceding chapter). This one appeared in a popular national weekly newspaper called *Grit,* running on January 21, 1923. The photo is stiffly posed, its human figures arranged like a table setting. Some media, including *Literary Digest,* took a pass on this chintzy-looking shot when using the photo package offered by International News Reel, and they published other shots instead. But, warts and all, "GRAVES OF THE COLORED VICTIMS" helps to solve the big riddle.

How many people did the Rosewood atrocity really kill?

Of the human figures in the photo, none is in a grave. They are all quite alive. The photographer has herded together some obliging Sunday sightseers, all whites, and has lined them up like wide-eyed window dummies, staring into the camera. Though difficult to distinguish in the *Grit* printing, there seem to be 26 individual spectators, eight of them women, and eight apparently children or adolescents, ranging down to one infant being carried. The setting shows why the photographer needed this crowd as a prop. The "graves" promised by the caption aren't very spectacular. There are three oblong mounds of earth, marked by narrow stakes placed at either end, as with headstones and footstones. Who might lie beneath this ground is impossible to tell.

As to the children among the onlookers, some residents of the area would recall being brought to gawk at Rosewood's ruins in childhood, on adventurous daytrips from Cedar Key, Sumner or Otter Creek. And some of these children seemed to compete afterward for playground bragging rights, as to who could describe the largest number of corpses supposedly seen. One *raconteur* in Cedar Key continued for decades to tell neighbors about the horrors he viewed in Rosewood as a child—bodies everywhere, laid out like cordwood, stacked all along the road. When I found this poet and offered public reckoning, he grew evasive, trying to distract me with other tales. Finally when I insisted, he told a vague story so lacking in detail that the mystery of "cracking" once more reared its boastful head, posing the unseemly question: Was he ever really there at all?

Most of the Rosewood stories depicting great stacks of black corpses were even less authoritative, coming from people (always white) making no claim at all to firsthand observation. Such white tellers wouldn't have dreamed of consulting the African American survivors whose friends and families were supposedly being described as bodies in the stack. Whites shrugged that those survivors had disappeared without a trace, and could never be found.

But the International News Reel photo casts some circumstantial light here. Newsreel crews were known for being fiercely competitive.[632] The cameraman at Rosewood was not likely to pass up a juicy shot of stacked corpses if one was anywhere around. The goal was not to flatter local secrecy but to bring home the prize. A daredevil who will dangle from a bridge with a camera, risking or even sacrificing life and limb, is likely to go for the big shot. Arriving in Rosewood, this crew or individual would presumably have pressed for the most crowd-pleasing visuals that the site could offer. And rapport with white locals was apparently impressive, judging by the obedient window dummies. There were plenty of new friends to act as guides, showing where any bodies might be stacked.

A variety of clues suggest that the crew did find the hottest shot that was available—and that it was the one with the posers—the "GRAVES OF THE COLORED VICTIMS." If a heap of bodies existed anywhere at the scene, it evidently was right there, underground, beneath the mounds in the photo. This grave site was not a secret. By Sunday it was almost a picnic spot.

The "GRAVES" photo uses a set-up like that of its companion, the ashes-of-the-death-house shot (again, see preceding chapter). In both, prestige is added by posing a white male as a focal point. In "GRAVES," the hero adds extra drama by holding an axe, which is poised hammer-like above an upright wooden stake. Apparently the photographer's idea was to send a visual message: A grave is being marked. But logistics seem muddled and the axe is held with its blade, not its hammer head, facing down onto the stake. The hero didn't seem to understand the instructions, and the cameraman snapped anyway.

There seem to be a total of eight such stakes. The two mounds on either side received two stakes apiece, at head and foot, but the center mound received a double portion, with two stakes each at head and foot. At a glance, however, the stake posed under the hero's axe happens to be mostly obscured by another stake. The photo could easily look as though it has only seven stakes. *Grit's* short blurb accompanying the photo seemed to try to make sense of this:

"GRAVES OF THE COLORED VICTIMS"

> **"Seven persons were killed during a race riot at Rosewood, Fla., and the village destroyed by fire, following an attack by Jesse Hunter, convict, on a white girl. Twenty colored persons, heavily armed, barricaded themselves in a house and for some time fought off the attacking white mob. Two white officers were killed and five colored persons lost their lives, but Hunter escaped."**

Only if you read to the end does the math break down, in the next-to-last line: "five colored persons lost their lives." Now we have eight stakes, seven apparent stakes, three mounds, five black dead and seven overall dead. So how many people are really buried here?

First, it should be noted that the caption neatly sums up the uprising delusion as it came to be polished and condensed by dutifully repeating catch-up media: "Twenty colored persons, heavily armed, barricaded themselves in a house." As in the delusional scenario, the two dead whites are "officers," and Jesse Hunter, the disappearing phantom, is reified as a star player.

But more to the mathematical point are the first four words, matching the number of apparent stakes (along with an overall headline in *Grit*: "Seven Persons Killed When Attack on Girl...").

Excluding Sam Carter, who was killed on Monday, there were indeed five African Americans killed in the Rosewood events. But Mingo Williams was killed and buried in Bronson. Even if it weren't for the evidence in his death certificate, it would be a safe guess that whites were not going to truck the corpse of an indigent African American across twenty miles of swampland during a riot, simply so he could be symbolically buried at Rosewood (where he had not lived and had no connection).

In 1996, in preparation for a documentary about Rosewood airing on the Discovery Channel (in which I provided some of the narration),[633] ABC News Productions made extensive efforts to locate supporting Rosewood visuals. Venturing into a New York photo archive, their search unearthed an obscure scrap of paper, bearing multiple hallmarks of authenticity. This scrap seemed to be the original penciled field notation sent in by the 1923 newsreel crew, conveying the sender's background explanation of the mass grave photo.

The note becomes a formidable smoking gun, for it confirms what many other clues suggest—that the number of people buried in the photographed grave site was—not seven, and not five—but three. The field note says this specifically. It is possible that when a more formal caption was written for publication of the picture, aiming to enhance sales, a hasty reading of the wire-service stories was used as the guide, and not the photographer's own scrawled description.

Various threads of evidence suggest that stories of a mass grave at Rosewood boil down to three fatalities: Sarah Carrier, Sylvester Carrier and Lexie Gordon. Their remains were probably already covered over by Saturday when James Carrier was killed, possibly nearby, to be buried separately. A garbled news item about the James Carrier killing had him standing over the graves of his "mother and brother."[634]

As mentioned earlier, in 1994 the State of Florida mounted an extensive publicity campaign to locate any possible descendant of Rosewood residents not previously on the record, offering claimants a chance to share in a large monetary appropriation. A number of new claimants appeared, most of them said by the verified survivors to be illegitimate. Bizarre stories told by the dubious claimants underscored the hoaxing, leading to rejection of their claims. But even in this process, no claimant, real or pretended, presented any allegation whatever that a previously unacknowledged friend or relative had been killed, outside the deaths already documented—the six African Americans and two whites.

The "Rosewood Massacre"—unlike the real-life Rosewood atrocity—inhabits a dimension of media myth and pseudo-history, overlaid with promotional gloss and marketing spin. The more one examines the real evidence, the more overwhelming the conclusion becomes—that is, if one chooses to examine. The legends are based on a lack of information—and more profoundly, on an avoidance of information.

Each week in the early 1920s, Dr. James Turner of Bronson, Florida, left his comfortable home and climbed into an undignified vehicle. Coaxing a spark from a grimy gasoline engine, the physician would adjust the throttle, steady his gaze and roll down the tracks of the Seaboard Air Line Railway, piloting a railroad cart, or "motorcar."[635]

Dr. Turner used a railroad cart because he wore several professional hats. He was not only a private physician in Bronson but a company doctor for two different corporations, working for the railroad itself and for Cummer Lumber in Sumner. Practicing medicine since 1904, Turner was issued a motorcar by one of his employers, facilitating his far-flung rounds. Twenty miles from his home, little Minnie Mitchell in Rosewood also knew the rhythm. Twice a week the doctor's cart would breeze past her grandparents' home, a steady marker of routine—like the weekly ice delivery truck driving over from Sumner, or Mama's twice-weekly sweepings of the yard, or the nightly passenger train—or that lonely background hum, the Sumner whistle.

In company towns like Sumner there was always a company doctor. Besides repairing sliced fingers or crushed ribs, he would skeptically test stories told by workers claiming that they were too sick to work. An employee enjoying cheap company housing (almost free, though not quite) had to pull his weight, and malingering was investigated.

Being a company doctor could be a dreary slog in a godforsaken practice. Sumner had seen an unlikely series.[636] One fill-in, Dr. Gray, was completely deaf and spoke in sign language. Once a promising medical student, according to descendants, Gray had caught an ear infection in the dangerous era before penicillin. A botched operation followed, and in a heartbeat his life was ruined, sending him to the last refuge for an unmarketable young doctor, at the ends of the earth in Sumner.

The longest-standing doctor at Sumner, pensive Augustus Cannon, had apparently been sent as a public health official in the fight against malaria. He then was caught up in the movement that would collapse the local economy, the shift by Cummer Lumber to a new company town and a new tract of cypress forest three counties away. Though complete evacuation of Sumner would not come until 1926, by 1923 the move was underway, with the new mill at Lacoochee up and running. Cannon was said to divide his time between the two sites. Dr. Turner of Bronson came as back-up.

On Friday, January 5, 1923, as news of the Carrier shootout was spreading through Levy County, Turner's 14-year-old son, James Turner, Jr., stood watching the doctor prepare for his usual Friday trip. Young Jim Turner had heard the rumors pouring out of the Rosewood battle scene twenty miles down the line. He knew that his father's motorcar route to Sumner would pass through the heart of the excitement.

An irrepressible, extroverted youth (by various informant accounts), Jim Turner longed to see the thrilling race riot for himself. Nor did his father seem to see much risk in the idea, or worry about any danger from supposed black rebels. The fourteen-year-old climbed aboard.

After twenty miles of chilly wind in their faces, the sputtering cart slowed. Jim Turner would remember being let off among whites loitering in the emptiness of Rosewood, guns cradled in their arms. He told how he became one more face among the deserted houses.

The prowling whites received him hospitably, and gave him the lowdown. A number of the faces were familiar. Doc Turner's boy was not just any sightseer but the son of the man who had treated half the county, and delivered babies for the rest. Moreover, Jim Turner, an affable Tom Sawyer of the hammocklands, was already moving toward a later career in local politics. He peppered the men with questions—and they offered a special peek.

In somebody's car, he would recall, he was taken southwest for a short distance, roughly in parallel to the railroad as it ran toward the Gulf, though in a path out of sight of the tracks, offering no distinctive landmarks to orient his sense of location in the woods. Then the car stopped. He would remember a thicket of pines. They got out. Inside the thicket, he said, the men took him to a pit, freshly dug, and not yet covered over.

The contents held him spellbound.

When I interviewed James Turner, Jr., in 1982, on two separate occasions, I was impressed by his credentials. The gregarious Tom Sawyer had grown up to become a Levy County sheriff—twice, in both 1944-1945 and 1956-1964. Additionally, in 1961 he was president of the Florida Sheriff's Association. When I met him at age 74 he was a calm, deliberative witness. Unlike some elderly whites who boasted defiantly, or seemed to crave attention, Turner spoke tersely but cooperatively, without adornment—specific answers to specific questions, no more—as if carefully testifying in court. Displaying no self-dramatization or swagger, he looked to me at that time like a man dutifully responding to the call of posterity, reporting unpleasant truths.

He said that when he was taken to the pine thicket as a 14-year-old, it went like this:

The opening in the ground seems to have been dug with shovels, though no shovels can be seen. The pit itself is what holds his attention, because of what is inside. The bodies are piled in haphazardly. He tries to count them, but gives up. The mass is too confusing. But some are women. He can see that. One or two wear coats, as if having fled into the cold. And some of the bodies are smaller. He sees the motionless forms of children. One is in a diaper. He will distinctly remember that.

All are black. They seem to have been shot. No other details will remain in his mind.

But his tour guides from the car provide him with some narration. They say a count has been made, and that the total number of corpses in the pit is eighteen.

In later years as duties in the sheriff's office caused Jim Turner to travel Levy County, he said, he would sometimes stop at a wooded spot where two lonely back roads converged, state highways 24 and 345. This spot, drastically changed and overgrown since 1923, was roughly where old Highway 13, the limerock ribbon, had curved past the edge of Rosewood. He said he would stop there because he kept thinking about it, that horrific pit. The thoughts drove him, he said, to push back into the undergrowth, searching for any sign of it. But the woods were thick. Each time he found nothing.[637]

The story told by James Turner, Jr., succinctly captures the informational maze presented by the Lynching Era, with its questions about horror, observation and memory. Here was direct testimony from an impressive source, displaying both credentials and a credible manner. And yet, when compared to massive agreement among other lines of evidence—evidence that this witness had never had reason to encounter in his long and illustrious career—the story he told could not be true.

Bear in mind that I know I'm putting my own credibility on the line by saying this. The evidence I refer to is so overwhelming that the step has to be taken. If I'm to remain true to the original quest that sent me into the Rosewood riddles in the first place—a quest simply to discover what's there—then I have to risk incurring audience suspicion if the evidence should insist on a difficult turn. The risk can't be helped. There is no way around this evidentiary mountain.

My initial Rosewood exposé in 1982 presented witness stories, including Jim Turner's, in the apologetic light of the incomplete evidence that was available at that time.[638] I had to tag the vignettes with coy warnings, presenting them as personal points of view, neither disprovable nor confirmable. That was a long time ago. Since then, Jim Turner's story, with its audience-grabbing shock effect, has been borrowed many times, as new media players referred to him as if they had interviewed him directly—though in fact they never met him (he passed away in 1986), and were selectively lifting from me, in my early portrayal from the two interviews of 1982. Typically, the borrowers were too hurried—or too excited—to seek background or examine the mass of evidence that had built up against the story. Sometimes they acknowledged me as the source but still screened out my subsequent findings. By the 1990s I had spent dismally long periods tracing every recorded name or remembered person with even a remote possibility of having disappeared from Rosewood. In the process, I was becoming much more familiar with the pitfalls of witness memory.

I was not delighted, over the years, to find more and more evidence against the sensational audience appeal that had seemed to beckon in the original Rosewood discovery. As evidence trickled in, the "Rosewood massacre" kept getting smaller—bad news for the journalist trying to approach new outlets with the story. The incident remained a landmark—an urgent and shocking violation of human rights—but its easiest shock value had fallen to the gremlins I insisted on awakening: the gremlins formed by the evidence.

Over the decades, Sheriff Jim Turner did not have to deal with the most important form of this evidence, for it was held in privacy by frightened African American survivors of Rosewood, most of whom settled far from Levy County. Like his shrugging white constituents, the sheriff thought these survivors had vanished, never to be found again.[639] From his vantage point there was no way to know what those survivors might be saying—though they, of course, knew their deceased relatives well, deeply grieving for them. And once located, these survivors spoke of no massive carnage.

It is astronomically unlikely that, in many independent conversations, all these forthright and soul-searching survivors would be conspiratorially hiding eighteen unrecorded killings of African Americans. Or, to put a finer point on the arithmetic, that they would be hiding twelve extra deaths, since that is the number that would be required to get a total of eighteen if added to the six African American dead on the roster.

It took time and effort to locate those survivors, and no little expense—and much more of the same to collate the extensive body of their combined testimonies. But once this was done, the conclusion was stark. No Rosewood residents had disappeared. This could be rechecked and reconfirmed from numerous new directions, again and again.

Five people were known to be dead, plus Mingo Williams killed in Bronson. Neither in Rosewood nor in surrounding black communities did other deaths appear. When I started investigating in 1982 it had seemed that the body count might climb much higher—though the garrulous old tales alleging this, and suggesting great killing fields, were told only by whites, and with notable vagueness.

Still, that did not mean those tales could be simply dismissed, on the grounds of smug assumption. It seemed indispensable that each be investigated, down to the last narrowing sinkhole of the most remote possibility—if the seriousness of the atrocity was to be done justice by a systematic accounting. Once this process was completed, of course, I could have concealed or glossed the results to ease the marketing of the story, continuing to shore up an illusion of a sensational death toll. But I was fascinated by trying to pinpoint what really happened in a time and place of secrets. I couldn't do that if I became one more concealer.

In the early years, when I first entered this maze, I had thought I was taking the measure of an atrocity—and perhaps planting a flag for justice. I failed to realize that the search would of necessity lead farther, to unmask a less familiar player, the ghost behind the atrocity—whether called "fever" or mass illusion or myth.

I was taking the measure of something larger than I knew.

Over the years since 1982, as the missing puzzle pieces of Rosewood have slowly surfaced, the 1923 residents who seemed at first to have disappeared turned out merely to have moved out of sight of one another. Minnie Langley, for example, heard that a granddaughter of Lexie Gordon, Frances Goins, was killed along with Lexie: "Frances wasn't no more than twelve or thirteen. They shot her on the front porch."

It developed that Minnie had heard this second or third hand. She was accurately portraying the rumor, but not the event. Frances Goins, very much alive and going about her life in ensuing years, was unseen by some groups of survivors in the confused and painful aftermath of the violence. The same process shaped another story about little Eloise King. Living north of Miami in the 1980s, Eloise King Davis was mildly amused to learn that she had been massacred in 1923. The old Mark Twain quote did not seem to her to be greatly exaggerated.

At any rate, few such mistakes about relatives and neighbors were made by the community's ex-residents. Their general understanding, repeated in many conversations by many voices, was that almost everyone escaped, and that few Rosewood residents were actually killed.

With very few exceptions (and those few are ruled out by other evidence), the populace of Rosewood has by now been traced, and can be shown to have survived the violence. Public information in 1923 badly distorted some aspects of the Rosewood events, but not all of them.

In the way of military propaganda, the ethnic propaganda in the newspaper stories used real-life details—some of them accurate—to flesh out a falsified theme (in this case the familiar theme of blame: *The blacks are running wild again!*). One of the details used by the 1923 media that turned out to be accurate was the body count.

Though modern tracing of the Rosewood population inevitably left some uncertainties, these, too, tend to make the point. Even if these uncertainties were to be accepted as remote (and very dubious) possibilities, and were added to the death toll, this still would not push the total past eleven or twelve—again undermining Sheriff Turner's puzzling mass grave story. Even by the wildest allowance of possibilities, you don't get eighteen dead. Relaxing the standards of evidence doesn't make up the difference.

At least two evacuees, Emma Carrier and a 17-year-old girl named Marie Monroe, were said to have died in the months following January 1923, possibly because of traumatic effects from the events. Another resident, James Hall (of uncertain age but apparently as old as eighty), was unnoticed by other survivors in later years and may conceivably have died in the violence, or as a result of its stress. There were also some names on the 1920 census that proved untraceable, though there were no direct allegations that these people were involved in the 1923 events at all. To add all of these candidates to the death toll still would not create the massacre depicted by enthusiasm, and there are compelling reasons to exclude most or all of them.

Also, Jim Turner's firmly stated memory of eighteen alleged corpses included deceased children, but no children can be discovered who were killed or disappeared. This is not said lightly. The idea that child deaths could have been covered up comes from the imagination of whites, musing that faceless pickaninnies might drop out of sight without anyone noticing. It scarcely needs saying that in real African American households, in the woods or anywhere else, children did not disappear without deep emotional wounds left behind, and agonized mourning.

Informants who knew James Turner, Jr., when he was a 14-year-old described the extroverted youth as being quick to tell an illustrative tale—and sometimes an imaginative tale. It seems far too condescending to say that perhaps somewhere in the course of a long life, adolescent tall tales became adult belief.

But there were other factors. Though dignified and serious when inter-viewed at age 74, this informant spoke with noticeably slurred speech. His replies were halting, sometimes telegraphic. Dignified reserve was only one part of the picture. The ex-sheriff had suffered prolonged, debilitating illness, with observable neurological effects. The recollection of the grave site was noticeably impoverished in detail. Acquaintances cited various severe stresses on this informant's memory. Some advised bluntly that his testimony be approached with caution.

The oral mystery of frontier America—the "cracking" dismissed by city slickers as tall tales—leads into a labyrinth beyond easy explanation, where assumptions become snares. Levy County's wilderness narrative tradition has been largely unfettered by literacy, even when individual narrators are firmly literate. A journey across this threshold necessarily reminds of what we don't know about the human mind, and of the places where forensic evidence grows feeble.

In 1998, as the 1997 Rosewood film was attracting new curiosity, a dramatization of Sheriff Jim Turner's alleged reminiscences was published as a short booklet, apparently by one of his younger relatives. The extraordinary booklet quoted Turner as having claimed that the Rosewood violence occurred in December 1924, that it started when a "Henry Carter" raped a "Nan Taylor," and that Rosewood was burned down by men on a stolen train.[640]

The ex-sheriff was quoted in the booklet as telling his relative-interviewer that "I'm eighty years old," though Sheriff Turner's October 17, 1986, death certificate shows his age at death as 78. It was unclear whether the booklet was using misquotes by an eager author and mediator or reflected original errors of memory in the source—that is, whether the strange statements came from Turner himself or from some other voice in his circle, usurping his persona in print. But without doubt there was extreme distortion. Riddles seemed to multiply around this outwardly impressive-looking witness.

There were no eighteen bodies in a pit. It could be that on an excited Friday a 14-year-old visitor was taken to the Rosewood cemetery—southwest of the depot crowd area, much as he remembered—to arrive at basically the same spot where an International News Reel crew would be taken later, by similarly helpful sightseers. On Friday as a railroad work cart passed through, the bodies might still have been exposed: the alleged ferocious rebels Sarah Carrier, Sylvester Carrier and Lexie Gordon (two shocking corpses of women, no children).

It is also at least possible, in view of peripheral clues, that the witness in this case may have only heard of the grave from others, with later life stresses embedding the traces as phantom memory. But whatever the degree of original observation, the overall picture—the view into the pit—works out much the same.

But was there a different kind of pit? Though African American survivors of Rosewood tended to be methodical and reliable on the issue of greatest pain—the issue of how many of their relatives or friends were killed—another discussion moved differently. There was the matter of keeping score, a distasteful twist of psychology particularly avoided by the keepers of American racial history, but nonetheless seen repeatedly after the "race wars" or lynching riots of the early twentieth century.

The pattern was preserved in print during the Chicago riot of 1919 on the front page of the *Chicago Defender*. The arrangement of information there was described by African American author Roi Ottley: "The front-page statistical reports of the dead and injured, clearly identified as 'white' and 'Negro,' appeared like box scores. It produced a feeling that the score must be kept even—that is, on an eye-for-an-eye basis."[641]

The idea of evening the homicidal score tended to produce post-event inflationary lore in riot after riot. Two separated cultures, black and white, sheltered opposite beliefs about how many of the other side were supposedly killed, though allegedly covered up officially.[642][643]

Some African American informants from Rosewood shrugged off such scorekeeping tendencies, but others were insistent. The real secret of the Rosewood conflict, the latter said, was not the number of blacks killed by whites, but the number of whites supposedly killed by blacks. Whites had the losing score, according to this view, but the losing whites were said to have hidden their fatalities in embarrassment, claiming victory by fraud.[644]

These stories, too, demanded investigation. Like other startling claims, they could not be dismissed simply on the grounds that they sounded contrived. Extensive searching was conducted in records and memories from white communities throughout the Rosewood area—and no suspicious deaths or disappearances of whites appeared. Even without this, other evidence has proved to be inescapable: the real white body count was two, Wilkerson and Andrews.

As in white-told massacre tales, the opposing black-told stories about dead whites described only a vague heap, a crowd, a faceless mass. In both racial groups the power of myth seemed to show an almost military competitiveness. *Our* side killed more of *them* than *they* killed of *us*. Our side won. It is not comforting to think of atrocity as gaining a second victory here, by sentencing some survivors to a mental prison of post-traumatic imagination, where they are always evening the score.

There was also mutual disproof. You could believe in a black massacre, or you could believe in a white massacre, but you couldn't believe in both at the same time, which created a double impasse. If you accepted the improbabilities in one side's massacre story, then the same rules should force acceptance of the other side's improbabilities—and this would mean twin massacres. Such was definitely not the point that either group of believers was making. Their point was that *only the other side* was massacred.

For decades the two story streams had little contact with one another, as racial segregation enforced the unlikelihood of either group having to deal with the inconvenient stories told by opposed believers. In a sense, two marginalized populations were collectively "cracking," compensating by means of grandiose boasts.

Among the oddities was a general similarity in alleged scores. White informant Jim Turner remembered eighteen dead blacks—but black informant Philomena Doctor remembered nineteen dead whites. The range—translatable as "not quite twenty"—emerged on both sides, and was repeated by African Americans in surrounding communities and in family networks. If this range didn't represent a real number of bodies, where had it come from?

The number of people inside Sarah Carrier's house at the moment of explosion was apparently between 15 and 17, with the uncertainty resting on two disabled men—James "Papa" Carrier and Willard "Big Baby" Carrier—who may or may not have been there. At most there were three adult males in the house, even if the two uncertainties are included. Certainly there were four women, three adolescents and seven smaller children.

These were: 1) Sarah Carrier, 2) Gertrude Carrier, 3) Bernadina Carrier, 4) Harry Carrier, 5) Philomena Goins, 6) Arnett Goins, 7)

George "Buster" Goins; 8) Emma Carrier, 9) Eddie Carrier, 10) Goldee Carrier, 11) Lonnie Carrier, 12) little James "J.C." Carrier, Jr., 13) Ruben Mitchell and 14) Minnie Mitchell.

And then there was Number 15—the only firmly agreed, fully functional adult male:

Sylvester Carrier.

When all is said and done, it has to be considered that a concrete descriptor—a range of "between fifteen and twenty"—might have been stripped from its original information context by stress, rumor or the news media, to then be moved, as a dream can move, onto a firmly believed mass of dead.

Chapter 39: Destinies

There is the question of contagion. When mass violence occurs, how likely is it to reach out and contribute to further mass violence?

Through the week of December 2-8, 1922, a racial rampage had run through Perry, Florida, two counties west of Rosewood, as the murder of white schoolteacher Ruby Hendry led to the burning of buildings owned or occupied by African Americans, then to a murder suspect being burned at the stake and the vigilante killing of at least two others.

A month later—almost exactly a month—the Rosewood violence would last for the same amount of time, spanning another neatly periodized week, this time January 1-7, continuing from its start as a home invasion alarm into a spree of murder and multiple arson.

Then, two weeks later and one county north, the echo process seemed to continue. In mid-January 1923 the town of Newberry, still recalling its Lynch Hammock rampage of 1916, revived its already established pattern of livestock theft retaliation. Around January 16, in an incident of which little is known, an African American identified as Abe Wilson was lynched near Newberry after being accused of stealing a cow.[645] The excuses for brutal bursts seemed to grow thinner with repetition: first the horrifically real murder in Perry, then a never-verified burglar in Sumner—and finally the cow.

This reminds that Newberry's 1916 case also seemed to fall into a series, occurring on the one-year anniversary of the 1915 Leo Frank lynching near Atlanta, and perhaps echoing forward in some way to Poly Wilkerson's doomed replay at Rosewood, fully six years later. There was the influence of World War I's ethnic rancors, spy-hunting vigilantism and African American migration, encouraging a wave of racial attacks in the eastern half of the United States, especially in 1919's "Red Summer" of race riots (or "race wars").[646] These, then, provided templates for the November 2, 1920, election day riot and racial cleansing at Ocoee, Florida, and the Tulsa, Oklahoma, riot of May 31-June 1, 1921. The extent of the Ocoee violence was never documented. The Tulsa case was confirmably very large. From all of this, mental images flickered toward Rosewood.

Not all prior incidents led to rampages. On July 4, 1922, when Alachua County deputy sheriff Frank Dunning was shot and disabled at an isolated home occupied by African Americans—in the same two-county area as Rosewood and Newberry—there were reports only of arrests, not lynchings. Arguably the arrests were excessive, but they seemed to be accompanied by no riot. Soon to come, however, were Perry, Rosewood and—again in sensitized Newberry—the Abe Wilson hanging in mid-January.

As lynching violence multiplied, local authorities in the two adjoining counties, Levy and Alachua, apparently feared a general breakdown. In late January, District Judge A. V. Long of Gainesville contacted Florida governor Cary Hardee, asking that a special prosecutor be sent to investigate both the Rosewood and the Newberry cases of that month.[647] Judge Long's message suggested that he was more irritated by the smaller Newberry case because it involved an upstart justice of the peace in a competing court, while the destruction of an entire community at Rosewood seemed to receive less emphasis from him. But the governor did respond. A state's attorney was recruited from downstate in central Florida to come and investigate. A general atmosphere of excited illusion was underscored when a grand jury was empaneled. A newspaper report portrayed Judge Long as telling the jurors to look closely at the Newberry lynching, in contrast to Rosewood, because, the judge reportedly instructed, the Newberry case was one of retaliation for cattle theft, and hence could not be condoned as being the defense of a white woman.[648]

The special prosecutor, George DeCottes, was known for his booming courtroom voice and bulldog tenacity, but his total investigation time in the two counties was reported to be three days.[649] The 25 witnesses said to be called before his grand jury were never named publicly. No Rosewood survivor would recall being sought, or knowing anyone who was.

The verdict was a customary one, seen also a half decade earlier at the Newberry mass lynching of 1916 and, during the Rosewood week, in the Sam Carter inquest of January 2: "Death by Hands Unknown." The DeCottes grand jury of February 1923 found that no perpetrators at either Rosewood or Newberry's Abe Wilson killing could be identified, and everyone went home. A local resident, Bertie Bryant, the daughter of a deputy sheriff, recalled the Levy County end of the proceedings: "They all went to Bronson in the courthouse. Nobody knew anything. They weren't gon' tell nothin'." In 1977 an elderly Alachua County resident, Frank Dudley, consented to be interviewed on the Newberry lynching of 1916, and confirmed a common story from that case, claiming that onlookers at the event were all forced to physically touch the hangman's ropes, in order to ritually acknowledge that they were complicit if they were present, and must never tell.[650] Whatever the mechanism, the secrecy was effective.

A white who remembered Rosewood said: "That's the way it was back then. You didn't know nothin', you didn't see nothin'. They [the Rosewood perpetrators] all had a bunch of kinfolks and you couldn't convict all of 'em. Somethin' could happen to you."[651]

Levy County Sheriff Bob Walker, who had tried to outwit mob power at Rosewood but was ultimately rendered powerless, seemed to suffer long-term effects. Afterward the once-legendary lawman showed signs of distraction, apparently making gross errors on two major criminal investigations. Running for re-election in 1924, Walker or a supporter placed a strange ad in a newspaper, phrased in the third person: "He may have made mistakes. So have you! If he made any mistakes they were those of the head and not of the heart."[652] When Walker lost the sheriff's race by a landslide in the July Democratic primary (the "white primary"), he resigned from office on the spot, and the rival who beat him had to be appointed to fill out his term until the general election.[653] Some of the influential whites who had stood with Walker in the Rosewood events, sheltering evacuees and attempting to outmaneuver the mob, would also meet somber outcomes. Whether haunted specifically by Rosewood or simply meeting the hazards of a dangerous world, their lives, too, entered deep vales.

Also in July 1924, the hearty train conductor Kay Bryce was on horseback at his Bryceville plantation. The horse reared suddenly, said to have been spooked by a shadow in a ditch. The rider was thrown against a tree. Severe lung injuries led to pneumonia.[654] At age fifty, and at a point two weeks after Sheriff Bob Walker resigned, the man who had everything was gone.

Walter Pillsbury, the charismatic Sumner mill superintendent who helped to save Aaron Carrier and numerous women and children, but who reportedly surrendered James Carrier to be murdered, would experience a sudden reverse in his promising career. After the Saturday hand-over and killing of the crippled hunter, Pillsbury evidently felt so tormented that his corporate superior and friend in Jacksonville, Arthur Cummer, felt compelled to write Pillsbury a reassuring letter. Cummer was one of the most powerful men in Florida, but took time on Tuesday, January 9, to stress to Pillsbury "the splendid manner in which you handled yourself and the company's interests under these very trying conditions." He seemed to agree that by that Tuesday the mob storm had passed, prefacing his remarks: "Now that the unfortunate affair of last week is over..."[655]

"I appreciated from the very start of the trouble that you would be faced with some very difficult problems, and that the responsibility of the situation, so far as the Company was concerned was entirely in your hands. And I knew, furthermore, that you would have to stand alone in the most important crisis of the whole affair. But, Walter, I have always had the greatest confidence in your good judgement and common sense, and frankly I felt sure you would work things out."

But not everyone was happy:

"The boys in the Office...tell me you are considerably disturbed over an anonymous letter which you received from Jacksonville. My judgement is that you should pay absolutely no attention to this first because a person who is not man enough to sign his name to a letter is a coward and a dog, second because you know in your own mind that you handled things in a fair and honest manner and that your conscience is clear and third because you have the unqualified approval of the Company in your entire actions."

The grievance in the anonymous letter was not specified. Possibly the letter writer was blaming Pillsbury for the death of a Cummer colleague, nightriding woods boss Henry Andrews. Whatever the subtext, it was apparently eating at Pillsbury—along with another matter.

"Of course the news papers in their mad desire to publish sensational stories did you an injustice in a great many instances—The same papers did the Company more or less of an injustice. But these things cannot be helped and I have found that the best thing to do is to ignore them. When a person gets before the public in any way he is sure to be misrepresented and he has practically no chance to state his side. This is one of the very unfortunate situations in our Country today, and one has only to read the papers to know how our very best men are black

guared [means "blackguarded," or reviled] and
abused.

"I do not blame you for being sore at some of
the reports which have been published—but
Walter the best thing to do is to pass them by as
unworthy of notice. You are clear in your own
mind that you have acted in a fair honest and
manly manner."

Arthur Cummer to Walter Pillsbury
January 9, 1923
(Collection of Jerry Peterson)

Arthur Cummer did not sound like a rough-hewn timber lord in this
letter, and indeed in the 1890s at the University of Michigan he was a
collegiate glee club singer and student of Literature, Science and the
Arts.[656] In Jacksonville he was a leading philanthropist.[657]

A closer match to the timber tycoon cliché might have been found
in Cummer's colleague and sometime partner, William O'Brien, head of
the controversial Putnam Lumber Company across the Suwannee from
Levy County. Also coming from the North Woods (though from
Wisconsin, not Michigan), Billy O'Brien was almost unknown in public
print, though he held 300,000 acres of Florida land, much of it in the
convulsive post-1921 county called Dixie.[658] O'Brien had worked his
way up, starting as a frostbitten timber cruiser with a natural genius for
estimating how much lumber a stand of trees might yield, despite hints
that his reading and writing abilities might be scant. A federal survey in
1912 placed Cummer Lumber as the eighth largest landowner in Florida,
slightly ahead of O'Brien's Putnam holdings.[659] Interlocking
directorships and joint ventures united a handful of such magnates,
including these two.[660] By 1923 Arthur Cummer, the sensitive tycoon,

was also vice-president of another empire, Florida's Barnett Banks, in competition with the Dupont fortune. He lived in a rarefied world.

Cummer's letter to Pillsbury, aiming for inspiration, revealed almost nothing about the material facts in the Rosewood events—one more instance of a taboo subject leaving only faint traces. Nor would any company records survive from Sumner.[661] The letter itself came to light only after a search of many years by a Pillsbury descendant, not surfacing until 2012. In the letter's bitterness about "these newspaper lies," and its effort to smooth troubled waters, it gave a foretaste of the cultural avoidance that would settle over Rosewood's remains.

It continued:

> **"It is my hope that this letter will set your mind at rest, and that you will agree <u>first</u> that so far as your own actions are concerned you are satisfied—the Company is more than pleased—and your friends are all proud of you—<u>second</u> that the best thing to do now is to drop the whole matter and not permit some low down mischief maker stir up any trouble."**

In 1926, Walter Pillsbury moved with the Sumner operation to the extensive new Cummer mill at Lacoochee in Pasco County. There he would rule a larger company town and live in a larger home, not a bungalow this time but a two-story haven with a clay tennis court. But the climb then ended. A cryptic feud arose with subordinate management at the new mill. Despite friendship with the Cummers, Pillsbury was allowed to resign.[662]

Moving his family back to Jacksonville, he went into business for himself, but was said to be swindled by associates. On a drive north of Jacksonville Pillsbury's automobile stalled in lonely country. With his customary energy, he climbed underneath to unclog a fuel line.[663] A curious child came to watch, providing a later witness. Reportedly the harried Pillsbury was stymied by the leak and climbed back into the driver's seat, composing himself by pulling out his pipe, and forgetting a soaking from the fuel line when he was under the car, as he struck a match. The freak fire reached hideous proportions. At age 51, the man who could do everything was gone.

484

Some of the survivors of Rosewood were brought to Kay Bryce's plantation at Bryceville, remaining there as long-term residents after Bryce himself had departed. But the majority of survivors were soon drawn hundreds of miles south, seeking jobs in the economic bubble called the Florida Boom, where the focus was southern Florida, in a time window around 1925-1926.[664] For a brief period, before the boom's collapse was sealed by the great hurricane of 1926, Florida real estate prices grew miraculously high, drawing speculators in a "fever" of excitement. Florida's 1920 population, about one million, would increase by 260,000 or more by 1925. "Contemporary accounts," said a *Harvard Business School* report, "describe a collective madness that consumed Florida investors."[665]

The first ripples of the boom had begun as 1923 arrived, and though southern Florida was the epicenter, there were hopes that distant northern Florida might boom as well, despite its unpredictable frosts. The Boston swindler Charles Ponzi, inventor of the Ponzi scheme, began selling godforsaken lots 65 miles west of Jacksonville, under the label "near Jacksonville."[666] In both Levy County and Suwannee County just up the magic river, a rash of oil well promotion manias broke out—quickly going dry.[667]

On the third floor of the Graham Building in Jacksonville, a Chicago investment firm set up a cadre of title lawyers to prepare for possible boom activity in an enormous swath of northern Florida, extending from Pensacola to Tampa, and thus seemingly including Levy County.[668] The county's leading lights had sensed opportunity as early in 1921, authorizing a $100,000 bond issue to improve the road out to Cedar Key.[669] This would eventually replace old Highway 13 with the present blacktop, Highway 24. Construction was ongoing in January 1923.[670] The new road, with its hope to pull stray boomers toward the Gulf beauty of Cedar Key, passed through a community that was not to realize the benefits: Rosewood.

Ultimately, only a few boomers would ever come to desperately shrinking Levy County, though the possibility remains that the boom could have influenced the 1923 mob cleansing, if for a moment the land looked promising. However, the few buyers of land along the new road (land that wound up never booming very much) tended to be individuals who, rather than aiding the 1923 rioters, had sided with Rosewood residents. One buyer of a few parcels was Justice L. L. Johns. Far from being a mob crony, Johns was the subject of angry stories among white woodsmen. They complained that he was a molly-coddler of the Negroes, because during the 1923 violence he had hidden a pursued

Rosewood suspect in his barn. Johns was said to have nearly gotten lynched himself.

The rioters of 1923 seemed to consist largely of small farmers and others not well placed for real estate speculation, though the boom could have moved them less directly. There was the old factor, the use of witch hunting by marginalized populations to protest their being left behind. As the boom very pointedly left behind the hammocklands, the overtly acknowledged panic came to be racial.[671]

For some of the Rosewood refugees, urban centers in Florida like Miami, Jacksonville and Gainesville would prove to be temporary stopovers, as they went on to join the greatest migration of their moment, that of black southerners going north, reportedly a half million migrants in the period from World War I into the 1920s. Members of the Bradley and Carrier families were drawn to Harlem.[672] Sam Hall's brother Wilson moved to Chicago's South Side.[673] In time, Lee Carrier would cross the continent and live in Seattle, though in a section little remembered by civic tradition, the city's bygone "Coon Hollow" ghetto. Today his descendants live 800 miles south of there in Oakland.

The two hardest-hit households in Rosewood were those of two sisters, Sarah and Emma Carrier. When Sarah Carrier and her son Sylvester were killed, Sarah's husband Haywood was said to be living in another town. On hearing the news he was said by multiple informants to lose his mind, apparently never recovering. The three grandchildren under Sarah Carrier's care entered a drifting existence in logging camps with their father George Goins, who was said to be employed later in the building of Gandy Bridge over Tampa Bay. A great-granddaughter of Sarah Carrier, Annette Goins Shakir, would be a college professor.

As to the second Carrier household, there was Emma Carrier, Minnie's "Mama," who was dealing with her gunshot wounds as she received news that her handicapped husband, James, had been murdered. Emma's life of discipline and industry had led at last to the loss of her husband, her home and nearly all of her material possessions. Within a year, according to granddaughter Minnie, Emma Carrier grew ill and passed away.

Minnie and her older brother Ruben lived with relatives in turpentine camps and elsewhere. Ruben had lost an eye. Minnie would mourn her beloved grandmother the rest of her life.

In advanced age, she was an elderly widow in a quiet ranch-style home at the wooded edge of the large Moncrief Park section of Jacksonville. There, well after the formal end of racial segregation, the population continued to be monolithically of only one race. For six decades, 1923 to 1983, Minnie Langley would receive no chance for public airing of her memories, which enveloped her home.

There was the cabbage palm in the front yard—like the shotgun-chewed sentinel of a Thursday night. There was the drainage canal trickling quietly in back, like the branch with the ghostly laughter. And there were the inside walls, painted soft pink, as if recalling the word.

In time, as Jacksonville grew, fewer chances arose to hear the owls behind her house at night, calling from a dark wall of trees just beyond the canal—as the dark wall of Gulf Hammock had once stood beyond her family pale. Through the Jacksonville trees came a faint industrial moan—not the Sumner work whistle this time but, in a residential area not heavily zoned, the moan of a neighboring flour mill.

In 1994 Minnie Lee Langley was asked about her plans for using the Rosewood claims money, of which she received a large share. She said she might buy a couch, so people could visit. Her lifestyle seemed not to change. As she passed age eighty, media activity surrounding the claims case began to test her patience. Hurried new questioners expressed enthusiastic but strange ideas about her lost hometown. The fighty little girl from the house with the swept yard sometimes snapped back at them sarcastically. They didn't seem to understand. She still missed Mama. And the commotion was making her think about that.

Her porch swing was left empty on December 16, 1995.

The symmetry in the timing could scarcely have been planned. Fannie Taylor's screams, whatever their other mysteries, could scarcely have come from any sort of conspiracy. They suggested no sinister cabal that might have been planning all along to burn down Rosewood.

And there were the irrational twists of Thursday night, looking like a drunken chain of blunders, not like calculated results from any sort of master plan. The two white nightriders, Wilkerson and Andrews, certainly were not planning to get themselves killed.

And yet the symmetry crept in: the way the timing sought symbolic periods on the calendar. The curtain went up around dawn on January 1—the first moments of the first day of the work week, and of the year. And then, in tidy periodicity, the play would continue for a week—almost precisely a week, until its day of rest, coming on Sunday afternoon, January 7. The seven days of Genesis were burlesqued, not creating but destroying.

Naturally, the thousands of people in the Rosewood events, including both participants and onlookers, were not all dreaming together as these symmetries were created. That would be a physiological impossibility. Each mind dreams alone. And yet the movements seemed somehow to align, to form symbol-rich patterns, too pat for mere coincidence—like a great flock of birds wheeling into momentary motifs—not exactly by accident, though not by plan.

The precipitating pressures on the agents were various, ranging from the nightmare life of alcoholic Bryant Hudson, the accused killer of Sam Carter, with his cursing and shouting—all the way up to the prayerful piety of the kingly figure at the top, the conflicted Walter Pillsbury.

All found themselves in a bubbling caldron of shadows and illusions. The show thrived on excited leaps of assumption and interpretation—leaps often small and personal—though converging at last in joint action—to create the shape, the week-long entity, which in retrospect would look so eerily measured out.

For some of the perpetrators, weeks more would be required—or years—to slowly wake from this dream and see what they had done. To see that the great crusade had been a sham, a sordid smashing of the helpless.

And, of course, some never woke.

The final shape was simple, not complex—perhaps not so hard a thing to cooperatively fashion, even if the fashioning was done without conscious plan. Starved of importance in the eyes of the world, the swampland had scripted its own grand opera, its stage play or minstrel extravaganza, its dance of masks.

Carter in his Cart.

The Carriers of Pride and Doom.

Fannie Taylor's Tale.

And Sylvester,

Man of the Woods.

The real events conveyed not only horror but something else—the prospect that in the great human storms that swirl constantly around the planet, there may be no clear boundaries between waking reason and the automatisms of dream.

This prospect whispered even in the word—that tightest, most explosively compressed of the patterns.

Lonely woodland beauty bleeding thorny pain, the would-be uprising that never rose, paradise rising in rose-colored glow—and all of it mundanely stenciled onto a weathered railroad depot sign. Eight letters. As if foreordained to encode.

Blooming from some origin too accidental for conspiracy, and yet too strangely ordered for blind chance—as if reality itself was somehow the dream, dreamed together, by us all.

The End

A Note on the Investigation

Looking out through her screen door, Minnie Lee Langley saw that a stranger had come. He said he was looking for people who had survived a long-ago atrocity, an event that had been kept out of official records. Then he rephrased it, saying: "I'm looking for people who lived at a place called Rosewood."

The frail widow kept her screen door latched as he talked, so that the stranger saw only a shadow behind the screen. But at the sound of the last word, "Rosewood," he heard a sharp intake of breath, and realized that she was stifling a sob.

That encounter came a year after the first clues had surfaced in the swamps. It had taken me a year to find her. It seems impossibly long ago now, merging with Rosewood itself in a lost world of the past.

We met in 1983—Reagan in the White House, the Cold War feeling hot, cell phones and laptops unknown, no Web, not even ATMs. She was 69. Just after the sob, a muffled rattling came from the latch on the door, and I was admitted into a world of memory.

For hours, then into the night, we sat in rapt conversation at her kitchen table, me fumbling with the questions, confused by the arcane details of her lost world—the swamp cabbage, chufa fields, great jungles called hammocks. The story came pouring out. I was so spellbound that I failed to notice as darkness crept in. I could barely see the reporter's notebook on the table as my pen kept scratching.[674] The darkness struck me only when I was startled by a sound coming through her open window from the wall of trees behind the house. I realized that it was the quavering of owls, as if the wilderness she once knew and was describing had returned in the intensity of our concentration, closing around us.

In countless interviews since then, with a labyrinthine list of informants, I would learn the pitfalls inherent in a cultural blind spot.[675] Here was the destruction of an entire community—an atrocity dwarfing the scale of an individual lynching—and yet official records had left it a blank, with no formalized profile at all. A scattering of race-baiting newspaper articles was little better, in many places so incoherent as to seem surreal.[676] [677]

So what really happened during a hidden week in January 1923? Was the erasure of an entire community to be a permanent blank?

Only one path led toward the answers. The Rosewood enigma could be investigated only by resort to the most notoriously flawed form of evidence, the fragile traces left in human memories. Here was a test case for a much-maligned form of information. On Rosewood's closed ground, a comprehensive picture could be compiled only from what living people held in their heads.

Historians have been known to complain about the headaches of dealing with living witnesses, saying that it's not their job to play psychiatrist. For the past three decades in the Rosewood maze I've learned what they mean. To gaze into these memories was to meet the turbulence of post-traumatic psychology, not to mention memory's more ordinary tricks. In a long-festering cultural wound, the tricks multiply.

Two early giants of lynching-era retrospective, Allen Grimshaw in 1959 and Elliott Rudwick in 1964, both explained that they had planned initially to use live informants to explore the old atrocities, but they changed their minds. Both said that interviews with witnesses grew perplexing.[678] Apparently they had met the psychological maze that builds a wall of illusion around communal trauma. Both retrenched and based their investigations mostly on paper sources, the traditional tools of historical investigation. These are much more easily managed than the shifting mental labyrinths of live informants, but they leave out whatever was not put down on paper. At Rosewood, what was not put down on paper was everything.

In 1970, historian William Tuttle again captured the way that bygone racial atrocities can be obscured by witness psychology: "Some spun spurious tales, others repeated rumors...and one Irish bailiff even claimed that he had killed a dozen blacks himself."[679]

This could be a catalog of the informant obstacles on Rosewood— yarns, rumors and boasts—though Tuttle could have added alibis, post-traumatic confabulations, childhood fantasies, senility, grandiosity, mild cognitive impairment and traps beyond diagnosis. When oral history meets violent crime, and communal avoidance meets mass atrocity, obtaining the raw testimony is only the first step.

It would turn out that sifting through the memories required a daunting process of corroboration, testing informant accounts against one another and against other evidence. The corroborating evidence could only be accumulated slowly, and often serendipitously, over a period of years, then decades.

In 1982-1983 as Rosewood was first tumbling from its cultural blind spot, there was little knowledge of a witness pitfall that is now notorious, the problem of "false memory syndrome" or "pseudo-memory."[680] Awareness of this dimension heightened as the Reagan years brought a series of collective panics or accusational trends. A "Satanic Panic" (envisioning non-existent child-sacrificing Satan worshipers) converged with "daycare hysteria" (envisioning similar hordes of sexual predators in commercial nurseries), along with a general controversy over "recovered memories."[681] It was shown that false memories can be weapons, if vulnerable witnesses, especially child witnesses, are pressured—or sometimes hypnotized—into "remembering" abuses that never occurred.

Child witnesses also bring up the age question. In 1993 the Florida Legislature appointed a committee of local academics to certify the Rosewood events for the claims case. Their report revealed that their reconstruction of the physical appearance of the community came from an informant remembering back to age three. By 1993, most of the reliable informants, being older, had passed on. The age-three reminiscence obligingly produced a nice dream: "She remembers the village as one of green forests." [682]

Experience with Rosewood suggests that age eight at the time of the events was about the limit for usable memories. The account in these pages has used a few seven-year-olds in passing, on minor points that were corroborated, but what is not seen is how many assertions from informants of that age had to be reluctantly passed over—because independent evidence dramatically revealed fantasies.

In a story like this, false memory is an adversary, but not an all-powerful one—because not all memories are false. Nobody but a lunatic (or perhaps a courtroom advocate or two) would try to say that memories can never be trusted. A mental map of the past does exist—fragile, treacherous in places, and certainly no videotape—but we *do* remember.

One antidote to illusions of memory in the Rosewood informant pool was in its sheer number of informants. Starkly differing viewpoints were found, allowing the contradictions and convergences to be compared. This was far different from using a lone *raconteur* to spin a convenient tale, or a selected few to tailor a melodrama. The comparison process was not perfect, and frustrating gaps in the event chain would remain. But the thing that had long stood in the shadows—the defiantly veiled atrocity—began to peer back from its lair. An overall silhouette emerged, in places rich in verifiable detail.

The second antidote was peripheral documentation. Though avoidant officialdom had left no description of the 1923 events in governmental files, there was an older body of documentation composed of the everyday paperwork that surrounds any rural community— marriage records, birth certificates, land records, census and tax rolls, World War I draft cards, the odd criminal indictment.. These predated January 1923 and did not directly illuminate the atrocity, but they provided ways to corroborate the witness memories, while presenting a vital picture of the community that was lost.

The Rosewood informants—more than a hundred of them including secondary and background sources—ranged from surviving atrocity victims to mob participants to bystanders, family members and peripheral authority figures.[683] Pensive, searching accounts given by some of the older informants sharply revealed imagined elements in stories offered by some others who in 1923 were young children.

And it made a difference that these voices came from living people, not lines of text in an oral history transcript. Live informants can be re-interviewed flexibly as new evidence reveals leads or contradictions. Surprise clues can be pursued on a tangent, then taken to other witnesses to clarify—as in a police investigation—though not so much as in the document-confined investigations better known to traditional history.

Inevitably, however, all of the procedures had to depend on an intangible, the attitude of the investigator. No matter how large the witness pool or how many corroborating documents, such an investigation can produce illusions if the examiner wants them. When I was drawn into the Rosewood puzzle I had plenty of misconceptions but no political point to prove. I was motivated by simple questions: Why? How did the Rosewood events occur? Why would people do this to one another?

When the answers began to appear, perhaps the hardest task was to find a way to communicate them, using only the evidence to paint a coherent picture, despite the maddening gaps that real evidence is going to have. In trying to meet that challenge I centered the story around the courageous figure of Minnie Lee Langley, who in 1923 was a nine-year-old tomboy named Minnie Lee Mitchell. Minnie was at a frighteningly central observation post, while proving to be one of those blessed informants who showed least effects from what might be called post-traumatic imagination. This, too, suggests the complexity of memory, for arguably at Rosewood she lost the most.

Appendix A

The Names

1) African Americans who lived in Rosewood either during the violence or prior to it.

Blocker, Annie ("Sis")—wife of John Blocker, separated; sister of Mary Jane Hayward; moved from Rosewood before 1923; living in Wylly, two miles northeast, at time of events.

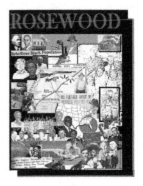

Blocker, Ernest—age 15, son of Annie Blocker; living with her in Wylly at time of events.

Blocker, Arthina—age 8, daughter of Annie Blocker, living with her in Wylly at time of events; later married name Arthina Bennett.

Bradley, Donarion ("Bishop")—age 19, son of Wesley and Virginia Bradley, living with his widower father in Rosewood; lumber stacker in Sumner.

Bradley, Ed—husband of Eliza Bradley, brother of Wesley and George Bradley, living with his wife in a two-person house-hold in Rosewood, retired logger, farmer.

Bradley, Eliza—age about 45, wife of Ed Bradley, living with her husband in two-person household in Rosewood, seamstress and laundress.

Bradley, George—age about 63, woodsman and hunting guide, living with wife Maggie and family in large building that was formerly Ford's Hotel, near the Rosewood railroad depot.

Bradley, Hoyt—son of Wesley and Virginia Bradley, living in Wylly two miles from Rosewood at time of occurrence.

Bradley, Lee Ruth ("Mossy")— age 7, daughter of Wesley and Virginia Bradley, living with her widower father in Rosewood, later married name Lee Ruth Davis; claimant in 1991-1992 original version of Rosewood legislative case.

Ages are for January 1923 unless otherwise stated. Sources: death certificates, census rolls, 1917 draft cards, Social Security Death Index, other documents; as well as oral confirmation of birth dates by witnesses. Some ages can be stated more precisely than others; the records often disagree; all ages should be taken as approximations.

Bradley, Maggie—wife of George Bradley, living with him in large building near the Rosewood railroad depot that was formerly Ford's Hotel.

Bradley, Raleigh—age about 24, son of George and Maggie Bradley, widower, living in his parents' home in Rosewood along with his small children; lumber stacker in Sumner.

Bradley, Virginia Carrier—wife of Wesley Bradley, sister of Haywood, James and Elias Carrier, died in childbirth ca. 1922.

Bradley, Wesley—age about 45, brother of Ed and George Bradley, widower of Virginia Carrier Bradley, logger, friend of Sylvester Carrier; full name of record: John Wesley Bradley.

Carrier/Carrol, Aaron—age 26*, son of James and Emma Carrier/Carrol, nephew of Haywood and Sarah Carrier, railroad tie-cutter, uncle of Minnie Mitchell, living with his wife Mahulda in a two-person household in Rosewood.

Carrier, Annie ("Sweety")—daughter of Haywood and Sarah Carrier, sister of Sylvester Carrier, absent from Rosewood at the time of the events, later married name Annie Oliver.

Carrier, Bernadina—age 20, daughter of Haywood and Sarah Carrier, living in the Rosewood home of her mother Sarah at the time of the events.

Carrier/Carrol, Eddie—age 17, son of James and Emma Carrier/Carrol, living in their home in Rosewood.

Carrier, Elias—brother of James and Haywood Carrier, preacher, age about 47 at time of death in church shooting in Rosewood around 1917.

Carrier/Carrol, Emma—age 52, sister of Sarah Carrier, wife of James Carrier/Carrol (two sisters had married two brothers, hence both had the married name Carrier), grandmother of Minnie Mitchell, who knew her as Mama.

Carrier/Carrol, Goldee—age 12, daughter of James and Emma Carrier/Carrol, living in their home in Rosewood

Carrier, Harry ("Little Brother")—age 14, son of Haywood and Sarah Carrier, living in the Rosewood home of his mother Sarah at the time of the events.

Carrier, Haywood—age 54, lumberjack and preacher, husband of Sarah Carrier and father of Sylvester Carrier, absent from Rosewood at the time of the events.

Carrier/Carrol, James, Sr.—age 56, husband of Emma Carrier/Carrol, brother of Haywood Carrier, brother-in-law of Sarah Carrier, handicapped by two strokes.

African Americans who lived in Rosewood during
January 1-7, 1923, or had lived there previously (continued

Carrier/Carrol James , Jr. ("J.C.").—age 8, son of James and Emma Carrier/Carrol, living in their home in Rosewood.

Carrier, Lellon ("Beauty")—daughter of Haywood and Sarah Carrier, sister of Sylvester Carrier, absent from Rosewood at the time of the events; professional singer; later married name Lellon Gurdine.

Carrier, Leroy ("Lee")—age 22, son of Ransom and Louisa Carrier, living in Rosewood home of his uncle Wesley Bradley after his father died and his mother remarried and moved away, lumber stacker in Sumner.

Carrier/Carrol, Lonnie—age about 12, son of James and Emma Carrier/Carrol, living in their home in Rosewood.

Carrier/Carrol, Mahulda Brown ("Gussie")—age about 24, wife of Aaron Carrier/ Carrol, schoolteacher, originally from the town of Archer 30 miles from Rosewood.

Carrier, Sarah J.—age 50, head of seven-person household in Rosewood including her married son Sylvester Carrier; laundress in Sumner.

Carrier, H. Sylvester—age 33, the central African American figure in the Rosewood events as of Thursday night, Jan. 4; tie-cutter and former logtrain fireman, nicknamed "Man," living in Rosewood in the home of his mother Sarah Carrier, with his wife Gertrude King Carrier.

Carrier/Carrol, Wade—age about 20, son of James and Emma Carrier/Carrol, resident of Wylly two miles from Rosewood, later a St. Johns County court bailiff in St. Augustine, Florida.

Carrier/Carrol, Willard ("Big Baby")—age about 20, son of James and Emma Carrier/Carrol, suffering from undiagnosed neurological or behavioral disorder, living with his parents in Rosewood.

Carter, Cornelia—age about 56, widow of Nebuchadnezzar Carter, mother of Sam Carter, caring intermittently for grandchildren on farm of 80 acres (no kinship relation between the Carters and the Carriers).

Carter, George—age about 22, son of Sam Carter; lumberjack, convicted of burglary and livestock theft.

Carter, Jesse—age 27, the missing son of Sam Carter.

Carter, Nebuchadnezzar—deceased husband of Cornelia Carter, father of Sam Carter, homesteaded the 80-acre Carter farm in the 1890s; barrel-maker (cooper) for turpentine distilleries.

*African Americans who lived in Rosewood during
January 1-7, 1923, or had lived there previously (continued*

Carter, Sam—age 45, widower, father of George Carter, son of Nebuchadnezzar and Cornelia Carter; blacksmith, spent a year in prison in 1900, lives alone in Rosewood on the 80-acre Carter family parcel.

Coleman, Emma Carrier—wife of trapper John Coleman and sister of Haywood, James, Elias and Virginia Carrier; living in Rosewood with her husband.

Coleman, John—aging trapper and hunter living in Rosewood with his wife Emma in a two-story home, briefly accused in 1911 of arson against Rosewood's A.M.E. church but exonerated.

Coleman, Warren—age 23 when shot to death in 1908, allegedly by Willard Carrier; was the son of John Coleman and Emma Carrier Coleman.

Davis, Hardee—age about 52, widower of Ella Carrier Davis, brother of Mary Ann Hall, living alone in Rosewood.

Edwards, Julia—wife of Ransom Edwards, living with her husband and three grandsons (Willie, Dewey and Nathan Evans) on their farm in Rosewood.

Edwards, Ransom—husband of Julia Edwards, farmer, ex-superintendent of Rosewood school, living with his wife and three grandsons (Willie, Dewey and Nathan Evans) on 28-acre farm in Rosewood.

Goins, Beatrice ("Bea")—age 9, daughter of Perry and Hattie Goins, living with her parents and siblings on 65-acre family farm; later married name Beatrice Frazier.

Goins, Arnett Turner—age 8, son of George and Willie Carrier Goins, staying in the Rosewood home of his grandmother Sarah Carrier at the time of the events.

Goins, Charlie—son of Ed Goins, brother of Perry and George Goins, absent from Rosewood at time of events.

Goins, Ed—former Rosewood turpentine operator, father of Charlie, Perry and George Goins, deceased in 1920.

Goins, George W., Sr.— son of Ed Goins, brother of Charlie and Perry Goins, husband of Willie Carrier Goins, heir to lost turpentine wealth, son-in-law of Sarah Carrier; logger, absent from Rosewood at the time of the events.

Goins, George, Jr. ("Buster")—age 4, son of George and Willie Carrier Goins, living in the Rosewood home of his grandmother Sarah Carrier at the time of the events.

Goins, Perry—son of Ed Goins, brother of Charlie and George Goins, living in Rosewood with his wife Hattie and children on 65-acre family farm and former turpentine distillery site; lumber stacker in Sumner.

Goins, Philomena—age 11, daughter of George and Willie Carrier Goins, staying in the Rosewood home of her grandmother Sarah Carrier at the time of the events; later married name Philomena Doctor.

Goins, Willie Carrier—daughter of Haywood and Sarah Carrier, sister of Sylvester Carrier, wife of George Goins, Sr.; absent from Rosewood at the time of the events.

Gordon, Lexie—age 55, widow, neighbor of Sam and Ellen King in Rosewood, living on 5.5-acre farm.

Hall, C. Bacchus—b. ca. 1848, d. 1919; married his young ward Mary Ann Hall in advanced age; owned store in Rosewood that functioned until around 1915; father of children named below.

Hall, Margie—age about 14, daughter of Bacchus and Mary Ann Hall, 1994 claimant in Rosewood legislative case; married name Margie Johnson.

Hall, Mary Ann—age about 42, died 1952, widow of Charles Bacchus Hall (deceased 1919), living in Rosewood with children Sam, Margie, Wilson, Charles and Mary, sister of Hardee Davis; had worked as lumber stacker at Sumner sawmill; grown children Stephen and Doshia no longer in Rosewood.

Hall, Mary Magdalene—age 3, daughter of Bacchus and Mary Ann Hall, 1994 claimant in Rosewood legislative case; married name Mary Daniels.

Hall, Sam—age 16, living with widowed mother Mary Ann Hall and younger siblings in home in Rosewood, family retains about 20 acres of formerly larger holdings, lumber stacker in Sumner.

Hall, Wilson—age 7, son of Bacchus and Mary Ann Hall, 1994 claimant in legislative case.

Hayward, Mary Ann—owner of 80-acre house site in Rosewood; married name Mary Jane Screen, sister of Annie Blocker, living with her children in Rosewood.

Hunter, Jesse—allegedly an escaped convict who attacked Fannie Taylor in Sumner, appears in no known official record.

Jones, Laura—age about 33, widow, living with her son Raymond Jones on 11-acre farm in Rosewood, near Sarah Carrier.

Jones, Raymond—age about 16, son of Laura Jones and her deceased husband Sam; friend of Sam Hall, lumber stacker in Sumner.

King, Sam—age about 44, living with his wife Ellen and adopted daughter Eloise in Rosewood on farm of 4.65 acres; lumberjack for Cummer Lumber.

King, Ellen—wife of Sam King, living with her husband and adopted daughter Eloise in Rosewood on farm of 4.65 acres; seamstress.

King, Eloise—age 8, adopted daughter of Sam and Ellen King, original name Eloise Carrier (daughter of Ransom and Louisa Carrier, sister of Leroy "Lee" Carrier)

McCoy, John—age about 63, owns largest African American-held farm in Rosewood (114 acres); lives there with wife Mary Ella and their youngest children.

McCoy, Lutie—age about 21, daughter of John and Mary Ella McCoy, married and living in Sumner at the time of the events; married name Lutie Foster.

McCoy, Mary Ella—midwife for Rosewood, wife of John McCoy; living with him and younger children on their 114-acre farm.

Mitchell, Minnie Lee—age 9, daughter of Daisy Carrier Mitchell (deceased) and Theron Mitchell (absent), living with her grandparents James and Emma Carrier/Carrol in Rosewood, later married name Minnie Lee Langley; claimant in original Rosewood claims case, 1991-1993, and in successful 1994 claims case.

Mitchell, Ruben—age 13, son of Daisy Carrier Mitchell (deceased) and Theron Mitchell (absent), living with his grandparents James and Emma Carrier/Carrol and his sister Minnie in Rosewood.

Sherman, Beulah "Scrappy" Carrier/Carrol—age 23, daughter of James and Emma Carrier, resident of Wylly two miles from Rosewood.

Smith, Nettie—age about 6, daughter of Virginia Smith, living in Rosewood with her mother and two brothers; later married name Nettie Joyner.

Smith, Virginia—age about 33, wife of absent logger Allen Smith, daughter of John and Emma Coleman, living in one-room cabin in Rosewood with her small children Nettie, Gilbert and Johnny.

Williams, Richard—former treasurer of Rosewood's A.M.E. church in 1911; acquitted of arson on the church. Husband of Janetta Carter, sister of Sam Carter; shooting incident with Sam Carter in 1900, resulting in a year of prison for Carter. The Rosewood church arson in 1911 remained unsolved.

2) African American non-residents of Rosewood relevant to the events and discussed in the text

Arnett, Benjamin W.—national bishop of the African Methodist Episcopal Church prior to his death in 1906; known for administering the oath of office to President William McKinley on March 4, 1897. Bishop Arnett's influence on A.M.E. church members in Rosewood was suggested by the naming of Rosewood resident Arnett Turner Goins, born 1913.

Abbott, Robert—founder and publisher of the *Chicago Defender*, whose January 13, 1923, story on Rosewood created a fictitious main character, later to become the central character of the 1997 motion picture *Rosewood*.

Cole, Ted—fictitious central character in the Rosewood events who was invented by the *Chicago Defender* in 1923, then transfigured into a character named "Mann" in the 1997 movie *Rosewood*.

Hurston, Zora Neale—writer and anthropologist born in Eatonville, Florida, in the Orlando area at the beginning of the twentieth century; went north to study at Howard and Columbia universities; wrote about the Ocoee violence of 1920 and the Florida timber culture, among other subjects.

Johnson, James Weldon—author, educator, lawyer, U.S. diplomat, songwriter, editorial page editor of the *New York Age*; in 1920 elected first African American executive secretary of the NAACP; born June 17, 1871, in Jacksonville, Florida.

Long, Boise—farmer in Newberry, Florida, 25 miles north of Rosewood, who in 1916 was accused of livestock theft, then was convicted of murdering Constable George Wynne and was hanged during the "Lynch Hammock" crisis, in which six neighbors and relatives of Long were lynched.

Missouri, Robert—employee of the Cummer Lumber shingle mill in Sumner; known for working double shifts and developing side businesses. Missouri had no direct link to the Rosewood community but knew a number of the residents. He exemplified the effects of segregationist rules that forebade promotion of African American workers.

Norman, Mose—resident of the voting precinct surrounding Ocoee, Florida, more than 100 miles south of Rosewood. His attempt to vote apparently initiated the Ocoee violence of November 1920.

Perry, Cain and Fortune—father and son, respectively, both hanged for the May 11, 1912, shooting deaths near Archer, Florida, of Alachua County Deputy Sheriff Charles Slaughter and civilian assistant F. V. White.

501

Perry, Julius "July"—orange grove manager or foreman in Ocoee, Florida, who was tortured and killed in the Ocoee "race war" of November 1920. Charges that he had started the hostilities were, apparently spurious.

Turner, Henry McNeal (1834-1915)—Bishop of the African Methodist Episcopal Church, the first such bishop elected from the newly emancipated South (1883); outspoken critic of the racial segregation system.

Williams, Mingo—resident of Bronson, Florida, 20 miles from Rosewood, employee of L. W. Drummond Naval Stores, murdered beside Highway 13 leading from Gainesville toward Rosewood on January 5, 1923, apparently by mob participants en route to Rosewood.

Wright, Charles—African American burned at the stake in the violence at Perry, Florida, during December 2-8, 1922, following the murder of white schoolteacher Ruby Henry (two counties away from Rosewood).

Young, Arthur—African American reportedly hanged during the violence at Perry, Florida, during December 2-8, 1922, following the rape and murder of white schoolteacher Ruby Henry.

---

3) Whites involved in or relevant to the Rosewood events

Andrews, Henry—age 43, logging superintendent or "woods boss" for Cummer Lumber and manager of its Otter Creek sawmill and quarters; known as "Boots" among African Americans for alleged abusive behavior.

Bryce, William Crighton ("Kay")—age 48, living in both Cedar Key and Bryceville near the Atlantic coast, landowner, turpentine operator, passenger train conductor.

Cannon, Augustus B.—company physician in Sumner for the Cummer corporation, reportedly treated both Fannie Taylor (Jan. 1) and white survivors of the Thursday night shootout (Jan. 4).

Cason, Jack—age about 47, turpentine woods rider, living in Rocky Hammock about nine miles from Rosewood with his 25-year-old wife, seven children and five step-children.

Davis, Robert W. "Colonel"—age 73, editorial page editor of the *Gainesville Daily Sun* 50 miles from Rosewood, writer of 1923 opinion pieces on Rosewood and the Ku Klux Klan.

DeCottes, George—special prosecutor from Deland, Florida, assigned to investigate the Rosewood events in late January-February 1923.

*Whites involved in or relevant to
the Rosewood events*

Dunning, J. S.—deputy sheriff of Alachua County, Florida, one county away from Rosewood, badly wounded in shootout on July 5, 1922, raising racial tensions.

Green, Truman—age 20, junior at the University of Florida in Gainesville, 50 miles from Rosewood; City Editor of the *Gainesville Daily Sun*, apparent source of 1923 wire service articles describing the Rosewood violence.

Hardee, Cary A.—Governor of Florida, 1921-1925, ordered special prosecutor to Rosewood in late January 1923

Hendry, Ruby—schoolteacher in Perry, Florida, two counties away from Rosewood, who was raped and murdered on December 2, 1922, setting off a week-long manhunt and racial frenzy there.

Hudson, Bryant—son, age 24, brother of Mannie Hudson, cousin of Bryan, Orrie and Garrett Kirkland, woodland farmer, army veteran.

Hudson, Columbus—father of Bryant and Mannie Hudson, woodland farmer, resident of Janney area north of Sumner.

Hudson, Mannie—age 27, woodland farmer, resident of Janney area north of Sumner.

Hudson, Perry—logger for Cummer lumber, resident of the Fowler's Bluff logging camp, cousin of Bryan and Mannie Hudson.

Hudson, Punk—resident of Cedar Key, woodland farmer, friend of Pat Taylor.

Jacobs, Charlie—original settler of Rosewood around 1879, notary public, storekeeper and community leader.

Jones, Richard Lloyd—owner and editor of multiple newspapers across the South and elsewhere; involved in distorting and provocative racial articles in both the Tulsa race riot of 1921 (*Tulsa Tribune*) and the Rosewood events in 1923 (*Jacksonville Journal*); cousin of architect Frank Lloyd Wright.

Kirkland, Bryan—age about 30, woodland farmer, resident of the Geiger Creek area west of Sumner, son of Orrie Kirkland, nephew of Garrett Kirkland, cousin of Bryan and Mannie Hudson.

Kirkland, Fred—age 14, living with his family in the Geiger Creek area west of Sumner, brother of Orrie Kirkland, nephew of Garrett Kirkland, cousin of Bryan and Mannie Hudson.

Kirkland, Garrett—resident of the Otter Creek area, brother of Orrie Kirkland, cousin of Bryan and Mannie Hudson.

*Whites involved in or relevant to
the Rosewood events*

Kirkland, John—resident of woodland area near Rosewood, owner of an 80-acre parcel inside Rosewood, cattle rancher, brother of Orrie Kirkland, uncle of Bryan and Fred Kirkland, cousin of Bryan and Mannie Hudson.

Kirkland, Orrie—age about 51, woodland farmer, resident of the Geiger Creek area west of Sumner, father of Bryan and Fred Kirkland, brother of Garrett Kirkland, cousin of Bryan and Mannie Hudson.

Johns, Lutie Luconie ("L. L.")—age 42, justice of the peace in Sumner, farmer, former timber company security officer, elected sheriff of Levy County in 1924.

McKenzie, Daniel ("D. P.", "Mac")—owner of Wylly turpentine operation, later a Florida legislator.

Pillsbury, Edward—age 17, son of Cummer Lumber superintendent Walter Pillsbury in Sumner; later a police detective in Jacksonville, Florida.

Pillsbury, Martha—age 14, daughter of Cummer Lumber superintendent Walter Pillsbury in Sumner; married name Martha Thompson.

Pillsbury, Walter—age 47, top management official for Cummer Lumber in Sumner, living there with his wife Grace and five children, born near Cadillac, Michigan.

Ramsey, Perry—sheriff of Alachua County, Florida, during the Rosewood events, reportedly went to the scene.

Studstill, Minor ("Cephus")—age 23, lumber inspection foreman for Cummer Lumber, living in Sumner.

Taylor, Bernice ("Barney")—three-year-old son of James and Fannie Taylor, with infant brother named Addis.

Taylor, Fannie—age 21, wife of James Taylor, living with her husband and two small sons, Addis and Bernice Taylor, in company-owned housing in Sumner.

Taylor, James—age 24, husband of Fannie Taylor, millwright in Sumner sawmill, brother of Pat and Henry Taylor of Cedar Key.

Taylor, Pat—age 22, brother-in-law of Fannie Taylor, brother of James Taylor, living in Cedar Key and later town marshal.

Turner, James, Sr.—company physician for both the Cummer corporation and the Seaboard Air Line Railway as well as private practice; alternated with Dr. Cannon in Sumner; later a Florida legislator.

Whites involved in or relevant to
the Rosewood events

Turner, James, Jr. ("Jim")—age 14, son of Dr. James Turner of Bronson; later sheriff of Levy County and president of the Florida Sheriff's Association.

Walker, Elisha R. ("Bob")—age 52, Levy County Sheriff for more than two decades, living in Bronson 20 miles from Rosewood.

Wilkerson, D. P. ("Poly")—age 41, ex-deputy sheriff and ex-quartersboss, still serving as district constable in Jan. 1923; living in Sumner with wife Mattie and children; said to be an employer of Sarah Carrier, related by marriage to Henry Andrews.

Williams, Clarence—deputy sheriff and quartersboss in Sumner, newly arrived.

Wright, John—age 52, Rosewood's only remaining storekeeper; husband of Mary Wright; landowner.

Wright, Mary—wife of storekeeper John Wright, widow of Charlie Jacobs.

Wynne, George—District constable in Newberry, Florida, 25 miles north of Rosewood, killed at the beginning of the "Lynch Hammock" events in August 1916.

4) Witness Participants
(Witnesses present during the 1923 events who were:
a) over the age of seven at that time, and
b) interviewed in the 1980s and/or 1990s)

Name	Age in 1923	Residence in 1923
Cannon, Marshall	22	Sumner
Carrier, Leroy	22	Rosewood
Carrol/Carrier, Lonnie	12	Rosewood
Cason, Lloyd	8	Rocky Hammock
Coburn, Frank	24	Cedar Key
Davis, Eloise (King)	8	Rosewood
Doctor, Philomena (Goins)	11	Rosewood
Evans, Willie	16	Rosewood
Faircloth, Allen	30	Cedar Key
Foster, Edith (Surls)	16	Sumner
Foster, Lutie (McCoy)	22	Rosewood until 1917, then Sumner
Frazier, Bea (Goins)	9	Rosewood.
Goins, Arnett	9	Rosewood
Hodges, Randolph	8	Cedar Key
Hall, Sam	16	Rosewood
Hawkins, Thelma (Evans)	19	Rosewood until ca.1919
Hudson, Charles	13	Janney, north of Sumner
Hudson, Perry	20	Fowler's Bluff camp
Jenkins, Eva (Marshall)	13	Gainesville, b. Rosewood
Johnson, Margie (Hall)	13	Rosewood
Jones, John Paul	10	Gainesville
Kirkland, Fred	14	Geiger Creek
Langley, Minnie (Mitchell)	9	Rosewood
McElveen, Jason	27	Sumner
McPhail, Billie (Zetrouer)	8	Sumner
Missouri, Robert	30	Sumner
Parham, Ernest	18	Sumner
Thompson, Martha (Pillsbury)	14	Sumner
Turner, James	14	Bronson
Smith, Elizabeth	29	Sumner
Washington, Lillie (Burns)	12	Lennon, b. Rosewood
White, John	21	Otter Creek

5) Secondary Informants

(In addition, more than 80 other individuals were interviewed who can be considered informants on aspects of the Rosewood events. Affected individuals who were aged seven or younger in 1923 are included in this group—as only secondary informants, owing to repeated demonstrations of "pseudo-memory." Also here are descendants who were privy to family stories about the events, holders of general background knowledge about the local area, and others.

Abraham, Louis
Alexander, Gertrude
Alford Nellie
Ames, Marie Monroe
Andrews, Guy
Atkins, Charlie
Baylor, Woodrow
Beauchamp, James
Bennett, Arthina (Blocker)
Bishop, James
Black, Janie Mae
Blocker, Ernest
Booth, George
Bradley, Queen
Bryant, Bertie
Cannon, Kenneth
Cannon, Margaret
Jones, Troy, Jr.
Kennedy, Bertha
Kent, Joy Cason
Kirby, Ruth (Ingram)
Lancaster, Leola
Leviston, Mim
Manley, Queen
McKenzie, William
Miller, Oliver
Monroe, Oren
Morrison, Mollie
Mortin, Allenetta (Robinson)
Norsworthy, L. W.
Pollard, Clarence

Carrol, Lucille
Cason, Lloyd
Cheeseborough, David
Christie, Catherine
Clyatt, S. C.
Cobb, Dogan
Cummer, Wellington
Davis, Jess
Doctor, Arnett
Dorsett, Naomi
Ellerbee, Helen
Glover, Leroy
Glover, Pompey
Goins, Angela
Goins, William
Gunnell, S. E.
Hall, Mary (Daniels)
Pruett, Mattie
Richburg, Willie
Rispus, Annie Belle
Robbins, G. T.
Roberson, Bill
Roberts, W. H.
Robinson, Theresa
Rountree, Preston
Scoggins, Doyal
Screen, Johnny .
Smith, Glen
Sparks, Oliver
Stephenson, Allen
Strong, Acie

Hall, Wilson
Hathcox, Willard
Hardee, Bascomb
Hardee, Haskell
Harris, Lula (Bradley)
Henderson, Lillie Belle
Hendricks-Frye, Helena
Henning, Helen
Herbert, Stella Pope
Howard, Mary Leona
(Bryce)
Ingram, Mertie
Johns, Charley
Johns, Kelton
Johnson, Elmer
Strong, Henry
Taylor, Addis
Taylor, Barney
Thompson, Wesley
Wiggins, Ella Mae
Wilder, Joseph
Wilkerson, Herbert
Wilkerson, James
Williams, Pat
Yant, Rufus
Yearty, John
Young, Bennie
Zetrouer, Aubrey
Zimmerman, Eugene

6) Households involved in the Rosewood violence

Sarah Carrier (husband **Haywood Carrier** living elsewhere)	James and Emma Carrier/Carrol
(grown or minor children at home) Sylvester Carrier (and wife Gertrude) Bernadina Carrier Harry Carrier	*(grown or minor children at home)* Willard Carrier Eddie Carrier Lonnie Carrier Goldee Carrier James "J. C." Carrier, Jr.
(grandchildren in household) Philomena Goins Arnett Goins George "Buster" Goins, Jr.	*(grandchildren in household)* Ruben Mitchell Minnie Lee Mitchell
(grown children living elsewhere) Lillian "Beauty" Carrier Annie "Sweetie" Carrier Willie Carrier Goins (apparently with husband George Goins, Otter Creek) Ruby Carrier	*(grown children living in Rosewood)* Aaron Carrier and wife Mahulda *(grown children living elsewhere)* Rita Carrier Williams (with husband Charles in Sumner) Beulah Carrier Sherman ("Scrappy," living in Wylly) Wade Carrier (with wife in Wylly)

Households of the three Bradley brothers

John Wesley Bradley (wife recently deceased: Virginia Carrier Bradley)	George and Maggie Bradley
(children at home) Donarion "Bishop" Bradley Marion "Soda" Bradley Wesley James Bradley Lee Ruth "Mossy" Bradley Ivory "Gal Baby" Bradley Clifford Bradley *(boarding in household, nephew)* Leroy "Lee" Carrier *(children living elsewhere)* Hoyt Bradley Callie Bradley Young Galvester "Nader" Bradley	*(one son at home)* Raleigh Bradley *(with his small daughters)* Lula Bradley Ruth Bradley *(absent grown children)* George Bradley, Jr. Rebecca Bradley Arthur Bradley Queen Bradley
	Ed and Eliza Bradley (no children; prior to 1923 cared for nieces Thelma Evans and Bertha Carrier)

Households Involved in the Rosewood Violence (continued)

The Goins brothers of M. Goins & Bros. Naval Stores (arrived in Rosewood 1895-1900, deceased before 1923)	
Martin(e) Goins (brother) (died 1905) and **wife Lydia** *Children of Martin and Lydia (none still in Rosewood in 1923)* Queenie Goins King (b. 1878) Sophie Goins Monroe (b. 1881) Hilton Goins (b. 1887) Florence Goins (b. 1896) *Grandchildren in Monroe family, possibly still in Rosewood in 1923:* Clara, Marie, Orion, Andrew, Earl (granddaughter Marie, above, reported deceased in Chiefland, late 1923, circumstances unclear) *Granddaughter:* Getrude King Carrier (daughter of Queenie Goins King and Thomas King, still living in Rosewood 1923 with husband Sylvester Carrier)	**Ed Goins** (brother) (d. 1920 in Rosewood) **(widower of Sarah)** *Son,* Perry Goins, living in Rosewood in 1923 with wife Hattie and children *Son,* George Goins, apparently living in Otter Creek with wife Willie Carrier Goins *Son,* Charlie Goins, location unknown, fugitive from justice *Son,* Jean Goins said to be living elsewhere by 1923, though wife Annie Belle Gordon Goins possibly there
Lucian Goins (brother) no descendants in 1923 Rosewood	*Son,* Will Goins, moved to Gainesville before 1923 *Daughter,* Agnes Goins Marshall, died 1917
Eli P. Walden (brother-in-law, died 1900) no descendants in 1923 Rosewood	*Daughters (not in Rosewood by 1923)* Rebecca, Pearl, Minnie, Rovenia

The Carters	
(two households on 80 acres) **Cornelia Carter** widow of Nebuchadnezzar Carter; cared for two grandchildren **Sam Carter** son of Cornelia Carter; wife Ida deceased; children: George, Pearlie, Jesse	Despite similar names, the Carters of Section 30 were not related to the Carriers of Section 29, by either blood or marriage.

Households Households Involved in the Rosewood Violence
(continued)

The Halls

Mary Ann (Davis) Hall
(widow of Charles Bacchus Hall; living on about 20 acres, remnant of larger prior holdings)
(children living at home)
Doshia Hall
Sam Hall
Margie Hall
Thomas Hall
Wilson Hall
Charles Hall
Mary Ann Hall
(grown son elsewhere)
Stephen Hall

James and Luvenia Hall
(separate household, James is brother of Bacchus Hall; no children)

Ransom and Julia Edwards
(living on 27-acre parcel)
(three grandchildren living in the home):
Willie Evans
Nathaniel Evans
Dewey Evans
(Another grandchild, Thelma Evans, had lived in the home of Ed and Eliza Bradley, but left Rosewood before 1923.)
(The Edwardses had also raised Sam King's wife Ellen.)

Lexie Gordon

(widow of M. B. Gordon, living on 5.5-acre parcel)
(one or two daughters living at home, and perhaps a grandchild or grandchildren)

Children all grown,
1923 locations unclear:
Annie Belle, Fonnie, Frank, James, Mary, Orlando, Rosa

John and Mary Ella McCoy

(living on 114-acre farm)
(children living at home)
Impie McCoy
Albert McCoy
Herbert McCoy
Martha McCoy
Mary McCoy
(and nine grown children living elsewhere, including Lutie Foster. The McCoys' earliest child, Bennie, was born in 1880.)

Hardee Davis (living alone on one acre) (widower of Emma Carrier Davis, sister of James, Haywood, Elias, Ransom and Virginia Carrier) (brother of Mary Ann Davis, widow of Bacchus Hall)

Laura Jones

(widow of Sam Jones, living with son Raymond on 11 acres)

Households Involved in the Rosewood Violence (continued)

White Residents of Rosewood

At least three households of whites were in Rosewood as it entered 1923:

John and Mary Wright—storekeepers running the community's only remaining store, which had passed down from Mary's first marriage to the late Charles Jacobs. A son from that marriage had grown up with the Wrights and moved away. Two children born to the Wrights themselves had died in early childhood.

Will and Mertie Ingram, farmers with several children.

Rob Ingram, Will's brother, lived nearby with and his wife and several children.

James and Fannie Taylor
(living in Sumner)

(children in household)
Bernice Taylor
Addis Taylor
(James's brothers in Cedar Key)
Pat Taylor
Jess Taylor
(brother-in-law in Cedar Key)
Mitch Wilder

Walter and Grace Pillsbury
(children, all at home)
Edward Pillsbury
Sopha Pillsbury
Martha Pillsbury
Joe Pillsbury
George Pillsbury
(future son-in-law)
Ernest Parham
(would wed Sopha)

Columbus and Virginia Hudson
(at Janney, north of Sumner)

(son at home)
Charlie Hudson
(grown sons living elsewhere)
Dave Hudson
Mannie Hudson
Bryant Hudson
(cousins)
Orrie Kirkland
Garrett Kirkland
John Kirkland
Bryan Kirkland
(Orrie's son)
Fred Kirkland
(Orrie's son)
Perry Hudson
"Punk" Hudson

Households Involved in the Rosewood Violence (continued

Two disputed households

The Robinson and Borden households were said by some survivors to have left the community before 1923, but others said they remained. Their 1923 residency cannot be conclusively established, though residents of both were accounted for after the 1923 violence.

Unoccupied Residences

As the Rosewood community entered 1923, vacant homes included those of Benny McCoy, Frank Burns, John Blocker, Will Marshall, John Monroe, Junius Coarsey, Suzy White, Raleigh Bradley and perhaps others.

>*Benny McCoy's sister Lutie Foster confirmed that he had left the community before 1923, though he continued to own his house site there.

>*Frank Burns's widow Mary Burns left after Frank's death of stroke and lived with a married daughter in a turpentine camp at Lennon.

>*After John Blocker became a fugitive, his wife Annie moved the family to Wylly.

>*Will Marshall moved to Gainesville after his wife Agnes died in 1917.

>*John Monroe, also a widower, had left the community to find work, though his children may have remained.

>*M. B. Coarsey, white, had run the Rosewood post office until his death, with his widow continuing until the post office closed in 1914. The Coarseys left a vacant brick residence across the railroad from the home of Sarah Carrier.

>*Suzy White, an elderly widow related to the Carters, moved to Gainesville.

>*Raleigh Bradley's wife Nancy died and he and his children moved in with his parents George and Maggie Bradley.

Other abandoned homes were no longer standing in January 1923, having burned accidentally in previous years, including those of Theron and Daisy Mitchell, Frank and Beulah Sherman and others.

Households Involved in the Rosewood Violence (continued

Two Goins cousins
(both deceased before the 1923 violence)

Agnes Goins Marshall was a college-educated daughter of Ed Goins, who was the brother of Martin Goins and a partner in M. Goins & Bros. Naval Stores. Agnes's husband Will Marshall was from coastal New Berne, North Carolina. Arriving in Rosewood in the late 1890s with the Goins turpentine migration, they brought a grand piano, which was left covered in their abandoned home after Agnes died in 1917. Will Marshall died three years later in Gainesville.

Sophie Goins Monroe was a daughter of Martin and Lydia Goins and attended St. Augustine College in Raleigh, North Carolina. In Rosewood, Sophie and her husband John Monroe received ten acres of the original 75-acre Goins parcel. Sophie, too, died in 1917. By 1918, her widower John listed as his nearest relative his daughter Marie.
Children living at home:
> Marie Monroe
> Andrew Monroe
> Orion Monroe
> Earl Monroe

By 1923 John Monroe was working elsewhere and the household may have moved, though the children may have remained in Rosewood. A death certificate for Marie Monroe puts her death in late 1923 in Chiefland, Florida, of unspecified causes, possibly related to chidbirth or flight from Rosewood. Marie left an orphaned infant, Roosevelt Grover Monroe, raised by Gertrude King Carrier, Marie's first cousin.

The deaths of Agnes Marshall and Sophie Monroe in 1917 were reportedly on the same day.

The Events

Incident Summary:
The Rosewood Atrocity

Incident Period: Seven Days
Onset: Sunrise (0726 hours), Mon., Jan. 1923
End: Sunset (1740 hours), Sun., Jan. 7, 1923

Site: Rosewood (unincorporated), Levy County, Florida
(50 miles from Gainesville, Fla., 120 miles from Jacksonville;
nine miles from Cedar Key; roughly halfway between Miami
and Atlanta); Gulf coastal littoral, hardwood hammock and
longleaf pine flats; seasonal swamp, six miles inland.
Latitude: 29° 14' 13.6638"   Longitude: -82° 55' 44.1516"

Incident Type: Forced De-population ("racial cleansing")
involving sequential homicides, torture, multiple arson)

Progression: initial home invasion alarm, manhunt,
escalation to torture, nightriding, armed resistance,
second-phase escalation to general riot.

Aggressing crowd at peak (Jan. 5): 300 to 1,000 members

Incidents of Torture: 3

Rescues by Law Enforcement: approximately 4 operations
(three using automobiles, the largest by train, involving
perhaps more than 50 female and children evacuees).

Threat of Deadly Force as Successful Deterrent: 2 occasions.

Form: Accusational panic escalating to uprising scare/riot
Initial questionable alarm by marginalized community member
triggered torture/inquisition spree climaxing in one impulse murder;
re-orientation lull of three days; disruption continued by nightriding
spree, homicide, home invasion, resulting in armed resistance killing

514

two nightriders, initial limited arson, forming secondary trigger to climactic phase of general riot, Jan. 4-7, interspersed with four more homicides; ending Jan. 7 with arson throughout target community; permanent forced de-population.

Size: Core De-population Area - Two Square Miles
Sections 29-30, T 14 S, R 14 E, Levy County, Fla.;
outlying involvement three miles west (in Sumner, Fla.);
related homicide 22 miles northeast (near Bronson, Fla.)

Core Target Area:
Total Community Population: fewer than 120
African American Population: fewer than 100
Number of African American Households: 18 to 22
Number of households burned: approximately 15 to 20
Effect: racially-selective de-population of target area, complete and permanent

Total Fatalities: Eight
(in chronological order, ages as recorded)
Samuel S, Carter, 43; Sarah J, Carrier, 50;
D. P. "Poly" Wilkerson, 41; Henry M. Andrews, 43;
Lexie Gordon, 55; H. Sylvester Carrier, 33;
Mingo Williams, 57; James Carrier, 56.
(Questions remain on unlocated subject Jesse Carter, and matters of definition on three evacuees apparently dying of non-violent causes within a year; such issues of remote possibility establish a margin of error on fewer than five ex-residents not firmly located by later tracing).

Injured Non-Fatalities: Four
Emma Carrier – one or two buckshot flesh wounds
Ruben Mitchell – blinded in one eye by flying glass in gunfire; other buckshot flesh wounds;
Mannie Hudson – severe buckshot facial wound
Aaron Carrier – threat of torture but stopped by rescue; no serious physical injury according to relatives

Contagion:
One month prior: murder/manhunt/racial rampage at Perry, Fla., 90 miles west, similar segmented incident period of one week, Dec. 2-8, 1922.
Two weeks post-event (mid-Jan. 1923): extra-judicial hanging of African American

Contagion *(cont.)*

reportedly named Abe Wilson, for cattle theft at Newberry, Fla., 40 miles north; included as part of larger breakdown in public order under grand jury investigation mandated by state governor in Feb. 1923.

Official Response

1) extensive manhunt, at least one investigation trip of 120 miles, fifty-dollar bloodhound rental fee paid by county commission;

2) approximately four rescue operations by law enforcement authorities;

3) two successful threats of deadly force to prevent mob violence, though by non-law enforcement personnel;

4) one justice of the peace inquest on initial homicide, verdict: "death by hands unknown;"

5) undocumented exchange of telegrams between Governor Cary Hardee and Levy County Sheriff E. R. Walker, declining Florida National Guard intervention;

6) February 1923 - Governor-mandated grand jury investigation by special outside prosecutor; 25 witnesses reportedly called; two-day session; verdict: "perpetrators unknown."

7) November 1923 - months after the event a series of irregular and incomplete death certificates were filed outside normal channels on five of the incident deaths;

8) Repeated research in later years by multiple investigators has confirmed that no known surviving governmental document contained any description of the events.

9) Modern Aftermath, Official Actions

a) July 1982, Florida Secretary of State's office declines to consider placing historical marker;

b) May 4, 1994, Rosewood claims bill signed by Florida Governor Lawton Chiles; Each of nine surviving ex-residents receives $150,000, minus controversial deductions taken by advocate/ intermediary; smaller payments to family members or descendants for reported loss of land, ranging individually from as low as $50 to $5,000 or higher; scholarship fund established for descendants of forced evacuees;

c) May 4, 2004, Florida Secretary of State's Office places $2,000 historical marker, dedicated by Governor Jeb Bush after emergency revision of badly flawed text, though questionable elements were left intact. including fact errors and the word "colored." The result would later become known among historical preservation officials as the most frequently vandalized historical marker in Florida.

_____

The Gun Photo

Photo of Sheriff R. E. "Bob" Walker
Model 1887 Winchester repeating shotgun
said to belong to Sylvester Carrier

As a long investigation began in 1982 and I wondered how to start searching for Rosewood witnesses, I was directed to two elderly brothers, whites, who lived 22 miles from Rosewood in Bronson.

Bascomb and Haskell Hardee were leading cattlemen. I had the impression that their holdings might be extensive, though they lived in unpretentious rural style, wearing comfortable clothes and giving me a hearty greeting.

Neither seemed defensive about the atrocity I was digging into—at that time such a secret that the University of Florida history library, only a few dozen miles away, had insisted to me that no such atrocity had ever occurred—or had even been heard of.

The Hardee brothers, though advancing in age, were not old enough to have participated in the 1923 event themselves, but they seemed fascinated by the buried mystery. Like everyone from their era in isolated Levy County, they knew that the event had occurred—in some form, behind a screen of rumors and legends. It was only official truth that had blanked out the traces, causing the disappearance of an entire community to disappear as well from the postcard picture of Florida's past.

At the early stage when I met the Hardees I had not been able to find any African American witnesses, or even a trace of them. Local culture for at least twelve miles around the vine-covered site of Rosewood had become monolithically white (with the exception of one isolated household, occupied by the adventurous Reynolds family, who had moved into a remote farm in the pines after Mr. Reynolds retired from a northern police department). In local white society the word on African American witnesses to the event was always the same: that Rosewood's attacked residents had fled into the woods and disappeared.

The implication, usually unspoken, was: "You know how those people are. They just wander off and can never be located." Whites also said that even if found, any African American survivors or their descendants would be too afraid to talk.

Soon, all of this would prove to be remarkably untrue. There were richly knowledgeable networks of black survivors living ordinary lives, some of them as near to the Rosewood site as Jacksonville and the Tampa Bay area (120 miles away or less), others in Miami, Pensacola and as far away as Chicago, New York or beyond (Lee Carrier's family lived for a while in Seattle, then moved to Oakland).

But that was all in the future as I talked to Bascomb and Haskell Hardee. Having been put in touch with them by phone by a minister in Cedar Key, I left my office chair in a newspaper office in St. Petersburg and drove a hundred miles north to Bronson and Bascomb's house. The two brothers were helpful throughout, though they came of the old segregated southern culture and felt at home in it. As I arrived and sat talking at a kitchen table to Haskell, Bascomb rose and said in his offhand way, "'Scuse me a minute, I've got to go out and pay the boy workin' in the yard." I never saw the "boy," but I think he was a grown man, another sign that I had entered a bygone world.

To me, a bearded newspaper reporter in a new Toyota on the heels of the Civil Rights era, the world of codified racial segregation seemed a distant place, almost unreal—though I would find in my search that in 1982 an occasional backroad café could still be found in Florida with a morbid back window or back door for black clientele.

As both Bascomb and Haskell Hardee sought to share with me the little they had heard about a 1923 atrocity of which they had no firsthand knowledge, it became clear that they had imbibed the uprising myth about Rosewood, which, I was to find, had permeated local white culture. This was the myth, taken up by confusing 1923 newspaper reports, that the Rosewood affair was a matter of some crazy, incoherent black savages at Rosewood rising up and challenging white authority, whereupon they had to be put down.

Haskell Hardee said helpfully: "One interesting thing about that thing, was how well armed they were [meaning the attacked residents of Rosewood], and how many guns they had, with so much ammunition." I didn't know that this was a variant of the common belief in the 1920s white South—repeatedly stated in newspapers—that dangerous blacks were amassing secret arsenals in places like churches, in preparation for some kind of spectacular take-over.

In the beginning stage of investigation I was wandering lost in a wonder-land of such statements and beliefs—not knowing what mix of fantasy and distorted truth might lie behind any one of them. Much less did I know that here, precisely, was a great doorway into a whole range of early twentieth-century myths, positing that one or another suspicious-looking minority group (not only blacks; often the conspirators were said to be white Catholics) was hoarding stockpiles of ammunition and planning for the day (which did not seem at all implausible to the many tellers) when that group would rise up in concerted rebellion, to run amok in the streets, massacring mainstream whites and taking over some piece of America. In the common anti-Catholic variant, America was to be taken over for demonic rule by the Pope. These beliefs often were held by reasonable-looking people who were unlikely to ever act on them. Haskell Hardee was a generous-spirited man and not some grumbling paranoiac, yet he lived in a world where the idea of insurrection by an underground minority conspiracy did not seem far-fetched.

The Hardees seemed enthusiastic about my visit as a symbol that the world beyond Levy County's woodlands, represented by an urban newspaper investigator, had taken an interest in their local history. They helpfully told me of other whites, older than themselves, who were said to have actually seen the Rosewood events. Soon they physically guided me to such whites.

Thus, I had my first of two interviews with former Levy County sheriff Jim Turner, who without doubt was present in at least the outskirts of the Rosewood violence as a fourteen-year-old boy. He did not participate in or even see the secretive violence itself, but was formidably positioned to reveal the context. It was Jim Turner (also former president of the Florida Sheriffs' Association) who would tell one of the most baffling stories I would encounter, about having personally seen a mass grave.

This was not only horrific but bewildering because in the coming years, as I found the African American survivors of Rosewood and slowly traced the former residents, it became clear that the very small casualty list they all confirmed did not match what Turner described having seen. I noticed that the two Hardee brothers seemed to grow nervous as Turner talked, and I thought the controversy of buried atrocity was the thing disturbing them. This informant seemed methodical and earnest in his description—though also I noticed there were signs of some kind of neurological impairment, as at times he spoke almost in monosyllables. There was also an elusive poverty of detail in what he described.

Later I was cautioned diplomatically by other old residents to take the words of this witness with a grain of salt. I found he was surrounded by a still more confusing halo of mythic portrayals on other fronts—though I never really knew how to interpret all this or what it meant. The mass grave he was describing flew in the face of all the other evidence, once that evidence had trickled in over future years—but how to characterize this contradiction remained an unanswered question. As with the uprising delusions, I seemed to have stumbled into unclassified backwaters of psychology—which in a sense is one of the themes of this book. Here was a world of oral tradition, racial belief and pressured memory that went far beyond the smug clichés I brought to the table about the easy job of digging up the past.

And in this stream, Bascomb and Haskell Hardee introduced me to the mystery of the gun.

Their chief personal knowledge of the Rosewood affair, they said, was indirect. In youth they had been hunting buddies with Earl Walker, the son of Sheriff Bob Walker. Looking back on this, they told a story that I was never able to verify through any other informant. Not for another fourteen more years, in the changed world of 1996, would I begin to see what they were talking about.

In the 1930s, they said, when they would go hunting with Earl Walker, he brought along a special shotgun, the one his father had confiscated after the blow-up at Rosewood.

Haskell and Bascomb talked about handling and using the gun themselves, and had no doubts about its existence. Moreover, they had picked up a specific name. This item was "Sylvester's gun," they said—the key weapon used by the 1923 uprising leader, an iceberg's tip of all those insurrection weapons that were supposedly stockpiled there somewhere.

The two brothers knew little about this desperado, but his ferocity seemed evident when they called him "Ol' Sylvester"—as one might say "a mean ole bear." In 1982 the federal census of 1920 was still under its customary 70-year-embargo (until 1990), and there was no Internet for steps like online searching of World War I draft cards. Not for many years would I see a draft card showing the age of "Ol' Sylvester," and saying that in January 1923 he was 31. Then many years more years after that would have to pass before I could survey a full panorama of documentary pieces, which revealed the draft card as just one more flawed record from a lost time and place. All other evidence said that in 1923 he was 33.

But what of this magical-seeming gun? The Hardee brothers told me that it had special properties. I couldn't quite grasp what they meant, or whether this was just some garnish on the tale. Moreover, the gun itself quickly became overshadowed as the story went on, for there was the fate of the gun's new owner.

Sheriff Bob's son Earl was also drawn into law enforcement, the brothers told me, and became a Florida Highway Patrol officer, in his case riding one of the early motorcycles. However, they said, Earl's beat had included the lonely highway through the bad swamps of outlaw fame, that no-man's land across the Suwannee from Levy County that was formed by Dixie County (which at its formation as a county in 1921 had not a single incorporated town).

One day in the 1930s, the brothers went on, Earl swooped out on his motorcycle at Cross City, an aptly named crossroads that became the county seat of Dixie County. There he told a rattletrap pickup to pull over, and inside were some of the area's fabled "hog and cattle people," wild folk who recognized no outside authority (this was the way it was told to me; I now know that records of the incident describe one occupant of the vehicle as a physician).

Earl told them they had a back tail light out, and to follow him up the road to the courthouse (there were allegations or suggestions that he had warned them before). Their response was gunfire. Earl managed to shoot two of them as he lay dying. The tale grew increasingly grim. Laced throughout was the implication of a curse—an evil aura surrounding the object Earl had come to possess, the magical-seeming but demonic gun, which now had brought its old train of carnage to its new owner.

I was meeting one of the many ways by which local culture strained to make sense of the 1923 upheaval, whose dread and recrimination seemed never to resolve (none of us had reflected that the original story of the Pharaoh's Curse, adhering to Lord Carnarvon and a train of woe, also had its origin in 1923).

I wanted to weave this richness into my original story on Rosewood, published in *Floridian,* the Sunday magazine of the *St. Petersburg Times,* on July 25, 1982. But the story of Earl Walker and the gun seemed off to the side, an intriguing but irrelevant patch of background detail, merely showing the obvious, that the backwoods could get trigger-happy—and that it told big tales. Rosewood posed urgent riddles of human rights and atrocity, and it was hard enough just to piece together what had materially happened in the 1923 events. The fable of the doomed son and the enchanted gun was a distant postscript to those riddles.

Over ensuing years, however, I noticed that survivors of the Rosewood violence mentioned another cryptic detail, something about Sheriff Bob Walker getting his picture taken with Sylvester's gun. Nobody could seem to explain the mentions any more definitely than that. The idea of an actual photograph from the Rosewood violence seemed too much to hope for. The few known photos were bland almost to the point of blankness. In one cryptic shot an unidentified white man gazes down noncommittally at the smoking ruins of a house (see Chapter 37, Arson for the Camera). And none of these known photos depicted the sheriff, with or without the gun.

Then in 1996, as Rosewood went through its publicity cycle of the 1990s (swelling from the 1991-1994 claims case and not to peak until the 1997 Warner Brothers motion picture *Rosewood*), I was contracted by David Tereshchuk of ABC News Productions, and provided some of the narration for a documentary on Rosewood that aired on the Discovery Channel. From this experience (as in 1983 when I took the story to "60 Minutes" and was their background reporter), I found my naiveté enlightened about the lens distortions enforced by the video age.

Tereshchuk patiently explained to me that various elements in the story—which to me seemed crucial to understanding the Rosewood events—could not be used in his documentary because there were no visuals to go with them. On TV, said the patient explanation, if a name is mentioned, the screen demands that a picture go with it. So if you don't have the visual, you had best avoid that slice of the truth (the explanation didn't quite put it that way).

The 1996 documentary, as it turned out, added shock value by inflating Rosewood's 1923 population by a factor of three. But it was a remarkably thorough effort in many ways—much more faithful to the facts than the next video depiction, the big-screen film *Rosewood* a year later, which seemed constrained by hardly any facts at all. Among the impressive efforts made by Tereshchuk's team was their tireless search for usable images. In this search an ABC researcher would at last discover, in the Corbis-Bettmann Archive in New York, the long-lost solution to the Sheriff-and-gun riddle.

As described in the preceding text here, the end of the Rosewood violence on Sunday, January 7, 1923, found a silent-movie newsreel crew making its way to the remote site on the hope of getting some blockbuster images. No one has ever been able to find any motion-picture footage that that International News Reel crew may have shot, (again see Chapter 37), but they left a more lasting monument in another form, for they also apparently shot still photographs, which were sent out laboriously by mail to weekly or monthly publications, which might still be interested in a news event days or weeks old, and could run the snail-mail photos.

This was how the man-looking-at-smoking-ruins photo came to be preserved—because it was published by slow-loop weekly media in 1923. At least four photos apparently taken by the crew saw publication

that way. The crew itself left no written documentation other than a few sentences of photographer's notes scrawled in pencil. By chance, however, there was one more photo which, though never published, wound up in the archive package. This was the strange picture of Sheriff Bob Walker posing obligingly as he prominently displayed the gun.

Details in the background suggest that he was standing in front of the old John Wright house, at ground-zero in the ruins of a racially cleansed community. The hints about this photo over the years suggested that Walker did this posing as one more of his attempts at crowd control. The hints are strong that he was seeking to convince lingering white rioters to go home, by proving to them that their main target, "Ol' Sylvester," was certainly dead. For here was his famous gun.

What the photograph did not explain was that Walker's two-handed display of the gun enables conclusive identification. It confirms the informant stories that the gun was a Winchester pump shotgun—though of an odd kind, not with an under-the-barrel slide or pump, but with an older-style lever mechanism in the trigger guard, like the one seen in actor Chuck Connors' specially adapted, flip-cocking rifle in the 1960s TV series "The Rifleman." Sylvester Carrier's gun, however, was not a repeating rifle. It was a repeating shotgun—hence the awe-stricken stories about its ability to mow down a crowd.

There is no doubt that the gun in the photo is a Winchester Model 1887—a relic even in Sylvester's day—though it was a relic with formidable technology, devised by Utah gunsmith John Browning in the 1880s under contract with the Winchester Repeating Arms Company.

The technology was only part of the riddle. It explained why the gun had such a reputation for firepower, but a deeper question lay in Bob Walker's posing for the camera with it, and then retaining the gun for long-term use by his ill-fated state patrolman son, Earl.

The crux of this mystery lies in stories which, in later years, began to multiply among some of the Rosewood survivors, saying that in the depths of the 1923 event, Sylvester Carrier became one more official illusion in a hall of mirrors. These stories insisted that the central combatant in the violence was not really killed, as all the newspapers said he was—when they repeated the sheriff's announcement of the death.

The stories said that Sylvester was secretly smuggled out of the ruins, still alive, and that another body was substituted to make it seem he had been killed—which enabled the wily trickster to then live, triumphantly, to a ripe old age in some distant and highly secret location. Sometimes he was said to be New Orleans, or Texas, or (for whatever reason) Kentucky, while less ambitious stories had him hidden away in south-central Florida or even at a secluded farmstead in Alachua County, a few miles from his grand trick.

My search for him over the years went as far afield as digging into local archives in Texas and checking records and memories for any sign of him in other places. Through all this, not the slightest hint emerged that Sylvester Carrier did in fact escape, while an avalanche of circumstantial evidence seemed to confirm that the escape story was one more myth.

Some of the tellers were knowledgeable, however. They said that once the trickster had slipped away, he continued hiding his identity by assuming his mother's maiden name, Lewis. This was an impressive detail for such a tale to include, for many people in Rosewood, including some relatives, assumed that Sylvester's mother's maiden name was Robinson, since she had been raised by a family named Robinson. But records confirm that both Sarah Carrier and her older sister Emma had joined the Robinsons through adoption, and were born Emma and Sarah Lewis. In hard years after 1923, Sylvester's younger brother Harry Carrier did verifiably take Lewis as his publicly affirmed surname (he died decades later in New York, according to his nephew Arnett Goins and others). It was possible that Harry's name reversal had influenced the stories about Sylvester in some way.

No trace of a "Sylvester Lewis" has ever been found in any of the alleged places of exile. Like the story told by former sheriff Jim Turner about the mass grave, the story about the hero's miraculous escape does not resolve into a neat forensic package. It reminds that if a realm of experience—or a community—is exiled from official truth, any later digging to unearth it may lead into the predictable cavern—that is, the uncharted depths of reality construction, both individual and cultural, where material evidence can seem to melt into the contours of a dream.

So the question remains: Did Sylvester Carrier really escape his attackers on the night of January 4-5, 1923? Has the tale of his resistance to mob bullying produced a satisfying and romantic ending after all— more satisfying than official truth wished to admit? Henry Sylvester Carrier, an extraordinary individual even when the myths are stripped away, might have been just the kind of escape artist to have pulled off such a *tour de force*—though this doesn't mean it happened.

The photo itself is taunting. Does it really prove that he was dead—because here was Sheriff Walker displaying the dead man's prized possession, the crowd-killing repeater shotgun?

Or does it prove just the opposite? Is the pose so forced, the message so blatant, that it says Walker is trying to cover up something here? In his customary behind-the-scenes way, was the shut-mouthed sheriff actually trying to help the secretly-escaped Sylvester, by engineering a show-and-tell session to fool the mob?

According to one's desires—and one's beliefs—the picture can be turned either way. This, too, is the tantalizing message coiled with such explosive force in an eight-letter word.

Bibliography

Books

Abbott, Lynn, and Seroff, Doug, *Ragged But Right: Black Traveling Shows, Coon Songs, and the Dark Pathway to Blues and Jazz*, University Press of Mississippi, Jackson, 2009.

Ames, Jessie Daniel, *The Changing Character of Lynching, Review of Lynching 1931-1941*, AMS Press, New York, 1942.

Aptheker, Herbert, *American Negro Slave Revolts*, New York, International Publishers, 1943, 1974.

Archer, Jules, *Riot! A History of Mob Action in the United States*, Hawthorn Books, New York, 1974.

Associated Press
Breaking News, How the Associated Press Has Covered War, Peace, and Everything Else, Princeton Architectural Press, New York, 2007.
M.E.S., His Book, A Tribute, (internal commemoration) 1918.

Baker, Ray Stannard, *Following the Color Line, An Account of Negro Citizenship in the American Democracy*, Corner House Publishers, Williamstown, Mass., 1908, 1973.

Bartram, William, *Travels Through North and South Carolina, Georgia, East and West Florida...*, printed by James & Johnson, Philadelphia, 1791; Mark Van Doren ed., 1928.

Bisson, Terry and Davenport, John, *Nat Turner, Slave Revolt Leader*, Infobase Publishing, 2009.

Bleyer, Willard G., *Newspaper Writing and Editing*, Houghton Mifflin Co., Boston, 1913, 1923.

Bloodworth, Bertha E. and Morris, Allen C., *Places in the Sun, The History and Romance of Florida Place-Names*, University Presses of Florida, Gainesville, 1978.

527

Boyer, Paul, and Nissenbaum, Stephen, *Salem Possessed: The Social Origins of Witchcraft*, Harvard University Press, Cambridge Mass, 1974.

Bremmer, J. Douglas, and Marmar, Charles R., *Trauma, Memory and Association*, American Psychiatric Association Press, Washington, D.C., 1998.

Brundage, W. Fitzhugh, *Lynching in the New South: Georgia and Virginia, 1880-1930*, University of Illinois Press, Urbana, 1993.

Brown, Nelson C., *Timber Products and Industries*, John Wiley & Sons, New York, 1917.

Brown, Richard Maxwell, *Strain of Violence, Historical Studies of American Violence and Vigilantism*, Oxford University Press, New York, 1975.

Buchholz, F.W., *History of Alachua County, Narrative and Biographical*, The Record Co., St. Augustine, Fla., 1929.

Bushnell, Amy, *Situada y Sabana, Spain's Support System for the Presidio and Mission Provinces*, Anthropology Papers of the American Museum of Natural History, No. 74, University of Georgia Press, Athens, 1994.

Cahn, E. J., *The World According to Swope, A Biography of Herbert Bayard Swope*, Simon and Schuster, NY, 1965.

Carnes, Mark C., *Secret Ritual and Manhood in Victorian America*, Yale University Press, New Haven, 1989.

Cash, W. J., *The Mind of the South*, Vintage Books, New York, 1941, 1991.

Cash, William T., *The Story of Florida*, The American Historical Society Inc., New York, 1936.

Chalmers, David Mark, *Hooded Americanism, The First Century of the Ku Klux Klan, 1865-1965*, Doubleday, Garden City, N.J., 1965; Duke University Press, 1981.

Clark, Christopher, *The Sleepwalkers: How Europe Went to War in 1914*, HarperCollins, New York, 2013.

Clinchy, Everett Ross, *All in the Name of God*, The John Day Co., New York, 1934.

Cockrell, Dale, *Demons of Disorder, Early Blackface Minstrels and Their World*, Cambridge University Press, Cambridge, U.K., New York, 1997.

Cooper, Dennis R., *The People Machine*, General Telephone Company of Florida, Tampa, 1971 (PKYL).

Conant, Luther, *The Lumber Industry*, United States Bureau of Corporations, U.S. Government Printing Office, 1914.

Courtwright, David T., *Violent Land, Single Men and Social Disorder from the Frontier to the Inner City*, Harvard University Press, Cambridge, 1996.

Crooks, James B., *Jacksonville After the Fire, 1901-1919, A New South City*, University of North Florida Press, Jacksonville, Fla., 1991.

Cutler, James Elbert, *Lynch-Law, An Investigation Into the History of Lynching in the United States*, Negro University Press, New York, 1905, 1969.

Daniel, Pete, *The Shadow of Slavery, Peonage in the South, 1901-1969*, University of Illinois Press, Urbana, 1972.

David-Menard, Monique, *Hysteria from Freud to Lacan, Body and Language in Psychoanalysis*, Cornell University Press, Ithaca, 1989.

Davidson, James W., Lytle, Mark H., *After the Fact, The Art of Historical Detection*, Alfred A. Knopf, 1982.

Davis, Jess G.
History of Gainesville, Florida, Biographical sketches of families, typescript, 1966, University of Florida Digital Collection.

History of Alachua County, Board of Commissioners, Alachua County, Gainesville, Fla., P. K. Yonge Library of Florida History, University of Florida.

Day, P. H., *Destination Cedar Key*, "as told to and written by Jennie Stevens," 2002 (Cedar Key Historical Society Museum).

Dees, Jesse Walter, Jr. and Vivian Flannery Dees. *Off the Beaten Path: The History of Cedar Key, Florida, 1843-1990*. Rife Publishing, Chiefland, Fla., 1990.

Detwiler, Frederick German, *The Negro Press in the United States*, University of Chicago Press, 1922.

Dinnerstein, Leonard, *The Leo Frank Case*, University of Georgia Press, Athens, 1968, 1990.

Dodd, Jean Hall, *Arthur Gerrish Cummer*, Cummer Museum of Art and Gardens, Jacksonville, Fla., 1996.

Dollard, John; Miller, Neal E.; Doob, Leonard; Mowrer, O.H.; and Sears, Robert R., *Frustration and Aggression*, Yale University Press, New Haven, 1939.

D'Orso, Michael, *Like Judgment Day, The Ruin and Redemption of a Town Called Rosewood*, G. P. Putnam's Sons, New York, 1996.

Dorson, Richard M. *America in Legend, Folklore from the Colonial Period to the Present*, Parthenon Books, New York, 1973.

Douglas, Marjorie Stoneman, *Florida, The Long Frontier*, Harper & Row, New York, 1967.

Ellis, Edward Robb, *Echoes of Distant Thunder, Life in the United States 1914-1918*, Coward McCann & Geoghegan Inc., New York, 1975.

Ellsworth, Scott, *Death in a Promised Land, The Tulsa Race Riot of 1921*, Louisiana State University Press, Baton Rouge, 1982.

Bibliography

Emerson, Ken, *DOO-DAH! Stephen Foster and the Rise of American Popular Culture*, Da Capo Press, New York, 1998,

Evans, Harold ed., *The American Century*, Knopf, New York, 1998.

Ewen, David, *History of Popular Music*, Barnes & Noble Inc., New York, 1961.

Fay, Bernard, *Revolution and Freemasonry, 1680-1800*, Little, Brown & Co., Boston, 1935.

Fairclough, Adam, *Race & Democracy, The Civil Rights Struggle in Louisiana 1915-1972*, University of Georgia Press, Athens, 1995.

Federal Writers Project, *Florida: A Guide to the Southern-Most State* ("The Florida Guide"), U.S. History Publishers, 1939

Feldman, Glenn, *Politics, Society, and the Klan in Alabama, 1915–1949*, University of Alabama Press, Tuscaloosa, Ala., 1999.

Fickle, James E., *Mississippi Forests and Forestry*, University Press of Mississippi, Jackson, 2001.

Fielding, Raymond, *The American News Reel, 1911-1967*, University of Oklahoma Press, Norman, 1972.

Fischer, David N., *Albion's Seed, Four British Folkways in America*, Oxford University Press, New York, 1989.

Fishburne, Charles C., Jr.
A History of the Cedar Keys to 1900, Cedar Key Historical Society, Cedar Key, Fla., 1972.
The Cedar Keys in the 19th Century, Seahawk Publications, Quincy, Fla., 1983.

Flynt, J. Wayne, *Cracker Messiah, Governor Sidney J. Catts of Florida*, Louisiana State University Press, Baton Rouge, 1977.

Frasca, John, *The Mulberry Tree*, Prentice-Hall, Englewood Cliffs, N.J., 1968.

Fraser, Walter J., *Charleston! Charleston!, The History of a Southern City*, University of South Carolina Press, Columbia, 1989

Fromkin, David, *Europe's Last Summer, Who Started the Great War in 1914?*, Alfred A. Knopf, New York, 2004.

Gannon, Michael,
Florida, A Short History, University Press of Florida, Gainesville, Fla., 1993.
(ed.), *The New History of Florida*, University Press of Florida, Gainesville, Fla., 1996.

Gerlach, Larry R., *Blazing Crosses in Zion*, Utah State University Press, Logan, Utah, 1928.

Gilje, Paul A., *The Road to Mobocracy, Popular Disorder in New York City, 1763-1834*, University of North Carolina Press, 1987.

Gold, Daniel Pleasant, *History of Duval County, Florida*, The Record Co., St. Augustine, Fla., 1928.

Graham, Hugh Davis, and Gurr, Ted, *Violence in America Historical and Comparative Perspectives*, National Commission on the Causes and Prevention of Violence, 1969.

Gramling, Oliver, *AP, The Story of News*, Farrar and Rinehart, Inc., 1940.

Green, Charlotte Hinton, *Birds of the South*, University of North Carolina Press, Chapel Hill, 1933.

Gunnell, S. E. ed., *Search for Yesterday, A History of Levy County, Florida*, Levy County Archives Committee, published serially, 1977-2000.

Handy, W. C., *Father of the Blues, An Autobiography*, Da Capo Press Inc., New York, 1941, 1969.

Harper, Kimberly, *White Man's Heaven: The Lynching and Expulsion of Blacks in the Southern Ozarks, 1894-1909*, University of Arkansas Press, 2010.

Bibliography

Harrison, Alferdteen ed., *Black Exodus, The Great Migration from the American South*, University Press of Mississippi, Jackson, 1991.

Heaps, Willard A., *Riots, U.S.A. 1765-1970*, The Seabury Press, New York, 1970.

Hedges, Chris, *War Is a Force That Gives Us Meaning*, Public Affairs, New York, 2002.

Hickman, Louise, *Ocali Country, Kingdom of the Sun, A History of Marion County, Florida*, Part Two, Marion Publishers, Ocala, Florida, 1966

Horowitz, Donald L., *The Deadly Ethnic Riot*, University of California at Berkeley Press, Berkeley, 2001.

Howard, Kennie L., *Yesterday in Florida*, Carleton Press Inc., New York 1970.

Howell, Arthur H., *Florida Bird Life*, Florida Dept. of Game and Freshwater Fish, Tallahassee, 1932.

Hurston, Zora Neale
    Jonah's Gourd Vine, J. B. Lippincott Co., Philadelphia, 1934;
    Mules and Men, J. B. Lippincott Co., Philadelphia, 1935;
    Their Eyes Were Watching God, J. B. Lippincott Co., Philadelphia, 1937;
    Dust Tracks on a Road, An Autobiography, J. B. Lippincott Co., Philadelphia, 1942.
    I Love Myself Whey I Am Laughing...And Then Again When I Am Looking Mean and Impressive: A Zora Neale Hurston Reader, Feminist Press at CUNY, New York, 1979.

Hutchinson, Earl Ofari, *Betrayal, A History of Presidential Failure to Protect Black Lives*, Westview Press, Boulder, Colo., 1997.

Jackson, Kenneth T., *The Ku Klux Klan in the City, 1915-1930*, Oxford University Press, New York, 1967.

Jahoda, Gloria, *The Other Florida*, Charles Scribner's Sons, New York, 1967.

Janet, Pierre, *The Major Symptoms of Hysteria,* Hafner Publishing Co., New York, 1907, 1965

Jaspin, Elliot, *Buried in the Bitter Waters: The Hidden History of Racial Cleansing in America* (Basic Books, New York, 2008.

Johannes, Jan H., *Yesterday's Reflections, Nassau County, Florida,* Florida Sun Publishing Co., Callahan, Fla., 1976.

Johnson, Eldrie Lee Cozine et al, *Our Boley,* Vol. I, Dawn Publishing Co., Boley, Okla., 1984.

Johnson, James Weldon, *Along This Way, The Autobiography of James Weldon Johnson,* Viking Press, New York, 1933, 1961.

Kennedy, N. Brent, and Kennedy, Robyn Vaughan, *The Melungeons, The Resurrection of a Proud People,* Mercer University Press, Macon, Ga., 1994.

LeShan, Lawrence, *The Psychology of War, Comprehending its Mystique and its Madness,* Helios Press, New York, 1992, 2002.

Loewen, James W., *Sundown Towns: A Hidden Dimension of American Racism,* The New Press, 2005.

Luther, Frank, *Americans and Their Songs,* Harper and Brothers, New York, 1942.

Loftus, E.F. & Ketcham, Katherine, *The Myth of Repressed Memory: False Memories and Allegations of Sexual Abuse,* St. Martin's Press, New York, 1994.

Louisiana Wildlife and Fisheries Commission, *Louisiana Birds,* Baton Rouge, 1955.

Longstreet, Rupert J., *Birds in Florida,* Trend House, Tampa, Fla., 1969.

Lowes, John Livingston, *The Road to Xanadu, A Study in the Ways of the Imagination,* Houghton Mifflin Co., Boston, 1927.

Malone, Bill C., *Southern Music, American Music,* University Press of Kentucky, Lexington, 1979.

May, Ellis C.,

'Gators, Skeeters, and Malary, Recollections of a Pioneer Florida Judge, Vol. I, Vantage Press, New York, 1953.

From Dawn to Sunset, Recollections of a Pioneer Florida Judge, Vol. II, Florida Grower Press, Tampa, Fla., 1955.

McCarthy, Kevin M.
  Black Florida, Hippocrene Books, New York, 1995;
  Cedar Key, Florida: A History, The History Press, Charleston, S.C., 2007.

McGovern, James R., *Anatomy of a Lynching: The Killing of Claude Neal*, LSU Press, Baton Rouge, 1982.

McPhail, Clark, *The Myth of the Madding Crowd*, Aldine de Gruyter, New York, 1991.

McWhiney, Grady, *Cracker Culture, Celtic Ways in the Old South*, University of Alabama Press, Tuscaloosa, 1988.

Milanich, Jerald T., *Florida Indians and the Invasion from Europe*, University Press of Florida, Gainesville, 1995.

Monaco, C. S., *Moses Levy of Florida: Jewish Utopian and Antebellum Reformer*, Louisiana State University Press, Baton Rouge, 2005.

Monteval, Marion, *The Klan Inside Out*, Negro Universities Press, 1924

Morneweck, Evelyn, *Chronicles of Stephen Foster's Family*, Kennikat Press, New York, 1973.

Morris, Allen
  Florida Place Names, University of Miami Press, Coral Gables, 1974.
  The Language and Lore of Lawmaking in Florida, Office of the Clerk, Florida House of Representatives, Tallahassee, 1979.

Muraskin, William A., *Middle-Class Blacks in a White Society: Prince Hall Freemasonry in America*, University Press of California, Berkeley, 1975.

NAACP, *Thirty Years of Lynching in the United States 1889-1918*, Negro University Press, New York, 1919, 1969.

Newman, Katherine S., *Rampage, The Social Roots of School Shootings*, Basic Books, New York, 2004.

Newton, Michael, *The Invisible Empire: The Ku Klux Klan in Florida*, University Press of Florida, Gainesville, Fla., 2001.

Oates, Stephen B., *The Fires of Jubilee, Nat Turner's Fierce Rebellion*, Harper & Row, New York, 1976.

Ofshe, Richard, Walters, Ethan, *Making Monsters: False Memories, Psychotherapy and Sexual Hysteria*, University of California Press, Berkeley, 1994.

Okihiro, Gary Y., ed., *In Resistance, Studies in African, Caribbean and Afro-American History*, University of Massachusetts Press, Amherst, 1986.

Oppel, Fran, and Meisel, Tony eds., *Tales of Florida*, Castle, Seacaucus, N.J., 1987.

Osterweis, Rollin G., *The Myth of the Lost Cause, 1865-1900*, Archon Books, Camden, Ct., 1973.

O'Sullivan, Maurice, and Lane, Jack, eds., *Florida Reader: Visions of Paradise*, Pineapple Press, 1994

Ottley, Roi, *The Lonely Warrior, The Life and Times of Robert S. Abbott*, Henry Regnery Co., Chicago, 1955.

Outland, Robert B. *Tapping the Pines: The Naval Stores Industry in the American South*, LSU Press, Baton Rouge, 2004.

Pickard, Ben, and Morrison, Sally, *Dudley Farm: A History of Florida Farm Life*, Alachua Press, Gainesville, Fla., 2003.

Pickard, John B., *Florida's Eden: An Illustrated History of Alachua County*, Maupin House, Gainesville, Fla., 1994.

Pember, Don R., *Mass Media in America*, Science Research Associates, Chicago, 1974, 1987.

Powell, John C., *The American Siberia, Fourteen Years Experience in a Southern Convict Camp*, M J. Smith & Co., Chicago, 1891.

Polk, Noel ed., *Outside the Southern Myth*, University Press of Mississippi, Jackson, 1997.

Powdermaker, Hortense, *After Freedom, A Culture Study in the Deep South*, Russell & Russell, New York, 1968.

Prince, Richard E., *Seaboard Air Line Railway: Steam Boats, Locomotives, and History*, Indiana University Press, 1969, pp. 101-102.

Pugh, M. D., *Collective Behavior, A Source Book*, West Publishing Co., New York, 1980.

Purkiss, Dianne, *The Witch in History, Early Modern and Twentieth Century Representatives*, Routledge, London, 1996.

Quinn, Jane, *Minorcans in Florida*, Their History and Heritage, Mission Press, St. Augustine, Fla., 1975.

Raper, Arthur, *The Tragedy of Lynching*, University of North Carolina Press, Chapel Hill, 1933.

Reinhardt, Richard, *Workin' on the Railroad: Reminiscences from the Age of Steam*, American West Publishing Co., Palo Alto, CA; University of Oklahoma Press, Norman, 2003.

Rerick, Rowland H., *Memoirs of Florida, Embracing a General History of the Province, Territory and State*, Vol. II, The Southern Historical Association, Atlanta, 1902.

Robinson, John R., *Born in Blood, The Lost Secrets of Freemasonry*, M. Evans & Co., New York, 1989.

Romans, Bernard, *A Concise Natural History of East and West Florida*, University of Florida Press, Gainesville, 1962.

Rudwick, Elliott M., *Race Riot at East St. Louis July 2, 1917*, Southern Illinois University Press, Carbondale, 1964.

Sade, Stanley, *The New Grove Dictionary of Music and Musicians*, Vol. 6, MacMillan Publishers Ltd., London, 1980.

Schall, Peter, *Sanford As I Knew It 1912-1935*, self-published, Orlando, Fla., 1970.

Schultz, Duane P., *Panic Behavior, Discussion and Readings*, Random House, New York, 1964.

Schwartz, Bennett L., *Memory, Foundations and Applications*, Sage Publications, Thousand Oaks, Ca., 2014.

Seneschal, Roberta, *The Sociogenesis of a Race Riot, Springfield, Illinois, in 1908*, University of Illinois Press, Urbana, 1990.

Shirer, William L., *20th Century Journey, A Memoir of a Life and Times, The Start 1904-1930*, Bantam Books, New York, 1985.

Shorter, Edward, *From Paralysis to Fatigue, A History of Psychosomatic Illness in the Modern Era*, The Free Press, 1992.

Siegel, Ronald K., *Fire in the Brain, Clinical Tales of Hallucination*, Dutton, New York, 1992.

Slavney, Phillip R., *Perspectives on "Hysteria,"* Johns Hopkins University Press, Baltimore, 1990.

Smelser, Neil J., *Theory of Collective Behavior*, Free Press, Glencoe, Ill., 1962.

Southern Biographical Association, *Men of the South*, New Orleans, 1922.

Spaeth, Sigmund, *A History of Popular Music in America*, Random House, New York, 1948.

Spiegel, Herbert and Spiegel, David, *Trance and Treatment, Clinical Uses of Hypnosis*, Basic Books, New York, 1978.

Stampp, Kenneth M., *The Peculiar Institution, Slavery in the Ante-Bellum South*, Alfred A. Knopf, New York, 1956.

Staub, Ervin, *The Roots of Evil: The Origins of Genocide and Other Group Violence*, Cambridge University Press, 1989.

Steele, Ronald, *Walter Lippmann and the American Century*, Atlantic Monthly Press, Little Brown and Co. Boston, 1980.

Stern, Jessica, *Terror in the Name of God, Why Religious Militants Kill*, HarperCollins, New York, 2003.

Stone, Melville, *Fifty Years a Journalist*, Doubleday, Page and Co., New York, 1921.

Strachan, Hew, *The First World War*, Viking, Penguin Group, New York, 2004.

Swanberg, W. A., *Citizen Hearst*, Charles Scribner's Sons, New York, 1961.

Swanton, John R., *Early History of the Creek Indians and Their Neighbors*, Smithsonian Institution, Bureau of Ethnology, U.S. Government Printing Office, Washington, D.C., 1922

Tasker, John, *Stephen Foster, America's Troubadour*, Tudor Publishing Co., New York, 1945.

Tindall, George B., *The Emergence of the New South, 1913-1945*, Louisiana State University Press, Baton Rouge, 1967.

Tolnay, Stewart, Beck, E. M., *A Festival of Violence: An Analysis of Southern Lynchings, 1882-1930*, University of Illinois Press, Urbana and Chicago, 1995.

Trevor-Roper, H.R., *The European Witch-Craze of the Sixteenth and Seventeenth Centuries and Other Essays*, Harper and Row, 1956, 1967.

Turner, Ralph H., and Killian, Lewis M., *Collective Behavior*, Prentice-Hall, Englewood Cliffs, N. J., 1957, 1972, 1987, 1993.

Tuttle, William M., *Race Riot, Chicago in the Red Summer of 1919*, Atheneum, New York, 1970.

U.S. War Department, *The War of the Rebellion, A Compilation of the Official Records of the Union and Confederate Armies*, Series 1, Vol. 49, Part I, Government Printing Office, Washington, D.C., 1897.

Uttley, Francis Lee, Bloom, Lynn Z., and Kinney, Arthur F. eds., *Eight Approaches to William Faulkner's "The Bear,"* Random House, New York, 1964, 1971.

Verrill, Ruth, *Romantic and Historic Levy County*, Storter Printing Co, Gainesville, 1976.

Villard, Oswald Garrison, *The Disappearing Daily: Chapters in American Newspaper Evolution*, Alfred A. Knopf, New York, 1944.

Wade, Wyn Craig, *The Fiery Cross: The Ku Klux Klan in America*, Oxford University Press, New York, 1996.

Weigall, T. H., *Boom in Paradise*, A. H. King, New York, 1932.

White, Walter, *A Man Called White, The Autobiography of Walter White*, Viking Press, New York, 1948.

Wilbanks, William, *Forgotten Heroes: Police Officers Killed in Early Florida, 1840-1945*, Turner Publishing Company, 1998.

Williams, Loretta J., *Black Freemasonry and Middle Class Realities*, University of Missouri Press, Columbia, 1980.

Wilson, Charles R. and Ferris, William, *Encyclopedia of Southern Culture*, University of North Carolina Press, Chapel Hill, 1989.

Wilson, Charles Reagan and Ray, Celeste eds., *The New Encyclopedia of Southern Culture: Vol. 6, Ethnicity*, UNC Press Books, Chapel Hill, 2007.

Wright, Gavin, *Old South, New South, Revolution in the Southern Economy After the Civil War*, Basic Books Inc., New York, 1986.

Wright, James Leitch, *Creeks & Seminoles: The Destruction and Regeneration of the Muscogulge People*, University of Nebraska Press, 1990.

Wright, Bishop R. R., Jr., *The Encyclopedia of the African Methodist Episcopal Church*, 2nd ed., published by the Book Concern of the AME Church, Philadelphia, 1947.

Woodward, C. Vann

    Tom Watson, Agrarian Rebel, MacMillan Co., New York, 1938;

    The Strange Career of Jim Crow, Oxford University Press, New York, 1966.

Wyatt-Brown, Bertram, *Southern Honor, Ethics and Behavior in the Old South*, Oxford University Press, New York, 1982.

Journal Articles, Dissertations, Reports

Benford, Robert D, "Dramaturgy and Social Movements: The Social Construction and Communication of Power," *Sociological Inquiry*, Winter 1992, p. 36.

Carper, N. Gordon

    The Convict Lease System in Florida, 1866-1923, dissertation, Florida State University, Tallahassee, 1964;

    "Martin Tabert, Martyr of an Era," *Florida Historical Quarterly*, Oct. 1973, p. 115.

DeSantis, Alan D. "A Forgotten Leader: Robert S. Abbott and the *Chicago Defender* from 1910-1920." *Journalism History*, Vol. 23, No. 2, Spring 1997, 63-71.

Dabbs, Lester, "A Report of the Circumstances and Events of the Race Riot on November 2, 1920 in Ocoee, Florida," thesis, Stetson University, 1969.

Drobney, Jeffrey A., "Where Palm and Pine Are Blowing: Convict Labor in the North Florida Turpentine Industry, 1897-1923," *Florida Historical Quarterly*, Apr. 1994.

Duncan, Hannibal Gerald, *The Changing Race Relationship in the Border and Northern States*, University of Pennsylvania, 1922.

Florida Department of Law Enforcement, *Report to the Florida Legislature, the Florida Department of Law Enforcement Investigation of the Rosewood Violence of 1923*, Tallahassee, Fla., December 23, 1994.

Florida State University System, *A Documented History of the Incident at Rosewood, Florida in January 1923*, Investigative Team: Maxine D. Jones, Larry E. Rivers, David R. Colburn, R. Tom Dye, William W. Rogers, commissioned by the Florida Legislature and submitted to the Florida Board of Regents, Dec. 22, 1993.

Froelich, Jacqueline, and Zimmerman, David, "Total Eclipse: The Destruction of the African American Community of Harrison, Arkansas, in 1905 and 1909," *Arkansas Historical Quarterly*, Summer 1999, p. 131.

Grimshaw, Allen D., *A Study in Social Violence: Urban Race Riots in the United States*, dissertation, University of Pennsylvania, 1959.

Hale, Grace Elizabeth, *Making Whiteness: The Culture of Segregation in the South 1890-1940*, dissertation, Rutgers the State University of New Jersey, New Brunswick, N.J., 1995.

Holmes, William F.
"Whitecapping: Agrarian Violence in Mississippi, 1902-1906," *Journal of Southern History*, Vol. 35, p. 165
"Whitecapping: Anti-Semitism in the Populist Era," *American Jewish Quarterly*, May 1974
"Whitecapping in Georgia: Caroll and Houston Counties," *Georgia Historical Quarterly*, Winter 1980, p. 388.

Jennings, Warren A., "Sidney J. Catts and the Democratic Primary of 1920," *Florida Historical Quarterly*, Jan. 1961, p. 203.

Johnson, Michael, "Denmark Vesey and His Co-Conspirators," *William and Mary Quarterly*, Oct. 2001, p. 915.

Bibliography

Jordan, Winthrop D., "The Charleston Hurricane of 1922; Or, the Law's Rampage," *William and Mary Quarterly*, Jan. 2002, p. 175.

Morgan. Philip D., "Conspiracy Scares," *William and Mary Quarterly*, Jan. 2002, p. 159.

NAACP, *Papers of the NAACP, Special Subject Files, 1912-1939*, UPA microform, University Publications of America, Bethesda, Md.

Paisley, Clifton, "Wade Leonard, Florida Naval Scores Operator," *Florida Historical Quarterly*, Apr. 1973, p. 381.

Pease, John H., and Pease, William, "The Blood-Thirsty Tiger: Charleston and the Psychology of Fire," *South Carolina Historical Magazine*, 79, Oct. 1978, p. 281.

Prescott, Stephen R., "White Robes and Crosses: Father John Conoley, The Ku Klux Klan, and the University of Florida," *Florida Historical Quarterly*, Vol. 71, No. 1, July 1992.

Ripley, C. Peter, "Intervention and Reaction: Florida Newspapers and United States Entry into World War I," *Florida Historical Quarterly*, Jan. 1971, p. 255.

Rogers, O. A., Jr., "The Elaine Race Riots of 1919," *Arkansas Historical Quarterly*, Summer 1960, p. 142.

Shofner, Jerrell H.
"Florida and the Black Migration," *Florida Historical Quarterly*, Jan. 1979, p. 267;
"Judge Herbert Rider and the Lynching at LaBelle," *Florida Historical Quarterly*, Jan. 1981, p. 292.

U.S. House of Representatives, *The Ku-Klux Klan: Hearing Before the Committee on Rules, House of Representatives, Sixty-Seventh Congress*, U.S. Government Printing Office, 1921.

Weitz, Seth A., *Bourbon, Pork Chops, and Red Peppers: Political Immorality in Florida, 1945-1968*, Florida State University, dissertation, 2007, Electronic Paper 1195.

Wolf, Charlotte, "Construction of a Lynching," *Sociological Inquiry*, Winter 1992, p. 83.

Zarur, George L., *Seafood Gatherers in Mullet Springs: Economic Rationality and the Social System*, dissertation, University of Florida, 1975.

Oral History Projects

American Life Histories, Federal Writers' Project 1936-1940
    Interview of W. G. Leonard, by Glenn H. Lathrop, Spokane, Wa., Forest History Society, Durham, N.C.;
    Interview of Marc L. Fleishel, by Elwood R. Maunder, April 4, 1960;
    Interview of Earl Porter, by Elwood R. Maunder, Feb. 7, 1964.

Forest History Today, "Memoirs of Martin Hoban, Logging Florida's Giant Cypress," by Bayard Kendrick and Barry Walsh, Spring/Fall 2007, p. 47.

Jacksonville Bar Association, Jacksonville, Fla., Interviews of Judge Warren L. Jones, by U.S. District Judge Gerald B. Tjoflat (three days) Aug. 15-17, 1989.

Livestock Weekly, "Gilbert Tucker Shares Stories Of Early Days On Florida Ranch," Interview of Gilbert Tucker, by Colleen Schreiber, Mar. 8, 2001.

Matheson Historical Museum Oral History Program, Gainesville, Fla., Interview of James Perry Ramsey, Jr., by Mary Ann Cofrin, Feb 6, 2003 (UFDC).

Samuel Proctor Oral History Program, University of Florida
    Interview of William N. Barry, by Jeff Charbonnet, July 19, 1984, AL 90;
    Interview of Thomas Bryant, by Steve Kerber, Jan. 19, 1980, FP 45 (UFDC).

Interview of Myrtle Dudley, by Lisa Heard, add. Sally Morrison, Feb. 25, 1992, AL 143 (UFDC).

Interview of John Paul Jones, by Ford Risley, Feb. 20, 1993, UF227 (UFDC) [also interviewed by author, 1994].

Collections

Alachua County Historic Trust: Matheson Museum, Inc., Gainesville, Fla.

Carrie Meek-James N. Eaton, Sr. Southeastern Regional Black Archives Research Center and Museum, Florida A&M University, Tallahassee, Fla.

Hagley Museum and Library, Wilmington, Del.

Levy County Circuit Clerk's Office, Bronson, Fla.

P. K. Yonge Library of Florida History, George Smathers Library, University of Florida, Gainesville, Fla.

Schomburg Center for Research in Black Culture, New York, NY.

State Archives of Florida, Tallahassee, Fla.

Florida Memory collection of historic Florida photos

State Library of Florida, Tallahassee, Fla.

The Seven Days *(day-by-day summary)*

[End of Day-by-Day Summary]

Topics and Names

Notes

Introduction

[1] The Rosewood re-examination process has been cited as having helped inspire the efforts of the Tulsa Race Riot Commission, 1997-2001 (report Feb. 28, 2001, investigating 1921 events in Oklahoma), the Wilmington Race Riot Commission, 2000-2006 (report May 31, 2006, investigating 1898 events in North Carolina) and the Elaine scholars' colloquium of 2000 (*Arkansas Review*, Aug. 2001, reviewing 1919 events in Arkansas).

[2] "[W]itness testimony presents the investigator with a kind of three-dimensional chess, in which each bit of evidence sheds light on many other bits. To collate the kaleidoscope of fragments, returning to the witnesses with more enlightened questions, has been a work of years, during which I also worked as an investigative reporter in Central America, interviewing survivors at remote massacre sites, which provided insights relevant to Rosewood." (*Synopsis of Research, The Destruction of Rosewood, Florida*, by Gary Moore, presented in academic team report to the Florida Legislature, Dec. 1993, pp. 417-418, Appendices, Attorney General's Rosewood File, Curington files, Vol. 30).

[3] The Rosewood claims case was conceived and begun in 1991 by tabloid television promoter Michael McCarthy, who optioned two Rosewood survivors and sought backing, unsuccessfully, from the Southern Poverty Law Center and the NAACP. McCarthy then turned to the pro bono office of Holland and Knight, the largest law firm in Florida, whose partner for pro bono cases, Stephen Hanlon, successfully took the groundbreaking case to a $1.2 million award by the Florida Legislature in 1994, after the claimant pool was expanded to include all Rosewood survivors then living, and the original promoter was no longer in the process, amid controversies over false statements.

[4] See Thucydides, ca. 400 B.C.: "My conclusions have cost me some labor from the want of coincidence between accounts of the same occurrences by different eyewitnesses, arising sometimes from imperfect memory, sometimes from undue partiality for one side or the other." (quoted by Alice M. Hoffman, "Reliability and Validity in Oral History: The Case for Memory," *Today's Speech*, Vol. 22, Issue 1, 1974; Hoffman also quotes Cornelius Ryan, author of *The Longest Day*, who said he conducted six thousand interviews on the 1944 D-Day invasion, but "discovered that interviewing is not reliable...unless it can be substantiated by documents supporting the testimony.").

Chapter 1: Lay of the Land

[5] Sarah Carrier was presented by the 1997 motion picture *Rosewood* as a heroine without complications, obscuring a complex personality described by family members and neighbors. *Informants:* L. Carrier, M. Langley, E. Blocker, L. Davis, L. Foster.

[6] World War I Service Cards (SAF-FMP): George Goins inducted Mayo, Fla., June 21, 1918, overseas service Aug. 26, 1918-July 30, 1919; Soldiers and Sailors Discharge Record (Book 1 p. 72, LCCH). Aaron Carrier's Service Record has been posted online in the Florida Memory photo collection of the State Archives of Florida. *Informants:* B. Frazier, M. Langley, S. Hall, P. Doctor, A. Goins, V. Hamilton, L. Carrol

[7] *Informants*: (who were adopted): L. Carrier, E. Davis, T. Hawkins, W. Evans, L. Carrol, A. Goins, M. Langley. Other informants: S. Hall, M. Johnson, L. Harris, L. Washington, V. Hamilton, L. Davis. 1920 Federal Census. Sarah and Emma Lewis, born around 1872 and 1869, had been adopted by 1880 by a family named Robinson, then in 1887 and 1886 married two brothers, Haywood and James Carrier. By middle age, leading up to 1923, Sarah Carrier and Emma Carrier both were raising grandchildren, the adoptive grandparents in both cases called Mama and Papa.

[8] A lifetime later, Arnett Goins and Minnie Langley would both remember the childhood jousts, though in different ways.

[9] *Informant*: L. Foster (daughter of Rosewood midwife Mary Ella McCoy). Cobwebs were commonly used anti-hemmorhagics in pre-1923 Rosewood. Minnie Langley recalled a visit from the iceman's truck from Sumner, where a sawmill generator ran an ice machine; as the iceman sawed off a block at his tailgate in front of her house, she snatched too closely at bits of ice flying off the saw. As she screamed, her grandmother rushed out of the house with cobwebs to staunch the bleeding of the finger.

[10] A difference on Sylvester Carrier's birth date appears between his World War I draft card, signed in 1917 and saying he was born September 7, 1892, and the 1900 Federal Census, which listed birth dates and said he was born in September 1889. Context information, including the censuses of 1910 and 1920, suggests that the 1889 birth date is correct, putting his age at the time of the 1923 events at 33. Acquaintances said he seemed to be in his thirties. If the draft card shaved three years off his real age, the reason is left to speculation.

[11] Dec. 27, 1899, sale by J. C. and M. J. Carson of one-half acre to H. J. and Sarah Carrier (Book 5, p. 212, LCCH).

[12] "Florida became a haven for Confederate deserters and those avoiding conscription." ("Battle of Olustee," Fla. Dept. of Environmental Protection, Olustee Battlefield Historic State Park Citizen Support Organization). "[A] malaria-cursed desert, a barren wilderness swarming with poisonous snakes and repulsive reptiles." (*Oranges and Alligators*, by Iza Hardy Ward and Downey, 1887, p. 83; Hardy added that such a doomsday picture was overblown). "[F]ar, very far, from corroborating the flowery sayings..."—John James Audubon, 1867 ("The River Returns, Stories of the Great St. Johns," Florida Memory Project, SAF). "A land of swamps..."—Sen. John Randolph, 1841 (*Touched by the Sun*, by Stuart B. McIver, Pineapple Press, 2008, p. 167).

[13] "One story and a jump"—*Dust Tracks on a Road, An Autobiography*, by Zora Neale Hurston, J. B. Lippincott Co. Philadelphia, 1942, p. 27. The term's reach is suggested by a retrospective on isolated Southampton County, Virginia, at the time of its landmark event, the 1831 Nat Turner slave rebellion: "Many whites occupied low-slung, wood-frame dwellings known as 'a story and a jump'" ("Untrue Confessions," by Tony Horowitz, *The New Yorker*, Dec. 13, 1999).

[14] *Informants:* L. Carrier, A. Goins, P. Doctor, M. Langley, L. Davis, S. Hall, F. Smith. "The Florida Cracker Vernacular Architectural Aesthetic," by Joshua Berry, Academia, p. 12: "Occasionally, additional rooms would be added directly behind the existing rooms on the first floor" in the "piecemeal fashion employed by pioneering Crackers."

[15] Historian Scott Ellsworth said of the Tulsa race riot of 1921: "Perhaps the most lasting effects of the riot are the twin oral traditions—one set white and the other black" (*Death in a Promised Land: The Tulsa Race Riot of 1921*, by Scott Ellsworth, Louisiana State University Press, 1992, p. 104).

[16] Sumner Quadrangle, Florida-Levy County, U.S. Geological Survey Map, Department of the Interior, 7.5-Minute Series (Topographic) 1955, 1993. The extent of Rosewood is collated from Levy County property records of land owners considered by survivors to have been living in the Rosewood community (LCCH).

[17] Cornelia Carter, widow of Nebuchadnezzar Carter, Homestead Certificate 13055, 80 acres comprising the west half of the southwest quarter of Section 30, Township 14-S, Range 14-E (LCCH).

[18] Aaron and Mahulda Carrier apparently either did not own their land or had not registered it or paid taxes on it. Witness agreement on the geographical position of their home, however, is further confirmed by its list position in the Federal Census of 1920: "Arion Carrer," Household 115.

[19] Farms beyond Cornelia Carter to the west were owned by whites and not

considered to be inside Rosewood; beyond Aaron Carrier to the east were open fields leading into another community, Wylly. There, the home of Joe Robinson, though he was related to Sarah Carrier, was considered to be in Wylly, and was not within the span of the 1923 Rosewood destruction.

[20] *Informants on house styles:* W. Evans, N. Joyner, B. Frazier, S. Hall, M. Johnson, M. Daniels, L. Carrier, M. Langley, L. Carrier, A. Goins, P. Goins, E. Davis, L. Davis, T. Hawkins, L. Washington.

Chapter 2: The Company Town

[21] Official sunrise Cedar Key, Fla.: Sunset/sunrise and moon data, Astronomical Applications Dept., U.S. Naval Observatory (USNO).

[22] The 1996 book *Like Judgment Day* began with a description of alleged extraordinary weather at Rosewood on the fateful New Year's Day, January 1, 1923. The book's opening page is devoted to a dramatic description of a purported ice storm ("crystals of rime" encasing palm and pine) on what it called "the coldest day anyone could remember." Though presented explicitly as fact, with a lead-in sentence intoning, "This much is known," the passage is fantasy. All witnesses old enough to have adult or adolescent memories agreed with meteorological records on this point: Nothing about the weather that day was extraordinary. Later in the week a cold spell would make temperatures more bitter, though they remained above freezing, with no ice storm. *Like Judgment Day* took as its central narrator Rosewood descendant Arnett Doctor, who was born in 1943 and had no eyewitness experience of Rosewood. As a self-appointed Rosewood spokesman to the media, Doctor announced at one point that Rosewood was made up of "mansions" with "manicured lawns" and at another that thirty women and children were "buried alive" in the Rosewood events (public speech, tape recorded). The statements came during the excitement of the Rosewood claims case in the 1990s, and left lasting confusion about the real nature of the community and its end. On May 23, 1996, the *Los Angeles Times* noted that *Like Judgment Day* "follows Doctor back into Florida history"—though in fact it follows him into his mind. Regarding more recent information on the 1990s claims case, the book is an important source, but on earlier events, and not just in 1923, it contains passages that are dramatized or imagined but are presented as fact. Enthusiasts have cited these as if they represent real history. The mythic version of Rosewood repeatedly reminds of the general way that excitement over racial controversy can suspend even basic evidentiary standards. By portraying a fantasized ice storm as a "known" fact, *Like Judgment Day* provides an introductory storm warning on fantasies later in its text, more seriously distorting the 1923 events.

[23] The Cummer Lumber Company, headed by brothers Arthur and Waldo Cummer and their brother-in-law J. L. Roe, had various corporate branches across Florida, and also conducted business as Cummer Cypress Company. (*Florida Gazetteer and Business Directory 1925*, Sumner, Fla.: "Cummer Cypress Co., A. G. Cummer pres., W. E. Cummer sec-treas.") An older name, sometimes given as Cummer & Sons Cypress Company, dated from Canadian-born patriarch Wellington Cummer, the corporate founder and father of Arthur and Waldo Cummer. Wellington Cummer died on December 25, 1909. Rosewood survivors, including those who received bi-weekly paychecks from the later firm, knew it as "Cummer Lumber."

[24] Capacity of the Sumner sawmill as 60,000 board-feet of lumber per day:
***Predating the Sumner mill in the Rosewood area was the Tilghman Cypress Company mill at Lukens, near Cedar Key, said to cut about 30,000 board-feet per day, and closing in 1918. ("Memoirs of Martin Hoban, Logging Florida's Giant Cypress," by Baynard Kendrick and Barry Walsh, *Forest History Today*, Spring/Fall 2007, p. 47).
***The Cummer sawmill at Lacoochee, replacing Sumner after 1926, was said to have a capacity of 100,000 board-feet per day.
***A larger production area lay in the wilderness counties across the Suwannee River, first in Taylor County, then after 1928 in less populous Dixie County. In Taylor County near the town of Perry were four cypress sawmilling giants. After 1914, the mammoth Burton-Swartz mill was said to have a capacity of 200,000 board-feet per day (1926 Burton-Swartz brochure, Florida Memory, State Archives of Florida, http://www.floridamemory.com/items/show/153293), while capacities of 100,000 board-feet per day were ascribed to each of the other three mills: Weaver-Loughridge, Taylor County Lumber and Standard Lumber. Another 200,000-capacity mill, that of Brooks-Scanlon, would move to Taylor County in the late 1920s.
***In Dixie County after 1919, Putnam Lumber conducted logging but shipped out its logs for remote milling in Jacksonville (at a Cummer facility) until 1928, then opened a new mill in Dixie County that some reports placed at a capacity of 200,000 board-feet per day, though that included pine as well as cypress. This mill was sometimes called the largest cypress sawmill in the world (*Gainesville Sun*, Nov 10, 1982).
***In the overall progression sketched above, the Cummer mill at Sumner can be seen as an intermediate step in a movement into new technology from 1900 to 1930, a process extending across Florida, and leveling most of the state's old-growth cypress by the end of the 1950s.

[25] A rumor-like repetition among hurried Rosewood examiners came to assert that the area's cedar boom ended in 1890. All credible sources and records agree that this was not the case. In matters of communal economic trends like Rosewood's, an error of a few years can cause significant distortion. The 1910 Federal Census found various Rosewood residents still employed at the Charpia

cedar mill, while larger cedar pencil mills at Cedar Key were still operating when hit by a September 1896 Gulf hurricane. (Fishburne, Charles C., *A History of the Cedar Keys to 1900*, Cedar Key Historical Society, Cedar Key, 1972; "Early Cedar Key Days," by "Captain T. R. Hodges," *Tampa Tribune*, February 21, 1954, PKYL).

[26] July 3, 1911, Charpia cedar mill, saws and other equipment sold at auction (LCCH).

[27] "Everybody else had left..."—*Informant:* E. Foster

[28] "More than five thousand acres" of Gulf Hammock—The Federal Writers Project in 1939 classified all the coastal hardwood hammockland between the Suwannee and Withlacoochee rivers in Levy County as comprising 10,000 acres, and called this "Gulf Hammock." However, both local parlance and maps distinguished "Suwannee Hammock" (north of the Seaboard Air Line Railway) from "Gulf Hammock" (the seasonal swampland south of the tracks and abutting Rosewood). "More than five thousand acres" is a rough total resulting from separation of the two. (*Florida: A Guide to the Southern-Most State, by the Federal Writers Project*, Works Projects Administration (The Florida Guide), Oxford University Press, 1939, p. 419).

[29] William S. Yearty, b. July 2, 1877 (typescript memoir, PKYL), said the deer were hunted for market and sold to agent Tom Yearty at Otter Creek, who shipped to the Duval Hotel in Jacksonville. The alleged killing of 1,300 was said to occur over the course of two September-March seasons.

[30] *Informants* on whistle schedule and Sumner: E. Parham, R. Missouri, E. Foster, L. Carrol, S. Hall, F. Smith. M. Thompson, E. Johnson, F. Kirkland, J. Yearty.

[31] Both the beginning point of "Jim Crow" racial segregation and the name itself are open to discussion.
The 1896 *Plessy v. Ferguson* decision in the U.S. Supreme Court, often cited as opening the way for standardized or codified racial segregation throughout the South, was a case begun in 1892 on a state law in Louisiana that was passed in 1890, mandating racially segregated railway passenger cars, known from still earlier times as "Jim Crow cars." This followed a similar state law in Florida in 1887. An oft-repeated statement that the term "Jim Crow law" was not used until 1904 is misleading in that the similar use of "Jim Crow car" as a phrase dates back at least to 1841, occurring in formal segregation of railway coaches in Massachusetts, not long after that state first acquired railroads. The term "Jim Crow" as a label for monolithic southern segregation after the 1890s may have been used more by critics of the system than by its enforcers (who tended to use terms such as "white supremacy"). Much of the confusion over when

segregation really began dates from the Civil Rights Era in the 1950s-1970s, when efforts to dismantle the distorted but entrenched system sought to portray it as being more of a temporary aberration in American culture than the real record may suggest. An earlier group of mainstream historians at the turn of the twentieth century ("the Dunning School") had sought to portray oppressive racial developments in the post-Civil War South in a positive light, while Civil Rights Era history took an opposing view, influenced by more current political trends. Between the two agendas, efforts to look back into the real roots of racial segregation face a prism of differing contentions. In general, Rosewood's many riddles remind of the words of Arnold Toynbee: "Each generation is apt to design its history of the past in accordance with its own ephemeral scheme of thought."

Chapter 3: The Spark

[32] The Tulsa race riot of 1921, unlike Rosewood in that it was an urban event leaving many sources of documentation and a concentrated witness population, was studied for decades by historian Scott Ellsworth and in the late 1990s by an official commission, yet even some fundamental dynamics remained concealed. Mainstream white folklore insisted that the white rioters in 1921 were "poor white trash"—or even Mexicans—while by contrast a black-readership newspaper of the 1920s, the *Chicago Defender*, was so eager to tar the white mainstream for the rioting that it insisted even Boy Scouts were involved. The reality remained successfully screened. Ellsworth would note: "The specific historical evidence on who the white rioters were is far from great." (*Death in a Promised Land: The Tulsa Race Riot of 1921*, by Scott Ellsworth, Louisiana State University Press, 1982, p. 104; *Chicago Defender*, June 13, 1921).

[33] The appearance of the triggering figure in the Rosewood violence was described most concisely by Sumner resident Ernest Parham, though others who knew her seemed to agree. *Informants*: E. Parham, F. Smith, E. Foster, S. Herbert.

[34] *Informants* on the Taylor household and neighborhood: A. Taylor and B. Taylor (the two sons); F. Smith, E. Foster, E. Parham, S. Herbert, E. Johnson, P. Doctor, A. Goins, R. Kirby.

[35] Position of the Taylor house in Sumner. *Informants:* M. Cannon, F. Kirkland, J. Yearty, F. Smith, E. Foster.

[36] Two former neighbors. *Informants:* F. Smith, E. Foster.

[37] Sigmund Freud's diagnostic category, "anxiety neurosis," with its sexual baggage, began to be obviously superseded in the late 1950s, when some forms

of what was then thought to be schizophrenia showed surprising response to drug therapy. Not until 1980 was the entity "panic disorder" added to the official diagnostic manual (DSM-III) of the American Psychiatric Association, specifying two-tiered symptoms: not only disabling momentary panic attacks, but intense secondary anxiety about unexpectedly becoming disabled by such attacks, contributing to avoidance of public places and a confined lifestyle.

[38] "Yes, Fear Can Kill You," by Jeff Wise, *Psychology Today*, Apr. 7, 2010: "People who have suffered panic attacks—and I'm one—know that fear can be so intense that you feel like you're going to die..."

[39] Background on James and Fannie Taylor: Federal Census, 1910, 1920, 1930; marriage record, LCCH. *Informants:* Baylor, A. Taylor, B. Taylor, F. Kirkland, J. McElveen, F. Smith, E. Foster, F. Coburn.

[40] *Informants:* F. Smith, E. Parham, M. Thompson, L. Carrier, R. Missouri.

[41] Frances Smith's story of rescuing Fannie Taylor's baby was described in the present author's original 1982 exposé of the Rosewood secret, with a caveat included, saying that it was only Smith's opinion and could not be confirmed. Various later recaps of Rosewood have used the story in Web-rumor fashion, repeating it as established fact. (*Floridian, St. Petersburg Times*, July 25, 1982).

[42] "housewives in the neighborhood"—*Gainesville Daily Sun*, Jan. 2, 1923. The *Tampa Morning Tribune* used the same wording, apparently in a state wire-service story from the *Sun*. But the *Florida Times-Union* in Jacksonville was more careful, changing the wording enough to weaken the unsupported impression that neighbor women had verified the attacker: "Her screams brought the ladies of the neighborhood to her assistance. In the meantime, the black brute escaped to a nearby hammock."

Chapter 4: The News

[43] *Florida Times-Union*, Jan. 2, 1923, p. 8.

[44] "History of the Telephone Service in Cedar Key," by Elizabeth Hughes Griffis, in *Destination Cedar Key*, P. H. Day, Jennie Stevens, 2002, p. 5 (CKHS).

[45] *The People Machine*, by Dennis R. Cooper, General Telephone Company of Florida, Tampa, 1971, p. 76, PKYL (Bradenton is about 150 miles south of Cedar Key).

Chapter 5: Toil and Trouble

[46] Wages. *Informants:* E. Parham, R. Missouri, J. White, F. Smith, L. Carrier, S. Hall; "Memoirs of Martin Hoban, Logging Florida's Giant Cypress," by Baynard Kendrick and Barry Walsh, *Forestry Today*, Spring/Fall 2007, p. 46.

[47] Pillsbury's clean-up. *Informants*: E. Parham, M. Thompson, F. Smith.

[48] The information on Edith Surls Foster, including birth date, comes from interviews in 1982 and 1983. The small photo of Surls as a young woman is from *Search For Yesterday, A History of Levy County, Florida*, Levy County Archives Committee, 1980, Chapter 9, p. 8.

[49] *Informants* on the Taylor sons: A. Taylor, B. Taylor, F. Smith, E. Surls, S. Herbert, P. Doctor, W. Baylor. In adulthood as an office supply salesman in Jacksonville, Bernice Taylor used the name "Barney," as he confirmed when interviewed in 1982.

[50] The house across the street from the Taylors' original residence continued a verbal pattern of strange clanging or synchronicity that crept through a semi-literate wilderness and through a regimented milltown; at the time of the alarm, both the facing houses at the end of the street were occupied by Taylors, though they were not related. Across the street from James and Fannie was the household of Clint Taylor, whose World War I draft card shows his full name as James Clint Taylor, while Fannie's husband was Henry James Taylor—putting two James Taylors in facing homes. After Clint James had apparently moved on, the remaining Henry James reportedly moved his family over to the departed Clint James's house, and installed bars on the windows. However trivially, Fannie Taylor's home ground seemed filled with word games.

[51] Since cross-racial sexual assault charges formed a major trigger for atrocities in the lynching years, the veracity of such charges and any indications of fakery have been objects of controversy as our own era has looked back. Unfortunately, the urgency of the questions has injected a layer of confusing contradictions and misportrayals into modern retrospectives. As only one example, a key prelude case to the Atlanta race riot of 1906 (an anti-black pogrom or lynching riot),was that of Annie Laurie Poole, a 15-year-old white, whose accusation resulted in the killing of a black stranger whom she identified. Later attempts to exhume the case and examine the veracity of its accusation vary markedly in the concrete details they say were true. At least some of the later examiners seem to be fantasizing, since they can't all be telling the truth at once in opposing versions. The research efforts that would be required to deconflict such narratives are far beyond practicality for the typical interested member of the public, and challenge even specialized investigation. Repeatedly, an atmosphere of excited illusion appears to echo from such cases into supposedly objective modern

analysis.

[52] The second grandchild who came on washday trips with Sarah Carrier was Arnett Goins, who in later years recalled that Sarah's youngest son, adolescent Harry Carrier, sometimes was a third helper.

[53] 1910 Federal Census; *informants*: T. Hawkins, P. Goins, L. Davis, S. Hall.

[54] The animated neon washerwoman icon stood above Long's Laundry at the East Main Street entrance to Tupelo Fairgrounds in Tupelo, Mississippi. Presley played an outdoor stage there at the Mississippi-Alabama Fair and Dairy Show on September 26, 1956.

[55] Mary McLeod Bethune's Daytona Educational and Industrial Training School for Negro Girls was founded in 1904. Its successor is now Bethune-Cookman University in Daytona. Informants on the attendance of Ruby "R. C." Carrier at the school: L. Carrier, P. Doctor, L. Davis, W. Evans. Zora Hurston moved north from Florida first to Howard University in Washington, D.C., then in 1925 to Columbia University's Barnard College in New York. The African American literary, artistic and cultural flowering known as the Harlem Renaissance, also called the New Negro Movement, was associated with New York in the 1920s.

[56] Philomena Doctor's son, Arnett Doctor (b. Jan. 5, 1943), told of first hearing his mother's story on Christmas Day, 1949 (D'Orso, pp. 27-28), when he was five. The memory he described was remarkably detailed for a decades-old impression retained from the age of five, but other Rosewood survivors who had heard Philomena Doctor's story seemed to generally agree that it did emerge in such later years, and not at the time of the events. Arnett Doctor's description of his mother's psychological depression and its severity was consonant with descriptions by others.

[57] In rumors, which became folklore, Fannie Taylor's alleged attacker had many faces. Some who claimed he was really a secret boyfriend said that he was a railroad employee, others said he was a fish peddler. Some said the attacker was really Fannie's husband, who was abusive, they said, and beat her. Some said he was really her father, who went running to Cedar Key after the attack and cried rape. Some said he was really Sarah Carrier's son, but got clean away. One story said he was a crafty white man who put the blame for the attack on a black man who went to pick up his check. Another said he really was black, but the mob thought he was kin to the laundress, who (this story said) was named Bradley. Some said he looked black because he had blacked his face. Some said Sylvester Carrier picked him up in a wagon.
Clearly, many people found Fannie Taylor's attack story to be suspicious, though the majority of local residents, both black and white, seemed to accept

what Fannie said, feeling that it was self-evidently the truth, and that an African American stranger really had broken in and attacked her. The later folklore showed a striking capacity to branch into contradictory explanations without comparing them. By 1993, what might be called a marketability factor had winnowed the many dubious versions back down to one that could be promoted publicly, with the greatest audience appeal. Mass media began to repeat that chosen story—which was the one about the secret white boyfriend—as if it were the only version that had ever been told. This story-of-greatest-appeal then took a next leap into a Special Master's hearing in the Florida Legislature in February-March 1994, and was endorsed there as if it were proven truth.

[58] Email correspondence Sept. 23, 2013. Former Peace Corps instructor David Fleischer, now a university professor, provided a persuasively detailed description of the Cedar Key encounter with the Rosewood mystery in the fall of 1967. Other sources recalled it more vaguely.

[59] George Zarur, Ph.D., oral history interview, Feb. 18, 1975, by John K. Mahon, University of Florida, tape recording in possession of author. Zarur conducted field research in Cedar Key in March-August 1974.

[60] *To Kill a Mockingbird*, the novel by Harper Lee, was published in 1960, received a Pulitzer Prize in 1961 and in 1962 was made into a widely seen motion picture starring Gregory Peck (characters Mayella Ewell and her abusive father lie about an attack by a black man). *In the Heat of the Night*, a 1965 novel by John Ball, became a similarly popular motion picture in 1967, starring Sidney Poitier and Rod Steiger, and was so influential that the television spin-off series ran for years. (Here, as in *To Kill a Mockingbird*, the abusive rural white father, Lloyd Purdy, is satisfyingly sacrificed to violent death in the plot). Sidney Poitier's famous line, "They call me *Mister* Tibbs," became national lore, while *To Kill a Mockingbird* has seen enduring use as a classroom teaching tool.

[61] "The Ominous Numinous, Sensed Presence and 'Other' Hallucinations," by J. Allan Cheyne, *Journal of Consciousness Studies,* 8, No. 5-7, 2001. "A Case of Sleep Paralysis with Hypnopompic Hallucinations," by David E. McCarty, M.D. and Andrew L. Chesson, Jr., M.D., *Journal of Clinical Sleep Medicine,* Feb. 15, 2009; 5(1), pp. 83–84. "The frequency and correlates of sleep paralysis in a university sample," by N. P. Spanos, C. DuBreuil, S.A. McNulta, et al., *Journal of Research in Personality,* 1995, 29, pp. 285–305. "Factors related to the occurrence of isolated sleep paralysis elicited during a multiphasic sleep-wake schedule," by T. Takeuchi, K. Fukada, Y. Sasaki, et al. *Sleep,* 2002: 25, pp. 89-96.

[62] The Web is laced with discussions of sleep paralysis and its folk names in various cultures. One summary refers to terminology from Turkey, Vietnam,

Hungary and elsewhere. ("Ridden by the Hag, My Sleep Paralysis Visitors," by Jenah Shaw, 2013).

[63] A first-person account, told by a psychologist and showing parallels between sleep paralysis hallucination and Fannie Taylor's attack story, can be found in *Fire in the Brain, Clinical Tales of Hallucination*, by Robert K. Siegel, Penguin Books, 1992: Chapter 5: "The Succubus."

[64] An extensive list of nations and their local terms for "traditional nocturnal pressing spirit attacks" can be found on page 14 of *Sleep Paralysis: Nightmares, Nocebos, and the Mind-body Connection*, by Shelley R. Adler, Rutgers University Press, 2011.

[65] *Following the Color Line, An Account of Negro Citizenship in the American Democracy*, by Ray Stannard Baker, Corner House Publishers, Williamstown, Mass., 1908, 1973. This subject—that of real or phantom cross-racial sexual attacks—is far from being solid ground, even in Baker's investigation. There were details in his original magazine reports on Atlanta, in *The American Magazine*, April 1907, that raise questions about descriptions of the same events in his book taken from those articles a year later. Post-millennial literature also presents some suspiciously soft or seemingly contradictory reporting on who was imagining what in bygone cross-racial violence.

[66] *Folk Devils and Moral Panics: The Creation of the Mods and Rockers*, by Stanley Cohen, MacGibbon and Kee, London, 1972. For later development of the concept: "Moral Panics and the Social Construction of Deviant Behavior: A Theory and Application to the Case of Ritual Child Abuse," by Jeffrey S. Victor, *Sociological Perspectives*, Vol. 41, No. 3, 1998, p. 541.

[67] "Hypnagogic and hypnopompic hallucinations during sleep paralysis: neurologiocal and cultural construction of the night-mare," by J. A. Cheyne, S. D. Rueffer and I. R. Newby-Clark, *Conscious Cognition*, Sept. 1999. p. 319.

[68] Lynching riots in both Mexico and Guatemala (e.g., Huejutla 1998 and Todos Santos 2000) have resulted in mob torture-murders of strangers or targets of opportunity on the basis of accusations made by lone accusers later shown to display symptoms resembling temporal lobe epilepsy. This disability can give rise to mental absence, confabulated memories and hallucinations. In the Latin American cases, mob fury swept aside and then concealed the shaky original nature of the accusations, none of which focused on racial issues. Racial accusation frenzies in the United States would seem to be local variants of a human universal.

[69] "[T]he oft-cited correlation between ISP [Isolated Sleep Paralysis] and anxiety disorders."—"A Case of Sleep Paralysis with Hypnopompic Hallucinations," by David E. McCarty, M.D. and Andrew L. Chesson, Jr., M.D., *Journal of Clinical Sleep Medicine*, Feb. 15, 2009, pp. 83–84.

Chapter 6: The Scent

[70] *Informants* describing Sheriff Bob Walker: F. Kirkland, M. Cannon, E. Parham, E. Foster, W. Baylor, M. McCain; biography sketch "Robert Elisha 'Bob' Walker," by Leigh Williams Kitchens, 2006.

[71] Sheriff H. S. "Cap" Sutton's firing: *Search for Yesterday*, Levy County Archives Committee, Chapter 13, *Levy Times-Democrat*, Sept 10, 1903; *Levy County News,* July 10, 1924. *Search for Yesterday*, Levy County Archives Committee, Chapter 8, p. 8, citing *Levy County Times Democrat*, Sept 10, 1903.

[72] The Lewis case: *Search for Yesterday*, Levy County Archives Committee, Chapter 8, pp. 8, 10 (citing *Levy County Times Democrat*, Sept 10, 1903). Repeating stories, *informant:* W. Baylor.

[73] "Colonel" William J. Simmons of the Ku Klux Klan explained his phantom rank in 1921 to Congress during hearings on the newly influential Klan. (*The Ku-Klux Klan: Hearings Before the Committee on Rules, House of Representatives*, Government Printing Office, 1921. p. 67). Simmons, an energetic fraternal organizer, explained: "I was at one time senior colonel in command of five regiments of the uniform rank of Woodmen of the World....I was under a colonel and I found how the colonels do." An earlier congressman, "Private" John Allen of Mississippi, had made a career of ridiculing the faux-colonel process, humorously insisting to voters that they call him, not "Colonel" or "General," but "Private." There is a gray area in the matter of faux colonels because some came by their titles through non-military appointment. In Florida as in many other states, incoming governors would appoint key supporters as "lieutenant colonels" on an honorary staff, which meant largely that they could wear exotic uniforms at the governor's inauguration and ever afterwards call themselves "Colonel." Some did so for the rest of their lives. The information climate surrounding Rosewood in 1923 saluted this hierarchy in imagination; at least three of the state's major newspapers in 1923 were run by such make-believe "colonels."

[74] Hurston on "colonel" and "governor": *Dust Tracks on a Road, an Autobiography*, Zora Neale Hurston, J. B. Lippincott Co., Philadelphia, 1942, p. 220. *Life on the Mississippi,* by Mark Twain, Harper & Brothers, New York, 1883, 1901, p. 328 (Mark Twain complained, apparently only half in jest, that

the South's bogus military promotions derived originally from the epidemic popularity of romantic novels such as *Ivanhoe* by Sir Walter Scott).

[75] The ceremonial trimmings of "colonels" and "cap'ns" suggest that the segregation-era white South might be viewed as a regional laboratory for Anthony F. C. Wallace's paradigm of the revitalization movement (1956). Mark Twain (above) explained: *"Then comes Sir Walter Scott with his enchantments, and...sets the world in love with dreams and phantoms; with decayed and swinish forms of religion; with decayed and degraded systems of government; with the sillinesses and emptinesses, sham grandeurs, sham gauds, and sham chivalries of a brainless and worthless long-vanished society. He did measureless harm...in our South they flourish pretty forcefully still."*

[76] Florida displayed borderland extremes on various racial issues, such as lynchings per capita. It would be almost the last southern state to abolish convict leasing, by stages at the state level in 1919 then in all forms as a result of the Martin Tabert revelations in the spring of 1923 ("Florida and the Black Migration," by Jerell H. Shofner, *Florida Historical Quarterly*, Jan. 1979, p. 283; "Where Palm and Pine Are Blowing: Convict Labor in the North Florida Turpentine Industry, 1877-1923," by Jeffrey A. Drobney, *Florida Historical Quarterly*, April 1994, p. 431). State convict leasing ended in Louisiana in 1901, Mississippi in 1906, Oklahoma in 1907, Georgia in 1907, Texas in 1910, but in Florida not until 1923. Alabama retained the practice until 1928.

[77] Florida state senator T. J. Knabb was still using leased convicts in his Baker County turpentine camps up until the practice was outlawed in May 1923; health and punishment conditions in the senator's camps were found to be abysmal (*The Convict Lease System in Florida, 1866-1923*, by Gordon N. Carper, Florida State University, 1964; "Murder, 'Convict Flogging Affairs,' and Debt Bondage," by Vivien M. L. Miller in *Reading Southern Poverty Between the Wars 1918-1939*, ed. Richard Godden and Martin Crawford, University of Georgia Press, 2006; Alachua County Commissioners Minutes 1923, p. 20149).

[78] *Cool Hand Luke*, by Donn Pearce, Scribners, 1965; film 1967 directed by Stuart Rosenberg, starring Paul Newman and George Kennedy (depicts Florida prison life in the 1940s-1950s; Pearce himself had spent two years in a Florida prison for burglary). "Chain Gang," by Sam Cooke, RCA Victor, 1960.

[79] Informants on Walker opposing Klan: B. Hardee, H. Hardee, J. Yearty.

[80] Levy County Fair. *Hooded Americanism: The History of the Ku Klux Klan*, by David Mark Chalmers, Duke University Press, 1981, p. 227.

[81] The folklore may get a bit carried away here. More documented accounts of

the Lewis double murder do suggest that face-blacking was involved, but say that the two killers blacked their own faces originally, in order to commit the crime. The practice of white minstrels blacking their faces apparently began in the late 1820s, around the same time that street mobs of the Jacksonian era sometimes used similar blacking—which was perhaps half-disguise, half primeval abandon. Which form of face-blacking, mob or minstrel, may have inspired the other is one of history's orphaned questions. ("Murder in Levy County, The Lewis Murders," by Ty Starkey, blog post, July 2003; *Demons of Disorder, Early Blackface Minstrels and Their World*, by Dale Cockrell, Cambridge University Press, Cambridge, UK, New York, 1997; *Informant:* W. Baylor).

[82] Shipment of bloodhounds. *Informants*: J. McElveen, F. Kirkland. Levy County Commissioners Minutes, Jan. 2, 1923 (LCCH).

[83] "The Bloodhound's Amazing Sense of Smell," Nature, WKNO-PBS. http://www.pbs.org/wnet/nature/episodes/underdogs/the-bloodhounds-amazing-sense-of-smell/350/ http://www.dc.state.fl.us/oth/timeline/1927a.html. In 1925 Rockwood Kennels, owned by prominent breeder V. G. Milliken of Kentucky, reportedly sold bloodhounds in the $100-$200 range (or more than a fourth the cost of a Model T). Florida prison guards earned $50 a month in 1925: *Nineteenth Biennial Report of the Prison Division of the Department of Agriculture of the State of Florida for the years 1925 and 1926*, Florida Department of Corrections.

[84] *Informants* on beginning of manhunt: M. Cannon, F. Smith, F. Kirkland, E. Johnson, J. Yearty, J. McElveen, E. Foster., L. Davis.

[85] Description of Deputy. *Informants*: E. Parham, F. Kirkland, M. Thompson.

[86] The works of Hurston on Florida timber camps as well as 1994 interviews by the present author with Dixie County camp veteran Cliff Clark and others confirmed that Levy County descriptions of the quarters boss function reflected a pattern seen widely in Florida.

[87] Taylor County Commissioners Minutes, Jan. 1, 1923: $425 payment approved to Rockwood Kennels in distant Lexington, Kentucky, the most noted bloodhound kennel in the nation; Perry, Florida's 1922 chase was a manhunt deluxe. *Gainesville Daily Sun*, Dec. 3-9, 1922. Interview in 1994 with Walter Peacock, witness to the December 1922 events in Perry.

[88] "An 'always tired' feeling is one of the signs of a mild case."—Rockefeller Sanitary Commission for the Eradication of Hookworm Disease, chairman Wyckliffe Rose. "Unhooking the Hookworm: The Rockefeller Foundation and Mediated Health," by Marina Dahlquist, Stockholm University, Sweden, 2012. "...[T]he climate [of the South] has operated through the hookworm to make

many half-invalid." (*Life and Labor in the Old South*, Ulrich Bonnell Phillips, Little, Brown and Co., 1929, 2007 edition University of South Carolina Press, p. 5).

[89] Newberry's plunge from boomtown to near-ghost town occurred as World War I blocked previously heavy demand in Germany for Newberry's mined phosphate, used in fertilizer. (Oral history interview of William N. Barry, by Jeff Charbonnet, July 19, 1984, Samuel Proctor Oral History Collection, University of Florida Digital Collection).

[90] The birth of Sumner as a company town seemed to leave no known record, as was not unusual in migratory timber operations, which in some cases marked their departure from a decade-long local site with mysterious mill fires and insurance controversies, further wiping out traces. Wellington Cummer III, descendant of the 1920s Cummers stated specifically that no records were left from Sumner, as did Cummer Museum of Art and Gardens in Jacksonville. As at many points in this story, the history is left to the local informants, who on Sumner's founding agreed: J. McElveen, S. Herbert, T. Jones, Jr., E. Parham, F. Kirkland.

[91] Marshall Cannon's barbershop (interviews 1982) stood in Sumner's area of freehold shops near the Seaboard tracks, well away from the sawmill area and beyond the property line of Cummer Lumber.

[92] "A vagabondish convict" was denounced by the *Gainesville Daily Sun*, January 10, 1923, merging two demonic images, that of the escaped convict and the predatory hobo: "a lawless and criminal negro vagabond. He was loafing over the country, shirking work, violating law and was a disgrace to his race."

[93] *Informant:* M. Cannon.

[94] *The American Siberia, Fourteen Years Experience in a Southern Convict Camp*, by John Powell, M J. Smith & Co., Chicago, 1891, p. 310.

[95] Mythic portrayals of Rosewood in the 1990s falsely depicted M. Goins & Bros. Naval Stores as being still in operation in 1923, causing the 1923 remnant community to appear larger and more robust than it was in fact. All informants agreed with Levy County Courthouse records on the trajectory of Goins turpentine, while Martin Goins's headstone remains from his 1905 death, a stone still visible in undergrowth at the site of Rosewood.

[96] Aunt Sissy. This was Rosewood resident Virginia "Sissy" Smith, née Coleman, whose husband Allen Smith had taken a job in Otter Creek and did not return, according to their daughter Nettie Smith Joyner, and confirmed by

niece Bea Goins Frazier.

[97] *Informants:* Arthina Bennett, née Blocker; Ernest Blocker (brother). Annie "Sis" Blocker, their mother, was born into the comparatively prosperous Hayward household in Rosewood, in a two-story home with a parlor piano like some others. Annie Hayward's marriage to John Blocker failed as Blocker became a fugitive from justice, apparently on bootlegging-related charges. His wife and children moved into the turpentine quarters at Wylly. Annie's sister Mary Jane Hayward had also married and continued to live on the family's eighty-acre farm on the western edge of Rosewood.

[98] Feb. 15, 1912, sale of one acre by W. A. and Sally (or Sallie) Sauls to the trustees of the First A.M.E. Church of Rosewood, Book 14, p. 113 (LCCH). *Informants*: T. Hawkins, L. Foster, M. Langley, L. Davis, L. Carrier, W. Evans.

[99] Magnolia Lodge #148, F.&A.M. deed, March 22, 1910, Book 4, p. 450 (LCCH). *Informants*: E. Davis, E. Jenkins, M. Langley, L. Davis, L. Foster.

[100] "Rosewood Massacre: The Untold Story," produced by David Tereshchuk, ABC News Productions, aired on The Discovery Channel, 1996.

[101] "Early Cedar Key Days," by "Captain" T. R. Hodges, *Tampa Tribune*, February 21, 1954 (PKYL).

[102] Wright General Merchandise (LCCH; *informants:* S. Hall, L. Carrier, J. Turner, L. Davis, M. Thompson. E. Parham, W. Baylor, F. Kirkland, A. Goins, P. Doctor).

[103] Scent sources used by bloodhounds: *Dogs Against Crime*, by Albert Orbaan, John Day Co, New York, 1968.

[104] "He had secured a bottle of turpentine some way and sat on the bank rubbing turpentine on his feet. That is supposed to destroy the scent."—This statement, about a fugitive hunted in Mississippi in 1919, said "supposed" because the alleged trick did not deter the dogs. ("In the Delta—The Story of a Man-Hunt," by Beulah Ratliff, *Atlantic Monthly*, April 1920).

[105] In mid-January 1923, dogs lost the trail of a murderer in the Brown Tisbee case sixty miles east of Rosewood in Alachua County (*Gainesville Daily Sun*, Jan. 19, 1923). A more spectacular occasion found a hot trail suddenly going cold after a horrific mass murder in Villisca, Iowa, in 1912. Even the era's fabled Sherlock Holmes of bloodhound trainers, Capt. Volney G. Milliken of Kentucky (he was a real captain, with rank in the police) sometimes found the best noses outfoxed by unknown means, as when "[t]he hounds promptly took

up the scent at Mr. Devere's home and followed it for several miles into a thicket where it suddenly stopped." (*Lexington Leader*, Apr. 8, 1908).

Chapter 7: Aaron's Ghosts

[106] *The American Siberia, Fourteen Years Experience in a Southern Convict Camp*, by John Powell, M J. Smith & Co., Chicago, 1891, p. 310.

[107] Marriage record, Aaron Carrier and Mahulda Brown, LCCH.

[108] "Action at Station Four, Florida," Feb. 13, 1865—*The War of the Rebellion, A Compilation of the Official Records of the Union and Confederate Armies*, Series I, Vol. 49, Part I, pp. 40-43, U.S. War Dept., Government Printing Office, Washington, D.C., 1897 (Fishburne, p. 94).

[109] A nationally known stereotype of panic in a purported African American context was provided in the segregation years by Florida-born actor Lincoln Perry, known in Hollywood as Stepin Fetchit. On-camera in Charlie Chan's haunted house scenes, Perry would quake in demented caricature of black fright. In Minnie Mitchell's world in Rosewood, real people did not act like that—except, at times, perhaps her uncle Aaron.

[110] *Informant* descriptions of finding Aaron Carrier's empty house: M. Cannon, F. Kirkland, L. Carrier, S. Hall, M. Langley, L. Davis.

[111] The fabled bloodhound wizard of the early twentieth century, Capt. Volney Milliken of Kentucky, found that even lowly chicken thieves could pull this trick, as his dogs trailed a gang only to a road, where apparently they were picked up by a vehicle and the scent disappeared (*Lexington Leader*, Kentucky, June 30, 1904). More germane to the theorizing at Aaron Carrier's house, an unconfirmed though persuasive-sounding narrative of a torture-fraught manhunt near Drew, Miss., in 1919, was sent to *Atlantic Monthly*. It told in graphic detail of frustrations and harsh actions that occurred when manhunters became convinced that an accomplice had given a fleeing man a ride on a mule, hiding the scent. ("In the Delta—The Story of a Man-Hunt," by Beulah Ratliff, *Atlantic Monthly*, April 1920).

[112] Tracking of closed vehicle: "Experts Answer FAQ About Bloodhounds," Jimmy Ryce Center for Victims of Predatory Abduction": "Can a bloodhound follow the scent of a child inside a car by means of the faint scent expelled through the car ventilation system?"

[113] Local sympathizers with the Monday torturers, perhaps having heard third-hand versions of the events, tended to differ on material details when retelling

what they thought was the story of the capture of Aaron Carrier, but they consistently imputed a dignified sense of purpose and righteousness to the torturers. A source of glory had been found, a cause.

[114] World War I Service Cards (SAF-FMP): Aaron Carrier. *Informants:* Theresa Robinson (Mahulda Brown Carrier's sister), M. Langley, L. Carrol.

[115] "History of Heart Attack…," http://www.epi.umn.edu/cvdepi/essay.asp?id=10; "Paul Dudley White: The Father of American Cardiology, by J. Willis Hurst, M.D., *Clinical Cardiology*, 14, 622, 1991.

[116] Another son of Orrie Kirkland, Jennings Bryan Kirkland, was documentably present as the Rosewood violence progressed on Thursday night, January 4.

[117] Though the Emancipation Proclamation was announced in September 1862, it was a war measure declaring that slaves in any state remaining in rebellion after a given deadline were to be considered freed. The deadline was January 1, 1863. Thus, the first minute after midnight, opening 1863, brought a rush of excitement into churches where celebrators waited up for that moment. The more final prohibition on slavery throughout the United States did not come until the Thirteenth Amendment to the Constitution in 1865.

[118] " 'Oh, in Florida! Hank! / Oh, let's shake it! Hank! / Oh, let's` break it! Hank! / Oh, let's shake it! Hank! / Oh, just a hair! Hank!' / The singing liner cuts short his chant. The strawboss relaxes with a gesture of his hand. Another rail spiked down. Another offering to the soul of civilization whose other name is travel." —*Dust Tracks on a Road, An Autobiography*, by Zora Neale Hurston, J. B. Lippincott Co., 1942.

[119] The story of Aaron Carrier being poisoned for allegedly poaching hogs is from Fred Kirkland and Sam Hall, persuasively capturing it from opposite perspectives, with more general support from others, including John Yearty and Lonnie Carrol.

[120] Florida did not receive a fence law, officially ending its frontier life as open range, until 1949. By then an intolerable clash had developed between the old frontier ways and incoming seekers of sunshine, as 1947-1948 reportedly brought auto collisions with free-roaming stock that killed 24 people, while injuring 257 others (counting only the human casualties).

[121] *Florida: A Guide to the Southern-Most State* ("The Florida Guide"), Federal Writers' Project, U.S. History Publishers, 1939, p. 383.

[122] The Newberry mass lynching of August 1916 arose out of charges of poached hogs, allegedly by African Americans in the isolated community of

Jonesville. However, later in the 1930s, after 1916's vicious action was said to have solved the problem, a white lawman in Newberry killed a white ex-lawman, and the alleged motive was that one of them was running a hog-theft ring. The pattern of hog poaching was largely white-on-white. This was also shown when Randolph Hodges told how his hog claim near the site of Rosewood was poached in the 1930s. By then, local African Americans had been driven out, so the poaching could not have been done by them.

[123] *Informants*: S. Hall, F. Kirkland, confirming the story from opposite perspectives, one of them in the targeted African American community, the other in the accusing white community.

[124] Mass strychnine poisoning near Hempstead, Texas: *New York Times*, Jan. 30, 1886. Another case in frontier Florida was described as occurring near future Cape Kennedy. Millionaire rancher Gilbert Tucker recalled his father poisoning poachers of ear-marked hogs with strychnine: "The children in one family got deathly ill....Word got around about that incident, and the stealing stopped." ("Gilbert Tucker Shares Stories Of Early Days On Florida Ranch," by Colleen Schreiber, *Livestock Weekly*, Mar. 8, 2001). Also, the notorious Hatfield-McCoy feud in West Virginia is customarily traced back to an origin in "Devil Anse" Hatfield's poached hog.

[125] 1910 Federal Census, Sylvester Carrier and Haywood Carrier, occupation: "cedar mill." *Informants:* S. Hall, L. Carrier. Auction in 1911 of Charpia cedar mill equipment: LCCH.

[126] 1920 Federal Census, Sylvester and Gert Carrier in Sumner. *Informants:* L.. Carrier, S. Hall, L. Davis, M. Langley, L. Norsworthy, P. Glover, R. Missouri.

Chapter 8: The Fast Shuffle

[127] International News Reel photos, Jan. 1923; *Levy County News* July 10, 1924. *Informants*: F. Kirkland, M. Cannon, M. Hogan, E. Parham.

[128] *Informants*: E. Parham, J. McElveen, M. Cannon, F. Coburn.

[129] "The Rosewood Massacre," 60 Minutes, produced by Joel Bernstein, voiced by Ed Bradley, Dec. 11, 1983 (the author proposed the segment to executive producer Don Hewitt and was background reporter and witness liaison).

[130] *Informants* on Jack Cason: L. Cason, J. Cason Kent, S. Hall, L. Davis, M. Langley.

[131] Turpentine woods rider duties. *Informants:* Cliff Clark (Dixie County), C.

Atkins, J. Turner, W. McKenzie, L. Washington. Two woods riders who were not white were Will Marshall (in Rosewood itself in the first years of the twentieth century) and Bud Campbell (at the Lennon camp 25 miles from Rosewood). At most camps the woods rider was a solitary white among wide-ranging black crews.

[132] *Informants*: M. Langley, A. Stephenson, L. Carrier, L. Carrol.

[133] The Hardy Boys (Frank and Joe) were fictional teen-aged detectives in the novels of Edward Stratemeyer, introduced in 1927 and ghostwritten by various authors in later years.

[134] *Tom Sawyer, Detective* (Mark Twain, 1896) was a sequel to *The Adventures of Tom Sawyer* (1876) and *The Adventures of Huckleberry Finn* (1884). Baden-Powell's boy detectives in 1908: *A Companion to Crime Fiction,* ed. Charles J. Rzepka and Lee Horsley, John Wiley & Sons, 2010, p. 323.

[135] The story of Edward and Bert, the quizzical "Hardy Boys" of the Rosewood incident, comes from various narrators, but principally from Edward Pillsbury's sister Martha Thompson, with support from L. Carrier, S. Hall, E. Parham, F. Kirkland, E. Foster, F. Smith and others.

[136] "The first theorist to discuss the problem of panic in unorganized groups was William McDougall in his book, *The Group Mind* (1920)."—*Panic Behavior, Discussion and Readings*, by Duane P. Schultz, Random House, 1964, p. 13. Also see *The Behavior of Crowds, A Psychological Study*, by E. D. Martin, Harper & Brothers, 1920. Gustave Le Bon's still older notion of "crowd mind," depicting angry masses as behaving like beasts or automatons, is now widely criticized.

[137] Corruption involving jook quarters bosses: Samuel McCoy Papers (FSL), letter describing jook rake-offs at Putnam Lumber in Dixie County; Frederick Cubberly Papers (PKYL), reports of U.S. Bureau of Investigation agent John Bonyne and others. *Informants*: E. Parham, R. Missouri, Cliff Clark (Dixie County). "Memoirs of Martin Hoban, Logging Florida's Giant Cypress," by Baynard Kendrick and Barry Walsh, *Forest History Today*, Spring/Fall 2007.

[138] As the Florida frontier modernized from 1900 to 1920, the Tilghman Cypress company town at Lukens, preceding Sumner in the vicinity of Cedar Key, was apparently a rougher place: "The Quarters Boss kept a certain amount of order in the jook, because of a large blacksnake whip that he wielded with a skillful and powerful hand, plus the fact that he controlled the moonshine, gambling, and all other concessions. Still, it's a mystery to me why stray bullets, if nothing else, hadn't penetrated him years before." ("Memoirs of Martin Hoban, Logging Florida's Giant Cypress," by Baynard Kendrick and Barry Walsh, *Forest*

Notes

History Today, Spring/Fall 2007; Martin J. E. Hoban interviewed 1966).

[139] A cypress lumber company town at Osceola, south of Orlando and more than 160 miles from Sumner, showed the same basic blueprint: ten houses down each side of a main white quarters street, electricity from an on-site generator each night until 10 p.m., and, set apart, "a juke joint" (in the imposed terminology of a later commentator: (http://www.weirdus.com/states/florida/abandoned/osceola_bank_vault/). How many jooks may have existed in company-town Florida is an interesting question. At the time of the two jooks in Sumner and Wylly, another happened to be described in print more than twenty miles away by a criminal indictment at the L. W. Drummond turpentine camp. There were probably various others in Levy County alone—all at a time when alcohol sale and consumption for entertainment were illegal under both local and federal law, raising still further questions about statewide economic networks and the supply of alcohol. The word "jook" (it was not pronounced "juke") was used across the South, though perhaps only in a brief window in time between the world wars, both of which drew many African Americans northward, as southern employers sought to offer enticements at their workplaces without increasing wages. Plantations at least as far away as Mississippi had "jooks" operating in shanties or other buildings. More than 250 miles south of Sumner, a Tidewater Cypress camp in Collier County, Florida, had "the Jerome Juke" in "an old two-story building." ("African Americans And The Sawmills Of Big Cypress—A Brief History," by Frank and Audrey Peterman, Earthwise Productions, Inc., for Big Cypress National Preserve).

[140] "He tells Lumber Company it is only way he can keep help as they will not live in such towns without [a jook]."—letter to *New York World* reporter Samuel McCoy during the Martin Tabert case of 1923, referring to logging superintendent William Fisher of Putnam Lumber in Dixie County (Samuel McCoy papers, FSL). "Any old-time operator will tell you that back in those days you couldn't run a sawmill out in the wilderness and keep colored help without a jook."—former Tilghman Cypress superintendent Martin Hoban, interviewed in 1966 ("Memoirs of Martin Hoban, Logging Florida's Giant Cypress," by Baynard Kendrick and Barry Walsh, *Forest History Today*, Spring/Fall 2007).

[141] "The jook at Lukens was a large, barn-like structure set slightly off on the edge of town. It was furnished with chairs, knife-scarred tables, a roof of Swiss cheese appearance due to bullet holes from many weekend brawls, and half-a-dozen curtained cubicles at the rear" (referring to Tilghman Cypress Company jook at Lukens, about six miles from Sumner, closed down in 1918: "Memoirs of Martin Hoban, Logging Florida's Giant Cypress," by Baynard Kendrick and Barry Walsh, *Forest History Today*, Spring/Fall 2007; Martin J. E. Hoban interviewed 1966).

[142] "Conspiracy of Silence Shrouds 1916 Lynchings," by Ron Sachs, *Gainesville Sun Sunday Magazine*, Nov. 6, 1977. The interviewee was listed as "Dr. William Berry," meaning pharmacist William N. Barry of Newberry.

[143] *The Godfather*, 1972, screenplay by Mario Puzo and Francis Ford Coppola, directed by Coppola.

[144] Frederick Cubberly Papers, PKYL, reports of Bonyne et al. The sawmill superintendent reporting the misconduct also gave a separate oral history interview on the timber industry: Marc. L. Fleishel, interviewed by Elwood R. Maunder, Forest History Society, Apr. 4, 1960.

[145] Attempt to recapture Aaron Carrier at Sumner jail. *Informants*: F. Kirkland, L. Carrier.

Chapter 9: Gang Rape

[146] Phone number and details of the *Gainesville Daily Sun* in January 1923 come from the *Sun* itself, and from *History of Gainesville, Florida, with Biographical Sketches of Families*, by Jess Davis, Alachua County Historical Society, 1966 (Chapter 9).

[147] *Gainesville Daily Sun*, Jan. 2, 1923.

[148] As the *Gainesville Daily Sun* expanded its illusion of two, three, then four or more attackers (though not even enraged whites at the scene described more than one) there were shocking precedents to be drawn upon, formed by cases known *Sun* readers. Two hard-drinking whites had committed Levy County's infamous Lewis double murder in 1902, but there were also notorious horrors committed by multiple black perpetrators against whites. A white family in Savannah, Georgia, was murdered *en masse* in 1905 in a treasure hunt similar to the 1902 case, and whatever the overlays of resulting hysteria, it does seem clear that a conspiracy among at least two black attackers was involved. White reaction then spilled into a panic. Before horrific lynching death, one suspect said there was an organization of such conspirators called the Before Day Club—almost certainly a myth, though the idea was inflated by white panic into a regional specter, as towns across Georgia began reporting Before Day Club clues, causing some African Americans to be killed. Afterward the supposed evidence evaporated and the footprints of panic were revealed. The 1905 Before Day Club excitement spread south into Florida, where at least one killing occurred.
Perhaps still more vivid as a template were memories from 1912 and nationwide news made by Forsyth County, Georgia, just north of Atlanta, where a particularly macabre rape and murder of a young white woman, Mae Crow,

caused a frenzy that spread across a number of counties. The apparent multiple perpetrators, accomplices or facilitators were jailed and delivered fragments of murky confession. One was lynched and two more hanged legally, while an ethnic cleansing movement developed among whites, driving a large number of African Americans permanently from their homes—a thousand dispossessed in Forsyth County alone, by some counts. Others were driven out of adjacent counties. Much as at Rosewood, this spasm would be largely wiped from public memory by the time the 1980s arrived, though it was publicized in 1987 by a protest event and confrontation, and more systematically by the 2008 book *Buried in the Bitter Waters: The Hidden History of Racial Cleansing in America* (Basic Books), by investigative journalist Elliot Jaspin. In 1923, memories of news and rumors from incidents such as Forsyth County in 1912 were positioned to echo behind images of gang attack.

[149] *Informant:* Theresa Robinson. Ms. Robinson's daughter Lizzie Jenkins has also written of the involvement of her aunt, Mahulda Carrier, in the Rosewood events.

[150] Theresa Robinson's account must be approached with care; it is a lone witness report without corroborating evidence, and the timing it describes raises questions. Robinson stressed that the arrival occurred at sundown, though sundown occurred at 5:30 that time of year and by 6:00 it was fully dark. The only known timetable for the local passenger train has the train departing Gainesville at 6:15 p.m. and arriving in Archer in about a half hour. The train was often late but seldom early.

[151] The definitive overview of lynch mobs thwarted by southern law enforcement can be found in "Judge Lynch Denied: Combating Mob Violence in the American South, 1877 –1950," by E. M. Beck, *Southern Cultures*, Vol. 21, No. 2, Summer 2015, pp. 117-139. Beck, a professor of sociology at the University of Georgia, is known for his previous inventory of lynching cases compiled with Stewart Tolnay of the University of Washington, in which more than 3,100 lynching incidents have been identified. More recently, for the article cited above, he spent five years cataloging known instances of lynchings that were threatened or attempted but prevented by authorities, finding 3,246 such preventions across the lynching-era South. The subject is also discussed at q nearer point in time by Arthur Raper in *The Tragedy of Lynching* (University of North Carolina Press, 1933), in his Part Seven, "Foiling the Mob," p.441.

Chapter 10: Bridge of Ghosts

[152] Levy County Commissioners Minutes, Jan. 2, 1923 (LCCH).

Chapter 11: At the Store

[153] Sunset/sunrise and moon data, Astronomical Applications Dept., U.S. Naval Observatory (USNO).

[154] Virginia Carrier's death was described by Wesley Bradley's daughter Rosetta Bradley Jackson in an interview with Maxine Jones and William Rogers, Sept 25, 1993 (Attorney General's Rosewood File, Vol. 26, Curington Files). *Informants*: L. Davis, L. Carrier, L. Washington, M. Langley.

[155] Baseball game festivities and singing by Lellon "Beauty" Carrier and Annie "Sweetie" Carrier. *Informants*: S. Hall, W. Evans, T. Hawkins. As the segregation decades produced tent shows with genuine African American performers in parallel to the twilight of white minstrelsy in blackface, Beauty Carrier was said to have used her singing in one of the traveling troops, recalled by one informant, Willie Evans, as being the well-known Florida Blossoms. Later in the Cummer company town of Lacoochee, where various Rosewood survivors went to live after 1923, Beauty's niece, Vera Goins Hamilton, was said to run a jook where she also sang, while Beauty herself became admired as a church soloist in Lacoochee. Philomena Doctor, Beauty's niece and Vera Hamilton's sister, was noted for singing in church in St. Petersburg, Florida.

[156] Though Sylvester Carrier's World War I draft card states that he was born Sept. 7, 1892, three federal census and other evidence seem to agree that the card is in error. Anomalies on stated birth dates were not isolated occurrences in World War I draft cards of the Levy County area. The 1900 Federal Census lists Sylvester Carrier's birth year as 1890, and this seems to agree with all evidence except the draft card.

[157] Winchester Repeating Arms Co., Model 1887 Lever Action Repeating Shotgun.. *Informants:* L. Carrier, L. Carrol, B. Hardee, H. Hardee.

Chapter 12: The Carter

[158] Nov. 8, 1916, acceptance of homestead claim by Nebuchadnezzar Carter, 80 acres in southwest quarter of Section 30. Claim apparently filed 1897 (Book 12, p. 661, LCCH).

[160] Age and descriptive details on Sam Carter: 1900 Federal Census (b. June 1874); *Informants:* S. Hall, L. Carrier, F. Kirkland, R. Hodges, J. Yearty, E. Davis, J. McElveen, E. Parham. C. Hudson, P. Doctor, L. Glover, P. Glover. J. Screen.

[161] LCCH: indictment of Sam Carter, 1900, for attempted murder of Richard

Williams, who was married to Carter's sister Janetta. Carter testified that Williams had shot at him first, and at his sister. This was a glimpse of internal violence that would embroil the community, since in 1911 Williams was reportedly fired as treasurer of the First A.M.E. Church of Rosewood, which then was burned down. Williams was accused but not convicted of the arson.

[162] LCCH, Criminal Record Book #1, 1867- 1926, Archive room, administrator Donna Cicale, June 2014.

[163] Details on Cornelia Carter: Sale of Carter land, 1925 (LCCH); *informants*: L. Foster, W. Evans. It should be pointed out that one Rosewood survivor who came forward in the 1990s to join the claims case had lived in Cornelia Carter's household, as confirmed by the 1920 census. The author was assigned by the Florida Attorney General's Office to interview this claimant for authenticity of residence, since other survivors objected that she had moved away before the 1923 violence struck. After the interview it was clear that the claimant had certainly lived in Rosewood at one point, but most of her descriptions greatly contradicted all other testimony. It seemed that the claimant might have had only very early childhood experience at Rosewood, generating almost no long-term memories, and that heavy confabulation was filling in the gaps. As more years passed and media continued seeking Rosewood survivor interviewers in the 2000s, this claimant became the last survivor still alive, and thus received great attention. Her startling statements—such as a description of Rosewood as being filled with roses—were accepted enthusiastically by credulous reporters and were published as if the statements had some basis. The claimant in question is not used as a source in these pages.

[164] Last stretch of Florida Railroad, Sumner to Cedar Key, completed March 1, 1861: *Tallahassee Floridian*, Railway and Locomotive Historical Society, The Florida Railroad Company, Inc. A schedule was issued before completion that showed trains leaving Fernandina on the Atlantic at 12:45 p.m., then arriving in Gainesville at 6:40 p.m., then as far as Bronson in Levy County at 8:40 p.m., a trip of just over eight hours if all went as scheduled (which often was not the case).

[165] Only in the most general terms did the slave crews constructing the Florida Railroad enter the records. Construction began in 1856, proceeding slowly and under financial difficulty. Work was re-contracted to J. Finnegan & Co. under Joseph Finnegan (later the victorious Confederate general at the Battle of Olustee: *A Short History of Florida Railroads*, by Gregg Turner, Arcadia Publishing, 2003). Also in charge of contracting slave work crews was William Phelan: "the energetic contractor, Mr. Phelan, is pushing the work forward vigorously with an efficient force of one hundred hands." (*Tallahassee Floridian*, Apr. 14, 1860). That the first African American settlers of Rosewood

had been slaves, and not free people of color, is suggested by the following: "In all Florida in 1856 there were between eight and nine hundred free Negroes, about 300 of whom were in Pensacola, 125 in Key West, 75 in St. Augustine, and 70 in Tallahassee."—"Florida in 1856," by Herbert J. Doherty Jr., *Florida Historical Quarterly*, Vol. 35, No. 1, July 1956 (citing state census of 1855; total state population: 110,000). Leon County (surrounding Tallahassee, the state capital) had 9,120 slaves, the largest recorded slave population of any Florida county at the time, and had 3,499 whites. Florida's largest city was then Pensacola with a total of 2,500 residents. The first census listing names of African Americans at Rosewood, in 1870, places their origins in South Carolina. Tradition in the family of Rosewood resident John Wesley Bradley pinpointed the South Carolina city of Beaufort and said that earlier family roots were in the West Indies. A similar tradition existed in the Carrier family. Minnie Langley said that her grandmother Emma Carrier (born Emma Lewis, sister of Sarah Lewis Carrier) spoke with a West Indies accent. Information is said to be sketchy on the early history of the Florida Railroad because in the late 1800s the headquarters of its successor line burned (interview, John Leynes, the Florida Railroad, March 3, 2008).

[166] Moses Levy established his 1,000-acre Pilgrimage Plantation in Alachua County in 1822-1823, just after Florida became a U.S. Territory in 1821 (*Moses Levy of Florida: Jewish Utopian and Antebellum Reformer*, by C. S. Monaco, Louisiana State University Press, 2005, pp. 101-102). His son, David Yulee Levy (who changed his named to David Levy Yulee) incorporated the Florida Railroad Company on Jan. 8, 1853 (*Johnson et al. v. Atlantic, Gulf & West Indies Transit Co. et al.*, No. 77, March 4, 1895).

[167] "Wade Leonard, Florida Naval Stores Operator," by Clifton Paisley, *Florida Historical Quarterly*, Vol. 51, No. 4, Apr. 1973, p. 381; "Naval Stores Industry," *New Georgia Encyclopedia*.

[168] In addition to family and official records and memories, the arrival of Martin Goins in the Rosewood area was described by William Samuel Yearty (b. July 2, 1877) in a typescript memoir (PKYL): "About 1895 or 96, the turpentine operators came to the Sumner section. A colored man or he claimed to be was Negro by name of Martine [sic] Goins put up a still between Rosewood and Sumner. He came out to see Dad about leasing his timber…Goins to have his crew, box timber, and Dad work it and Goins buy raw gum."

[169] Arriving in Rosewood, Martin Goins and three partners, his brothers Ed and Lucian and his brother-in-law Eli Walden, set up a turpentining company after selling a similar firm in North Carolina in 1895. There, local records show, a firm called Goins Brothers had owned 4,447 acres of land in the old Murchison area (largely subsumed after 1913 by federal purchases for Ft. Bragg). When this was sold and operations were moved to Florida, the new enterprise at

Rosewood was called M. Goins & Bros. Naval Stores. Turpentine stand depleted in 5-10 years: *Encyclopedia of Southern Culture*, eds. Charles Reagan Wilson and William Ferris, University of North Carolina Press, 1989, p. 39. (Rosewood informants tended to say six years or more: J. Turner, C. Atkins. C. Clark).

[170] "Wade Leonard, Florida Naval Stores Operator," by Clifton Paisley, *Florida Historical Quarterly*, Vol. 51, No. 4, Apr. 1973, p. 381; "Naval Stores Industry," *New Georgia Encyclopedia*. The naval stores industry left its imprint in North Carolina in the nickname "Tar Heel," and in Georgia in Joel Chandler Harris's Uncle Remus story of the Tar Baby.

[171] On Jan. 1, 1903, the Cedar Key Town Company leased to M. Goins & Bros. Naval Stores "all the pine timber on Sections 2, 3, 5, 6, 7, 8, 9 and 10" of Township 15-S Range 13-E "for making turpentine," for a period of three years (LCCH). This was a substantial holding, but, in the myth process that has inflated the population and economic size of 1923 Rosewood, the Goins property has also undergone inflation. During the 1990s claims case, the land that was only leased was portrayed as being owned. This was further inflated in 2013 by a prestigiously published book (from the University Press of Florida) claiming that the Goins family had constituted the largest landholding interest in Levy County (the book was later repudiated by its publisher in an extraordinary step, for reasons stated as "scholarly misconduct").
In reality, the Levy County site owned by the Goins family comprised less than eighty acres. Some African American farmers in Rosewood itself had larger parcels, and various white holdings across the county were much larger. The Goins family had bought their Rosewood tract (originally 80 acres) from John and Mary Wright in 1903, then later carved off a small part for a daughter, leaving about 65 acres as the headquarters for the family business. In 1923, though the business had ceased operations years earlier, Ed Goins's son Perry continued to live on the tract with his wife and children.

[172] *Informants*: E. Jenkins, B. Frazier, L. Foster, L. Carrier, J. Yearty, E. Blocker, R. Missouri. The 1900 Federal Census, listing birth years, seems to pinpoint the beginning of the Goins movement to Florida in 1894-1895, as shown by birthplaces listed for children. Some family members or associates seemed to continue arriving through 1900 or perhaps later, and some, including Eli Walden's wife Rebecca, remained in North Carolina.

[173] Records on the Goins and Walden families as well as the 1900 letter from Eli Walden were found through the persistent efforts of family genealogist Helena Hendricks-Frye.

[174] The damaged gravestones of both Martin Goins and his brother-in-law, E. P. Walden, are at this writing still extant at the site of Rosewood (Martin Goins:

June 15, 1842 - Dec 16, 1905; E. P. Walden: Sept 25, 1842 - Nov 15, 1900).

[175] E. Walden fought on both sides. *Informant*: H. Hendricks-Frye.

[176] *Charlotte* (North Carolina) *Observer*, Dec. 31, 1905, p. 10, obituary found by Goins family historian Helena Hendricks-Frye, 2015 (collection of Marie Ames).

[177] *Informants*: W. Evans, L. Foster.

[178] *Informant*: J. Yearty, referring to his father Will Yearty, author of the memoir cited above.

[179] George Carter indictments, 1916, 1919 (LCCH).

[180] Folklore version of the cattle theft. *Informant*: F. Kirkland.

[181] *Informants*: E. Foster, L. Glover, J. McElveen. L. Carrier, S. Hall.

[182] The story of borrowing Deputy Williams's car is from *informant* Ernest Parham.

[183] *Informants:* W. Baylor, F. Kirkland.

[184] Parham's description essentially matches those of *informants* J. McElveen, M. Cannon and F. Kirkland.

[185] Stories about capture of Carter. *Informants:* L. Davis, L. Carrier, S. Hall, W. Baylor.

[186] 1900 Federal Census; *Soldiers and Sailors Discharge Book* (LCCH); World War I Service Cards (SFA-FMP): discharged Dec. 5, 1918; 1921 indictment (LCCH). Informants: C. Hudson (brother), P. Hudson (cousin), M. Cannon.

[187] *Informants:* B. Young, F. Kirkland, M. Cannon.

[188] *Gainesville Daily Sun*, Jan. 3, 1923.

Chapter 13: Tuesday

[189] Newberry lynching: Sachs, *Gainesville Sun*, Nov. 6, 1977.

[190] The 1920 Federal Census confirms Minnie Langley's recollections of the household of Frank Sherman and Beulah "Scrappy" Carrier Sherman (though

the census enumerator rendered "Beulah" as "Beauty").

[191] Buck dancing, a lightly stomping solo dance similar to clogging, was among various dance forms featured by traveling tent shows, which after about 1900 were the African American heirs to the tradition of white minstrels in blackface. Perhaps the highest-profile tent show in Florida was the Florida Blossoms, whose "coon song" genre might shock modern ears (an impressive exhibit on "coon songs" has been assembled at FAMU Black Research Archives in Tallahassee, Fla.). Florida Blossoms star Katie Price, "the Georgia Sunbeam," was billed in 1909 as a 'soubrette, coon shouter and buck dancer.' Later blues singer Bessie Smith was said to join the Blossoms in 1915 (*Ragged But Right: Black Traveling Shows, Coon Songs, and the Dark Pathway to Blues and Jazz*, by Lynn Abbott and Doug Seroff, University Press of Mississippi, 2009, pp. 292-293, 298-299). Informants from Rosewood agreed that Rosewood resident Lellon "Beauty" Carrier (daughter of Sarah Carrier and sister of Sylvester Carrier) left the community to become a professional singer before 1923, traveling with a show. Lellon Carrier Gurdine later returned to live in the Cummer milltown of Lacoochee three counties south of Rosewood—where the Florida Blossoms performed for a large crowd in 1925 (*Ragged But Right*, p. 335). Rosewood informant Willie Evans, unprompted, recalled an impression that it was the Florida Blossoms that Beauty Carrier had joined.

[192] Some ten miles from Wylly at the Gulf, a jook had operated in the company town of Lukens (Tilghman Cypress Company) until operations ceased there in 1918. A company superintendent alleged: "Every Saturday evening, the Seaboard Railroad brought in a carload of colored ladies from points north, some of them from as far away as Jacksonville. By midnight the jook joint was really jumping. It usually closed in the wee small hours with a fusillade that reminded one of the trenches of World War I." ("Memoirs of Martin Hoban, Logging Florida's Giant Cypress," by Baynard Kendrick and Barry Walsh, *Forest History Today*, Spring/Fall 2007; Martin J. E. Hoban interviewed 1966).

[193] The jook at Lukens up to 1918 was apparently less well appointed, with "half-a-dozen curtained cubicles at the rear." Hurston described some timber town jooks of the 1930s that had no such facilities, forcing liaisons to occur outside in the dark on the ground ("Memoirs of Martin Hoban, Logging Florida's Giant Cypress," by Baynard Kendrick and Barry Walsh, *Forest History Today*, Spring/Fall 2007; Martin J. E. Hoban interviewed 1966).

[194] *The Jazz Singer*, directed by Alan Crosland, starring Al Jolson, produced by Warner Bros. The film's finale has Jolson singing his signature song, "My Mammy," in blackface (https://www.youtube.com/watch?v=PIaj7FNHnjQ). "Jolson's very last recording sessions, in 1950, were devoted to eight [Stephen] Foster tunes" (*DOO-DAH! Stephen Foster and the Rise of American Popular Culture*, by Ken Emerson, Da Capo Press, 1998, p. 12).

[195] Spaeth, Sigmund, *A History of Popular Music in America*, Random House, New York, 1948, p. 110; Ewen, David, *History of Popular Music*, Barnes & Noble Inc., New York, 1961, pp. 21, 27-28; *Encyclopedia of Southern Culture*, eds. Charles Reagan Wilson and William Ferris, University of North Carolina Press, 1989, p. 1089.

[196] "Swanee," music by George Gershwin, lyrics by Irving Caesar, 1919, originally written in a parody spirit, but adopted more neutrally by Al Jolson and recorded for Columbia Records, becoming a hit that "penetrated the four corners of the earth," Gershwin said. "Alexander's Ragtime Band," by Irving Berlin, 1911, met controversies that it had been borrowed from a draft by Scott Joplin.

[197] Spaeth, Ewen, ibid.

[198] Bankruptcy proceedings, Suwannee Valley Land Corporation, assets bought at auction by Rosewood storekeeper John Wright (Chancery Progress Docket, LCCH).

[199] "Winter Shooting in Florida," by Campbell Moller, 1889, in *Tales of Old Florida*, eds. Frank Oppel and Tony Meisel, Castle, Seacaucus, N.J., 1987. The Suwannee Inn Hotel was still operating in Wylly in 1911, with Samuel B. Goldberg as secretary-treasurer (*Levy Times-Democrat*, Oct. 19, 1911, in *Search for Yesterday*, Levy County Archives Committee, Chapter 13, March 1983).

[200] *Informants*: S. Hall, M. Johnson, W. Hall, M. Daniels, D. Gummer, L. Davis, L. Carrier, Langley, E. Blocker.

[201] *Informants*: B. (Zetrouer) McPhail, A. Zetrouer.

[202] *Informants*: M. Thompson, E. Parham, F. Smith; *Jacksonville Journal*, Jan. 5, 1923; *Gainesville Daily Sun*, Jan. 13, 1923 (quoting *Levy Times-Democrat*); letter Arthur Cummer to W. H. Pillsbury, Jan. 8, 1923 (collection of Jerry Peterson).

[203] W. H. Pillsbury's 1882 edition of *Paradise Lost*, collection of Martha Thompson/Jerry Peterson. *Informant*: M. Thompson.

[204] *Informants*: K. Johns, E. Parham, F. Kirkland; Carter inquest (LCCH).

[205] *Levy County News*, July 10, 1924.

[206] Levy County Commissioners Minutes, Dec. 1922-Jan. 1923; *Informant*: F. Kirkland.

207 Indictment Dec. 17, 1921, Bryant and Dave Hudson charged with assault (LCCH); Bryant Hudson death certificate (FBVS); *Informants*: M. Cannon, C. Hudson.

208 *Soldiers and Sailors Discharge Book* (LCCH): Bryant Hudson.

209 The irregular death certificates filed belatedly by incoming Justice of the Peace R. Machen Middleton covered five persons killed in the Rosewood violence. The irregularities were discovered by the Florida Department of Law Enforcement during investigation mandated March 4, 1994, by the Florida Legislature (investigator John Stevens, case supervisor Eric Ericson, report Dec. 23, 1994: Attorney General's Rosewood files, Vol. 13, Curington File; FBVS).

Chapter 14: The Convict

210 Lull period in mass violence: *The Deadly Ethnic Riot*, by Donald L. Horowitz, University of California at Berkeley Press, Berkeley, 2001, p. 71 "...the violence may be interrupted for a period, which I call the *lull*..."; p. 16: "...the *lull*, a time of apprehensive quiet during which rumors and warnings may circulate..."

211 *Informants*: R. Hodges, E. Parham, J. Turner. The Florida Department of Agriculture kept records of convicts leased to private employers, noting the Marshburn turpentine camp at Rosewood in 1905, though by 1906 that camp was no longer noted and the only Levy County leasing seemed to be at the Lennon Naval Stores Company of Bronson. At Otter Creek, J. S. Fisher & Co. operated a lease stockade during 1910-1913, also recalled by informant J. Yearty, but this seems to have ended by 1915. By 1917, amid growing pressure to build automobile roads, convict labor in Levy County seemed to concentrate in county road gangs, as in: "The convict gang was brought up Tuesday near Cedar Key to build the hard surface road between Bronson and Williston" (*Levy Times-Democrat*, March 1, 1917, cited in *Search for Yesterday*, Levy County Archives Commission, Chapter 13, March 1983).

212 *New York Times* (Associated Press), Jan. 6, 1923: "...escaped from a road gang in Levy County."

213 Besides his interview with the author in 1982, J. McElveen was recorded in a separate session by the Cedar Key Historical Society as he described the Rosewood events. The eerie racist atmosphere during that session is startlingly apparent in strange snickering and giggling repeatedly heard in the background as atrocities were bombastically described.

214 Aug. 18, 1925, sale of 80 acres in west half of southwest quarter of Section

30 to N. R. Reynolds by heirs of Nebuchadnezzar Carter (Book 20, p. 141, LCCH).

[215] Florida Death Index: Black male deceased in Levy County, 1923 (Vol. 203, No. 15619).

[216] *Informant*: M. Langley: "They was workin' on that road when we was there. The chain gang was somewhere up the road. I don't know where exactly....They used to have prisoners comin' by the house there, in trucks, carry 'em in to the road....They carry 'em down this way somewhere, and then they carry 'em back down that way somewhere. They was workin' on the hard road right behind our house...Them people was out there workin' on that hard road, them chain gang people."

[217] Six days before the Fannie Taylor incident the *Gainesville Daily Sun* published one of its periodic race-baiting police-court stories, ridiculing defendants from "Darktown," in the kind of back-page descent that was viewed as clever in some journals of the place and time. On Dec. 26, 1922, the target at the *Daily Sun* was "Marvin James, colored," whose last name seemed to fascinate an unnamed wordsmith in the newsroom—presumably city editor Truman Green, age 20, the paper's only reporter. The piece chuckled: "...James, true to his name, was trying to exert the daring and bravery of the Jesse James of olden days." A dreamily lax information environment was toying with the notions of "black desperado" and "Jesse James." Then six days later came the hunter of women who became the hunted quarry of the Monday manhunt, "Jesse Hunter." It was an interesting coincidence. Some elements in the *Daily Sun's* Rosewood coverage were verifiably invented—or "expanded," to use the local journalistic term—and there is no way to say how far the clever (or sloppily accidental) word games might have progressed. On Jan. 7 the *Sun* drove the possibility home, changing Jesse Hunter's name in tune to the Jesse James myth: "Hunt for James Hunter—Wanted for Assault on White Woman is Being Continued." Note the slip: Jesse and James are now transposed—or merged—in a context of journalistic free association.

[218] *I Love Myself Whey I Am Laughing...And Then Again When I Am Looking Mean and Impressive: A Zora Neale Hurston Reader*, Feminist Press at CUNY, 1979, p. 51.

[219] *Informants*: J. Screen, S. Hall. L. Carrier.

[220] *Florida Times-Union*, Jan. 7, 1923; *Washington Post*, Jan. 6, 1923.

[221] *Laws of Florida*, 1921, Vol. 2, p. 230, Special Acts: Levy County bond issue of $100,000 for roads. "for the building of a road and necessary bridges into Cedar Key, Florida." Right-of-way was granted across the property of John

McCoy, Mary Ann Hayward, Cornelia Carter, John Wright and others (LCCH).

[222] The unexplained name in the Florida Death Index, a black male deceased in Levy County in 1923, is identified as "Jesse Carey."

Chapter 15: Stranger in Paradise

[223] The cracker barrel image was cemented when a future Florida governor visited a phosphate boomtown and said he spied the justice seated before a plank laid across two barrels, with the constable in attendance. (*Napoleon Bonaparte Broward: Florida's Fighting Democrat*, by Samuel Proctor, University of Florida Press, Gainesville, 1950, pp. 49-50).

[224] *Miami News*, January 25, 1957.

[225] *Informant*: Willard Hathcox. World War I draft card confirmation: Poland Italy Hathcox, born Jan. 17, 1875. Poland Italy's sister Cuba was married to Cummer Lumber logging superintendent Henry Andrews, who entered the Rosewood sequence on January 4, 1923.

[226] Perhaps the most notorious—and specific—allegations of jook corruption arose across the Suwannee River from Levy County in the Dixie County no-man's land created in 1921. There, quarters boss W. Alston Brown ("Cap'n Brown") was fired by superintendent Marc Fleishel after reportedly siphoning off $981.84 in jook profits that should have gone to the company, Putnam Lumber, according to Fleishel. So many murders and disappearances of African American employees occurred in the Dixie County chaos that the U.S. Bureau of Investigation (forerunner of the FBI) sent a multiple-agent team to investigate. A 1923 letter sent to journalist Samuel McCoy of the *New York World* alleged that the Putnam Lumber jook was the second largest building in Dixie County (after Putnam's company hotel), forming a formidable revenue source. Rake-offs alone were alleged to total $500 per month, and to accrue to logging superintendent William Fisher (later indicted for murder but not convicted). Eventually an African American jook manager disappeared and apparently became yet another murder victim, in order to prevent his testimony. Dixie County Sheriff Sam Chavous then went to prison. (Samuel McCoy papers, FSL; Cubberly papers, Agent E. J. Cartier report, May 17, 1921, pp. 1-2, PKYL; Dixie County Commissioner Minutes, 1921; Dixie County *informants*: Cliff Clark, Perry Hill, Preston Chavous).

[227] "To assist in supplying the heavy demands of the United States government at this time, the Cummer Lumber Co., with offices and mills in this city [Jacksonville] is establishing a sawmill on the Okeechobee line near Daytona, Fla." (*Lumber World Review*, Oct 10, 1917, p 35).

228 *Informants*: E. Johnson, S. Herbert, E. Parham, L. Carrier.

229 *Informants* on influenza epidemic: E. Parham, T. Hawkins, B. McKenzie, M. Thompson; "Memories of Otter Creek," by Charles F. Kimble, *Search for Yesterday,* Levy County Archives Committee, Chapter 7, p. 15. (Also see: *The Great Influenza,* by John M. Barry, Viking Penguin, 2004, p. 4: "Epidemiologists today estimate that influenza likely caused at least fifty million deaths worldwide, and possibly as many as one hundred million." Many of the deaths were said to occur between mid-September and early December 1918; there were said to be more deaths in one year than the Black Death of the Middle Ages had caused in a century.

230 *Informant*: J. McElveen; *The Florida Buggist*, Official Organ of the Florida Entomological Society, University of Florida, June 1919, Vol. III, No. 1, p, 34, by U. C. Lofton: A half dozen *Gambusia affinis* top-minnows were said to be able to eat more than a hundred mosquito larvae in two hours.

231 "They take it as a matter of providence that everyone in the South should have it [malaria] and that it does not amount to much" (Florida Buggist, ibid.; *Technology and Culture*, Vol. 47, No. 2, April 2006, review by Darwin H. Stapleton of *The Mosquito Wars: A History of Mosquito Control in Florida*, Gordon Patterson, University Press of Florida, 2004.

232 *Informants:* J. H. Wilkerson, J. Turner, J. Yearty. Testimony of James Herbert Wilkerson, Florida Legislature, March 18, 1994 (Box 5, first folder, Administrative Files, Vol. VIII, pp. 748-795, FAMU).

233 The magnetic pole of the Suwannee-Rosewood riddle is here left unnamed. Seekers may walk 102,650 paces NNE of the Baird Buried Treasure Hole and listen for the Lord God birds.

234 *The Road to Xanadu, A Study in the Ways of the Imagination*, by John Livingston Lowes, Houghton Mifflin Co., Boston, 1927.

235 "Kubla Khan," Samuel Taylor Coleridge, first published in 1816 but apparently written in the 1790s, reportedly under the influence of opium-based laudanum in a dream, on which we have only the word of the poet in 1816.

236 *Travels Through North and South Carolina, Georgia, East and West Florida...*, by William Bartram, printed by James & Johnson, Philadelphia, 1791; ed. Mark Van Doren, 1928.

Chapter 16: Poly's Fall

[237] A jook at the sawmill company town of Lukens, cutting cypress until 1918 some six miles from Sumner at the Gulf, was described by the company superintendent there: "By midnight the jook joint was really jumping. It usually closed in the wee small hours with a fusillade that reminded one of the trenches of World War I," leaving "a roof of Swiss cheese appearance due to bullet holes from many weekend brawls." ("Memoirs of Martin Hoban, Logging Florida's Giant Cypress," by Baynard Kendrick and Barry Walsh, *Forest History Today*, Spring/Fall 2007, p. 47).

[238] The position of the company-town jook at Sumner as a bootleg liquor hub was stated specifically by white informant Ernest Parham, but less clear was any mutation as Sumner changed from its initial culture (1911-1919, when it was a more lawless frontier outpost), into its post-1919 form after devout superintendent Walter Pillsbury was sent in, apparently for clean-up (and as National Prohibition posed an extra embarrassment for unmolested jook commerce). Poly Wilkerson's tenure as quarters boss had grown from the old culture, and Wilkerson was eventually fired by Pillsbury or his ally Sheriff Bob Walker. Liquor machinations under Wilkerson were suggested obliquely by a memoir from the nearby cypress camp-town of Lukens, whose own bootleg liquor traffic at the Lukens jook was portrayed almost as feeding off Sumner's vice: While "bringing liquor in from Sumner," an African American was stopped by a white deputy sheriff and killed, nearly causing a riot between blacks and whites, according to Lukens's company superintendent. In typical company towns such a local deputy would also have been company quarters boss, as in Sumner and elsewhere. The memoir left unexplored the Lukens deputy's protectiveness of moonshining boundaries. "[T]he very next Saturday night, the deputy was waiting for him when the train came in [from Sumner]. When the man got off the train, the deputy was there and asked him to open up his bag...so it could be searched for contraband liquor. The man started to run, instead of obeying, and the deputy sheriff just pulled his gun and shot him down dead in the back, just a few yards from the train." ("Memoirs of Martin Hoban, Logging Florida's Giant Cypress," by Baynard Kendrick and Barry Walsh, *Forest History Today*, Spring/Fall 2007, p. 48).

[239] Informants on Robert Missouri: A. Doctor, P. Doctor, T. Hawkins, V. Hamilton, J. McElveen, E. Parham. Draft card signed June 5, 1917, at Lukens near Sumner, where Missouri worked for Tilghman Cypress Company until its 1918 closing, then moved to Sumner. Born Aug. 14, 1891, Crescent City, Fla.

[240] Descriptions of illegal but enforcement-exempt company jooks ranged across early twentieth-century Florida.
*In the sawmill company town of Osceola, 160 miles southeast of Sumner, a

jook serving Lee Tidewater Cypress Company was "a big house by the river."
*Deep in the Big Cypress Swamp, more than 300 miles south of Sumner, a company camp jook was "an old two-story building."
*In the opposite direction, 70 miles northwest of Sumner, Tide Camp of Burton-Swartz Cypress Company had "plenty of fighting and a quarter boss to keep the Negro quarters straight. They'd dance all Saturday night and most of Sunday night."
*Moving back closer to Sumner, though still 40 miles northwest across the Suwannee River, perhaps the most notorious camp, at Clara, had its "dance, gambling and drinking emporium."
*Still closer to Sumner, Putnam Lumber Company's apparently ambitious operation at Shamrock, Dixie County, used "the second largest building in Shamrock...of two stories," allegedly producing a "rake of [rake-off] amounting [to] $500/00 each month."
*Closest to Sumner was Tilghman Cypress Company at Lukens (until its logging ceased in 1918), where the jook was "a large, barn-like structure set slightly off on the edge of town...furnished with chairs, knife-scarred tables, a roof of Swiss cheese appearance due to bullet holes from many weekend brawls, and half-a-dozen curtained cubicles at the rear."
(Sources: "The Osceola Bank Vault," http://www.weirdus.com/states /florida /abandoned/osceola_bank_vault/; "African Americans And The Sawmills Of Big Cypress—A Brief History," by Frank & Audrey Peterman, Earthwise Productions, Inc., for Big Cypress National Preserve, Ochopee, Fla.; Oral history interview of Earl Porter, former executive of Burton-Swartz Cypress Company, interview by Elwood Maunder, Forest History Society, Oct. 1963; *Miami News*, May 14, 1923; letter April 26, 1923, to editor of the *New York World*, Samuel McCoy papers, SLF; "Memoirs of Martin Hoban, Logging Florida's Giant Cypress," by Baynard Kendrick and Barry Walsh, *Forest History Today*, Spring/Fall 2007, p. 48).

[241] Indictment of Gertrude King, accused of murder "at the Jook, in the quarters," Aug. 7, 1921 (LCCH). (At almost the same moment and 35 miles northwest, in notorious swamps across the Suwannee, another of the rare official renderings of the word "jook" into written letters was occurring. U.S. Bureau of Investigation agents, perhaps impelled by 1921's "murder farm" peonage scandal in Georgia, converged on newborn Dixie County with its Putnam Lumber criminal mysteries. The puzzled agents, however, were outsiders, not to mention being city folk. and met a world which Zora Hurston two decades later (also in Cross City) portrayed as resembling the Stone Age. The G-men in 1921 wrote the word as "juke," not "jook." (Cubberly Papers, PKYL).

Chapter 17: Billy and Broad

[242] *Gainesville Daily Sun*, Jan. 1, 1923.

[243] "The High Sheriff" is the title of Chapter 9 of the Levy County Archives Committee's exploration of local history called *Search for Yesterday*, published in sections over more than two decades beginning in 1976. Chapter 9 contains reminiscences on bygone sheriffs and their departments. In the Rosewood inquiry, informants of both races repeatedly said "sheriff" when they meant a local deputy and "high sheriff" when they meant the sheriff.

[244] Montgomery Ward & Co., catalog 1894-1895, Follet Publishing Co.: "Genuine Black Raccoon Muffs" for $3.75, "Genuine Mink Muffs" for $8.00, "Men's Genuine Plymouth Buck Gloves" for $1.25.

[245] "The Standard Manufacturing Company…was on the eastern tip of the island. In the heyday of the Standard Manufacturing Company the U.S. had only two other fiber factories, one in Jacksonville, and one in Sanford, Florida" (*Cedar Key, Florida, A History*, by Kevin McCarthy, The History Press, 2007, p. 54). *Florida State Gazetteer and Business Directory 1925*: Standard Manufacturing Co., Cedar Keys. Interview, Galina Binkley, Cedar Key Historical Society Museum, 2014 (the museum is in the former home of the Standard Manufacturing Company's founder). Minnie Lee Langley would spend much of her adult life working at the brush manufacturing plant in Jacksonville.

[246] Census records confirm that Emma and Sarah Carrier, sisters, were born Emma and Sarah Lewis. Under circumstances apparently not preserved by family stories, they were both adopted into a neighboring family, the Robinsons, causing some neighbors to know them as Emma and Sarah Robinson. The two sisters would marry two brothers, James and Haywood Carrier, thus giving them the same married surname.

Chapter 18: Sending Word

[247] White *informant* Fred Kirkland also repeatedly used the term "raising sand," as did other local residents. In Rosewood claims case testimony in 1994, Minnie Langley's use of the term on the witness stand puzzled an examining attorney:
Ms. Langley: "…And he said, 'Aunt Emma, you better get ready because I think these people are going to try to raise some sand.' "
Attorney: "Raise what?"
Ms. Langley: "Raise up at us tonight. So Mama, she was slow getting ready because she did not want to go. But she went anyway. So he said, 'You better

come on where I can save you.' " (Feb. 25, 1994, Box 4, Folder 11, page 43, FAMU).

[248] Arnett Goins testimony, Florida Legislature, Feb. 25, 1994 (Box 4, Folder 11, pp. 65-100, FAMU).

Chapter 19: Christmas

[249] *Florida Gazetteer and Business Directory 1911-1912*, R. L. Polk & Co., Jacksonville, shows "saw mill" owned by H. E. Charpia (PKYL).

[250] 1911-1912 *Gazetteer* ibid.: Rosewood, population 300; lists seven stores, including two turpentine commissaries, as well as "Hall, C. B. & Co., general store." The *Gazetteer* of 1918 then shows all of that gone, except for a lone entry: "Wright, J. M. general store."

[251] *Informants* on the old Rosewood community ca. 1911: L. Carrier, L. Foster, S. Hall, M. Johnson, L. Washington, T. Hawkins, L. Carrol, B. Frazier, W. Evans (confirmed by Levy County Courthouse records).

[252] *Informants*: L. Davis, M. Langley, W. Evans, P. Doctor, T. Hawkins, A. Stephenson. Evans alone had a specific memory of the group perhaps being the well-known Florida Blossoms. Lellon "Beauty" Carrier also appears in D'Orso, page 95. Florida Blossom Minstrels: *Ragged But Right, Black Traveling Shows, 'Coon Songs,' The Dark Pathway to Blues and Jazz*, by Lynn Abbott and Doug Seroff, University of Mississippi Press, 2007, p, 7.

[253] Informant Lutie McCoy Foster's recollection seems to refer to *The Juvenile and Gem Lesson Papers*, a periodical mailed to A.M.E. churches from the organization's national Sunday school headquarters in Nashville, Tennessee (*The Encyclopedia of the African Methodist Episcopal Church*, 2nd ed., Philadelphia, Compiled by Bishop R. R. Wright Jr., published by the Book Concern of the AME Church, 1947, p. 513).

[254] The description of regional tithe flow is from *informant* Lutie Foster, and seems confirmed by Wright ibid., 1949, p. 383, describing the Eleventh Episcopal District of the A.M.E. Church covering all of Florida.

[255] *Informants* on the Christmas shooting and George Goins: L. Foster, L. Carrier, S. Hall, E. Jenkins, E. Blocker, L. Davis, M. Langley, L. Washington. World War I Service Card (SFA-FMP): George W. Goins; born Southern Pine, North Carolina; residence: Cedar Key; Army serial no. 2959548; Inducted at Mayo, Fla.; Served overseas from Aug. 26, 1918, to July 30, 1919; "Race/Ethnicity: White." Compare to Service Card for Aaron Carrier,

"Race/Ethnicity: Colored." George Goins would be listed on a war memorial in Pasco County, Florida, in the "colored" column.

[256] Marriage record, George W. Goins and Willie R. Carrier, Sept. 29, 1910, (LCCH). This was a month after the wedding of George's brother Perry Goins to Hattie Coleman, on Aug. 21, 1910.

[257] Confirmed by 1870 Federal Census, when James was five, Haywood three and Elias aged seven months. The 1910 Federal Census showed the Elias Carrier family in household 10 of the Rosewood area. He is listed as aged 39, with wife Mary, 28, three daughters and two sons. By 1920 the family is no longer recorded in the area.

[258] Interview at Floyd Care Nursing Home, Bartow, Florida.

Chapter 20: Going to Sarah's

[259] James Herbert Wilkerson, one of Poly Wilkerson's sons, b. Dec. 9, 1915, told the story of the woman on the porch in sworn testimony before the Florida Legislature on March 18, 1994 (Box 5, first folder, Administrative Files, Vol. VIII, pp. 748-795, FAMU). Wilkerson also told the same story separately to the author. In the legislative testimony, cross-examination by attorney Stephen Hanlon for the Rosewood claimants demonstrated weaknesses in the story.

[260] *The Klan Inside Out*, by Marion Monteval, Negro Universities Press, 1924, p. 67: Testimony of Judge Erwin J. Clark, former general counsel for the Ku Klux Klan in Texas.

[261] NOAA, Special Observer's Meteorological Record, Gainesville, Fla., Jan. 3-4, 1923.

Chapter 21: Moonlit Ride

[262] Henry Andrews, logging superintendent; Minor "Cephus" Studstill, lumber inspection foreman; Jennings Bryan Kirkland, farmer; Mannie Hudson, farmer. (News accounts and informant recollections agree on their presence).

[263] "Raised in the woods so he knew every tree / Kilt him a b'ar when he was only three / Davy, Davy Crockett, / King of the wild frontier!" For a coonskin-cap moment in the 1950s, a nation was reintroduced to the cracking ritual of frontier boasting ("The Ballad of Davy Crockett," lyrics by Tom Blackburn, music by George Bruns, from the 1955 film *Davy Crockett,* produced by Walt Disney).

[264] One British observer on the early American frontier was the often-shocked Frances Trollope, who found frontier bluster intruding even into Congress in Washington: "[We were] extremely amused by the rude eloquence of a thorough horse-and-alligator orator from Kentucky, who entreated the House repeatedly to 'go the whole hog.'" On a riverboat, Ms. Trollope never doubted a frontiersman's sad-eyed tale (told with a straight face and the appearance of full belief) about "an enormous crocodile" eating an entire family. The story appeared in her book as unquestioned fact, allegedly demonstrating the shocking dangers presented by frontier America (a more pressing danger being perhaps that one might get lied to, rather than eaten by a crocodile). (*Domestic Manners of the Americans*, Frances Trollope, Whittaker, Treacher & Company, 1832, p. 184. p. 39).

[265] *Informant*: G. Andrews, Starke, Fla.

[266] Death certificate (FBVS): Henry M. Andrews.

[267] Emerson, the Massachusetts philosopher and essayist, came south in 1826 at age 23 because of health problems ("stricture in the chest" and "bronchial ailment," interpreted in some biographies as referring to tuberculosis). His journal showed a ten-week stay in St. Augustine starting in January 1827, after arrival from South Carolina, though Emerson's poem commenting on the city's Minorcan population is a fragment titled, "Written in St. Augustine In 1826" (*Florida Reader: Visions of Paradise*, eds. Maurice O'Sullivan and Jack Lane, Pineapple Press, 1994, p. 63; also see examiner.com, "Writer...Recorded His Impress-ions...," by Rhonda Parker, Sept. 28, 2011).

[268] *Informants*: G. Andrews, L. Norsworthy; "From the river to the Sea...," by Sandie A. Stratton and Stacey A. Cunnington, Florida History Online; "Corsicans to Florida - 1767 - The New Smyrna Colony - St. Augustine." http://corsicacorsica. homestead.com /newsmyrnacolony.htm. *Mullet on the Beach: The Minorcans of Florida, 1768-1788*, by Patricia C. Griffin, St. Augustine Historical Society, 1991.

[269] Letter to William Emerson, in "Ralph Waldo Emerson in Florida...," by Mrs. Henry L. Richmond, *Florida Historical Quarterly*, Vol. XVIII, No. 2, Oct. 1939; *Sarasota Herald-Tribune*, Nov. 12, 1939.

[270] Navy tradition, Admiral David Farragut at the Battle of Mobile Bay, Aug. 5, 1864 (a "torpedo" was a tethered mine); "John Brown's Body," Stephen Vincent Benet, 1928.

[271] Henry Andrews's gravestone can still be seen near Starke, Florida. Family history and land grant: *Informant* L. Norsworthy.

²⁷² Federal Census: 1910 Lafayette County, Fla., 1920 Jasper County, S.C.; *Logging Railroads in South Carolina,* by Thomas Fetters (Jasper County Library, Ridgeville, South Carolina).

²⁷³ The piney woods Klan violence of the 1960s made direct reference to earlier "whitecapping," an ethnic cleansing movement around 1903 in the same area, also centered around the timber industry. (*Mississippi Forests and Forestry,* by James E. Fickle, University Press of Mississippi, 2001, pp. 85, 108). *Outside the Southern Myth,* by Noel Polk, University Press of Mississippi, Jackson, 1997, p. 134, quotes William F. Winter: "[I]n the late 1950s and early 1960s, probably the highest incidence of Ku Klux Klan activity occurred in some of the predominantly white counties of the Piney Woods." See "Whitecapping: Agrarian Violence in Mississippi, 1902-1906," by William F. Holmes, *Journal of Southern History,* May 1969, Vol. XXXV, No. 2, p. 165). In the 1960s the Crown-Zellerbach papermill in the pine belt at Bogalusa, Louisiana, was a "direct descendant" of a mill which in the southern timber boom at the turn of the century had been called the largest sawmill in the world. By 1964 the Bogalusa mill was said to have a Klan cell of "at least 100 members and probably many more" out of a total workforce of 2,900. At least 800 klansmen were said to live in Bogalusa (nicknamed "Klantown, USA"), with "more Klansmen per square foot than...heard of anywhere in the South."(*Race & Democracy, The Civil Rights Struggle in Louisiana 1915 – 1972,* by Adam Fairclough, University of Georgia Press, Athens, 1995, p. 350).

²⁷⁴ *Klandestine, The Untold Story of Delmar Dennis and His Role in the FBI's War Against the Ku Klux Klan,* by William Mcilhany, Arlington House Publishers, New Rochelle, NY, 1975.

²⁷⁵ "Spectacular and strenuous activity" (Long-Bell Lumber Company pamphlet, quoted in Fickle, p. 101).

²⁷⁶ *Informants:* Allen Stephenson, Cliff Clark and Walter Peacock (Dixie County); Frederick Cubberly papers (PKYL); "Bully Bob Sullivan," by Michael Browning, *Miami Herald,* Nov. 30, 1977; Correspondence, Michael Browning, May 24, 1996; W. Alston Brown death certificate 1933 (FBVS).

²⁷⁷ "Martin Tabert, Martyr of an Era," by N. Gordon Carper, *Florida Historical Quarterly,* Vol. 52, No. 2, Oct. 1973, p. 116. Samuel McCoy Papers (FSL).

Chapter 22: Man

²⁷⁸ *Informant:* John Paul Jones, former executive secretary of the Florida Press Association and University of Florida journalism professor; interview 1994.

[279] The "race war" theme remained active in some quarters. In the 1960s "Mississippi Burning" violence, FBI informant Delmar Dennis described Klan Imperial Wizard Sam Bowers diagramming on a blackboard a plan to start a race war (McIlhany, ibid., pp. 53-54).

[280] *From Slavery to Freedom: A History of American Negroes*, by John Hope Franklin, Alfred A. Knopf, 1956, p. 472 (quoted in *The Emergence of the New South 1913-1945*, by George Brown Tindall, Louisiana State University Press, 1968, pp. 151-152).

[281] *The Encyclopedia of the African Methodist Episcopal Church*, 2nd ed., Philadelphia, Compiled by Bishop R. R. Wright Jr., published by the Book Concern of the AME Church, 1947, p. 562. "Henry McNeal Turner (1834-1915)," by Stephen Ward Angell, *New Georgia Encyclopedia*.

[282] *Informant*: S. Hall.

[283] Aug. 12, 1911, mortgage of two oxen and two mules by Sylvester Carrier to First National Bank of Gainesville (Mortgage Book 2, p. 394; Book 2, p. 236, LCCH).

[284] May 9, 1911, Sylvester Carrier tried and acquitted of selling alcoholic cider, annotated indictment (LCCH).

[285] Indictments of John Coleman and Richard Williams for burning First A.M.E. Church, tried sequentially, both acquitted (LCCH).

[286] Sale by W. A. and Sally Sauls of a triangular parcel of one acre to trustees of First African Methodist Episcopal Church of Rosewood (Book 14, p. 113, LCCH).

[287] *Informant* Sam Hall confirmed Florida prison records and courthouse records, recalling Sylvester Carrier as being sent "to prison" and not to a local jail. *Informant* Leroy Carrier recalled the sentence as being served at a Perry County timber camp. The court record shows Rosewood farmer John McCoy as one of the witnesses against Haywood and Sylvester Carrier.

[288] *Informant*: E. Jenkins.

Chapter 23: All at Once

[289] The narration of events at the house is principally from Minnie Langley, though is generally confirmed by the three other surviving witnesses from inside

the house: Arnett Goins, Philomena Doctor and Lonnie Carrol (Carrier). There was additional confirmation from second-hand accounts passed down from Gert Carrier through informant Ella Mae Wiggins and others. General discussion occurred among surviving family members after the violence, and all seemed to confirm this narrative. The one witness demonstrably fantasizing on some other points, Philomena Doctor, had little to say about events inside the house. Her sensational claims were made about what she said happened after she left there (19 dead white men on the front porch; nine days hiding in the swamps). On events inside, she, too, seemed to confirm Minnie Langley's impressions.

[290] *Soldiers and Sailors Discharge Book* (LCCH): Bryan Jennings Kirkland; World War I Service Cards (SFA-FMP), discharged Dec. 10, 1918.

[291] *Informants*: E. Parham, J. McElveen, E. Foster, F. Kirkland, M. Thompson.

[292] During World War I, Levy County recorded military inductions of 212 white soldiers, eight white officers, 214 African American soldiers, 31 sailors and three marines. Its casualty records showed 12 dead and two wounded: four black and eight white fatalities and one wounded from each race.

[293] One of the irregularities left unexplained in the indictments of Haywood and Sylvester Carrier was a months-long lapse between arrest and trial, and another long period before imprisonment. The first could have been explained by infrequent court sessions.

[294] 1920 Federal Census, Precinct 9, Sumner, Levy County, Fla.

[295] *Dust Tracks on a Road, An Autobiography*, Hurston, 1942, p. 20.

[296] "For four days groups of white and Negro rioters waged race war in the streets of the capital until federal troops and driving rains ended the affrays" (Tindall, p. 152). A *Washington Post* retrospective of March 1, 1999, describing the 1919 riot, had it "triggered in large part by weeks of sensational news coverage...The headlines dominated the city's four daily papers—the *Evening Star*, the *Times*, the *Herald* and *The Post*—for more than a month. A sampling of these July headlines illustrates the growing lynch-mob mentality: 13 SUSPECTS ARRESTED IN NEGRO HUNT; POSSES KEEP UP HUNT FOR NEGRO; HUNT COLORED ASSAILANT; NEGRO FIEND SOUGHT ANEW."

[297] *AP, The Story of News*, by Oliver Gramling, Farrar & Rhinehart, New York, 1940, p. 30 (book prepared for the 1938 retirement of Frank Noyes as Associated Press president; Oliver Gramling was an AP manager).

[298] *20ᵗʰ Century Journey, A Memoir of a Life and Times, The Start 1904-1930,* by William L. Shirer, Bantam Books, New York, 1985, pp. 223-224: "We would pitch in to enlarge one hundred words of cable from home into several thousand words. That was where one's imagination came in." Also p. 225: "All of us around the copy desk became more or less proficient at this sort of 'expansion' of the news."

[299] "The Diallo Verdict," *New York Times*, Feb. 26, 2000. A wave of protest in New York claiming intentional police brutality in the shooting was attributed by some to media assumptions: "The Diallo crisis was a manufactured one—an unparalleled example of the power of the press, and, above all, the *New York Times*, to create the reality it reports." ("Diallo Truth, Diallo Falsehood," by Heather Mac Donald, *City Journal,* Summer 1999). Similar controversies followed night shootings by law enforcement anti-bandit squads on the California-Mexico border in the 1990s, also with signs of target panic.

[300] *Informants*: E. Wiggins, L. Davis, L. Carrier.

Chapter 24: The First Battle

[301] Two examples from outside the South suggest the scope: in the Omaha, Nebraska, riot of 1919 a white mayor was hanged and nearly killed by a mob that burned the local courthouse as they sought a black suspect; in the Springfield, Illinois, riot of 1908 a white restaurateur's business was destroyed because he tried to help African American targets.

[302] The author's initial exposé on Rosewood (*Floridian* magazine, *St. Petersburg Times*, July 25, 1982) was written in an early stage in the search for missing evidence, when some white informants, whose eyewitness status later proved doubtful, alleged mass killing of "30 to 40" African Americans. One extreme speculation, musing about "150, maximum," came from a local resident not born until 1925, and the lack of credibility in this statement was made clear in print. None of these high-number sources claimed to have actually seen the killings, or could name specific victims. As the article was published, the long process of finding African American survivors had just begun, and those survivors, once found, would prove that the death toll was much smaller than white legends portrayed, and further, that the killing was serial in nature, not occurring in simultaneous massacre form. However, the author's 1982 article was titled "the Rosewood Massacre," using a term from one informant (others used phrases such as "that riot" or "that thing at Rosewood").
Despite new evidence, the phrase "Rosewood Massacre" would become a genie impossible to put back into the bottle. In 1983 the author proposed the Rosewood story to "60 Minutes" and served as background reporter on the resulting segment (aired Dec. 11, 1983), but was not involved in writing the

script or title—which again was "The Rosewood Massacre." During taping, as correspondent Ed Bradley was speaking on-camera at the Rosewood site, the author heard a large death toll being described and pulled aside the field producer, reminding that resources provided by "60 Minutes" had enabled the location of additional witnesses, who were increasingly confirming that the death toll was small. The harried producer's response could have been an epitaph on attempts to staunch the massacre myth. He said, "*NOW* you tell me." The segment as aired used an unobtrusive switch, beginning with an opening voice-over: "Perhaps as many as forty people died here"—which the scant evidence at that time could still warrant as an extreme possibility. But at the end came a wrap-up with the switch, saying flatly: "Forty people died here." The shift to certainty was not warranted by the evidence then known.

The power of myth would continue over the years, until the 1997 motion picture *Rosewood* closed with a screen note claiming a death toll of "40 to 150," and further claiming that this was the opinion of Rosewood's survivors—which it was not. If the "40" in the film's distortion was taken from "60 Minutes" in 1983, and the "150" from the fantasy indulged in passing in 1982, then both figures were from the present writer, and had long ago been refuted by his later work. The movie's creators had obviously run a literature search, and hence knew of my article in *Tropic,* the Sunday magazine of the *Miami Herald,* on March 7, 1993, which explained that mounting evidence proved the Rosewood death toll to be no more than around twelve—and probably fewer. Viewers of the movie were not positioned to see what the movie left out. The shocking screen note looked serious, and many sophisticated viewers were convinced. The art, however, was in its persuasiveness, not in its concern for truth. In many ways over the years, the Rosewood "Massacre" has taken the measure of video magic.

[303] *The Deadly Ethnic Riot,* by Donald L. Horowitz, University of California at Berkeley Press, Berkeley, 2001, p. 376. Referring to intensive studies on 1960s riots, to the earlier era of lynching riots, and to communal violence in India, Horowitz said that examination showed "how the riot depends on conditions that assure safety for those who pursue the violence. At bottom, rioters are risk-averse actors." Also p. 385: "The risk aversion of rioters is well reflected in the balance of casualties, which is generally overwhelmingly favorable to the aggressor"; p. 384: "Possible [riot] sites can be evaluated from the standpoint of the probable safety of those attacking. Rarely do they choose the least safe areas to do their killing, even if the payoff to them there might be great; and when they do choose risky locations, they are readily dissuaded by displays of force. Generally, however, they do not choose the areas safest to themselves. They tend to take some risk, but typically a moderate one, and they can be moved quickly from greater to less risk" (cf. *I Investigate Lynchings,* by Walter White, *American Mercury,* Jan. 1929: "boastful people who practice direct action when it involve[s] no personal risk").

---

[304] *Atlantic Monthly's* iconic Delta manhunt story, purportedly a true eyewitness account from the Mississippi Delta, begins with an African American pedestrian pulling a pistol and firing coldly and randomly at a passing car, striking the white driver, which then caused various black bystanders to be tortured in a hunt for the shooter. No surprise seemed to be expressed by any of those involved that the fugitive possessed a gun in the first place. ("In the Delta—The Story of a Man-Hunt," by Beulah Ratliff, *Atlantic Monthly*, April 1920 (of events near Drew, Mississippi, in 1919). The 1919 Elaine racial rampage in the Arkansas Delta, just across the Mississippi River, found numerous sharecroppers' cabins well-armed simply for hunting, with the guns then becoming a confusing focus of uprising accusations.

[305] The first photo, in black and white, was apparently taken on January 7, showing Sheriff Bob Walker displaying the gun allegedly used by Sylvester Carrier on Thursday night; Walker seems to be displaying the gun to give public proof that the shooter was indeed deceased, so the mob would go home (in retrospect the photo can be taken as an opposite proof, for there were later tales of subterfuge aiding Sylvester's escape). The second photo, in color, shows a preserved Winchester Model 1887 repeating shotgun, leaving no doubt that the gun held by Walker is that model, closely fitting descriptions of the gun that were given by Rosewood survivors. *Informants* Bascomb and Haskell Hardee, cattlemen and friends of Sheriff Walker's son Earl in their youth, told how the gun remained with Walker and was used by Earl Walker on hunting trips. The two informants recalled handling the gun themselves in the late 1920s or early 1930s.

[306] "Winchester's Remarkable Model 1887," by Holt Bodinson, *Guns Magazine,* 2014; *The Winchester Book,* by George Madis, Taylor Publishing, 1971.

[307] The 1958–1963 ABC TV series *The Rifleman* featured Kevin Joseph "Chuck" Connors as Lucas McCain, using a modified Winchester 1892 44-40-caliber rifle. The TV series was supposedly set in the 1880s—before such guns were made. Two stand-in rifle props were used in the series, each with a rapid-fire pin modification for firing without pulling the trigger.

[308] *Informants*: J. McElveen, S. Hall.

[309] In 1917, 20,000 trench guns were purchased for the U.S. Army. These were modified Winchester pump shotguns with shorter barrels, fittings for bayonets and heat shields so the user could grasp the barrel during bayonet thrust. On Sept. 19, 1918, the government of Germany protested that the use of these guns violated the rules of war ("Joint Service Combat Shotgun Program," by Hays Parks, *The Army Lawyer*, Oct. 1997, p. 17; "The 1897 Winchester Trench Gun:

An old broom knows all the corners," Guns.com, 2014). After the 1918 German protest there was a curt reply referring to German poison gas, and the protest was dropped.

[310] A Model 1887 repeating action shotgun was brandished by actor Arnold Schwarzenegger in the 1991 film *Terminator 3 Judgment Day*, maximizing the dramatic flair inherent in the flip-cocking movement.

[311] "Conspiracy of Silence Shrouds 1916 Lynchings," by Ron Sachs, *Gainesville Sun Sunday Magazine*, Nov. 6, 1977. *Gainesville Daily Sun*, Aug. 16-21, 1916.

[312] On Jan. 5, 2002, four months after the 9/11 hijacking attacks, Florida high school student Craig Bishop, age 15, stole a Cessna 172 during a flight lesson and flew it into the 28th floor of the Bank of America Plaza building in Tampa. Bishop carried a note praising Osama bin Laden, calling him "absolutely justified in the terror he has caused on 9/11," though investigation found no conspiratorial links. Bishop was known as a quiet young man who kept to himself, apparently with no problems reported. He was also went by the name Charles Bishara and was Arab American, a background not generally mentioned in news of the event, apparently in fear of widening ethnic retaliations. The sole fatality in the 2002 crash was the pilot. Apparently the phenomenon represented emulation rather than conspiracy.

[313] The shooting is described by reminiscences filed at the Newberry branch of the Gainesville Public Library. According to the descriptions, Newberry Town Marshal Sug Beard (name of record not given) fatally shot former town marshal Dick Wright in front of a meat market on the east end of Main Street, Newberry, near the later location of Keene's Cabinet Shop. A rash of hog thefts is mentioned and the shooting is said to have occurred because the present town marshal and the meat market owner were involved in a theft ring. The shooting has apparently never been verified historically beyond this level, though the agreement of the memories seems at least to show that hog theft by local whites was a continuing problem, and not a special 1916 crisis occasioned by African Americans.

[314] *Gainesville Daily Sun*, Aug. 18, 1916.

[315] "Now boys, we only drink when we kill something" was a maxim allegedly spoken at a Levy County deer hunt (Will Yearty typescript memoir, PKYL). Before another remembered hunt, the drinking of "beer toasts" through the day was said to enliven anticipation ("Gulf Hammock Hunting Camp," *Search for Yesterday*, Chapter 16, p. 18).

[316] Myrtle Dudley, the niece of Constable George Wynne, said of his 1916

death: "He should have known better than going into a nigger's house in the middle of the night. He had somebody with him, but they both got shot"— sounding remarkably like comments by some whites after Constable Wilkerson's foray at Rosewood a half decade later (interview by Lisa Heard and Sally Morrison, Feb. 25, 1992, Samuel Proctor Oral History Program, AL 143, UFDC).

[317] *Gainesville Daily Sun*, Aug. 18, 1916: "...possessed of a mean disposition ...about 35 years old, height, five feet eight inches, weight, about 145 pounds, dark, bumpy skin, round face and stubby moustache."

[318] James Herbert Wilkerson testimony, March 18, 1994 (Box 5, first folder, Administrative Files, Vol. VIII, pp. 748-795, FAMU).

[319] James Street quoted by John H. Napier III in *Mississippi's Piney Woods*, ed. Noel Polk, University Press of Mississippi, Jackson, 1986, p 22. "Towns were gone..." (*Mississippi Forests and Forestry*, by James E. Fickle, University Press of Mississippi, Jackson, 2001, p. 119).

[320] *Mississippi Forests and Forestry*, Fickle, p. 66.

[321] Ibid., p. 103.

[322] *The Lonely Warrior, The Life and Times of Robert S. Abbott*, by Roi Ottley, H. Regnery Co., 1955, p. 177.

[323] "...[E]xtreme distortions of the numbers of deaths, insidious exaggerations that fostered a desire to even the score on the basis of 'an eye for an eye,' a white victim for a black victim, and vice versa." (*Race Riot, Chicago in the Red Summer of 1919*, by William W. Tuttle, University of Illinois Press, 1970, p. 47).

[324] Following the Tulsa race riot, the *Washington Bee*, an African American weekly, was said to headline: "Colored Rioters Poorly Armed. But Casualty List Favorable" (June 21, 1921). (*Black Power and the Garvey Movement*, by Theodore G. Vincent, Ramparts Press, Berkeley, 1971, p. 35).

[325] Foreword by John Hope Franklin, p. xvi, *Death in a Promised Land, The Tulsa Race Riot of 1921*, by Scott Ellsworth, Louisiana State University Press, 1982.

[326] Scorekeeping folklore repeatedly used nearby bodies of water to explain how large numbers of bodies could supposedly be hidden without a trace. After the Tulsa riot of 1921, secret dumping was said to have occurred in the Arkansas River; after Elaine, Arkansas, in 1919, in the Mississippi River or a swamp

called Snow Lake; after Chicago in 1919, Bubbly Creek; after East St. Louis in 1917, Cahokia Creek. The striking similarity in belief patterns, coupled with the lack of forensic evidence, could easily suggest an archetype in post-traumatic fantasy: *They were dumped in the water.*

[328] *Informant* Ernest Parham, who clerked at the Sumner commissary and sold shotgun shells, confirmed that in 1923, as today, a box held 25 shells.

Chapter 25: Man Down There

[329] Grace Elizabeth Hale titled her influential study of white supremacy "Making Whiteness": "Spectacle lynchings brutally conjured a collective, all-powerful whiteness" (p. 203, 1998). "Newspaper reporters and men around the stove at the crossroads store...all helped shape the stories of specific events into a dominant narrative..." (p. 206, 1998). (*Making Whiteness: the culture of segregation in the South*, by Grace Elizabeth Hale, Vintage Books, 1998; Knopf Doubleday, 2010).

[330] Specifically, Minnie Langley remembered her cousin Philomena going back up the stairs to rescue Buster, though this was also the moment (as everyone else remembered fleeing logically out the back door), when Philomena would portray herself as stepping over 19 dead white men on the front porch. If what Minnie said was true, a small moment of heroism by 11-year-old Philomena may have been obscured by the later mysteries of her own post-traumatic fantasy.

Chapter 26: To the Woods

[331] As white mainstream newspapers of the "race war" era created illusional black uprisings, those same illusions were taken up ironically and used by the black press in the North—and by later mainstream historians—to create opposite illusions. In this process the imagined uprisings are accepted facilely as fact, but are transformed to portray romanticized joint defense efforts allegedly made by the attacked communities. Preparatory to his 1967 survey of modern southern history, George Tindall encountered cryptic news items on Rosewood and accepted the uprising illusion without questioning it, while reversing the moral message that the newspapers had promoted. Tindall wrote: "Negroes had fought back in organized fashion not only in Washington and Chicago but in Charleston, Longview, Knoxville, Elaine, Tulsa and Rosewood; and the casualties included substantial numbers of whites." Without addressing the complexities and mysteries in the other cases (which remind of Rosewood in many ways, if examined closely), it can be said that witnesses from the one case at issue here agreed that the "organized fashion" boiled down to one man,

Sylvester Carrier.
Repeatedly the Rosewood witnesses revealed how tensions surrounding racial questions can erode the customary checks and balances of historiography with wishful thinking. Johns Hopkins University historian Michael Johnson, recipient of the ABC Clio Award from the Organization of American Historians, has warned that today's romantic invention of bygone uprisings extends back to the slavery era: "Much of the writing about slave conspiracies is based on assumptions about solidarity and community that have suffused slavery scholarship for the last forty years." (*William and Mary Quarterly*, Jan. 2002, p. 202; *The Emergence of the New South 1913-1945*, by George Brown Tindall, Louisiana State University Press, 1967, p. 155).
The process can be seen dramatically in retrospectives on the Ocoee, Florida, racial rampage of 1920. Though an investigation by Zora Hurston and all known witnesses who were interviewed later seemed to agree that central Ocoee protagonist July Perry was left to defend himself alone, historians have seemed to prefer the racist uprising illusions offered in the white press of 1920, if the polarity could be reversed to paint "uprising" as "communal self-defense." Wikipedia continues to say of Ocoee: "African-American residents fought back in an evening-long gunfight...."
Such glimpses are important not as real descriptions of Rosewood, Ocoee or other atrocity cases, but as revelations of a dream universe living within supposedly rigorous historiography. *American Historical Review* went so far as to endorse the fantasies in the 1997 film *Rosewood,* though even some former enthusiasts had jumped ship on that work, denouncing the movie's distortion of history. Not so *American Historical Review.* It cheered that "*Rosewood* [the movie] captures the often hidden story of black resistance," by depicting "blacks forced to defend home and family from the inhuman fury of the mob."
This was not how the surviving African American witnesses depicted the 1923 events. The lynching era did produce real cases of solidarity and resistance, but the creation of false cases reminds that something is badly distorted in historiographical standards on this emotion-laden ground. Arnold Toynbee's sigh bears repeating: "[E]ach generation is apt to design its history of the past in accordance with its own ephemeral scheme of thought."

[332] This picture of the Wesley Bradley household combines memories from *informant* Lee Carrier, who lived there, with those from Lee Ruth Davis, Wesley's daughter, who was among the children taken to Wright's.

[333] *Informants*: W. Evans, N. Joyner, L. Foster, B. Frazier.

[334] Other rampage incidents in the lynching era suggest that the white panic of Thursday night and Friday morning derived from what today might seem the least logical expectation. Whites believed that local African Americans (who in reality were fleeing or staying out of sight) might conspire to massively retaliate. Such fears reached a point in the Atlanta race riot of 1906 (a pogrom consisting

of whites attacking blacks) that a white child, hearing the retaliation fears expressed by adults, brought her father his ceremonial sword so that he could defend his family against the envisioned hordes. The child was future novelist Margaret Mitchell, starting early on the imagination required for *Gone With the Wind.*

335 *Race Riot in East St. Louis, July 2, 1917*, by Elliott M. Rudwick, University of Illinois Press, 1964, p. 71.

336 Ibid., p. 72.

337 Ibid., p. 55.

338 *Informants*: L. Carrier. L. Davis, L. Harris, E. Wiggins.

339 *Informants*: M. Langley, P. Doctor, A. Goins, W. McKenzie, L. Carrier, L. Washington.

340 *Informants:* N. Joyner, L. Cason.

341 *Informants*: E. Davis, B. Frazier, F. Smith, M. Thompson.

342 Mob "frenzy," as social scientists have often pointed out, does not necessarily involve wild-eyed motor dyscontrol. Rioters may appear quite deliberate, or almost inert and bored. The "frenzy" is often internal, an invisible shift into a willingness to do the previously unthinkable. After the Leo Frank lynching of Aug. 17, 1915, a prominent member of the crowd, Robert E. Lee Howell, brother of the editor of the *Atlanta Constitution*, rushed forward and began screaming about vengeance, while maniacally kicking the corpse. This was such a departure that despite the secrecy of that event, news of Howell's behavior surfaced publicly. Here was classic "frenzy," almost a seizure or a fit. Even some of the lynchers in the Frank case seemed to consider it a bizarre exception.

343 *Informant*: L. Washington.

Chapter 27: Left Behind

344 All informants agreed on the dismantling of Sumner after it had lived out the lifespan of a company timber town, in this case from 1911 to 1926. Fred Kirkland, one of the left-behinds in the woods, would tell of the deserted site of Sumner after 1926. Ernest Parham explained how lumber turned out by the Sumner mill before 1923 was already being sent to Lacoochee to build the new mill, which was in operation before 1923. "…the mill, which dominated life in

Lacoochee from 1922 to 1959...." (*Tampa Tribune*, Oct. 24, 2008). The life span of Sumner as a transitory company town seemed to be more or less standard regionally: "an Alabama lumberman remembered: 'At no time before 1935 did the management of the company ever believe they would be able to operate longer than eight or ten years.'" (*Mississippi Forests and Forestry*, by James E. Fickle, University Press of Mississippi, Jackson, 2001, p. 103).

[345] Fickle, ibid., p. 117.

[346] *Terror in the Name of God: Why Religious Militants Kill*, by Jessica Stern, HarperCollins, 2009, pp. 233, 283.

[347] The lore on marginalized backwaters displacing their frustrations into violence extends into cinema fiction, ranging from the sublime to the ridiculous. There was Black Rock (the dying desert town that hid an ethnic atrocity) found by the 1955 Spencer Tracy film *Bad Day at Black Rock*, and, at the absurd extreme, Valkenvania, a junkyard nightmare enclave found by tourists Chevy Chase and Demi Moore after a wrong turn off the New Jersey turnpike (*Nothing But Trouble*, 1991). More seriously, at the time that the phosphate boomtown of Newberry, Florida, was converting into nearly a ghost town in 1916 when World War I closed its phosphate markets, Newberry produced its mass lynching.

Chapter 28: Footprints of Panic

[348] *Little Green Men, Meowing Nuns and Head-Hunting Panics: A Study of Mass Psychogenic Illness and Social Delusion*, by Robert E. Bartholomew, McFarland & Company, Jefferson, N.C., 2011, p. 20.

[349] *The War of the Worlds*, 1898, "scientific romance" novel by H. G. Wells: radio adaptation by Howard E. Koch, directed and with narration by Orson Welles, The Mercury Theatre on the Air, CBS Radio, Oct. 30, 1938.

[350] *The Invasion from Mars: A Study in the Psychology of Panic*, by Hadley Cantril, Hazel Gaudet and Herta Herzog, Princeton University Press, Princeton, N.J., 1940; *Getting It Wrong: Ten of the Greatest Misreported Stories in American Journalism*, by Joseph W. Campbell, University of California Press, Berkeley, 2010, pp. 26-44.

Chapter 29: The Last Stand

[351] *Informant*: J. McElveen.

[352] *Informant*: J. Yearty.

[353] *New York Times*, Jan. 6, 1923; *informant*: E. Parham.

[354] *Informant*: J. Yearty.

[355] "Willard Carrier, the little Negro boy who shot and killed Warren Coleman, a Negro man at Rosewood, was given a preliminary hearing before Judge Friedman on Monday. Since he was only about six years old, he was released under a $200 bond." (*Levy Times-Democrat*, May 28, 1908, quoted in *Search for Yesterday*, Levy County Archives Committee, 1983, Chapter 13, p. 9. Indictment, Willard Carrier, May 11, 1908, LCCH.

[356] "Lot of stroke in the family," said Lonnie Carrol (he pronounced and wrote the name "Carrier" as "Carrol," speaking of "Sylvester Carrol" for example). Besides the cerebral stroke of Lonnie's father, James Carrol/Carrier, Lonnie cited a stroke leading to the death of his brother Eddie in 1945; Lonnie was also with his older brother Aaron in 1965 when Aaron suffered a stroke, collapsing on a back road in Volusia County, Florida, as he and Lonnie were tie-cutting in the woods. The above list of statements, as well as Lonnie Carrol's recitation of death years for other siblings, made it clear that his own stroke had left his mind clear in many ways, yet his speaking was labored, and the sharpness of thought seemed to come and go.

[357] The *Florida State Gazetteer and Business Directory* for 1907-1908 listed three separate turpentine operations at Rosewood at that time: 1) "M. Goins & Bros.," 2) "S. H. McKinnon" and 3) "M. T. Marshburn and Co." Moreover, what may have been a fourth firm, the Dean operation, was mentioned in two different records, those of a landmark U. S. Supreme Court case *Clyatt v. U.S.* of 1901-1905, and, in 1900, an indictment of a figure later to appear in 1923—Sam Carter—one of whose witnesses was "at J. R. Deans Turpentine Still about eight miles from Rosewood." (Box 11, Historical Felony Records, LCCH). Apparently as pines at Rosewood were exhausted, Marshburn and McKinnon merged and moved to Wylly, forming M. & M. Naval Stores, which then was bought by Daniel P. McKenzie, the owner of the Wylly operation in 1923. The Goins firm may have found fewer options because its surviving owner, Ed Goins, was African American. The original managing partner in the firm, Martin Goins, Ed's brother, died in 1905, and Ed Goins continued managing a remnant of the business for several years more, though it seemed to disappear after about 1916. For comparison, in 1911-1912, The *Gazetteer* found Rosewood's H. E. Charpia "saw mill" still operating, as well as another sawmill operated by William B. Mozo (a mill that may have been nearer to the site of later Wylly). By then, however, only two turpentine operations were listed at Rosewood: "Edward D. Goins" and "A. M. Dorsett." The 1918 *Gazetteer* found all businesses of any kind gone from the site, except for John Wright's store.

[358] The *Gazetteer* listings of three turpentine camps at Rosewood help to solve two mysteries. First, rather elaborate brick ruins were found at the site of Rosewood by the Florida Department of Law Enforcement in 1994, on the Gulf Hammock side of the old railroad right-of-way and not matching site descriptions or land records of the Goins operation. And second, there was Rosewood's other landmark event in history. On Feb. 11, 1901, two black turpentine workers who had escaped from debt bondage in Georgia were working in Levy County when they were kidnapped and taken back by their former employer, with the aid of Levy County Sheriff H. S. "Cap" Sutton. They then disappeared and were feared killed as punishment. This became a test case for an 1866 federal anti-peonage law that had been devised for Spanish hacienda abuses in New Mexico, but in the new instance was applied by Federal Magistrate Frederick Cubberly to Florida. The alleged kidnapper, Samuel Clyatt, was prosecuted and convicted under the statute. In 1905 the U.S. Supreme Court ruled on the case, by then known as *Clyatt v U.S.*, and approved use of the anti-peonage law—a step that has sometimes been called the opening for federal intervention in southern segregation-era racial abuses in the twentieth century, a precedent now taught in law schools (there were other such openings in the same years). The camp where the two workers were found and kidnapped was in Rosewood. It was not the Goins operation, however, and was said to be run by a man named Deen or Dean, who protested the kidnapping but was brushed aside. The camp in question may have been either the Marshburn or the McKinnon operation, and perhaps also gave rise to the brick ruins found in 1994. Whatever the details, a great sweep of history involving federal action toward racial abuses, and finally leading to climax in the Civil Rights era and the death of Jim Crow segregation, leads back to a tiny place in the woods, seemingly a magnet for mysteries.

[359] On Sept 11, 1905, State Supervisor of Convicts N. A. Blitch reported 11 prisoners working in Rosewood for turpentine contractor M. T. Marshburn: "Sanitary conditions good. Food ample. No sick and no punishments" (SAF). The Otter Creek camps had a larger convict presence, as late as 1913 recording 37 black male prisoners, eight guards and eight dogs, while the 1910 Federal Census found 54 prisoners at Otter Creek (all but one prisoner black), a warden, ten guards and four "water boys." All such convict leasing was apparently gone from the area before 1923, but earlier, during the childhood of Willard Carrier, harsher conditions prevailed.

[360] William Samuel Yearty (b. July 2, 1877) typescript memoir (PKYL).

[361] *Informants*: T. Hawkins, M. Langley, S. Hall.

[362] "Memoirs of Martin Hoban, Logging Florida's Giant Cypress," by Baynard Kendrick and Barry Walsh, *Forest History Today*, Spring/Fall 2007, p. 47.

[363] "Nathanial Abraham, back in prison…," Associated Press, April 22, 2012; *Boys Among Men: Trying and Sentencing Juveniles as Adults*, by Daniel L. Myers, Greenwood Publishing Group, 2005, p. 1.

[364] The Jonesboro shooters came from a hunting-oriented culture and stole their grandfather's guns; Nathaniel Abraham was surrounded by Detroit's bizarre "devil's night" custom of arson and vandalism preceding Halloween (more than 500 fires set in a three-day period some years, peaking in 1994). When arrested, Abraham's face was said to be painted for a Halloween party. All of these child shooters lived among patterns that could invite emulation.

[365] *Informant*: B. Bryant. This was apparently a story that the informant had been told by family members, from a time when she was too young to remember well herself.

[366] The screenplay of the 1997 Warner Bros. film *Rosewood* used at least 22 names of real persons from the 1923 events, while placing those names on imagined personalities and actions, and interweaving them with at least 26 other names of characters wholly imagined—though somehow the result was endorsed as "history" by talk shows and even some legislators. The character designated by the screenplay as "Big Baby" (actor Ken Sagoes) was placed in a remarkably degrading pornographic sequence which in real life had never occurred. Nothing like it was mentioned or even hinted by any real survivor.

[367] Oct. 11, 1910, W. A. and Sallie Sauls sell to Sam and Ellen King (Book 1, p. 542, LCCH); Feb. 7, 1919, four acres owned by Sam King (Book 14, p. 19, LCCH); "Sam King—4.06 acres" (1922, 1926 tax rolls, LCCH).

Chapter 30: First Flames

[368] The description of the King household and the events there on the night of Jan. 4, 1923, is from *informant* Eloise King Davis, adopted daughter of Sam and Ellen King.

[369] The boundary, not marked on the ground but traced by property divisions, separated sections 29 and 30, T 14-S, R 14-E, Levy County, running north and south to intersect the SAL railroad at the Masonic tract (USGS, Sumner Quadrangle, 1955, 1993; LCCH).

[370] Federal Census, 1870, 1880, 1900, 1910. *Informants*: L. Carrier, S. Hall, T. Hawkins, N. Joyner, W. Evans, L. Foster, L. Davis, J. Yearty, F. Kirkland; William Samuel Yearty (b. July 2, 1877) typescript memoir (PKYL); *Florida Gazetteer and Business Directory*, 1890, 1908, 1911-1912, R. L. Polk & Co.,

Jacksonville; property records, LCCH.

[371] "Melungeons," *The New Encyclopedia of Southern Culture: Vol. 6, Ethnicity,* Celeste Ray and Charles Reagan Wilson eds., UNC Press Books, Chapel Hill, 2007. Informant Margaret Cannon referred to the light-skinned tri-racial residents of western Rosewood as "Croatans," a term perhaps surviving from the Roanoke Island mystery of 1590. The area of light-complected people on the western side of the Rosewood community was known as "Goins," or as "Hilton Station" (apparently for Martin Goins's son Hilton Goins) and, according to survivor Margie (Hall) Johnson, it was sometimes sarcastically called "Yallertown," in reference to "high yellow" skin tone.

[372] Aug. 19, 1908, sale of 3.5 acres to M. B. and Lexie Gordon (Book 14, p. 9, LCCH); Oct. 11, 1910, sale of adjoining 2.2 acres to M. B. and Lexie Gordon by W. A. and Sallie Sauls (Book 6, p. 296, LCCH); tax rolls 1922: 5.5 acres owned by M. B. Gordon (Cassette Vol. 2, LCCH).

[373] The equation of a crow's hoarse croaking with whooping cough could be characterized as sympathetic magic, going beyond the chemical or herb applications of "like cures like" associated with homeopathy. A white storekeeper at Otter Creek in the same era reported a similar belief: If a chicken hen crows like a rooster, kill it or the family will get sick (William S. Yearty, b. July 2, 1877, typescript memoir, PKYL).

[374] *Informants*: M. Johnson, E. Wiggins, A. Doctor, M. Ames, H. Hendricks-Frye, B. Frazier, O. Monroe; W. Yearty memoir, ibid., PKYL.

[375] On July 14, 1937, Rob Ingram's brother Will, still living in the area, would be arrested for stealing a hundred-pound hog from another white. Rob stood witness for his brother, stating that the free-roaming hog in question was really Will's, and "that the hog was raised by the Defendant from a pig." Obviously, someone's idea of truth was a bit lax. In such livestock quarrels, an atmosphere of transgression and deception lay waiting to be projected into the most explosive realm of misperception, that of race (*State of Fla. v. Will Ingram,* historical felony records, LCCH).

[376] Sympathetic magic was described well in the following terms:
"If we analyze the principles of thought on which magic is based, they will probably be found to resolve themselves into two: first, that like produces like, or that an effect resembles its cause; and, second, that things which have once been in contact with each other continue to act on each other at a distance…The former principle may be called the Law of Similarity, the latter the Law of Contact or Contagion. From the first of these principles…the magician infers that he can

produce any effect he desires merely by imitating it." [as with a voodoo doll]: *Ethnographische Parallelen und Vergleiche,* by Richard Andree, J. Maier, Stuttgart, 1878.

[377] Aug. 19, 1908; March 22, 1910; sale of one acre with 356 feet of railroad frontage by W. A. Sauls to Magnolia Lodge #148, F.&A.M. (Book 4, p. 450, LCCH). *Informants*: L. Davis, E. Davis, T. Hawkins, L. Carrier, S. Hall.

[378] *Informants*: E. Jenkins, E. Davis, M. Langley, M. Johnson.

[379] A happenstance in the property record for the Rosewood Masonic lodge causes that building to be one of the few vanished Rosewood structures whose approximate site can be deduced on the ground today. This is because the Masonic plot lay where the discernible north-south line between map sections 29 and 30 met another marker that is still visible: the path of the bygone Seaboard railroad. Guided by these lines in 2009, archaeologists Edward Gonzalez-Tennant and James Davidson pinpointed the one-acre area where the Masonic lodge would once have stood, though to the naked eye the area seemed featureless, covered in vegetation and long since found to be unpromising in terms of any archaeological remains. However, the two archaeologists learned that theirs was not the only effort at the Rosewood site. Around the same time a former Florida university professor, Marvin Dunn, arranged for a South Florida investor to purchase, for $44,000, five acres of ground in another part of the overgrown Rosewood area, stating hopes that the state could be persuaded to build a park there. The retired professor, Dr. Dunn, then obtained $48,703 from the state as an historical preservation grant in order to dig into his five acres, saying he was seeking ruins of the Rosewood railroad depot—though all witnesses, records and other evidence agreed that the depot site was not at that location, or anywhere near. The five acres Dr. Dunn had obtained lay in an area of seasonal swamp, often-submerged empty woodland where no one had ever lived. In essence, the $48,703 grant from the state was spent in reconfirming that emptiness, for nothing was found. However, Dr. Dunn then convinced the state to pay another $49,975, now making a total of nearly $100,000 paid to him in public funds, to dig at another site—the Masonic plot that Gonzalez-Tennant and Davidson had earlier deduced. His digging there was depicted in a video, showing Dr. Dunn at a pit dug in the ground with no visible labels, stakes, strings or other signs of systematic investigation. Davidson eventually distanced himself from the effort, saying that its philosophy was that "all you needed was a shovel and a site." State funding was not deterred, however, and Dr. Dunn received yet a third grant of nearly $50,000, bringing the total paid to him from public funds to nearly $150,000.

By 2011, Dr. Dunn reported proof that his efforts were vindicated, because, he said, he had unearthed the remains of a ceremonial sword used in Rosewood's Masonic initiation rites. Davidson said in a telephone interview that the find was only an oblong mass of corroded metal that could as easily have been a discarded automobile tie rod. Dr. Dunn announced the finding of the alleged sword in another promotional video, but it later seemed to disappear from public mention. By that time, Dr. Dunn had convinced the University Press of Florida, the state's premiere outlet for scholarly information, to publish a book by him that would showcase the archaeological finds, including the alleged sword. This led to a two-year editorial process in which all mention of the archaeological finds were excised from successive versions of a changing manuscript. A copy editor told superiors of discovering that substantial parts of the text had been plagiarized.

This failed to deter University Press, however, and its director suggested a romantic title for the developing manuscript: "The Dark Heart of Florida." The drafts were to be "whipped into shape," a project editor wrote in an internal email. Another editor emailed on October 4, 2012, that the project "has been a mess at every stage."

In February 2013 the results were published under the title *The Beast in Florida: A History of Anti-Black Violence*. Six months later a copy was bought by criminologist Margaret Vandiver, who noticed that one of the photographs in the book seemed to be falsely labeled, whereupon the present author was asked to examine the book for other irregularities. A challenge to the book then resulted in an outside judge, historian Canter Brown, finding so many instances of plagiarism in this extraordinary work that Brown said he stopped counting, as he advised the press that the book was unsalvageable. So many different sources had been plagiarized that the results merged confusingly. In addition, the falsely labeled photograph was shown to be surrounded by a large number of other fact errors.

Once more, as in the Rosewood claims case of the 1990s, a disowned atrocity had attracted a process of false appearances. In December 2013 *The Beast in Florida* was repudiated by University Press of Florida for "scholarly misconduct" and its contract was canceled, though copies already in libraries were left there with no explanation to scholars or the public as to what had happened, or which information in the book should be approached with caution. The State of Florida had lost nearly $150,000, the taxpayers were never told of the debacle and there was no public reflection on what this process suggested about the Sunshine State's difficulties in examining its buried past. Somewhere, a forgotten archive box may still hold an unrecognizable length of corroded metal labeled as a Masonic sword.

[380] The third degree of freemasonry marks the all-important elevation from journeyman to master Mason. Its initiation rite involves a harrowing interrogation ceremony somewhat like a hard-boiled police interrogation, which has bequeathed to American culture the term "getting (or giving) the third degree."

[381] The paths of Masonry and another influential institution, the Church of Jesus

Christ of Latter-day Saints, crossed fatefully in 1842, when Mormon church founder Joseph Smith also founded a Masonic lodge, and, incorporated Masonic symbols into Mormon church ceremonies. By 1848, however, with Smith and his followers settled in frontier Illinois, he was accused of dictatorial social control, then was jailed and attacked in the settlement of Carthage. A mob of angry non-Mormons, reportedly with blacked faces (as was not uncommon among rioting mobs in that period) was said to contain some fellow Masons. Stories would persist that Smith tried to signal them by shouting a secret Masonic distress phrase: "Oh, Lord, my God, Is there no help for the Widow's Son?"—though if so, the appeal failed, for the attack continued, and Smith was killed.

[382] *Informants*: S. Hall, M. Johnson, W. Evans. In its 1994 Rosewood investigation (report Dec. 23, 1994), the Florida Department of Law Enforcement located surviving Teacher's Daily Registers for 1921-1923 in schools for white children at Sumner and Wylly, but could find no surviving written record from the public school for African Americans that had once existed at Rosewood, a school pre-dating the community's private subscription school in its Masonic hall. The only known documentation of that public school that still survives (aside from witness recollections) seems to consist of five words. On Dec. 3, 1923, a parcel of land was bought at the Rosewood site, and was described as "Joining Negro School House Lot" (Book 17, p 276, LCCH).

[383] Jan. 1, 1923, Cedar Key Town Company leased to M. Goins & Bros. Naval Stores eight square miles of pinelands for three years, including sections 2, 5, 7, 8, 9 and 10 of Township 15-S, Range 13-E (LCCH).

[384] As shown by the square and compass symbol on Martin Goins's obelisk-style Masonic gravestone, still extant at the site of Rosewood, approximate coordinates: 29.236494,-82.929492.

[385] *Informants*: W. Evans, L. Davis, E. Jenkins, M. Langley, E. Davis, T. Hawkins.

[386] *Levy Times-Democrat*, Oct. 14, 1911, cited in *Search for Yesterday*, Levy County Archives Committee, 1983, Chapter 13, p. 11.

[387] This long-lived dispatch also appeared in publications as diverse as the *Nashville Tennessean* (Jan. 6), the *New York Age* (Jan. 13) and the *Literary Digest* (Jan. 20). Thus it was particularly well represented in archives in the 1960s when historian George Tindall found it.

[388] Four vacant homes:
    1. Frank Burns home. Sept. 1, 1913, sale of Lot 5, Block 2 of the town

of Rosewood, and other property, by Mrs. L. L. Charpia to J. T. Tatum (this was apparently the site of the defunct Charpia cedar mill; Book 8, p. 772, p. 331). The abandoned rooming house that had served the cedar mill then became home to the Frank and Mary Burns family, as recalled by witnesses including their daughter Lillie Washington, who lived there. After the death of Frank Burns, Mary Burns and the rest of the family moved 25 miles northeast to Lennon, where a son-in-law was woods rider at a turpentine camp, thus leaving the Burns home vacant to meet the 1923 violence.

2. Fred Edwards home. Oct. 11, 1910, sale of two acres by W. A. and Sallie Sauls to Fred and Josephine Edwards, along railroad next to Gordon plot (Book 6, p. 428). Informants agreed that this home, standing between the Burns and Gordon homes, had fallen vacant well before the 1923 violence. Later descendants also agreed; in 1994 they received state compensation for the holding as part of the Rosewood claims case.

3. Benny McCoy home. Feb. 13, 1912, sale of two acres by W. A. and Sallie Sauls to B. F. McCoy (Book 6, p. 337). Sept. 8, 1916, sale of two acres by Minnie Gordon to Benny McCoy (Book 11, p. 580). Benny McCoy was a married son of farmer John McCoy, whose 114 acres lay farther north of the railroad. Benny's sister Lutie Foster said that her brother and his family were untouched by the 1923 violence, apparently having moved away from their home just north of the railroad, near the Masonic lodge, at a time well before 1923.

4. Will Marshall home. No separate property record has been found for the abandoned home of Will and Agnes Marshall, and it may have stood on the Goins family plot. It was well remembered, along with its vacant condition after 1917, by informants Eva Jenkins (who had lived there), Willie Evans and others. After Agnes Marshall died in 1917, her daughter Eva explained, as others agreed, the widower, Will Marshall, took the surviving family to Gainesville, where he, too, was said to have died, around 1920. The house was described as a comfortable one-story dwelling on the north side of the railroad, with rockers on the porch and swings in the yard.

[389] *Informants*: E. Foster, T. Hawkins, L. Carrol, L. Davis, W. Evans, G. Alexander, C. Pollard, L. Washington, E. Davis.

> 1900 Federal Census: head of household M. B. Gordon, "turpentine farmer," and wife "Mexie" Gordon, born Sept. 1867, with five children. The children's listed birthplaces confirm a move from North Carolina around 1895 (son Frank was born in N.C. in Sept. 1894, but daughter Mary born in Fla. in Jan. 1898. Daughter "Fonnie," born Oct. 1898, was apparently still living with widowed Lexie Gordon around the time of the violence in 1923.

1910 Federal Census: head of household B. Minner Gordon "sawmill laborer;" wife Lexie Gordon, age 47; six sons and daughters, including Annabella, age 24; Mary, age 14; Fonnie, age 11 and Rosie, age eight.

1920 Federal Census: head of household Lexie Gordon, widow, age 52; son-in-law "John" Goins; daughter Annabelle Goins, age 31; grandson Walter Goins, age 2; granddaughter (Sarah) Goins, age 7; granddaughter Elvira Robinson, age 15; daughter (Fonnie Benbow?), age 21; grandson (Hilton Benbow?), age 11 months; daughter Mary Johnson, age 24; granddaughter (Elutsie?) Johnson, age 8.

(By Jan. 1923, family members agreed, most of Lexie Gordon's live-in daughters had moved away with their families, leaving Lexie alone with perhaps one daughter, Fonnie, and perhaps Fonnie's small son).

[390] The East St. Louis riot: "...[S]mall gangs lighted torches, joking while waiting for Negroes to flee from the furnaces that had been their homes. Residents faced a terrible decision—to remain inside and await incineration or to risk slaughter by gunfire outside." (*Race Riot in East St. Louis*, July 2, 1917, by Elliott M. Rudwick, University of Illinois Press, 1964, p. 46).

[391] Widow Laura Jones and her son Raymond lived across the railroad from the house where Minnie Mitchell lived with her grandparents James and Emma Carrier. Minnie remembered the Jones household as an unpretentious place, the recipient of any killed opossums that James Carrier might bring home from hunting. His wife Emma was too fastidious to eat possums, being repelled by their habit of scavenging dead carcasses, and Minnie was sent to take them across the tracks to Miz Laura, who didn't seem to mind. However, Laura Jones was not destitute, cultivating a patch of sugar cane beside her house and owning the 11 acres where she lived, according to the county's 1922 tax rolls (LCCH).

[392] A recurring story from the Newberry, Florida, mass lynching of 1916 said that its secrecy was enforced by requiring all onlookers to come forward and touch the hangman's ropes, thus to certify partnership in the crime and an obligation not to tell who did it. The same rationale has sometimes been put forth as the reason for the riddling of a lynching victim's corpse with bullets, ostensibly to make all the shooters claim a share in the illegal execution. There have been few polls to assess more impulsive reasons. (Sachs, *Gainesville Sun*, Nov. 6, 1977, quoted an elderly informant from Newberry who repeated the rope-touching story).

[393] *See Appendix C:* "Photo of Sheriff Bob Walker with Sylvester Carrier's Gun."

[394] Arnett Goins, Philomena Doctor's younger brother, said in 1993 that he did not believe his uncle Sylvester had been killed in 1923 because at a family funeral in the 1950s, a messenger came to Sylvester's immediate family and said they should attend to a residence near Palatka, Florida, where Sylvester was said to have died while hiding out. However, Arnett Doctor (Philomena Doctor's son) said the family was still receiving postcards from Sylvester in the 1960s—coming from a hiding place in Louisiana. There are other examples. Each story is improbable internally but barely possible. When compared they erode this small space of possibility and act as mutual disproof.

[395] Rosetta Bradley Jackson, a daughter of Rosewood survivor Wesley Bradley, born Jan. 21, 1924, gave the following account: "I never heard he [Sylvester Carrier] was wounded, but I understand that the Masons—at that time Masons were a very strong and very religious organization. They helped him escape and that he died years later, and they said he went to Texas and then he died later....There was a small article in the Louisiana paper that he had died, but he had changed his name." (interview for Rosewood claims case by William Rogers and Maxine Jones, Sept. 25, 1993, Attorney General's Rosewood files, Curington file, Vol. 26, p. 280). This account can be compared to another from informant Allen Stephenson, who heard about the 1923 violence from eyewitnesses when he lived in Wylly just after the events, and alternative beliefs had apparently not had time to grow. Stephenson said: "His own people—his sister—they all know. They'll tell you. He didn't escape."

[396] *Biography of Power: A History of Modern Mexico, 1810-1996,* by Enrique Krauze, HarperCollins, 1997, pp. 303, 825: "As always happens when the heroes of a people die, extravagant stories begin to spread. The corpse exhibited in Cuautla was said to lack a small wart on the face or the birthmark of a hand on its chest...Or the little finger Zapata once had injured was intact and unscarred on the corpse. People swore they had seen him at night, mounted on [his famous horse] *As de Oro.* Much later there were reports of an old man glimpsed behind the walled up door of a jailhouse in Anenicuilco—it had to be Zapata. Nineteen years later there was somebody who said, 'I saw his body...the one they killed was not Don Emiliano, but his *compadre* Jesus Delgado.'" A eighty-year-old *zapatista* veteran said: "The day before [the shooting] he read a telegram from his other *compadre,* the Arab. Now Zapata is dead, but he died in Arabia; he sailed to Arabia from Acapulco."

Chapter 31: Crow's Thrice

[397] Matthew 26:34, King James Version: "Verily I say unto thee, That this night, before the cock crow, thou shalt deny me thrice."

[398] Four surviving eyewitnesses from this group—M. Langley, L. Carrol

(Carrier), P. Doctor and A. Goins—would confirm directly what a number of other informants said about their flight.

[399] Their sister, Lee Ruth Davis, confirmed the nicknames and names of record of Marion (Bishop) and Donarion (Soda) Bradley, as did other informants. Donarion "Bishop" Bradley b. Sept. 15, 1903, d. May 5, 1982; Marion "Soda" Bradley d. March 1974 (Box 3, Folder 6, FAMU).

[400] *Panic Behavior, Discussion and Readings*, by Duane P. Schultz, Random House, 1964, p. 6 (citing Quarantelli, 1954, p. 272). and pp. 57-58 (citing Freud, 1921).

[401] *Informants*: L. Carrol, T. Evens. M. Langley, L. Carrier, L. Davis. "Wade Carrol," born Feb. 5, 1903, 5 feet 5 inches tall, 185 pounds, nine years in public school in Levy County (St. Johns County Sheriff's Department, employed as court bailiff in post-Rosewood years, by telephone, 1982). Marriage record, LCCH.

Chapter 32: Road Shadow

[402] 1925 Florida state census: Gainesville, Fla., population 8,466 (p. 84).
1920 Federal Census: Gainesville, Fla.. population 6,860.
1925 state census reported entire Alachua County population as 32,084 (p. 16).
"We have easily, ten thousand inhabitants and for peace and good order we will match it against any city or town anywhere on the created earth."—Col. Robert Davis, editorial page editor, *Gainesville Daily Sun*, Jan. 3, 1923.
"By 1920 the city's population soared to over 10,000."—"A History of Gainesville, Florida," by Historic Gainesville Incorporated (Web site). It was reported in the 1920s that the 1920 Federal Census originally undercounted Gainesville, giving it 5,000 inhabitants, until irate city fathers forced a recount, which then produced the 6,860 figure. Even some of the most basic details of the 1923 Rosewood setting (like Gainesville's real size) are lost in official murk, as if visible only through an unfocused camera lens.
By 2007, the university city of Gainesville, Florida, had come a long way, to be ranked the Number One place to live in North America by Cities Ranked and Rated.

[403] *Gainesville Daily Sun*, editorial, January 19, 1923.

[404] *Gainesville Daily Sun*, Aug. 13, 1922, p. 6: "COLONEL 'BOB' NAMED AS GREATEST ORATOR STATE HAS PRODUCED."

[405] "Man's instinct to kill remains uncontrolled." (*Gainesville Daily Sun*,

editorial, Jan. 14, 1923); "Shooting Doves" (Jan. 22, 1923). "The editor of the Sun, looking back through a vista of more than seventy years, sees the good old colored 'Mammy' who nursed us in childhood....It is strange how the very mention of the old time colored people touches the hearts of the better class of the southerners ...[t]hose of us who recall the real old black Joe of slavery days..." (Jan. 18, 1923).

[406] "A brutish negro made a criminal assault on an unprotected white girl. As a result of this, two officers of the law were killed* and many others wounded. Houses were burned, indignation, vengeance and terror ran riot. We do not know how to write about it. We feel too indignant just now to write with calm judgment and we shall wait a little while." (*Gainesville Daily Sun*, editorial, Jan. 6, 1923). *This interpretation of the deaths of Poly Wilkerson and Henry Andrews during a home invasion (calling them "officers of the law") could be interestingly compared to arguments blaming the slaves for the Civil War.

[407] Ambassador James Gerard reportedly said: "The Foreign Minister of Germany once said to me 'your country does not dare do anything against Germany, because we have in your country 500,000 German reservists who will rise in arms against your government if you dare to make a move against Germany.' Well, I told him that that might be so, but that we had 500,001 lamp posts in this country, and that that was where the reservists would be hanging the day after they tried to rise." ("American Leaders Speak, Recordings from World War I and the 1920 Election," National Forum Series, Library of Congress, http://memory.loc.gov/ammem/nfhtml/)

During World War I, mob hostility toward German-Americans was widespread in Florida: "Acts of reprisal against German Americans were as common as rumors of activities of German spies. In Plant City a man was arrested and his baggage searched for vials of typhoid and yellow fever germs, which, according to rumor, were to be deposited in the county water supply. In Tampa a rooming house was fire-bombed, reportedly because two of its lodgers who were 'unnaturalized Germans' had been talking about the United States in a way that...stirred considerable feeling." ("Intervention and Reaction: Florida Newspapers and United States Entry into World War I." by Peter C. Ripley, *Florida Historical Quarterly*, Jan. 1971, p. 265).

The sawmill town of Sumner was not exempt. Shingle mill worker Robert Missouri recalled a story that a German saboteur was caught red-handed trying to poison the water tower that stood over the Sumner mill; Missouri did not doubt the story's accuracy. A more horrific tale said that at Cummer operations in Jacksonville a German-American worker who cheered too loudly for the Kaiser was pushed into a furnace and never seen again. Jason McElveen recalled that in the euphoria at war's end in 1918 he climbed to the top of the Sumner water tower and triumphantly planted the flag. Racial passions merged with war passions during the war; African Americans were said by rumors to be bribed by German agents to become saboteurs—a modernizing of the slave insurrection panic rumor. Amid World War I's fears, Home Guards were reportedly placed around a drinking-water reservoir in Tampa against alleged black poisoners. Nationwide, the kindled mob impulses of World War I led into a "Red Summer" of epidemic "race wars" in 1919 (25 separate riots that year, according to Tindall, p. 152).

[408] *The Other Florida*, by Gloria Jahoda, Charles Scribners Sons, NY, 1967, p. 228: "The naval stores saga has been written in blood. 'Don't you ever mess with no teppentine folks,' Negro Floridians of the towns warned me over and over. 'They savages without a God.' "

[409] A mysterious racial confrontation in Sapulpa, Oklahoma, made national news for a moment at the same time as Rosewood, then disappeared from the news without explanation. Today, even in Sapulpa itself there are few clues as to what happened.

[410] *Chicago Daily News*, Jan. 5, 1923; *Washington Post*, Jan. 6, 1923; *New York Amsterdam News*, Jan. 12, 1923.

[411] Florida state census 1925, p. 80. *Florida State Gazetteer and Business Directory 1925*, R. L. Polk & Co., Jacksonville. *Search for Yesterday*, by Levy County Archives Committee, published in sections 1977-1983. *Informant*: J. Turner.

[412] The Florida state census of 1925, p. 59, placed Levy County's African American population at 4,032. In 1920 the county's African American population was reportedly 3,960.

[413] Scraping: "Wade Leonard, Florida Naval Stores Operator," *Florida Historical Quarterly*, Jan. 1971, p. 381. *Informants*: C. Atkins, J. Turner.

[414] During Rosewood claims case testimony on March 7, 1994, legislative special master Richard Hixson pointed out that census figures on Levy County's African American population showed no significant decrease between 1920 (when 4,032 African American residents were counted) and 1925 (when a state census counted 3,960). This population plateau endured despite steady outward migration for economic reasons, seeming to confirm that the forced depopulation suffered at Rosewood was confined to a small area (Cassette 1, testimony recordings, FAMU).

[415] On June 1, 1994, the Civil Rights Division of the Florida Attorney General's Office began extensive advertising in newspapers large and small, seeking any unaccounted for Rosewood survivors and descendants, and offering financial rewards from funds allotted by the legislature. Civil Rights officer Guy

Robinson reported charting family trees from Rosewood covering more than 400 people, including descendants. The present author was assigned to review claimants for 1923 residency status in Rosewood. The search continued until a deadline of Dec. 31, 1994. No stories of previously unknown deaths appeared. (Associated Press, May 9, May 31, 1994; *Los Angeles Times*, Feb. 12, 1995).

[416] A similar aid to assessing exaggerated body-count stories was provided after the Atlanta race riot of 1906. Repentant municipal authorities in Atlanta made a blanket offer to pay funeral expenses for any African American fatality. It was pointed out that this gave incentive for any additional deaths to be reported. None were.

[417] A summary presented in the 1994 claims-case hearing demonstrated how a single roadside killing, that of Mingo Williams, could be expanded in imagination by excited assumptions. The summary said of the Rosewood violence: "Black people walking down streets in towns twenty miles away were gunned down. The sanitized news accounts of the day reported seven people dead. The people who were there place the number at over 100." In fact, no "people who were there" gave such accounts. Only rumors among some whites—who were distant from the scene—said anything similar. The summary's phrase "twenty miles away" was apparently a reference to Mingo Williams, but led to a disguised assumption—almost racist in tone—that if one African American were killed there must have been dozens of others in a culture too confused for counting (Box 3, Exhibit 1, FAMU).

[418] William Crighton "Kay" Bryce, the conductor on the passenger train running through Rosewood, was said by his daughter, Mary Leona Howard, to have had a childhood friend, an African American, who was killed by an anonymous roadside shooter, never identified. Howard said her father remained haunted by the event. The large sample of Rosewood informants yielded various stories of three-R homicides (Random Roadside Racial), rarely investigable in a morass of folklore, forgetfulness and criminal guilt.

[419] *Gainesville Daily Sun*, Jan. 5, 1923. Via wire service, this announcement about Deputy Dunning appeared at least as far away as the Orlando, Florida, *Sentinel* on the same day, where local readers would have been at a loss to know the deeper significance back in Gainesville. Alachua County Commissioners Minutes for 1922-1923 show that Deputy Dunning received a special payment of ten dollars per month, apparently for his disability after the July 4, 1922, shooting.

[420] *Gainesville Daily Sun*, July 6, 1922, p. 1: "Deputy Sheriff Shot and Badly Wounded by Negro Moonshiners."

[421] "A brutish negro made a criminal assault on an unprotected white girl. As a

result of this, two officers of the law were killed...." Davis apparently found it easy to believe that Poly Wilkerson and Henry Andrews were lawmen as with Deputy Dunning six months earlier, the imagined climax to an epidemic of black-on-white shootings of officers (*Gainesville Daily Sun*, Jan. 6, 1923). On Jan. 7 Davis wrote that "Rosewood...was no 'Southern Lynching Outrage.' It was caused by the shooting down and killing of two officers of the law and the wounding of another. These law officers were shot down by negroes, barricaded in a house where a brutish beast was supposed to be sheltered and this brute had criminally assaulted a white woman."

[422] *Gainesville Daily Sun*, Jan. 7, 1923.

[423] The series of inter-racial shootings of officers included the following:
> May 11, 1912—Deputy Charles Slaughter and helper F. V. White killed, Deputy J. A. Manning wounded;
> Sept. 15, 1913—Jacksonville police officer Napoleon Hagan killed;
> Aug. 17, 1916—Alachua County Deputy/Constable George Wynne killed, helper Lem Harris wounded;
> Aug. 10, 1917—Jacksonville police detective Frank Hagan killed (he was a brother of Napoleon Hagan above);
> Sept. 26, 1919—Jacksonville police officer Charles Turknett killed;
> June 18, 1921—Alachua County Deputy Robert Arnow killed;
> July 4, 1922—Alachua County Deputy Frank Dunning wounded, permanently disabled.

(In addition, two white officers were killed by whites during the same period: Jacksonville police officer Henry Everett in 1920 and Lake City Police Chief Hardy Revels in 1922). The period's racial tensions were underscored in 1919 by Florida Governor Sidney Catts, who in a March 28 letter scolded the NAACP, telling it "to [teach] your people not to kill our white officers and disgrace our white women."

[424] *Forgotten Heroes: Police Officers Killed in Early Florida, 1840-1925*, by William Wilbanks, Turner Publishing Co., 1998, p. 115. Wilbanks's work brought to light the seldom-examined Slaughter-White killing and revealed the contra-dictions in the attendant newspaper conspiracy theory.

[425] As a Jan. 13 retraction of Davis's earlier errors on the "two lawmen," the *Sun* ran an item from Levy County's small weekly, the *Levy Times-Democrat*, demonstrating the error and criticizing it. Unfortunately, no original 1923 copies of that newspaper have been found.

[426] Special deputies' lists have modernized along with other institutions. Today the Alachua County Sheriff's Office continues to maintain a Reserve Deputies Program with certified criminal justice standards. As to the special "colonels"

appointed by Florida governors in the early twentieth century, these were officially called "lieutenant colonels," with no military authority, though many proudly referred to themselves as "colonel." Three "colonels" ran Florida newspapers at the time of the Rosewood events, deploying their journalistic troops at the *Tampa Morning Tribune,* the *Orlando Sentinel* and the *St. Augustine Evening Record.* On the grandest scale, one of the architects of the modern global political map, working at the Versailles conference after World War I, was President Woodrow Wilson's close advisor, "Colonel" Edward House of Houston, Texas. "Colonel House" was another faux southern warrior, appointed honorarily by a governor with no real military rank. Not only news writers but the crowned heads of Europe called him "Colonel House."

[427] Although the names of the two alleged killers of Mingo Williams were provided by an informant, that party could cite only second- or third-hand knowledge without corroboration, while displaying credibility issues on other points. This allegation would seem too thin for a public murder accusation against named individuals. Despite repeated attempts to find corroboration of the allegation through other sources, none has emerged. The names are not given here.

[428] Legislative testimony in 1921 described the 1920 promotional contract that allowed the phenomenal spread of the previously small Ku Klux Klan, Inc., expanding it from Georgia into much of the rest of the nation. The contract was said to be signed in June 1920. Soon afterward a newspaper item appeared in a logical area of expansion, nearby Florida. Wording in the article (in the *Bradford County Telegraph,* 74 miles northeast of Rosewood) suggested that the item was placed by the Klan itself, with a news dateline of August 4 and saying that the organization had begun seeking Florida members. This may have marked the first known evidence of the revamped Klan's official entry into the state. By the time of the Ocoee riot on November 2, 1920, Klan activities in Florida were growing rapidly. As a Georgia corporation, the Knights of the Ku Klux Klan, Inc., was said to have been born originally in a pact signed on October 26, 1915, amid excitement in Atlanta over the August lynching of Leo Frank and the upcoming Atlanta premiere of *The Birth of a Nation* (called America's first full-length motion picture), which presented the then-extinct Ku Klux Klan of Civil War Reconstruction as the film's collective hero. In recent years former *Tampa Tribune* reporter Billy Townsend has described evidence of occasional Ku Klux Klan phraseology or emulation in Florida as early as 1918, though generally the small organization of that moment was considered to operate only in Georgia, and to a minor extent in Alabama (*The Ku-Klux Klan: Hearing Before the Committee on Rules, House of Representatives, Sixty-Seventh Congress,* U.S. Government Printing Office, 1921, pp. 150, 180, 148, 121; *Bradford County Telegraph,* Aug. 20, 1920: "Aug. 4—Work of organizing branches Knights of the Ku Klux Klan throughout Florida already has been started....it was announced today.").

[429] *Gainesville Daily Sun*, Jan. 1-2, 1923.

[430] The New Year's Eve error was repeated in 2001 (*The Invisible Empire: The Ku Klux Klan in Florida*, by Michael Newton, University Press of Florida: "On New Year's Eve, Gainesville Kluxers staged a cross-burning rally..."), though the present author dismally found an earlier example in his own work, occurring in his March 7, 1993, overview of Rosewood in *Tropic*, the Sunday magazine of the *Miami Herald*. The seemingly small difference of a day—January 1 switched to December 31—would loom larger in 2001, when it was used to imply that the Rosewood violence was a proven Klan project. In fact, no evidence has ever been found to demonstrate a Klan presence at Rosewood. The rectifying of the New Year's Eve sequence removes the last prop to any such suppositions. The evidence on the real link between the Ku Klux Klan and the Rosewood violence, if any link ever existed, has yet to be found.

[431] *Gainesville Daily Sun*, Jan. 19 and 21, 1923; "White Robes and Crosses: Father John Conoley, The Ku Klux Klan, and the University of Florida." by Stephen R. Prescott, *Florida Historical Quarterly*, Vol. 71, No. 1, July 1992, p 18.

[432] At this writing even the Wikipedia entry on the *Gainesville Sun*, recapping that newspaper's history, prominently uses the allegation that Robert Davis said he was a 1920s Ku Klux Klan member, as if this were a landmark in the paper's development. In fact no such confession occurred. Wikipedia says: "...in 1922...an editor at the paper openly admitted his membership in the Ku Klux Klan and praised the Klan in print," making it clear that Davis is the editor meant. Davis did praise the Klan at one point and in 1923 said he had long ago been in the bygone Klan just after the Civil War (when he was still in adolescence), but in 1923 (at age 73) he grew increasingly troubled by the Rosewood events and related violence, then changed his Klan endorsement to pointed criticism, while also admitting errors of fact he had made on Rosewood. The Wikipedia entry cites as its source a 1997 academic paper claiming that Davis confessed Klan membership in a *Sun* editorial on December 30, 1922. There is no such editorial. The allegation is an illusion. The nature of the real racism at the 1923 *Gainesville Daily Sun* becomes masked if discourse resorts to simplistic falsehoods.

[433] "Colonel" Samuel T. Salisbury, who for a year was chief of police in Orlando, Florida, and was a leader in the opening phase of the Ocoee violence of Nov. 1920, was interviewed for a master's thesis in 1969, and said that "ninety percent of all law enforcement officers, judges, public servants and lawyers" in Winter Garden and Ocoee, Florida, were in the Klan, including Salisbury himself. ("A Report of the Circumstances and Events of the Race Riot on

November 2, 1920 in Ocoee, Florida," by Lester Dabbs, Stetson University, 1969).

[434] Burial arrangements for James Elmer McDaniel, killed Nov. 2, 1920, at Ocoee. Undertaker's Memoranda, Nov. 2, 1920, The Carey Hand Funeral Records, Special Collections Department, University of Central Florida Libraries, Orlando, Florida: "Interment at Destination Cemetery, City Stone Mountain, State Georgia." Ritual significance of Stone Mountain: "[in the early 1920s] Picnics, barbecues and outdoor sports were popular with local Knights, who met regularly on Thursday evenings and usually held initiations in Piedmont Park on Stone Mountain. On solemn occasions, such as the death of a fellow member, Atlanta kluxers would approach the bier, offer the Klansman's prayer, and leave a wreath in the shape of a cross."—*The Ku Klux Klan in the City*, 1915-1930, by Kenneth T. Jackson, Rowman and Littlefield, 1967, p 37.

[435] *The Ku-Klux Klan: Hearing Before the Committee on Rules, House of Representatives, Sixty-Seventh Congress*, U.S. Government Printing Office, 1921, pp. 150, 180, 148.

[436] *Hooded Americanism: The History of the Ku Klux Klan*, by David Mark Chalmers, Duke University Press, 1981, p. 226.

[437] *Informants*: H. Hardee, B. Hardee, W. Baylor.

[438] *Informants*: E. Parham, P. Hudson, F. Kirkland, L. Carrier, S. Hall.

[439] Three *informant* stories about the Ku Klux Klan in the Sumner area help to demonstrate the ambivalent nature of its profile there. One account had a former white resident of Rosewood, Junius Coarsey, whipped by the Klan for a romantic liaison that broke up a family, with no mention of racial issues (told by E. Foster). Another had Sumner's lauded worker Robert Missouri driving his new Model T past a robed and hooded Klan procession, which made him nervous but seemed to cause no violence at the sight of an African American showing his independence in his car (told by Missouri himself). A third story named Sumner resident Jason McElveen as a Klan sympathizer or member, as McElveen seemed to confirm, though he was also apparently among sawmill personnel who helped guard Sumner's black quarters *against* the 1923 white mob (told by R. Kirby, and separately by McElveen).

[440] Creek and Miccosukee, the two related languages of Seminole groups in Florida, both belong to the greater Muskogean language group that once extended across the southeastern United States, especially as pockets of other groups shrank or died out under European encroachment, including Siouxan, Iroquoian and Algonquian groups. Four of the "Five Civilized Tribes" of the old South were Muskogean, using similar-sounding but divergent word structures.

Among the Seminoles the word closest to *"mingo"* would be *"micco."* The "mingo" variant was a common word, but in another of the southern groups, the Choctaws, not the the Seminoles.

[441] "The Menéndez Marquéz Cattle Barony at La Chua and the Determinants of Economic Expansion in Seventeenth Century Florida," by Amy Bushnell, *Florida Historical Quarterly*, Apr. 1978, Vol. 56, No. 4, pp. 420, 428, 430. *Early History of the Creek Indians and Their Neighbors*, by John R. Swanton, Smithsonian Institution, Bureau of Ethnology, U.S. Government Printing Office, Washington, D.C., 1922.

[442] *Florida: A Guide to the Southern-Most State*, by the Federal Writers Project, Works Projects Administration, (The Florida Guide), 1939, Oxford University Press 1976, p. 418: "Its present name, as familiar as that of any river on the continent, is a Negro corruption of San Juanee, meaning 'Little St. Johns.'"

[443] Death certificate, Mingo Williams, Jan. 5, 1923 (FBVS).

[444] Choctaw Museum, Philadelphia, Mississippi, telephone interview, Bob Ferguson, April 17, 1995.

[445] *A dictionary of the Choctaw language*, by Cyrus Byington, Smithsonian Institution, Bureau of Ethnology, Bulletin 46, U.S. Government Printing Office, Washington, D.C., 1915, p. 137: "a minko or mingo…a sachem [chief, leader], a sagamore [chief]." Pushmataha, sometimes called "the greatest of all Choctaw chiefs," was known as Mingo Pushmataha, and was mingo/chief of the Choctaw Six-Towns district. Pushmataha died in 1824 in Washington, D.C., protesting settler encroachment, 42 years before Mingo Williams was born.

[446] *Dust Tracks on a Road, An Autobiography*, by Zora Neale Hurston, J. B. Lippincott Co., Philadelphia, 1942, p. 243.

[447] *Informant*: W. Hall. (Hall's sister, Mary Hall Daniels, also recalled similar stories). Compensational stories about royal roots were not exclusively African American on the harsh Florida frontier. Myrtle Dudley, born in 1901 to one of the more prosperous white land-owning families in the Newberry area, recalled to an interviewer in 1992: "I hate to tell you why Grandpa came here. Grandpa and the queen of England were in love. She was going to marry Grandpa, and it was against the law for English to do it. Somehow he got word that they were going to kill him. One brother was with him, and the other one came later. But they drifted off to Miami." Like the younger Hall children in Rosewood, Myrtle Dudley forty miles away seemed never to guess that the romantic epic she was apparently told in childhood might have been a wilderness form of fairy tale. There were many such examples. (interview by Lisa Heard and Sally Morrison,

Feb. 25, 1992, Samuel Proctor Oral History Program, UFDC).

[448] *Gainesville Daily Sun,* January 19, 1923, murder of Brown Tisby: "The murder of the aged 'conjur' doctor last week brought to light some almost unbelievable evidences of negro superstition. Tisby was known among negroes and some white people it is said, as a 'conjur' doctor with peculiar powers...it is claimed...that he could ward off the work of the devil, protect human life from injury and drive away evil spirits...He was unable to read or write and could not distinguish between certain denominations of currency. Negroes, however, rarely ever cheated him for services, they say, as he was believed to control their destinies in his own hands."

[449] Hurston, ibid., p. 199.

[450] *Birds of America,* 1840-1844, by John James Audubon, p. 227: "...it removes from one [tree] to another, cackling out its laughter-like notes, as if it found delight in leading you a wild-goose chase in pursuit of it...Often when you think the next step will take you near enough to fire with certainty, the wary bird flies off before you can reach it."

[451] "Lord god" as a folk name for *Hylatomus pileatus,* the pileated woodpecker, is confirmed by regional texts: *Birds in Florida,* by Rupert J. Longstreet, Trend House, Tampa, 1969; *Florida Birds,* Florida Game and Fresh Water Fish Commission, 1931; *Birds of the South,* by Charlotte Hilton Green, University of North Carolina Press, Chapel Hill, 1993. In Audubon's time, the original folk name was apparently "log cock," but oral repetition smoothed and polished it, including repetition among slaves, to produce a richer vessel of meaning: "lord god." Slightly different versions of this result, including "log guard" and "lord-to-god," were heard across the South: *Alabama Birds.* by T.A. Imhof, State Of Alabama, Department Of Conservation, Game And Fish Division, University Of Alabama Press, 1962, p 331; *Louisiana Birds,* Louisiana Wildlife And Fisheries Commission, Louisiana State University Press. Baton Rouge, 1987, p. 354.

Also see *The Civil War and Reconstruction in Florida,* by William A. Davis, Columbia University, Longmans Green & Co,, 1913, p. 6: "You catch occasionally the strident whooping of the swooping, red-headed 'Lawd Gawd'—the biggest woodpecker that flies in America."

[452] *Bear, Man, And God: Eight Approaches to William Faulkner's "The Bear,"* eds. Francis Lee Uttley, Lynn Z. Bloom and Arthur F. Kinney, Random House, New York, 1964, 1971. *Go Down Moses,* by William Faulkner, Random House, 1942, p. 202. "The Bear" first published as "Lion" in *Harper's Magazine,* 1935.

Chapter 33: Paradise Lost

[453] *Los Angeles Times*, Jan. 5, 1923: "POSSE HUNTS NEGRO MORON / Florida Town Stirred Over Girl Attack /...By AP NIGHT Wire."

[454] Letter from Arthur Cummer to Walter Pillsbury, Jan. 9, 1923, Jerry Peterson Collection, quoted in Chapter 39.

[455] Though it was taken as a given in Walter Pillsbury's family that his mother, Martha Howd Pillsbury, of Millbrook, Michigan, was Native American, few specifics on her have come down through family stories or emerged from investigation. She was said to have married Edward Pillsbury on Dec. 27, 1873, with their son Walter born March 25, 1875, Edward then dying on July 13, 1882, and Martha Howd Pillsbury apparently soon afterward. Their son Walter would name two of his own children for his deceased parents, Edward and Martha. *Informants*: Martha Pillsbury Thompson, Jerry Peterson, Joseph Pillsbury.

[456] Quotations from John Milton's *Paradise Lost* are from Walter Pillsbury's 1884 reprint, an album-sized book with Gustave Doré illustrations, passed down to Pillsbury's daughter Martha Thompson and to her grandson Jerry Peterson.

[457] National Prohibition, forbidding the production, sale and transport of alcohol for entertainment purposes, began in Jan. 1919 with the ratification of the Eighteenth Amendment to the Constitution, then took effect on Jan. 17, 1920, with the Volstead Act, or National Prohibition Act, providing for enforcement.

[458] National Prohibition was a triumph for the Anti-Saloon League and the time of reform known as the Progressive Era, exemplified by President Theodore Roosevelt, muckraking journalists (whom Roosevelt disliked), the Pure Food and Drug Act, graduated income tax and other attempts to better society by law. It could be said that in this varied combination lay also the codification of "Jim Crow" racial segregation in the states of the South, which after the 1890s took previous *de facto* segregation and enshrined it in state laws. Thus the early twentieth century arguably became a time of the two great "shuns"—Segrega-*shun* and Prohibi-*shun*—milestones in the history of attempts to reshape the national culture by force. Walter Pillsbury of Sumner, the fervent corporate dynamo sent to clean up a company town in 1919, knew the spirit of this age.

[459] A. J. Studstill, the suitor in the orange peel story, was remembered as being the younger brother of Minor "Cephus" Studstill, the 23-year-old lumber inspection foreman wounded at Rosewood.

[460] *Gainesville Daily Sun*, Jan. 5, 1923: "25 Negroes Barricaded in House, Defy

Armed Posse and Open Fire on Whites." The St. Augustine, Florida, *Evening Record* reported "25 or more heavily armed negroes" in the uprising fortress (emphasis added). The *New York Times* (Jan. 6) said "estimated at 25"—and suspected that the mysterious brute Jesse Hunter was among the 25 warriors. Details in the stories would shift but the impression of an uprising cadre remained firm, lasting for more than a week after the events. On Jan. 21, the nationally-distributed weekly tabloid *Grit* summed up: "Twenty colored persons, heavily armed, barricaded themselves in a house..." Little Minnie had become a bandoliered cutthroat.

[461] Lee Carrier would recall that as he walked, an African American porter on a train tried to talk him into climbing aboard and riding to Newberry. He bitterly remembered the cajoling tone, and said it looked like one of the slaving traps, a ploy to have him arrested on trumped-up hobo charges in Newberry (presumably with a commission to the porter), then to be shipped across the river into the Dixie County lease camps. There was no proof that this was the porter's aim, but the view of the danger across the river seemed to be general in Rosewood. Lee Carrier was not obsessively suspicious, and described another African American met on his flight who helped him, hiding him in a barn and packing a bag of food to be taken on the walk.

[462] Lee Ruth "Mossy" Bradley was the youngest daughter of Wesley Bradley, in whose home Lee Carrier also lived. In 1992, Lee Ruth (Bradley) Davis was approached by media promoter Michael McCarthy at her home in the Liberty City section of Miami and became the first of two claimants in the original incarnation of the 1990s Rosewood claims case. The present author first met her a decade earlier in 1982.

[463] Buck fever: *Killing Tradition: Insight Hunting and Animal Rights Controversies*, by Simon Bronner, University Press of Kentucky, 2008, pp. 52-53, quotes a psychologist as saying buck fever exhibits "signs of an anxiety attack." In old Levy County, Florida, "[t]he anticipation for opening of hunting season would build up a crescendo of feverish excitement as the great day approached," with some men starting to wear their hunting caps and coats well in advance. ("Gulf Hammock Hunting Camp," *Search for Yesterday*, Chapter 16, p. 18). Even solemn Dr. J. W. Turner of Bronson was said to tap a bottle of Canadian Club and caution, "Now boys, we only drink when we kill something." (Will Yearty typescript memoir, PKYL).

[464] Property and census records: Calvin Dibble of Connecticut was the first Rosewood postmaster, and sold land to other northerners, among them Jacobs, Touliner, Sheldon, Burnham, Carson and Coarsey. Dibble was known to one informant, through passed-down tales, as a "Jew or Eye-talian or somethin'." A memoir characterized another founder as a "Jew named Jacobs at Rosewood,"

saying that just after the Civil War there were two cedar stations on the railroad, Rosewood and Otter Creek (Will Yearty memoir, PKYL). As such seekers arrived, only a half century farther back in the past was a pioneering utopian community built in nearly trackless wilderness fifty miles away. This was the disaster-wracked project conceived by visionary financier Moses Levy, who dreamed of a refuge for Eastern European Jews. The project was already failing when it was destroyed in the Seminole Wars, forming a stratum of buried history predating Rosewood.

[465] First appearing in records in the Federal Census of 1870, but apparently already established at the site, early African American settlers of Rosewood, including the Carriers, Bradleys, Halls, Edwardses, Williamses and others, may have arrived as enslaved railroad workers, but there is another possibility. At the time of the Civil War, a white pioneer identified vaguely as "Major Chambers" was said to have a plantation at the site of what would be Rosewood, growing cotton in the rich soil of Gulf Hammock. The Federal Census of 1860, though not listing slaves by name, showed a John E. Chambers as the largest slave-holder in Levy County, with 73 slaves.

[466] Historians generally consider it doubtful that in real life Harriet Beecher Stowe, author of *Uncle Tom's Cabin; or, Life Among the Lowly* (1852) was approached by President Lincoln and told drolly, as often repeated afterward: "So you're the little lady who wrote the book that started this great war." Coming to Florida after "this great war," Stowe moved into a kind of fairy castle partially carved into the monstrous trunk and roots of a great liveoak in the new citrus town of Mandarin (now in metro Jacksonville). She had resources for her subtropical citrus project; her 1852 book was called the most successful bestseller of the nineteenth century, behind only the Bible.

[467] The citrus paradise-seekers after the Civil War seemed particularly deluded, for just before the war, in January 1857, a disastrous freeze had destroyed northern Florida's orange crop. It was as if the trauma of war had swept everything before it, and memory started new. "Florida will certainly be the garden of the continent," the *Jacksonville Press* enthused in 1876. A factor perhaps helping to blind the 1880s citrus boomers to the risks in northern Florida's climate lay in their product itself. Oranges were enjoying epidemic new popularity in the late 1800s and, symbolically, they were the color of gold. "An 'orange fever' swept Florida in the 1870s and 1880s, and thousands of new settlers poured through Jacksonville" ("Coming of Age, Foundations of Modern Florida: 1880-1900," by Gary Mormino, *The Florida Grower*, Aug. 2000). Thus began a Florida rhythm that might help explain both the blindness that covered the Rosewood atrocity during one period (the racial segregation years), and the impassioned exaggerations cloaking the case in another (after rediscovery, especially in the 1990s). Both informational trends on Rosewood, though

opposite in philosophy, exhibited selective blindness. A historian has spoken of Florida's "manic cycles of boom and bust," as if selective blindness might be a local folkway (*History of Duval County, Florida*, by Daniel Pleasant Gold, The Record Co., St. Augustine, Fla., 1928, p. 196).

[468] Whether by climate cycle or bad luck, the years 1895-1900 chilled northern Florida's soul. "The freeze in 1895 did away with the citrus industry in this part of the state. It was quite a shock. In 1897 we moved...," said State Representative Thomas Bryant (born March 28, 1890, interviewed Jan. 19, 1980, by Steve Kerber for the Samuel Proctor Oral History Program, UFDC). "It is said that the 'Big Freeze' of 1898 completely wiped out every trace of any orange trees there. Eventually the remains of the homes of the grove owners also vanished." ("East Pasco's Heritage," by Lorise Abraham, History of Pasco County). "The citrus industry that had been the basis of the local economy was totally destroyed by the Great Freeze of 1894/95." (Website for Floral City, Fla.). And this was not to mention the "Great Arctic Outbreak" of 1900.

[469] A particularly ill-timed business concern, the Gulf Hammock Orange and Vegetable Company, was established in Levy County in 1894, just prior to the freezes (*Search for Yesterday, A History of Levy County, Florida*, by the Levy County Archives Committee, Chapter 6, p. 14). "Churches filled with people, praying, some were there all day and others came from time-to-time, making a continuous prayer-meeting. It was one long prayer—'God save our trees.'" (*Yesterday in Florida*, by Kennie L. Howard, Carleton Press, New York 1970, p. 188). Also see: *Dunnellon—Boomtown of the 1880s, The Story of Rainbow Springs and Dunnellon*, by J. Lester Denkins, Great Outdoors Publishing Company, St. Petersburg, Fla., 1969; *Ocali Country, Kingdom of the Sun, A History of Marion County, Florida*, by Eloise Robinson Ott and Louise Hickman Chazal, Perry Printing Company, Ocala, Florida, 1966.

[470] Will Yearty memoir, PKYL. *Cedar Key, Florida, A History*, by Kevin McCarthy, The History Press, 2007, p. 47: "The thirty-mile-long devastation up the Suwannee Valley ruined so many turpentine stills and stacks of pine that some 2,500 people lost their jobs. With the loss of so much pine, turpentine, cedar and sponges, the importance of Cedar Key as a port declined, and the railroad reduced its schedule to the town."

[471] 1900 Federal Census: head of household, John Wright, son John A. Wright, born Sept. 1898; son Norman Wright, born May 1900. *Informants*: B. Bryant, W. Hall. L. Carrier. *Levy Times-Democrat*, Nov. 10, 1908, cited in *Search for Yesterday*, Levy County Archives Committee, March 1983, Chapter 13, p. 9.

[472]Arnett Goins's daughter, Annette Goins Shakir, also confirmed the impression, saying that her father "talked about Mr. John Wright who

was the gentlemen who owned a store. And he often said that when they went into his store he never let any of the children leave unless he gave them something, whether it was a little piece of candy or something of that nature." (interview by Larry Rivers, Sept. 25, 1993).

[473] In the 1997 film *Rosewood*, he became "The penny-pinching, adulterous town grocer John Wright" (as seen by the *New York Times)*. "Wright screws his black help in the store's back room and his sons sass their stepmom" (as seen— skeptically—by Bill Stamets, reviewing for the *Chicago Reader)*. "The sexploitative storekeeper, John Wright" (as seen by Cineaste). *People* magazine—no skepticism here—enthused that the Wright character in the movie was "a reality-based character." Mark Caro of the *Chicago Tribune* interviewed John Singleton, the film's director, and asked him about the suspiciously villainous portrait, remarking (skeptically), "The first you see of John Wright...he's cheating on his wife with a young black clerk at his store." In response, wrote Caro, Singleton laughed. "That affair was imagined, Singleton says, but adds with a chuckle: 'You never know.'" Less amused was Rosewood survivor Wilson Hall, who rejected the movie angrily: "'That's a damn lie,' [Hall] says. 'How could they release something like that? This is history. This is something that should be taught. People should be ashamed.'" (*Chicago Tribune*, Feb. 21, 1997).

[474] *Informants*: E. Parham, P. Hudson.

[475] Historian Elliott Rudwick said of the East St. Louis lynching riot in 1917: "Invariably when firmness was shown the mobs fell back..." (*Race Riot in East St. Louis*, July 2, 1917, Rudwick, University of Illinois Press, 1964, p. 79). However, the success of firmness can depend on strength of numbers, as Pillsbury seemed to consider with his improvised platoon.

Chapter 34: The Sergeant

[476] Apparently the first national attention to the Rosewood violence came on Wednesday, Jan. 3, 1923, when the *New York Tribune* ran a one-sentence wire-service item on the Sam Carter killing, with no mention of a place called Rosewood. The snippet was datelined "Bronson," and its garbled information said the killing had happened "here," meaning in Bronson. Occasional historians in later years would find this nugget and use it as documentation for surveys of lynching violence, dutifully listing the scene of the crime as Bronson.

[477] In 1959 when Allen Grimshaw conducted a landmark study of twentieth-century American racial violence, he disfavored the idea of finding elderly living witnesses who had actually seen the events."[S]uch interviews have more

frequently been suggestive of points of interpretation than as direct sources of data," he said. Grimshaw turned instead to a more manageable source for his view of history, using "complete coverage" found in back issues of the *New York Times*. Today, a half century later, it can be said that anyone attempting to analyze the Rosewood case from its 1923 coverage in the *New York Times* (on Jan. 6, 7, and 8), would be analyzing an illusion. Were there really savage uprisers in a fortress? In the *Times* there were. Was the fallen logging boss Henry Andrews really a virtuous lawman? A reader of the *Times* would have seen him that way. Large pieces of this illusion were eventually confessed at the source by the *Gainesville Daily Sun*, but no retraction would creep a thousand miles north to appear in the *Times* (or three times as far to the other *Times*, which carried the same illusions to readers in Los Angeles). The racial filters influencing the mainstream press in 1923 did not work in all papers all the time, but Rosewood demonstrates that they were pervasive. The *New York Times* of that era was not as ranting as, for example, the *Washington Post* of the same period (a different paper than the *Post* of later years), but the *Times* of 1923 did not escape the gremlins of its age. Racist wire-service stories from shadowy aeries like the upstairs office of the *Gainesville Daily Sun* flooded into chattering Morkrum mass-telegraph machines at the *Times*, and—if Rosewood is any indication—such stories might run with scarcely a word being questioned. If not for the presence of living witnesses on Rosewood—with all their imperfections—the secrets hidden by this atrocity would be lost.

[478] Examples of the three time-labeled dispatches ran in the *Florida Times-Union*, sequentially on January 5, 1923. Two were datelined Gainesville and one Cedar Key. The Cedar Key dispatch and one of those labeled Gainesville were credited in print to The Associated Press. Though by 1923 Associated Press rules required that its dispatches be credited to AP in member papers, in practice many such items ran without any mention of their wire-service origin.

[479] *A Report by the Oklahoma Commission to Study the Tulsa Race Riot of 1921*, presented to the Oklahoma Legislature, February 28, 2001, p. 58: "The *Daily Tribune*, a white newspaper that tried to gain its popularity by referring to the Negro settlements as 'Little Africa'…said that a mob of whites was forming in order to lynch the Negro. Adjutant General Charles F. Barrett, who led National Guard troops from Oklahoma City into Tulsa the next day, recalled that there had been a 'fantastic write-up of the…incident in a sensation-seeking newspaper.'" *Tulsa Tribune* editor Richard Lloyd Jones wrote after the Tulsa riot: "But there is a bad black man who is a beast. The bad black man is a bad man. He drinks the cheapest and the vilest whisky. He breaks every law to get it. He is a dope fiend. He holds life lightly. He is a bully and a brute. A dozen of such collect[ed] at the Tulsa County Courthouse with firearms when they heard the lynching rumor." (Jones wrote this for the *Chicago Tribune*, June 2, 1921). The riot provocation in Jones's *Tulsa Tribune* was seen by some observers as a national pattern: "[J]ust the sort of thing done by the Tulsa 'Tribune' is being

done every day all over the country and especially by the South." (James Weldon Johnson, *New York Age*, June 18, 1921, quoted by Frederick G. Detweiler, *The Negro Press in the United States*, University of Chicago Press, 1922, p. 86). Richard Lloyd Jones's arrival in Florida was described in *Editor and Publisher*, June 3, 1922: "FLORIDA METROPOLIS CHANGES HANDS, John H. Perry and Richard Lloyd Jones, New Owners, Also Announce That They Are Associated in Tulsa Tribune." A description of Jones becoming editor of the *Jacksonville Metropolis* in 1922 and changing its name also occurred much later, in the *Florida Times-Union*, June 11, 1997).

[480] The Tulsa case was one of several from the era in which provocative newspaper articles, generally remembered as having encouraged the violence, were later removed from archives by unknown hands. There is now only the proof of memory that the title to Richard Lloyd Jones's editorial in the May 31, 1921, *Tulsa Tribune* said "to lynch Negro tonight," or some variation thereof. Repeated searches by various investigators have found no surviving copy of the article.

[481] *Dictionary of Unitarian and Universalist Biography*, "Richard Lloyd Jones."

[482] *Jacksonville Journal, Jan. 5, 1923.*

[483] By Jan. 1923, Richard Lloyd Jones and his entrepreneurial partner, John H. Perry, had acquired or were in the process of acquiring a total of seven newspapers, four of them in the South, including the Charleston, South Carolina, *American* and the Pensacola, Florida, *Journal*. The acquisitions began in June 1922 when Perry bought half interest in Jones's *Tulsa Tribune,* which then became "the 'mother' sheet of the syndicate." The partners expressed a hope to acquire a total of ten papers by the end of 1923, and spoke grandly of someday owning four newspapers in each state of the Union. In a fast-changing journalism world, John Perry also sold the *Seattle Post-Intelligencer* to the Hearst corporation *(The Fourth Estate,* Jan 6, 1923). Living out some of his predictions, Perry would eventually control "organizations which serve 11,000 weekly and 300 daily newspapers. His journalistic influence reached to Great Britain, Canada, Mexico, Nova Scotia, Norway, Denmark and Sweden." *(Pittsburgh Press,* Dec. 5, 1952, obituary of John H. Perry). As to Richard Lloyd Jones, after his 1922-1923 venture into Florida he retrenched to center his operations at his Tulsa stronghold. Regarding his role in helping provoke the Tulsa race riot a year and a half before the Rosewood incident, it can be said that Jones, like his Florida colleague, "Colonel" Robert Davis at the *Gainesville Daily Sun,* was not a stereotyped tobacco-chewing racist. The trait that both these gatekeepers of southern information seemed to share (besides their racial excitement) was a sermonizing flair for theatrics and soaring oratory. They seemed enthralled by things grandiose. Jones, a native of Wisconsin, was not

only an editor but the founder of Tulsa's All Souls Unitarian Church, and "used his newspaper as a pulpit, regularly preaching to his readers in editorials printed under the banner, 'Saturday Sermonette.'" (*Dictionary of Unitarian and Universalist Biography*). Davis, an Old South orator with antebellum roots, was reflected in a euphoric headline: "COLONEL 'BOB' NAMED AS GREATEST ORATOR STATE HAS PRODUCED... that grand old man of Florida...the most flowery speaker, the best word painter and most pleasing orator [in] the state...." (*Gainesville Daily Sun*, Aug. 13, 1922). Davis had been Speaker of the Florida House of Representatives and served four terms in U.S. Congress. In the matter of provoking race riots through the media, something in the ancient fire of oratory seemed to tend toward a rhetorical "fever" (Davis himself used the word) that could spiral into "lynch fever."

[484] *AP: The Story of News*, by Oliver Gramling, Farrar & Rhinehart, New York (prepared for The Associated Press), 1940, p. 313. In 1906, evening or afternoon newspapers were also a major factor in the Atlanta race riot. A white grand jury investigating the 1906 riot was angry and blunt: "[T]he sensationalism of the afternoon papers in the presentation of the criminal news to the public prior to the riots of Saturday night, especially in the case of the *Atlanta News*, deserves our severest condemnation." (*Following the Color Line*, by Ray Stannard Baker, Doubleday Page, 1908, p. 18).

[485] *Jacksonville Journal, Jan. 5, 1923.*

[486] "American Negroes Run 113 papers": *New York Times*, July 30, 1922. The Department of Labor study, announced July 29, found that 96 of the 113 papers "owned and directed by negroes" were "secular," 23 were religious and eight were fraternal; published weekly, monthly or daily, in addition to 14 magazines.

[487] "There are left 253 [African American-run] periodicals to be called newspapers. All these are first and foremost 'race papers.' In other words, they all keep race interests pre-eminent." (*The Negro Press in the United States*, by Frederick G. Detweiler, University of Chicago Press, 1922, p. 4). "True, many of the papers cover a small area...the figures for circulation...in some cases do not exceed 3,500 and are sometimes quoted as low as 1,000" (Detweiler, p. 11).

[488] Detweiler 1922, ibid., pp. 1-24. "The figures given out by the Census Bureau show that, in 1920, there were 6,211,062 Negroes over ten years of age who could read and write. At the rate of one copy to five readers a total circulation of a million and a quarter would be enough for all [African American newspapers in the early 1920s] (ibid., pp. 11-12). Movement to the North (Ibid., p. 14). The *Chicago Defender* selling two-thirds of its issues outside Chicago (Ibid., p. 15).

[489] A rare acknowledgement of this dimension came in Florida in a 2007 doctoral dissertation: "Only occasionally was adequate information regarding

lynching available, and at times the northern press had to decipher, if not imagine, what actually occurred." (*Coming from Battle to Face a War: The Lynching of Black Soldiers in the World War 1 Era*, by Vincent P. Mikkelsen, p. 139, Department of History, Florida State University, supervising professor Maxine Jones). Mikkelsen cited two examples of post-World War I atrocity news reports which, though widely repeated by later commentators as fact, seemed to be embellished if not invented.

[490] *War Is a Force that Gives Us Meaning*, by Chris Hedges, Random House, 2002, p. 7. Hedges's concept of Mythic War vs. Sensory War, based on work by army psychologist Lawrence LeShan, could be viewed as central to the Rosewood events. Here is the "fever" that had Colonel Bob Davis at the *Gainesville Daily Sun* sounding the battle cry, while Davis's later waking from the glorious dream, in his anguished editorial of April 29, 1923, denouncing the "barbarity," sounds like waking from a thrilling state of consciousness ("Mythic War") to find the reality of gore and ruins ("Sensory War").

[491] Dateline: "(Special to the Amsterdam News), Rosewood, Jan. 9 [1923]." Headline: "22 KILLED IN FLORIDA RACE WAR, Armed Warfare as Whites Attack Negro Community..."

[492] *Mass Media in America*, by Don R. Pember, Science Research Associates, Chicago, 1974, 1987, p. 33; *After Freedom, a cultural study in the deep South*, by Hortense Powdermaker, Viking Press, 1939, 1968, pp. 319-320; *Lonely Warrior: The Life and Times of Robert S. Abbott*, by Roi Ottley, Henry Regnery Co., 1955.

[493] In an essay for the fiftieth anniversary of the *Chicago Defender*, Langston Hughes, poet and *Defender* columnist, applauded his employer as "the journalistic voice of a largely voiceless people." (*Langston Hughes and the Chicago Defender: Essays on Race, Politics, and Culture, 1942-62*," Langston Hughes, comp. Christopher C. De Santis, University of Illinois Press, 1995, p. 13). "The Mouthpiece of 14 Million People," *Chicago Defender* headline displayed on front page, image appearing in "Newspapers, The Chicago Defender," www.pbs.org/.

[494] *The Lonely Warrior, The Life and Times of Robert S. Abbott*, by Roi Ottley, H. Regnery Co., 1955, pp. 206, 221, 227).

[495] For example, no other news medium, for either racial audience, seemed able to match a spectacular revelation made by the *Chicago Defender* about the Tulsa race riot of 1921. The *Defender*, and no other medium, discovered that African American residential areas in Tulsa were being aerially bombed as if in World War I, by white men in airplanes: "Bombs Hurled From Aeroplanes in Order to

Stop Attacks... Airplanes rained bombs down on the few hundred of our men fighting there." (*Chicago Defender,* June 5, 1923). This theme seemed to work so well that in the following weekly edition of the *Defender*, on June 13 (though there were still no other media reports of any such miracles), the paper brought out a more detailed report on Tulsa's spectacular air war, "expanding" the details of the supposed aeronautics of June 1:

> "With the coming of daylight, airplanes from the local aviation field, in which the Cadillac company is interested, directed the movements of the oncoming army. At 6:15 a.m., men in the planes began dropping fire bombs of turpentine and other inflammable material on the property. Women and children running from their burning homes were struck dead by the incessant machine gun fire from the hills or burned to death by the liquid fire poured down from the airplanes...The whites stormed the church, the defenders putting up a game fight until the airplanes bombed the structure and all within were driven out to the mercy of the mob."

This remarkable epic contained miracles of chemistry, avionics and pyrotechnics, as well as miracles of information. Yet the thrilling images would reach across future decades. In the 1950s, historian Allen Grimshaw placed the *Defender's* aerial bombing in his oft-cited masterwork as if it were fact (*A Study in Social Violence: Urban Race Riots in the United States*, by Allen D. Grimshaw, dissertation, University of Pennsylvania, 1959, pp. 105-108). The *Defender* story that the historian found so credible continued:

> "Men fought with utter abandon against the human devils above and around them. As the scorching, white fire from airships above was poured upon them, the defenders of their homes made a valiant effort to stave off the bloodthirsty passion of the hounds who killed them. Men slipped and fell in the blood of their brothers...One man, leaning far out of an airplane, was brought down by the bullet of a sharpshooter and his body burst upon the ground. Men were hideouts. Women were evil. Judgement was in the air and the multitude perished." (*Chicago Defender*, June 13, 1921).

With its biblical prose, the aerial bombing of Tulsa became a permanent exhibit in American historical gullibility. In 1982 a subsequent historian, Scott Ellsworth, compiling a valuable and extensive look at the Tulsa race riot, had little choice but to deal with the thrilling air war, though very diplomatically: "As is the case with many aspects of the riot, there is some confusion over the use of airplanes."
During the Tulsa violence, police did commandeer private airplanes to fly over the city. On the issue of whether any bombing was done, Ellsworth could find only one surviving observer—and no media reports besides the *Defender's*. The lone observer (the best Ellsworth could come up with after an assiduous search) spoke only of "a great shadow in the sky" and mentioned no bombs or even gunshots coming from this "shadow." Ellsworth then acknowledged that this

"only implies that planes may have attacked the area"—and yet instead of concluding that all evidence was thus against the *Defender's* hoax, Ellsworth then cited the *Defender* as if its view of things might be equally credible: "but the *Chicago Defender* reported directly that black neighborhoods in Tulsa were bombed from the air by a private plane equipped with dynamite" (*Death in a Promised Land: The Tulsa Race Riot of 1921*, by Scott Ellsworth, Louisiana State University Press, 1982).

The emotional climate perhaps affecting the views held by such later examiners is suggested by their own further distortions of the *Defender's* original distortion. The *Defender* (the only source on the aerial apocalypse) never seemed to mention any dynamite. Yet the historians (both Ginzburg and Ellsworth) dropped in this touch, as if seeking to rationalize the irrationality they were endorsing. The *Defender's* original miracle story depicted the sky-cruising devils as "dropping fire bombs of turpentine and other inflammable material" and pouring down "liquid fire" and "scorching, white fire from airships"—not dynamite.

Thus progressively laundered, the story would echo into *Parade* magazine in 1983: "Tulsa, Okla., became the first U.S. city to be bombed from the air." ("First U.S. City To Be Bombed From the Air," *Parade*, March 13, 1983). And perhaps inevitably, it would meet the 1990s media excitement over Rosewood, as the Florida Legislature's "university team" provided a summary of atrocities contemporary with Rosewood, to give the Rosewood claims case added weight. They said of Tulsa: "white men who have been deputized raid a munitions dump for dynamite, commandeer some airplanes, and drop dynamite from the air on a black neighborhood." The laundering was by then complete (magical turpentine bombs laundered to become more logical dynamite)—and the dynamite was worth saying twice in the same sentence. (*A Documented History of the Incident at Rosewood....*, Dec. 23, 1993, p. 98). The period of Rosewood excitement did not rest with reimagining Florida, but reached out a thousand miles to join the *Chicago Defender's* fantasy universe.

[496] Florida's 1993 legislative-academic committee on Rosewood should be given its due. While it accepted the Grimshaw/*Defender* vision of aerial dynamite bombs at Tulsa and similar material, its credulity balked at the extremes in the *Chicago Defender's* story on Rosewood itself—because anyone viewing even fragments of the Rosewood evidence could see how blatantly the *Defender's* story had been faked. The team said flatly: "The *Defender's* account seems to have been largely fictional." (*A Documented History of the Incident at Rosewood....*, Dec. 23, 1993, p. 21, Attorney General's Rosewood Files, Peters files, Vol. 1).

[497] The pattern of media hoaxers seeming to taunt their audience (that is, blatantly alluding to deception in works that are themselves blatantly deceptive) forms one of the mysteries in the personalities of fabricators. The journalistic

hoaxer Stephen Glass crippled the *New Republic* in 1998 after it gullibly defended his remarkable fake stories ("We extended normal human trust to someone who basically lacked a conscience")—though Glass had been feeding veiled clues to his editors all along—in his complex mentions of deception inside the deceptive stories, as if taunting the gullible reader. For example, one of his hoaxes said straight out that it involved "Werty, Iowa—a fictitious town." Glass also gloated in print about how he had tricked a story source by using fictitious credentials, saying he was from an "Association for the Advancement of Sound Water Policy"—as pointed out by the *Chicago Reader*, July 10, 1998, in an analysis by Mike Miner: "Once again Glass—at least in retrospect—had shown himself to be so enamored of deception that he plotted a con in the fiction he was passing off as journalism." Miner also cited another case of such hinting, in the *Boston Globe* columnist and eventually disgraced hoaxer Patricia Smith. "Smith wasn't the absurdist that Glass was, but like him she calls attention to deception while deceiving," as when Smith wrote: "So we've established that Stephen Fagan, he of the forehead-hugging hair, palm beach preening, and makeshift social status, is the most pathological of pathological liars." Smith wrote about a cancer victim whose cancer was "something false and foreign growing inside her." Here, a pathological liar was tauntingly bringing up the subject of pathological lying, as if fascinated by it—or as if half-dreaming. The mental world enfolding Robert Abbott at the 1923 *Chicago Defender* is unlikely to be analyzed by history, as history strains, eyes tightly shut, not to question Abbott's dreams.

[498] Ottley, ibid., p. 221. As Ottley described it, the babbling imposture was apparently not a joke but a striking intrusion of fantasy role-playing in an individual otherwise impressively functional and financially successful.

[499] In the "Red Scare" of 1919, the *Chicago Defender* was among the organizations targeted for investigation of subversive or Bolshevik sympathies by the U.S. Bureau of Investigation, the forerunner of the FBI. A by-product of this was a list of the *Defender's* 1919 marketing outlets in states across the country. A principal sales area seemed to be in Mississippi (as sociologist Hortense Powdermaker would also suggest later), but three outlets were in Florida: 1) a dealer called Florida News in an unspecified Florida city, ordering 25 copies of the *Defender* in 1919; 2) a dealer called the News Depot in Tampa, ordering 35 copies; and 3) a dealer named Harold Finley in the town of Palatka, ordering 100 copies. Palatka was a sawmill town 45 miles west of Gainesville; Tampa lay 130 miles south. Rosewood exile Philomena Goins (Doctor) would be taken to live in the Tampa Bay area. Her cousins in the Wesley Bradley family fled Rosewood to Palatka.

[500] "Nineteen Slain in Florida Race War," *Chicago Defender,* Jan. 13, 1923. It was a long story, presenting a labyrinth of different fictional segments.

[501] "A Forgotten Leader: Robert S. Abbott and the Chicago Defender from 1910-1920," by Alan D. DeSantis, *Journalism History*, Summer 1997, Vol. 23, No. 2, p. 63.

[502] *Voices of Revolution: The Dissident Press in America,* by Rodger Streitmatter, Columbia University Press, 2013, pp. 153-154.

[503] *Chicago Defender*, Jan. 6, 1923, p. 1.

[504] Ibid., Feb. 10, 1923, p. 1.

[505] Ottley, p. 129.

[506] *The First Waco Horror: The Lynching of Jesse Washington and the Rise of the NAACP*, by Patricia Bernstein, Texas A.&M. University Press, 2006, p. 133. *The Voice of the Negro 1919*, by Robert T. Kerlin, E. P. Dutton & Co., 1920, p. 75.

[507] *Race Riot, Chicago in the Red Summer of 1919*, by William M. Tuttle, Atheneum, New York, 1970, p. 49.

[508] *The First Waco Horror: The Lynching of Jesse Washington and the Rise of the NAACP*, by Patricia Bernstein, Texas A.&M. University Press, 2006, p. 133.

[509] Ottley, pp. 140-141.

[510] *AP, The Story of News*, by Oliver Gramling, Farrar & Rhinehart, New York, 1940, pp. 284-286; *New York Times*, May 3, 1918. In their rush, media pirates could be a bit short-sighted. Melville Stone, head of The Associated Press in 1919, had begun his career running the *Chicago Daily News*, where in 1876 he fought news thieves in a competing paper by embedding a trap in a story, quoting a mayor in the distant nation of Serbia as saying, *"Er us siht la Etsll nel lum cmeht."* When his rival paper stole the story and ran it as its own, Stone made them a laughingstock by pointing out that the phrase (which they had also stolen, verbatim) was not Serbian at all, but English spelled backwards, saying, "The McMullens will steal this sure." (The McMullen brothers ran the rival paper). Nearly a quarter of a century later the ploy was used again, this time between two "yellow journalism" rivals, the *New York Journal* (Hearst) and the *New York World* (Pulitzer) in 1898 during the Spanish-American War, with the *Journal* planting a fake story: "Colonel Reflipe W. Thenuz, an Austrian artillerist of European renown…was so badly wounded that he has since died." As expected, the *World* then stole the story—only to have the *Journal* do the laughing, for the foreign-sounding name "Reflipe W. Thenuz" was a scrambled version of "We pilfer the news." ("Property, Natural Monopoly and the Uneasy

Legacy of *INS v. AP*, by Douglas G. Baird, Coase-Sandor Working Paper Series, University of Chicago Law School, 2005, pp. 5-6; *Citizen Hearst*, by W. A. Swanberg, Charles Scribner's Sons, New York, 1961, pp. 148-149).

[511] Melville Stone affidavit, *AP v INS*, complaint 1917, p 20. "Associated Press Seeks Injunction," *Editor and Publisher*, Jan. 13, 1917, Vol. 49, Issues 27-39.

[512] "Associated Negro Press," *Encyclopedia of the Harlem Renaissance, A-J*, Taylor & Francis, 2004, pp. 57-58. "Abbott complained to a friend that [Claude Barnett of ANP] was 'stealing my news and selling it to other papers for a profit'....[I]n general, historians...agree with Abbott's accusation."

[513] "[The film] 'Rosewood' spends the bulk of its 142 minutes battering viewers with vivid depictions of lynchings, rioting and suffering without giving the action any shape....Not helping matters are [director John] Singleton's concessions to showbiz. The romance between Mann and a young teacher, a subplot involving whether Wright's children will accept their stepmom and climactic horseback and train-chase heroics are such obvious Hollywood hooey that they undermine the movie's more serious purposes" (*Chicago Tribune*, Mark Caro, Feb. 21, 1997). Other opinions made clear that they took the movie as real history: "John Singleton had done much to enhance the public's historical education" (*American Historical Review*. April 1998). The movie was shown at Duke University's 2004 Black History through Film Movie Event. Duke Law School's internal newspaper the *Herald* then told its readers indignantly that at Rosewood "between 70 and 250 people were killed"—which not even the movie's enormous exaggeration of the Rosewood death toll had said.

[514] *Chicago Tribune*, Mark Caro, Feb. 21, 1997.

Chapter 35: The Bargain

[515] *Dudley Farm, a History of Florida Farm Life*, by Ben Pickard and Sally Morrison, Alachua Press, 2003, p. 60: "Myrtle Dudley, then fifteen years old, recalls frightened African American families sought protection and comfort from Fannie Dudley at the homestead itself. Throughout the community other African Americans also sought and received protection from their white neighbors." Dudley Farm Historic State Park, 333 acres, was acquired through donation by Myrtle Dudley in 1983, at a site near Newberry, Florida, 13 miles west of Gainesville.

[516] "A Century Later, A City Remembers," by Jim Auchmutey, *Atlanta Journal-Constitution*, Sept. 17, 2006.

[517] *Gainesville Daily Sun*, Jan. 5, 1923.

[518] *Informant*: Guy Andrews.

[519] Otter Creek resident Will Yearty was a storekeeper at the time of the Rosewood events, living 12 miles away. In 1931 he was elected to the Florida Legislature and considered himself part of the rural clique later known as the Porkchop Gang. Yearty said in a memoir that their aim was to keep taxes down, and that his motto was: "If you can't understand a bill vote against it and you will be right nine times out of ten" (typescript memoir, PKYL). Later the porkchoppers were associated with fighting for racial segregation and, in the McCarthy climate, were known for an anti-communist and anti-homosexual witch hunt under the ill-starred Johns Committee. Former Florida governor Charley Johns, the head of the committee, was once a flagman for the Seaboard Air Line Railway and knew personally some of the 1923 Rosewood participants, including conductor Kay Bryce and logging boss Henry Andrews. *Informant*: C. Johns. *St. Petersburg Times*, April 19, 1963; July 27, 1962, by Martin Waldron: "'Our state has grown tremendously under a Pork Chop Senate,' said Sen. Dewey Johnson of Quincy. 'It has held down spending and it has held down taxes.' The 22 Pork Chop Senators represent about half the state's land area but only about 18 per cent of the state's population....Rayburn Horne, the small loan lobbyist, owns a fish camp where Pork Choppers hold regular meetings ...The Pork Chop Gang is ruthless in its power." (cf. "Bourbon, Pork Chops, And Red Peppers: Political Immorality In Florida, 1945-1968," by Seth A. Weitz, Florida State University, 2007, p. 3: "Allen Morris claimed the name originated in 1955 when a group of North Florida Senators took a 'blood oath' at a fishing camp called Nutall Rise on the Aucilla River." Cites "Reconsideration: Second Glances at Florida Legislative Events," by Allen Morris, Office of the Clerk, Florida House of Representatives, 1982, p. 172).

[520] W. Randolph Hodges, born Feb. 5, 1914, was not quite nine years old when the violence occurred in 1923, and said he received his news of it at Ben Rowland's barbershop in Cedar Key. He was elected to the Florida Senate in 1952 and served 12 years, twice being president pro tempore. "Randolph Hodges... will then become titular head of the majority bloc—the small country faction often referred to by opponents and by themselves as 'the porkchoppers.'" (*Miami Herald*, Sept. 2, 1959).

[521] *Informant*: J. Yearty; Will Yearty memoir (PKYL).

[522] *Collective Behavior*, by Ralph H. Turner and Lewis M. Killian, Prentice-Hall, 1957, 1987, p. 8: "The redefinition of right and wrong that we identify by the term emergent norm can range from permissive to obligatory."

[523] 1922 tax rolls, LCCH.

[524] The report's discussion of Rosewood's size and appearance began on page 10 with a remarkable entry, which formed its only look at the community's physical aspect:

> "Elsie Collins Campbell, a white woman of Cedar Key, once lived at Rosewood, and was about three years old at the time of the disturbance. She remembered the village as one of green forests. This view is shared universally by blacks and whites when they describe the community's dominant features."

The statement could be viewed a champion of scholarly obfuscation. Ms. Campbell did not live at Rosewood "at the time of the disturbance," when she was three, and certainly no community was there after "the disturbance," so if she ever lived there at all it must have been before age three. However, the report uses this memory from a presumable infant for its only bird's-eye view of Rosewood: a place of "green forests." That the forests were green is presented as a valuable detail. And that "this view is shared universally by blacks and whites" becomes a parody of scholarly balance, as if to show that whites did not think the forests were purple or azure, or that blacks did not say there were no forests at all. Behind the statement was a crusade to promote the Rosewood claims case of 1991-1994. (Attorney General's Rosewood file, Peters File, Vol. 1, "Documented History of the Incident Which Occurred...," submitted to the Florida Board of Regents, Dec. 21, 1993, pp. 10-11).

[525] "[W]hat Atlanta is today...manicured lawns": Rosewood descendant Arnett Doctor, quoted in the *Tampa Tribune*, May 16, 1993, which explained: "Doctor describes it as a thriving, upper middle-class community. 'Rosewood was nicknamed the "Black Mecca." Rosewood was to the Southeast, and especially Florida, what Atlanta is today. Two hundred to 300 people lived in Rosewood in 60 to 70 well-built homes with manicured lawns.'" In an interview on Sept. 23, 1993, an academic-committee member seemed to prompt ex-resident Lillie Washington to paint a picture of Rosewood as a "thriving" community, but Washington would not cooperate:

Question: 'Was Rosewood a thriving community, that is, were people doing different kinds of things. There were very few people just sitting around idle. They did a variety of things. Was it a busy working kind of place?'

Answer: 'No, but most of them didn't work in Rosewood because it wasn't any work. They worked in Sumner, Florida.'" (Attorney General's Rosewood files, Curington file, Vol. 29).

[526] The 2013 book *The Beast in Florida: A History of Anti-Black Violence*, recalled by University Press of Florida a year after publication for "scholarly misconduct," contained a statement that Rosewood was physically filled with roses. Besides repeating errors from the 1993 academic report (with footnotes saying "DeGrandy and Larson," though they were not the report's authors), the book retold the confabulated anecdote about Aaron Carrier being dragged

behind a car (pp. 101-102), footnoting it to a 1990s source (D'Orso, 1996, p. 4), as if that made it true. The book also puzzlingly said that Sam Carter was a "business advisor or accountant" (p. 102) on the strength of an informant who arose in the 1990s (and was disputed by the verified survivors). Sylvester Carrier became "a veteran of World War I" (p. 105, also from a 1990s misstatement) when in fact he was a prison inmate. These were only a few of the 1990s mythic assertions that were extracted and repeated as fact in the 2013 rendition, suggesting that the myths, having been fleetingly endorsed in a time of media excitement a generation earlier, might continue to be resurrected by new enthusiasts.

[527] *Informants*: M. Howard (Bryce's daughter); M. Thompson, J. Turner, R. Hodges, C. Johns, S. Hall, E. Davis, M. Langley, L. Carrier.

[528] A photo on file at the Cedar Key Historical Society (three-story house complete with windmill) was said in 1982 to depict the Bryce house. Other views of the house and windmill, unlabeled except for "Cedar Key," are on file at the State Archives of Florida, viewable online in the Florida Memory collection. Martha Pillsbury Thompson, who as a child spent time in the summers at the home of her father's friend Kay Bryce in Cedar Key, recalled the windmill specifically.

[529] *Informant*: M. Thompson.

[530] *Informant*: M. Langley.

[531] *Gainesville Daily Sun*, Jan. 6, 1923.

[532] *Informants*: M. Langley, L. Davis, E. Davis, S. Hall, R. Missouri, L. Carrier, V. Hamilton, T. Hawkins, L. Carrol, L. Cason.

[533] *Informants*: S. Hall, M. Daniels, M. Johnson, M. Langley, L. Davis, L. Carrol, V. Hamilton.

[534] Sam and Ellen King were still alive and at the Cummer mill town of Lacoochee in the 1940 Federal Census. Their daughter Eloise (King) Davis described Sam King's death.

[535] *Informant*: E. Davis, presenting record of the 1952 bill of sale, photocopied by author.

[536] March 25, 1925, the sale record for parcels in Section 29 by Cedar Key State Bank, pres. J. W. Turner, to D. W. Daughtry, shows at least five errors, internal contradictions or anomalies on land amounts, names and dates (Book 18, p. 344,

LCCH). By 1926, "McIntyre Trustee" was penciled beside 20 acres belonging to "C. B. Hall Estate" (the remaining 20 acres of larger holdings once possessed by Charles Bacchus Hall, the late father of Sam, Wilson, Mary Ann, Margie and other Hall siblings). The same procedure was used on 10 acres belonging to African American Rosewood resident John Monroe. Meanwhile, the 80-acre Goins tract (though the tax rolls showed it as 65 acres) was recorded sold in sequential transactions by heirs from April 18 to Sept. 8, 1925 (Book 9, p. 318; Book 18, p.344, LCCH). It is difficult to see whether some of the questions raised come of customary informalities, or from the examiner's ignorance of local procedure or perhaps more dismal reasons. The largest African American-owned parcel in Rosewood, John McCoy's 114 acres (originally 120) was recorded sold on May 5, 1923, to L. L. Johns and H. B. Rogers, who apparently held a 1920 note on the property (Book 16, p. 568). Four months later on Sept. 15, 1923, the same buyers were recorded acquiring the 80 acres of family property retained by Mary Jane Hayward (the sister of Annie "Sis" Blocker in Wylly), whose married name was Mary Jane Screen (Book 16, p. 659). Another 80-acre parcel, originally homesteaded by Sam Carter's father Nebuchadnezzar Carter, was recorded sold by the Carter heirs on Aug. 26, 1925, to N.R. Reynolds (Book 20, p. 141). Nearly all African American-owned property in the area considered to be Rosewood was recorded sold by the end of the Florida Boom in 1926 (the King parcel was an exception). A chief acquirer, John McNulty, would also become receiver in 1931 for the entire town of Cedar Key, after Florida's early entry into the Great Depression in 1926, due to the burst real estate bubble, forced the Cedar Key municipality into bankruptcy. Chaotic tensions and pressures helped to both cause and obscure the forced dispossession at Rosewood.

[537] Advertisement in the Scranton, Pennsylvania, *Republican*, of July 9, 1925: "Scores of Scrantonians are Flocking to Florida / To Make Big Fortunes in That Land of Gold / Everybody Wins and Failure is Unknown...There Is No Bubble About the Florida Boom." Two-thirds by mail: "Florida in the 1920s, The Great Florida Land Boom," floridaHistory.org. As an example, on March 21, 1925, Joseph and Lillie Robinson (of Wylly, living beyond the Rosewood area of destruction but related to the Rosewood victims) sold their land to "John McNulty, of the county of Hamilton, in the state of Ohio" (Book 17., p. 402, LCCH).

[538] Three examples, out of many, were lynching incidents at Huejutla, Mexico, in 1998, and San Cristóbal and Senahú, Guatemala, in 1994 and 2001. At San Cristóbal, American tourist June Weinstock, accused suddenly and without reason of being a child-snatcher allegedly selling children's body organs for transplants, was beaten nearly to death while military rescuers were within reach, as they held back from challenging the mob at its peak. The full mob process in the Weinstock attack took so long that national news cameras were able to arrive and film the crowd. In the Senahú case, Guatemala's *Prensa Libre*

said on March 15, 2001: "Lynching...Could Have Been Avoided."

[539] At Huejutla in 1998 (above), military interveners waited until after two hapless traveling peddlers had been hacked to death before the eyes of perhaps a thousand spectators, on an accusation, as with June Weinstock in Guatemala four years earlier, of being baby-stealing organ snatchers, a modern version of the hunted witch. Once the crowd had satisfied itself and was wandering away, military units that had apparently been watching rushed in and made some symbolic arrests, of scant importance to the two savaged peddlers.

[540] Also known as the Rodney King riots, the April 29, 1992, Los Angeles event continued in bursts for days. Death counts depend on definitions of what was riot-related. The most common death tolls cited were 52 or 53. A *Los Angeles Times* study (April 28, 2012) found "more than sixty people lost their lives" over five days. By any criteria that incident had the highest number of officially reported deaths of any mob outbreak in twentieth-century America, topping the previous contender, the East St. Louis "race war" of 1917. At least three other candidates—Tulsa in 1921, Chicago in 1919 and Elaine, Arkansas, in 1919— have been presented by some advocates as being more lethal because of alleged secret fatalities. No such secret masses of dead seem ever to have been tied to any specific named disappearances, while they also present other reasons for doubt.

[541] Videotaped attacker Damian Williams served four years, was released, then was convicted in the murder of a drug dealer and sent back to prison. The others identified on videotape in the Denny assault were set free after trial resulted in a hung jury.

[542] The author's original exposé on Rosewood (*Floridian, St. Petersburg Times,* July 25, 1982) accepted a lone informant story saying that the Rosewood events had involved two Bryce brothers, not just William Crighton "Kay" Bryce but also his brother John. Subsequently, as other informants spoke only of Kay, it became clear that he alone was the rescuer, as the author specified in subsequent accounts. Bryce's daughter, Mary Leona Howard, confirmed: "Uncle John wasn't in it." However, the original depiction of two brothers was apparently enticing, and the 1997 Rosewood movie dropped in John anyway, using their name, "Bryce," on a heroic train duo. The fantasy brother act was then embraced as real history by a 2013 book from University Press of Florida, further slurring the image by calling them "the Bryce brothers, James and Creighton," while an advocacy summary in the 1990s claims case said they were dashing northern tycoons who had come south to run a railroad; the real Bryce family had been southern for generations and did not own the railroad.

Chapter 36: Jump Jim Crow

[543] *Americans and Their Songs*, by Luther Frank, Harper & Brothers, New York, 1942, p. 80.

[544] May 28, 1883, Book E, p. 781 (LCCH).

[545] Dec 23, 1886, James Carrier wed Emma Lewis. (*Search for Yesterday, A History of Levy County, Florida*, Levy County Archives Committee, Chapter 5, p. 7).

[546] *Romantic and Historic Levy County*, by Ruth Verrill, Storter Printing Co., Gainesville, 1976, pp. 102-103 (PKYL), contains a persuasive account of a hunter in 1941 bringing in two specimens of the "dogkiller" (*Eira barbara*), a bushy-tailed member of the weasel family, officially said to be confined in range to Latin America. The book said in that era the Florida Department of Conservation knew these animals as "Teyra cats," adding that "many do not know of this wily predator and its existence in Florida, but it has been in the state many years, having, it is said, come in from Louisiana." *Informant*: M. Cannon.

[547] Bob Walker bear hunting in 1908: *Levy Times-Democrat*, Nov. 10, 1908, cited in *Search for Yesterday, A History of Levy County, Florida*, Levy County Archives Committee, Chapter 13, p. 9. Teddy Roosevelt's "teddy bear" in the Mississippi canebrakes: The *Washington Post*, Nov. 16, 1902, ran Clifford Berryman's editorial cartoon depicting a soft-hearted President Roosevelt refusing to shoot a captive bear while on a hunt near Onward, Sharkey County, Mississippi, on Nov. 14, 1902, inspiring a Brooklyn store owner's idea for stuffed toy bears ("Real Teddy Bear Story," Theodore Roosevelt Association; "The Story of the Teddy Bear," Theodore Roosevelt Birthplace, U.S. National Park Service). Despite the president's restraint in the Mississippi cane-brakes, the real story behind the teddy bear incident was not sentimental. Local hunters, including the state's governor, were instilled in a ritualistic tradition that a hunter who fails to kill is worthy of ridicule, so on the Mississippi hunt the empty-handed president was presented with a captive target to slay, a pathetic small bear that had already been beaten nearly to death, on which Roosevelt was expected to save his ritual pride by blasting point-blank. Reportedly this was the courtesy he refused. The bear was finished anyway. "Largest fur coat, duck and leather coat...": Sears, Roebuck and Co., 1908 catalog, p. 1093.

[548] Carbon bisulfate: "Gilbert Tucker Shares Stories Of Early Days On Florida Ranch," by Colleen Schreiber, *Livestock Weekly*, March 8, 2001. *Informants*: C. Hudson, R. Hodges, L. Lancaster. "Genuine Black Raccoon Muffs": Montgomery Ward & Co., 1894-1895 catalog, Follet Publishing Co. (Also offered for sale, at 75 cents a pair, were "Men's Domestic Dogskin Gloves"). *Informant*: L. Carrier. Folktales in Cedar Key told of a local lay-about who was

said to keep a souvenir ear from a lynching (though not from Rosewood), preserving it in white powder against bugs. *Informant*: M. McCain.

[549] *Informant*: M. Langley.

[550] *New York World*, April 2, 1923: "A million people..." The *World*, owned by Ralph Pulitzer and edited by Herbert Bayard Swope, would send reporter Samuel Duff McCoy to Florida in the spring of 1923 to cover the Martin Tabert scandal involving murderous slave camps on the county line between Dixie and Taylor counties. The *World* was awarded the 1924 Pulitzer Prize for the story (Samuel McCoy papers, FSL; *The World According to Swope, A Biography if Herbert Bayard Swope*, by E. J. Cahn, Jr. Simon and Schuster, 1965, p. 243; "Martin Tabert, Martyr of an Era," by N. Gordon Carper, *Florida Historical Quarterly*, Oct. 1973, p. 115).

[551] *Informants*: E. Parham, J. McElveen, M. Thompson, F. Smith, F. Kirkland

[552] *Gainesville Daily Sun*, Jan. 7, 1923:
"Returning to the negro quarters of Sumner, three miles away, early Saturday morning after having spent the night in nearby woods, the negro appealed to W. H. Pillsbury, superintendent of the Cummer Cypress Company mill there, for protection. Mr. Pillsbury locked him in a shanty on the outskirts of town.
"Later in the morning when members of the mob heard that the negro was being held there, an immediate demand was made for his body. Fearing possible violence near the mill, Mr. Pillsbury turned the man over after receiving a promise that no outbreak would take place within the village. The negro was led to the scene of earlier violence and there shot to death after questioning by his captors."

[553] Aphasia was first identified by pioneer French physician and surgeon Pierre Paul Broca in 1861, on a patient whose cerebral lesion left him able to say only one syllable, "Tan." In 1864 a Paris medical professor suggested replacing Broca's term for the impairment, aphémie (aphimia) with the word *"aphasie"*— or in English, "aphasia." The 1870 Federal Census found James Carrier in Rosewood at age four, suggesting that he was born around 1866.

[554] *Informants*: E. Foster, F. Kirkland; *Gainesville Daily Sun*, Jan. 7, 1923; *New York World*, Jan. 7, 1923: "When he refused to reveal the names of the Negroes who did the shooting, the white men, officers were informed, led him to the Negro graveyard and made him stand on the newly dug graves of his brother and mother, also victims of the fighting."

[555] *New York Times*, Sunday, Jan. 7, 1923. This is obviously the same wire-

service dispatch that ran in the same day's *Gainesville Daily Sun,* a thousand miles south of the Times Building, though the wording was changed slightly.

[556] *Florida Times-Union,* Sunday, Jan. 7, 1923.

[557] Sheriff Walker's descendant Leigh Williams Kitchens has documented the reasons why his name caused confusion. Walker's father's name was Elias Walker, then the sheriff himself, born Jan. 6, 1869, was named Elisha Walker. However, this could get tangled with his father's name so in time he adopted an additional name, Robert, which his nickname shortened to Bob. Though some assumed he had been "Robert Elisha Walker," all along, Kitchens photographed his gravestone, which reads simply "E. Walker" ("Robert Elisha 'Bob' Walker," by Leigh Williams Kitchens).

[558] *Florida Times-Union,* Jan. 7, 1923: "several white men." *New York Times,* Jan. 7, 1923: "twenty-five or thirty men."

[559] Discharge book 1, p. 71 (LCCH): During World War II, Patrick I. Taylor joined the U.S. Army at age 39 for one month, then was discharged for unspecified illness.

[560] In 1890 President Benjamin Harrison's administration sent a revenue cutter and a detachment of U.S. deputy marshals to restore order in the isolated port of Cedar Key, Florida (then called Cedar Keys), because the U.S. Collector of Customs there (who was also the president's half-brother) had been run out of town by local violence, as town government fell into the hands of thugs. *New York Times,* May 17, 1890:

> "CEDAR KEYS, Fla., May 16. -- Cedar Keys during the past week has been in a condition not short of a siege. The place has virtually been in the possession of Mayor Cottrell and a band of armed men, and business has been at a standstill. Men and women have been confined to their houses, not daring to leave for fear of their lives." (Also see *Off the Beaten Path, The History of Cedar Key, Florida. 1843-1990,* by Jesse Walter Dees Jr. and Vivian Flannery Dees, Rife Publishing, Chiefland, Fla., 1990, p. 78; Congressional Edition, U.S. Congress, Vol. 2688, p. 369; "Crisis at Cedar Keys," by Master Chief William R. Wells II, *Naval History,* April 2002).

White Cedar Key, with its 1923 indignation painting Rosewood as a black outlaws' roost, was obscuring its own history as a smugglers' roost. A sawmill superintendent's memories from the company town of Lukens, which stood a few miles from Cedar Key until 1918, said that whites would come over from Cedar Key on weekends and use trumped-up charges to jail his African American laborers in what amounted to blackmail. In its isolation—and coastal beauty—Cedar Key harbored a violent legacy that was another part of the secret behind the Rosewood violence.

561 *Informants*: R. Hodges, F. Kirkland, J. Turner, E. Zimmerman, J. McElveen, M. McCain, W. Baylor, N. Dorsett.

562 *Sarasota Herald-Tribune*, Nov. 28, 1932: "THREE MEN DIE AS CEDAR KEY JAIL IS BURNED...(AP) Three prisoners, members of a Greek sponge fishing fleet from Tarpon Springs, were burned to death today when flames, said by authorities to have been started by the men in an effort to burn holes in the floor through which to escape, destroyed the city jail here." Again a locally-generated Associated Press story of that time and place is shown to be a hasty mask. Another AP story, coming much later (*St. Petersburg Times*, Aug. 9, 1944), revealed what the first report had masked: The three fishermen were hijacked by Cedar Key's drunken Justice of the Peace, T. W. Brewer, in a dispute over a woman, then in jail they were murdered and a fire set to cover the traces. The burned bodies revealed stab wounds, and one man was apparently still living when burned. The Justice of the Peace and a deputized accomplice received life prison terms.
At the time of the murders, Cedar Key had just lost its rail link to the outside world, cementing its entry into the ranks of dead towns, as it also passed into municipal bankruptcy. The three bodies were examined by Dr. J. W. Turner, the father of Rosewood informant and future Levy County sheriff Jim Turner. ("Murders at Kiss-Me-Quick: the Underside of International Affairs," by Jerrell H. Shofner, *Florida Historical Quarterly*, Vol. 62, No. 3, Jan. 1984, p. 332-335; *Cedar Key, Florida, A History*, by Kevin McCarthy, The History Press, 2007., p. 71).

563 Discharge book 1, p. 71 (LCCH), Patrick I. Taylor, "carpenter." *Informants*: J. Taylor, A. Taylor, B. Taylor, J. Turner, N. Dorsett.

564 *Informants*: R. Hodges (FDLE interview, 1994), J. Turner, W. Baylor.

565 *Informant*: R. Hodges.

566 W. Randolph Hodges, president *pro tempore* of the Florida Senate, 1959; president, 1961. *Miami Herald*, Sept. 2, 1959, cited in *Cedar Key News*, obituary. *Informant*: R. Hodges.

567 *Informants* on Punk Hudson: C. Hudson, J. Turner, A. Faircloth, F. Kirkland, M. McCain, F. Coburn, R. Hodges.

568 *Informant:* J. Turner.

569 *Informants*: E. Zimmerman, G. Booth, R. Yant.

---

[570] Chicago White Sox star outfielder Joseph Jefferson "Shoeless Joe" Jackson was associated with though apparently not a main conspirator in the fixing of the 1919 World Series, resulting in the "Black Sox" scandal that left Jackson and seven others banned from major league baseball. It is said to be a myth that a disillusioned child fan pleaded with Jackson during trial: "Say it ain't so, Joe."

[571] Rosewood survivors were generally conservative in estimating the death toll among African Americans. and tended to be closely confirmed by other evidence. However, one exception was the shooting and arson at the King and Gordon homes. Certainly one murder did occur there, that of Lexie Gordon. This trauma rippled through survivor networks to result in stories that more deaths had occurred in that one nexus. Named as one of the alleged victims was Frances Goins or, alternatively, Eloise King, both children at the time. In the most extreme version of these stories, Lonnie Carrol, who was badly disabled by stroke when interviewed in 1983, though still lucid on some issues, said: "Gordon, all the whole family of them got kilt. Was a crew of 'em in the family, three houses along there. All of them got kilt. They wasn't no kin to us. They were neighbor people. Killed her over the porch and kicked her out doors. All the whole family got kilt."

When this statement was made, and others about Frances Goins being killed, the decades of cover-up and official avoidance had left open the possibility that multiple disappearances might indeed have occurred at these two homes (not three homes as the statement said). The 1920 federal census found 10 persons in household 107, headed by Lexie Gordon, including Lexie herself, and next door at the King home (household 108), three persons: Sam, Ellen, and their small daughter Eloise. As survivor networks were located in 1982-1983. the Kings were accounted for, and could be seen to have survived, but nine of the 1920 census residents of the Lexie Gordon household remained ciphers, as yet untraced and hence possibly victims of concealed murders.

It would take another decade of slowly pursuing clues in survivor groups to find interlocking testimony confirming that all or nearly all of these people had moved out of Lexie Gordon's home and away from Rosewood before the 1923 violence. All were accepted as a matter of course within their own families as having survived the violence. There was no morbid furtiveness such as might have characterized some kind of (extremely improbable) family cover-up of additional deaths. Lexie's own murder had produced deep anguish in the family and any additional disappearances would presumably have had the same effect.

This impression was reinforced by other allegations that only one small girl was killed, with some stories saying this was Eloise King, but others that it was Frances Goins. By 1983, Eloise King Davis had been located in Opa-Locka north of Miami. It took longer to locate Frances Goins, also alive. These were the only stories among African American survivors about alleged unrecorded killings of black victims in the 1923 violence. The rest of such stories traced back to boast-like tales told among whites, referring to dimly envisioned masses of alleged black dead, none identified by name. The Gordon/King tracing showed how chaos and emotional pain could provide spurious indications of apparent unrecorded killings.

[572] *Informants*: J. Yearty, H. Strong, L. Glover, P. Glover, J. White.

[573] "Nits Make Lice: Drogheda, Sand Creek, and the Poetics of Colonial Extermination," by Katie Kane, *Cultural Critique*, No. 42, Spring 1999, p. 97: "Additionally, the vehicle implies a second image, the usual practical response of humans to insect parasites—eradication."

[574] Kane, ibid., pp. 84-85: At Drogheda in September 1649 a member of Cromwell's force reported "3,552 of the enemy slain and 64 of ours" with "none spared." Cromwell's official report said he "forbade to spare any that were in arms in the town and, I think, that night they put to the sword about 2,000 men...I am persuaded that this is a religious judgment of God..." The killing of children was not mentioned, but might be inferred.

[575] Ibid., pp. 86-87: The earliest mention of the phrase seemed to be in a 1675 poem, *The Moderate Cavalier* ("Did kill the Nits, that they might not make Lice"), and a comment by a historian of the period, John Nalson, saying he had talked to a relative in the army who, at third-hand, was said to have heard soldiers saying disdainfully: "Nits will be Lice, and so would dispatch them."

[576] "New Perspectives on the West, Philip Henry Sheridan," http://www.pbs.org/weta/ thewest /people/s_z/sheridan.htm

[577] *The American Way of War: A History of United States Military Strategy and Policy*, by Russell Frank Weigley, Indiana University Press, 1977, p. 158.

[578] Memphis, July 31, 1862, W. T. Sherman to his wife Ellen: "The North may fall into anarchy first, but if they can hold on the war will soon assume a turn in extermination, not of soldiers alone that is the least part of the trouble, but the people."—*Home Letters of General Sherman*, by William T. Sherman, ed. M. A. DeWolfe Howe, C. Scribner's Sons, 1909, p. 230. The same letter (p. 229) said: "...As to freeing the negroes, I don't think the time is come yet. When negroes are liberated either they or masters must perish. They cannot exist together except in their present relation, and to expect negroes to change from slaves to masters without one of those horrible convulsions which at times startle the world is absurd."

[579] "[E]arly September or late in August last I heard Colonel Chivington in a public speech announce that his policy was to 'kill and scalp all, little and big, that nits make lice.' ("Nits Make Lice: Drogheda, Sand Creek, and the Poetics of Colonial Extermination," by Katie Kane, *Cultural Critique*, No. 42, Spring

1999. p. 83, citing "Affidavit of S. E. Browne sworn before the United States Senate in 1867, 'The Chivington Massacre,' *Reports of the Committee*, 71). Kane's extremely thorough search for mentions of the phrase "Nits make lice" in the Chivington case seemed to turn up only one other account of the pre-massacre speech. A 1959 book (*An Informal History of Denver and the Rocky Mountain News*, by Robert L. Perkin, p. 269) said the speech was "warmly applauded and the phrase became a fighting slogan for the Third," a reference to the Third Colorado Territory Regiment, which committed the Nov. 29, 1864, massacre under Chivington. The power of the phrase in capturing an extreme of evil may have found it used, both in Ireland with regard to Cromwell and in the U.S. regarding Chivington, more by opponents of its philosophy than by actual believers—as after-the-fact narrations of the Pat Taylor atrocity at Rosewood may perhaps have used the phrase more than Taylor himself did. In 1854, the monstrosity at Sand Creek demanded a metaphor once publicity swelled in the late 1860s, and S. E. Browne's witness recollection of the horrific phrase in the speech—"that nits make lice"—served to carry the sense of revulsion, regardless of what Colonel Chivington may actually have said. Kane pointed out (p. 100): "No recorded copy of the speech exists." She noted the original meaning of "metaphor"—"'to carry over' (*meta*, over + *pherein*, to carry)." Atrocity engenders a swarm of shocking images, whose power can make them deceptive images.

[580] Ironically, the phrase "Jim Crow segregation" seems to be another backlash metaphor, apparently used more by the system's detractors, to express its monstrosity, than by the actual implementers of the system, to whom the phrase is tacitly imputed by the critics. The real architects of "Jim Crow segregation" tended not to call it "Jim Crow" but used more self-aggrandizing phrases, notably "white supremacy."

[581] "African Americans continued to live and work in Cedar Key until the fiber factory closed in 1952." (*Cedar Key, Florida, A History*, by Kevin McCarthy, The History Press, 2007, p. 61). Stories in Cedar Key portraying the Rosewood events of 1923 as the explanation for the town's monolithic whiteness by 1982 were conflations. Cedar Key's remarkable palm fiber factory, retooled from an oyster cannery in 1909 with machinery made at Archer just up the railroad, would provide an economic lifeline through hard decades. Prior to 1923, Minnie Langley would recall, she would go with her grandfather James Carrier in their ox cart as he took palm buds to sell to the fiber factory, nine miles from Rosewood at Cedar Key. The 1952 closing of the factory, deepening the left-behind seclusion of Cedar Key, occurred after technology changed, but also after a hurricane. Once again, local white supremacy boasts were obscuring a larger demon, in this case the devil's bargain in Florida paradise: the weather.

[582] *Axis Rule in Occupied Europe: Laws of Occupation - Analysis of Government - Proposals for Redress*, by Raphael Lemkin, Carnegie Endowment

for International Peace, Washington, D.C., 1944. Lemkin's coining of the word, borrowing from both Greek and Latin, seems to have come in 1943, the year of the book's preface. Writing in 1955, British historian Arnold Toynbee found the term "genocide" still so new that he put it in quotation marks: "The subsequent 'genocide' of the Jews carried out by the German National Socialists..." (*A Study of History, Abridgement of Volumes VII-X*, by Arnold Toynbee, Oxford University Press, 1957, p. 177).

[583] Patrick I. Taylor died March 3, 1950 (death certificate 4711-1950, FBVS), less than a decade after he enlisted briefly in the army during World War II but was discharged for illness (Discharge book 1, p. 71, LCCH).

[584] Rice's song and dance number was so popular, especially in the North, that a dissenter complained: "Tis Jim Crow here, Jim Crow there—Jim Crow every where." (*Demons of Disorder, Early Blackface Minstrels and Their World*, by Dale Cockrell, Cambridge University Press, 1997, p. 66).

[585] *Americans and Their Songs*; by Frank Luther, Harper & Brothers, New York, 1942, p. 80.

[586] *John Brown's Body*, by Stephen Vincent Benét, Elephant Paperbacks, Chicago, 1928 (Pulitzer Prize for Poetry. 1929).

[587] *Demons of Disorder, Early Blackface Minstrels and Their World*, by Dale Cockrell, Cambridge University Press, 1997, pp. 62-63; *Southern Music, American Music*, by Bill C. Malone and David Stricklin, University Press of Kentucky, Lexington, 1979, p. 21.

[588] Not among lovers of minstrelsy was Frederick Douglass, who condemned: "the 'Virginia Minstrels,' 'Christy's Minstrels,' the 'Ethiopian Serenaders,' or any of the filthy scum of white society, who have stolen from us a complexion denied to them by nature, in which to make money, and pander to the corrupt taste of their white fellow-citizens." (*The North Star*, Frederick Douglass, Rochester, Oct. 27, 1848, http://utc.iath.virginia.edu/minstrel/miar03bt.html).

[589] Two different autopsies on the appeal of blackface minstrelsy can be compared. *Demons of Disorder...*, by Dale Cockrell, above, noted minstrelsy's rebellious release of inhibitions similar to carnival misrule and Jacksonian-era torchlight riots. Meanwhile, *DOO-DAH! Stephen Foster...*, by Ken Emerson, also cited above, observed that minstrelsy offered a young society of recent immigrants an avenue for finding group identity, by feeling part of a great white whole through distancing from the black Other. Emerson (p. 12) spoke of "the American identity they were eager to assimilate," but also saw the dysinhibition: "blackface... represents a certain freedom to whites—freedom from bourgeois

conventions and expectations" (p. 16). The white identity motivation reminds of Grace Elizabeth Hale's view of spectacle lynching, that it was a way of "making whiteness."

590 "[A] Jim Crow mania has seized on all classes of the community" (*London Satirist*, quoted in Cockrell, p. 68).

591 Ibid., p. 66.

592 *The Changing Race Relationship in the Border and Northern States*, by Hannibal Gerald Duncan, University of Pennsylvania, 1922, pp 55-56; "Jim Crow railroads in Massachusetts," by Louis Ruchames, *American Quarterly*, Vol. 8, No. 1, Spring 1956, pp. 61-75.

593 Duncan, ibid.

594 Ibid.

595 *History of Popular Music*, by David Ewen, Barnes & Noble, New York, 1961, pp. 27-28.

596 *With Amusement for All: A History of American Popular Culture Since 1830*, by LeRoy Ashby, University Press of Kentucky, 2006, p. 19: "[M]instrelsy's theatrical attack included two main characters: 'Jim Crow' and 'Zip Coon.' In 1834, George Washington Dixon...introduced 'Zip Coon'—'Zip' serving as the abbreviated version of 'Scipio,' then a common African American name. Whereas the shuffling, ragamuffin Jim Crow was the caricature of a slave, Zip Coon personified a northern urban dandy, a swaggering parody of fashion and pretense."

597 "I Wish I Was in Dixie Land," by Daniel Decatur Emmett, 1859 (other contributors or collaborators were claimed). "The familiar expression on which the song was founded was not a southern phrase, but first appeared among the circus people of the north....As the cold weather approached, the performers would think of the genial weather they were headed for...'Well, I wish I was in Dixie.'" (*The Minstrel World, Vol. 68*, by J. Alfredo Novello, 1888, p. 976). As with Stephen Foster's 1851 blackface hit about the Suwannee, "Old Folks at Home," Dan Emmett's 1859 hit blackface song "Dixie" was soon said to have been "sung, whistled and played in every corner of the globe," as it became a juggernaut of behavioral contagion (*New York Clipper*, Aug. 10, 1861, cited in *Dan Emmett and the Rise of Early Negro Minstrelsy*, by Hans Nathan, University of Oklahoma Press, 1962, p. 269). The geography of the 1923 Rosewood tragedy reprised two southern metaphors, Dixie and "Swanny," though etching them in grim relief. Rosewood's figurative horizon was bordered by the feared river of no-return, the Suwannee, which in the minds of

Rosewood's black pioneers was not a sign of paradise. On its far bank lay the newly formed outlaw county named Dixie, known for peonage abuses and slaving traps. The nostalgic Florida Legislature had seen fit to name the new county Dixie in 1921 when they created it, as if erecting a never-never-land for the Lost Cause.

Chapter 37: Arson for the Camera?

[598] "[B]orn in a log cabin…grew up on a farm about four miles from Perry. He began his education in a log building known as the Pine Grove School. The desks were the tops of wooden boxes…Split logs with pole legs served as seats. Classes were held whenever they would not interfere with planting, hunting, or harvesting. School was in session less than forty days a year. He finished his education at the Perry School, a four mile walk from the farm…..received his license to teach in 1893… In 1897 he was appointed principal of the Perry School…", then was apprenticed to his brother's law office in Perry while he was principal. ("Cary Augustus Hardee, Spokesman for Educational Progress," by James D. Catron, Jr., professor of political science, North Florida Junior College, SAF): "Cary Augustus Hardee-Florida Governors," Florida Dept. of State, Division of Historical Resources. *Informant*: C. Hardee III.

[599] Even before the Florida Boom of the mid-1920s, Tallahassee was apparently smaller than Gainesville. The capital city's small-town cliques linked directly to the Martin Tabert slaving scandal that made nationwide news in April-May 1923. Governor Hardee's physical appearance: *St Petersburg Times*, May 12, 1986, article by former Florida governor LeRoy Collins on Hardee: "He regularly walked from the mansion to the Capitol in the morning…Hardee in the '20s was a picture of neatness and gentlemanly distinction. His clothes were immaculate, his silver hair well groomed. He had a gold-capped cane, that he would swing in perfect rhythm with his stride. He was recognized by the public as a conscientious, careful conservative."

[600] Suwannee-Madison County, Fla., Archives Biographies, "Hardee, Cary Augustus," citing *The History of Florida, Past and Present, Vol. II*, The Lewis Publishing Co., 1923, p. 3. *'Gators, Skeeters, and Malary, Recollections of a Pioneer Florida Judge, Vol. I*, by Ellis C. May, Vantage Press, New York, 1953. *The History of Florida, Past and Present*, 1923.

[601] *Florida, From Indian Trail to Space Age: A History. Vol. I*, by Charlton W. Tebeau and Ruby Leach Carson, The Southern Publishing Company, Delray Beach, Florida, 1965, p 61. *Boom in Paradise*, by T. H. Weigall, A.H. King publisher, New York, 1932.

[602] Forced labor ploys involving Dixie and Taylor counties continued until they

happened to net a misguided white youth from a large family farm in North Dakota, whose idea of the grand tour turned into hoboing into Florida on a freight. Once caught, Martin Tabert was essentially worked and whipped to death, with the results written off as malaria. His family had the persistence and influence to force an investigation. Ensuing publicity mentioned other cases of men who had disappeared into northern Florida's labor camps, but a full accounting of victims was never made. The great majority of victims were African American.

603 *Dixie County informants*: Cliff Clark, Preston Chavous, Perry Hill, Allen Stephenson U.S. Bureau of Investigation reports, Frederick Cubberly papers (PKYL).

604 Putnam Lumber reported the start of its logging in Dixie County as being in 1918-1919, but until 1928 it shipped logs out by rail to be sawn at a Jacksonville mill leased from the Cummer corporation. In 1927-1928 Putnam built its own sawmill in its new company town, Shamrock, in Dixie County. a mill sometimes called the largest cypress sawmill in the world. In the late 1920s Putnam's total timber holdings were described as being 242,000 acres, most of it in Dixie and Taylor counties. Other counts said 300,000 or 350,000 acres. Dixie County comprises a total of more than 450,000 acres in non-submerged area. The percentage of that area owned by Putnam Lumber in the 1920s is not clear.

605 *Tallahassee Democrat*, April 27, 1923: Sheriff J. R. Jones of Leon County, which includes Tallahassee, and Tallahassee's Judge B. F. Willis were removed from office after revelations that they were involved in trumping up charges against transients in order to jail them and send them into a Dixie County slave camp run by Putnam Lumber, where at least two convicts died under oppressive conditions. Historically, Putnam had done its logging in a joint operation with nearby major timber corporations called the Carbur Logging Company. Whether the slave camps might have involved unacknowledged corporate partners was one of countless questions in the Tabert scandal that apparently went unexplored.

606 April 25, 1921, Dixie County's creation by the Florida Legislature was announced by newspapers on April 26, Confederate Memorial Day. (Confederate Memorial Day was originally positioned as April 26 by the Ladies Memorial Association of Columbus, Georgia, in 1866, because that date saw General Johnston surrender to General Sherman in North Carolina, 17 days after Lee's surrender at Appomattox.

607 *Florida Times-Union*, May 30, 1923: "SHERIFF OF DIXIE COUNTY BEFORE GOVERENOR TO ANSWER CHARGES FILED." (Carper, N. Gordon, "Martin Tabert, Martyr of an Era," *Florida Historical Quarterly*, Oct. 1973, p. 115).

608 *Literary Digest*, June 16, 1923, p. 38.

609 *Jacksonville Journal*, Jan. 5, 1923. The *Journal's* new editor, Richard Lloyd Jones, knew about troops in a riot, since in 1921 he was running the *Tulsa Tribune* when it was accused of helping start the Tulsa riot. The officer leading National Guard troops into the riot denounced the *Tribune* as "a sensation-seeking newspaper."

610 *Gainesville Daily Sun*, Jan. 6, 1923.

611 Guide to the Records of the Florida State Archives, 1988: "Due to the absence of correspondence and other records from this period, Governor Hardee's scrapbook contains the best source of information on his term available at the Archives." The two governors of the boom period—Cary Hardee (1921-25) and John Martin (1925-1929)—left no papers ("Fortune and Misfortune, the Paradoxical Twenties," by William W. Rogers, *The New History of Florida*, ed. Michael Gannon, University Press of Florida, 1996, p. 294).

612 *Informant*: Cary Hardee III.

613 One example was sightseeing after the East St. Louis riot of 1917: "Hundreds of visitors from St. Louis, Mo., across the river, came to look over the acres of charred debris which formerly was 'Black Valley.'" (*Tulsa World*, July 5, 1917, p. 1).

614 Killed when a sightseer truck overturned were two occupants, Ann Grady, 20, and Hershell Parker, 23, both from a town 30 miles away. The collateral accident occurred on Sunday, April 12, 1936, a week after the storm, as National Guard troops opened the site to general traffic and "more than 100,000 people drove through the storm area during the day"—quite a Sunday drive (*Tupelo Daily News*, April 13, 1936). The town's mayor had announced angrily: "Sightseers cannot help us. They get in our way." (*Memphis Commercial Appeal*, April 7, 1936).

615 *Informants*: E. Johnson, M. McCain, J. Yearty, E. Foster.

616 In 1914, as D. W. Griffith's 165-minute *The Birth of a Nation* was demonstrating the power of film narrative, William Randolph Hearst's news organization branched out into silent newsreels, competing with Pathé, then merging to form Hearst-Pathé, then divorcing again while also dropping the Hearst name from the continuing Hearst newsreel effort, as Hearst had become associated with pro-German sentiments in World War I. From this process came Hearst's International News Reel, in tandem with his International News Service

(which was successfully sued by The Associated Press in 1917-1918 for pirating AP news stories). That a crew or individual from International News Reel did come to Rosewood in January 1923 is beyond reasonable doubt. The resulting photos show no definable landmarks, but one photo does capture a recognizable Rosewood figure (Sheriff Walker), and there are other confirmations. The newsreel format, replaying large or exotic news events, would become central to the Hearst legend because of the 1941 movie *Citizen Kane*. "The greatest film of all time" was a thinly disguised, fictionalized portrait of then-aging press lord Hearst, and it was structured around a "News on the March" newsreel. The movie's plot unfolds as reporters, spurred by the newsreel, try to track down the meaning behind a single strange word, uttered mysteriously in the dying breath of power-mad media mogul "Charles Foster Kane." The pursuit of this word becomes his biography: "Seventy years of a man's life. That's a lot to get in a newsreel." "When Charles Foster Kane died, he said just one word: Rosebud."

[617] *The American News Reel, 1911-1967*, by Raymond Fielding, University of Oklahoma Press, Norman, 1972, p. 132.

[618] Fielding, ibid., pp. 103, 221, 144-145.

[619] The journey of the International News Reel photos from Rosewood has been long. In 1933, archivist Otto Bettmann fled Nazi Germany with two steamer trunks filled with old photos, which were not seized by German customs agents (unlike his money) because the photos seemed worthless, though they would become the foundation of the Bettmann Archive, a rental library of 16 million iconic images. In 1996 this was sold to Corbis Corp., owned by Bill Gates of Microsoft. That same year a search was underway, for ABC News Productions was making a TV documentary about the Rosewood events. Where others had failed, ABC's researchers in New York located the trove of original International Newsreel photos which had found their way into the Corbis-Bettmann Archive. With the photos were the photographer's original field notes.

[620] Fielding, p. 99: "Footage was transported from camera to laboratory by every known means of transportation—airplane, train, boat, automobile, and even dogsled. Some companies owned and operated their own aircraft."

[621] Ibid., p. 96: "Much of the newsreel coverage of World War I was faked by film studios"; p. 140: "All the companies were engaged in piracy, of course."

[622] Ibid., p. 145: "Fox Newsreel editor Ray Hall admitted faking a sequence showing a Fox cameraman photographing a rum-running operation off the coast of New England." p. 145: "large amounts of bogus footage." p. 148: "[A]mong techniques for faking footage were the staging and manipulation of participants and re-enacting of events that had already occurred, as well as manufacturing an entirely false event, 'a gag.' "

[623] Ibid., p. 96: *Literary Digest*, Nov. 13, 1915. The birth of cinema special effects was a long one, traceable back to the invention of moving pictures by Thomas Edison in the 1890s. Almost immediately, in 1898, naval battles in the Spanish-American War were faked by using toy ships, flash powder and cigar smoke, for presentation in the first two-minute newsreels.

[624] *New York Times*, Jan. 8, 1923.

Chapter 38: The Mass Grave

[625] "Rosewood (1997)," Review Summary, by Michael P. Rogers, *the New York Times online,* http://www.nytimes.com/movies/movie/154623/Rosewood/overview.

[626] Comparison can be drawn between two streams of mass media fantasy, in 1923 and 1997. In the *Gainesville Daily Sun* of Jan. 6-10, 1923, "Colonel" Robert Davis, wrote editorials so divorced from material fact that they soon had to be repudiated, first on Jan. 13 ("WE WERE MISINFORMED") and again on Jan. 19 ("threw us all into a fever of excitement"). The racist assumptions thus revealed would seem at first glance to be quite different from a media lapse in a future age, in 1997, when reviewer Michael Rogers informed readers of the New York Times online that "[i]n reality, between 70 and 250 people were killed at Rosewood." The 1923 illusion, evidently believed with great fervor at the *Daily Sun*, demonized the African American subjects of the portrait, while the 1997 media fantasy demonized their attackers. In the latter, an enormous massacre was somehow created in the writer's imagination, then was presented as fact in the *New York Times* online, though such massive carnage had never really occurred. It could be mentioned that the 1997 lapse occurred not in a news story or editorial but in a review of a movie, but still the account took on journalistic authority as it purported to detail the historical reality on which the movie was based ("in reality"). As in the "fever of excitement" in 1923, some kind of psychological mystery seemed to enfold the 1997 writer, since the apocalyptic fatality numbers, "between 70 and 250" did not come from any Rosewood source, not even the most distorted. The sympathies of the 1997 writer seemed deeply opposed to those of Colonel Davis in 1923, not assailing African Americans but advocating for them, and yet the phrase "fever of excitement" might still apply, in the sense of an emotional state that causes startling leaps of imagination in supposedly serious and sophisticated portrayers of a disturbing scene. The commonality in both cases, 1923 and 1997, would seem to be the temptation to demonize, to heroically elevate one's own self in imagination by discovering a perfectly odious demon to destroy—or in other words, the ancient constant that survives many changes in fashion and politics: the fervor of the witch hunt.

627 "Jesse Carey," black male, deceased in Levy County in 1923 (Florida Death Index, Vol. 203, No. 15619). The reader may recall that after the Rosewood violence some whites, especially those close to Fannie Taylor, insisted that her attacker was eventually found and killed, though no public word of this emerged, and those alleging the death could supply no details, while clearly they were not eyewitnesses. Meanwhile, a son of Sam Carter did seem to drop from official sight by 1925 and seemed to be deceased. His first name, like that of the alleged convict sought in the Taylor manhunt, was Jesse. Officially, there seemed to be no record of a Jesse Carter being killed, though there was the record given above, for a "Jesse Carey." These could conceivably add up to a ninth Rosewood fatality—or merely to a dance of coincidence.

628 Other very remote possibilities only serve, ironically, to cinch the case that the death toll was small. There was Sam Hall's uncle Jim Hall, apparently in his eighties, who lived alone with his wife Luvenia. Memories are unclear as to whether James Hall was seen alive after the violence, and the stress—or more direct attack—might conceivably have proved fatal. However, no family excitement surrounded the issue, and no specific story of killing arose. Also Marie Monroe, age 17, died ten months after the violence (death certificate 12345-1923, FBVS) and this may, or may not, have been hastened by malaria or other illness contracted while fleeing or hiding in the swamps, leaving the death as open to question, though only very barely so. The vanishing probabilities in such cases serve to close the larger question because even if one or two such instances were to be included as possible fatalities for margin of error (though not because any evidence supports them), the straining picture would still fall far short of the numbers of alleged deaths in local lore—such as 17, 19 or "30 or 40" deaths. Again, any evidence that might superficially seem to hint at a higher death toll only does so until pinned down. Pursuing such allegations to specifics tends to show their baseless nature. Belief in the mythic interpretations would seem to rely on being too avoidant to seek out the facts.

629 The possible Tulsa provenance for an imagined Rosewood death toll can be seen on the Web: "the 1921 Tulsa race riot...resulting in the death of anywhere from 75 to 250 people." ("Now Tulsa Does Care," "History Matters, The U.S. Survey Course on the Web"). "FACTS: 75 to 250 people were killed. Many lives changed." ("Tulsa Race Riot – 1921," prezi.com). "The total number of people killed during the [Tulsa] riot is debatable – estimates range from 27 to over 250." ("Tulsa Race Riot, 1921," BlackPast.org), Oklahoma legislator Don Ross wrote that around 1930 when he was attending Tulsa's Booker T. Washington High School his teacher insisted that in the riot, then a decade past, "300 people died." Rep. Ross recalled that as proof, the teacher displayed a photo album containing "a yellowing newspaper article [describing] block after block of destruction – '30, 75 even 300 dead.'" The desire to prove an epic death toll at Tulsa was demonstrated by the Tulsa Race Riot Commission of 1997-2001. When no evidence of previously concealed bodies was found at

local sites alleged by rumor, the commission went to the expense of using ground-piercing radar to elaborately continue looking. When the radar search started it was heralded with media fanfare, but then seemed to drop from the news—because once again the illusions were disproved. In the commission's final report the results of the radar search are difficult to find and were not phrased emphatically, but the essence was that the search came up empty. In 1921, official sources placed the death toll in the Tulsa riot at 36. A higher number, the 75 in the wide range found in Web repetitions, may result from inferences drawn about a funeral home ledger (p. 24, commission report), though in the climate of expectation suggested by the radar summary and other aspects of the inquiry, that inference, too, may be open to question. (*Tulsa Race Riot, A Report by the Oklahoma Commission to Study the Tulsa Race Riot of 1921*, Feb. 28, 2001, pp. v, 124-131: p. 131: "Examination of select areas as Newblock Park and Booker T. Washington Cemetery through use of ground penetrating radar failed to reveal any features suggestive of a mass grave....Initial study of Oaklawn Cemetery with ground penetrating radar revealed individual internments [sic] but no mass grave." (at Oaklawn, much was made of an anomaly found by radar where, it turned out, "cemetery records [showed] an adult white male buried there shortly before the riot."

[630] The movie's closing screen note said in full: "The official death toll of the Rosewood massacre, according to the state of Florida, is eight...two whites and six blacks. The survivors, a handful of whom are still alive today, place the number anywhere between 40 and 150, nearly all of them African American." (*Rosewood*, Warner Brothers, 1997, ellipsis in original).

[631] In 1982, as investigation into Rosewood was just beginning, elderly white informants were found who vaguely alleged "30 to 40" deaths. Meanwhile, two other whites (one a child in 1923, the other as yet unborn) agreed that certainly the death toll must have gone no higher than 150: "150, maximum." A 1983 segment about Rosewood on "60 Minutes" (for which the author was background reporter but had no input into the script) used the rumors for a flat assertion: "forty people died here"—which not even the legends had presented so finally.
From 1982 into the 1990s, emerging information on what had been a cultural secret continually sharpened the picture of what had happened in 1923, replacing gossip and official avoidance with evidence. In this process, African American ex-residents of Rosewood were found who conclusively refuted the legends told among whites—though the 1997 movie's screen note turned all this around, claiming that its misleading numbers came from "the survivors" themselves.

[632] *The American News Reel, 1911-1967*, by Raymond Fielding, University of Oklahoma Press, Norman, 1972, p. 138, described "intense competition among

producers and cameramen to scoop their rivals."

[633] "The Rosewood Massacre: the Untold Story," ABC News Productions, David Tereshchuk director, airing on the Discovery Channel 1996. Again, though I provided some of the narration for this documentary, no one consulted me on the title (and at any rate the production could argue that the word "massacre" is accurate if used figuratively). A strange sequel occurred in WorldCat, an online catalog to libraries worldwide, when it listed me as lead author of the documentary, while slighting Tereshchuk, the real author, by placing him as an also-ran. The gibberish that can arise from automated or mindless Web repetitions was further shown because the entry making me lead author linked to Gary Moore the blues guitarist, as if that was me, too—so that I became both ABC author and string virtuoso at once. Other Web gossips didn't seem to mind, as my fame in these new directions then echoed. A site called: "Reel American History," associated with a university, seemed to like the cluelessness and made me lead author as well: "Rosewood Massacre: The Untold Story. Gary Moore, Jack Smith, and David Tereshchuk. New York: ABC News Productions, 1996." The muddled info-profile of Rosewood may result from ideological excitement, but technology alone can sometimes seem to encourage a waking dream.

[634] *New York Times*, Jan. 8, 1923.

[635] *Informant*: J. Turner (Dr. J. W. Turner's son). Other informants confirm the physician's energetic rail schedule, and that he was company doctor for employees of both the Cummer Lumber sawmill in Sumner and the Seaboard Air Line Railway.

[636] In the Martin Tabert legislative hearing and court trials of 1923, a camp doctor in Dixie and Taylor counties was denounced for misdiagnosing Tabert's failing health during convict servitude. The pivotal cause of Tabert's death was apparently his being whipped to death, though the proximate cause may indeed have been malaria, brought on by physical collapse both from the whipping and slave labor. The convict doctor, T. Caper Jones, came under still greater criticism as he defended himself by maintaining that the clearly beaten Tabert was really being idealized, and had died of a venereal disease. The craven picture presented by that camp physician, whose practice lay in remote swamps, was sharply different from the respect enjoyed by the company doctors in better organized Sumner.

[637] The same general area was searched by the Florida Department of Law Enforcement in 1994, as part of their Rosewood investigation mandated by the legislature during the Rosewood claims case. The FDLE's thorough examination found some bricks and foundation stones not previously known, apparently remaining from a turpentine still, but in terms of anything resembling a grave

site no indication was found.

[638] "The people who remember often disagree in their recollections." ("Rosewood Massacre," *Floridian, St. Petersburg Times,* July 25, 1982, p. 6). That article said of James Turner: "He remembers nothing special about the way the corpses were dressed. the women wore dresses. Some wore coats. It was cold.
"He remembers the diapers. 'There were little chillun...suckin' babies...six months old...shot.' "
I was new in those days to the ways that traumatized witness reminiscence can require corroboration. At that early stage in collating the witness testimony there was little way to classify any one informant's credibility. Official avoidance, which had caused no authoritative records to be left on the Rosewood events, thus left no pre-existing standard of veracity. A standard would have to be elaborated informally and gradually, over a period of years, from the overall picture presented by areas of greatest agreement among all the witnesses and other evidence. Even now—after more than three decades of learning—I see no best way to characterize the profound mysteries in James Turner's earnest testimony, though I see that in 1982 I might have probed more deeply into the reasons behind his halting speech and other neurological signs. Without independent information on the overall credibility of this informant, one can only insist on what all other evidence confirms: At Rosewood in 1923 no children disappeared. The only two specific allegations of children killed at Rosewood posited a lone victim, in some tellings Eloise King, in others her next-door neighbor Sarah Goins. These stories were very persuasively answered by the words of the alleged victims themselves, once they were found, still quite alive, in later years.

[639] White informant Frances Smith moved with her husband from Sumner to the Cummer corporation's new sawmill at Lacoochee, as Sumner was replaced in 1926. The Smiths eventually ran a store in Lacoochee and Frances noted that some of the Rosewood survivors, whom she recognized vaguely from earlier days, eventually moved to Lacoochee as well. "Some of old Sarah Carroway's grandchildren moved here," Smith said (meaning Sarah Carrier), " and they'd deny they ever lived at Rosewood." Smith was missing a nuance as she specifically referred to Vera Goins Hamilton, the younger sister of Arnett Goins—who indeed had *not* lived at Rosewood. If Hamilton told Smith this in later years she was describing a reality, not being evasive. Some survivors may have been too frightened to talk, but others discussed the memories readily among family and friends. Sylvester Carrier's wife Gert, for example, was said to talk about the Rosewood events repeatedly.

[640] *High-Sheriff Jim Turner, High Times of a Florida Lawman,* by David T. Warner, Black Belt Press, Montgomery Alabama, 1998 (PKYL). This

mystifying booklet purports to describe the Rosewood events in James Turner's own words, after interviews with him by a relative. It fantastically rearranges real Rosewood names, invents incidents and merges fantasies—as if in homage to the Rosewood movie's similar approach. Whether the result slandered Turner and distorted what he had told the narrator a decade earlier, or whether it somehow captured a real delusional process in the original informant, the fantasy was apparently not noticed by the booklet's few reviews, as by Alabama Public Radio: "Warner sat with his distant cousin, James Turner, who was eighty at the time and had been elected sheriff of Levy County five times....These are stories Turner told Warner, now recast in Sheriff Turner's voice as reminiscences of his adventures. Are they fictionalized? It doesn't matter....The Rosewood massacre is described by Turner, who was *there* [italics in original] with his physician father." The theme of racial violence seems to evoke a perplexing indulgence of falsehood, couched as an article of faith: "Are they fictionalized? It doesn't matter."

[641] *The Lonely Warrior, The Life and Times of Robert S. Abbott*, by Roi Ottley, H. Regnery Co., 1955, p. 177. On the Chicago Riot of 1919, Ottley's characterization was reprised by Tuttle, who found that wildfire rumors carried "extreme distortions of the numbers of deaths, insidious exaggerations that fostered a desire to even the score on the basis of 'an eye for an eye,' a white victim for a black victim, and vice versa. (*Race Riot, Chicago in the Red Summer of 1919*, by William M. Tuttle, Atheneum, New York, 1970, p. 47).

[642] Historian William Tuttle noted a boast made after the Chicago race riot of 1919: "one Irish bailiff even claimed that he had killed a dozen blacks himself." The layers of illusion that could complicate such boasts were captured by NAACP assistant secretary Walter White after the Ocoee, Florida, rampage of 1920: "A white citizen of Ocoee with whom I talked in front of the Post Office but whose name could not be learned, said... 'I do know that 56 were burned up. I killed 17 myself." ("Election Day In Florida." by Walter White, *The Crisis*, Jan. 1921, Vol. 21, No. 3). The illusions were layered here because White's separate internal report on the same 1920 incident ("Report of Walter F. White," NAACP papers UPA, Par. 11, Series Reel 4, Frame 708), portrayed the 56 figure as coming only from hearsay told by his hired driver at Ocoee, while he had the 17 figure coming from an entirely separate hearsay source, an attorney. The "white citizen...in front of the Post Office" who became the public face of all this in *The Crisis*, the NAACP's monthly magazine, was apparently not only dubiously boasting but may himself have been an invented composite, imposed on information from rumor.

[643] Elliott Rudwick, writing about the East St. Louis riot of 1917, noted the prevalence of scorekeeping myths about supposed secret white dead. Allegedly these bodies could not be viewed or identified because they had been dumped into Cahokia Creek. Such stories seemed to reverse the evidence even at

prestigious levels, Rudwick said, as when W.E.B. Du Bois wrote: "The Negroes...piled the white dead on the street." (*Race Riot at East St. Louis, July 2, 1917*, Rudwick, Southern Illinois University Press, Carbondale, 1964, pp. 54-55, citing *Darkwater*, by W. E. B. DuBois, Harcourt Brace, 1920, pp. 94-95). Four years later on the Tulsa riot of 1921, the *Chicago Defender* was convinced of a high score: "Soldiers guarding prisoners in the ball park told them that three times as many whites were being killed as our men" (June 11, 1921). Scott Ellsworth wrote of a black witness to the Tulsa event who was convinced of the score because of "the large number of whites which he saw get shot by black snipers." As late as 1999 when an official commission was looking back into the Tulsa riot, a mysterious, never-named interview subject was said to speak of a group of elderly black men (supposedly willing to talk only to the secretive interpolator) "who know where some mass graves are where whites are buried." A commission member concluded, on no more evidence than this, that the report was believable (telephone interview, Eddie Faye Gates, Tulsa Riot Commission, March 29, 1999). John Hope Franklin, who moved to Tulsa as a ten-year-old not long after the riot, found that "the collective wisdom in the black community" said that "many more whites were killed during the riot than any whites were willing to admit...These conclusions seemed necessary for the continued self esteem of Tulsa's black community. Whether or not the conclusions were valid, they had the desired effect." (Foreword by John Hope Franklin, *Death in a Promised Land, The Tulsa Race Riot of 1921*, by Scott Ellsworth, Louisiana State University Press, Baton Rouge, 1982, p. xvi).

[644] One Rosewood survivor, aged seven in 1923 but later privy to family stories, was a kindly, soft-spoken woman, active in her church in the Liberty City area of Miami. But on the matter of scorekeeping a coldness appeared. Not only was it insisted that many whites were killed at Rosewood and kept off the record, but this informant sought to shave down the number of blacks killed, using harsh logic. When enumerating the African American fatalities she would acknowledge only two, Sarah Carrier and Sam Carter, though naturally the others—Sylvester Carrier, Mingo Williams, James Carrier and Lexie Gordon—were known to her. Reasons were found to exclude them from the scorekeeping. One candidate was removed by the Sylvester-secretly-escaped stories. And Mingo Williams didn't live in Rosewood, so you couldn't count him. But what about James Carrier, she was asked. The kindly voice grew less kindly. "That old man was crippled," she said, with unfathomable disdain. "He was nearly dead anyway." And if it were to be doubted whether this theme really represented scorekeeping—the self-treatment of unseen emotional pain by re-imagining an atrocity—there was one more exclusion to come. What about Lexie Gordon? Wasn't she killed, too? The voice replied: "She was almost white. She didn't count against our side."

Chapter 39: Destinies

[645] *Florida Times-Union*, Jan. 18, 1923, p. 5: "NEGRO HANGED FOR STEALING CATTLE, Scene of Lynching Was Famous Lynch Hammock." Of Wilson it was said only that he "owns a farm on the Gainesville-Newberry road" and "was arrested last Sunday afternoon (Jan. 14) on a charge of cattle stealing." Local sentiments among whites were expressed in another line: "For years it has been impossible for a white man to raise cattle in that section with any success, on account of thieves. It will be remembered that it was in this section that some hogs were stolen some seven years ago." The degree of substance behind white beliefs in African American livestock thieves was never publicly demonstrated.

[646] Among the spy-hunters during World War I was Florida Governor Sidney Catts (1916-1921), who found a way to combine war fever, anti-Catholicism and racism into a single stream. Catts was purportedly connected to a rumor claiming that Catholic monks at St. Leo Monastery near Tampa were plotting to arm African Americans, take over Florida for the Kaiser and then deliver it to the Pope ("St. Leo, Florida: A Catholic Anomaly in Protestant 'Cracker' Country," by Harry J. Schalerman, Jr., and Dewey M. Stowers, Jr., *The Florida Geographer*, Vol. 22, 1988, p. 36).

[647] *Florida Times-Union*, Jan. 31, 1923.

[648] Ibid.

[649] *Sanford as I Knew It 1912-1935*, by Peter Schall (sports editor for the *Sanford Daily Herald)*, self-published, Orlando, 1970 (PKYL). *Florida Times-Union*, Feb. 16, 1923: "NO INDICTMENTS OF MOB MEMBERS BY THE GRAND JURY."

[650] "Conspiracy of Silence Shrouds 1916 Lynchings," by Ron Sachs, *Gainesville Sun Sunday Magazine*, Nov. 6, 1977. Frank Dudley died in 1989. He was a nephew of Constable George Wynne, whose killing on Aug. 17, 1916, set off the Newberry rampage.

[651] *Informant*: W. Baylor.

[652] *Levy County News,* May 22, 1924 (article found by the Florida Department of Law Enforcement in its 1994 Rosewood investigation, investigators Eric Ericson and John Stephens).

[653] Sheriff Bob Walker resigned July 8, 1924, "following the result of the local primary," and the victor in the primary, L. L. Johns, then filled out the unoccupied term until the general election on November 7, 1924. Naturally, few

people voted in that election. Of the 629 who did, 624 voted for Johns. A lone vote was cast for Walker.

[654] *Informant*: M. Howard. Gravestone: William Crighton Bryce, Bryceville, Fla., died July 23, 1924.

[655] Letter in the collection of Jerry Peterson, Bryceville, Fla., passed down by his grandmother Martha Thompson, Walter Pillsbury's daughter.

[656] *Arthur Gerrish Cummer*, by Jean Hall Dodd, Jacksonville, Fla., 1996, p. 2 (CMA).

[657] Today, the Cummer Museum of Art and Gardens on Riverside Avenue in Jacksonville remains an admired civic fixture. As the Cummers helped level the old-growth cypress forests of Florida, they, unlike some others, also gave back. Their Jacksonville operation, the largest employer in the city in 1911, is remembered as operating a pioneering kindergarten for employees' children. Their Sumner commissary seemed not to use debt to ensnare laborers as, for example, a preceding corporate sawmill at Lukens, nearby on the Gulf, was said to have done. According to the Jacksonville Historical Society, after the city's great fire of 1901, the Cummer family (headed by Arthur's father Wellington Cummer) opened their home to refugees.

[658] Putnam Lumber Company, "Our Heritage," http://www.putnamlumber.com/company _Our_Heritage.html "He and his associates acquired about 300,000 acres of land that had been sold by the State of Florida. Originally Putnam Lumber Company was formed as a timber holding company and did not undertake manufacturing operations until 1919." Between 1919 and 1928, Putnam Lumber's logs from Dixie County were shipped to Jacksonville by train for milling in a Cummer-owned facility; by 1928 Putnam had built its own mill at Shamrock in Dixie County, alternately called the largest sawmill in Florida and "the biggest cypress sawmill in the world." (*Gainesville Sun*, Nov. 10, 1982). In the late 1930s timber executive W. G. Leonard described Putnam's tract as comprising 242,000 acres ("American Life Histories: Manuscripts from the Federal Writers' Project, 1936-1940" January 20, 1937, Spokane, Washington: "Sawyer County, The Timber Business," W. G. Leonard interviewed by Glenn H. Lathrop).

[659] *The Lumber Industry*, by Luther Conant, United States Bureau of Corporations, U.S. Government Printing Office, 1914, pp. 217-222: Cummer Lumber was calculated to hold 318,000 acres, compared to a calculation for Putnam of 238,000 acres.

[660] One of the most impressive combines of the large timber firms in Florida, including Cummer, O'Brien's Putnam, Burton-Swartz, Brooks-Scanlon and

Sears interests, formed in the early 1930s when they joined together to explore their Florida timber holdings for another kind of treasure: petroleum. Had the big oil strike ever been made, the shape of the future might already have been determined. ("Burton-Swartz Cypress Company of Florida," by Drew Harrington, *Florida Historical Quarterly*, April 1985, 63: 423).

[661] No company records left from Sumner: "They just sort of disappeared" (interview with Jean Hall Dodd, Cummer Museum, 1996). The Cummer Museum in Jacksonville was created in the donated home of Arthur Cummer and his wife Ninah May Holden Cummer after they died in 1943 and 1958. Corporate documents tracing the history of the razing of Florida's forests were not included in the collection. Wellington Cummer III, grandson and namesake of the original family patriarch, confirmed when contacted in 1982 that after the last Cummer cutting was completed in the 1950s company records were not preserved. Speaking of the Rosewood incident, he said: "It was deliberately hushed up."

[662] *Informants*: M. Thompson, E. Parham.

[663] The horrific story of a star-crossed executive and a clogged fuel line was told vaguely, at a distance, by informant Fred Kirkland, but in much more detail by Walter Pillsbury's daughter Martha, who saw the results during her father's last moments at a Jacksonville hospital. The fatal fire was so freakish, and Pillsbury's history of conflict with a mob in 1923 had been so severe, that foul play instead of an accident might easily be suspected. However, Pillsbury's son Edward would become a Jacksonville police detective, in a prime position to investigate, and the possibility of arson seems never to have been raised. The family accepted that a curious child from the nearby countryside happened to be watching, but otherwise, at the moment when a man of destiny met his end, they said that only one individual was present, the man himself.

[664] For example, the family of logger John Wesley Bradley managed to reassemble after a time in the Florida logging town of Palatka, then in 1925 Bradley was drawn to booming opportunities in the Miami area, where he became a carpenter amid epidemic housing construction. The Carters, selling the Rosewood land from which they were dispossessed, were drawn to one of the new boom cities being built in the Palm Beach area, though Kelsey City, as it was called, was hit by hurricanes in 1926 and 1928 as well as by financial weather. Its remains lie in what is today Lake Park.

[665] "The Forgotten Real Estate Boom of the 1920s," Baker Library, Harvard Business School, Harvard University, 2012, in "Real Estate History: An Overview and Research Agenda," by Marc A. Weiss, *Business History Review* 63 (1989), pp. 241–282. "When one thinks of Florida during the 1920s, it is usually the 'land boom' which comes to mind. The astronomical increase in

property values, the population explosion, the fantastic advertising, and then the cataclysmic hurricane in September 1926..." ("Judge Herbert Ryder and the Lynching at La Belle," by Jerrell H. Shofner, *Florida Historical Quarterly*, Jan. 1991, p. 292). Migration was so frenetic during the Florida Boom that the U.S. Post Office in Savannah, Georgia, was said to have received 6,000 change of address orders, as the *Miami Herald* claimed that Savannah had lost 20,000 residents (*Florida, From Indian Trail to Space Age*, by Carson Tebeau, The Southern Publishing Company, Delray Beach, Florida, 1965, p. 61).

[666] Tebeau, ibid., p. 60.

[667] Aside from newspaper reports on the oil promotion boom in Levy County and upriver in Suwannee County, there are witness recollections. Minnie Langley: "They was tryin' to pump that oil in Lukens, Florida (six miles from Rosewood). They had the pump down there tryin' to dig the oil. But they couldn't find no oil." Edith Foster: "They tried a boom here one time, you know, between here and Cedar Keys, and they surveyed out a lot of land, and I think people bought a lot of land. Then they claimed they were drillin' for oil between here and Cedar Key. You notice the big old pipe out there in them scrub places. And I think people bought some shares in it. They didn't find no oil. Just ole real estate doin'."

[668] Oral history interview of Judge Warren L. Jones, conducted Aug. 15, 1989, by U.S. District Court Judge Gerald B. Tjoflat, Jacksonville:
Q: "And how many title lawyers were you bossing?"
A: "Oh, I don't know. At one time, there were 10 or 12 of them."
Q: "You were down, where, in the Graham Building? Was this space in the Graham Building?
A: Yeah, in the Graham Building, on the third floor. Then we had space on another floor.
Q: Warren, what were they in the midst of doing then?
A: Examining the titles to a tract in West Florida extending from around Pensacola down to way south of Tampa. I don't know how many thousands of acres of land they had under contract." (confirmed in interview with Judge Tjoflat, 1996).

[669] *Laws of Florida*, 1921, Vol. 2, p. 230, Special Acts: Levy County bond issue of $100,000, "for the building of a road and necessary bridges into Cedar Key, Florida."

[670] Abandoned limerock borrow pits for road-building can still be seen near Florida Highway 24 in its passage through the site of Rosewood. *Informant* Sam Hall recalled pre-1923 dynamiting for limerock which, he said, caused a shower of stone that killed one of John McCoy's chickens. Minnie Langley recalled

construction on "the hard road" that was taking shape north of her grandmother's fields.

[671] "Floridians and their southern neighbors were feeling the forces of unwelcome change [as the 1925 boom] convinced many white Floridians that their way of life was being threatened by forces which they could not control." ("Judge Herbert Ryder and the Lynching at La Belle," by Jerrell H. Shofner, *Florida Historical Quarterly*, Jan. 1991, p. 292).

[672] Donarion "Bishop" Bradley, Raleigh Bradley, Harry Carrier and others from Rosewood would migrate to New York. *Informants*: L. Harris, P. Williams, L. Davis, L. Carrier. Legislative testimony 1994: Arnett Goins.

[673] Wilson Hall's mother, Mary Ann Hall, lived in Chicago until her death in 1952 (FAMU, Box 3, Folder 2). Wilson himself eventually returned to Florida and lived not far from Bryceville in the Jacksonville area, where his sisters Margie, Mary Ann and Doshia also settled. Their brother Sam lived just north in Brunswick, Georgia.

A Note on the Investigation

[674] As we talked in that first interview, Minnie Lee Langley held in her lap a newspaper telling of an April 18, 1983, bombing in Lebanon at the U.S. Embassy (prelude to a more disastrous event at the Beirut Marine barracks in October). Forgetting the newspaper in the intensity of her story, the 69-year-old narrator unconsciously kept creasing and recreasing the tightly gripped newspaper, as if to bring some kind of order to the story of helplessness and pain she was relating.

[675] Two other racial rampages help to illustrate the mysteries behind the phrase given here as "cultural blind spot." The 1920 Ocoee ethnic cleansing riot in Florida was large and horrific, but half a century later in 1968, when a local sheriff was interviewed by graduate student Lester Dabbs, he said he had been a deputy there in 1920 and had no memory of any such riot occurring. The 1921 Tulsa, Oklahoma, race riot was still larger, laying waste to more than 30 city blocks with a death toll still in dispute, but just over a half century later in the 1970s, when historian Scott Ellsworth interviewed local prosecutor Bill LaFortune, the latter said he was born and raised in Tulsa and had never heard of any such riot. In local white culture of the era such oblivion was not uncommon. In 2008, journalist Elliot Jaspin would locate a number of such geo-historical blindspot areas, sites of "racial cleansing" episodes in the lynching era, perhaps the largest formed by a multi-county, myth-cloaked area just north of Atlanta, centered on Forsyth County, Georgia. These "cultural blind spots" were not just matters of courthouse cover-up or a fudged record here and there. They suggest

patterns of mass psychology in which social science joins the avoidance by omission, and history is ill-equipped to penetrate the consequences ("A Report of the Circumstances and Events of the Race Riot on November 2, 1920 in Ocoee, Florida," by Lester Dabbs, Jr., Master's Thesis, Stetson University, 1969; *Orlando Weekly*, Edward Ericson, Jr., Oct. 1, 1998; *Death in a Promised Land: The Tulsa Race Riot of 1921*, by Scott Ellsworth, Louisiana State University Press, 1982; *Buried in the Bitter Waters: The Hidden History of Racial Cleansing in America*, by Elliot Jaspin, Basic Books, 2008).

[676] In a hearing on March 3, 1994, in the Rosewood claims case, an academic committee assigned by the Florida Legislature to verify the Rosewood incident was rebuked for their inability to produce any official record that the 1923 event had occurred. The legislature's hope had apparently been that once mainstream professors from the state university system were put on the case, their expertise might unearth documentation previously overlooked. Instead, the "university team" verified to a surprised Special Master running the hearing that there was nothing. On multiple levels, official Florida had produced a massive omission. Though voluminous evidence on the incident did exist, it was informal in nature, consisting mostly of witness memory and confusing newspaper accounts. Official files, which should have been the first line of preservation, were empty. Professor William Rogers told the hearing that "it was just a bitter disappointment that we could not" find any official documentation. (Southeast Regional Black Archives Research Center and Museum, Florida A.&M. University, Rosewood claims case files, cassette 1, side A).

[677] For his influential 1905 study of lynching, James Cutler sent questionnaires to local officials in efforts to obtain informant input, but got back such answers as "In answer to the above I will say that I don't know anything about it." Cutler then turned to newspaper sources, though making it clear that he trusted them only for general data, on which a reporter was "less likely to indulge his imaginative powers" (*Lynch Law: An Investigation into the History of Lynching in the United States*, by James E. Cutler. New York: Longmans, Green, and Co., 1905, pp. 156, 159). The NAACP, founded in 1909, sent field investigators to dangerous lynching areas. John Shillady was beaten on a trip to Texas and the trauma seemed to influence his resignation soon afterward. His successor, Walter White, described various witness encounters, though an atmosphere of advocacy and polemics left many questions about the veracity of the NAACP material, questions seldom examined. In 1930, the newly formed Southern Commission on the Study of Lynching probed twenty sites, with such success that its director, Arthur Raper, wrote: "The identification of lynchers can usually be accomplished without great difficulty. The Commission's field workers secured fairly definite information about many of the persons who took an active part in 1930's lynchings." (*The Tragedy of Lynching*, by Arthur F. Raper, Southern Commission on the Study of Lynching, 1933, 2003, pp. 10-11).

[678] Grimshaw wrote that "...such interviews have more frequently been suggestive of points of interpretation than as direct sources of data," hence he resorted to newspaper reports. To Rudwick "...it became apparent that interesting interviews are not always illuminating ones...memory distorts events..." (*A Study in Social Violence: Urban Race Riots in the United States*, by Allen Grimshaw, doctoral dissertation, University of Pennsylvania, 1959: *Race Riot at East St. Louis July 2, 1917*, by Elliott M. Rudwick, Southern Illinois University Press, Carbondale, 1964, p. ix).

[679] *Race Riot, Chicago in the Red Summer of 1919*, by William M. Tuttle, Atheneum, 1970, p. 269.

[680] The term "pseudomemory" (rendered here as "pseudo-memory") refers to impressions about past experiences that are mistaken by a subject for real memories, but are in fact imagined insertions. The term is associated with University of Washington psychologist and memory expert Elizabeth Loftus, who began studying deceptive memory in the 1970s. The term "false memory syndrome" is of later origin, though in much the same stream of controversy. The term is credited to mathematician Peter Freyd in the 1990s, after he was accused of childhood sexual abuse by his grown daughter Jennifer, herself a psychologist, and Freyd and his wife Pamela founded the False Memory Syndrome Foundation. Freyd's daughter wrote: "In 1991 there was no false memory movement or noisy debate about recovered memories. A lack of information prevailed." (*Betrayal Trauma: The Logic of Forgetting Childhood Abuse*, by Jennifer J. Freyd, Harvard University Press, p. 197).

[681] "The satanism scare has been to the 1980s and early 1990s what the religious cult scare was to the 1970s" ("Satanism: The New Cult Scare," by David G. Bromley, in *The Satanism Scare*, eds. James T. Richardson, Joel Best and David G. Bromley, Aldine de Gruyter, 1991, p. 49). Said to begin in the 1970s with conspiracy-theory presentations in growing fundamentalist church circles, the satanism scare took force from fears of social breakdown in reaction to women's rights reforms, counterculture movements and related trends. Boosts came from the 1979 founding of the Moral Majority by Rev. Jerry Falwell, and in 1980 the publication of *Michelle Remembers*, a book by psychiatrist Lawrence Pazder and his wife/ex-patient Michelle Smith, who said Pazder's therapy had awakened her to repressed memories of horrific abuse by a satanic cult as a child. The book was later discredited, but by 1983 a growing current of angry belief led to the McMartin Pre-School case in Manhattan Beach, California, whose sensational court proceedings ran to 1990. Called the longest and most expensive criminal trial in American history, McMartin reportedly cost $15 million and publicized the ritual-abuse accusation stream nationally. A number of other daycare centers were targeted by what became runaway prosecutions based on evidence later debunked. After missionaries carried the stream to

Guatemala (where perhaps forty percent of the population had turned from Catholicism to other Christian denominations), rumors spread through a remote province, Huehuetenango, saying that a worldwide convention of satanists would meet there on a specific weekend in April 2000. On the foretold weekend, two busloads of tourists, not from America but Japan, happened to make a routine trip to a mountain village in Huehuetenango, then were accused of being the satanists. A 43-year-old businessman on holiday, as well as a Guatemala tour bus driver, were hacked and beaten to death. "Satanic Panic" was the title of a book about the scare pattern by sociologist Jeffrey Victor (*Satanic Panic: The Creation of a Contemporary Legend*, by Jeffrey S. Victor, Open Court, Chicago, 1993).

[682] *A Documented History of the Incident at Rosewood*: "Elsie Collins Campbell, a white woman of Cedar Key, once lived at Rosewood, and was about three years old at the time of the disturbance. She remembers the village as one of green forests. This view is shared universally by blacks and whites when they describe the community's dominant features" (submitted to the Board of Regents of the Florida State University System for deliberations by the Florida Legislature, Dec. 22, 1993, p. 20).

[683] The difficulties in classifying the Rosewood informants into levels of relevance (Who qualified as an eyewitness? Who had been old enough to have credible memories? Whose hearsay information was verifiable?) reminds of the many obstacles presented by Lynching-Era secrecy. The term "eyewitness" becomes open to interpretation. In 1993 an academic report on Rosewood used alleged memories from a three-year-old as major evidence; see previous note. Less extremely, an informant who was an eight-year-old living twenty miles from the events was an eyewitness to the general atmosphere, but was hardly co-significant with a twenty-year-old experiencing the events themselves. Moreover, an age threshold appeared. In 1982 as this investigation began, the term "pseudo-memory" was still new or unknown in discourse, but the 1980s would bring tragic demonstration that childhood impressions can be molded and misused by insistent interrogators. Among Rosewood informants, the age of eight seemed to be the earliest formation point for consistently verifiable memories. Many confirmable details could emerge from age seven or below, but they seemed to blend with fantasy—with "pseudo-memory"—often enough to preclude their use as narrative anchors. Considering this threshold, there came to be ten central survivor-witnesses to the Rosewood events, all located in 1982-1983, though one would not declare until 1994: Minnie Lee (Mitchell) Langley (1983), Beatrice Goins Frazier (1982), Philomena Goins Doctor (1982), Sam Hall (1983), Leroy Carrier (1983), Eloise King Davis (1982), Lonnie Carrol (1982), Margie Hall Johnson (1983), Willie Evans (1983) and Arnett Goins (1994). In addition, important information came from ex-residents of Rosewood who had moved away from the community shortly before the destruction of

1923, including Thelma Hawkins (1982), Ernest Blocker (1982), Lutie Foster (1983), Lillie Washington (1983) and Eva Jenkins (1993). Survivors Lee Ruth Davis, Nettie Joyner and Lula Harris provided important information but were aged seven or below in 1923, and in at least one case demonstrated pseudo-memory intrusions requiring careful corroboration. Since the 1990s, news media and other inquirers have extensively used child survivors Mary (Hall) Daniels and Allenetta (Robie Robinson) Mortin without consideration of age-related or other complications, which in one of those cases grew extreme, with results that might be called bizarre, precluding use of that informant here. Beyond the core African American informants, levels of significance radiate outward to include residents of Sumner, a main event-node in 1923, including many white ex-residents with detailed memories. Here, too, the passions and haste of some examiners have endorsed some clearly fantasizing witnesses, sometimes to almost humorous degree. In all, as the circle expands to include background informants, descendants and corroborative witnesses—many with important information—the number of intersecting viewpoints collated for this study passes the one-hundred mark, generating a level of detail rarely seen in retrospective investigation of rural Lynching-Era mysteries.

Made in the USA
Las Vegas, NV
08 February 2023